AF479157

The Counter-Arts Conspiracy

Art and Industry in the Age of Blake

MORRIS EAVES

The Counter-Arts Conspiracy

Art and Industry in the Age of Blake

CORNELL UNIVERSITY PRESS

ITHACA AND LONDON

Published with the assistance of the Getty Grant Program.

First published 1992 by Cornell University Press.

International Standard Book Number 0-8014-2489-5
Library of Congress Catalog Card Number 92-52749
Printed in the United States of America
Librarians: Library of Congress cataloging information appears on the last page of the book.

♾ The paper in this book meets the minimum requirements of the American National Standard for Information Sciences—Permanence of Paper for Printed Library Materials, ANSI Z39.48-1984.

To Harmon and Louise Eaves,
my much-loved parents, without whom nothing

CONTENTS

Illustrations ix
Preface xv
Abbreviations xxi
Cast of Some Contemporary Characters xxiii

I. NATION: The Making of an English School of Painters 1
The State of the Arts and the Ocean of Business, 1810 1
The Problem of the English School 3
The Ancients 8
The Vasari Canon and Its Extensions 9
Patronage and the English Inheritance 12
Institutions of Art: The Royal Academy 14
The Argument 21
Patronage in a Commercial Country 25

II. COMMERCE: A New Maecenas 33
Why the English School Painted Shakespeare 41
An Era Ends 56
English Engravers Meet an Enterprising English Tradesman 63
English Tradesman: Same Song, Second Verse 70
On the Discrimination of Anticommercialisms 92
Hazlitt's "Enquiry": A New Look at an Old Club 96
Cunningham's *Lives*: The Graphic Spirit of His Country 101

III. RELIGION: A Christian History of Engraving 107

The Pentateuchal Plot 112

Bezaleel and Aholiab 117

The Golden Hall of Urizen 121

The Heart of the Pharisee 124

The Argument 133

The Alpha of Omega: The Old, the New, and the Original 147

IV. TECHNOLOGY: The Artistic Machine 153

Addressing a Public 156

Arts Counter Arts 158

Vulgar Fellows and Ignorant Journeymen 168

The Space of Translation 175

Technohistory 182

The *Tout-ensemble* 237

A Republican Art 259

Works Cited 273

Index 281

ILLUSTRATIONS

1.1. James Barry, *An Inquiry into the Real and Imaginary Obstructions to the Acquisition of the Arts in England*, 1775, title page. Collection of Robert N. Essick. 4
1.2. William Blake after Joshua Reynolds, *The Graphic Muse*, engraved frontispiece to Hoare's *Inquiry*. Collection of Robert N. Essick. 5
1.3. Prince Hoare, *An Inquiry into the Requisite Cultivation and Present State of the Arts of Design in England*, 1806, title page. Collection of Robert N. Essick. 5
1.4. Benjamin Haydon, *Some Enquiry into the Causes Which Have Obstructed the Advance of Historical Painting, for the Last Seventy Years in England*, 1829, title page. By permission of the British Library. 6
1.5. James Barry, self-portrait, mezzotint, c. 1802. By permission of the Trustees of the British Museum. 7
1.6. Annibale Carracci, *The Dead Christ Mourned*, oil, 1603–1604? By courtesy of the Trustees, The National Gallery, London. 11
1.7. C. Bestland after Henry Singleton, *The Royal Academicians Assembled in Their Council Chamber [1793], to Adjudge the Medals to the Successful Students in Painting, Sculpture, Architecture, and Drawing*, engraving, 1802, and key. By permission of the Trustees of the British Museum. 16
1.8. Roger de Piles, *The Principles of Painting*, 1743, title page and pages 297, 298. The Beinecke Rare Book and Manuscript Library, Yale University. 18
1.9. A. C. Pugin, Thomas Rowlandson, and J. Bluck, *The Great Room of the Society for the Encouragement of Arts*, etching and aquatint from Rudolph Ackermann's *Microcosm of London*, vol. 3, 1809. Yale Center for British Art, Paul Mellon Collection. 24
1.10. Pietro Martini after J. H. Ramberg, *The Exhibition of the Royal Academy, 1787*, engraving, 1787. By permission of the Trustees of the British Museum. 29
2.1. William Woollett after Benjamin West, *The Death of General Wolfe*, engraving, 1776. By permission of the Trustees of the British Museum. 32

2.2. James Gillray, *Shakespeare Sacrificed;—or—The Offering to Avarice,* etching and aquatint, 1789. By permission of The Huntington Library, San Marino, California. 36
2.3. Anker Smith after Francis Wheatley, *The Death of Richard II,* engraving, 1793. Memorial Art Gallery of the University of Rochester; Marion Stratton Gould Fund. 37
2.4. William Blake, *The Portland Vase,* engraving for Erasmus Darwin's *The Botanic Garden,* part 1, *The Economy of Vegetation,* 1791. Collection of Robert N. Essick. 39
2.5. James Barry, *Commerce or the Triumph of the Thames,* 1777–1784, 1801. Royal Society of Arts, London. 48
2.6. James Heath after J. S. Copley, *The Death of Major Peirson,* engraving: (*A*) preliminary etched state, 1788; (*B*) published state, 1796; (*C*) key. *A* and *B* by permission of the Trustees of the British Museum; *C,* Tate Gallery, London/Art Resource, New York. 50
2.7. Francesco Bartolozzi, engraved ticket of admission to the 1791 exhibition of Copley's *Siege of Gibraltar* (facsimile of ticket by unidentified artist). By permission of the Trustees of the British Museum. 53
2.8. S. Rawle, *View of the Shakespeare Gallery,* etched frontispiece to the *European Magazine,* vol. 46, 1804. By permission of the Trustees of the British Museum. 54
2.9. Francis Wheatley, *The Opening of the Shakespeare Gallery, 1790,* watercolor, 1790. Victoria and Albert Museum. 55
2.10. William Blake after John Opie, *Romeo and Juliet,* engraving, 1799. Collection of Robert N. Essick. 59
2.11. Valentine Green after Josiah Boydell, *John Boydell,* mezzotint, 1772. By permission of The Huntington Library, San Marino, California. 71
2.12. J. Parry after Anthony van Assen, *Alderman Boydell,* engraving, 1804. By permission of the Trustees of the British Museum. 72
2.13. John Landseer after Philippe Jacques de Loutherbourg, *The Angel Binding Satan,* engraving, 1797. By permission of The Huntington Library, San Marino, California. 76
2.14. A. C. Pugin, Thomas Rowlandson, and J. Bluck, *The Interior of the British Institution, Pall Mall,* etching and aquatint from Rudolph Ackermann's *Microcosm of London,* vol. 1, 1808. By permission of The Huntington Library, San Marino, California. 77
2.15. William Blake after John Flaxman, *Letter to the Committee for Raising the Naval Pillar,* plate 3, engraving, 1799. By permission of The Huntington Library, San Marino, California. 82
2.16. James Gillray, *Design for the Naval Pillar,* etching, 1800. By permission of the Trustees of the British Museum. 83
2.17. J. M. W. Turner, *The Battle of Trafalgar,* oil, 1822–1824. National Maritime Museum, Greenwich. 85

2.18. William Blake, *The Spiritual Form of Pitt Guiding Behemoth,* tempera, 1805–1809. Tate Gallery, London/Art Resource, New York. 86
2.19. William Blake, *The Spiritual Form of Nelson Guiding Leviathan,* tempera, 1805–1809. Tate Gallery, London/Art Resource, New York. 87
3.1. William Blake, *The Book of Urizen,* title page (copy G), relief etching, 1794. From the Lessing J. Rosenwald Collection, Rare Book and Special Collections Division, Library of Congress. 115
3.2. William Blake, *Milton,* plate 40 (copy A), relief etching, c. 1804–1808. By permission of the Trustees of the British Museum. 123
3.3. William Blake, *The Marriage of Heaven and Hell,* plate 24 (copy D), relief etching, c. 1790. From the Lessing J. Rosenwald Collection, Rare Book and Special Collections Division, Library of Congress. 125
3.4. William Blake, *Illustrations of the Book of Job,* plate 11, engraving, 1825–1826. Collection of Robert N. Essick. 129
4.1. William Blake, *Jerusalem,* plate 81 (copy D), relief etching, c. 1804–1820. By permission of the Houghton Library, Harvard University. 185
4.2. Type in chase. 186
4.3. William Blake, *America a Prophecy,* 1793: (*A*) fragment of relief-etched copperplate, detail; (*B*) plate *a,* printed impression. From the Lessing J. Rosenwald Collection, Rare Book and Special Collections Division, Library of Congress. 187
4.4. Joshua Reynolds, *King George III,* oil, 1780. The Royal Academy of Arts, London. 188
4.5. Joshua Reynolds, *Queen Charlotte,* oil, 1780. The Royal Academy of Arts, London. 189
4.6. Bate's New Process: engraving of *The Friends,* 1848, after a statue by William Behnes, and detail. 190
4.7. Printed text in pixels. 192
4.8. Halftone screen. 193
4.9. Gilbert Stuart, *George Washington,* oil, detail: (*A*) magnified halftone; (*B*) line shot; (*C*) halftone. White House Collection. 193
4.10. Computer-generated block portrait of George Washington: (*A*) out of focus; (*B*) in focus. Courtesy of Leon D. Harmon, by permission of the estate of Leon D. Harmon. 194
4.11. Computer-generated block portrait of Abraham Lincoln: (*A*) out of focus; (*B*) in focus. Courtesy of Leon D. Harmon, by permission of the estate of Leon D. Harmon. 196
4.12. A dollar bill, magnified; normal size. 197
4.13. William Blake, *Christ Blessing,* tempera, c. 1810, reproduced by circular screen, and detail. Courtesy of The Fogg Art Museum, Harvard University, Cambridge, Massachusetts; bequest of Grenville L. Winthrop. 198
4.14. Dudesert after Claude Mellan (1649), *The Sudarium of St. Veronica,* engraving, 1735, detail. By permission of the Trustees of the British Museum. 200

4.15. Nicholas Beatrizet (active 1540–1568) after Girolamo Muziano, *The Sudarium of St. Veronica,* engraving. By permission of the Trustees of the British Museum. 200
4.16. Dudesert after Claude Mellan (1649), *The Sudarium of St. Veronica,* 1735. By permission of the Trustees of the British Museum. 201
4.17. Signatures: (*A*) Claude Mellan, *The Sudarium of St. Veronica,* detail; (*B*) William Blake, *The Antiquities of Athens,* 3:16, plate 21, 1792, detail. *A* by permission of the Trustees of the British Museum; *B,* the Blackader-Lauterman Library of Architecture and Art, McGill University; photo courtesy of Christopher Heppner. 201
4.18. Marcantonio Raimondi (c. 1480–1530) after Raphael, *Adam and Eve,* c. 1512–1514. By permission of the Trustees of the British Museum. 203
4.19. Raphael, *Venus,* drawing, c. 1512. By permission of the Trustees of the British Museum. 204
4.20. Marcantonio Raimondi after Raphael, *Venus and Cupid,* engraving, c. 1512–1514, and detail. By permission of the Trustees of the British Museum. 204
4.21. Cornelis Cort after Titian, *Tarquin and Lucrece,* engraving, 1571. By permission of the Trustees of the British Museum. 208
4.22. Titian, *Portrait of a Man,* oil, c. 1512. By courtesy of the Trustees, The National Gallery, London. 209
4.23. James Gillray, *Titianus Redivivus,* etching and aquatint, 1797. By permission of the Trustees of the British Museum. 210
4.24. Hendrik Goltzius, *Farnese Hercules,* engraving, c. 1591 (pub. 1617), and detail. By permission of the Trustees of the British Museum. 211
4.25. Peter Paul Rubens, *Moses with the Brazen Serpent,* oil, c. 1630. By courtesy of the Trustees, The National Gallery, London. 214
4.26. Schelte Adams van Bolswert after Peter Paul Rubens, *Moses with the Brazen Serpent,* engraving, probably after 1633. By permission of the Trustees of the British Museum. 215
4.27. Robert Nanteuil after Philippe de Champaigne, *Charles Benoise, Conseiller au Parlement de Paris,* engraving, 1651, and detail. By permission of the Trustees of the British Museum. 217
4.28. Robert Nanteuil, preliminary drawing for *Marin Cureau de la Chambre,* c. 1656. National Gallery of Art, Washington, Rosenwald Collection. 218
4.29. Robert Nanteuil, *Marin Cureau de la Chambre,* engraving, 1656. By permission of the Trustees of the British Museum. 218
4.30. William Hogarth, *The Idle 'Prentice Betray'd by His Whore,* plate 9 of *The Idle Apprentice,* engraving, 1747. By permission of the Trustees of the British Museum. 220
4.31. Tom Cook after William Hogarth, *The Idle 'Prentice Betray'd by His Whore,* 1795(?), from *Hogarth Restored,* 1806. By permission of the Trustees of the British Museum. 221

4.32. Details: (*A*) Hogarth, *The Idle 'Prentice;* (*B*) Cook after Hogarth, *The Idle 'Prentice.* By permission of the Trustees of the British Museum. 222
4.33. Robert Strange after Guido Reni, *Miserere,* engraving, 1753, and detail. By permission of the Trustees of the British Museum. 225
4.34. Francesco Bartolozzi after Annibale Carracci, *Clytie,* engraving, 1772, and detail. By permission of the Trustees of the British Museum. 227
4.35. William Woollett after Cornelis Dusart, *Jocund Peasants,* engraving, 1767: (*A*) early state, detail; (*B*) published state. By permission of the Trustees of the British Museum. 228
4.36. William Sharp after John Opie, *Edward Long:* (*A*) preliminary etched state; (*B*) before all letters, after insignia; (*C*) before letters, after frame and insignia; (*D*) published state, 1796. By permission of the Trustees of the British Museum. 230
4.37. Robert Graves after William Sharp after John Opie, *Edward Long:* (*A*) copperplate (back); (*B*) engraving, c. 1813. By permission of the Trustees of the British Museum. 233
4.38. Francesco Bartolozzi after Annibale Carracci, *Head of a Young Monk,* stipple in imitation of chalk, unpublished state and detail, c. 1796. By permission of the Trustees of the British Museum. 234
4.39. Anonymous, *A Connoiseur [sic] Admiring a Dark Night Piece,* engraving, 1771. By permission of the Trustees of the British Museum. 235
4.40. Rembrandt van Rijn, *Christ Healing the Sick* (the Hundred-Guilder Print), etching and drypoint, c. 1649. By permission of The Huntington Library, San Marino, California. 238
4.41. Captain William Baillie's restoration of Rembrandt's Hundred-Guilder Print, 1775. Davison Art Center, Wesleyan University. 239
4.42. Rembrandt van Rijn, *Adoration of the Shepherds,* etching, c. 1652. By permission of the Trustees of the British Museum. 240
4.43. Rembrandt van Rijn, *Student at a Table by Candlelight,* etching, c. 1642. By permission of the Trustees of the British Museum. 241
4.44. R. Williams after Godfrey Kneller, *Theophilus Hastings, Seventh Earl of Huntingdon,* mezzotint copperplate, 1687, detail. By permission of the Trustees of the British Museum. 244
4.45. R. Williams after Godfrey Kneller, *Theophilus Hastings,* mezzotint (strengthened with the burin), 1687. By permission of the Trustees of the British Museum. 245
4.46. Valentine Green after Joseph Wright of Derby, *Experiment on a Bird in the Air Pump,* mezzotint, 1769. By permission of the Trustees of the British Museum. 249
4.47. William Blake after Henry Fuseli, *Head of a Damned Soul in Dante's "Inferno,"* line engraving, first state, c. 1789, and detail. By permission of the Trustees of the British Museum. 252

4.48. William Blake after Jean-Antoine Watteau, *Morning Amusement,* stipple with line and flick work, second state, 1782, and detail. By permission of the Trustees of the British Museum. 253
4.49. William Blake, *Joseph of Arimathea among the Rocks of Albion,* engraving: (*A*) first state, 1773, detail; (*B*) second state, c. 1810–1820, detail; (*C*) second state. *A* and *B,* Fitzwilliam Museum, Cambridge; *C,* collection of Robert N. Essick. 257
4.50. William Blake, *Chaucers Canterbury Pilgrims,* engraving, third state, c. 1810–1820, and detail. By permission of the Trustees of the British Museum. 258
4.51. Thomas Cockson, *Robert Devereux, Second Earl of Essex,* engraving, c. 1599. By permission of the Trustees of the British Museum. 260
4.52. Louis Schiavonetti after William Blake, *Deaths Door,* engraving, from Robert Cromek's 1808 edition of Robert Blair, *The Grave.* Collection of Robert N. Essick. 262
4.53. William Blake, *Deaths Door,* white line etching, only known impression, 1805. Collection of Robert N. Essick. 263
4.54. William Blake, *Illustrations of the Book of Job,* plate 12, engraving, 1825–1826, and detail. By permission of the Trustees of the British Museum. 264
4.55. William Blake, *The Wrath of Elihu,* pen and watercolor drawing, 1821: (*A*) detail; (*B*) detail, magnified halftone. Courtesy of The Fogg Art Museum, Harvard University, Cambridge, Massachusetts; bequest of Grenville L. Winthrop. 265
4.56. William Blake after Robert Blake, *The Approach of Doom,* relief etching, only known impression, c. 1792, and detail. By permission of the Trustees of the British Museum. 267
4.57. William Blake, *Jerusalem,* relief etchings, c. 1804–1820: (*A*) plate 99 (copy J); (*B*) plate 53 (copy A); (*C*) plate 76 (copy A). *A,* The Beinecke Rare Book and Manuscript Library, Yale University; *B* and *C* by permission of the Trustees of the British Museum. 268
4.58. William Blake, *The Man Sweeping the Interpreter's Parlour,* relief etching and/or engraving, second state, c. 1822. By permission of the Trustees of the British Museum. 269
4.59. William Blake, *Satan Calling Up His Legions:* (*A*) tempera, c. 1795–1800; (*B*) tempera, c. 1800–1805. *A,* Victoria and Albert Museum; *B,* Petworth House (Egremont Collection), The National Trust. 270
4.60. Frederic Shields, *Blake's Work-Room and Death-Room,* monochrome wash drawing, c. 1880–1890. Collection of Robert N. Essick. 272

PREFACE

In the mid-1960s the distinguished art historian Ellis K. Waterhouse began his lectures to the American Philosophical Society by observing that "the whole history of art in Britain is still surprisingly underexplored" (1). Despite some exceptional advances, the situation remains essentially unchanged. Certainly most of the little that has been written about the theory of the visual arts in Britain has been anemic. The typical mode has been unintegrated paraphrase, the typical manner a high-handed lassitude exemplified by Frederick J. Cummings's remark that "Reynolds' ideas were so completely out of date by the time he repeated them to his students that it is almost impossible to find any freshness in them" (152). As rich and varied as the accomplishments of traditional English art history have been—and they have been—it has often robbed theory and history to pay for its devotion to "the objects." Even histories of key institutions such as the Royal Academy have been one-dimensional because it was apparent in advance that the findings would not repay the time of an expert historian of art working under the traditional covenant.

As a reminder of how little engaged traditional English art history has been with the issues of theory and cultural history, one has only to reread, at the risk of belaboring the obvious, the eighteenth- and nineteenth-century volumes in the Oxford History of English Art. Joseph Burke's volume on the earlier century gives John Locke a single mention, and T. S. R. Boase's on the later century never brings up Charles Darwin. Burke gives short shrift to the histories and theories of art that the Royal Academicians beginning with Sir Joshua Reynolds expounded at length, and Boase leaves their nineteenth-century counterparts virtually untouched. As far as those magisterial surveys of the English school of painting were concerned, the picturemakers wasted all the words they spent trying simultaneously to grasp the "crisis" (as their predicament was usually characterized) of the country's visual arts and to invent and sustain a competitive English school of painting. No analysis of the historical situation of English artists, including the history of their art history or the historical situation of their theories, emerged from these standard and quite representative twentieth-century "histories." A reader who wanted to find out where one of William Blake's harsh reactions to Reynolds came from and where it led would face a dead end. Burke and Boase did not find such questions on their agenda, which was preoccupied by questions of style and genre as represented by individual contributions to a canon of masterpieces.

As everyone who follows the fortunes of art history has heard by now, the worm has to some extent turned. Though there will necessarily be serious losses to make up later, there are new opportunities for gains. Scholars such as Albert Boime have begun to attend to the culture, class, and politics of the period, while others of a more literary bent, such as John Barrell, have offered revised interpretations of the documents of the period—including, of course, the paintings—based on close inspections and an enhanced sense of the relevant contexts. If my own investigation has a neighborhood, it is this "new" art history, and its next-door neighbor may be Barrell's *Political Theory of Painting from Reynolds to Hazlitt*, in which we find (for the first time) careful readings of some key theoretical statements in the mainstream of English writing about art undertaken for the purpose of defining their respective positions in a discourse of "civic humanism" more extensive than art theory.

A measure of the deficiencies of traditional art history has been its halfheartedness in the face of Blake's ideas about art. In their 1893 edition of Blake, Edwin Ellis and W. B. Yeats recorded that "these are supposed to be mere nonsense, the result of ignorance and irritability" (2:308), and sound scholarship on his theories of art still seemed impossible well after Blake's installation in the literary canon. Historians of theory from the literary side declared that he had no such theories, only an epistemology (Wimsatt and Brooks 424), while art historians were sometimes wont to label his theory "strict academic doctrine" (Butlin, *William Blake* 16)—stricter, that is, than the more eclectic doctrines that Joshua Reynolds expounded in some twenty years as first president of the Royal Academy and published as his *Discourses on Art.*

Indeed, one of the clearest instances of the problem has been the chronic failure to distinguish the academic Reynolds from his self-declared archantagonist Blake, never a member of the Academy, on meaningful theoretical grounds. Even E. K. Ellis admitted to being long "puzzled" by Blake's "savage—and apparently isolated—criticism of Reynolds" (77) before concluding that Blake's antagonism had something to do with differences over the American Revolution. Even Barrell has furthered this conventional confusion, albeit in an unconventionally sophisticated way. His determination to extract a civic-humanist interpretation from the statements of Blake and Reynolds brings them together under false pretenses, and the stubborn one is clearly not Reynolds, who succumbs easily, but Blake. Despite the similarity, the difference between the two was great. One local source of the problem is easy to identify. Because of the contrariousness of Blake's thought—"Both read the Bible day & night / But thou readst black where I read white," he wrote in *The Everlasting Gospel*—it is seldom enough to show what Blake meant by showing what others in his community of discourse—or, more adequately, in one of his communities of discourse—meant. But the ultimate failure of discrimination occurs not at the comparison-and-contrast level, where the differences between Blake and Reynolds may seem to lie mainly in the temperature of the rhetoric, but in the deeper strata where syntax, metaphor, and narrative are achieved simultaneously.

The study of Blake has so far benefited relatively little from the waves of interest in theory and history that have touched if not swept the coasts of English art history, and neither students of Blake nor historians of English art have been finding much more use for one another than they ever have, yet certainly one of the most interesting things about English art history is Blake, and, it has to be said, one of the most interesting things about Blake is his place in art history or arts histories. Thus it occurred to me to observe what each might contribute to the health of the other under the coercion of some newly conceived relationships: narratological and pedagogical ones, commercial, religious, and technological ones. Hence in this book I experiment with fresh initiatives and models in the hope of stretching old limits in ways that may benefit the study of Blake as well as one or more of the art histories capable of telling his story as part of its own. I have pilfered material and approaches from here and there; much of what I try out on the Blake–art history combination comes from theories of narrative, theories of metaphor, and cultural studies. In the process of applying them, I have aimed at a working eclecticism that, at least for a scholarly audience, does not need elaborate theorizing beforehand.

As I saw it, the interpretive challenge was to place Blake's ideas about art in the most useful narrative contexts, which were, it inevitably seemed, other English ideas about art. This may seem too obvious to be called even a hunch, but these ideas are the very ones that have been neglected in conventional art history. And that neglect, itself an obstacle to scholarship, has allowed a mistaken attitude toward Blake's theory to gain credibility: that his ideas about art can be explained without reference to other nearby ideas, as if his own had no contemporary contexts or targets or as if their real contexts were in Plotinus, Paracelsus, and Boehme. These distortions cultivated the impression that Blake was not joining a contemporary conversation but starting one or talking to himself and the ancient dead; and that impression reinforced another, that Blake was in the rhetorical position of a religious fanatic harassing passers-by on a street corner. This is indeed one possible position, but it is only occasionally Blake's. The far more consequential truth is that he was joining an important conversation with a history. It was, as one would naturally expect for a painter-engraver, a conversation about painting and engraving, and it had subtopics relevant to the working artists of the time: the national situation of their arts, the commercial viability of their products, the usefulness of their ideology, the adequacy of available technology to their technological requirements, and so on. Further, I speculated that those issues would be defined and situated by reference to narratives telling the histories of ancient and modern art illustratively, selectively, and advantageously. And I hoped that these contexts would help to explain even Blake's most outrageous claims: that Reynolds was "Hired to Depress Art"; that he with his "Gang of Cunning Hired Knaves" had conspired to starve out original artists "under pretence of Encouraging" what they were actually "Endeavouring to Depress"; that, in short, English art was controlled by powerful political and commercial interests that had conspired to exploit and repress original artists with a system of "Counter Arts."

I have named this conversational intersection English-school discourse, after the lingering crisis that occasioned one of these theoretical forays after another. Confronting the conspicuous failure to establish an English school of painting that could compete successfully with the continental schools, writers groped for explanations and solutions. My introductory section, "Nation," analyzes narratives that they created about the past, in order to explain both the present crisis in England and the successes of other schools elsewhere, and about the future, in order to envision a prosperous English school. In later sections, using categories suggested by the structure of the discourse—business especially, but also academization, nativism, imperialism, and so forth—I rotate these narratives through several angles by relabeling the crisis: in a political crisis the critical factors may emerge in the narratives of civic humanism; in a technical, educational, or commercial crisis, the key narratives are likely to be different. And all of these narratives, as well as others, offer a view of the whole, in which painting can be seen as an integral segment of political discourse, or educational or commercial or philosophical discourse, each of which also intersects with the others.

One needs little exposure to Blake to realize that if he listened to such a conversation, he would soon have theories and histories of his own to contribute. My preliminary discussions are prompted by the claim that his ideas about art, and many of his ideas about literature as well, are profoundly indebted to this discourse. The ideas are not, as often supposed, private. They have an internal coherence, but they also rely on the coherence of the discourse on the English school of painting as it had evolved over the course of the eighteenth century. To put it simply, Blake can annotate Reynolds's *Discourses* because both the discourses and his annotations belong to the larger English-school discourse. While these generalizations account for the norm, they leave out of account Blake's deviation from the norm. I propose that much of it can be attributed to his introduction of a secondary discourse, this one Christian, into the primary one. In "Religion" I show that the resulting change is registered clearly in such key components of the discourse as the history of art that it reports. For more than a century the challenge had been to narrate a history of art in general capable of accommodating the history of English art in particular—at least as a coherent episode, perhaps even as the climactic phase. Blake's retelling of the more extensive history incorporates Christian elements, drawn, for example, from biblical narrative, in such a way as to reformulate the conditions under which English art had failed to thrive (and most writers agreed that it had failed) and the conditions under which it could expect future success.

Blake's Christian history of art advances new critiques of the old topoi in the English-school discourse, including, among others, the training of artists, the role of patrons, the history of England, the obligations of the audience. But to do so it leans heavily on yet another history, the history of the print technologies of which the graphic arts are a branch. Though the eighteenth-century contributors to English-school discourse had often written about the craft of painting and engraving and had sometimes criticized commercial arrangements that threatened to reorganize familiar materials and methods of production, no one before Blake had delivered so trenchant a critique of the technological histories in which the histories of art are always implicated. Two essays of 1977, "Blake and the Artistic Machine: An Essay in Technology and Decorum" and "What Is the History of Publishing?" were earlier attempts of mine to explore this difficult terrain. But even then it seemed to me that my formulations, as appealing as they were to me at the time, would finally have to be posited within a broader context. Hence, as the culmination of this book, "Technology" submits revised assessments of Blake as the engraver who hated Rembrandt and adored Dürer. I investigate the ties that bind technical concepts, such as "line," "color," and "harmony," not only to the organization of the workplace but also to republican politics, Protestant Christianity, and the axis of class and gender.

The guiding proposition throughout all the sections and subsections of exposition, analysis, illustration, and commentary has become trite but remains inescapable: "William Blake" as we have him at the moment is the product of multiple converging histories that we must know if we are to understand what we are talking about when we speak of "Blake's art" or "Blake's ideas." I am not competent to tell nearly all of it, but I have ventured to trace significant aspects of the story by which Blake attempted to orient himself to the contemporary situation, leaving us a history of technology, commerce, religion, and art—that is, a consolidated history of organized work, of buying and selling, and of theory and practice in poetry, painting, and engraving—all saturated by and saturating the Christian religion. My aspiration has been to establish a history of production, along with the myths that are integral to any such history, in which Blake's illuminated books might have a conceivable place.

Finally, then, this book, inspired by the difficulties of Blake's example, is intended as a challenge to the most significant traditional ways of narrating the history of English art. I could not have done without those traditions, and I have drawn on them regularly. But in the search for a satisfactory way of counting Blake in, so to speak, and of accounting for his striking but finally peculiar self-positioning, I have tried to devise a different kind of reporting with new, or at least newly construed, fields of analysis. Although I do want to make some claims for the general advantages of these new narratives, I certainly do not claim to have written anything like a comprehensive survey. Despite what the length of this book might suggest, I have had to be extremely selective and have understood all along that I could not produce a definitive study on settled premises. So, recognizing that I too was joining a conversation that would continue, I have settled for suggesting routes and advancing proposals without taking full adult responsibility for conveying my tolerant readers to the very door of an edifice I could not build.

This book, long in progress, trails many debts. It owes a great deal, much of it probably incalculable and invisible, to the example, work, conversation, and assistance of David Bindman, Detlef Dörrbecker, David Erdman, Robert Essick, Michael Fischer, Northrop Frye, Jean Hagstrum, Nelson Hilton, W. J. T. Mitchell, Morton Paley, David Simpson, and Joseph Viscomi.

For primary research, I could not have done without months in the British Museum and other British collections in 1977–1978 and 1983–1984. Writing began in earnest in 1984–1985 at the National Humanities Center, where I was blessed with the unforgettable advantages of its hospitality, peaceable comforts, and intellectual energies. The staff of this scholarly pleasure dome are truly among the wonders of the academic world. I learned much from the inspiring union of intellectual lives there, though my principal obligation during that fellowship year is to my friend and colleague David Simpson, ever fine to argue with, who knows the difference between a razor and a blunt instrument.

As I might have predicted, returning to the National Humanities Center to teach with Paul Hunter and Myra Jehlen in the three summers of 1988–1990 produced some of the finest teaching and learning experiences of my life, including several relevant to this book. Meanwhile, Robert Essick and Joseph Viscomi, whose knowledge of the graphic arts of Blake's time is daunting, have kept me informed up to the last second. I hope I have made adequate use of what they have tried to teach me. As readers of the final drafts of the manuscript, Nelson Hilton and Mary Lynn Johnson were extremely helpful—in catching errors, of course, but also in making creative suggestions that have turned this into a better book than it could otherwise have been.

Since I arrived at the University of Rochester in 1986, Patricia Neill has tolerated the many intrusions of this book into her official reponsibilities as managing editor of *Blake/An Illustrated Quarterly* with unfailing resources of grace, wit, cooperation, and skill. My research assistants Angela Jones and Laura Sebastian have somehow managed to provide many hours of expert and efficient help in the midst of their demanding schedules as graduate students, teachers, and scholars of romanticism and Irish culture, respectively. Meanwhile, superb colleagues, plus the social and professional skills of Nancy Hall, master administrator, and Rosemarie Hattmann, department secretary, are the only things that have made it possible for me to be the chair of an academic department and still look myself in the eye in the morning. And from past experience I knew it would be, as it has been, a privilege to work with Cornell University Press's Bernhard Kendler, one of the paragons of his profession. In her exacting profession, Barbara Salazar, senior manuscript editor at Cornell, has proved similarly helpful; the book has benefited greatly from its education first at her hands and then at the hands and eyes of designer Richard Rosenbaum, who calmly accepted the challenge of devising a readable form for this heap of text, notes, commentary, legends, and pictures.

Photographs are an integral part of this study, and I thank the people who were kind enough to help me gather them: Robert Essick, Joseph Viscomi, and Morton Paley all again, along with Frances Carey, Paul Dove, Obadiah Eaves, Thomas Lange, William Pressly, and Jules Prown.

In a much earlier dedication I gratefully called my wife, Georgia Eaves, and my sons, Dashiell and Obadiah Eaves, friends for life. As I have not been able to invent any more faithful characterization, neither have I been able to imagine a real life, least of all this intellectual one, without these brilliant and exciting companions.

Morris Eaves

Rochester, New York

ABBREVIATIONS

anno.	Blake's annotations to [Reynolds, etc.]
DC	*A Descriptive Catalogue of Pictures*
DNB	*Dictionary of National Biography*
E	*The Complete Poetry and Prose of William Blake,* ed. David V. Erdman. Newly rev. ed. Berkeley and Los Angeles: University of California Press, 1988.
EG	*The Everlasting Gospel*
FZ	*The Four Zoas*
J	*Jerusalem*
MHH	*The Marriage of Heaven and Hell*
OED	*Oxford English Dictionary*
PA	*Public Address*
R.A.	Royal Academy
VLJ	*A Vision of the Last Judgment*

CAST OF SOME CONTEMPORARY CHARACTERS

James Barry (1741–1806) (fig. 1.5), advocate and exponent of English history painting, was born in Cork, Ireland, studied in Italy under the sponsorship of Edmund Burke and others in the late 1760s, and worked in London thereafter, initially with success. In 1776 he painted a corrective version of Benjamin West's *Death of General Wolfe* in classical dress, and in 1777–1784 he painted his *Progress of Human Culture* series in the Great Room of the Society of Arts (figs. 1.9, 2.5). Elected to the Royal Academy in 1773, he was named professor of painting in 1782, and in 1799 he was expelled.

Francesco Bartolozzi (1727–1815), engraver, studied painting in his native Florence and engraving in Venice. Urged to come to England by Richard Dalton, engraver and librarian to George III, Bartolozzi arrived in London in 1764. In 1768 he was a founding member of the Royal Academy, and for decades he was its only professional engraver with first-class status. That honor, and his association with the fashionable "chalk manner" of stippled engravings in imitation of drawings (fig. 4.38), won him the unremitting opposition of Robert Strange. With the help of many assistants Bartolozzi producted a vast number of engravings, including plates after old masters (fig. 4.34) and popular contemporary artists, especially Angelica Kauffmann and his old friend Giovanni Battista Cipriani. Leaving England in the very depressed market for engraving after the turn of the century, he spent the last years of his life in Lisbon, in charge of the National Academy of Portugal.

James Basire (1730–1802), engraver known for correct drawing and firm lines, was Blake's master during his apprenticeship. In 1763 Richard Dalton, engraver and librarian to George III, took Basire to Italy and on that journey apparently made the connection that brought Bartolozzi to England. Basire succeeded George Vertue as engraver to the Society of Antiquaries in the early 1760s and became engraver to the Royal Society a few years later. In 1771, the year before Blake began his apprenticeship, Basire engraved *Pylades and Orestes* by Benjamin West, who generally preferred William Woollett.

John Boydell (1719–1804), engraver, printseller, alderman, and lord mayor of London, got into the printselling business by publishing a volume of views of England and Wales in 1746. In 1761 he published Woollett's engraving of Richard Wilson's *Destruction of the Children of Niobe* and in 1776 the fantastically successful engraving by Woollett of West's *Death of General Wolfe* (fig. 2.1). The epoch-making Shakespeare Gallery (figs. 2.8, 2.9), which he inaugurated in 1786, contained more than a hundred pictures before it was sold by lottery in 1804.

John Singleton Copley (1738–1815), Boston-born American painter, made a splash in London when his *Boy with a Squirrel* was exhibited there in 1766. Benjamin West urged him to come to London. After a period in Rome, he settled permanently in England in 1775. He was elected to the Academy after the exhibition of his *Death of the Earl of Chatham*, engraved by Bartolozzi, which was followed by his successful *Death of Major Peirson* (fig. 2.6) and *Siege of Gibraltar* (fig. 2.7).

Robert Hartley Cromek (1770–1812), engraver, editor, and publisher, studied engraving with Bartolozzi and engraved a bit after Thomas Stothard. He launched several publishing ventures that required contacts with artists, engravers, and writers. He was associated with Allan Cunningham in collecting "old" Scots songs, some composed by Cunningham. In 1808 he published an edition of Robert Blair's *Grave* with Blake's drawings engraved by Louis Schiavonetti (figs. 4.52–53). In 1807–1809 Cromek tirelessly exhibited Stothard's painting of the Canterbury pilgrims—the idea for which Blake believed Cromek ("Screwmuch") and Stothard ("Stewhard") had stolen from him (fig. 4.50)—to procure subscribers to a proposed engraving by Schiavonetti ("Assassinetti," E 503–4). The engraving was not finished until 1817, by James Heath, seven years after Schiavonetti's death and five years after Cromek's.

Allan Cunningham (1784–1842) was apprenticed as a stonemason to his brother in his native Scotland. Eventually, in London, he became superintendent of the works for the very successful sculptor Francis Chantrey. Simultaneously he pursued a life in letters. Robert Cromek, on a song-collecting trip to Scotland, paid Cunningham for some of his "old" (fake) Scots ballads, and it was very likely Cromek who helped persuade him to move to London, where, beginning in 1810, Cunningham tried his hand at many popular literary forms. The first edition of his *Lives of the Most Eminent British Painters, Sculptors, and Architects,* with an entry on Blake, was published in Murray's Family Library, 1829–1833. His last major work, an eight-volume edition of Burns, came out in 1834.

John Flaxman (1755–1826) (fig. 2.15), artist and sculptor, Blake's friend, promoter, and patron, was better known in Europe than any other English artist. Son of a castmaker, he began a productive association with Josiah Wedgwood after a stint in the Academy schools. Designs for Wedgwood ware popularized Flaxman's version of neoclassical simplification and purity. After a Wedgwood-sponsored stay in Rome from 1787 to 1794, he produced illustrations for the works of Homer, Aeschylus, and Dante (some engraved by Blake) that traveled well and reinforced his position as a standard bearer for international neoclassicism. His reputation as a sculptor of monuments increased until he had a huge practice. In 1810 he was elected the first professor of sculpture at the Royal Academy.

Henry Fuseli (Johann Heinrich Füssli) (1741–1825), ordained Zwinglian minister, painter, and author, first came to London in 1764, then, encouraged by Reynolds, studied painting in Italy from 1770 to 1778. Back in England he painted his best-known work, *The Nightmare,* in 1781, and began his long association with the sensational, the bizarre, the intense, and the extreme (fig. 4.47), which bordered, it was often said, on insanity. He was elected to the Academy in 1790 and contributed heavily to the Shakespeare Gallery even as he worked on his solo Milton Gallery, which finally opened (briefly) in 1799. From 1799 to 1805 he was professor of painting at the Academy; he was elected keeper in 1804, and in 1810 he was reelected professor of painting. Among his students were Thomas Lawrence and Edwin Landseer.

George III (1738–1820) (fig. 4.4), king of Great Britain and Ireland from 1760 to 1820, studied drawing and architecture as a young man and collected books, art, and furniture. He patronized the Royal Academy at its founding in 1768 and was Benjamin West's regular patron until 1801. Inevitably associated with the loss of the American colonies, he also oversaw the wars with France that followed the French Revolution, the union of Ireland and England in 1800, and the defeat of Catholic emancipation in 1801. Mental instability led to the regency of the prince of Wales (later George IV) in 1811.

Valentine Green (1739–1813), mezzotint engraver (figs. 2.11, 4.46), achieved success shortly after he arrived in London in 1765. In 1775 he became mezzotint engraver to George III. He engraved frequently after Reynolds, and he did Benjamin West's *Return of Regulus to Carthage* and *Hannibal Swearing Eternal Enmity to the Romans,* the largest history paintings ever executed in mezzotint up to that time. In 1805 he became the first keeper of the new British Institution.

Benjamin Haydon (1786–1846) (fig. 1.4), painter, writer, lecturer, attended the Academy schools but, in his ardent if outmoded championing of idealized history painting, ultimately became the Academy's vociferous antagonist. He had extensive connections with literary people. His huge painting *Christ's Entry into Jerusalem* (1820) incorporated portraits of contemporaries including Wordsworth and Keats. With characteristic intensity he promoted the state's acquisition of the Parthenon frieze sculptures (the "Elgin marbles") in 1816. Despondent over professional failures and incessant financial problems that landed him in debtors' prison four times, he committed suicide in his studio.

William Hayley (1745–1820), though best remembered as Blake's possessive patron from 1800 to 1803, when Blake was his artist-engraver in residence in Felpham (Sussex), was a prolific if sometimes ridiculed dramatist, poet, editor, and biographer who refused the laureateship in 1790.

Friend and neighbor of William Cowper, he wrote a biography of that poet and another of Milton. He befriended and freely advised painters, before Blake Joseph Wright of Derby and George Romney, whose biography he also wrote. Before his early death in 1800, Hayley's illegitimate son Tom was apprenticed to Flaxman.

William Hazlitt (1778–1830), painter, essayist, lecturer, philosopher, political commentator, and drama critic, lived mostly by his pen, though he had come to London in the late 1790s to work as a portraitist. Encouraged by Wordsworth and Coleridge, among others, he left off painting (to which he periodically returned) for writing and is best known for collections of essays on various subjects—*Table Talk* (1821), *The Spirit of the Age* (1825), and *The Plain Speaker* (1826). His last book, *Conversations of James Northcote* (1830), returns for a final time to the subject of painting via the anecdotes and opinions of Reynolds's erstwhile assistant, portraitist, and contributor to the Shakespeare Gallery.

James Heath (1757–1834), engraver born the same year as Blake, like Blake began his career engraving Stothard's illustrations for the *Novelist's Magazine.* In 1794 he was appointed historical engraver to George III. With a variety of assistants he completed numerous large and small projects, including work for the Shakespeare Gallery, Copley's *Death of Peirson* (fig. 2.6) for Boydell, West's *Death of Nelson,* and a reengraved Hogarth. It was Heath who in 1817 finally completed the engraving of Stothard's *Canterbury Pilgrims* painting, left unfinished at Schiavonetti's death in 1810.

Prince Hoare (1755–1834) (figs. 1.2, 1.3), painter and writer, was the son of the fashionable Bath portraitist William Hoare. After training in the Academy schools, he, like Fuseli and Northcote, studied with Anton Mengs in Rome in the late 1770s. Returning to England in 1780, he painted for a few years but stopped exhibiting after 1785 to concentrate on writing instead. His first play was a tragedy performed in Bath in 1788 (at Drury Lane in 1796), but he also wrote, and saw produced, musical farces, operas, and comedies. He published poetry and several works about art, some of them in his official capacity as honorary foreign secretary to the Royal Academy beginning in 1799.

John Landseer (1769–1852), engraver, historian of engraving, and father of the engraver Thomas and the painters Charles and Edwin Landseer, worked in the 1790s for the proliferating galleries of this and that, engraving after Philippe de Loutherbourg (fig. 2.13). Later he engraved some of J. M. W. Turner's landscape drawings. He wrote and published a good deal of antiquarian scholarship on subjects allied to the history of engraving. He fought fiercely to have engravers admitted to the Academy on equal terms with painters, though without success in his lifetime.

John Opie (1761–1807), painter, began as a traveling portraitist in Cornwall and then, as the protégé and partner of the physician-satirist John Wolcot ("Peter Pindar," author of *Lyric Odes to the Royal Academicians* and editor of Matthew Pilkington's *Dictionary of Painters*), made his debut in London as a natural phenomenon, "the Cornish wonder." He contributed to the major galleries of the 1790s;

painted portraits of numerous cultural luminaries, including Dr. Johnson, William Godwin, Charles James Fox, Edmund Burke, and Fuseli; and was elected professor of painting at the Academy in 1805. He was buried in St. Paul's Cathedral.

John Pye II (1782–1874), engraver, assisted his father on engraving projects in Birmingham before becoming James Heath's assistant in London, a specialist in landscape engraving, and eventually J. M. W. Turner's favorite engraver. His *Patronage of British Art* was conceived as a major foray in his long battle against the Royal Academy, especially its treatment of engravers as second-class members.

Joshua Reynolds (1723–1792) (figs. 4.4, 4.5), the most important English painter of his time, settled in London for life in 1753 after periods of study and work in Devon (his home), London, where he was apprenticed to the portrait painter Thomas Hudson, and Italy, where Venetian coloring captivated him. His London practice was always successful, and his eminence made him an easy target of attacks. In 1768 he was elected first president of the new Royal Academy and knighted. As a member of a lettered circle that included Burke, Oliver Goldsmith, and Dr. Johnson, he was well placed to conceive the annually delivered discourses that aspired to give English art the respectability that comes with an articulated theory. After a visit in the early 1780s to Holland and Flanders, where he studied Rubens, his health gradually failed, and in 1790 he delivered his final discourse. He was the first painter since van Dyck to be buried in St. Paul's Cathedral.

Luigi ("Louis") Schiavonetti (1765–1810) (fig. 4.52), of Bassano, Italy, came to England (with his brother, also an engraver) to assist an architectural engraver, Gaetano Testolini, for whom Schiavonetti engraved plates in imitation of Bartolozzi. After Testolini's ruse was exposed, Schiavonetti became, oddly or not, one of Bartolozzi's assistants and later set up an independent shop to produce engravings in his style. Besides engraving Blake's illustrations of Blair's *Grave* for Cromek, he was commissioned, again by Cromek, to engrave Stothard's *Canterbury Pilgrims* painting but died before he could finish it.

William Sharp (1749–1824) (figs. 4.36, 4.37), engraver, son of a gunmaker, got his start as a writing engraver. He, like Blake and Heath, engraved Stothard's illustrations for the *Novelist's Magazine.* Sharp's work was highly regarded both in Britain and on the continent, and he engraved major work for American painters in London. He completed *The Landing of Charles II,* left unfinished by Woollett at his death, for West and *King Lear in the Storm* for the Shakespeare Gallery. His delinquent engraving of Copley's *Gibraltar* (fig. 2.7), published almost two decades after the commission, is perhaps the epitome of all such misguided speculations.

Martin Archer Shee (1770–1850), portrait painter, studied painting in Dublin before coming to London, where Burke introduced him to Reynolds in 1788. In 1799 he placed himself as George Romney's successor by taking over his London house; the next year he was elected to the Academy.

His literary ambitions caused Byron to link "Shee and Genius" in *English Bards and Scotch Reviewers.* In 1805 and 1809 Shee published his *Rhymes on Art,* in 1814 *The Commemoration of Sir Joshua Reynolds, and Other Poems,* and in the 1820s a tragedy accepted at Covent Garden but never produced. In 1830 he succeeded Thomas Lawrence as Royal Academy president. He was later knighted.

Thomas Stothard (1755–1834), painter, was apprenticed to a designer of patterns for brocaded silks, and he was always willing to work on mundane assignments—tickets, house decorations, and the like. Most of his enormously prolific, skillful output was in book illustrations, some of the earlier of which Blake, Heath, and Sharp engraved for *Novelist's Magazine.* He contributed to the Shakespeare Gallery in the 1790s, was elected to the Academy in 1794, and became Academy librarian in 1812. We do not know what Stothard, a great admirer of Rubens, made of Blake's accusation that Cromek and Stothard had stolen his original idea for the *Canterbury Pilgrims* project, which was to help liberate English art from Rubens, but Stothard's painting was a popular success in the years when Blake's was not.

Robert Strange (1721–1792), Scots engraver, put his art to work in the Jacobite cause, engraving a portrait of the Pretender and banknotes for the anticipated regime. From his refuge in France, where he studied engraving with Jacques-Philippe Le Bas, he returned to London and eventually went to Italy, where he, like Basire, was one of the engravers associated with Richard Dalton, the king's librarian, who recruited Bartolozzi, Strange's rival thereafter. Back in London the conflict over Bartolozzi's inclusion in the Academy despite its rules barring engravers precipitated Strange's *Inquiry* of 1775. Many of his projects involved reproductions of old masters with the express aim of educating English tastes (fig. 4.33). With West's help he gained access to some van Dycks, which he engraved with great success. He was knighted in 1787 upon engraving West's *Apotheosis of Prince Alfred and Prince Octavius.*

Josiah Wedgwood (1730–1795), potter and industrialist, was from a family of Staffordshire potters. By 1769 he was sufficiently successful to build new works with a classical name, Etruria, and take a partner, Thomas Bentley, who tended mainly to the London end of the firm's operations. Wedgwood was a vastly energetic artisan, engineer, and organizer and an inveterate experimenter. His goal was to devise refined products for an upscale clientele and new techniques for marketing them. With Flaxman as his well-chosen lead designer in the 1780s, he was able to join a fashionable aesthetic, neoclassicism, with innovative methods and materials that transformed utilitarian objects into collectible decorative items (fig. 2.4). He was also one of Wright of Derby's patrons.

Benjamin West (1738–1820) of Pennsylvania, after studying and working as a painter in Philadelphia and New York and spending three years in Italy, established himself permanently in London. In the early 1770s the controversy over his use of modern dress in *The Death of General Wolfe* (fig. 2.1), as it made his work a commercial success, also helped set new goals for history painting in England. Soon after, in 1772, he was appointed history painter to George III, his patron until 1801. Among the founding members of the Royal Academy, West was Reynolds's successor as president from 1792 to 1820.

William Woollett (1735–1785), the first English engraver widely admired on the continent, established his reputation for landscape work with *The Destruction of the Children of Niobe,* engraved after Richard Wilson and published by Boydell in 1761, and enlarged that reputation to include history painting with his *Death of Wolfe* (fig. 2.1; also fig. 4.35) after West, on the strength of which the king made Woollett his historical engraver in 1775.

Joseph Wright ("Wright of Derby") (1734–1797) began, like Joshua Reynolds and John Mortimer, as a pupil of the portraitist Thomas Hudson in London. But for most of his life he worked around Liverpool and Derby, where Wedgwood was among his major patrons. In an enterprising environment of burgeoning industrialism and progressive science, in the 1760s he began to paint his "candlelight pictures" (fig. 4.46), dramatic chiaroscurist experiments usually emphasizing technical, commercial, and scientific subjects, often in combination with group portraits. He preceded Blake as an object of William Hayley's regard, advice, and help. It was Hayley who helped Wright get commissions from Boydell for the Shakespeare Gallery.

The Counter-Arts Conspiracy

Art and Industry in the Age of Blake

I NATION
The Making of an English School of Painters

. . . the print-shops are filled with vague trumpery smearings, contemptible caricatures, and nonsensical transparencies.

—John Landseer, *Lectures on the Art of Engraving* (1807)

The State of the Arts and the Ocean of Business, 1810

In the years 1809 and 1810, Blake seems to have been thinking even more than usual about the history of art. He took the occasion of his 1809 exhibition to write a *Descriptive Catalogue of Pictures* assessing the present state of painting in relation to its history. Shortly afterward he painted a Last Judgment that he called, oddly, "a History of Art & Science" (E 562). But even Blake seems to have suspected that the point might be lost on viewers if he did not explain himself in words. Thus "For the Year 1810" he wrote some "Additions to Blakes Catalogue of Pictures &c," the document that editors now title *A Vision of the Last Judgment,* which explains how a canvas that seems to depict a single event in the future history of the world as reported by Christians can tell the entire history of art and knowledge by revealing at once the mental pattern behind all such history at all levels. For Blake this ability seems to be the special power of what we ordinarily think of as "religion," which helps to explain, I hope, why essays on the English school of painting and on art and commerce are followed by an essay on the Christian history of engraving.

Blake had used his painting of "Sir Jeffery Chaucer and the nine and twenty Pilgrims on their journey to Canterbury" to focus the greatest part of the discussion of painting in the *Descriptive Catalogue.* It seems natural that the decision to engrave the painting (fig. 4.50) would inspire him to extend his assessment of painting to engraving, and indeed, as we shall see, the histories of painting and engraving are inextricable one from the other. Thus in 1809 or 1810, writing in his notebook, Blake seems to picture himself as the engravers' Joshua Reynolds, standing before a gathering of his colleagues to deliver a public address—pointed with "Anecdotes of Artists"—concerning the state of their particular art as an indicator of the state of art generally. He declares it "a Public Duty respectfully to address myself to The Chalcographic Society & to Express to them my opinion. . . ." He reminds them of his qualifications to offer such an opinion, "the result," he says, "of the incessant Practise & Experience of Many Years." He renders his verdict: "That Engraving as an Art is Lost in England" (*PA*, E 571–72).

No generation is without its prophets of doom to send posterity black reports of every human effort. We may wonder whether Blake's severity is therapeutic, a matter of blaming the times to maintain self-respect. At fifty-three, he has seen every artistic project launched under his own name fail. And since every project has been floated on the same optimistic enthusiasm, no doubt every sinking has struck him with proportional force. In late 1799, writing George Cumberland to thank him for his attempt—"tho it has faild of success"—to pair Blake with a prospective customer, Blake marks the approaching turn of the century, "now Exactly Twenty years since I was upon the ocean of business," with a survey of his fortunes to date. The worst that can be said is that "I am laid by in a corner as if I did not Exist & Since my [43 engravings, based on a selection from 537 preliminary watercolors, all by Blake, for an edition of] Youngs Night Thoughts have been publishd [by R. Edwards in 1797] Even [Joseph] Johnson [the bookseller] & Fuseli [the painter] have discarded my Graver." But, as an artist over forty, "having passed now near twenty years in ups & downs" and about to sail through the straits to a new century, he wants to think that from experience he has learned to "wait with Patience" for the goddess Fortune who "Alone is the Governor of Worldly Riches" (E 704).

When Blake comes to compose his *Public Address* a decade later, he finds himself waiting still. Meanwhile, he has added to his list of grievances three bad years with William Hayley in Felpham (1800–1803); a battle with the entrepreneur Robert Cromek over the illustrations of Robert Blair's *Grave* (1805–1808); Cromek's theft, as Blake imagined, of his idea for a painting of the Canterbury pilgrims, of which Thomas Stothard, as (in Blake's account) receiver of stolen conceptions, made a great success (1806–1807);[1] and a solo exhibition of his art, complete with *Descriptive Catalogue* and featuring—too late—his Chaucer painting, all of which failed miserably (1809).

"This Day is Publishd Advertizements to Blakes Canterbury Pilgrims from Chaucer. Containing Anecdotes of Artists. Price 6^{d}" (*PA*, E 571). Looking back with Blake here in 1810 over the ocean of business now stretching not twenty but thirty years to the horizon, and knowing as he must that the Canterbury pilgrims engraving—"Engravd by William Blake tho Now Surrounded by Calumny & Envy" (E 571)—is as sure to fail as all his other enterprises to date, we cannot be surprised to hear him confess that "Resentment for Personal Injuries has had some share in this Public Address" (E 574).

So even Blake admits that the severe verdict

[1] Read's "Rival *Canterbury Pilgrims*" and Ward's "Canterbury Revisited," reliable and judicious accounts based on fresh examinations of Blake's dealings with Cromek and Stothard during this period, have cast serious doubt on Blake's accusations of theft. But Bentley's "Blake Reconfigured" carefully examines the evidence once more—to Blake's benefit. Gage, apparently unaware of Read's and Ward's findings, has covered some of the same ground and added some new facts in "An Early Exhibition."

of the *Public Address* is indeed partly self-defense. But far more than the resentment of an aging engraver embittered by three decades of bad business supports the conclusion that English engraving is lost in 1810. Though Blake's conclusion is not the only possible one, it makes him a man of his time, participating in a controversy that has been growing for a century before he arrives, continues vigorously while he is on the scene, and remains active for decades afterward. To put his pessimistic account into broader perspective, we need to sample enough of the background to show that the issues he addresses and the occasions for taking positions on them are both familiar even if his positions on those issues are not—not quite. No voice in the wilderness, then. The discourse is thick.

At the surface, for example, is Blake's simple mention of "Anecdotes of Artists." Beneath it—I cite now only the most direct and obvious connections—lie Edward Edwards's *Anecdotes of Painters Who Have Resided or Been Born in England, with Critical Remarks on Their Productions* (1808); Edwards's erstwhile collaborator Horace Walpole's *Anecdotes of Painting in England* (1762–1780); the collection of anecdotes of early English artists compiled from 1713 to 1756 by George Vertue, whose manuscripts are the core of Walpole's volumes; Roger de Piles's *Art of Painting, and the Lives of the Painters,* to the translation of which Bainbrigg Buckeridge appended a small collection of the lives of English painters (first published 1706); and the master anecdotalist Giorgio Vasari's *Lives of the Painters,* eleven of which were first translated into English by William Aglionby (1685). Blake's themes, points of reference, allusions, and lexicon signal that he is not starting a game but joining one in progress. Further, as my example from Blake shows, arguments about English engraving are part of a larger argument about English painting. Engravers belong to the argument as members of a reproductive ratio in which engraving is to painting as printing is to writing. We shall begin, then, with the English-school controversy.

The Problem of the English School

Peter Gay has shown that England was often the standard against which the French philosophes measured the condition of their arts. England stood for the arts flourishing in conditions of liberty, France for the arts stagnating under class and court tyrannies (222–23, 228–38). Gay does not point out that English critics typically took the opposite view as they pondered the vexing case of the English school of painting, a thing known chiefly, like the dog in the nighttime, by its absence. "I cannot forbear adding to this little *Reproof,* an *Observation* that I have made abroad; which is, That of all the *Civilized Nations* in *Europe,* we are the only that want *Curiosity* for *Artists,*" wrote William Aglionby, the first English translator of Vasari and the author of some early dialogues on painting, in 1685 (Preface, n.p.).[2] Not long afterward Jonathan Richardson wrote of "the English school of Painting" as "a thing as yet unheard of, and whose very name (to our dishonour)

[2] Though we draw on different assortments of sources with different aims, Lipking's chapters on "the ordering of painting" are often relevant to the present discussion in a variety of complementary ways, perhaps most directly in "Horace Walpole's *Anecdotes* and the Sources of English History of Art" (127–63). On the present point see, for instance, the brief discussion of Aglionby (112).

has at present an uncouth sound." But his hopes were high: "who knows to what heights it may rise? for the English nation is not accustomed to do things by halves" (194). Contemporary witnesses sometimes agreed with twentieth-century historians that "the second part of the eighteenth century saw the establishment of a true English school of painting" (Hind, *John Raphael Smith* 5), yet those on the scene nonetheless dwelled on its failures rather than its achievements. Inferiority is a stock topic in the discourse about English art well into the nineteenth century. A standard gloomy vocabulary of urgencies, inquiries, trials, perils, and crises keeps the temperature of the rhetoric hovering around the boiling point: "The present moment is considered by artists as teeming with the crisis . . . of the destiny of their Art in England" (Hoare 211) (figs. 1.1–1.4).

From the continent word had come that, no matter what England's success had been in other areas of learning, "in the Polite Arts, we are struck dumb, and scarcely a paltry city on the continent but insults our weakness in that vulnerable part" (Green 32). The continental writers claimed that the problem was endemic and irremediable: England is a cold country for cold, gross, calculating—as opposed to warm, refined, emotional—temperaments. The notion that *raisons naturelles* affect everything from racial and personal characteristics to systems of government and artistic accomplishment is ancient, but the cries of protest from English writers blame three influential writers, the "pious priests" Jean Baptiste Dubos, Montesquieu, and Johann Joachim Winckelmann, for giving the old notion new force in "the monstrous doctrines of 'British incapacity for arts'" (W. B. S. Taylor 2:132).

In his *Critical Reflections on Poetry, Paint-*

AN

INQUIRY

Into the Real and Imaginary

OBSTRUCTIONS

TO THE

ACQUISITION of the ARTS

IN

ENGLAND.

BY JAMES BARRY,

Royal Academician, and Member of the Clementine Academy of Bologna.

Navigia, atque Agri culturas, Mœnia, Leges,
Arma, Vias, Veſteis, & cætera de genere horum,
Premia, delicias quoque vitæ funditus omneis,
Carmina, Picturas, & dædala ſigna polire,
Uſus, & impigræ ſimul Experientia mentis
Paullatim docuit pedetentim progredientes.
Sic unum quicquid paullatim protrahit ætas
In medium, ratioque in luminis eruit oras.
Namque aliud ex alio clareſcere corde videmus
Artibus, ad ſummum donec venêre cacumen.

LUCRETIUS, lib. V.

LONDON,

Printed for T. BECKET, Corner of the Adelphi, Strand.

MDCCLXXV.

1.1. James Barry, *An Inquiry Into the Real and Imaginary Obstructions to the Acquisition of the Arts in England,* 1775, title page.

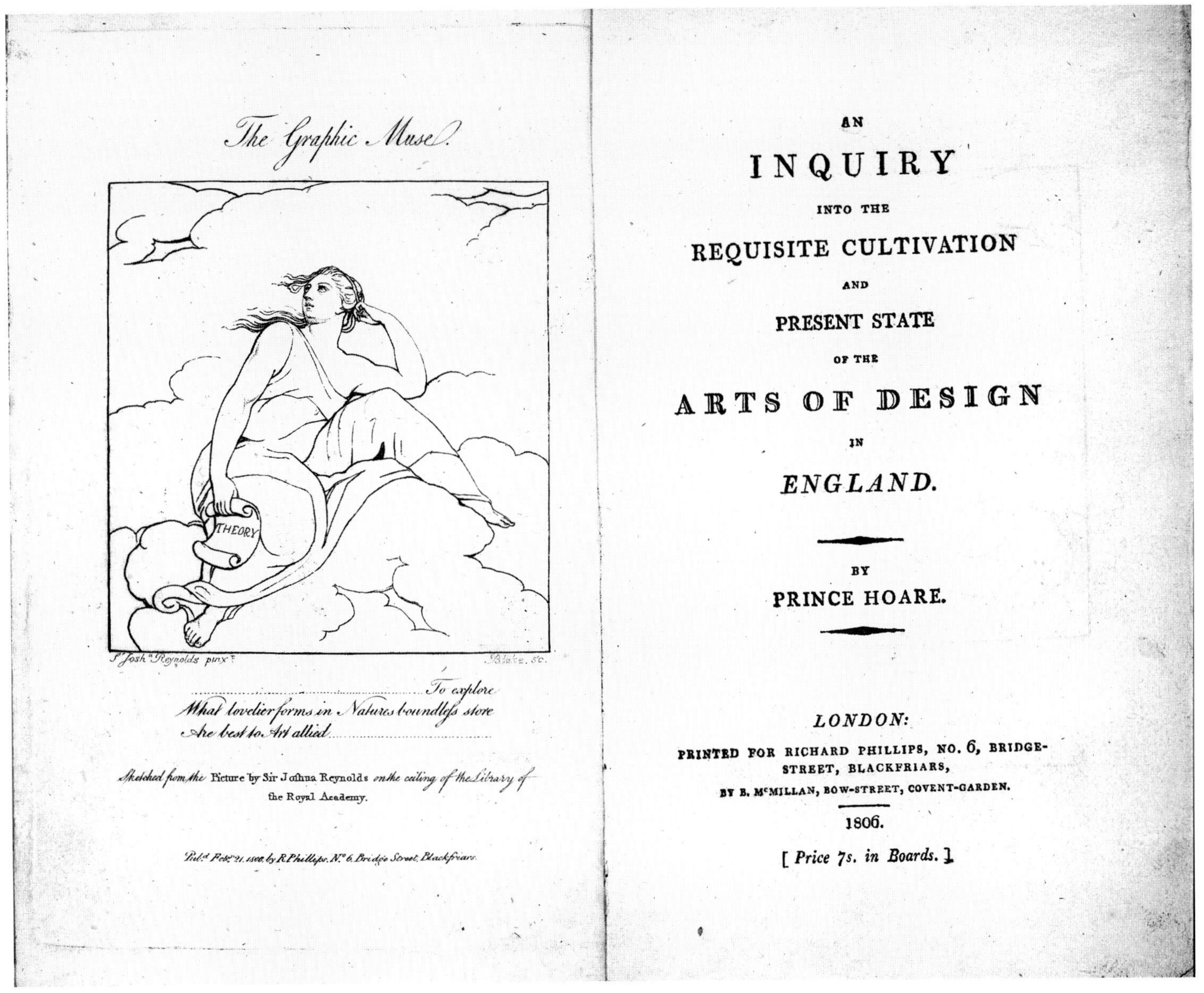

The Graphic Muse.

THEORY

Sr. Josh.a Reynolds pinx.t

Blake. sc.

................To explore
What lovelier forms in Natures boundless store
Are best to Art allied................

Sketched from the Picture by Sir Joshua Reynolds on the ceiling of the Library of the Royal Academy.

Pub.d Feb.y 21. 1806. by R.Phillips. N.o 6. Bridge Street, Blackfriars.

AN

INQUIRY

INTO THE

REQUISITE CULTIVATION

AND

PRESENT STATE

OF THE

ARTS OF DESIGN

IN

ENGLAND.

BY

PRINCE HOARE.

LONDON:

PRINTED FOR RICHARD PHILLIPS, NO. 6, BRIDGE-STREET, BLACKFRIARS,

BY B. M'MILLAN, BOW-STREET, COVENT-GARDEN.

1806.

[*Price 7s. in Boards.*]

1.2. William Blake after Joshua Reynolds, *The Graphic Muse,* engraved frontispiece to Hoare's *Inquiry.*

1.3. Prince Hoare, *An Inquiry into the Requisite Cultivation and Present State of the Arts of Design in England,* 1806, title page.

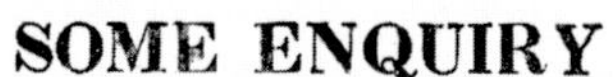

SOME ENQUIRY

INTO THE

CAUSES

WHICH HAVE

OBSTRUCTED THE ADVANCE OF
HISTORICAL PAINTING,

FOR THE LAST SEVENTY YEARS IN ENGLAND.

BY B. R. HAYDON,

HISTORICAL PAINTER.

"Nor stony tower, nor walls of beaten brass,
Nor airless dungeon, nor strong links of iron,
Can be retentive to the strength of spirit."—*Shakspeare.*

London:
PUBLISHED BY RIDGWAY, PICCADILLY;
AND AT B. R. HAYDON'S EXHIBITION ROOM, WESTERN
EXCHANGE, OLD BOND STREET.

1829.

1.4. Benjamin Haydon, *Some Enquiry into the Causes Which Have Obstructed the Advance of Historical Painting, for the Last Seventy Years in England,* 1829, title page.

Inquiries span the half century, centered on the French Revolution, in which the "present state" of the visual arts in England seemed in a crisis of "cultivation," "acquisition," and "obstruction." Haydon's self-composed epitaph employs one of the most prominent themes of English-school discourse, the need for state patronage, to cast himself as the (representative) victim of government neglect.

> HERE/LIETH THE BODY/OF/BENJAMIN ROBERT HAYDON/An English Historical Painter, who, in a struggle to make the People, the Legislature, the Nobility, and the Sovereign of England give due dignity and rank to the highest Art, which had ever languished, and until the Government intervenes, ever will languish in England, fell a victim to his ardour and his love of country; an evidence that to seek the benefit of your Country by telling the Truth to Power, is a crime that can only be expiated by the ruin and destruction of the Man who is so Patriotic and so imprudent. [Quoted in Eric George 307]

Hoare's *Inquiry* of 1806 bore a frontispiece engraving of *The Graphic Muse* by Blake after a painting by Joshua Reynolds, widely acknowledged as the founding father of the English school. Reynolds did his painting for the ceiling of the library in Somerset House (premises of the Royal Academy), where it was surrounded by allegories of nature, history, allegory, and fable in the four coves. The scroll that reads "Theory" in the engraving reads "The-

ing, and Music, first translated in 1719 and reissued several times, Dubos (1670–1742) used England prominently to document his claim "*That physical causes have probably had also a share in the surprizing progress of arts and sciences*" (2:107). No matter how much Henry VIII, Elizabeth, and Charles I loved painting, said Dubos, from their time to this "England has not hitherto produced so much as one painter, who deserves to be ranked among the artists of the first, or even of the second class" because the climate has been too cold and too wet for painters, though "warm enough" for "good musicians," "excellent poets," and "eminent men in most sciences and professions" (2:113). In *The Spirit of Laws,* translated into English in 1750, Montesquieu (1689–1755) laid down a speculative but systematic analysis "Of Laws in Relation to the Nature of the Climate" in books 14–19. Though Montesquieu was interested in English government, not English painting, *The Spirit of Laws* gave new life and credibility to older claims such as Dubos's.[3] Winckelmann (1717–1768) applied what he learned from Montesquieu about *raisons naturelles* to art history. Winckelmann proposed that a temperate climate and a moderate government "will account for the progress of the arts in Athens, in a similar state of things at Florence" (*Writings* 108)—a sequence that we shall meet again. To friends and visitors, including James Barry, Winckelmann apparently spoke ill of English prospects in the fine arts so often that his views became widely known (Leppmann 237).

Coming as they did insistently from several influential sources, these charges struck an English nerve and the pain persisted. W. B. Sarsfield Taylor, writing as late as the 1840s, cites "the Winkelmann and Du Bos problem, of our 'unhappy climate' and 'Boetian dulness,'" as a formula. He claims that the problem has been "finally solved"—by exhibitions of "*merely* British pictures" in 1818 and 1819—but the extravagance of his protests suggests that the humiliation, if less, still lingered (2:245–47). Earlier, in 1806, a year that will have a special place in our history, Prince Hoare had struck the same note: "It has been, and yet remains, a theme of triumph in the mouths of other nations, that England has not been able to exhibit any incontestable proofs of power" in painting and that the cause may be simply that "the national intellect of the English *is not disposed* to eminence in the plastic arts." If so, "all attempts" and "all hopes" must "terminate in despair" (Hoare 155–56). Most native writers felt obliged to retort directly (see, e.g., Hoare 204–5), usually with the formula that the problem was not "Genius" but "opportunity" (Green 36) or "means" (Northcote 1:398).

We can establish basic points of reference through James Barry's several analyses of the problems of English painting. By the time he sends *A Letter to the Dilettanti Society, Respecting the Obtention of Certain Matters Essentially Necessary for the Improvement of Public Taste, and for Accomplishing the Original Views of the Royal Academy of Great Britain* (1798), Barry has battled his way through nearly a half century of fierce disputes inspired by events, often disappointing events, in his own life as a working painter (fig. 1.5). Though his writings are

[3] Montesquieu's highly favorable account of British government appears in bk. 11, chap. 6, of *The Spirit of Laws.* He spent eighteen months in England during 1729–1731 and recorded his impressions of the country, mostly negative, in his "Notes on England." The "Notes" do not comment on English painting.

ory is the knowledge of what is truly Nature" in the painting (Hutchison 66, Penny 284 and color pl. 112). In view of Blake's attitude toward Reynolds's "theory" as well as his practice, the ironies of the conjunction are manifold.

In 1802, late in a life that spanned sixty-five years and ended in 1806, James Barry began this mezzotinted self-image. The ravages of a life lived in stubborn resistance have replaced the thoughtful intensity of earlier portraits.

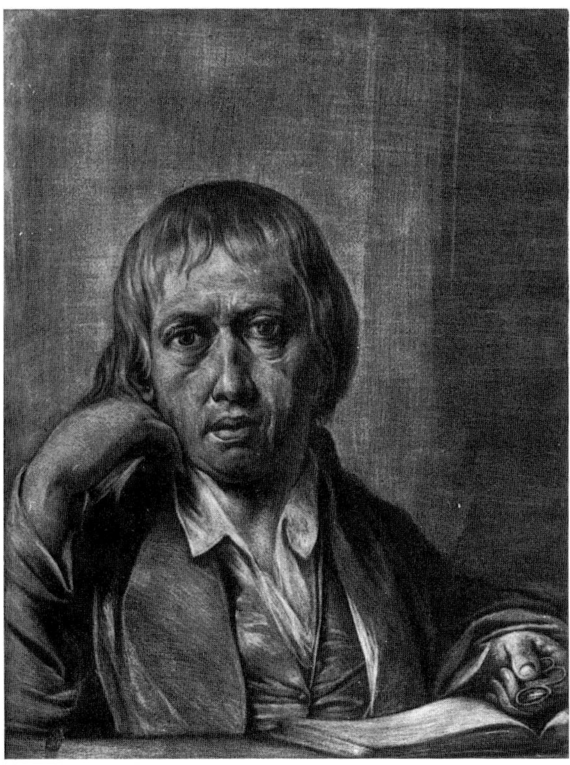

1.5. James Barry, self-portrait, mezzotint, c. 1802.

anything but cool and detached, they have real virtues and uses. They are fairly comprehensive and representative, if memorably hyperbolic and indignant. They change generally with the times and particularly with the occasion, and, although they can be aggressively inconsistent, they show after all a fundamental consistency.

The Ancients

The historical scope of Barry's arguments increases steadily over the years, but the plot is implicit from the start. It is well summarized in one of John Brown's titles: *A Dissertation on the Rise, Union and Power, the Progressions, Separations and Corruptions, of Poetry and Music* (1763). Barry substituted the more familiar sister arts of poetry and painting, but the story of a decline from a unified origin is the great commonplace. His *Letter* puts English art at the end of a historical narrative that begins as far back as a pre-Greek "Master Art." Since this ancient art is supposed to have been essentially pictorial rather than poetic, "Painting . . . is the real art of wisdom, and Poetry is only an account or relation of it" (64). Barry is probably thinking of hieroglyphics, the subject of much speculation at the time: "the arts of design," he says in his Academy lectures, are "the first, the universal and natural written language" (Wornum 83). ("Thus we see the common foundation of all these various modes of WRITING and SPEAKING, was a PICTURE or IMAGE, presented to the *imagination* thro' the eyes and ears," claims William Warburton in *The Divine Legation of Moses* [3.4:120]. "The first and most natural way of communicating our thoughts by marks or figures, is by tracing out the images of things" [3.4:71].) This myth of origins and the first-is-best logic that supports it are evidences, if evidence is needed, of the Enlightenment interest in the origins of evolutionary processes.

Furthermore, the pictorial master art is Barry's contribution to the persistent effort to raise painting—degraded by its association with manual labor in the service of the spectator's sense experience—to the level of its sister art, poetry, which had been traditionally dignified by its role in the reader's moral and philosophical education through ideas in language. Nonetheless, as we shall see, Barry's master art is not a particularly coherent part of his general view. He is going the usual poet-painter analogy one better but has little use for it in his broader argument. His earlier declarations that "little is known of the original state of any thing. . . . We can never decompound sufficiently so as to discover these stamina [at the origin of various characters and national groups] in their simple and naked state" (*Inquiry* 83–84) are more consistent.

Extending his history backward beyond ancient Greece, Barry imagines a society that delivered knowledge directly, which is to say optically in pictures that also served as words, rather than indirectly through words about images; and delivered it wholly rather than partially: "all these knowledges existed together, in a more complete and united state" (*Inquiry* 64). The subsequent history of art thus becomes a tale of fragmentation and corrupt transmission alternating with strenuous attempts at reintegration, accounting for the apparent rise and decline of painting at different periods. Homer, Plato, Pythagoras, and Thales, among other painters manqué, bring fragments of this original pictorial knowledge into Greece (62). In most accounts, such as George Turnbull's *Treatise on Ancient Painting* (1740), the ancient arts peak in Periclean Athens. In Barry's history, however, the Greek cycle peaks in the reign of Alexander. At some point in Barry's scheme between the pre-Greek and the Hellenistic periods, decline turns to progress. Barry's *Letter* is short on reasons for the reversal, but in earlier writings he described the "slow progress" (*Inquiry* 40) by which the ancient Greeks "perfected" (41) art as a movement from line to color to tone. "Here we find them beginning with an outline. . . . A Corinthian and his followers first attempt to fill up this outline with one colour. . . . Others come to have an idea of light and shadow.—They no longer use simple colours."[4] These are the words of William Aglionby, but Barry is not disputing them. When he asserts in his Royal Academy lectures that we must "reject as fabulous . . . early accounts of the progressional discovery of the art in Greece" (Wornum 71), he simply means that Greece cannot claim all the credit. Progressional discovery is as essential to his story as the internationalism implicit in his refusal to allow that any one nation might have a special genius.[5]

As we expect in a history patterned by improvement, technique becomes the most obvious sign of progressive change and artists appear as specialist inventors identified with technical advances: "Apolodorus is distinguished for a judicious choice of nature. Zeuxis for good colouring. Parhasius is first remarkable for symmetry and expression. Pamphilus joins the study of mathematics to art. Pausias excells at fore-shortening his figures. Euphranor introduces majesty; and Apelles, grace. . . . [I]n whatever way we take it [the history of art], it was equally a work of progressive and accumulated experience" that improved upon a beginning always "dry, cold, meagre, and wooden" (*Inquiry* 41–43, 45). Barry uses his narrative of "acquisition" (48), as he calls it elsewhere, to counter the explanations from "genius" or "climate" (64) with which the continental critics had dismissed England's chances of producing great painters.

The Vasari Canon and Its Extensions

For several good reasons the next cycle, in Italy rather than Greece, is the real center of Barry's narrative, from which both the Greek past and the English future have been pro-

[4] This narrative of Greek technical progress is ancient. Cf. Quintilian 4:451 (bk. 12, chap. 10.2–6). Perhaps it first appears in English writing with Aglionby's description of Greek painters "*contenting themselves with drawing the out lines of one* Colour, *and shadowing them within: Some time after,* Cleophantus *of* Corinth *Invented Variety of* Colouring" (36).

[5] Cf. Fuseli's similar attitude toward the myth of Greek progress—"If ever legend deserved our belief" (Wornum 394)—and its transferability. Fuseli describes the Greeks' step-by-step advancement from "skiagrams" to "polychroms" (Wornum 350–51).

jected. He sees the Italian school through Vasari's *Lives* as a steady technical progression from primitive dryness and linearity to an advanced richness of color and tone. Most of the third chapter of Barry's 1775 *Inquiry into the Real and Imaginary Obstructions to the Acquisition of the Arts in England* consists of a long quotation from Vasari describing the three ages in which Italian art advanced from a "low beginning" to "the top of perfection" (19–20).[6] Reading the Vasari canon back into ancient Greece, Barry finds the same pattern of acquisition and finds it again in the recent history of art, which seeks to extend the canon through the synthetic program of the Carracci, "uniting the Grecian with the Italian art, which had been the unremitting object of my own attention." The result is "the true sublime style of historical art, *founded* upon the Greek purity of design, and *blended* with whatever was great and estimable in the celebrated leaders of the Italian schools" (my emphasis, 50) (fig. 1.6).

At its most optimistic and symmetrical this is a history of Chinese boxes, each containing and replicating but enlarging the scope of the others: Greek art moves from line to color and tone but its characteristic virtue is line (purity of design), while the leading characteristics of Italian art, which moves through a similar pattern, are color and tone. The goal of modern art is to move again through the pattern, blending Greek and Italian excellences at a higher level. George Turnbull, whose subtitle includes the expected *Rise, Progress, and Decline,* calls the relation between cycles "Analogy" (xxii). The relation and its predictive tendency are reminiscent of typological interpretation—if Apelles has his Raphael and Zeuxis his Titian, who are to be their English counterparts?—except that this typology has been rationalized with a heavy dose of Locke, as we shall see. In Turnbull, furthermore, the specialization of skill is given a negative turn through human imperfection. Raphael and Apelles lacked coloring skills as Zeuxis and Titian lacked drawing. This is a common rationale for specialization: Fuseli and John Opie both use it in their Academy lectures.[7] But since improvement lies nonetheless with comprehensiveness, Turnbull promotes the pedagogy by which all painters try to combine all skills.[8]

[6] Alsop discusses the Vasari canon and the associated idea of art history as a "progression, consisting of a long series of triumphant solutions of technical problems" (111; also 110–15 and in passing). Alsop, whose interest is mainly in the influences of Vasarian art history on collecting, is also able to show how the canon was extended into the past to include the "primitives" Cimabue and Giotto as well as forward to include, among others, Veronese, Tintoretto, Rubens, and Poussin.

[7] Opie and Fuseli in Wornum 259 and 381. See also "Formulas of Augmentation" in Eaves, *Blake's Theory* 138–45. See also, however, Fuseli's criticism of Vasari and of Carracci eclecticism (Wornum 342–43, 394–98, 548–49) for the lowest-common-denominator mediocrity they encourage. But Fuseli restricts his criticism to theory only: "Separate the precept from the practice, the artist from the teacher; and the Carracci are in possession of my submissive homage" (Wornum 396).

[8] Turnbull explores the analogy between classical and Italian art in chap. 2, 18–48.

Charles Dempsey has argued that in Bologna during the early 1580s—a generation after Vasari—the three Carracci founded the Carracci Academy on a program of combining Venetian/Northern naturalism with Roman/Tuscan idealism: "to assimilate to this [Roman] canon the naturalistic and illusionistic canons of Venice and Emilia, exemplified with the examples of Titian and Correggio, and in so doing render the ideal with convincing verisimilitude" (247). Paintings so made would aspire to delight and instruct by appealing to viewers at the level of the natural and then elevating them to the level of the ideal. As Dempsey indicates, the debate in which the Carracci Academy participated reached well beyond local practice, even as far as Counter-Reformation disputes over artistic skill and philosophical truth in the art of Michelangelo. Annibale Carracci's *Dead Christ Mourned* arrived in England in 1797 as part of the famous Orléans stock, first exhibited in London and then sold on the confused and hectic art market created by the French Revolution (and the failure of the Boydell Shakespeare Gallery). Though the financial maneuvers behind the sale were complicated, the reserve price of this pietà, 3½ times greater than that for Raphael's

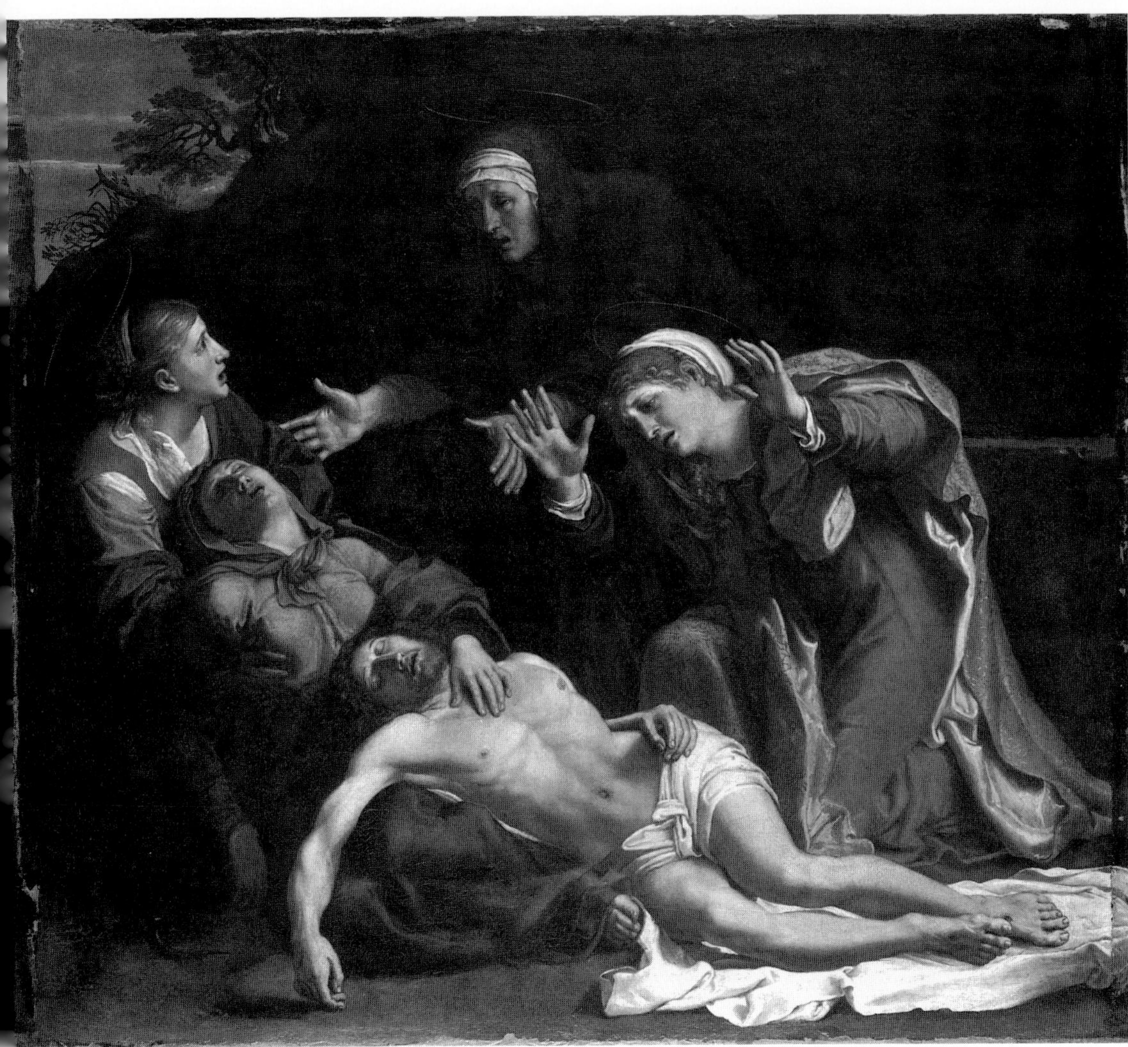

Madonna and Child, gives some indication of the value placed on it at the time (see Dempsey 293 and Reitlinger 1:32).

1.6. Annibale Carracci, *The Dead Christ Mourned,* oil, 1603–1604?

Patronage and the English Inheritance

We have been isolating a history of production from the history of consumption that is necessarily coordinated with it. As the lists of names in previous passages show, artists control the former, audiences the latter. The commonplace modern personification of an audience in a purchaser who drops by the selling place, the bookstore or gallery, to buy products, books or pictures, before returning home to finish off the act of consumption is too watery a notion to be of much use when we discuss the history of a national art. Traditionally, from the artist's point of view, the audience is personified in the patron, who in the most potent incarnation lives up to the rather overwhelming parental promise of his etymology. As father, advocate, defender, and patron saint, he may well have the power to dictate the form of the product that he will then consume. Furthermore, the special cultural status of artworks can make them, for the patron, an investment, since they are not consumed in their consumption but preserved as collectibles for reconsumption, often at a higher rate than the one originally paid to the artist. Under the circumstances it is not surprising that patrons and patronage were never far from the minds of writers concerned with the health of the English school of painting, and we can hardly expect to account for the discourse without acknowledging the central role of patronage in it.

Barry persistently coordinates successful art with successful patronage. The high place of Hellenistic art in his scheme, for instance, is apparently the combined product of unobstructed technical progress and unobstructing patronage in the person of "the unboundedly generous, magnanimous, unenvious" Alexander the Great, the unpatronizing patron who encouraged "unrestrained display" of "unrestrained abilities of the heroes, of every species" (*Letter* 42; see also Wornum 77). (Compare Quintilian: "It was, however, from about the period of the reign of Philip down to that of the successors of Alexander that painting flourished more especially, although the different artists are distinguished for different excellences" [4:451–53; bk. 12, chap. 10.6]. Pliny's Alexander is a magnanimous showoff who allows good painters to correct his ideas on art and gives them his favorite mistresses [9:325; bk. 35, chap. 36.84–87].) The Periclean and Hellenistic ideals are more alike than they may appear. Both stand for the conditions of liberty under which the fine arts have flourished. In Winckelmann's *History of Ancient Art,* Alexander forces the Greeks into the state of "disarmed freedom" that, along with luxury and munificence, brings about "the epoch of the highest refinement in art" (4:225; bk. 10, chap. 1). When Alexander is demoted as a patron, as he is by Fuseli, it is usually for the tyranny that squelches art: "When the spirit of liberty forsook the public, grandeur had left the private mind of Greece . . . and Alexander was become the representative of Jupiter" (Wornum 370). Liberty is a critical element in the analogy because it was felt to be, with commerce, an English specialty.

Patronage is equally important in Barry's account of Italian art, epitomized by Leonardo da Vinci, who would have been "able to dispute the palm with the stoutest of those Greeks"

(*Letter* 43) had it not been for the interference of envious patrons: "the Medici family was the real *blight* which interrupted the further growth of Art at Florence" (49). The best patronage of the day came from the church, which at just the right moment in European history "opened a new and large field for the exercise of the arts" (30). Despite serious "abuses," the power of Roman Christianity "derived from intellect" (32). Barry asserts the "infinite importance of such a government as the Papal to the arts which humanize society" (29). The contrast between tyrannical individual patrons who impose upon painters and institutional patronage that opens new fields for exercise will reappear in Barry's analysis of English art.

Barry, like most writers who want to avoid a diagnosis of England's chronic artistic backwardness based on fixed conditions of climate or native talent, tells instead a story of artistic development interrupted by anti-artistic events. In *The Present State of the Arts in England* (1755), Hogarth's French friend André Rouquet had acknowledged the interruption of the development of English arts by "intestine divisions," "civil broils," and "foreign wars" (12). For Barry the Reformation is the great divide that prevented England from receiving, as it otherwise would have done and as France did, the artistic benefits of Italian painting and its system of patronage: "the accidental circumstance of the change of religion . . . gave us a dislike to the superior and nobler parts" of art to be found in "Christian story" (*Inquiry* 64–65).

In the long run this turned out to be a compelling and immensely useful explanation. Some thirty years later Prince Hoare's *Inquiry into the Requisite Cultivation and Present State of the Arts of Design in England* (1806) also blames the Reformation for a "general depression" (266) in the visual arts under Elizabeth I (see also Shee 105–8n). The "dislike," as Barry calls it, took the form of an immense displacement in which English art vacated the central place that art had occupied in Italian Rome. In flooded the schismatics, who abandoned the main ideas of Christian story to brawl over the peripheral minutiae of Christian doctrine, leaving would-be history painters without an approved, which is to say a patronizable, subject. At the same time the Protestant confusion of visual representation with idolatry forced English artists out of the main traditions of history painting open to Raphael and Michelangelo and into the narrow byways of "landscape, portrait, and still life . . . the artists were then naturally led to practice only the baser and lower branches" (*Inquiry* 65). Published more than half a century after Barry's *Inquiry*, Benjamin Haydon's 1829 *Enquiry* (fig. 1.4) once again identifies "the mere accident of the Reformation" as the turning point in English painting for giving portraiture, "having no counter-balance" (15), a self-sustaining monopoly: "the Reformation destroyed the equilibrium of patronage" (35) and thus threw the artistic economy of production and consumption out of kilter.

Barry, like almost everyone else who reviews the history of English patronage, extols the energetic "attempts" by Charles I "to introduce arts and elegance into the kingdom" (*Inquiry* 70). Barry is in no position to praise Charles too highly. He cannot share Charles's enthusiasm for Rubens, whose painting Barry criticizes harshly (57–59), or for Charles's court painter, Sir Anthony van Dyck, whom Barry dismisses with "Lely, &c." as just one more well-trained portrait painter (70). For one who regards England as the heir of Greek and Italian history painting, Charles's Flemish connections are diversions from the main road of

European art. And Charles in any case made little difference to English art history because all his progress was wiped out when the "zeal for religious canting and reformation" (70) re-asserted itself in the Puritan revolution.

Valentine Green's enthusiasm for Charles's achievements is more typical:

> In England, too, the flame had begun, and its heat was promoted by the casual visit of Rubens to the Court of London . . . in the Character of Envoy from the States of Brabant. At his leisure, those works were produced which embellish the Chapel of Whitehall, and a few other Pictures. . . . But his pupil Vandyck, whose residence here was of long duration, and whose employment being so much about the Person of the King, and those of the Royal Family, that Dobson, Cooper, and Johnson . . . exerted themselves so successfully, as to procure them the approbation of their own, and the admiration of the present times. [8]

The more successful Charles's encouragements are made out to be, the more drastic and unnatural the interruption seems: "And had not the *Bloody-Principled Zealots,* . . . under the pretext of a *Reformed Sanctity,* destroyed both the Best of Kings, and the Noblest of Courts, we might to this day have seen these *Arts* flourish amongst us; and particularly, this of *Painting,* which was the *Darling* of that Vertuous *Monarch*" (Aglionby, Preface, n.p). Green concludes that "the national troubles" (8) of the revolution forced painting again to serve "local purposes, and the gratification of private taste" (35)—coded phrases that in this discourse usually mean "portraits." For Green, "local" and "private" oppose "national" and "public," as expressed through "national policy" (34) by the government on the model of France under Louis XIV.

Institutions of Art: The Royal Academy

> And whereas we have thought fit to establish in this our City of London a Society for the purposes of cultivating and improving the Arts of Painting, Sculpture & Architecture under the Name and title of the Royal Academy of Arts, and under our own immediate Patronage and Protection.
>
> —George III, from the diploma awarded to academicians upon election to the Royal Academy

> England, so far as we have yet seen, obtained her Royal Academy under yet better auspices: here was no flourish of princely donation; for, except for a *loan* of a few thousand pounds, since *paid back,* I believe, the British academicians remain to this day unloaded with any overwhelming burden of gratitude. . . .
>
> —"Irish Artists II," *New Monthly Magazine,* 1824

Prince Hoare also declared that "the experience of ages has shewn that on the genius of existing governments depends the state of the Plastic Arts." Nearly comatose under Elizabeth, they "revived" under Charles, "were again beaten down by the revolutionists," and, "as if stunned . . . they remained languid and prostrate until the present reign [of George III]. . . . Never did any art, in any country, strive so long against persecution and neglect" (266–67).

"The present reign" was a long one. It began in 1760—Hoare is writing in 1806—and would not end, at least officially, until 1820. The notion that English painting did not rise and walk until the middle of the eighteenth century was standard. Hoare allows the first half of the century only one bright spot, an "untimely spring" associated with St. Paul's and thus with the architect Sir Christopher Wren and the painter (of the cupola) Sir James Thornhill in the reign of Anne, followed, however, by "an ungenial damp" and "clouds of darkness" (114). The darkness settled in until the founding of the Royal Academy in 1768, featuring Joshua Reynolds as "the Aeneas of the hour" (117) (fig. 1.7).

Hoare is repeating the myth that served for decades as the reigning account of the founding of the English school. It is well represented in Burke's obituary of Reynolds: "He was the first Englishman who added the praise of the elegant arts to the other glories of his country" (quoted in Cunningham 1:328). This plain assertion gradually acquires its more extravagant form, as here from Cunningham's own revision of Pilkington's often-revised *Dictionary of Painters:* "It has been well observed, that after Kneller, painting fell in England into a state of barbarism, each artist wandering in darkness, till Reynolds, like the sun, dispelled the gloom. . . . Hence it may justly be said, that the English School was of his foundation. To the grandeur, truth, and simplicity of Titian, and the daring strength of Rembrandt, he united the chasteness and delicacy of Vandyck. Delighted with the picturesque beauties of Rubens . . ." (493). Reynolds's eclecticism is translated into mythical powers of assimilation. Shining forth as father of the race, he becomes an all-sufficient point of origin for the English school.[9]

Reynolds's importance to the founding of the English school lies at least as much in his institutional roles, as first president and de facto ideologue of the Royal Academy, as in his successes as a painter. As the quotation indicates, he symbolizes the kind of internationalism and eclecticism that make academic education viable. The theory of painting that he offered in his annual presentations to the Academy was not merely tolerant in spirit. Its inclusiveness was programmatic. Because "students should not presume to think themselves qualified to invent, till they were acquainted with those stores of invention the world already possesses, and had by that means accumulated sufficient materials for the mind to work with," the recommended exercises for "forming the mind of a young Artist" emphasize amalgamation: "begin with such exercises as the Italians call a *Pasticcio* composition of the different excellencies which are dispersed in all other works of the same kind" (dis. 12, 222).

That is, the narratives of the Vasari canon and its extensions are, among other things, pedagogical programs that readily adapt to systemization and institutionalization. That is why Jonathan Richardson, the most enthusiastic early promoter of education as the basis for the formation of an English school of painting,

[9] Cf. Fuseli's description of Reynolds, Wornum 406. Though I am quoting from the edition of Pilkington that Allan Cunningham revised, I am not proposing that Cunningham brought the *Dictionary* entirely into line with his own *Lives.*

(OVERLEAF)

Henry Singleton's painting *Royal Academicians Gathered in Their Council Chambers, 1793, to Judge the Work of the Students* (1795) shows the institution beginning its second phase after the death of Reynolds in 1792. According to the key published by C. Bestland with his engraving of 1802, many of the artists with whom we are concerned appear in this group portrait, including Barry, Fuseli, Stothard, Opie, Bartolozzi, and Northcote. The Pennsylvanian Benjamin West (near the center with his hat on), George III's favorite history painter, at least until 1810, was elected president to replace Reynolds. (This is the year West thought he was learning the "Venetian secret" from Mary Anne Provis and her father. See the commentary to fig. 4.23.) Thomas Lawrence, who had been elected a member of the Academy just the year before, is sitting at front left with his legs crossed. He would become president at West's death in 1820. The American painter John Singleton Copley (with cane) and Lawrence's friend Joseph Farington (facing Copley), whose diaries are a major source of information about the period, are standing in front of the Laocoön cast that Blake came to the Academy to sketch for his engraving for Rees's *Cyclopaedia,* probably in 1815 (Essick, *Separate Plates* 99–100 and pls. 51–53). According to Frederick Tatham, while Blake was drawing the Laocoön, Fuseli—long associated with the Acad-

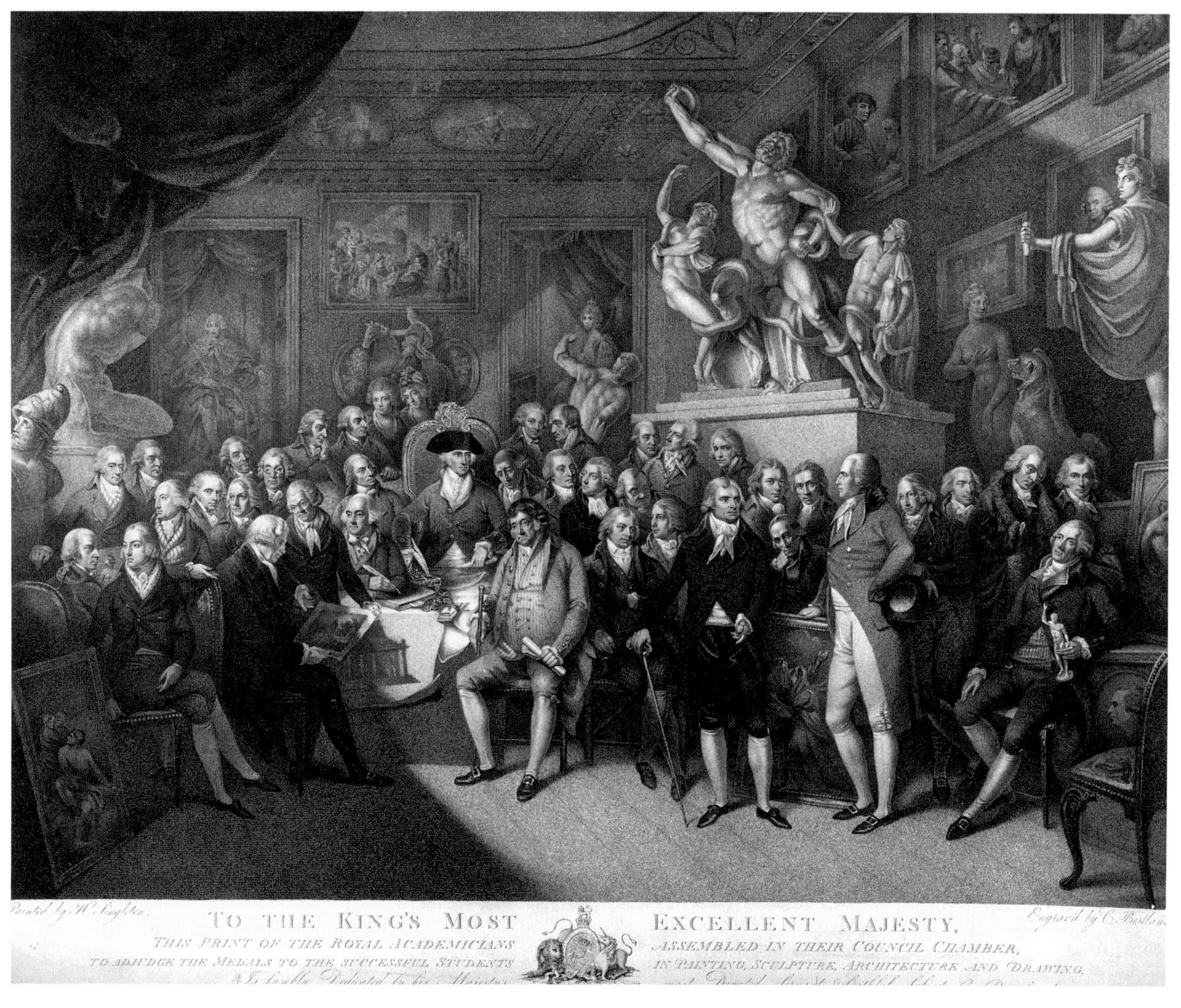

1.7. C. Bestland after Henry Singleton, *The Royal Academicians Assembled in Their Council Chamber [1793], to Adjudge the Medals to the Successful Students in Painting, Sculpture, Architecture, and Drawing,* engraving, 1802, and key.

emy as professor of painting and, since 1804, keeper—remarked, "You a student you ought to teach us" (quoted in Essick, *Separate Plates* 99).

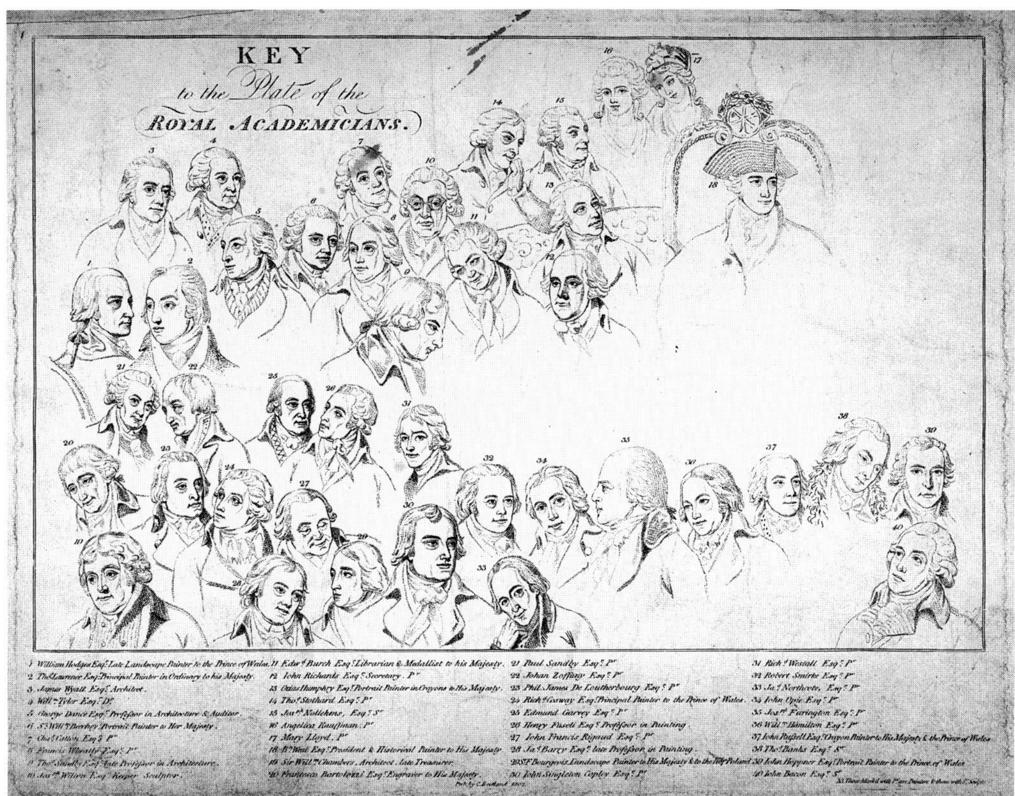

found Roger de Piles's *balance de la peinture* so useful.[10] The *balance* is a pedagogical distillation of the Carracci program (fig. 1.8). Art histories of "acquisition," such as Barry's tale of the development of Greek art from line to color and tone, arrange the elements of de Piles's *balance* in narrative form. When the elements are extracted from the narrative and arranged as categories on a grid, or scorecard, they reveal new uses in teaching, learning, and judging. Although as de Piles presents it the *balance* is rudimentary, the rudiments can be extended, refined, and applied at any level of production or consumption to analyze a painting, or the cumulative oeuvre of a painter, or potentially any conceivable body of work, into components that can be scored separately by number, then totaled.

Jonathan Richardson seems to have under-

[10] See "The Uncomplicated Richardson," which includes a discussion of de Piles's *balance* (Lipking 109–26). More recently, Gibson-Wood has argued persuasively that Richardson, looking to modernize, methodize, and rationalize, deliberately anchored his "eminently learnable" (44) connoisseurship in a Lockean epistemology that was later obscured by his son's editorial alterations in 1773 and 1792. I have, however, cited the edition of 1792 instead of earlier ones because of its availability to Blake's contemporaries. Gibson-Wood discusses Richardson and de Piles on 44–46.

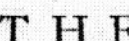

THE

PRINCIPLES

OF

PAINTING,

Under the HEADS of

Anatomy	Contraft	Harmony	Paffion
Attitude	Colouring	Hiftory	Portraiture
Accident	Defign	Invention	Sculpture
Architecture	Difpofition	Landfkip	Style
Compofition	Draperies	Lights	Truth
Claro-obfcuro	Expreffion	Proportion	Unity, &c.

In which is Contained,
An Account of the *Athenian*, *Roman*, *Venetian* and *Flemifh* SCHOOLS.

To which is Added,
The BALANCE of PAINTERS.
BEING
The Names of the moft noted PAINTERS, and their Degrees of Perfection in the Four principal Parts of their ART: Of fingular Ufe to thofe who would form an Idea of the VALUE of *Paintings* and *Pictures*.

Written Originally in *French* by Monf. *DU PILES*, Author of *The Lives of the Painters*.

And now firft Tranflated into ENGLISH.
By a PAINTER.

LONDON:
Printed for J. OSBORN, at the *Golden Ball*, in *Pater-nofter Row*. M.DCC.XLIII.

The Balance *of* PAINTERS. 297

A

CATALOGUE

OF THE

Names of the moft noted PAINTERS, and their Degrees of Perfection, in the Four principal Parts of *Painting*; fuppofing abfolute Perfection to be divided into twenty Degrees or Parts.

NAMES.	*Compofition.* Deg.	*Defign.* Deg.	*Colouring.* Deg.	*Expreffion.* Deg.
A.				
Albano	14	14	10	6
B.				
Barocchio	14	15	6	10
Baffano, Jacomo	6	8	17	
Belino, John	4	6	14	
Bourdon	10	8	8	4
Le Brun	10	16	8	16

C.

stood that de Piles's four meager categories are the core of a universal pedagogy that could improve both supply and demand, or production and consumption, by teaching the artists through academies and simultaneously teaching the "nobility, and gentry" to be "lovers of Painting, and connoisseurs" (196).[11] Artists could paint individual works by it (starting with line and moving toward harmony, re-

[11] See Dubos's laudatory critique of de Piles's *balance* (1: 224–25). He complains only that de Piles's four categories should be five.

298 *The* Balance *of* PAINTERS.

NAMES.	*Composition.* Deg.	*Design.* Deg.	*Colouring.* Deg.	*Expression.* Deg.
C.				
The *Caracches*	15	17	13	13
Da Caravaggio, Polydore	10	17	0	15
Correggio	13	13	15	12
Da Cortona, Pietro	16	14	12	6
D.				
Diepembeck	11	10	14	6
Dominichino	15	17	9	17
Durer, Albert	8	10	10	8
G.				
Giorgione	8	9	18	4
Giofeppino	10	10	6	2
Guerchino	18	10	10	4
H.				
Holbein, Hans	9	10	16	13
I.				
Jordano, Luca	13	12	9	6
Jourdaens, James	10	8	16	6
L.				
Lanfranco	14	13	10	5
Van Leyden, Lucas	8	6	6	4
M.				
Michael Angelo Buonarotti	8	17	4	8
Michael Angelo da Caravaggio	6	6	16	0
Mutiano	6	8	15	4
P.				
Palma the elder	5	6	16	0
Palma the younger	12	9	14	6

Par-

1.8. Roger de Piles, *The Principles of Painting,* 1743, title page and pages 297, 298.

In Roger de Piles's *balance,* Rubens and Salviati tie for first with 65, the Carracci come out very well with a 58, while Holbein (48) outstrips Michelangelo (37), largely because Holbein received a higher mark for coloring, 16 versus 4. The pleasures of de Piles's method were infectious. Many readers, such as the one who marked up this copy of *The Principles of Painting,* were drawn into the competition, computing totals, disputing de Piles's judgments, and adding new painters and categories.

capitulating the history of Greek art) or develop entire oeuvres according to it (as Reynolds in his first discourse says that Raphael progressed from an early dry manner to the grand style of painting); institutions could teach from it (a "method of study," Barry calls his progression [*Inquiry* 49], and the Academy curriculum roughly corresponded); the public could learn true taste from it, critics could judge paintings by it, and the pattern of art history could be described with it. By the end of the century de Piles's *balance* no doubt looked like the relic of a simpler age that had hoped to reduce complex masterpieces to simple rules, but in fact by then the principle of the *balance* was embedded in well-established art histories, curricula, and institutions.

As the theoretician of the Academy, Reynolds extends the boundaries of eclecticism far beyond Barry's, finding a secondary theoretical place—which for Reynolds always means a pedagogical place—for Rembrandt, Rubens, and van Dyck alongside the Italians. He does so, however, in the standard way: extending the Vasari canon by tracing the lineage of Rembrandt, Rubens, and van Dyck to the Venetians and especially to Titian, who was to color what Raphael was to line and what Michelangelo was to expression. Reynolds's famous final discourse, which studies the contradiction between Reynolds the theorist and Reynolds the painter, shows how ambivalent he could be about the influence of his eclecticism on his own practice. But then after all he was a born compromiser and combiner—a born president of the Royal Academy—for whom the exclusive pursuit of Michelangelesque purity belonged to the fantastic realm of farewell speeches and deathbed regrets. The pedagogical inclusiveness of his penultimate discourse, which finds a legitimate if peripheral place even for the likes of Hogarth and Gainsborough, is more faithful to his premises: "The less we confine ourselves in the choice of examples, the more advantage we shall derive from them; and the nearer we shall bring our performances to a correspondence with nature and the great general rules of Art" (dis. 14, 247).

In the background of his first discourse, which presents a rationale for the establishment of the Academy, lies an assortment of familiar themes drawn from the ongoing dispute over the English school. He begins with the key theme, belatedness (problem) and arrival (solution)—"why . . . so long" (13). In the hallowed tradition of Jonathan Richardson, Reynolds pairs that theme with the equally familiar one of ignorance and education. English art is late because England's Academy, the institutionalized form of education ("Institution . . . to advance our knowledge of the Arts" [14]), is late, and it in turn is delayed because of "that slow progression of things, which naturally makes elegance and refinement the last effect of opulence and power" (13). With the adverb "naturally" Reynolds is attempting to break down the stubborn opposition between "a commercial nation" and "the Polite Arts" with a fable of cultural evolution that binds commerce, art, and the class structure into a single system through education (13). The evolution moves not from commerce to art but from a rudimentary commercial system that will support only manufactures to a more advanced one that will also support embellishment and ornament. As Reynolds put it later in his dedication to the discourses: "The regular progress of cultivated life is from necessaries to accommodations, from accommodations to ornaments" (3). We might imagine that he is trying to find a way of optimizing the advantages for artists in the severer scheme of development outlined by Adam Smith:

> Every man is rich or poor according to the degree in which he can afford to enjoy the necessaries, conveniencies, and amusements of human life. . . . But after the division of labour has taken place. . . . the far greater part of them he must derive from the labour of other people, and he must be rich or poor according to the quantity of that labour which he can command, or which he can afford to purchase. The value of any commodity, therefore, . . . is equal to the quantity of labour which it enables him to purchase or command. [1:47 and n.1].

With education, through the Academy, as coordinator, Reynolds more playfully synchronizes the founding of the Academy with the *natural* alliance of commerce and art, the *regular* progress of cultivated life, the cyclical pattern of history, and what has been called the westering of culture, a geographical pattern favorable to England and to the present moment: "It has been observed, that the Arts have ever been disposed to travel westward . . . but, as if the ocean had stopped their progress, they have for near an age stood still, and grown weak and torpid for want of motion. Let us for a moment flatter ourselves that they . . . have at last arrived at this island. Our Monarch [George III] seems willing to think so, having provided such an Asylum [the Academy] for their reception, as may induce them to stay where they are so much honoured" (dis. 1, 14n).[12] (Martin Archer

[12] Pressly relates Reynolds's statement to Barry's use of the sunrise in *The Phoenix or the Resurrection of Freedom,* an aquatint of 1776. By means of an inscription on a scroll in the print, Barry connects republican institutions with favorable conditions for the arts and extends the westward movement from England—a new country, as he says elsewhere—to America, an even newer one: "Every like loves his like, Or 40 reasons why the shallow and half characters were in very Art so peculiarly selected & Patronized in this Reign" (quoted in Pressly, *Life* 78; see also pl. 57). The

Shee is merely extending this line of apologetic optimism concerning the belatedness of English painting when he declares that "poetry appears to be the first powerful product of human genius, painting, the last and most delicate of its offspring" [114n].)

With the Vasari canon of progressive acquisition as a bottomless reservoir of pedagogical examples, Reynolds adapts the familiar analogy between Italian and English art to the Academy program. Even when the analogy fails at precisely the critical point—the Academy itself—the momentum of the analogical argument sends out metaphors to span the gap: "Raffaelle, it is true, had not the advantage of studying in an Academy; but all Rome, and the works of Michael Angelo in particular, were to him an Academy" (15). The remainder of the first discourse expounds the appropriate pedagogical sequence, "method of proceeding," or "method of education" by which the learner, carried along by the virtues of "industry" and "assiduity" (19), "acquires" habits, is "advancing" toward knowledge and making "progress" (20). Reynolds's heavy investment in the cycle of rise, progress, and decline brings him back to the analogy of classical to Italian to English art for an optimistic climax: "that the present age may vie in Arts with that of Leo the Tenth; and that *the dignity of the dying Art* (to make use of an expression of Pliny) may be revived under the Reign of GEORGE THE THIRD" (21).

The Argument

At this point we can risk some generalizations about fundamental elements in the English-school narrative as it evolved over the course of the eighteenth century in reaction to practical failures at home and theoretical opposition from the continent. The progressive nature of art, as expressed in the Vasari canon and the Carracci program, has striking advantages over other forms of apology for the English school, and it had been favored from the beginning, when Aglionby labeled his Vasari (augmented with three dialogues) a "Remedy" following "the *Course* of the *Arts Improvement*, beginning with *Cimabue*, and going on with all those who were, as it were, the *Inventers* and *Perfecters* of it by degrees" (Preface, n.p.). The progressive pattern favors modern art in general, puts English art on a plane at least level with the art of other nations, and readily adapts to the introduction of empirical elements that give it the look and feel of a thoroughly modern theory. (Reynolds, for example, makes extensive use of a kind of empirical Platonism in the pedagogy he recommends for students in the *Discourses*. The Platonic-sounding "central form" is actually a product of the Lockean tradition, probabilistic logic, and generalization by averaging. That is, the central form is the goal of an educational program that can be systemized.)

Furthermore, the progressive pattern suggests that English art may recover from even the

history of "Liberty" corresponds to the usual republican, or civic-humanist, history of artistic accomplishment, moving from ancient Athens to ancient Rome to Renaissance Florence to modern England to new America (see Barrell, and the text from the margins of the print quoted in Pressly, *Life* 77).

longest detours merely by returning to the path of progress. Although decline, the phase with which the cycle of improvement was sometimes supposed to end, was a common topic—in poetry, certainly, writers of the century after Shakespeare and Milton often depressed themselves with the possibility of having cycled into an age of criticism—writers on the English school generally had little use for it in reference to their own situation. Having never stood on a high place, they had little fear of falling. Decline is brought in to describe what happened in Greece and Italy, and, more important, it provides an occasion for England to lead a new climbing expedition. Jonathan Richardson's notion that painting had been in a steep decline since the death of Raphael is opportunistic. Richardson proposed that the chances for a new cycle might be best in England—a "new country," as Barry later says (*Letter* 52), where the sun does not have to learn to rise in the twilight of past ages.

The discourse is nationalistic insofar as it envisions modern English art as a national effort threatened by time (old masters) and distance (foreign artists protected by foreign intellectuals). But this is an international or secondary nationalism that must remain open to the claims of both time and distance. Writers who harp on the English connoisseurs' "blind Admiration" of the old masters and the invasion of home territory by "the Labours of the present Foreigners" (Barry, *Inquiry* 32) issue their complaints on the basis of an essential continuity that gives English painting a place in the historically and geographically continuous program of artistic mastery, old as well as new. Although the "accidental circumstance" of the Reformation diverted England's art history, "another *accident*" kept the cultural memory of continuity alive, "our *cultivation* of Greek, Italian, and French literature, where we unavoidably *acquired* something of a just taste for the fine arts" (my emphasis, 65). With accident, cultivation, and acquisition Barry again promotes progressive historical explanations of the fate of English art over the essentialisms of the continental critics. The sequence "Greek, Italian, and French" follows the historical sequence of great painting as Barry construes it. His hope that the fourth term will be "English" rests on the notion that acquisition tends to spread from a well-informed core of spectators who "have all their faculties at command" (*Account* 39) to "build" the taste of the more extensive public: "if picture knowledge is new in England, it will not be always so; we ought not to build too confidently on the ignorance of the public. . . . The higher exertions of Art . . . require . . . not only some degree of information in the spectator, but also that he consider them with some attention and study . . ." (23–24).

When Barry, then, claims Giles Hussey as his immediate predecessor, he does so because he supposes Hussey to have been the English messenger for the Carracci.[13] And when Barry looks back over his century from the vantage point of 1798, he sees other continuities, such as the "Titianesque" manner that links the "long and uninterrupted chain of the great successors of the Venetians, in Rubens, Joardans, Rembrandt, and Vandyk; it is often found, and in a

[13] Giles Hussey, 1710–1788, whose portrait Barry included in his *Elysium* in the Adelphi sequence, used work by the Carracci to illustrate his theories of the relation between cosmic, mathematical, musical, and optical harmonies. After a period of painting portraits in London for financial reasons, Hussey inherited enough money to be able to give up painting in 1768. In 1787 he began to live as a self-styled religious recluse.

high degree, in Reynolds and Greuze, and always in the finished pictures of [Richard] Wilson" (*Letter* 3). Such continuity is a coherent feature of Barry's history of painting as a "gradual" ideological and technical "progress"—the kind systematically arrayed in his own sequence of paintings, for the Society of Arts at the Adelphi, on "human culture" from savagery to Elysium (fig. 1.9).

In sum, the typical argument for the English school is broadly economic in motivation, historical in form, and prospective or open in vantage. The object of the argument is to construct a diagnostic, remedial, and prognostic narrative that grants English art an honorable place in European art history. The most influential versions of that narrative have four leading features, the first pair of which give meaning to the second. In the first pair, an argument by analogy is driven by a principle of improvement that is transferable across historical periods and across cultures. In the second, a list of obstructions is supplemented by a list of countermeasures. The two pairs dovetail in a single prospective history: when the obstructions are removed and the countermeasures implemented, the principle of improvement will be able to operate freely, and the heretofore partial analogies will emerge in increasingly comprehensive forms.

Although stakes deepen, issues complicate, and implications multiply as the decades pass, the favorite arguments continue to be analogical. As *X*, so England, with *X* usually being ancient Greece, whose grace is often extended sequentially to ancient Rome and Renaissance Italy. That historical sequence is the product rather than the origin of a more profound idea, that all past artistic success manifested a fundamental evolutionary pattern. The pattern, a gradual development based on the cumulative acquisition of concepts and skills, arrives in many alternative and overlapping forms: institutional (the spread of academic education), historical (the Vasari canon), theoretical (de Piles's *balance*), practical (the Carracci program), and far too many more to represent fully here.

Most solutions to the problems of the English fine arts proposed before and during Blake's lifetime depend fundamentally on the cyclical analogy and the principle of improvement. The founding of the Royal Academy in 1768, after years of less successful attempts to organize painters in a professional society, is exemplary.[14] On the whole it was promoted as the modern institutionalized re-creation of a system of progressive acquisition that had existed *in some sense* in Athens, Rome, Florence, or Venice. The new Academy would attempt to increase the efficiency of development by institutionalizing the very principle of development deduced from the art history of earlier periods.

These were, however, only the uplifting forms of unrealized hope and possibility, while the debate was conducted in the ominous rhetoric of national disaster. A string of highly visible practical failures in the present made it easy to spot the ironies, not to say mockeries, in the theoretical optimism about the future. Knowledge of patterns of development, after all, can be either cheering or depressing depending on one's position. At a conference on the prospects of economic development in the Third World, insiders, those who feel that the pattern already applies to them, may empha-

[14] Pears 121–22 and Hutchison 26–41 usefully list the Academy's predecessors.

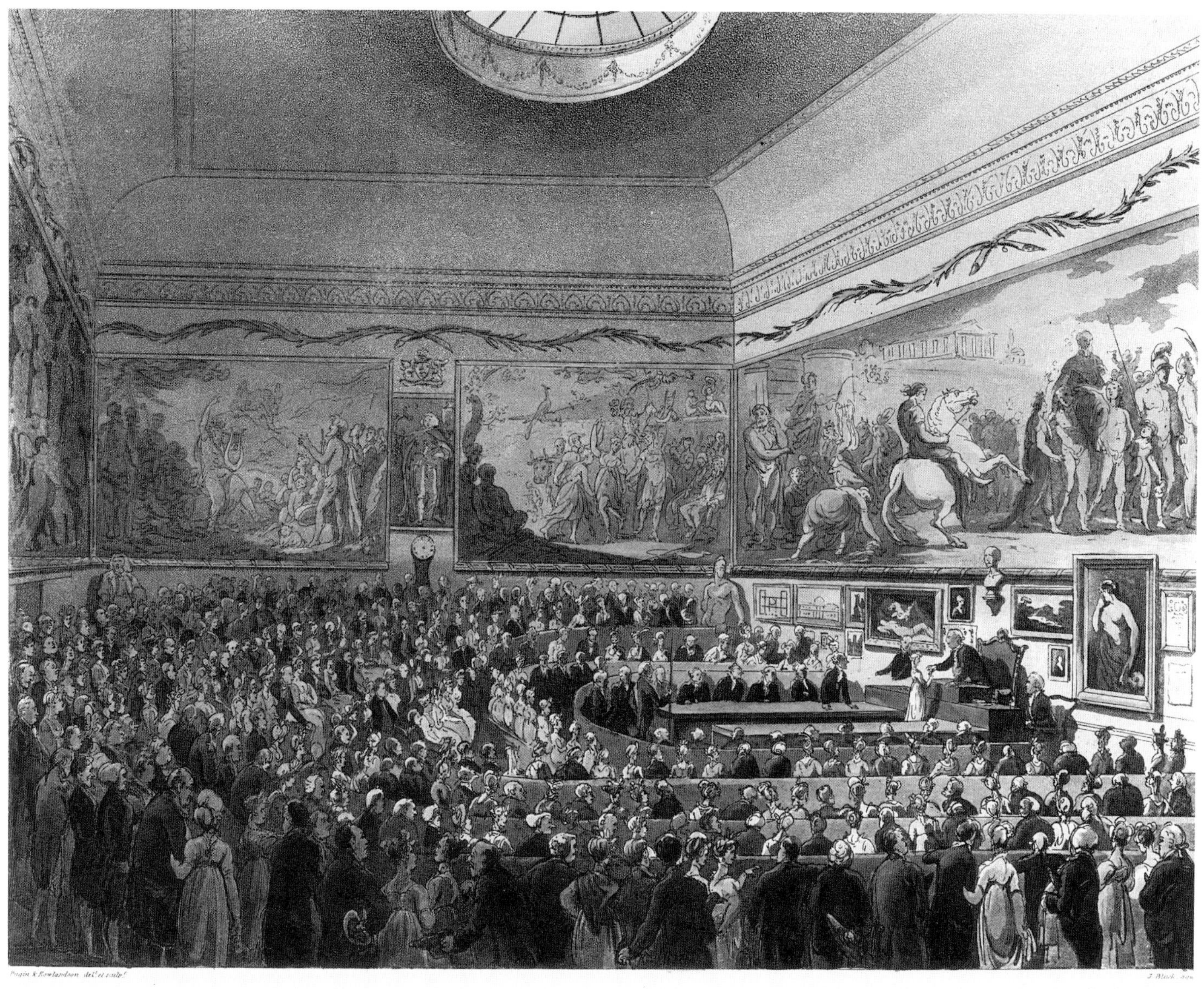

1.9. A. C. Pugin, Thomas Rowlandson, and J. Bluck, *The Great Room of the Society for the Encouragement of Arts*, etching and aquatint from Rudolph Ackermann's *Microcosm of London*, vol. 3, 1809. (This aquatint was published as a separate print.)

size preconditions that outsiders cannot meet; outsiders may emphasize the transferability of the pattern itself. In arguments about the development of art history, eighteenth-century continental writers tend to behave as insiders. Consolidating and defending, they assure themselves that they are correct by rediscovering the pattern of artistic improvement in classical art and in their own. Negatively, they discover that wherever great art is missing, as in England, the pattern of improvement has been blocked. In this respect, the English artists end up in the position of Montesquieu's Indians: "It has been discovered that the savages of America are immune to discipline, incorrigible, and incapable of any enlightenment or instruction. Indeed, trying to teach them something, trying to bend their brain fibres, is like trying to make totally crippled people walk" (435).

But still, the pattern of improvement itself makes the underlying bias toward nurture over nature compelling enough to encourage English writers, behaving as outsiders at the periphery of an inner circle, to transfer it to their own situation. In this respect, Montesquieu's vast devotion to the efficacy of "education," which "we find . . . among civilized peoples" (435), becomes the solution to the problem posed by his own *raisons naturelles.* English writers do not deny that England's artistic development has been obstructed, but they give themselves grounds for optimism by insisting that the development is natural and the obstruction unnatural. Once the real obstructions to the acquisition of the arts, as Barry significantly put it, are removed, the stream of progress will begin to flow.

Patronage in a Commercial Country

The progress, when it comes, will necessarily flow through economic channels. People will exchange more money for more English paintings more often, and painters will begin to live in better parts of town and sit down to better food. Though the English-school discourse can be clear and direct on aesthetic ignorance and education, it turns evasive in regard to the bottom line. When Fuseli, following the procedures of Winckelmann and Montesquieu, outlines the conditions under which Greek art came to be great, he mentions religion as "the first mover of their art," along with climate and civil and political institutions, but he omits economic institutions entirely (Wornum 349). Again, though he would tie artistic to social progress, he omits commercial arrangements from that account (552–53). But we can safely say that the narrative of the English school was embedded not only in the myths of Western art history that we have been analyzing but also in the socioeconomic myths of feudalism and aristocracy. The founding of the Royal Academy is again indicative. One great difference between the loosely organized network of clubs, societies, and schools through which the English art trade had been conducted and the new centralized Academy was its royal sponsorship. "GEORGE THE THIRD" ends Reynolds's inaugural lecture because the monarch and his analogical peers are the economic focus of the hope embodied in the myth on which the rest

According to Ellis K. Waterhouse, the "first temporary exhibition of the work of living artists ever to be held in London" (49) opened on 21 April 1760 in the Great Room of the Society for the Encouragement of Arts, Manufactures, and Commerce. There was talk of English painters' decorating the Great Room. Eventually Barry undertook the project alone, working on location to produce six murals, *The Progress of Human Culture,* in about six years (1777–1783). Blake read the circumstances as a comment on Barry's heroism and English "encouragement":

> Who will Dare to Say that Polite Art is Encouraged, or Either Wished or Tolerated in a Nation where The Society for the Encouragement of Art. Sufferd Barry to Give them, his Labour for Nothing A Society Composed of the Flower of English Nobility & Gentry—Suffering an Artist to Starve while he Supported Really what They under pretence of Encouraging were Endeavouring to Depress.—Barry told me that while he Did that Work—he Lived on Bread & Apples [Anno. Reynolds, E 636]

Barry built his *Progress* series on the standard analogy of classical to modern English culture, by which the progress attributed (in a trio of canvases) to the former is transferred expectantly (in a second trio) to the latter. Pugin, Rowlandson, and Bluck's aquatint shows how the room looked around 1809. The murals are still on view today.

of the lecture draws. Because it was expected that artistic progress would flow through the traditional channel of so-called great-man patronage, the English-school discourse is studded with references to artistically minded kings, emperors, popes, and cardinals with big pockets in other times and places. The Royal Academy would provide an institutional meeting ground for practitioners of the "polite" arts and the educable "polite" class.

This illusion, perhaps fostered by the analogical myth itself, was a major distraction for several decades. Its anachronistic influence led artists up any number of blind alleys in search of "support" and "encouragement." Certainly to our ears Barry sounds sadly confused and out of date when in one of his early writings he recommends that every English nobleman protect himself from the bad advice of dealers by taking "an Artist in his Service, by Pension or otherwise, whose Judgment and Instruction they could always have recourse to" (*Call* 29).[15] (He forgets to explain why the patron would have the judgment to choose a good artist as adviser.) The negative side of his proposal is equally revealing. Before the old-style wealthy patron can be rehabilitated, Barry says, the dealer must be banished from the scene. The unfavorable treatment of the dealer, who personifies commerce, as the source of lies and misinformation that obstructs a direct relationship between artist and patron typifies the tendency to delete or disguise mercantile elements in the discourse.

If good patrons of the great-man type, such as Alexander the Great, selflessly provide autonomy, bad patrons, obsessed with "self-importance," use painters to "communicate [the patron's] ideas and teach, rather than run the danger of being themselves taught." Consequently, says Barry, they sponsor "pimps and buffoons" instead of independent artists: "great artists . . . have but seldom received benefit or assistance from any individual of very shining talents. I say individual, for it may be different when that individual acts in community, as in a Society . . . or . . . subordinately as a trustee" (*Letter* 35).[16] As Barry hints, the solution most often proposed as an alternative to great-man patronage before 1790 and after 1800 was institutional patronage. Though the line between aristocratic and state patronage is thin, the emphasis is different. Barry was not the only one who supposed that the contemporary counterpart to the church in former times was French patronage, the institutional character of which had made it far superior to English: "And how much are you, David, to be envied, blest as you are, amongst a public . . . which, even in its worst times, was habitually exercised in honestly and urbanely meeting the efforts of art with an indulgence, estimation, and reception, so adequate, and so generous!" (47).[17] This sort of English admiration of French patronage was widespread.

[15] Lippincott makes excellent use of Arthur Pond's career to illustrate the multiple pursuits of ambitious artist-dealers at mid-century. Her account can be extended with the studies of Pointon and Bennett. Bennett documents Stothard's willingness and ability to adapt to the demands of fashion, patrons, technologies of reproduction, etc.

[16] Cf. Pears on the patron-painter collaboration that was often held up as an ideal (143, 162–63).

[17] For Barry's admiration of the French see also *Letter* 28–29. Writing, in this instance, in 1798, he speaks of "this momentous crisis of Revolutions." Barry's politics are not clear to me, but surely it is worth noting that he was an Irish Catholic working in London, and that 1798 was the year of Wolfe Tone's final attempt to lead a French invasion of Ireland (to assist the 1798 rebellion) and of his suicide after he was convicted of treason.

George Turnbull, though he prefers Pericles to Alexander and the French state as a paragon of patronage, agrees at a deeper level with Barry and Valentine Green that institutions, rather than individuals, are the proper measure of artistic encouragement. Periclean Athens demonstrates, Turnbull says, "how necessary a free, generous publick-spirited Government or Constitution is to produce, but more especially to uphold and promote, the Liberal Arts and Sciences; and how amicably they all conspire to illustrate and perfect one another" (110). Of course Turnbull means to suggest by analogy that if the arts have a better chance of thriving in English constitutional liberty than in continental tyranny, England may be the new Athens. Nonetheless, in narratives shaped largely by analogy with the art of other cultures at earlier times, commerce is difficult to accommodate. It has its own narratives, one of which I shall discuss in due course, but those are not easily harmonized with the stories that otherwise seemed most encouraging to English hopes of founding a proper school of painting. In the commerce narratives English painting is an English product analogous to other products; but in the analogies that control the English-school narratives commerce is a form of patronage, or, synonymously, a form of "encouragement" or "support" for art (fig. 1.10).

Barry's attempts to tell the story of English patronage show the extent of potential conflict. Narrating as usual by analogy, he seems to suggest that the integrated system of institutional patronage, based on religion, that (at its best) connected ideas and artists in Vasari's Rome had been supplied in "this commercial country" (*Inquiry* 146) by the institutions of commerce. He is not the first, of course, to associate commerce with England's stunted artistic growth. As early as 1755 André Rouquet had built an explanation around a polar opposition between commerce and art, claiming that commercial and artistic success have different "sources" (6)—commerce in memory and judgment, the polite arts in memory and imagination. Furthermore, commercially inclined people have "rule and compass always in hand; . . . they require the test of strict demonstration. This geometrical rigour, so agreeable to the nature of commerce, is a damp to genius. . . . It was therefore natural that the English should busy themselves chiefly in geometry, in mechanics, and commerce; while the French and Italians found their principal amusement in the polite arts" (7).

In his *Review of the Polite Arts in France, at the Time of Their Establishment under Louis the XIVth, Compared with Their Present State in England* (1782), the mezzotint engraver Valentine Green criticizes more specifically than Rouquet the commercial system of production and marketing that supports English art in lieu of institutional patronage. Instead of working on grand projects financed by kings and peers, English artists paint subjects that they hope will have a lively sale when engraved. They solicit subscribers to the prints at a guinea apiece, forcing the painters, "in addition to their own *speculative* labours," to "*venture* on the heavy expences attending the laborious operations of Engraving them" (my emphasis, 50). Green's anticommercial rhetoric—the metaphors of the South Sea Bubble—puts painters in the shabby role of speculators-against-their-will who venture capital in hopes of gain, who must stoop to the "humiliating Practice" of "offering those Works to public view" for a shilling. The system is "making *Marchands d'Estampes* [print merchants] of our first men of Genius, and reducing the study of their Profession to *Connoisseurship in proof impressions from Engravings*" (50–51). Green writes of "opening a free passage to a current which has been too long obstructed by the blindness of prejudices" (34). Commerce, associated with "Arithmetical calculations" and "contracted optics" (57) with an eye on quick profit, seems inherently unable to open passages. It only strengthens, by exploiting, the localism, privatism, blindness, and prejudice that block the current. Green compares English commerce to the French "system" by which both patron and artist operate with "Ministerial Protection" and "under the eye of the Sovereign." Close ties to noblemen in the government seem to give French artists regular access to "the first employments of the State" (11–12). Contrasting French successes with English failures, Green calls for "National Patronage" (46).[18]

For many critics, the chief indicators of the difference between continental governments and English commerce as sources of patronage were the excessive English encouragement of portraiture and a corresponding lack of encouragement of history painting. The handwriting had been on the wall a long time. Late in the seventeenth century Aglionby recommended his translation of Vasari with the observation that "we never had . . . an English Man, that pretended to *History-Painting.* I cannot attribute this to any thing but the little Encouragement it meets with in this Nation, whose Genius more particularly leads them to affect Face-Painting" (Preface, n.p.). A century later Gainsborough used the theme to point out a contradiction between English economic reality and the program of the new Academy: "[B]etwixt Friends Sir Joshua either forgets, or does not chuse see [sic] that his Instruction is all adapted to form the History Painter, which he must know there is no call for in this country." And Gainsborough went on to observe that the contradiction reappeared in the rift between Reynolds's theories and his practice: "Therefore he had better come *down to Watteau* at once . . . and let us have a few Tints; or else why does Sir Joshua put tints equal to Painted Glass . . . when the great style would do. Every one knows that the grand style must consist in plainness & simplicity . . ." (96–97).[19]

Barry associates Italian history painting with "Christian story," which, because "derived from intellect," is parallel to the intellectual arts of ancient Greece. In Barry's history of progressive intellectual acquisition, Christianity requires learning, and painting falls among the

[18]The sense of English inferiority to the French in patronage may have been largely an illusion; see Locquin. Bruntjen maintains (without qualification) that "Boydell's private patronage of history painting in England achieved greater success than the various combined efforts of the French government in its patronage of historical art in France during the eighteenth century" (250n13), a point difficult to assess without some definition of "success" and "French government." Boydell's role is discussed below.

[19]Gainsborough's comment comes in a letter to "Mr. Hoare," perhaps Prince Hoare or his father the portrait painter. The letter is undated; a probable date would be the early 1770s, since Gainsborough is commenting on a copy of Reynolds's fourth discourse (first delivered in 1771), which Hoare seems to have sent. Perhaps it is needless to add that Sir Joshua's position as father of English history painting and of the corresponding Academy ideology (oriented toward history painting) was hardly without supporters: "Nor is it easy to do justice to the merits of one, who being the first Painter of eminence that this country has produced, has by his excellent instructions, and professional skill, formed an English Historical School of Painting, which bids fair to rival those of Rome and Florence in their best days," wrote the Rev. John Whitehouse in introducing his *Elegaic Ode* to Reynolds's memory (iii–iv).

The annual exhibitions of the new Royal Academy—the first of their kind in England—were important social and pedagogical occasions constructed quite deliberately on a commercial base. They were a great "opportunity" and "encouragement" to artists, and the printseller John Boydell and the pottery manufacturer Josiah Wedgwood tried to reproduce them on a smaller scale in their London shops. Here, beneath exuberantly overhung walls of canvas, Reynolds, with ear trumpet, is escorting the Prince of Wales (later George IV) through the crowded exhibition of 1787. They are standing in the top-lit Great Room of the new Academy premises at Sir William Chambers's Somerset House.

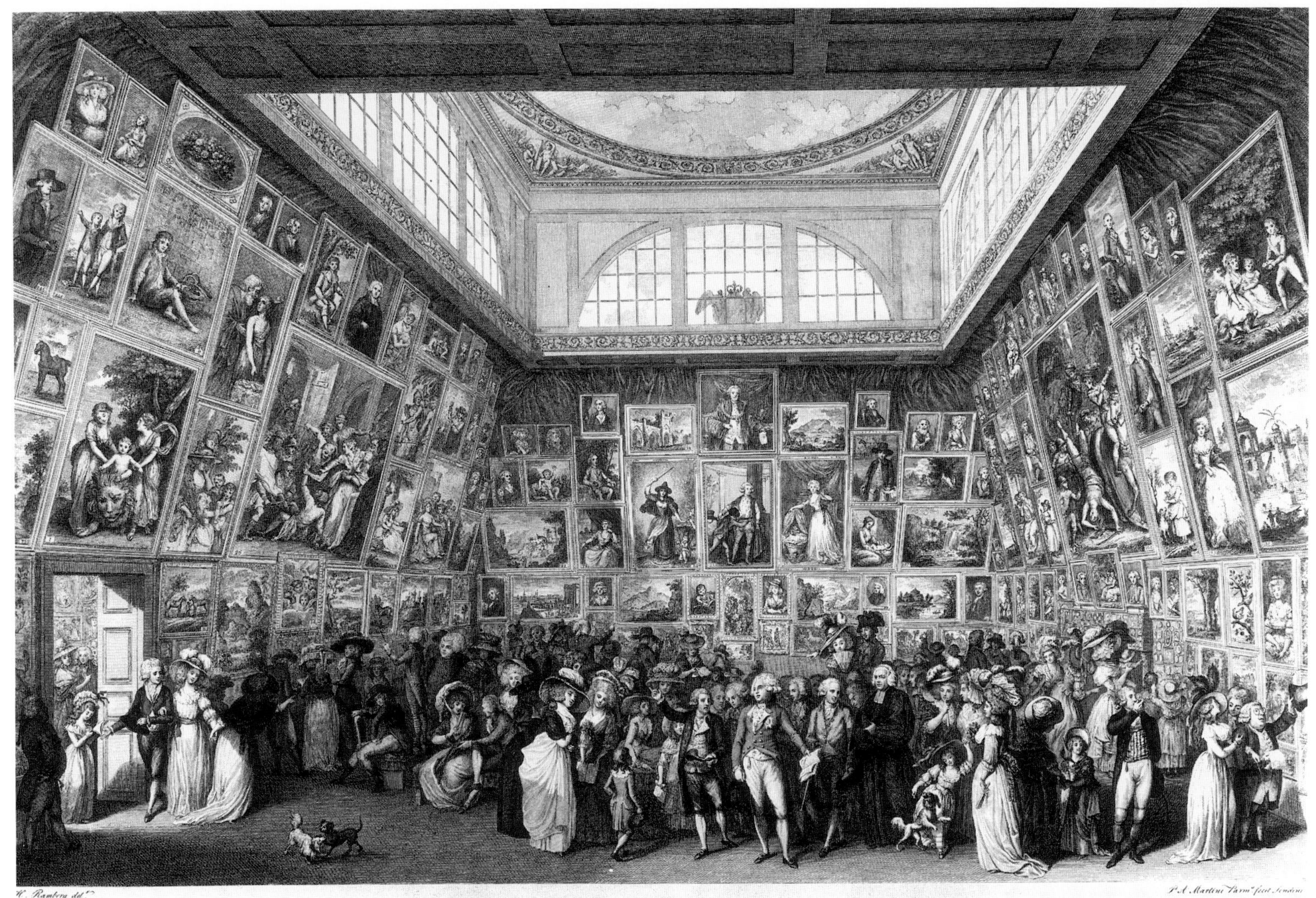

1.10. Pietro Martini after J. H. Ramberg, *The Exhibition of the Royal Academy, 1787*, engraving, 1787.

teaching arts. Acquisition occurs gradually, it seems, on all fronts: as painters acquire skills, paintings improve, and members of the public acquire improved tastes. The system of patronage ensures the smooth continuous operation of this economy of knowledge by encouraging the "few *artists*" capable of maintaining "the dignity of the *art*" to produce works that correspond with "the interest and wishes of the *public*" (my emphasis, *Inquiry* 146).

Commerce naturally operates in reverse, with a stake in original ignorance rather than the progressive exercise of intellect. Since ignorance is emptiness, or "vanity," which looks only at itself, the expression of ignorance in painting is portrait, which thrives on "vanity and folly" (Barry, *Account* 12). In the standard complaint, if the patron is vain, then the portrait painter is "a mighty flatterer," as Cunningham later describes Reynolds (1:325). The image of a supplier returning to the demander an image of the supplier's face for money belongs to a group of anticommercial images of the relationship between artist and audience that depict a closed, private cycle of sensual or emotional need and gratification.

Barry calls the trade in portraiture "an artificial consequence" (*Account* 12), artificial apparently because the progressive acquisition of knowledge is natural. The commercial economy of knowledge operates on the perversions of improvement, debasement, and depravation (the *OED* quotes Burke for 1795: "If this be improvement, truly I know not what can be called a depravation of society"). Its effects gradually spread to all elements of the system: as "the trade of portraits" in England has "much depraved" the "public taste for the arts" on the one side, it has "shamefully debased" the "mind of the artist" on the other (11). The measure of commercial success is profit, a good idea in commerce being a profitable idea. Portrait painting thus falls among the "true commercial ideas . . . and the annual profits of it are the only estimates of it which generally come under consideration" (12).

To describe the changes that occur when commerce replaces Renaissance religious patronage in the analogy, Barry transfers the lexicon of commerce to painting, which becomes a form of "manufacture" (*Account* 13) carried on by a "contemptible Mechanick" (*Call* 19), while erstwhile "patrons" become "more properly the employers of the artists" (*Account* 7). Catalogues become advertising hype, "exaggerated puffing catalogues, and other frauds of auctioneers, and mercenary picture-dealers" (Wornum 214), while the Royal Academy becomes a training school supplying "mechanical culture" to "base, uneducated, indigent people" who, as artists, "destroy and contaminate every thing valuable" and end by reducing "this liberal art . . . to a mere trade" (*Account* 97).[20]

As we expect in a history that values progressive acquisition aiming toward the restoration of a comprehensive master art, the commercial reduction comes in the form of contraction and fragmentation. As early as 1773 Barry formulates the opposition between an acquisitive art and a divisive commerce. Instead of "expanding our minds" to an "enlarged" idea of art, he complains, "we have looked upon the arts, as we do upon trades, which may be car-

[20] Pointon's statistics on Academy exhibitions from 1781 through 1785 clearly establish the predominance of portraiture (see charts on 189–91). She suggests that the "successful portrait painter . . . employed the Royal Academy as his chief publicity agent" (191).

ried on separately" (*Inquiry* 140–41). In production, "our practice, until lately, has been rather to contract the art itself, to split it into pieces, and to portion it out into small lots, fitted to the narrow capacities of mechanical uneducated people" (140). "Until lately" is a formula for rhetorical optimism that Barry often employs only to return a few years later with a heightened version of the same complaint. In his Royal Academy lecture on composition, first delivered in the 1780s, he describes the division of art by commerce. "As art is of a two-fold nature, consisting of the *ideal* and the *mechanical,*" it succumbs to "men of mean intellects, who, incapable of meddling with the *ideal,* will operate solely with these mechanical principles, as their entire stock of trade, and thus bring about a separation between the body [execution] and soul [idea] of art, with very little hope, with very little prospect of their being happily re-united afterwards" (Wornum 173–74).

Since, in Barry's scheme, intellectual acquisition threatens commercial acquisition, the agents of profit must thwart the agents of knowledge. It is at this point, as his analysis comes closest to a full-fledged conspiracy theory, that he may seem to earn his contemporary reputation for paranoia in tirelessly dwelling on the "secret workings and machinations of these interested men"—the artists who depend upon the maintenance of "public ignorance" (*Inquiry* 147) to achieve "greater profits" (146). But, as we shall see, Barry is not alone in his paranoia, if that is what it is. More important, the extension of the narrative from the blackhearted dealer to an equally malevolent co-conspirator from the artist's side of the plot is a logical, or perhaps mythological, development to which we shall return.

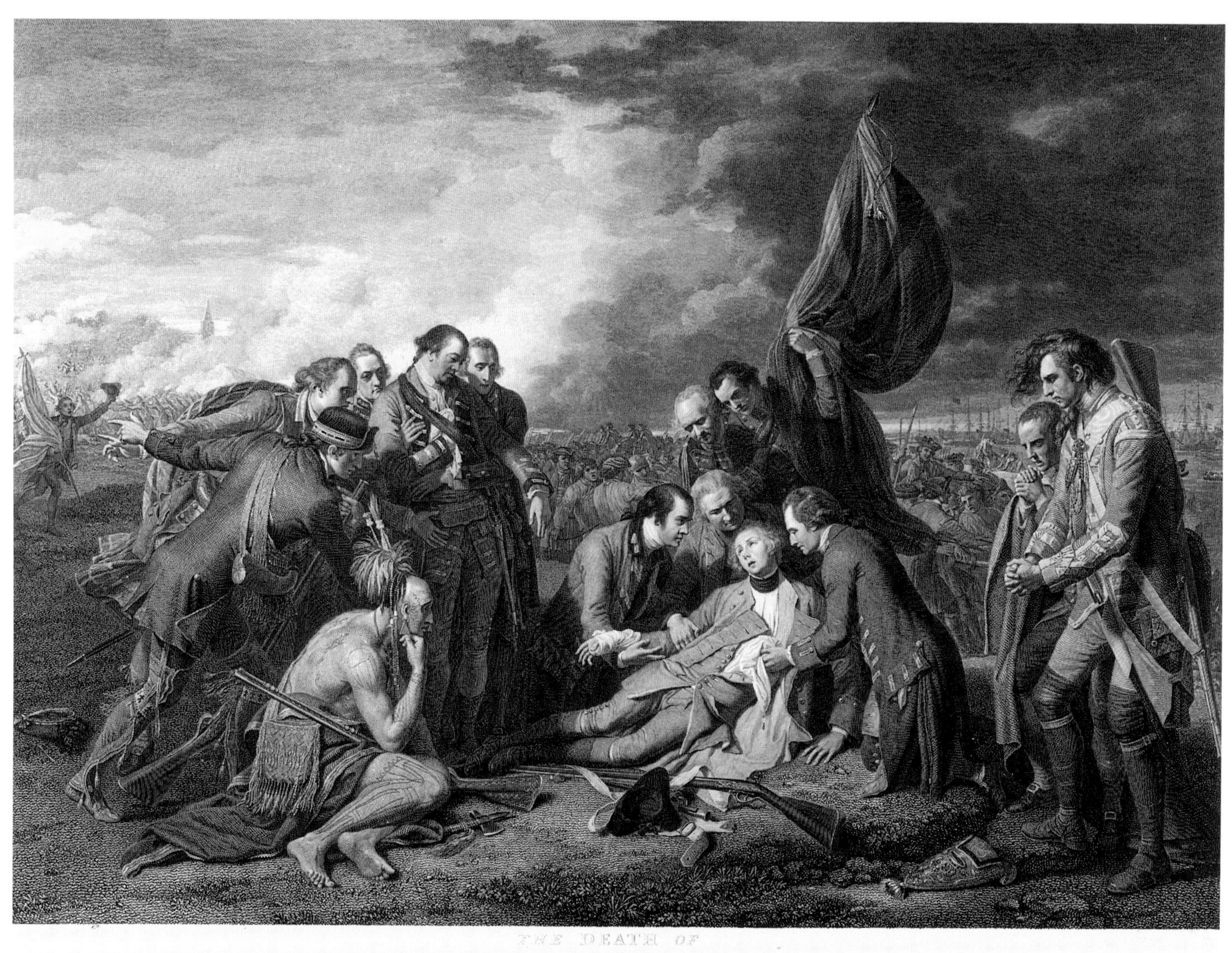

2.1. William Woollett after Benjamin West, *The Death of General Wolfe*, engraving, 1776.

II COMMERCE
A New Maecenas

> But the greatest news relating to virtu is Alderman Boydel's scheme of having pictures and prints taken from those pictures of the most interesting scenes of Shakespear, by which all the painters and engravers find engagements for eight or ten years; he wishes me to do eight pictures, but I have engaged only for one. He has insested [sic] on my taking earnest mony, and to my great surprise left upon my table five hundred pounds—to have as much more as I shall demand.
>
> —Joshua Reynolds to the Duke of Rutland, 13 February 1787

> . . . mercy on us! *Our* painters to design for *Shakespeare!* . . . Piranesi might dash out Duncan's Castle—but Lord help Alderman Boydell and the Royal Academy!
>
> —Horace Walpole to Lady Ossory, 15 December 1786

To Rasselas, say, following the polite arts in England from Abyssinia through the printed word, it may have appeared that the honorable members of the new Academy were awaiting the arrival of a monarch to match Louis XIV, of a Protestant archbishop to equal a French cardinal, of English aristocrats newly alerted, perhaps through the annual Academy exhibitions, to the benefits of good taste—and found instead, as the consummation of their hopes, a commercial Maecenas. In the anti-commercial context of the English-school discourse as I have outlined it, the onset of what can only be called the Boydell era may seem surprising, since its appearance on the horizon signaled unmistakably, as nothing before ever had, the arrival of commercial patronage as a force to be reckoned with. But from another angle there is no surprise. The Boydell era seems inevitable, and the only wonder is that it did not arrive sooner, as part of the shift memorialized in Oliver Goldsmith's observation that "the author, when unpatronized by the Great, has naturally recourse to the bookseller" (108)—the often-noted shift from a "client economy" in which the middle class live as clients of the aristocracy to an economy in which an entrepreneurial middle class strive to open up larger markets (Brewer 197–202). John Boydell's operations were part of the "disentangling of production and distribution" that David Alexander has linked to the "redeployment of labour skills" (236) in the hundred years after 1750. If, as Louise Lippincott has demonstrated, the jack-of-all-trades Arthur Pond, who not only painted, engraved, and

General James Wolfe led British troops against the French (under Montcalm) at Quebec in 1759, virtually ensuring that Canada would be British. Benjamin West painted his first of at least six or seven pictures of Wolfe's death a decade later and in 1771 exhibited it at the Royal Academy, where its rich combination of the exotic, the heroic, and the modern in a historical fabrication with classical underpinnings created a sensation. But it took William Woollett's print from the painting and an engraved key—not published until 1776 by Boydell—to establish West's reputation, along with Woollett's and Boydell's. That coalition of patriotic subject, history painter, printmaker, and publisher held the potential for

sold but also supplied copies of paintings to furnish houses and perfomed customs and shipbroking services, typified the aggregated commerce of the early Georgian period, John Boydell was the disaggregated new middleman. To grasp some, at least, of the era's significance, we shall scrutinize both its successes and its strains from a variety of perspectives.[1]

The Bastille fell in the summer of 1789, and the Assembly adopted the Declaration of the Rights of Man and Citizen soon afterward. A few months earlier, in April, at the annual dinner of the Royal Academy in London, Edmund Burke jotted a few words on a slip of paper that he passed to Joshua Reynolds, now sixty-six years old and the president of the Royal Academy for two full decades. Approving what Burke had written, Reynolds passed the slip on to the Prince of Wales, who proposed a toast: "This end of the table, in which, as there are many admirers of the art, there are many friends of yours, wish to drink an English tradesman, who patronizes the art better than the Grand Monarque of France: 'Alderman Boydell, the Commercial Maecenas.' "[2] It would be difficult to exhaust the implications of the toast to "Alderman" John Boydell, to become lord mayor of London in 1790, himself an engraver but also printseller, entrepreneur, publisher, purveyor of England's art to the world and of the world's art to the English.[3]

Even for Boydell, who had begun as an independent engraver in 1746 and had been working very successfully in the printselling trade for decades, 1789 was a red-letter year not only for his business and personal prestige but also for English engraving and the English school of painting. Three years earlier he had first announced his Shakespeare Gallery scheme, aiming ultimately to publish illustrations of Shakespeare's plays (in one format) and an illustrated edition of the plays (in another). The illustrations would be engraved versions of paintings produced specially for the occasion by England's best painters. The project would be financed through an expanded version of a system that Boydell had used successfully in the past: commission paintings and engravings, pay the painters and engravers partly or wholly in advance, and recoup the investment plus profit upon publication of the reproductions (fig. 2.1). Capital for the commissions would come from Boydell's pocket, considerably supplemented by money made from advance sales

[1] Marilyn Butler touches perceptively on the Boydell-Blake connection as an important element of the social situation in which Blake's work of the 1790s was composed, though I find that her attempt at a three-way coordination of the 1790s, "the Boydell years," the "years of Blake's great achievement," and the years of "revolutionary ferment," requires an unacceptable flattening and forcing of complexities (Butler 39–53).

[2] "Maecenas" is Gaius Maecenus, Roman statesman, patron of Horace and Virgil. Details of the occasion differ considerably—on whether the dinner was the lord mayor's or the Royal Academy's, whether the toast was delivered by Reynolds or the prince, whether the toast did or did not include the term "Commercial Maecenas." Whitley, who does not give his source, has the prince proposing the toast at the R.A. dinner but omitting reference to Boydell as Maecenas (2:112). Cf. the anonymous author of "Comparative Merits," who has Reynolds in the presence of the prince propose the toast to "Alderman Boydell, commercial Mecaenas [sic]" (57). For other interesting variants, see the event as reported by Hudson (199), Leslie and Taylor (2:532–33), Pye (*Patronage* 211), and Stannard (n.p.). The most reliable report is very likely the one in the *London Chronicle* of 25–28 April 1789 (see Burke 5:465). Two years later, in 1791, Boydell made himself the first lord mayor to have the Academy to dinner.

[3] For information on Boydell I am indebted principally to Bruntjen, but also to a variety of other primary and secondary sources, including Balston, Boydell himself (as presented by Jones), the *DNB*, W. H. Friedman, and Whitley.

commercial success that Boydell—who claimed to have made £15,000 on an investment of £200 to £300 for *Wolfe*—later tried to organize and magnify with his Shakespeare Gallery project. It seems just to conclude with Richard Godfrey that "West is a central figure in the history of English engraving, for he understood that history painting could only be subsidized by the sale of engravings, and was at pains to cultivate the friendship of the best engravers" (45; see also Alexander and Godfrey 33). Woollett's prints after West were so well regarded that the engraver's name often supplanted the painter's, and Gilbert Stuart's portrait of Woollett justly shows *Wolfe* in the background (reproduced in von Erffa and Staley 213). Three decades after *The Death of Wolfe* and a year after the death of Boydell, West was trying to repeat his success when he teamed up with the engraver James Heath to produce a painting and print showing the death of Nelson at Trafalgar (reproduced in von Erffa and Staley 130). (The *Nelson* print was executed as a same-size companion to the *Wolfe*. The technological gap persisted: the painting took considerably less than a year to complete, the engraving five years.) After the royal patronage of West ceased in 1810, he reverted to the patronage of the public, charging admission to see his huge paintings *Christ Rejected* and *Death on the Pale Horse*—more than twenty feet wide—in premises rented for the purpose (see also Altick 132, 135).

of the Shakespeare works by subscription. As they were finished, the paintings and engravings would be shown and the related Shakespeare products would be sold at the gallery, located in Pall Mall, in the "polite" end of town. Boydell hired the architect George Dance the Younger to turn what had once been the bookshop of Robert Dodsley into the Shakespeare Gallery, complete with imposing facade. Since a major commercial advantage of the Shakespeare project was its broad appeal in two markets—for buyers who wanted the most recent and lavish edition of Shakespeare's text *and* those who wanted the latest work by the current generation of English painters—Boydell had to organize not only the painters and engravers with whom he was accustomed to dealing but also the typographers (to design special typefaces), printers (William Bulmer created the Shakespeare Printing Office), editors (George Steevens edited the plays), and publishers. These daunting complications came out of Boydell's resolve to magnify demand—existing, latent, and new (cf. McKendrick, "Commercialization" 71)—and to benefit from the economies of international scale that his earlier successes in continental markets encouraged him to contemplate.

By 1789, the year of the toast, the commercial apparatus was in place, subscriptions for the Shakespeare were brisk, the gallery held its first exhibition, and Boydell's nephew Josiah was supervising a "manufactory at Hampstead" that the *British Mercury* claimed was filled with engravers toiling away at their Shakespeare copperplates (quoted in Bruntjen 141n).[4] Most of the prominent English painters, including Reynolds, had been brought into the project to keep the Hampstead engravers and others who worked independently busy for some time to come. Though public criticism of the gallery started early (fig. 2.2), hopes for the biggest and best project of English commercial patronage ever were running high and already inspiring imitators. Thomas Macklin's Poets' Gallery got under way in 1788, to be followed by Macklin's Bible project in 1790, Fuseli's Milton Gallery the same year, and William Bowyer's Historic Gallery in 1792 (fig. 2.3). All the schemes except Fuseli's used the Boydell formula, which included combinations of commissioned paintings by various hands; engravings of the paintings; a publishing venture—editions of Shakespeare, the poets, the Bible, Hume's *History of England*—underwritten by subscription; and an exhibition gallery. Although Fuseli's solo Milton Gallery, which had no major publishing/engraving project as its focus, was financed by individual patrons, its entrepreneurial spirit was as Boydellian as its name: "I am determined to lay, hatch, and crack an egg for myself too, if I can," Fuseli remarked to William Roscoe (17 August 1790, Knowles 1:174–75). Meanwhile, Fuseli was also a major contributor to the Shakespeare Gallery. Boydell, trying to occupy some of the Milton territory that Fuseli had left unguarded, eventually published three Milton volumes edited by William Hayley (1794–1797) (see Bruntjen 132n32).

Boydell's commercial strategy arises from

[4] Josiah Boydell (1752–1817), initially a painter by trade, joined his uncle's business in the 1780s but was never an equal partner. He was in charge of supervising the engravers for the Shakespeare Gallery project, among others. He succeeded his brother as alderman (of the Ward of Cheap, around Cheapside, the busy commercial area where the Boydell shop was located) from 1805 through 1809. In 1811 poor health forced him to retire from active business (Bruntjen 67n).

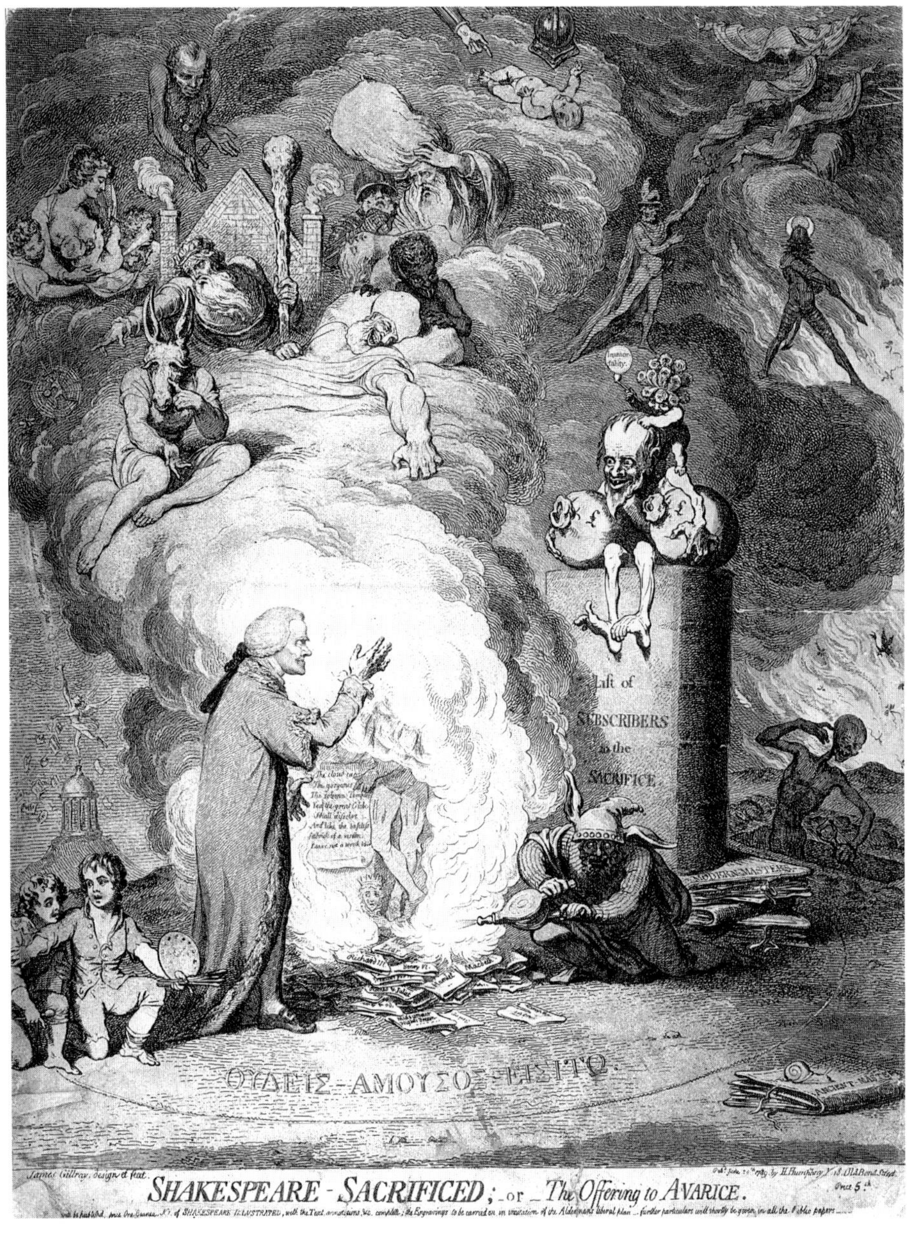

2.2. James Gillray, *Shakespeare Sacrificed;—or—The Offering to Avarice,* etching and aquatint, 1789.

Given the financial stakes that a hoard of artists and engravers had in his project, it is not hard to see why, from the inception of the Shakespeare Gallery, Boydell had to fight hard to maintain public confidence. Gossip began immediately among insiders. Among the first and best of the public attacks that began to appear soon after is James Gillray's aquatint *Shakespeare Sacrificed;—or—The Offering to Avarice,* published the year the gallery opened. Avarice, with money bags, sits on the altar—Boydell's list of subscribers—while Boydell, in his alderman's robes, burns Shakespeare's plays so that the English school's smoky chimeras can live for a time. The print is packed with allusions to paintings by West, Barry, Northcote, Fuseli, Reynolds, and Opie. In September 1788 Gillray tried to get Boydell to let him engrave a Northcote painting for the gallery. Boydell apparently refused, and *Shakespeare Sacrificed* was Gillray's revenge (W. H. Friedman 77–78).

In 1805, writing to William Hayley, Blake portrayed "all the time of Boydells Macklins Bowyers & other Great Works" as a past time of great economic opportunity in which his "Talents," plural, as painter and engraver, had been passed over (11 December 1805, E 766). Francis Wheatley (1747–1801), dead by the time of Blake's retrospection, had been one of those more favored. His large oil painting *The Death of Richard II* was ready to greet

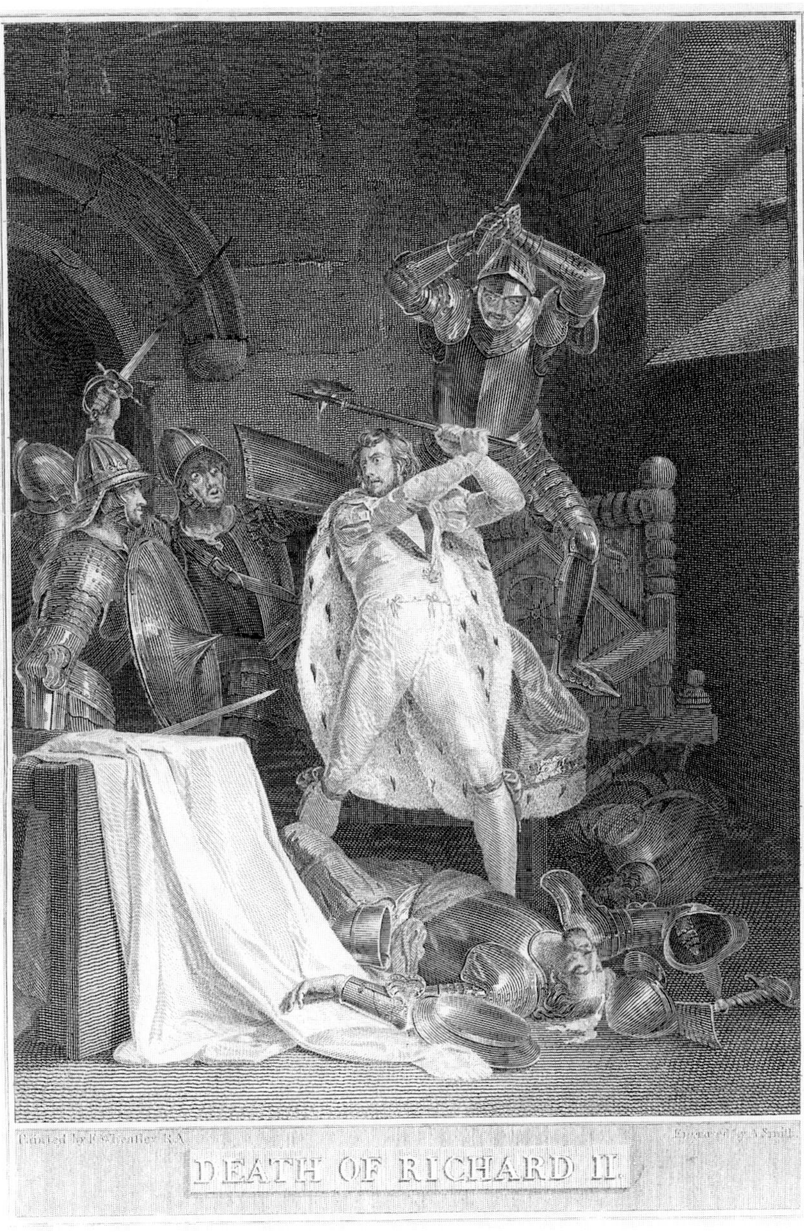

2.3. Anker Smith after Francis Wheatley, *The Death of Richard II,* engraving, 1793.

potential customers at the inaugural exhibition in 1793 of Robert Bowyer's Historic Gallery at 87, Pall Mall, not far from Boydell's Shakespeare Gallery at no. 52. Wheatley (who did the watercolor drawing of the Shakespeare Gallery opening reproduced in fig. 2.9) was very much a part of the Boydell era. He accepted thirteen commissions for the Boydell project, two for Bowyer's. The projects overlapped in many ways, not least in exploiting two veins of a burgeoning nationalism: Boydell's Shakespeare Gallery tried to capitalize on Shakespeare as the national poet; Bowyer's Historic Gallery entered the new market for constructions of English history. The overlap becomes obvious in *The Death of Richard II,* a title at home in both ventures. Bowyer claimed to base his gallery on the narrative of Hume's *History of England,* finished in 1762, but, as Bernard Barryte has shown in a well-informed essay on the Wheatley painting, dramatic departures from Hume were common. Hume suggested that Richard probably died of starvation in prison; Wheatley preferred the more extravagant visual opportunity offered by the popular story that he was bludgeoned from behind. Bowyer had copied Boydell in promising to donate Wheatley's *Death of Richard II* along with the other paintings in his gallery to the nation. As it happened, however, circumstances forced Boydell and Bowyer to imitate each other in a less public-spirited method of unloading property, a lottery (27 February 1805).

the thoroughly commonplace and persistent sense of misalignment voiced in the dedication of George Cumberland's *Essay on the Utility of Collecting the Best Works of the Ancient Engravers of the Italian School* to Baron Farnborough: "My Lord, That the Polite Arts may become, for the general benefit, as perfectly understood among us as the Arts of Commerce are, is a desire in which we mutually participate." The heart of Boydell's strategy lies in his ingenious, multifaceted attempt to transform two narratives that had often been opposed, the commercial and the aesthetic, into one. To the extent that Boydell would be a candidate for inclusion in any reasonably comprehensive history of art patronage, Burke was right to place him in a sequence with highly touted predecessors such as Maecenas. But as *commercial* Maecenas Boydell belongs to more than one history. In the history that he frequently encouraged others to tell, he competes with a patron such as George III, who supposedly was keeping Benjamin West too busy doing history paintings to contribute much to the Shakespeare Gallery. But in the more important history Boydell's closest contemporaries are not old-style patrons and certainly not monarchs, but such new-style merchandisers as Josiah Wedgwood (1730–1795), men who were learning how to coordinate complex systems of production and marketing and who wore the mantle of patron the way defense contractors wrap themselves in the flag—as a business strategy. In a confirmation of the shortage of traditional patronage in England, Iain Pears sharply distinguishes, for purposes of definition, patrons from customers and dealers (139–56). But one of the most important features of the period after 1760 is its search for ways to map the patron onto the customer and the dealer. Boydell and Wedgwood are archetypal.

Developing techniques that Boydell, though older, would repeat later, Wedgwood marketed his pottery as if it were of artistic significance.[5] To ride the crest of excitement over Herculaneum and the vogue for neoclassicism, he called his new factory Etruria, signed some of its early products *Artes Etruriae Renascuntur,* created such virtuoso showpieces as the Portland vase to add visual evidence to the claim of reviving Greek arts (fig. 2.4), and extended neoclassical styles from painting and sculpture, such as John Flaxman's, to pottery. In his drive to become "Vase maker General to the Universe" (quoted in Reilly 1:643), Wedgwood made much of his production techniques, including the revival of encaustic painting, sometimes going so far as to suggest that the ingredients were too rare to supply his needs indefinitely. He adopted the terminology of art collecting to product lines that he called "Historical Cabinets" (i.e., famous heads). He created showrooms appropriate both to the ancient-arts analogy that gave his products significance and to the upper-class clientele that bought them. He thought out the problems of showroom display by analogy with a "show, Exhibition, or rarity" in a setting that would be, as he described it to his London partner Thomas Bentley, "Elegant, extensive & Conven[ient]" (quoted in McKendrick, "Wedgwood" 419). Displays in their Greek Street showroom were organized on the principle of carefully regulated novelty to give people a reason for returning to the premises. Exhibition

[5] My information on Wedgwood's techniques of production and marketing comes from the extensive research of Neil McKendrick and Robin Reilly.

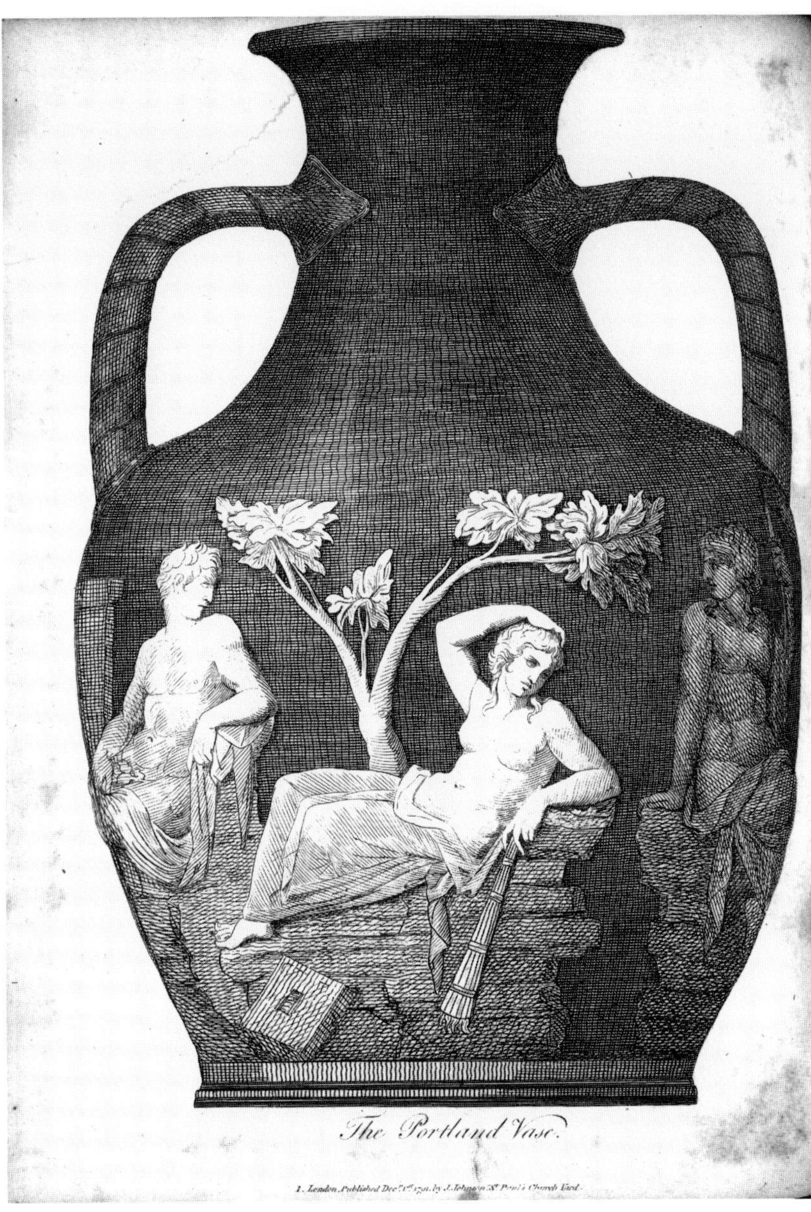

2.4. William Blake, *The Portland Vase,* engraving for Erasmus Darwin's *The Botanic Garden,* part 1, *The Economy of Vegetation,* 1791.

Josiah Wedgwood employed Blake's friend John Flaxman on numerous projects in the 1770s and 1780s, when Flaxman's brand of neoclassicism became the style most closely identified with the Wedgwood line of pottery, and then helped send him to Rome to supervise a group of artists working for Etruria, the Wedgwood factory. In 1784 Flaxman urged Wedgwood to rush to London to see the Portland (or Barberini) vase, "the finest production of Art that has been brought to England" (quoted in Reilly 1:663). By 1786 the vase was in Wedgwood's hands, on loan from the Duke of Portland, and for the next four years he labored to translate the vase into his famed "jasper ware" pottery. With great difficulty Etruria manufactured Portland replicas that crowned Wedgwood's campaign to enlist the status of classicism in the cause of marketing neoclassicism—a notable case of tradition authorizing novelty. As the applied chemistry of the pottery had supported Wedgwood's reputation as a man of science, the Portland vase completed his image as an Enlightenment-style antiquarian. The first perfect copy of the vase went to his friend Erasmus Darwin in 1789. The next year Wedgwood was charging admission to see a copy displayed at his London showroom (Reilly 1:673, 681, fig. 1037). And the next year four unsigned engravings of the vase appeared among the illustrations of Darwin's *Economy of Vegetation.* These unsigned engravings, first attributed to Blake by Geoffrey Keynes, were apparently com-

openings were timed to coincide with the introduction of spectacular new products that always had a powerful combination of social, historical, and artistic resonance. The social level of the spectacle was reinforced positively through the presence of prominent guests and negatively through ticketed admission, all in the service of "shewing that we are employ'd in a much higher scale than other Manufacturers" (quoted in McKendrick, "Wedgwood" 421)—upscale products for upscale buyers. Wedgwood understood the relation between the dynamics of class and the dynamics of marketing that produces emulative spending: "begin at the Head first, & then proceed to the inferior members" (quoted in Reilly 1:675). His exhibitions, like Boydell's, featured prototypes (the Russian service for Catherine the Great in 1774) that promoted the sale of copies.

Wedgwood's promotional schemes rest on two complementary metaphors that are made possible by his closeness to his products and his simultaneous distance from them. His position as a wealthy manufacturer overseeing the work of numerous artisans at Etruria ("to make *Artists*," as he said, of "mere *men*" [quoted in McKendrick, "Factory Discipline" 34]); commissioning and consulting such artists as Flaxman, George Stubbs, and Louis François Roubillac; claiming antiquarian knowledge through his copies of antique pottery but also through membership in the Antiquarian Society;[6] and sponsoring the revival of Greek art—all gave him the opportunity to play the patron. At the same time, however, his identification with his products through the control of production as well as marketing offered a supplementary opportunity. If products are marketed as art, then by extension of the metaphor the maker is an artist. A manufacturer whose products carried his name, Wedgwood reaped the benefits of the association with art and with the historical myth of the revival of ancient Greek arts in modern England through the agency of Wedgwood himself, during his lifetime and afterward. In 1866 Eliza Meteyard concluded the first full-dress biography of Wedgwood with the assertion that "IT WAS PATRONAGE WHICH SOUGHT THE GREAT POTTER: NOT THE GREAT POTTER PATRONAGE" (quoted in McKendrick, "Wedgwood" 412). Though the image of a Wedgwood so obsessed with "the creation of beauty" (431) that he had no time for mere patronage is Meteyard's mid-Victorian refinement of the material, the central image of Wedgwood the artist followed naturally from the associated image of Wedgwood ware as art. Now that it no longer has the commercial utility with which Wedgwood invested it, the image lives on in an encomiastic narrative tradition: "But Wedgwood was more than a mere chooser and employer of artists, a mere translator into clay of designs made by other hands in other materials, a mere copier of the antique. He possessed . . . an inventive faculty, which revealed itself . . . in the origination of new forms. Into his selected designs . . . he infused something of his spirit and temper . . . ," writes Arthur Herbert Church for the *Dictionary of National Biography*. The artistic image of Wedgwood as one identified with his work tends to reappear whenever he is praised.

[6] Wedgwood was elected to fellowship in the Royal Society in 1783, and in both the Antiquarian Society (now Society of Antiquaries) and the Society for the Encouragement of Arts, Manufactures, and Commerce in 1786.

missioned to replace an inferior set by Bartolozzi (see Essick, *Blake's Commercial Book Illustrations* 45–49).

Why the English School Painted Shakespeare

> Whatever Josiah's private sympathies, his public productions were designed to travel commercially in all directions.
>
> —Robin Reilly, *Wedgwood*

Although Boydell was eleven years older than Wedgwood, in the 1760s, 1770s, and 1780s the commercial Maecenas might have learned a lot from the potter about the uses of public myths, analogies, and roles in the marketing of the polite arts. The similarities are many, though the challenges that they turned into commercial programs were different. Wedgwood aimed to combine the utility of a craft with the sociocommercial advantages of an art. So did Boydell, at least insofar as his interest lay in associating engraving with its loftier cousin, painting. But Boydell found his greater challenge, and the centerpiece of his advertising strategy, in the problem of the English school: how to raise English painting to the level of continental painting. Thus from the beginning he placed the Shakespeare project squarely in the context of the English-school controversy. By 1789, pulling out all the stops, he was prepared to advertise his scheme as a solution to the problem of English painting as we have heard it described for a century and more:

> In this progress of the fine Arts, though Foreigners have allowed our lately acquired superiority of Engraving, and readily admitted the great Talents of the principal Painters, yet they have said with some severity . . . that the abilities of our best Artists are chiefly employed in painting Portraits . . . While the noblest part of the Art—HISTORICAL PAINTING—is much neglected. To obviate this national Reflection was, as I have already hinted, the principal cause of the present undertaking. [Preface to the 1789 catalogue of the first exhibition in the Shakespeare Gallery, quoted in Bruntjen 71]

The press echoed him. In 1789 Humphrey Repton, as the anonymous author of *The Bee, or A Companion to the Shakspeare Gallery*, praised one of John Opie's paintings as justifying "hopes that the Gallery will lay the foundation for an English School of Painting that shall equal, if not surpass, that of all the other countries" (quoted in Bruntjen 13–14). From the start the Boydell project was seen as a new kind of artistic opportunity, but also as one particularly appropriate to the English situation. Boydell crystallized the hope that commerce rather than aristocratic patronage would create an English school. "But, after all [of Joshua Reynolds's supposed influence], what or where is this vaunted patronage of the great?" asks the anonymous author of *Observations on the Present State of the Royal Academy:* "Nay, it appears to me, that the BOYDELLS, by their establishment of the SHAKESPEARE GALLERY, have a better claim to the homage of the arts, than the aggregate body of the nobility and gentry of Great Britain" (22).

Brief as it is, Boydell's public relations work has several features of interest. He invokes the "progress" theme in its commercial version, tying artistic progress not to specific artistic techniques but to a specific business venture.

He uses them-and-us characterization to cast England as the object of unfavorable world opinion. Consider the difference between Boydell and Aglionby, who a century earlier also offered his critique of English taste on the authority of continental opinion. Aglionby rhetorically identified with that authority, and the effect was to scorn native ignorance. But then he was looking for independent status as a connoisseur; Boydell is looking for customers. His formulation "Foreigners . . . they" suggests that foreign conclusions are drawn from an alienating distance and "with some severity." He has carefully chosen his words for the effect of foreign criticism, suggesting with his noncommittal "Reflection" a secondary image that may be a practical or diplomatic problem but not necessarily the whole truth. The message is that, while the foreign opinion of English painting may be excessively severe, to avoid further embarrassment the nation must demonstrate its full range of artistic power. Boydell lets the foreigners take the blame for negative judgments of English painting while reserving for himself the role of knowledgeable insider, which he establishes with personal pronouns that beckon toward "our . . . superiority" and "our best Artists." As an insider willing to reveal for the general good his special knowledge of what outsiders are thinking, he earns the authority to propose without seeming to impose a solution, this time with a personal pronoun that might otherwise seem overassertive—"as I have already hinted," he whispers, as if letting us in on a trade secret. He augments his authority with reminders that he has righted English artistic injustices before: "Foreigners have allowed our lately acquired superiority of Engraving." He means *I have seen to it,* tacitly identifying his widely recognized commercial success in the export of English engravings with a supposed reversal of continental opinion.

He makes his past success the first stage in a plot of artistic progress as follows. By convincing the foreigners of the superiority of English engraving—as he would have it, while others might say "by selling lots of English engravings"—he has taken one step in the right direction. And then the foreigners have already "admitted the great Talents of the principal Painters." "Admitted . . . Talents . . . yet": he puts England on the brink of victory. What stands in the way? Here again he draws on the terms of the English-school debate to characterize the obstruction as neither climate, temperament, nor talent but opportunity.

Boydell, in his effort to harmonize a commercial discourse with an aesthetic one, does not overlook the social affinities of the latter, which can make artistic progress a kind of social climbing. Instead of talking about producing, selling, and buying pictures, or even using the more familiar "encouraging," "promoting," and "supporting," he substitutes the symbolic opposition between portrait and history, which of course is far more than a choice of subject. The choice is between levels in the conventional hierarchy of decorum congruent with a social hierarchy—between "the noblest part of the Art," as Boydell puts it, and the most vulgar. Everybody has a face; few have significant histories. Portrait painting is poor painting, the peddler painter serving the self-indulgent. Portrait painting is also parochial painting; the images of the English ladies and gentlemen, wealthy merchants, and popular divines do not travel well. In the aesthetic translation, portrait does not deliver universal nature. In the commercial translation, portraits, despite their commercial utility, are local products for restricted markets. Portrait is diversion and neglect: when painters are neglected, they neglect history painting and paint portraits. And portraiture turns both painter and subject away from public virtue toward private vanity and flattery. Portraits establish a direct relationship between painters and clients; the painter doubles as the merchant and the subject as the customer.

It is essential to the design of Boydell's rhetoric that he speak not as a private individual but as a middleman, a public man whose eye is not on himself but on the public and the painters. As the common resort of painters needing funds, portraiture had long been synonymous with commerce. Boydell verges on paradox in proposing that his kind of commerce can solve the artistic problem often regarded as the very consequence of England's commercial proclivities. Insofar as his proposal embodies Reynolds's hope that the progress of a commercial nation and the progress of art may eventually converge, it is appropriate for the institution founded in that hope, the Royal Academy, to supply the trained labor force for Boydell's scheme. As jobs follow college, the Shakespeare Gallery follows Academy schooling, based on public values of consensus and an international style, with an appropriately extensive marketplace.

Only from this angle can we understand Boydell's appeal to patriotism, which defines the group to which he belongs as a national group subject to a "national Reflection" by "Foreigners." He even claims that patriotism is "the principal cause of the present undertaking." But his commercial aims make his patriotism less parochial than emulative. He appeals to the English desire to beat other nations at their own game, history painting. Portrait painting is not a viable candidate for "national" artistic superiority in Boydell's sense, which to be complete must be "international." In that competition Boydell again casts himself as the middleman, operating from a national base but as the source of an international perspective from which English painting can be judged superior. In his life of Northcote, Allan Cunningham later formulated accurately this side of the Shakespeare project's appeal: "The aim of that generous patron of the fine arts was to establish a market all over the world . . . and so diffuse at one and the same time a knowledge of our history, our poetry, and our fine arts, among all nations" (6:75).

Shakespeare fits this scheme in two important ways.[7] First, Boydell wants Shakespeare's Englishness—our poet to make a match for our painters and engravers. At the same time, of all English poets Shakespeare is the one for whom international claims can be most forcefully made, the one who raises English history, in the extended sense required by history painting, to the level of history with a capital *H:* "The encouragement he himself [Boydell] would endeavour to find if a proper subject were pointed out. Mr. Nicol replied that there was one great National subject concerning which there could be no second opinion, and

[7] Paulson usefully relates Boydell's choice of Shakespeare as a subject to the English painter's plight in "Shakespeare and the Englishness of English Art" (25–36). For a broader, more pragmatic account of the nationalism that fed Shakespeare's reputation in the 1790s and after, see Gary Taylor, who observes accurately that "Boydell set out to alloy Shakespeare, patriotism, and the profit motive" (124). "Patriotism," however, must be understood here in its twentieth-century sense (cf. Hugh Cunningham, "Language of Patriotism"); the term would have meant something quite different to Boydell's contemporaries.

mentioned Shakespeare" (Graves 143). Thus, in Boydell's terms, which are the only terms that make Shakespeare useful to "the present undertaking," Shakespeare is the most commercial English poet.

Second, the choice of Shakespeare allows Boydell to exploit the strongest formulation of the poet-painter analogy. If the best long-term answer to continental skepticism about the future of English painting had been the analogy of historical cycles, the best short-term response had been a second tier of analogy: as one art, so another. The analogy of the arts has of course many uses. Armed with the commonplace that "Poetry addresses itself to the same faculties and the same dispositions as Painting, though by different means" (dis. 13, 205), Reynolds argues for the legitimacy of artistic combinations such as opera, though on other grounds he also maintains that "no Art can be engrafted with success on another art" (dis. 13, 210). The same formula can be turned into a national defense of painting: as English poetry, the greatness of which seems undeniable, so English painting. The continental critics talk "as if the Genius of a Painter was one Kind of Essence, and the Genius of a Poet another; and as if the Air and Soil which had given Birth to a Shakespear and a Bacon, a Milton and a Newton . . . could be deficient in any Species of Excellency whatsoever," wrote the anonymous author of *The Plan of an Academy* in 1755 (vi).

In this hopeful formulation English painting becomes, in Valentine Green's characteristic figure, "the last offspring of a parent that had filled the world with the renown of all her other progeny" (37)—the sister arts in their English-school clothes.[8] Though neither earliest nor most cohesive, Barry's use of the analogy as an answer to Winckelmann in the *Inquiry* of 1775 is the best known. The fable of an original master art suggests that the separation of verbal from visual arts is itself temporary. The "peculiar advantages and disadvantages" (108) of each of the two, different objects produced under different circumstances, account for the good fortunes of English poetry and the bad fortunes of English painting. Michelangelo required the Sistine Chapel, whereas *Paradise Lost* "required neither a palace nor a prince, and is as much within the purchase of the mechanic, as of the sovereign." Paintings are "unique" and "confined to the possession of some one great employer or purchaser" (*Account* 19). However, the knowledge that "the essence and ground-work of poetry and painting is in every respect the same" (*Inquiry* 107) reassures Barry that when opportunities are equal, the arts will be equal—and, at least by implication, reunited as one.

The strength of these otherwise thin and vaguely Horatian commonplaces becomes more understandable when we notice their persistent alliance with a moralized empiricism. It comes out early and unmistakably, for example, in George Turnbull's 1740 *Treatise on Ancient Painting*. To deepen the familiar assertion that "the Climate cannot be too cold, nor the Air too gross, to bring forth an *Apelles* or a *Raphael*, that produced a *Milton*" (110), Turnbull levels all the arts to languages that "convey into the mind Ideas" either "sensible" or "moral." We might object that, if the arts are the

[8] The relation of painting to poetry is a standard topic in the tradition, if that is the term, of *ut pictura poesis*. See esp. the two chapters on "English neoclassicism" in the first part, "The Tradition," of Hagstrum. Although Hagstrum's emphasis, as his subtitle indicates, is on pictorialism in poetry, the earlier chapters in "The Tradition" are broadly relevant to several issues that I take up, including the socio-intellectual status of poets and painters.

same, why do we need Raphaels when we already have Miltons? He answers that the more means of conveyance there are, the stronger the impression: "they must necessarily have a multiplied Force" (ix).

Turnbull's argument, like Barry's, replaces continental pessimism about fixed climates and temperaments with a dynamic educational optimism. Turnbull boldly assimilates the pattern of improvement exemplified by the Vasari canon to a Baconian-Lockean epistemology, thus making all the arts part of one vast scheme to train the mind to natural knowledge and to virtue through experience: "What are Landscapes or Views of Nature, but . . . Samples and Experiments in natural Philosophy? And moral [i.e., history] pictures . . . are they not . . . Samples or Experiments in moral Philosophy?" (145).

Turnbull's treatment of painting is far more leveling and Lockean than Barry's, but they are more alike than different in essentials. Both exemplify an inclination to justify art as a component in a vast pedagogical scheme of individual and social improvement whose germinal episode is the "experiment" or sample experience and whose end is natural and moral knowledge, or what Hoare, reciting the standard idea, later calls "advancement in mental elegance" and "the improvement of *mental pleasure*" (20). The expanded Vasari canon fits neatly into the scheme, helping the arts find their place alongside philosophy and science in a harmony of pedagogical means (mythologized in Barry's master art). Natural and moral knowledge can be harmonized because external nature is treated as if in tune with human nature. Since the movement in this program is from ignorance to knowledge, any nation can play. The only possible handicap is some form of forced preconception, or tyranny, and England's liberty gives it, if anything, an advantage.

The importance of education as deep advertising cannot be overemphasized. Turnbull's empiricism supplies the mechanism by which a member of the English audience may move, or must move, from an appreciation of poetry to an appreciation of painting. From this point of view, Boydell's Shakespeare project provides the educational materials through which the mechanism will operate—thus solving the problem of the English school while doubling the market.

The commercial usefulness of the analogy between poetry and painting shows up explicitly in one of the catalogues of Boydell's competitor Thomas Macklin, when he comes to offer "some apology for his presumption" in making a "humble effort" to "present the public with an entertainment of this kind." Macklin's apology draws on the "natural alliance between the Fine Arts" to explain that, as the "object of all the Arts is precisely the same" though the means of attaining the object are different, poetry and painting are naturally supplementary. Poets give painters all their "happiest subjects," while painters "reflect a lustre" on poems. Consequently the best way for a humble middleman to pursue "the encouragement of the Artists" is by "this mode of illustrating the authors of our own Country." Since this manner of construing the analogy emphasizes mutual supplementation and variety, Macklin can extend the spirit of generosity to his financial liberality: "in the encouragement . . . I made it my uniform practice to act as liberally as my means would possibly admit, relying only for remuneration on a generous Public." He can use the same spirit to distinguish his project from Boydell's: "I did not confine my views to any particular author [as Boydell did], because I conceived that, by embracing them all, a more extensive field presented itself for the exertions of fancy, and afforded room for a more diversified display of excellence" (*Catalogue of the Third Exhibition of Pictures Painted for Mr. Macklin, by the Artists of Britain* [1790], iii–iv; quoted in Bruntjen 152–53n109).

Another feature of Boydell's project that commercializes a prominent theme of the English-school discourse is the gallery itself. Asking where their work could be seen had become a standard way of focusing attention on the English painters' special plight. Writers on the English school routinely noted the gravity of the problem and proposed solutions. Here again we recognize at least two distinct though related aims of such proposals, the commercial and the pedagogical. Painters and sculptors wanted work, and they wanted what we now call exposure in order to get more work. Public displays of art provided work and exposure. But displays also provided the occasion for instruction. An exhibition of old masters would create no work for English painters, but it might teach both the painters and the public more about correct taste.[9]

The gallery phase of the Shakespeare project thus belongs in a well-established line of argument about the English school. In the system of analogy that supplied, at least in prospect, a history of English painting, the Shakespeare Gallery of course fell under the rubric of *opportunity,* which was supposed to be chronically lacking. The Italians had their churches and their palaces to paint for; what analogous opportunities did the English painters have? This figure of thought inspired any number of ingenious proposals and gave them at least some moral force. There is no room here for a complete record, but any list of landmarks of the genre must include Hogarth's scheme for decorating the Foundling Hospital in the 1740s—often regarded as the first exhibition of contemporary art in England—followed eventually by the annual exhibitions at the Royal Academy, which were a, perhaps the, major emphasis of the Academy's original program. Louise Lippincott has shown how the Academy institutionalized on a larger scale the clubs through which business had been conducted and commercial schemes hatched (or, in the vocabulary of this discourse, opportunities created) in earlier decades. A good example is the proposal to decorate St. Paul's with paintings by six academicians. Accounts differ, but according to Barry the idea was first broached "in a conversation at one of our [Academy] dinners" (quoted in Pressly, *Life* 42) and was pursued by means of a letter from Barry to the Duke of Richmond in August 1773. By October, after the dean and chapter of St. Paul's had approved the plan, the archbishop of Canterbury and the bishop of London had rejected it (Pressly, *Life* 42–43). Thereafter, beginning with Barry's own *Inquiry* in 1775, the lament over Protestant iconoclasm becomes a stock motif in the English-school debate and the church hierarchy's rejection of the Academy plan becomes a long-lived case in point.[10]

[9] The first extended attempt of which I am aware to record and understand the institutional history of art in the eighteenth century is W. B. Sarsfield Taylor's in 1841. Much of his second volume, esp. chap. 15, develops the argument that institutions, including the exhibitions that they sponsored, provided the "continuity of purpose" hitherto lacking in a history in which there had been "nothing steady, nothing consecutive" (2:129, 128).

[10] Pressly notes that as late as 1807 Robert Southey—of a new generation—expresses regret over the rejection (*Life* 211n53), and still later regrets could surely be found. For a fuller account of the late eighteenth-century effort to intro-

Most of the proposals for public exhibitions on a large scale have the double aim of giving English painters the chance to do history paintings and of educating the public. The education is of two kinds: the moral instruction associated with arts and letters and the instruction in taste associated with exposure to correct works of art. The proposers were of course aware that opportunity and education are related. Education of the public is, among other things, a commercial tactic for opening a new market by creating a new supply (from painters educated into the skills of history painting by the Academy) matched to a new demand (from a public educated into the taste for history paintings by exhibitions), and history painting was, among other things, an underdeveloped market in England. "Taste" is not only aesthetic judgment but also educated yearning—often accompanied by an exchange of goods and money. The effort to put English painting into the path of the "progression of the arts" is, by the end of the century, a commercial effort to achieve a coordinated progression of skills, taste, and money strong enough to motivate an economic takeoff in the painting industry. Of course the discourse is usually silent on these indelicate matters.

After the collective effort to win approval of the St. Paul's scheme had failed, Barry decided to go it alone in a similar project, the decoration of the Great Room of the Society of Arts at the Adelphi, on which he spent several years during the 1770s and 1780s (see Pressly, *Life*, 86–122). The *Progress of Human Culture* paintings are, as his descriptions of them show, Barry's independent contribution to a national *educational* collection of art that culminates in the founding of the great public museums (fig. 2.5). The Adelphi sequence is progressive not only in its depiction of the history of knowledge but also in its doubly pedagogical purpose of letting some light into the dark minds of English artists and the English audience. Barry attempted to capitalize on the public opportunity provided by the Adelphi paintings by using them to support various private commercial ventures in the manner of the time. He won permission from the Society for exhibitions, and he executed and sold prints after the paintings. Similarly, the Academy group had offered to decorate St. Paul's gratis, as a public service, understanding that the value of the publicity would have been far greater than any fee they might have charged. Joshua Reynolds was clearheaded about the motive: "For the sake of the advantage which would accrue to the Arts by establishing a fashon of having Pictures in Churches" (to Lord Hardwicke, 16 October 1773, *Letters* 37). The painters would also have anticipated a profit from reproductions. In 1783 Barry did for his Adelphi pictures what he doubtless would have done for the St. Paul's paintings: he wrote a catalogue (*An Account of a Series of Pictures*) tied to a proposal for reproductions (*Proposals for Publishing by Subscription, Six Engraved Prints, from the Above-Mentioned Series*). In the lexicon of "opportunity" and "encouragement," Barry later maintained that sale of the engravings helped to support the painting: "Mr. Barry also takes this Opportunity of offering to the Notice and Encouragement of a high spirited, liberal Public, an improved Renovation of some other Engravings, by the private Sale of which, he was enabled to devote almost Seven Years Applica-

duce art into English churches, culminating in George III's ultimately aborted plan for a Chapel of the History of Revealed Religion at Windsor, with paintings by West, see Dillenberger; also Pears 47, 139.

(OVERLEAF)

The most interesting of Barry's six *Progress of Human Culture* murals in the Great Room is *Commerce or the Triumph of the Thames,* which began as a tribute to British trade afloat and then moved with the age toward nationalistic imperialism in the postrevolutionary years. (Though *Commerce* is a way of declaring that England is the most commercial nation in the world, deep misgivings about commerce surface in Barry's discussion of the picture [*Account* 59–70, esp. 60–61].) Allowed by the Society to clean the Great Room pictures in 1801, Barry took the opportunity to make some changes, among them the tower added to the background at right: this is his contribution to the competition, announced in 1799, to design a monument exalting British naval victories over the French (see figs. 2.15 and 2.16)—doubtless the competition that inspired Opie to propose, in 1800, a British Pantheon that would employ British painters and sculptors to produce works on British subjects. Barry died in 1806, the year of Hoare's *Inquiry* and the founding of the British Institution, before he could execute another intended addition to the *Commerce* mural, the figure of Lord Nelson (Pressly, *Life* 101–5 and *Artist as Hero* 82–83).

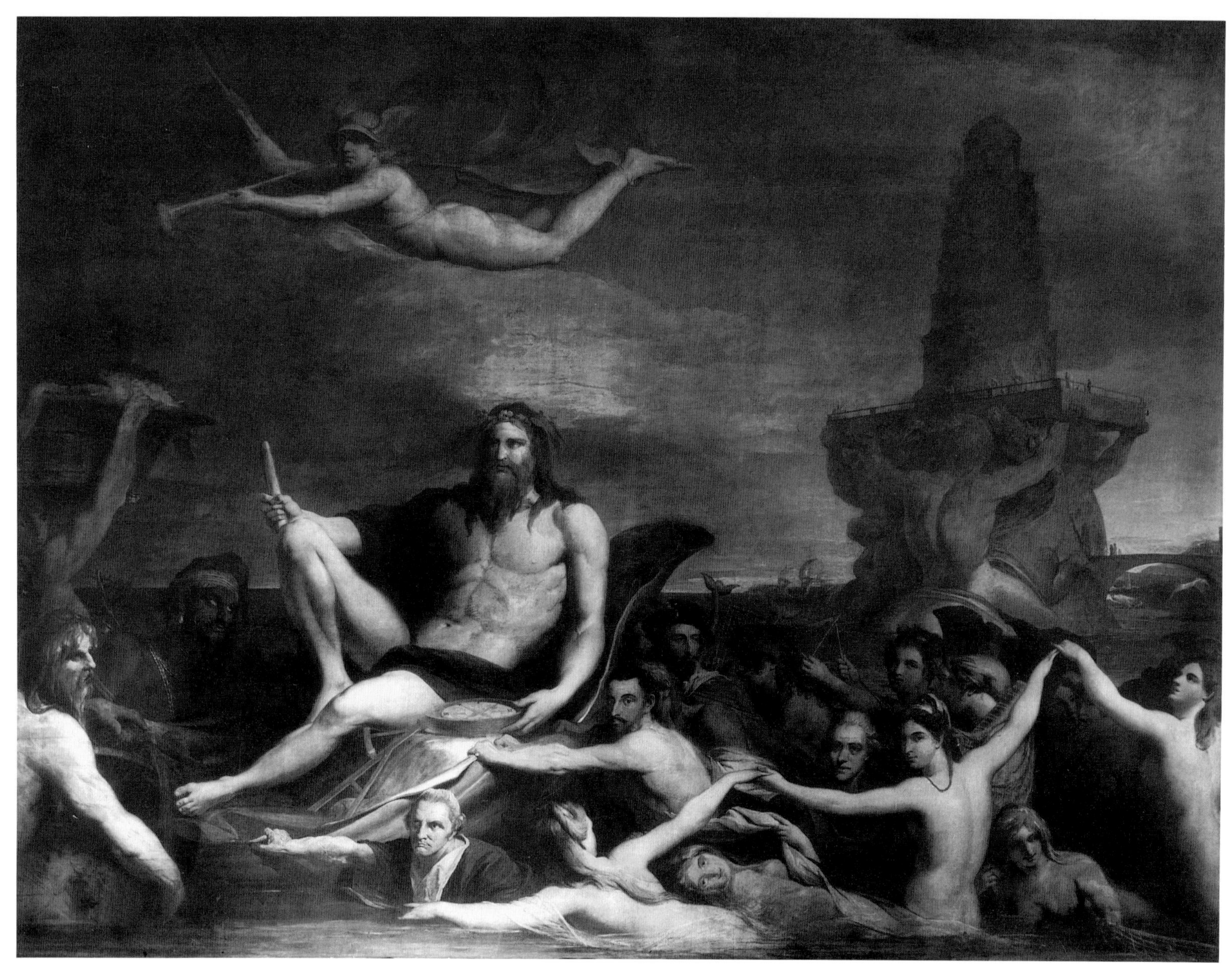

2.5. James Barry, *Commerce or the Triumph of the Thames*, 1777–1784, 1801.

tion in carrying on that very extensive and laborious Work of Painting at the *Adelphi*" (quoted in Pressly, *Life* 129).

One important context for Boydell's gallery, then, is the evolution of the public exhibition as a form of commercial opportunity or encouragement for artists. While for convenience we may designate the two major kinds of exhibition public and private in their ownership, both are public in access. Though private galleries seldom acknowledge their historical responsibility and public collections even more seldom acknowledge their commercial role, they are closely related nonetheless; witness the continuous line of development toward a national public collection of pictures from the Foundling Hospital days to the creation of the National Gallery with government funds in 1824. The line of development of course includes Boydell's additions to the list of proposed collections: one, with the Shakespeare Gallery paintings as part, in Green Park (a rather oversubscribed spot that Blake's friend George Cumberland also proposed, in the 1790s, for a collection of Greek antiquities that would mold English taste); and a second in Guildhall (Bruntjen 226–28). Furthermore, the way had been well prepared by several decades of experiments by Hogarth, the Academy, Barry, West, and Copley, among others, in devising ways to get English paintings into public settings, with the aim of profiting not only from the paintings but also from exhibitions and prints (figs. 2.6, 2.7). English painters had been slowly discovering how to make exhibitions do double and triple duty as forms of public service and forms of merchandising, married in the reverential rhetoric of education.[11] We have seen Boydell tying his project to the theme of public service, which allowed him to exploit the subthemes of the English-school debates. Not only was the neglect of English history painting supposed to be the "principal cause" of the Shakespeare project, but the "national honour" was said to be at stake in its success—along with "the advancement of the Arts" and (last) the "advantage" of the painters (quoted in Bruntjen 71). The language was contagious, and many commentators over the next few years would characterize Boydell's Shakespeare as (in Boydell's words) a "national attempt" (Bruntjen 149n; see also, e.g., Bruntjen 116, 127n, 128n, 129n).

The gallery was a key means to give the project a highly visible face that would legitimize Boydell's claims to public-spiritedness. One of the great advantages of St. Paul's for its would-be decorators had been its status as a central public institution. And, while no St. Paul's, the Society of Arts that Barry had ennobled with his *Human Culture* paintings was a public institution with walls appropriate to civic themes. Boydell cleverly bought into the spirit of such undertakings by creating an imitation of a public institution. First, he physically separated the gallery from his shop as if to distinguish public from private space. That distinction he reinforced with another between the earlier, commercial phase of his project and the later, noncommercial phase, which he symbolized by a promise to turn the gallery over to

[11] Boydell's opportunity to gain from his own patronage did not go unnoticed. Bruntjen quotes a broadside from 1790: "Mr. Alderman HUM'EM and Co. . . . propose to publish, by subscriptions, a most grand and pompous collection OF DESIGNS, to illustrate the immortal SHAKESPEARE" (92). Gillray's satirical prints, including *Shakespeare Sacrificed:—or—The Offering to Avarice* (1789) (see fig. 2.2) and *The Monster Broke Loose—or—A Peep into the Shakespeare Gallery* (1791), are the best evidence of Boydell's vulnerability to anticommercial mockery, which no doubt motivated him to bury the commercial aspects of his project even more deeply in public-service rhetoric.

(OVERLEAF)

In the last decades of the eighteenth century such painters as Benjamin West and his compatriot rival John Singleton Copley developed a commercially successful formula: paint an event of popular interest, exhibit it accessibly, charge admission, and solicit subscriptions for an engraving to come. Copley's titanic efforts—in both senses of the term—to make the formula work to his advantage during the 1780s and 1790s help to locate history paintings in the commerce of the period. After moving from Boston to London, Copley established himself professionally by advertising his work through the annual exhibitions of the new Royal Academy. In 1778 *Watson and the Shark* created a great sensation at the Academy, and he exploited it commercially with a print by Valentine Green the next year. For his next big project Copley applied for the commission to memorialize William Pitt, Earl of Chatham, who had died by stroke in the House of Lords in 1778. Denied the commission, he went ahead with the painting as a financial speculation. Instead of putting it in the Academy show, he solicited subscriptions for an engraving and exhibited *The Death of the Earl of Chatham* independently—but during the Academy's 1781 exhibition. Sensing a threat, the Academy reacted strongly. The architect William Chambers, leading the opposition, called Copley's exhibition a "raree

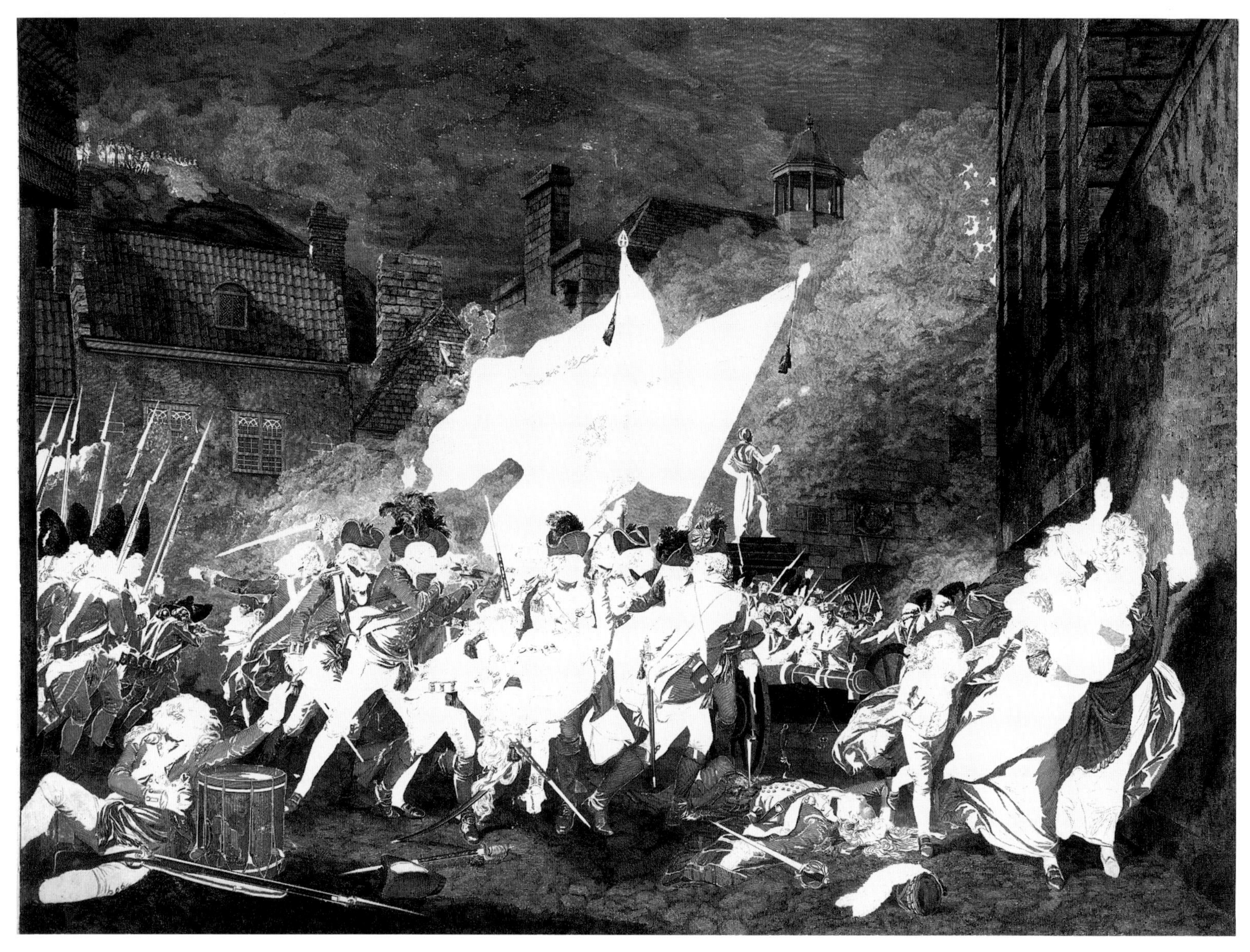

A

2.6. James Heath after J. S. Copley, *The Death of Major Peirson,* engraving: (*A*) preliminary etched state, 1788; (*B*) published state, 1796; (*C*) key.

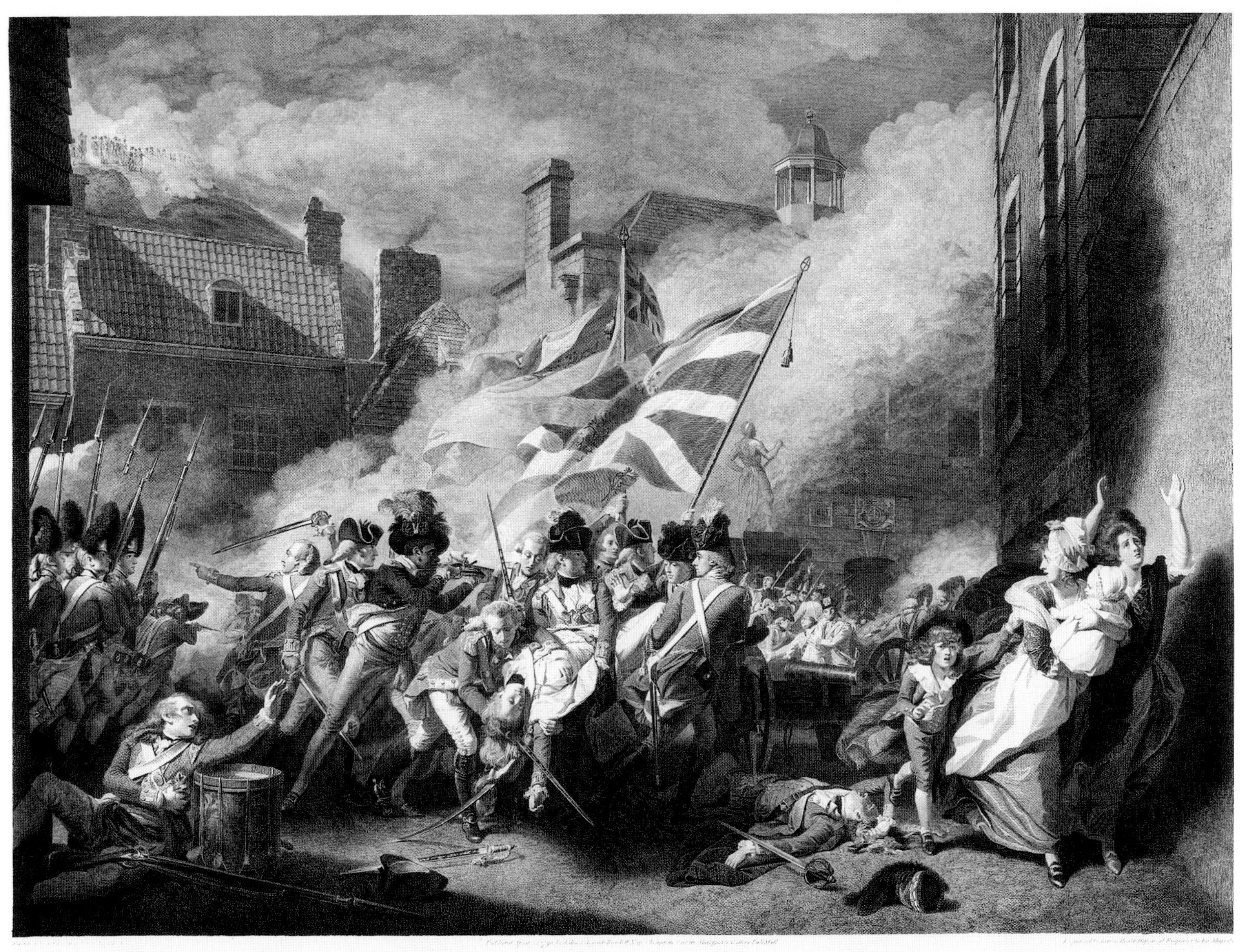

B

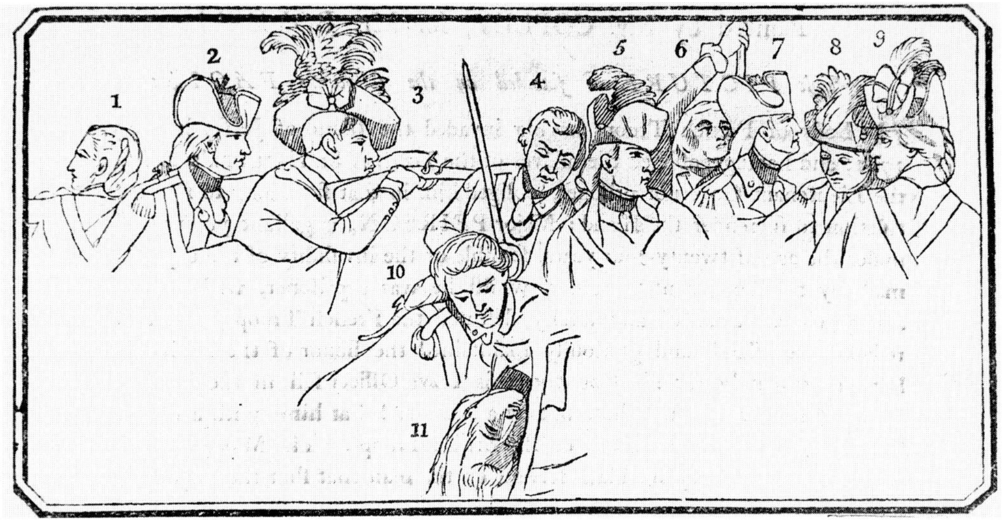

C

the public after the completion of the publishing projects. And finally, acting out his role as patron, he hired the architect George Dance to design not a picture dealer's or printseller's shop but a mock-public building, even a national building, complete with pilasters, pediment, and commissioned sculpture by Thomas Banks and Anne Damer.

By tying his project to a national problem (the reputation of the English school) and to an oft-proposed solution (the encouragement of history painting) that depended upon an international response; by tying his project to a national poet whose reputation was international and to a quasi-national institution that could claim to represent the nation's greatest poet through the work of its best painters and engravers, Boydell positioned himself to deploy the analogies that had supported such projects in the past. The abortive plan to decorate St. Paul's had been devised by analogy with the great European religious monuments; English painters would have attempted to make St. Paul's the Sistine Chapel of a modern commercial nation. Boydell's project was devised and promoted in that analogical spirit, which soon began to work in his favor. In the first flush of enthusiasm upon the opening of the Shakespeare Gallery in 1789, a London newspaper concluded that the gallery would "rank the name of Boydell with the Medici" (quoted in Bruntjen 91)—the gallery itself presumably being Boydell's Farnese. When Burke labeled Boydell the commercial Maecenas, he was merely extending the embrace of the analogy to the other sister art and the Romans. Boydell added credibility to the analogy by cultivating his image as a public man—sheriff, alderman, lord mayor—and for a time he vigorously expanded the lord mayor's role as patron of public architecture and painting at Guildhall, against the advice of his nephew Josiah (Bruntjen 197–240 and appendixes 2 and 3) (figs. 2.8, 2.9).

show"—accurately if pejoratively marking the business tactic that painters had learned from other exhibitors. The fear was justified: as Academy receipts declined by £1,000, Copley attracted 20,000 people in six weeks. He briskly followed up his success with *The Death of Major Peirson* (1784), commissioned this time by Boydell and exhibited in the Haymarket at a shilling per viewer with the increasingly standard promotional literature: printed explanation, key, and solicitation for a projected engraving (Prown 2: 275–91, 302–21). James Heath required twelve years and the work of many assistants to complete the engraving, but Boydell made a great success of it.

Copley continued to exploit his formula with *The Siege of Gibraltar,* commissioned in 1783 by the London Court of Common Council, which had denied him the commission for *Chatham.* When it was finally completed eight years later, the picture was so huge (almost 18 by 25 feet) that it had to be exhibited in a tent 84 feet long in Green Park. Because of complaints from wealthy residents about noise and crowds and the obstruction of their view, the tent had to be moved several times. The effort was worth the trouble:

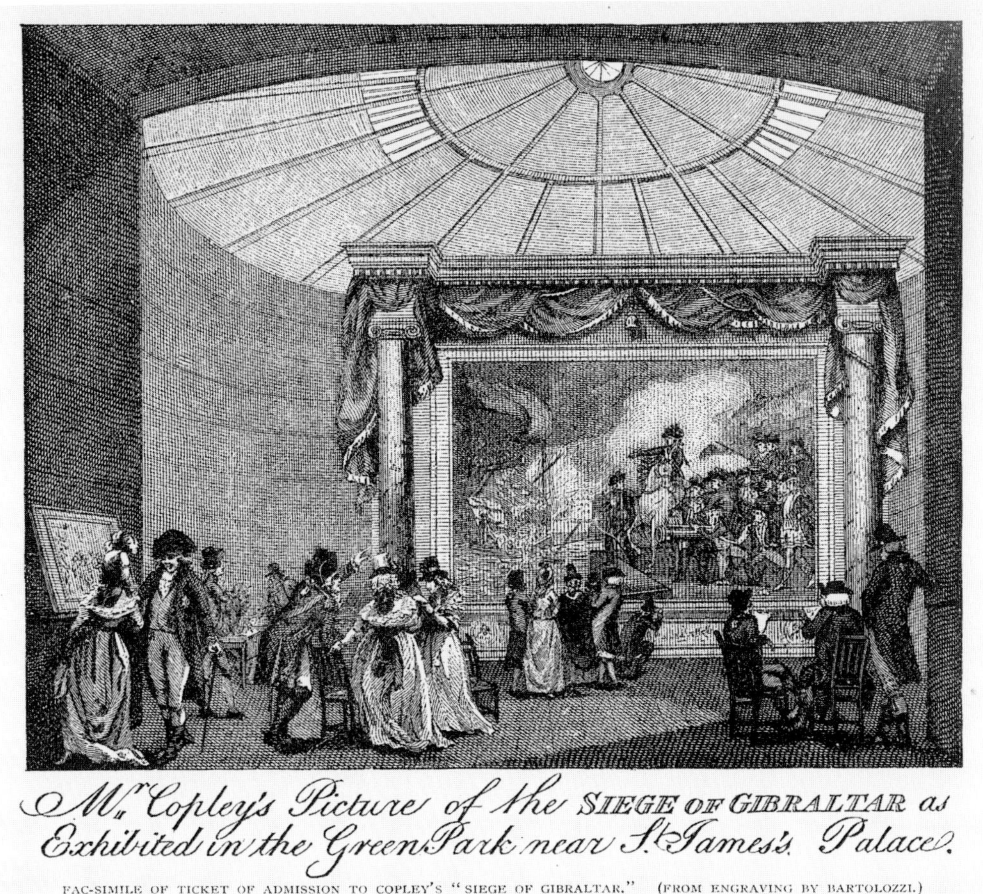

2.7. Francesco Bartolozzi, engraved ticket of admission to the 1791 exhibition of Copley's *Siege of Gibraltar* (facsimile of ticket by unidentified artist).

Copley claimed that 60,000 people came to see the painting. The admission ticket, engraved by Bartolozzi, suggests what such exhibitions were like. Boydell was heavily involved in some of these projects, and indeed Copley's formula was the one he recalibrated for the Shakespeare Gallery. He multiplied its private commercial potential, most obviously by enlarging scale and scope and combining the sale of engravings with the sale of a printed text, even as he emphasized its public or institutional aspects. The similarity of Boydell's and Copley's formulas is also revealed in the similarity of their difficulties: endless trouble with engravers—largely because of their inferior technology—and an unstable relationship among often conflicting private, state, and public interests. Thus Copley could never sell his *Death of Chatham:* painted as a public spectacle, it was ill suited for any other use, and, as the chorus of would-be history painters endlessly lamented, the opportunities to make paintings into dignified public spectacles were rare in England. Copley finally got rid of his *Chatham* by holding his own lottery in 1806—the year of Hoare's *Inquiry* and Landseer's aborted lectures on engraving, and the year after Boydell's and Macklin's lotteries. Copley, perpetually at odds with his engravers, could have told them a thing or two about the English school of engraving. And he understood that painters in England had to create their own "opportunities" (Prown 2:288, 322–36; Altick 105–6).

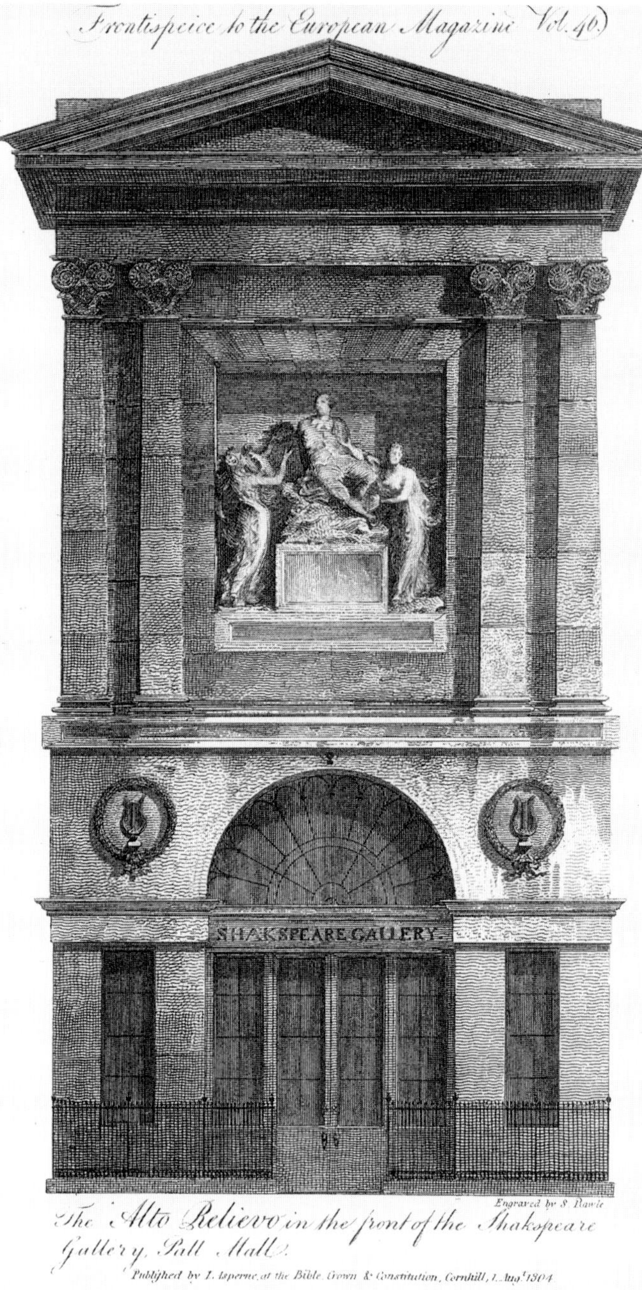

2.8. S. Rawle, *View of the Shakespeare Gallery,* etched frontispiece to the *European Magazine,* vol. 46, 1804.

On more than one occasion Boydell narrated a history of English art to show how it would appear with himself as hero. The history follows the familiar progressive pattern, though with an interesting commercial slant, pairing metaphors of "honour" and "reputation" with metaphors of "value," "support," and "advantage." In 1793 he explained to the Court of Common Council that

> in past Ages, and in all countries, it has been always acknowledged, that the Arts have been of infinite service to mankind. In Italy it has been their chief support; the Honour of being the first that brought the Arts, to a degree of perfection, never known before, has given them that character in the world, that every production coming from thence stamps a value upon it.
>
> From Italy the Arts spread into Germany, France, Spain and other parts of Europe, and have been the cause of their partaking of the Honour and advantage, which formerly appertained chiefly to Italy.
>
> Till latterly this Country had not gained any reputation in the Polite Arts; it was generally thought that the Genius of England, could not arrive to any degree of perfection. . . . Our Noblemen and Gentlemen of great fortunes, laid out large sums of money . . . furnishing their rooms with Italian and French productions.

At this point he introduces himself, implicitly, as the one responsible for the "first great improvement . . . employing and encouraging our engravers on proper subjects" to "bring that

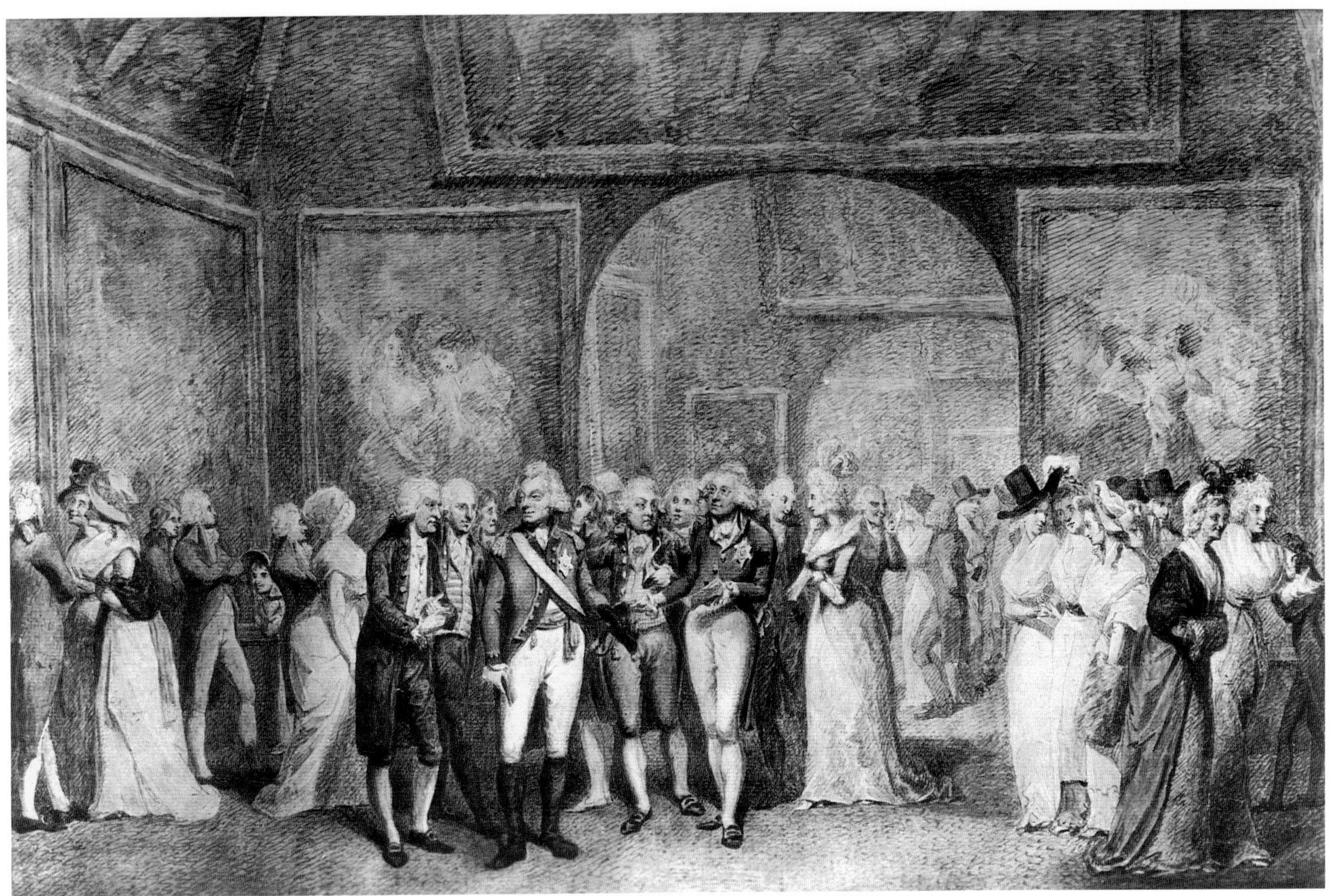

2.9. Francis Wheatley, *The Opening of the Shakespeare Gallery, 1790,* watercolor, 1790.

branch of the Arts to such a degree of perfection that would be of national advantage by preventing large sums going out [of the country], and a great balance in our favour; that time is happily arrived." With engraving as the foundation, "of late years, the same steps has [sic] been taken to encourage, and improve Historical Painting," with the foreseeable result that "we shall at least rival if not excell the greatest Masters of Italy and all other Countries" (from a speech of 31 October 1793, quoted in Bruntjen 273).

In the next decade, after the Shakespeare Gallery had failed, Boydell recast the narrative less modestly:

When I first began business, the whole commerce of prints in this country consisted in importing foreign prints, principally from France. . . . Impressed with the idea that the genius of our own country-

An Era Ends

> While this work was printing, the worthy Alderman paid the debt of nature. The Shakspeare Gallery did not long survive its founder; and circumstances have attended its dissolution sufficient to discourage in future all similar speculation, and deprive the arts of those resources which the spirit of trade supplied, when the spirit of taste lay torpid, and the spirit of patronage appeared to be extinct.
>
> —Martin Archer Shee, *Rhymes on Art*

> What is given in this last Prize, for the Sixty-second Drawn Ticket, has cost the Proprietors upwards of £30,000.
>
> —*Plan of the Shakespeare Lottery* (1804)

We can now understand Lippincott's inclination to rank Boydell "with Wedgwood and Boulton as one of England's heroic entrepreneurs" (146). But this is the point at which to add that, if Boydell had understood the interdependence of production and marketing as profoundly as Wedgwood did, the Shakespeare Gallery might have weathered the storms that sank it. Boydell's tactics, like Wedgwood's, were appropriate innovations in a commercial economy where conventional patronage—the commissioned work—could exist only in severely abbreviated form. In Boydell's economy, patronage was less often an isolated act than one transaction in a series of interdependent transactions that occurred in a relatively short time with rapid cash flow. The Shakespeare project was designed from the outset as such a series. It was a kind of game in which the limitations of capital were played against the limitations of time. The first announcements of the project came in 1786, the first published results in 1791, the beginning of the end in 1803. The two-volume *Collection of Prints* was published in 1805; the first number had appeared in 1791. Limited funds made time a critical factor: could Boydell begin to make money on the project before he ran out of money to invest in it?

The venture was full of perilous incalculables. At the production end, the printing press, a highly efficient machine that competent operators could keep on a daily schedule of work, was perhaps the most predictable element. But the printing depended upon the editor, Steevens, who was supplying the text of Shakespeare to be printed. The pictures, on which much of the project's special appeal rested and in which most of the optimism and money were invested, were in the hands of a trained labor force doing labor, unfortunately, to which they were largely unaccustomed. Many eighteenth-century portrait painters knew how to produce portraits systematically on a strict schedule. History painting can be systemized, but most of the painters in the Boydell project had had few occasions to paint history, much less to devise a system for painting it efficiently. Boydell put the lack of a uniform system in the best light when he tried to tie it to English liberty: "Every Artist, partaking of the freedom

> men, if properly encouraged, was equal to that of Foreigners, I set about establishing a School for Engraving in England. . . . By the blessing of Providence, these exertions have been very successful; not only in that respect, but in a commercial point of view, for, the large sums I regularly received from the Continent, previous to the French Revolution, . . . encouraged me to attempt also an English School of Historical Painting. . . . [T]he Shakspeare Gallery will convince the world that Englishmen want nothing but the fostering hand of encouragement to bring forth their genius in this line of art.

Nothing short of Napoleon could have stopped the advance of English art as delivered to the public through Boydell.

> This Gallery I once flattered myself with being able to have left to that generous publick . . . but unfortunately for those connected with the Fine Arts, a Vandalic Revolution has arisen, which, in convulsing all Europe, has entirely extinguished, except in this happy Island, all those who had the taste or the power to promote those Arts; while the Tyrant that at present governs France, tells that believing and besotted nation, that, . . . he is a great patron and promoter of the Fine Arts. . . . [T]his unhappy Revolution has cut up by the roots that revenue from the Continent which enabled me to undertake such considerable works in this country. [Preface to Boydell's *Collection of Prints from Pictures Painted for the Purpose of Illustrating the Dramatic Works of Shakspeare, by the Artists of Great-Britain*, 1803, in Bruntjen 148–51n]

of his country, and endowed with that originality of thinking so peculiar to its natives, has chosen his own road to what he conceived to be excellence, unshackled by the slavish imitation and uniformity that pervade all the foreign Schools" (quoted in Bruntjen 150n).

The inefficiency of painting was compounded at the next stage of the reproduction sequence by the inefficiency of engraving. The role of engraving in Boydell's marketing strategy was clear from the start. The paintings would create, at the top of a social pyramid, what has been called a demonstration effect, which would in turn spur emulative spending at lower levels. Boydell's experience had taught him that a dense social structure with its layers close together promotes emulation. His dispersive scheme was organized geographically as well: promotion and display start in London because sales start there and spread to the provinces. Unique paintings supply the top and center; engraved reproductions supply the rest.[12] Despite technical innovations and shortcuts, however, fancy engraving of the sort expected for history paintings was so slow that Boydell's first big commercial success, a print of Richard Wilson's *Destruction of the Children of Niobe,* had taken Woollett two years to finish—earning £150 for him and £2,000 for Boydell in two years at 5 shillings per copy (Bruntjen 18–20; W. H. Friedman 39). Later Woollett's engraving of West's *Death of Wolfe* (fig. 2.1) took four years, generating £15,000 in receipts by 1790 (Bruntjen 35–36; W. H. Friedman 39–40). Though Boydell's engravers for the Shakespeare project could cut some corners, nothing could bring letterpress printing and engraving into efficient coordination.

The gross inefficiency of this cumbersome system of production greatly increased the financial risk. The manufacturing time was too great, for instance, to allow an investor to calculate the value of timeliness, which is to say, of popularity. How does one exploit the interest of the moment if the interest may fade before a product can be manufactured to match it? Many otherwise promising collaborations of painter, engraver, and printseller failed just here, and the collaborators were left holding expensively produced prints depicting unfashionable costumes, outdated issues, barely remembered battles, and retired heroes. And those were small and isolated undertakings in comparison with Boydell's Shakespeare. Its very scale, in fact, was a way of making visible the project's claim to civic—national and international—significance. The Shakespeare Gallery would declare war on continental misunderstanding by mobilizing the best poet, the best editors, the best printers printing on the best paper, and the best painters, their works engraved by the nation's best engravers, in a production and marketing scheme supervised by a Maecenas who symbolized the national talent for commerce, all in the name of the English school. The lag between conception and execution brought about many changes. The best laborers and best techniques, even the best by the taste of the time, proved too expensive in the long run and were not often chosen; in the long run (and it was a very long run), Boydell came to rely instead on a few painters and a few engravers who had the very virtues that were missing from his original scheme: low cost, dependability, and uniformity. They lacked only superior ability. Meanwhile there

[12] McKendrick's "Commercialization" describes the effect of demonstration and emulation in an economy moving toward mass production.

was time for Boydell's choices to be noticed, and time for public criticism to increase and spread, as it did.

In maximizing the economic advantages of his project to so many groups, Boydell necessarily maximized the number of areas in which failure could occur and the span of time over which it might occur. Thus he designed into the scheme features meant to relieve cash-flow problems created by the long time span created in turn by inefficient production: the subscription system that would create income during the earliest stages, a stepped schedule of publishing in increments (numbers) to even out the cash flow over the middle period, and the gradual introduction of novel elements that would keep customers coming back to the gallery and keep them buying (as when he decided to introduce new designs into the small plates that illustrated the Shakespeare edition—rather than duplicate in a small size only the larger plates that had already been produced—in an attempt to increase orders for the Shakespeare text) (fig. 2.10).

Boydell needed Wedgwood's remarkable agility and capacity for invention. The potter worked constantly to anticipate changes in taste; thus he was able to ride the wave of interest in neoclassicism, and he marketed it across a range of international markets much broader than anything Boydell ever attempted. He worked equally hard at penetrating occasions—national and international events, new stars in the firmament, including French and American heroes—with his products. He figured out how to commercialize history, and he saw to it that time was on his side. But time eventually caught up with Boydell's Shakespeare Gallery. Most important, markets available in 1789 had changed drastically by 1803–1804, when the project was in its last phase. But the momentum of the project allowed only minor changes of course. The Gallery faltered in the 1790s, long before it failed, and all of Boydell's hastily improvised efforts to stop the downward slide could only slow it. The collapse of the Shakespeare project occurred not in splendid isolation, either, but as the largest of a depressing string of commercial failures. The paintings from Macklin's Poets' Gallery and his Bible project had been sold by lottery in 1797. By then the Shakespeare Gallery was already struggling for life.

In March 1801 Boydell sent an agent to the continent to promote sales and then in August tried to incorporate the Shakespeare project by selling shares. As early as 1803, the year the nine-volume text edition finally appeared, the Boydells began to sell off their own enormous stock, and in November the firm stopped payment on their debts (Bruntjen 115). In a letter to William Hayley, Blake describes a visit to Boydell in 1804 (the year of van Assen's portrait sketch, fig. 2.12): "I have also seen Alderman Boydel, who has promised to get the number and prices of all Romney's prints as you desired. He has sent a Catalogue of all his Collection, and a Scheme of his Lottery; desires his compliments to you; says he laments your absence from London, as your advice would be acceptable at all times, but especially at the present. He is very thin and decay'd, and but the shadow of what he was; so he is now a Shadow's Shadow; but how can we expect a very stout man at eighty-five . . . ? You would have been pleas'd to see his eyes light up at the mention of your name" (4 May 1804, E 748–49). "Lottery" is the method by which Boydell sold off his stock. The "Catalogue of all his Collection" is the 1803 catalogue of the Boydell

Just as Copley tried to make prints of his *Gibraltar* painting available at different prices for different pocketbooks, so Boydell had his Shakespeare paintings engraved in more and less expensive formats (larger, smaller, with and without the Shakespeare texts), usually by different engravers. Blake's sole work on the Shakespeare Gallery was a small print, after a painting by Opie, of act 4, scene 5, of *Romeo and Juliet,* engraved in 1799 and published about 1803. Curiously, though there is a large print by G. S. and J. G. Facius, there is also a second small print, engraved by Peter Simon, of the same design. Robert N. Essick has explained the du-

stock, consisting, according to Pye, of forty-eight volumes, arranged in artistic schools, comprising 4,432 prints from both the Cheapside shop and the Shakespeare Gallery in Pall Mall (Pye, *Patronage* 253n).[13]

The physiological explanation for Boydell's appearance may be his eighty-five years in this world. But Blake sees in the shadow's shadow the "thin and decay'd" soul of British commerce. In his double-edged description of this fallen Maecenas of the trade we see a Blakean spectre, once one of the formidable "fiends of commerce" (E 754; see also "Now Art has lost its mental Charms," E 479), now the shadow of its former self, whose lamplike eyes light up at the mention of old allies. Boydell died that December at the age of eighty-six. The next month, in January 1805, both the contents of the Shakespeare Gallery and the very building were sold off by lottery. The paintings in Bowyer's Historic Gallery were sold, again by lottery, the same year.

In another letter to Hayley only a few months earlier Blake described himself as an isolated commercial bust in the midst of a general boom: "Art in London flourishes. Engravers in particular are wanted. Every Engraver turns away work that he cannot Execute from his superabundant Employment. Yet no one brings work to me." He is still feeling that way almost a year later: "Money flies from me; Profit never ventures upon my threshold, tho' every other man's doorstone is worn down into the very earth by the footsteps of the fiends of commerce." The passing of another year brings yet another repetition of the belief that "my Fate has been so uncommon. . . . I was alive & in health & with the same Talents I now have all the time of Boydells Macklins Bowyers & other Great Works. I was known by them & was look'd upon by them as Incapable of Employment in those Works it may turn out so again notwithstanding appearances [of a change for the better, through Hayley]" (to Hayley, 7 October 1803, E 736; 7 August 1804, E 754; 11 December 1805, E 766–67).

But Blake was wrong if he really supposed

[13]For Boydell's interesting place in the history of avoiding bankruptcy by lottery, see Bruntjen 148n and Ashton.

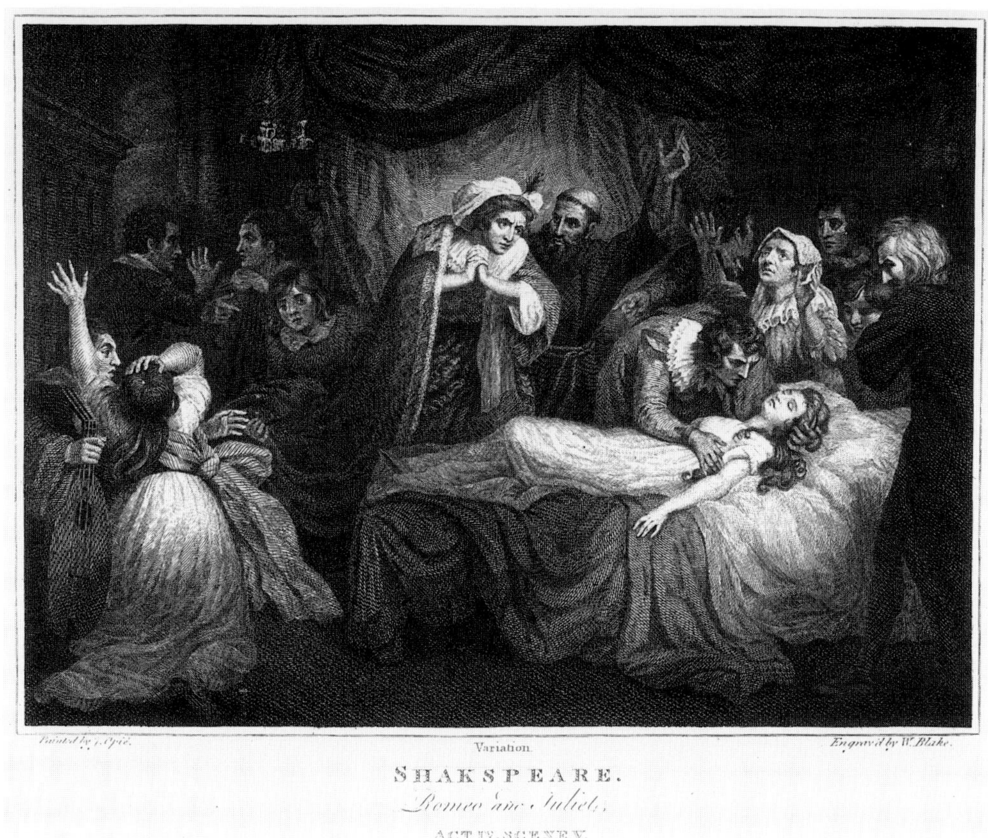

2.10. William Blake after John Opie, *Romeo and Juliet*, engraving, 1799.

plication: Blake was engraving an earlier version of the painting that included extra figures excluded from the later version that Simon copied (*Blake's Commercial Book Illustrations* 83). This is the only such variant in the series. (See also W. H. Friedman 231, Bruntjen 142–43n, Bentley, *Blake Books* 614–17, and Essick, *Separate Plates* 252–53).

that business was bad for him alone. In the post-Boydell era, the sense of failure and crisis was as general as the gloomy coda of Prince Hoare's 1806 *Inquiry* suggests: "Such . . . is the state of the Arts of Design in England, at a moment when they are declared to be in danger of perishing for ever. They stand therefore on the brink of splendour or annihilation; they plead before a profoundly reflecting nation; they demand a trial" (263). The outlook for the arts of design in England had changed, and with it the discourse on the English school.

After the Boydell experiment old voices blend with new ones, though even the old voices come across in a new way because they have become, for good or ill, voices of experience: it is one thing for Spenser to be an Anglican and a monarchist, quite another for T. S. Eliot. Likewise, it is one thing for Jonathan Richardson and Joshua Reynolds to use history painting as a benchmark of English accomplishment, but quite another for late arrivals such as William Blake, not to mention Benjamin Haydon. Nonetheless the history-painting lament continues to play a standard part in discussions of the English school well into the nineteenth century, long after the school had in fact established itself in areas other than history painting. When Hoare sounds the familiar theme in 1806—"Happy were it . . . if we could . . . remove the charge brought against us by other nations, of deficiency in history painting. It cannot be denied . . . that works in the higher provinces of this class, do not constitute the prominent feature of our school" (221–22)—his language is hardly different from Boydell's more than two decades earlier. Northcote is still repeating the old complaint in 1830: "Except in the department of portraiture, the art of painting in England has been obstructed or disregarded . . ." (1:398). But 1830 is not 1782, and there are new skeletons in the margins of the discourse. To name only two: the French Revolution had given new, perhaps apocalyptic, force to "history," while the portrait/history opposition had become considerably more symbolic and less real or, should we say, less adequate as a description of the painting actually being done. Not that the opposition had ever been without symbolism, nor had it ever been adequate. But the fit between the simplicities of official theory and the complexities of practice had become ill indeed; the margins were threatening to outgrow the text. In this respect landscape painting and the novel are analogues in their respective narratives. Neither is adequately credited in contemporary theories; both attempt status-seeking alliances with poetry and, somewhat later, science. Fielding's prefaces to *Tom Jones* exemplify the former; nineteenth-century efforts to affiliate the novel with narrative forms of scientific documentation, such as the case study, exemplify the latter.

Under that kind of pressure, as we might expect, the old themes are occasionally forced into new service. The opposition of portrait and history, for example, had long been supported by the analogy of poetry and painting: since poetry was aligned with history in such forms as epic, so painting, as the sister of poetry, should align itself with history. As we have seen, at one level deeper the sister-arts analogy itself had attracted some serious attempts at credible explanation and demonstration, usually along psychological lines. But as the sister-arts analogy generated explanations, the explanations in turn generated new analogies better suited to the cultural situation of painting in the early nineteenth century than the old analogy with poetry. From this perspective Prince Hoare is just loosely paraphrasing Turnbull's old Lockean arguments when he proposes that genius is not a monolithic trait but a combination of four factors: taste, judgment, imagination, and an "organic impulse" (such as a discriminating ear or eye). To demonstrate that art and poetry require the same combination of factors, he analyzes, at some length, scenes from Shakespeare's plays as word paintings "drawn" by his "pencil" (i.e., brush) (186). If "there have been English poets," we are driven to conclude that "England is capable of producing a painter" (189). Of course Hoare's choice of Shakespeare as the basis of his comparison is not accidental and in fact may have been inspired by the long-delayed publication of the two-volume *Collection of Prints* in the Boydell Shakespeare series only the year before.[14] But in any case the argument circles wearily back around to the point where Boydell started more than two decades earlier.

This conservative line of argument, however, has hidden potential that eventually moves the debates on English painting far beyond Boydell's exploitation of Shakespeare. A few years later John Constable can revise an argument much like Turnbull's and Hoare's to give art the status of science and replace history painting with landscape. Previously landscape had seemed a parochial and peripheral kind of imagery, mired, like portrait, in local circumstances. Its most successful theoretical strategy had been Poussin's and Claude's mythologized prospects, which gave ideologues such as Reynolds grounds for at least limited admiration.

Constable redirects the energy of the old argument. Painting "should be pursued as an inquiry into the laws of nature . . . a branch of natural philosophy, of which pictures are but the experiments." If eighteenth-century English apologists found the alliance of poetry and painting useful, their nineteenth-century successors, faced with a decline in the fortunes of poetry, acknowledge the advantages of a new union: "In such an age as this, painting should be *understood*, not . . . considered only as a poetic aspiration, but as a pursuit, *legitimate, scientific, and mechanical*" (Constable 69). While Constable carries on the venerable tradition of associating painting with the powers that be in the hope of sharing the wealth, the powers have changed. If art can claim science and mechanics as it once claimed poetry, in a country whose scientific and technological strengths are boosting the well-established strength of commerce, then painting may participate in the English success. Landscape can displace history as the best hope of English painting—and so Allan Cunningham treats it, in his lives of Wilson, Reynolds, and Gainsborough, with Reynolds again the loser. To his Hogarth, Cunningham adds "the truly English and intrepid spirit of Gainsborough": "His paintings have a national look. He belongs to no school; he is not reflected from the glass of man, but from that of nature . . ." (1:356).

Cunningham here exemplifies the amalgamation of nationalism with individualism that, with variations, begins to appear in the post-Boydell era. Among artists and their spokespersons there is at least a temporary disillusionment with the supposed national genius for commerce and a corresponding decline of faith in merchant patronage. They are replaced by a new fascination with the nation's recently demonstrated military genius and a flirtation

[14] The date on the title pages of both volumes is 1803, but Josiah Boydell's preface is dated 1805 (Bruntjen 112 and 146n).

with what Hoare calls "a more enlarged patronage" (152), meaning state support.

In Hoare's *Inquiry,* then, alongside the diplomatic tributes to Boydell, Macklin, and Bowyer for their exertions on behalf of English history painting, we find a bleak report on the results of their patronage. Hoare casts them as well-meaning merchants who aroused "hopes" that led to "consequences nearly fatal" (75). He notes the paradox by which "the employment afforded by the zeal and bounty of the printsellers" had in the long run "conducted to the depression of the historic art" (228). Painters who left "the household security of portraiture to follow the visions of fancy" conjured up by the printsellers in the 1790s "found themselves, on their dissolution, suddenly destitute of habitual employment, and had thus the task of beginning their career anew" (75). Hoare's point, implicit in the return of such old anti-commercial metaphors as "bounty," "depression," and "speculation" to the discourse, seems to be that individual and merchant patronage are economic systems that naturally favor the production of certain kinds of art but not the best kinds. Patronage "derived from employment established on commercial speculations," such as Boydell's Shakespeare Gallery, are "certainly not favorable to the severer process of art" (227–28), which cannot be sustained on the boom-and-bust curve of speculation. Hoare figures old-master collecting—conventionally associated with great-man patronage, often regarded as the genteel alternative to art merchandising—similarly, as a business that engages "the prudent considerations of property and commerce" (71). Buying an old painting "no more indicates a love of painting, than common transfers at the Bank do a love of the three, or four, per cents" (72). While Hoare dismisses the familiar objection that "a *commercial* people cannot direct its mind to the study of the liberal arts" (205), he does after all treat art and commerce as unnatural allies and their narratives as incongruent.

Then, without irony, he uses England's successes in battle as proof that commerce is not the nation's sole specialty. The move from merchandising to battle is, as Hoare sees it, on the road from individual patronage to that "more extended" institutional patronage. The modern institution of choice is not the church, which could be treated favorably as the curator of conceptual narratives that need communicating—I am thinking of Barry's account of the connection between great history painting and Christianity—but the state, treated as the sponsor of military heroism that needs imaging. The faith being promoted through imagery is no longer religious belief but patriotism. What might have been pagans in the Christian myth become foreign troops in the new analogy. Thus when Hoare tells his readers that England has at last "disdainfully sent home all auxiliaries" (216–17)—foreign artists—in portrait painting, the "meed" of which now "seems as truly our own as that of naval combat" (219), the metaphors are not incidental, nor, as we shall see, are they the only form that the league of art and empire will take.

English Engravers Meet an Enterprising English Tradesman

The changes we have been sampling can be traced at least partly to the experience of the Boydell era, which shaped the nineteenth-century discourse on the English school in ways that can be seen emerging in competing posthumous myths about Boydell himself. Both are reflected in Cunningham's life of George Romney, represented as the suspicious painter who pulled back from the Shakespeare Gallery as a project of "dealers and speculators," while Cunningham himself rises to the defense of "these worthy and generous men. They were tradesmen, and highminded ones, and never for a moment assumed the airs of patrons of art . . . and it was not unnatural to desire to gain rather than lose by speculations which supported art, and put money into the pockets of painters" (5:111). The underlying question was well put at least as early as 1808: "Whether Boydell knew, or mistook, its proper fulcrum—whether he employed it too much in coining money, and too little in raising the arts—or whether, like certain commercial statesmen, and certain Birmingham manufacturers, he really conceived these purposes to be inseparable—is yet to appear" (*Review of Publications of Art,* quoted in W. H. Friedman 215). Iain Pears has noted that in the early part of the eighteenth century, "the dealer frequently drew the lightning of social criticism from the painter, partially separating him from the taint of lucre and thus allowing the more idealised, intellectual aspects of the painting profession to attain greater emphasis" (96). As the process continued into the later decades of the century, the dealer Boydell became the era's most useful lightning rod.

It is hardly surprising that in one version of the history of engraving, and indeed, by extension, the history of the visual arts, Boydell becomes the heroic man of business who at a crucial moment pilots the chariot of the art to the top of the mountain of trade. Most twentieth-century accounts still reproduce this view of the man. "In 1786," writes Sven Bruntjen, "English artists, in the opinion of nearly every connoisseur except Boydell and the King [in patronizing West, presumably], were incapable of history. . . . This he changed in the twinkling of an eye. . . . Boydell's enterprise permanently freed English art from the dominance of portraiture. From 1786 to now there has always been a large English market for the other branches of painting" (20–21). These wondrous feats are said to be part of a general liberation from great-man patronage: "Functioning both as dealers and as patrons, these commercial men [publishers and printsellers] enabled a new breed of independent-minded artists to reach a large, educated public and thus to free themselves from dependence on aristocratic sponsorship which, in England, had been a meager resource to artists" (1).

In the 1790s "Anthony Pasquin" (John Williams) declared in his essay "The Royal Academicians" (1796?) that "until Mr. Boydell became a print-merchant, the works of our engravers did not constitute a material part of our commerce, nor were their names generally circulated or known upon the continent . . ." (14 [of second pagination, which begins after 64]). The 1812 edition of Alexander Chalmers's *General Biographical Dictionary* presents a Boydell who began his career at a time when "the arts were . . . at a very low ebb in this country" and became "certainly the greatest encourager of the art [of engraving] that this country ever knew" (6:304). In the 1820s Boydell's reputation remains intact. In *The Connoisseur's Repertory* (1824–1828?), a biographical dictionary of artists, Thomas Dodd looked back upon the second half of the eighteenth century as a time when the "chalcographic art"—engraving—"was reviving from a long apathetical slumber, under the spiritual auspices of the late venerable Alderman, who, by giving encouragement to every rising genius, no matter whether foreign or domestic, may be said to have laid the foundation for the cultivation and improvement of the fine arts in this country" (2: n.p.).

The metaphors are worth our attention. We recognize the English-school lexicon of "encouragement" and "improvement." Here engraving, as the art of reproduction, is a "foundation" for "cultivation" of "fine arts"—painting and sculpture. Boydell's encouragement is figured as the climax of a sleeping-beauty plot in which the engravers awake under his "spiritual auspices." Two decades later, when John Pye II came to write *Patronage of British Art, An Historical Sketch* (1845), Boydell had settled firmly into his position as the man of business whose speculations in printselling "turned the foreign print trade in favour of Great Britain" (58; cf. Chalmers 6:304, 305).[15] He had become the centerpiece in an interpretation of the history of English engraving that turns on an essential commercial adjustment of a system of marketing initiated by Hogarth and improved and completed by Boydell. We can reconstruct the history, from Pye and others, as follows.

The first period of English engraving extends all the way from the Anglo-Saxons to Hogarth. Through these centuries, no matter what the uses to which their skills were put, engravers subsisted as lackeys. The first engravers in England were the Anglo-Saxon goldsmiths, much of whose work was coin engraving. Responsibility for the coin of the realm connects the Anglo-Saxon artisans to their counterparts in imperial Rome, where the craft, at least according to some, was devoted largely to the minting of coins. The earliest English engraving to be accomplished "precisely in the same manner as a copper-plate is engraven" (Landseer, *Lectures* 101) produced the brass plates on English tombs. Eventually engravers added portraiture to their repertory. But the opportunity to display their skills to a wider audience was prevented by their humiliating dependence upon the stubborn structures of church and state privilege until 1733. In that year, according to Pye, there were still only two printshops in all of London, and those two limited their trade to foreign prints and to English portraits, most, no doubt, in the old stiff, dry, and hard "gothic" style to match the gothic financial arrangements under which the hapless engravers worked. The thaw began with *The Harlot's Progress,* which Hogarth published from his house in 1733. The *Progress* of that year helped to make prints popular as "furniture"—wall decoration—and new printshops began to open. Finally, by obtaining in 1734–1735 the passage of the copyright act that

[15] For an account of the import trade in paintings and prints during the pre-Boydell years (to 1774), see Pears 55 and his appendix of tables, 207–13. He suggests that the late 1760s may have "marked the turning point when England finally escaped the dominance of foreign production of prints"—especially from France—"and began to establish that superiority (partly based on highly advantageous customs tariffs) which led by the 1780s to France being a net importer of English works" (55).

covered engravings, "Hogarth's Bill," Hogarth saved the engraver from exploitation.[16] "And thus," Pye solemnly concludes, "the British public became honourably distinguished as affording the first source of real patronage enjoyed by the British artist" (*Patronage* 43).

At his death Hogarth left the elements of a new marketing mechanism in place: "The connexion thus in course of formation between painting, engraving, the printing-press, and the public, from 1733, proceeded under such favourable encouragement, that between 1740 and 1750, engraving began to develope considerable native talent, and young Englishmen commenced travelling abroad to study that art" (Pye, *Patronage* 54–55). Any sharp-sighted merchant scanning the decade for the main chance would have seen in printselling an opportunity waiting to be seized. John Boydell arrived on the scene with a combination of timing, skills, acumen, and desire to succeed that made his coming seem providential to nostalgic posthumous observers.

As "engraving, the printing-press, and the spirit of commercial enterprise combined to render designs articles of trade" (Pye, *Patronage* 160), Boydell led the effort to raise English engraving to the peak of its potential market value. Trade in engravings seems to have turned from an import to an export market in the 1770s (Bruntjen 38). Contemporaries remarked that England was the leading supplier of engravings to the continent, but with the corollary that the English bought far fewer prints than the Europeans, especially the French: "The calculation in all undertakings is on the foreign sale, being thrice above our own" (quoted in Whitley 2:72, from a document of 1787).

But then catastrophe struck: " . . . the storm of the French Revolution burst . . . shook the foundation of states, as well as of individuals, turned the attention of Britain from peace to war, and . . . suspended altogether that commerce by which British artists had been mainly enabled to live" (Pye, *Patronage* 252–53). In fact, faith in the French market had risen considerably with the commercial treaty signed by France and England in 1786. Wedgwood had been one of its most avid promoters. And since at first the Revolution itself had seemed only to improve the profit-taking opportunities, Etruria tooled up to celebrate the new era with plaques and medallions (Bindman, *Guillotine* 96–101; Reilly 1:118–27). No doubt the same eager anticipation had bolstered the toast to Boydell in 1789. But in the late 1790s large collections of paintings from the continent were ending up in England, and an "astonishingly great" number of continental paintings flooded the English market (Pye, *Patronage* 279),[17] while the export print trade collapsed (246). The war brought to bust the "booming industry" in colored prints that had been maturing during the last decades of the century (J. Burke, *English Art* 310). The profitable fashion for using prints as wall decoration faded away so completely that three decades were not able to revive it. Pye testified in 1836 that in France ordinary people were buying prints for furni-

[16] The first effective English copyright law for authors was the Act for the Encouragement of Learning, 1709, which defined copyright and established fines for infringement. Provisions of the copyright law for authors were strengthened twice in Blake's lifetime, in 1774 and 1814. See W. H. Friedman 35.

[17] W. B. S. Taylor discusses the Orleans gallery (on public display in 1798–1799 until dispersal), the collection of the French financier Charles Alexandre de Calonne, and others from the revolutionary and Napoleonic periods (2:367–78).

ture while "in England the same class of persons have not any." The serious consequence was that since the war years, opportunities for British line engravers had been limited "principally to the embellishment of books" (*Evidence* 45, testimony 26 July 1836).[18]

For those who picture Boydell as he pictured himself, bold architect of the international triumph of English engraving and painting, the French Revolution unnaturally intrudes on a smoothly developing mercantile romance that begins with English engravers shut away from the public, forced to serve the narrow artistic demands of an aging aristocracy. In the cyclical analogy, the Revolution reinaugurates the pattern begun by the Reformation and repeated in the Civil War. French radicals interrupt the progress initiated by Boydell as the Puritan radicals interrupted the progress initiated by Charles I. As Boydell explains,

> This Gallery I once flattered myself with being able to have left to that generous publick, who have for so long a period encouraged my undertakings; but unfortunately for those connected with the Fine Arts, a Vandalic Revolution has arisen, which, in convulsing all Europe, has entirely extinguished, except in this happy Island, all those who had the taste or the power to promote those Arts; while the Tyrant that at present governs France, tells that believing and besotted nation, that, in the midst of all his robbery and rapine, he is a great patron and promoter of the Fine Arts; just as if those Arts that humanize and polish mankind could be promoted by such means, and by such a man, you will excuse, my dear Sir, I am sure, some warmth in an old man on this subject, when I inform you, that this unhappy Revolution has cut up by the roots that revenue from the Continent which enabled me to undertake such considerable works in this country. [Quoted in Bruntjen 149n]

Boydell's admirers recognized in his birth and boyhood early anticipations of the remarkable bourgeois virtues that later gave him the power to exploit weaknesses of the old order with the strengths of the new. A combination of independent thinking, hard work, and efficient management helped him make the most of every opportunity to increase his trade. The benefits of that increase extended to his fellow engravers, who were thus delivered from their captivity by a species of enlightened self-interest operating to the mutual advantage of all who contributed to the system. The plot climaxes in the commercial triumph symbolized by the Royal Academy dinner at which the prince, as the latest generation of an old order that recognized the point of allowing itself to be reformed by the new, delivers a toast composed by a statesman-philosopher to honor the spirit of British commerce in the person of one of its great traders, whose success has been ratified by his rise into the ranks of civic authority. Presumably enlightened self-interest keeps the prince from flinching when he ventriloquizes Burke's analogy: the true counterpart of "the Grand Monarque of France" is "an English Tradesman."

The characteristic mood of Boydellian romance is the optimism that radiates from a sunny view of commerce of the sort traditionally inspired in patriotic breasts by a sight of the bustling Thames from an eminence:

> Rome only conquerd halfe the world, but trade
> One commonwealth of that and her hath made;

[18] See also Pye, *Patronage* 372. The notion that the postrevolutionary successes of English engraving were in book illustration was commonplace.

And though the sun his beame extends to all
Yet to his neighbor sheds most liberall;
Least God and Nature partiall should appeare
Commerse makes everything grow everywhere

[John Denham, *Cooper's Hill*][19]

The old militarism divided and conquered; the Roman victory was unnatural, thus forced and partial. The new commerce is like nature; it lights the world as completely and impartially as God's sun, and makes everything grow everywhere. The old emperor was housed in Rome; the new is the mammon in everyone, organizing a "commonwealth" by common wealth. However common its wealth, this universal new day is dawning in London. During Blake's lifetime, the identification of Albion with trade, the feeling that England had discovered its true character and destiny in its talent for commerce, became firmly fixed. While the Revolution left much of the commercial landscape temporarily in shadow, the example of the French nonetheless usefully reinforced the contrast between the destructive fires of revolution and the productive sun of English business shining on a nation of shopkeepers.

To its optimists, the spirit of commerce seemed utterly transparent. That is, viewed from within the system, "commerce" seemed less the name for a new way of doing things than the name for a new context of freedom in which people could do as they chose.[20] The code words for the principle of choice are "self-interest" and "self-love," which, given the appropriate context—the free market, for example—worked to maximize advantages. In the commercial romance, the trader-hero, who removes obstacles to free choice in the marketplace, is the leading agent of this liberty. The Boydell story shows how the pattern looks when it is applied to the special sector of the economy involving artists, works of art, and audience as producers, commodities, and consumers, respectively. The enabling trader liberates engravers from narrow and tyrannical relationships by opening a direct line to the audience at large. The feeling of artistic freedom that may result from this new access to markets is well represented by the claim of the London engraver Abraham Raimbach (1776–1843) that the only inducement to the pursuit of engraving is "independence of all patronage but that of the public, and its facilities of extensive distribution" (quoted in Pye, *Patronage* 375).[21] Benjamin West, looking back on his

[19] *Cooper's Hill* was first published in 1642. The lines on commerce were added after l. 192 of the 1668 edition. See Martz 2:239n and Osborn.

[20] Donald Greene skillfully documents the manifold alliances of liberty, commerce, poetry, and politics in eighteenth-century Britain. In *The Romantic Ethic and the Spirit of Modern Consumerism,* Colin Campbell aims to get at the roots of the changes in consumption—identified by McKendrick, Brewer, and Plumb—that accompanied the changes in production commonly designated the Industrial Revolution. Campbell proposes an integrative explanation that puts two "ethics" into complementary relation: the Protestant ethic coupled to the emergence of modern capitalism in Max Weber's influential work, and a romantic ethic similarly coupled to modern consumerism. Weber's theory of capitalism is "productionist" in its bias; thus the need for a theory of consumption to balance it. By defining the spirit of consumption as an "autonomous, self-illusory hedonism" (11) arising from the same cultural matrix as the self-denying Protestant ethic formulated by Weber, Campbell challenges the assumption that "modern cultural development is best characterized by ever-increasing rationality" (13). In his analysis "Protestant" and "romantic" are subtly intervolved, overlapping, and opposing terms. I regret that his study came to my attention too late for me to take full account of its implications for my own.

[21] Artists (and others) have often believed that the shift from private patronage to commerce was a shift to "public" support and have equated freedom from old-time pa-

years of dependence on George III, told Joseph Farington that if he had the last thirty-two years to live over again, "his choice wd. be *to depend upon the public rather than on an Individual*" (26 May 1804, *Diary* 6:2331). Once these facilities of distribution, which the public seems to own, are in place as a marketing system, the system can be regarded as autonomous. After the initial conquest of the old order, the Boydellian hero has only to act as a matchmaker between producer and consumer. Artists and public, previously frustrated in their attempts to locate one another, are guided by the manager into the system, where the true match is at last made. The manager, like the system, is transparent. The manager may act, as Adam Smith suggests, from self-love: "It is not from the benevolence of the butcher, the brewer, or the baker, that we expect our dinner, but from their regard to their own interest. We address ourselves [as consumers], not to their humanity but to their self-love, and never talk to them of our own necessities but of their advantages" (1:27). But self-interest is, in an important if paradoxical sense, disinterested, the essence of freedom of choice rather than an obstacle to it.

Since the commercial spirit in which the match is made is also the national spirit, the English merchant helps English art clarify its own identity. In the new Rome the improved Maecenas is commercial.[22] Boydell saw that English engraving had a special role to play as the intermediary between artist and audience, and he had the wit to cultivate engravers for this purpose. He, like Wedgwood, understood that his merchandising was part of a system that would respond as a system. His concern with engraving was no mere bias of his apprenticeship but a critical factor in his coordination of his own projects with the rest of the commercial system. The biographical dictionaries deliver the milktoast version of Boydell's insight: "He said he was certain from his success in encouraging engraving, that Englishmen wanted nothing but proper encouragement and subjects to excel in historical painting . . ." (Chalmers 6:306). In a speech that might well be a source of this remark, however, Boydell himself claimed that the development of engraving had been the "first great improvement" to bring England into the progression of the arts that had spread from Italy to the rest of Europe: "it was obvious to all, that pursuing with Industry the way proposed would bring that branch of the Arts to such a degree of perfection that would be of national advantage by preventing large sums going out, and a great balance in our favour . . ." (speech to the Court of Common Council, 31 October 1793, quoted in Bruntjen 273n; see also 149n).

Boydell realized that engraving was more than another department of the arts. It was the missing link with commerce: engraving, as it reproduces painting, makes painting commercial. Not that this insight had been utterly lost on others, whose many piecemeal schemes for

tronage with artistic freedom. Raymond Williams has discussed the confusion over the change from patronage to commerce in his studies of modern communication, especially *Communications*. See also J. W. Saunders for a historical survey of the development of literary professionalism and mass-market publishing out of Renaissance patronage. He captures well one aspect of what he terms "the romantic dilemma": "In the air, like so many other radical notions in this age of the French Revolution, was the hope that very soon writers might be able to write directly for the masses" (160).

[22] Dr. Johnson spoke often of the consortium of publishers that backed his *Dictionary* as *his* Maecenas.

selling history paintings through engravings showed that they would have understood what Barry meant when he wrote of "our engravers (whose works are now a considerable article of commerce)" (*Account* 91). The new thought behind the Shakespeare Gallery is that English history painting had not been commercial in any sustained, systematic way. Because engraving could potentially make it so, Boydell harps on the causal connection between the establishment of an English school of engraving and an English school of painting.

After the Boydell failure, then, pleas for the support of English engraving—"in which for a long series of years we have so particularly excelled," thus adding to the "wealth and reputation of the country," writes William Roscoe (55)—become a standard theme of English-school discourse. The revival of engraving, writes Hoare in 1806, would mean "the revival of another branch of revenue" (42–43). Before the Committee on Arts and Manufactures, Pye and others repeatedly credited the Boydell heritage with inculcating in English engravers a unique "commercial spirit" (*Evidence* 33, testimony of 5 July 1836) that had turned them into businesslike artisans historically allied with commerce instead of dangerous radicals or finical prima donnas. "It is the commercial spirit," Pye testifies, ". . . that has extended encouragement to engraving here [in England] more than any other." Boydell is Pye's model of the commercial sagacity that once understood how to put the now-neglected spirit of English engravers to good use. Pye is arguing that engravers, as traditional allies of English commerce, ought to be brought back into the system to contribute to and share in the "commercial wealth of the nation" (*Evidence* 30, testimony of 5 July 1836).

The key to first Hogarth's and then Boydell's success was the discovery of "the mass of the people," who "became the first source of patronage to native talent; hence, too, a new and vast channel of enterprise was opened to the commercial speculator; and the various powers of the painter's mind were applied, through the art of engraving, to advance the interests of trade, by cultivating and feeding the taste of the million, both at home and abroad" (Pye, *Patronage* 141). Pye images the trader as a channel builder. The channel unblocks the natural communication, called "enterprise," that flows between native artist and native audience, providing satisfaction to both parties as it provides, as a natural by-product, profit to the "commercial speculator." The artist is an agriculturalist "cultivating and feeding" the audience's "taste" through channels kept free and open by the trader. Notice that the artist is not envisioned as one who feeds already established appetites. That possibility is evaded, no doubt because it might conjure up frightening images of dangerously sensual appetites that "the million" might be supposed to have. Instead the artist's work is a crop that, having been cultivated, in turn cultivates as it feeds the mind of the audience. The image assimilates forms of communication and education to forms of transporting goods to market and eating. The Boydell figure is imagined as one whose activities have no independent effects. He is the enabler, providing the situation of liberty in which an unobstructed process of growing, eating, and learning becomes possible.

English Tradesman: Same Song, Second Verse

> Come ye—whate'er your creed—O waken all,
> Whate'er your temper, at your Country's call;
> Resolving (this a free-born Nation can)
> To have one Soul, and perish to a man,
> Or save this honoured Land from every Lord
> But British reason and the British sword.
>
> —William Wordsworth, "Lines on the Expected Invasion. 1803"

> During my illness a Mr Lanseer (an Engraver, I hear, who lectured last Season at the *R. Inst:*, but was dismissed for personal Invectives against Boydell) called. . . . When a little recovered, seeing his Card among many others I asked the old woman, who is Mr Lanseer (for I had never heard the *name* before). I am sure, I don't know (says she) but from what he said, I guess, he is a sort of a *Methody Preacher* at that Unstintution, where you goes to *spout,* Sir.
>
> —Samuel Taylor Coleridge, 1 February 1808

We must acknowledge the poetic symmetry of a toast to English commerce on the eve of the French Revolution. Boydell has liberated the engravers and with his new project will move on to liberate the painters. By organizing the producers and consumers around himself as middleman, he has struck the delicate balance of forces that makes commerce possible. As a result of his efficient management, the elements in the system are just beginning to produce some of the unlimited potential for mutual benefits that the system promises. Across that other Channel, in a nation whose failure to understand commerce has made it vacant at the center where commerce should be, the extremes inevitably clash. In this view the Revolution pits a senile aristocracy defending unearned privilege against "the million" in the form of an uncultivated and thus infantile mob jealously destroying the privileges of others because it lacks the initiative to create opportunity for itself. But for all that, the Revolution is an untimely and unruly, even Vandalic, disruption of the Dick Whittington plot of commercial romance that forms around the figure of John Boydell as its hero; and Blake, among others, testifies to the unpoetic, wraithlike survival of Boydell into a new century. After the Revolution had foiled the merchant's "*lines, channels & connections,*" as Wedgwood called them (quoted in McKendrick, "Wedgwood" 418), Boydell's plight was embodied in the very measure that allowed him to skirt bankruptcy—the lottery, an undignified parody of the prudent buying and selling within the intricate network that supports normal commerce (figs. 2.11, 2.12).

In one version of the story, then, Boydell remains unscathed as the "friend and patron" of artists whose merchandising "did more for

In 1769 Boydell published his first two-volume *Collection of Prints Engraved after the Most Capital Paintings in England,* which was firmly associated with his Englishness. The volumes appear in the portrait of Boydell by his nephew Josiah, engraved in mezzotint by Valentine Green (published 1772), where Boydell holds a print of St. George and the dragon. In 1773 Boydell presented the volumes to the Society of Arts, and the Society presented a gold medal to him in honor of his efforts on behalf of English engraving (Bruntjen 42).

As he cultivated his image as English Boydell, he developed the edifying narrative that accompanies it. As if instructed by Hogarth's Industrious Apprentice, he tells how, as a youth newly arrived by coach in London, he

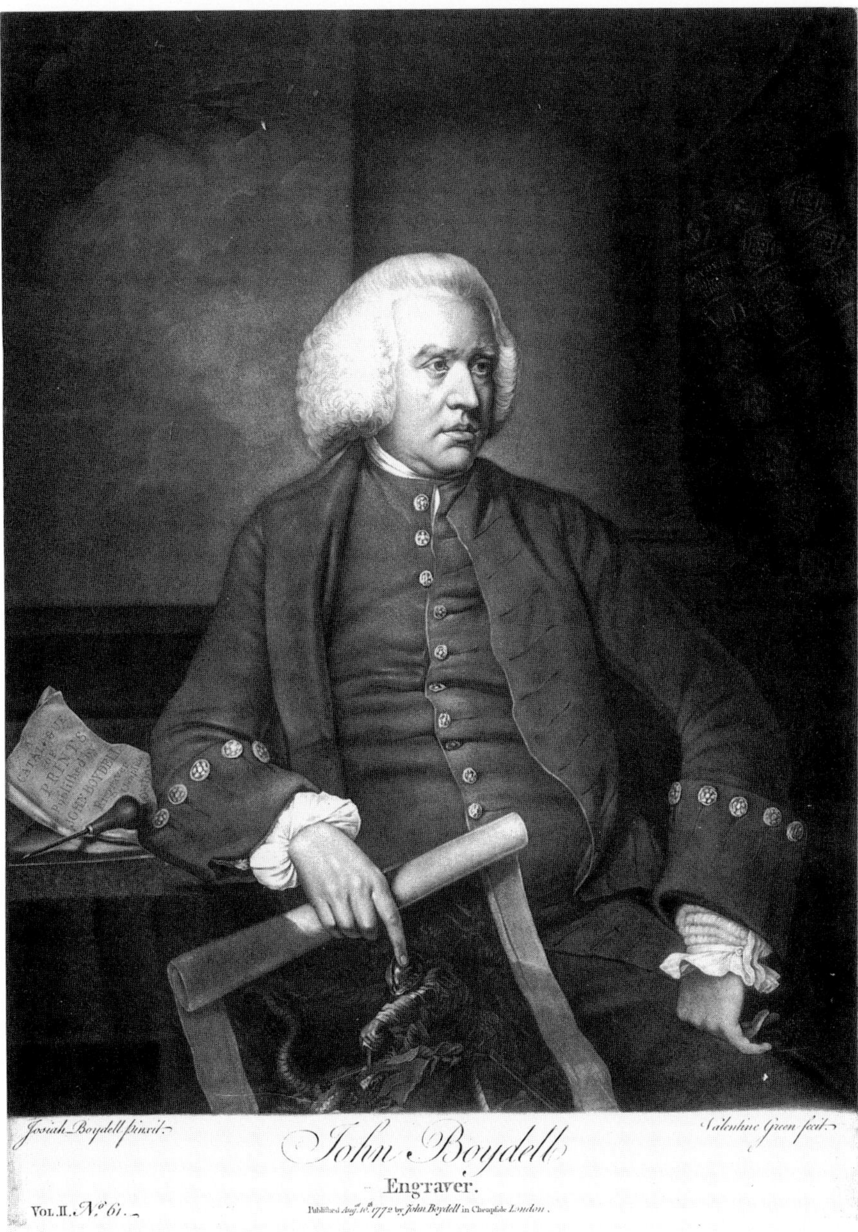

2.11. Valentine Green after Josiah Boydell, *John Boydell*, mezzotint, 1772.

"improved much in a little time. I resolved to be Industrious to have Patience, Perseverance Economy and trust to Providence for my future success," with a touch of Scrooge in his "dislike to such amusements which was better employed by my future pursuits." He picked up French—"which enabled me to Correspond with Foreigners"—from a clergyman's sermons. He resolved never to use tobacco "in any manner whatever" after calculating that one-quarter of a fellow artist's time was wasted in taking snuff and never to fall prey to the vices of free spending and loose women after seeing what happened to apprentices made of stuff less stern. He married with great thrift—"not one farthing spent upon acct of the Wedding, not so much as a glass of Wine or any addition of Clothes"—and a bit above his station, "little thinking I should be Lord Mayor of London and she, the Lady Mayoress." (His London landlord, checking the newlyweds over, observed that Mrs. Boydell "was fit to be Lady Mayoress.") (All quotations are from the manuscript autobiography by Boydell, printed with an introduction by W. Bell Jones.)

Summing up a life of rectitude in the preface to the catalogue that accompanied Boydell's presentation of pictures for Guildhall in 1794, he reminded readers that "honour, honesty and industry, are the Foundation of everything praiseworthy." Two of the pictures, depicting ceremonies by which lord mayors take office, are said to be "proofs of the consequence of In-

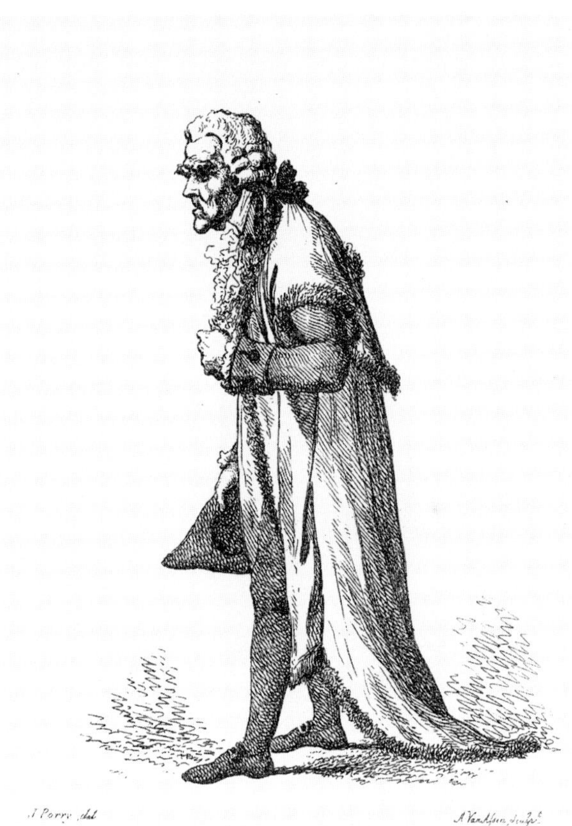

ALDERMAN BOYDELL.

London Pub.d Dec. 20. 1804 by J. Parry. No 5. Bentinck Street Soho

2.12. J. Parry after Anthony van Assen, *Alderman Boydell,* engraving, 1804.

the advancement of the arts in England than the whole mass of nobility put together," as the painter James Northcote put it in 1821 (quoted in *DNB* s.v. Boydell). But Boydell appears in a less flattering role at the center of an alternative history of English engraving. In his history of retailing, David Alexander has pointed out how "suspicious" consumers were of the "middlemen who fitted themselves in between producer and consumer" (231). The suspicion, of course, was precisely that the middleman's system of distribution was not transparent. Especially the people whom the system failed began to question the proposition that "a distribution system is only a mechanism for the exchange of goods and services between producers and consumers," which displays at least a remarkable "lack of curiosity about the organization of social systems" (3). The consumers' (and, we should add, the producers') suspicion of the middleman's "mechanism" of "exchange" was a symptom of sociocommercial change and misalignment that Boydell came to exemplify.

John Pye II, who in most respects was a Boydell partisan, in other respects favored a contradictory line of argument to the effect that spring may not be perpetual in the gardens of commercial paradise. In 1836, when the government established a committee to study causes and remedies for the inferiority of English arts and manufactures to the French,[23] the testimony concerning engraving included this exchange between a member of the committee and Pye:

> Mr. Brotherton.—Do you not think there are engravers of great merit who are little known?—[Pye] Most certainly. [Brotherton] Then anything that would have the effect of drawing them into public

dustry, Prudence, and Commerce," in that many of the people taking part in the ceremonies have "by their exertions . . . arrived to honour and riches; they have it in their power to be of particular service to their fellow citizens, and to the public, by their example, by their benevolence, and activity as magistrates, in relieving, advising, and assisting all around them, who merit their attention" (quoted in Bruntjen 215, 218; see also W. H. Friedman 31–32).

Within the decade after Boydell's death, these elements coalesced in a mercantile hagiography that honored Boydell's belief that his life "would impress all young men with the truth of what he had often held out to them, 'that industry, patience, and perseverance, if united to moderate talents, are certain to surmount all difficulties.' " "[W]ith that spirit and perseverance which he manifested in every succeeding scene of his life, he, at twenty-one years of age, walked up to the metropolis, and bound himself apprentice for seven years to Mr. Toms. . . ." With "an industry rarely to be paralleled" and "unconquerable perseverance" he took up the cause of English engraving until he "changed the course of the current" that earlier had carried "immense sums . . . out of the country" for foreign engravings. "He used to observe" that his earliest successful book of prints "was the first that had ever made a lord mayor of London." "Having been so successful in promoting the art of engraving in this

[23] This is the committee that issued the *Report on Arts and Manufactures* so highly recommended by the painter Benjamin Haydon—"no one with any pretensions to taste, should be without it." Haydon's remarks on the committee are part of his attack on the Royal Academy as a commercial monopoly ("Painting" 216–17).

notice, would be most beneficial to them?—[Pye] Unquestionably. At present, they are only drawn into notice through the medium of printsellers and booksellers. They have no direct patronage among the rich, as far as I know; I have known but one amateur patron of engraving in my day.

Commerce is conceived as a "medium" between engravers and their public. Conventional patronage is conceived as "direct." Brotherton questions the influence of the commercial medium:

[Brotherton] [Do you not think that] the engravers, perhaps, owe their fame to the recommendation of those who sell their prints, rather than to any merit they possess?—

Perhaps the influence of the medium is so great as to control even the eyes of the buyers, who may see only what the sellers tell them to see.

[Pye] I have already stated, as far as I know, except a few private patrons, no encouragement is extended to the art, besides that which comes through the printsellers; and if an artist be daring enough to publish anything for himself, he must make a sacrifice of sixty or seventy per cent, to get it placed before the world.

Pye considers, and rejects, the usefulness of independent publication as a way to restore the direct line from producer to public. The old English-school problem of public viewing—"to get it placed before the world"—reappears as a problem with commerce. Since the middlemen own even the space of display, "independent" publication is channeled through the commercial medium at the going rate. Brotherton seems to imagine that some more public kind of viewing space might be provided:

[Brotherton] Would it not tend very much to redeem the artist from the thraldom of the printseller, if he had an opportunity of exhibiting specimens of his art in public, on which public opinion could be passed?—

Pye backs away from Brotherton's logic:

[Pye] It is difficult to answer this question satisfactorily. I have already stated that which appears to me as being requisite to render justice to engraving. [Pye, *Evidence* 37–38, testimony of 5 July 1836]

Pye, though inclined to blame the dealers, was not sufficiently confident of his conclusion to single anyone out, and by the time he wrote *Patronage of British Art* in the next decade, his reticence had only increased: "And it may be questioned whether those circumstances which exposed the powers and genius of British artists to be estimated by the mercantile speculator, accordingly as they possessed the means of drawing money from the pockets of the public, constitute a fault for which any particular class can be deservedly reproached, or merely a national misfortune to be for ever deplored" (143). Pye was offering an explanation that has become familiar to everyone living with advanced technology: the faults are not faults but accidents and national misfortunes that lie neither in the system nor in the class of people who manage it.

But two weeks after hearing Pye's tactful evasions, the committee called an old engraver whose decades of experience had not mellowed his view of the recent history of English engraving:

That the dictations of ignorant capitalists, cooperating with those parts of the academical code

country, he resolved to direct his next efforts to the establishing an English school of historical painting . . ." (Chalmers 6:302–4). As a result of the "entire failure" of the "Shakspeare Gallery speculation" in the aftermath of the Revolution, the "venerable Boydell, in his patriotic endeavour to still further advance the interest of the arts of his country, made a wreck of his fortune" (Cunningham, quoting "one of Northcote's biographers," 6:82). In a final show of character, he insisted on being the first magistrate to arrive at the Old Bailey, before the fires were lit, caught a cold, and died as he lived, "by a too scrupulous attention to his official duties" (Chalmers 6:308; see also W. H. Friedman 33–34).

which respect the profession of engraving have produced these effects [of causing talented engravers to leave England for the better opportunities and tastes of the continent], and, in the general practice of engraving, the further effect of separating, in a great measure, the mechanical from the mental part of the art; is now but too obvious to persons of discernment. [Pye, *Evidence* 41, testimony of 19 July 1836]

"Those parts of the academical code which respect engraving" are the controversial rules of the Royal Academy barring engravers from membership with full status. The Academy rejected engravers at its founding, then again by unanimous vote in 1809 and 1812 (Pye, *Patronage* 200; see also Barry's *Letter*), while admitting, at least according to the most hostile accounts, flower painters, enamel painters, coach painters, sign painters, bricklayers, and foreigners. Pye's testimony communicates the outrage felt by engravers when the Academy finally agreed to compromise its standards by admitting a small group of six engravers to second-class membership as "*associates only* [thus not R.A. but A.R.A. or A.E.R.A.]*: but without the pleas of teaching, encouraging, protecting, or otherwise serving engraving;* and with the certainty of marking the professors of that art to be contemptuously pointed at" (*Evidence* 7).[24]

The witness of 19 July 1836 who lashed out at ignorant capitalists and the academical code was John Landseer (1769–1852, A.R.A. 1806), father of the engraver Thomas and the painters Charles and Edwin, and now approaching seventy years of cantankerous age. Landseer's professional experience as an engraver began with his work on the projects of Boydell's imitative rivals, Macklin and Bowyer, in the 1790s (fig. 2.13). In the next decade he unforgettably established his reputation as a hard man to deal with by launching a series of lectures "on the art of engraving" at the Royal Institution of Great Britain in 1806. The occasion was more auspicious than might at first appear. Boydell had died in December 1804, the lottery (to which all 22,000 tickets had been sold) had been held in late January 1805, and in December 1805 the winner had sold the Shakespeare Gallery in Pall Mall, with over 4,000 square feet of exhibition space, to the new British Institution, which had moved in, after redecorating, by early 1806 (Fullerton 63) (fig. 2.14). Landseer's lectures might have been, after all, a dignified tribute to Boydell's service to the art instead of an attack on ignorant capitalists.

Landseer's sponsor, the Royal Institution, had been founded by a Harvard-educated American, Count Rumford, as a society for the diffusion of useful scientific and mechanical knowledge. Its program of lectures, as they broadened far beyond the terms of the Institution's prospectus, became immensely popular. In its Albemarle Street theater, semicircular and warmed by steam, Humphry Davy lectured on chemistry, but so did his friend Coleridge on poetry, and Constable on landscape painting. A few blocks away in Pall Mall, the British Institution, by contrast, was founded as an institutional supplement to the Royal Academy.[25] It

[24] The rank of A.R.A. was created in 1770, and the first engravers were admitted that year (Hutchison 53–54). As indignant critics never failed to notice, special exceptions were made. Thus Francesco Bartolozzi, the Italian engraver who had emigrated to London in 1764, was a full-fledged charter member of the R.A., but he had been admitted as a painter. For the most reliable and detailed account of the engravers' struggle for recognition, see Fox.

[25] W. B. S. Taylor gives an appropriately patriotic early Victorian account of the founding and early years of the

was widely acknowledged that a supplement was needed. The Shakespeare Gallery had been designed as such, and as the gallery's failure became evident after 1800, Josiah Boydell circulated proposals for a national museum established on commercial principles, with provision for exhibitions, sales, premiums, engravings, and the like (Fullerton 60–61). The prospectus of May 1805 for a British Institution for Promoting the Fine Arts in the United Kingdom addressed two longstanding needs, for a public gallery of works not for sale and for a system of exhibition and sale of contemporary work. The prospectus emphasized the links between education, economics, and empire: "to improve and extend our manufactures, by that degree of taste and excellence which are to be exclusively derived from the cultivation of the Fine Arts; and thereby to increase the general prosperity and resources of the Empire" (quoted in Fullerton 61). To minimize the appearance of a territorial challenge at a time when the Academy was in disarray, the directors passed a law declaring that though the British Institution was "intended to promote the extension and increase the beneficial effects of the royal Academy," it was "by no means to interfere with it in any respect" (quoted in W. B. S. Taylor 2:214). Nevertheless, the spirit of competition between the two institutions was sometimes rancorous.[26]

But that directive leaves in question the role that the Institution might play. The preface to the second edition (1805) of Martin Archer Shee's *Rhymes on Art* radiates hope inspired by the founding of the new British Institution as a sign of "this patriotic sensibility arising in the minds of the public to the interests of the fine arts" (xlv). Much later W. B. Sarsfield Taylor will declare that the Institution is,

> next to the Royal Academy, the most important, and most serviceable establishment for the promotion of British art, and the encouragement of British talent, that has yet arisen in England; . . . its very form, constitution, and existence are pleasing and decisive evidences of the patriotic spirit which has displaced, in a very considerable degree, the anti-English prejudice, which had for so many centuries retarded the march of British genius in the arts, and had at length nearly succeeded in extinguishing it altogether. [2:214]

The calls on patriotism and the thumping emphasis on things English and British are clues to the kind of supplement the founders thought was necessary: a *British* Institution to intensify artistic nationalism. Taylor, writing from the perspective of the early 1840s, a decade after Cunningham had shown how to conceive a history of English art in nationalistic terms, associated the founding of the new Institution with a swerve toward intellectual independence "among the higher and better informed classes of society, who began to take the liberty"—not an unimportant word here—"of thinking for themselves." Taylor interestingly attributed this mental liberation to an effect of the French Revolution: "The revolutionary war, by putting a stop to the *grand tour,* left them to the direction of their own natural good sense; and no longer exposed to the insidious

---

British Institution (2:214–44). The most coherent and accurate account is Peter Fullerton's.

[26] Fullerton notes that the Academy censured Prince Hoare for writing too favorably about the Institution in his *Academic Annals* (66). Farington's diary entries for the period give a good sense of the hopes and fears that the Institution inspired in the Academy.

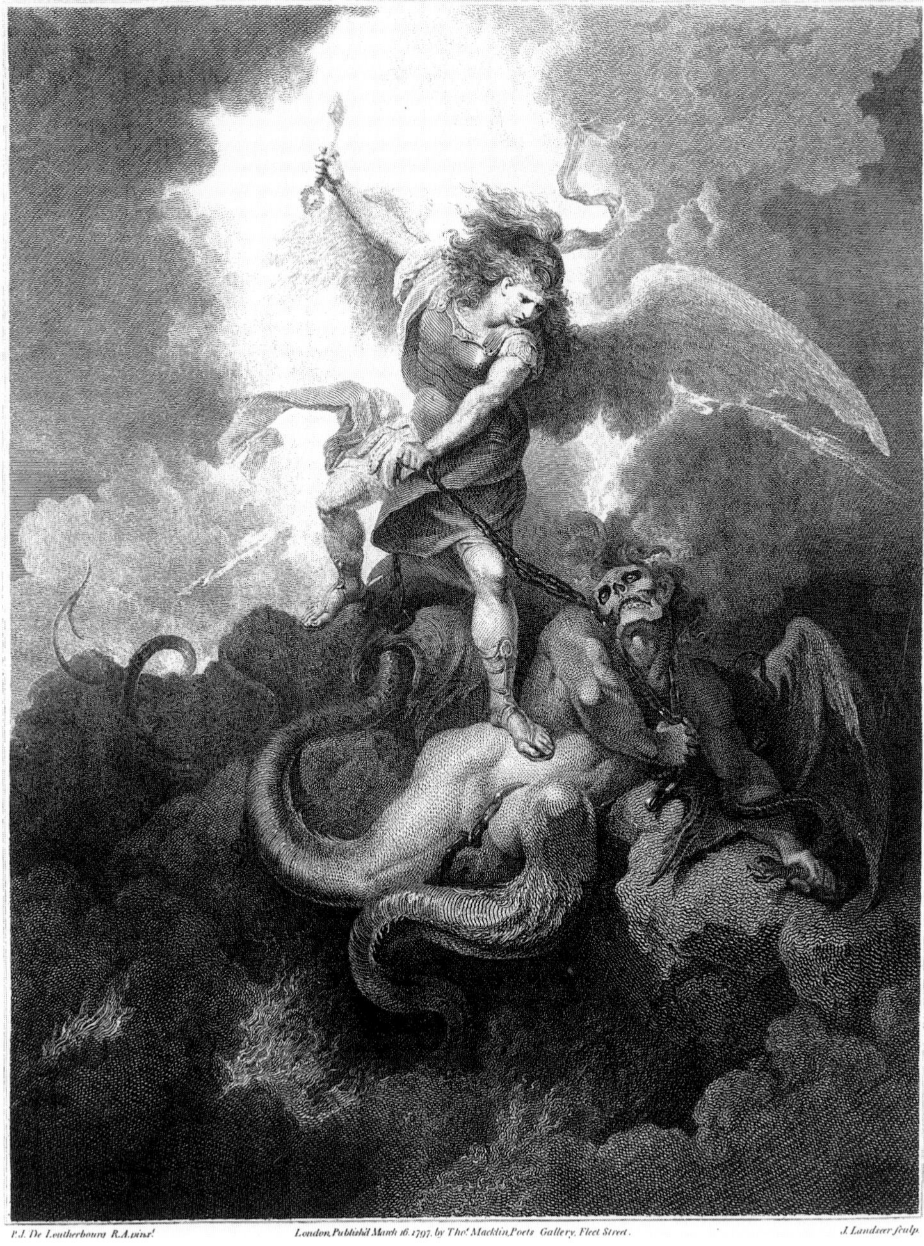

2.13. John Landseer after Philippe Jacques Loutherbourg, *The Angel Binding Satan*, engraving, 1797.

In the 1790s John Landseer worked as an engraver for Thomas Macklin, whose Poets' Gallery was an imitation of Boydell's Shakespeare Gallery. In the Poets' Gallery Macklin also exhibited paintings for his Bible project, which culminated in the publication of an illustrated six-volume Bible in 1800. The painter whom Macklin employed most frequently for his Bible project was Philippe Jacques de Loutherbourg, whose *Angel Binding Satan* (1792) was one of the pictures Landseer engraved for Macklin. (See Paley, *Apocalyptic Sublime* 58–61 & pls. 27, 29–31.) Nearly a decade after Landseer had created a furor by attacking Boydell in his lectures on engraving at the British Institution, Henry Crabb Robinson attended a series of Landseer's lectures on the philosophy of art at the Surrey Institution. Robinson's diary for 5 December 1815 records his impressions: "He is animated in his style, but his animation is produced by indulgence in sarcasms, and in emphatic diction. He pronounces his words in *italics;* and by colouring strongly he produces an effect easily" (1:505–6).

Materially, the "public" side of Boydell's aspirations is well illustrated by the ready transformation of the Shakespeare Gallery into the British Institution (cf. fig. 2.9).

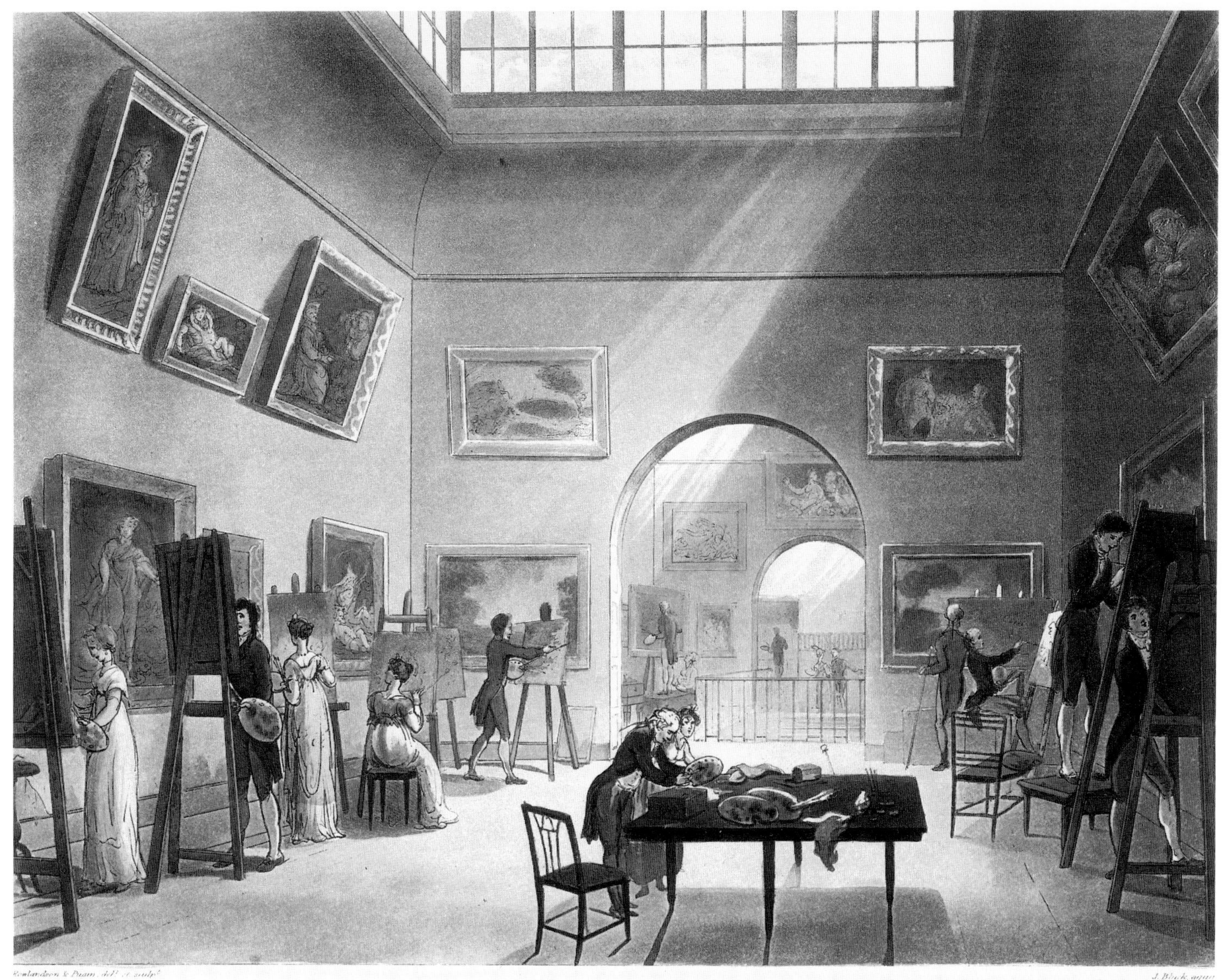

2.14. A. C. Pugin, Thomas Rowlandson, and J. Bluck, *The Interior of the British Institution, Pall Mall,* etching and aquatint from Rudolph Ackermann's *Microcosm of London,* vol. 1, 1808. (This aquatint was published as a separate print.)

advice and intrigues of foreign charlatans" (2:215).

A principle of compensation is at work. Boydell had given English artists and their engravers their last great chance to compete with continental artists on their own terms, albeit with the advantage of English liberty and commercial sagacity. In that sense the Shakespeare project was a national opportunity with international design and reach—and we know that Boydell did everything in his power to promote the national and public dimensions of his project over the entrepreneurial and private. Previous success in international markets allowed Boydell to design a commercial framework for the internationalist program symbolized by Royal Academy pedagogy.

But the Shakespeare Gallery and allied speculations had ultimately failed. The blame, so it was often said, lay neither with British artists and engravers nor with Boydell and the merchants. The plot that thickens out of this view is a bourgeois tragedy in which Boydell, whose "patriotic endeavour . . . made a wreck of his fortune," is sacrificed—to the French Revolution and, in Cunningham's treatment, to the mass audience, for whom "the love of art is not a common passion: every day we see the merest daubers patronised by the highest of the land. . . . The public runs after whatever is strange or new; . . . the gaping of the multitude lasts but for a season, and is ever ready to welcome new entertainers" (life of Northcote, 6:82, 81).[27] The British Institution is another element of a pattern of responses to the Boydell failure, as is Taylor's later attempt to see the founding of the Institution as an indirect benefit of the Revolution. The Institution's programmatic emphasis on the Britishness of British art seems to represent a new turn inward, toward the "natural good sense" of the "higher and better informed classes" of British society, reinforced by a defensive antagonism toward "foreign charlatans."

Furthermore, the changing artistic climate coincides with political changes. During the first years of the new century, the period of the French Consulate, Napoleon was at his most formidable and English fears of invasion were strongest. In 1804 he crowned himself emperor, and in 1805 he had his greatest victory at Austerlitz. But 1805 was also the year of a rousing demonstration of British naval power at Trafalgar and—important for our purposes—the year of the Shakespeare Gallery lottery. The chronological coincidence of artistic failure with naval success helps explain two things: why Prince Hoare published his *Inquiry* in 1806, and why he included in it a call for reconsideration of a Royal Academy scheme that the painter John Opie had first presented in 1800 in a letter to the *True Briton:* the Gallery of British Honour, a great circular naval monument modeled on the "Pantheon at Rome" (quoted in Hoare 47). Large pieces of sculpture—Neptune paying homage to Britannia, a statue of George III—would set the mythopolitical tone, while in a series of compartments around the circle statues of naval heroes would alternate with paintings of victories. The monument would inculcate patriotism with a visceral sublimity, giving "pleasure" through the "terror and admiration" of "Britain's thunder"—"fire, water, wind, and smoke, mingled in terrific

[27] For a detailed account of the range of effects that the Revolution had on Boydell's Shakespeare project—canceled subscriptions, loss of interest among would-be subscribers, difficulties with the export trade, especially to France (later in the decade to Germany as well), and changes in French taste after a redistribution of wealth—see Bruntjen 112–17.

confusion": "In the midst, British valour triumphantly bearing down all opposition, accompanied by humanity, . . . ready to succour the vanquished foe!" (quoted in Hoare 50–51).

The Gallery of British Honour was no isolated proposal but one episode in the continuing effort to locate the polite arts advantageously in the economy, and more particularly in the effort to create viable formats for commercial display. Shee relates the naval monument plan directly to the "danger of total annihilation, to which the failure of all private encouragement had exposed the higher classes of art" (84–85n), and renews the old complaint:

> No patriot acts adorn our public halls;
> No Gospel glories grace Religion's walls;
> No martial pomps in pictur'd lore allure—
> In taste alone is public spirit poor?
>
> [83, ll. 293–96]

During the early years of the Shakespeare Gallery, the apparent success of the private commercial galleries had given new impetus to proposals for public galleries. In 1793, Blake's friend George Cumberland urged the establishment in Green Park of two galleries filled with casts of "antique statues, bas-reliefs, fragments of architecture, fine bronzes, &c." (*Anecdotes* 15), with an informative text below each. Later in the decade, after the Boydell formula for using commercial galleries as the merchandising arm of the Royal Academy had begun to fail, writers conceived new schemes by which public galleries would take over part of that role: thus the title of Barry's *Letter to the Dilettanti Society, Respecting the Obtention of Certain Matters Essentially Necessary for the Improvement of Public Taste, and for Accomplishing the Original Views of the Royal Academy of Great Britain* (1798). Cumberland's gallery of ancient art appeals to the regressive or restorative aspect of the cyclical analogy—"in conjunction with my friend Cumberland to renew the lost Art of the Greeks" (E 701), as Blake put it rather craftily in 1799. And of course the primary task of public galleries is pedagogical, but the pedagogy has commercial extensions. Commercially, Cumberland's Green Park gallery would give public sanction to the market that has come to be called neoclassical—Wedgwood's market, and Flaxman's.

The pedagogical and commercial elements of Barry's proposal are somewhat different though equally familiar. The *Letter* of 1798 rehearses several commonplace themes in order to justify a public collection of old masters, which, when "separated [from each other], and in private hands," are "likely to perplex and retard the progress of good taste" (52). The ostensible reason for "this evil of old pictures" (53) seems to be less that they are kept hidden in the houses of the wealthy than that isolated masterpieces teach isolated excellences—Raphael drawing, Titian color, Michelangelo sublimity, and so on—instead of the Carracci blend, which "a national or academical gallery" would achieve "by arranging them together. . . . The work of each old master then becomes the corrective of the other . . ." (53).[28] The collection would thus illustrate the principle of progressive acquisition that Barry's own Adelphi sequence narrates.

Cumberland and Barry were two of many writers who continued to regard the need for a

[28] In his Academy lecture on coloring Barry also complains of the lack of a good public picture collection to assist in the forming of a true taste (Wornum 214).

public collection of masterworks as particularly urgent in "a new country like England, where happily this pre-occupation [by overwhelming numbers of pictures already in place, as in the churches of Italy] was prevented by our former religious bigotry, which kept out art of all kinds, except mere servile face-painting and a little landscape" (Barry, *Letter* 52). A new country is both artistic wilderness and frontier: while one part of the public has been fooled into believing that the only masterpieces worth hoarding are old and foreign, the other part has been deprived of the education that a public display of masterpieces can provide. Finally, Barry's national collection would have the commercial benefit of emptying the great houses of England of their old masters, thus creating demand for the new masters. Why not a new supply of old masters instead? Again Barry's commercial hope rests on a combined technical and intellectual progression. The national collection would inculcate a taste for a combination of excellences such as only the new generation of painters, working at the top of the curve of progressive understanding, could supply.

As a ploy for artistic patronage, Opie and Hoare's Gallery of British Honour seems as characteristic of its time as the proposal to decorate St. Paul's had earlier been of its. Some features remained constant. Opie's mention of the Roman Pantheon indicates that the cyclical historical analogy was still useful, however the Jacobinical manipulation of that analogy might have imperiled its credibility. The earlier projects and proposed projects, including Barry's Adelphi sequence, had also appealed to patriotic sentiments. Moreover, history painting, the generic basis of the projects, had long been domesticated, or perhaps nationalized. The famous arguments over dressing modern heroes in ancient or modern costume show the influence of historical analogy on local and national concepts of heroic dignity, but, whatever the drapery, *national* history became a standard source of subjects for history painting during the latter half of the century.

We can see a new tendency anticipated, however, in the historical context of Opie's initial proposal for the Gallery of British Honour in 1800. First, his timing, like Hoare's, seems intended to take advantage of a wave of national pride, no doubt intensified by fear, after the British defeat of Napoleon's expedition to Syria and Egypt in 1798–1799. Second, there is not one Pantheon but two. The one, created in the distant and revered artistic past at Rome, substantiates the historical analogy. (Young English artists doing their Italian stint would have visited it.) The other, newly constructed across the Channel in Paris, was intended to complete the analogy for France as the true heir of Rome. Though begun in 1759 as the Church of Sainte-Geneviève, it was not named the Panthéon until it was secularized during the Revolution. Reconsecrated, as it were, to revolutionary France, the new church, first proposed as a way of moralizing and generalizing the death of Mirabeau, was then decorated with patriotic sculpture and history painting. (In April 1791, Mirabeau was the first of the revolutionary heroes whose remains—his heart, in a lead urn—were placed there. Voltaire's were deposited in July, with even more neo-Roman pomp and circumstance.)[29] Speaking for the Department of Paris, which had proposed the Pan-

[29] See Schama's accounts (Mirabeau, 546–48; Voltaire, 561–66); the illustrations in Schama 562–63, 565, 567; and Leith 102–3, 120, 128.

théon, Rochefoucauld told the Constituent Assembly that rededicating the church to hero worship was in the best classical tradition, "so that the temple of religion might become the temple of the *patrie;* that the tomb of a great man might become the altar of liberty" (my trans., quoted in Leith 102). Clearly, Opie was proposing the Gallery of British Honour as a third Pantheon to serve as a public sign that Britain, not France, had inherited the analogy.

While Opie showed his hand by alluding to the Roman Pantheon, naming the British monument so would have seemed under the circumstances either imitative and vaguely blasphemous—in what the English considered to be the French manner—or demeaning, in view of the London Pantheons of his day.[30] Instead, he chose a name that would relate this public edifice to the great artistic projects of his decade—Boydell's Shakespeare Gallery, and the galleries of Fuseli, Macklin, and Bowyer, representing English secular and religious poetry, English Protestant faith, and English history respectively (fig. 2.3). The combination gives the Gallery of British Honour its moral axis. Hoare in effect suggests that the Boydell enterprise involved a moral failure manifested in printsellers' desperate attempts to lure customers: "at what shop-windows does he [Hoare's reader] most frequently find his passage impeded by crowds? Are they not invariably those of the printsellers?" (58n). By substituting the authorized thrills of battle for the sexual thrills of "licentious prints" sold by an "ignorant or profligate publisher" (56), the Gallery of British Honour would offer a moral alternative.

We note Hoare's strict separation between the reader who is the object of this appeal and the debased multitude under observation by that reader. Hoare addresses his reader not as a customer for the printsellers' products but as someone interested in improving the customers' morality. Money proferred by an audience at the level of the individual transaction—cash for prints—is being replaced by money from the state: money approved, as it were, and purified by its removal from the taint of individual desires. The resulting public echoes the separation in Hoare's rhetoric: on the one hand a social elite, represented by state and sovereign, that would sponsor a Gallery of British Honour, and on the other hand the crowds that would be diverted from the printsellers' windows to the legitimate pleasures of military adventure purchased for them by the state. The tasteless, immoral mob has of course not been invented for the occasion but reformulated in postrevolutionary circumstances. English military might, coded as national "honour," seems a natural addition and yet also a strong redirection of the sequence that encourages Hoare to image ultimate victory for the English school in military metaphors: "the meed of portrait-painting seems as truly our own as that of naval combat" (219), and "with the magnanimous spirit of a Chatham" we have "disdainfully sent home all auxiliaries" (217), all foreign portrait painters. In short, if the sea of portrait painting

[30] There were two relevant Pantheons in London: an elegantly decorated building that went up in Oxford Street in 1772, and the structure that replaced it after a dramatic fire in 1792. See Altick 85 and his illus. 17. According to Altick, both Pantheons were more notable for public and private assemblies than for exhibitions, though over the years they displayed numerous curiosities, such as Vincenzo Lunardi's balloon and other flying machines, some of Mary Linwood's famous needlework copies of paintings, a model of the town of Bath, and astronomical exhibitions. The architectural precedent might be relevant: the Oxford Street Pantheon was round in imitation of the Roman edifice, and Opie's 1800 proposal called for a round monument.

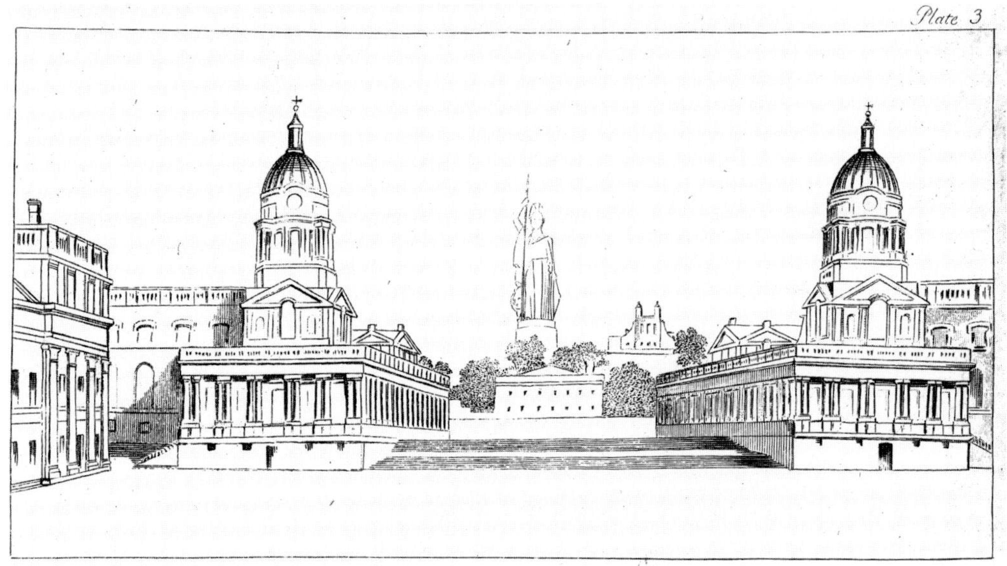

2.15. William Blake after John Flaxman, *Letter to the Committee for Raising the Naval Pillar,* plate 3, engraving, 1799.

is ours, can it be long before we take the land of history painting?

The increasing appeal of that redirection helps us understand Hoare's revival of the idea of a Gallery of British Honour in 1806, after the failure of all those other galleries but also after Nelson's popular victory. The sculptors had benefited enormously when the government voted in 1795 to fund monuments in Westminster Abbey and St. Paul's Cathedral to British heroes of the French wars; indeed, the very establishment of a professorship of sculpture at the Royal Academy in 1810, with Flaxman as the first professor, has often been credited largely to the decade and a half of state patronage that preceded it. Opie's notion of a Gallery of British Honour grew from a neighboring root: it attempted to enlarge the circle of patronage by adding projects funded by public subscription to projects funded with state money, and by adding painters to architects and sculptors, in a composite nationalist scheme. In fact, Flaxman first designed a triumphal column, *Britannia Triumphans* (figs. 2.15, 2.16), for the same naval monument competition and then, upon reading Opie's proposal for the Gallery of British Honour, wrote William Hayley that Opie's idea should be given "preference" because it would be "much more profitable to the public and beneficial to the arts of design than mine" West's and Copley's successes in the 1770s and 1780s confirm that patriotic, nationalistic, militaristic, and imperialistic subjects were (of course) not new to English—or, more imposingly, British—art in 1800. But the new wave of imperial spectacle stirred by reaction to the French Revolution kindled hopes for a profitable association between artists and the state. John Flaxman's career in these years illustrates how an artist's, and especially a sculptor's, "encouragement" might come from the surge of British nationalism. As Flaxman himself put it in his first Academy lecture, "native achievements had called the powers of native sculpture to celebrate British heroes" (quoted in Yarrington, "Nelson" 317). In 1799, entering a competition for a naval monument to commemorate British victories over the French, Flaxman printed his *Letter to the Committee for Raising the Naval Pillar,* accompanied by three designs, engraved by Blake, for a typically "*Colossal Statue*" of Britannia "*230 feet high; proposed to be erected on Greenwich hill.*" This is the competition that also stimulated two nonentries, as it were, Gillray's *Design for the Naval Pillar* and Barry's 1801 addition to *Commerce or The Triumph of the Thames* (fig. 2.5). In 1801 Flaxman exhibited the Britannia design at the Royal Academy. In 1805 he used the design in a monument to Lord North and in the same year designed the Trafalgar vase, inscribed "BRITONS STRIKE HOME" in block capitals on one side, "BRITANNIA TRIUMPHANT" on the other, with a sculpted British lion on

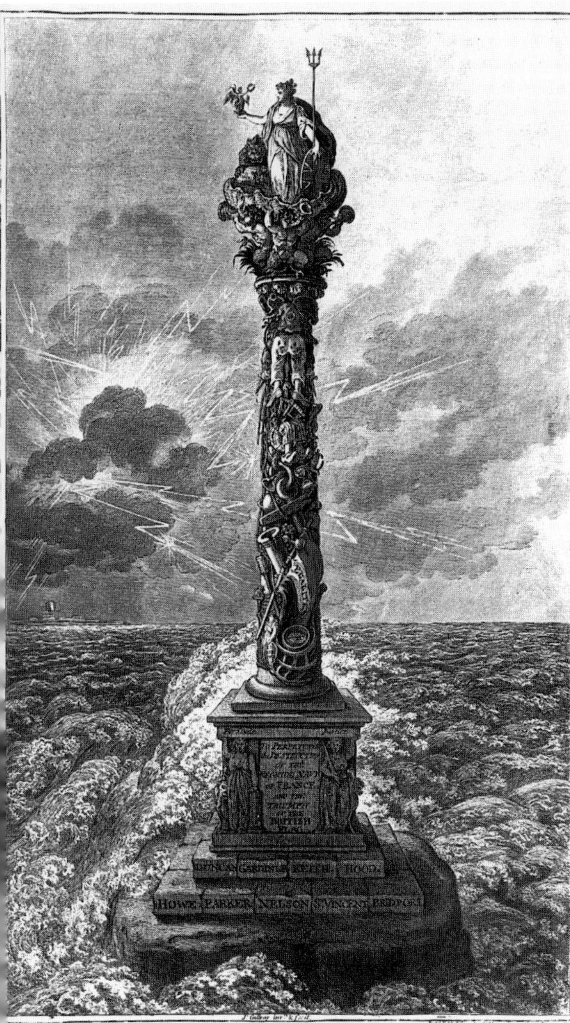

2.16. James Gillray, *Design for the Naval Pillar,* etching, 1800.

(quoted in Yarrington, *Commemoration* 340). It seemed that heroes and hero worship might come to the rescue of the English school.[31]

The new British Institution held its first exhibition in 1806, the year of Landseer's lectures. During the following decade the Institution devised various ways of promoting, and by promoting, shaping, English art. In 1813 the British Gallery, so called, the former Shakespeare Gallery, mounted its commemorative exhibition of Reynolds, which W. B. Sarsfield Taylor labels "the first public exhibition of the works of any individual British artist" (2:227)[32] and the first in a series of retrospective exhibitions featuring national artists. Reynolds was followed the next year by Hogarth, Wilson, Gainsborough, and Zoffany. The Institution also used the technique of association-by-juxtaposition to raise the status of the English work. As Taylor says, "The summer exhibition was composed from the five principal schools, including our own" (2:234), and Reynolds was hung alongside Rubens and van Dyck—just as Reynolds had once juxtaposed the names of English and continental artists in the *Discourses.* The Institution followed a parallel policy with the cover (more than sixty were presented to naval and military officers) (Bury 142). In the same year the *Gentleman's Magazine* printed letters urging that St. Paul's become the British Pantheon (Yarrington, "Nelson" 327n), and in 1808 Flaxman started work on a statue of Nelson that ended up eventually in St. Paul's stock of mammoth naval monuments.

[31] Alison Yarrington, *Commemoration,* connects Flaxman's professorship to the preceding years of state patronage and quotes Flaxman himself to good effect (ix). Yarrington also succinctly but helpfully discusses Opie's gallery proposal in the context of related ones (app. a, 338–45) before and after. See also the Introduction and chap. 1. Ada Earland treats Opie's proposal briefly (152–55).

[32] Taylor means, I take it, that the Reynolds retrospective was the first such exhibition sponsored by a public institution instead of by the artist. Individual artists had regularly held exhibitions of their own works: from that model derive both J. M. W. Turner's permanent gallery, which he opened in 1804 and remodeled in 1819, and Blake's temporary 1809 exhibition in his brother's shop. Joseph Burke 256–57 provides a useful summary of major independent efforts by Copley, Wright of Derby, Barry, West, Morland, and others for the period 1781–1827. For a documentary survey of exhibition and reviewing practices in the period 1785–1848, see Holt.

icy in acquisitions, buying Reynolds and West along with Veronese and Parmigiano. Beginning in 1807 living British painters (only) could win cash prizes for their current year's work. Until 1817 one of the standard prize categories for the exhibition was finished sketches representing recent successes of the British army and navy. From 1816 (the year after Waterloo) through 1826, of eighteen prizes given, five were for Waterloo battle pictures, with one Trafalgar and one Battle of the Nile (Fullerton 66, W. B. S. Taylor 2:243–44). As that imbalance suggests, the British Institution often chose to encourage not just British artists but a particularly British art by setting British themes—characters in British history, or British military victories—for some of its exhibitions. The Institution maintained the traditional hierarchy by encouraging history painting above all, but it moved history in the direction that West and Copley had successfully pioneered and that Cunningham would later articulate—away from "the monkish miracles and incredible legends of the church" that "the Italians" (life of West, 2:38) had squandered their canvases on, and toward a national mythos.

The nationalism that inspired the British Institution also moved private individuals. Taylor commemorates "patriotic and generous" citizens who set a "patriotic example" (2:245) by holding semipublic exhibitions of British art during the period. Sir John Leicester (1762–1827), for example, did "his duty to his country" (2:245) by organizing exhibitions that he supplemented with catalogues and commissions. Taylor treats Leicester and Walter Ramsden Fawkes (1769–1825), Turner's patron, as the leaders of a band of wealthy upper-class patrons who not only collected British art but also exhibited it to a "fashionable assemblage" and "the most competent judges of pictorial merit, probably, in Europe; we mean the nobility and gentry of this country" (2:245, 246) (fig. 2.17).

While the competing myths that form around the figure of Boydell reveal important shifts in the economic outlook of English-school discourse, they do not emphasize what may be the most far-reaching change: the retreat from the theory and practice supporting the notion that the English school would share a continuous, progressive tradition with the art of other nations. Landseer's anti-institutionalism, as expressed in the alliance of art with the "natural bent" of individual freedom and the opposition to institutionalized mercantile restraints, is indeed part of this retreat.

Taken altogether the evidence suggests that, following the failure of the academic-internationalist commercial projects, preeminently Boydell's, around the turn of the century, those with a stake in British art saw a new, or at least vastly improved, opportunity in hitching the wagons of the English school to the political and military strengths of the imperial lion (figs. 2.18, 2.19).[33] The failure of the commercial galleries helps to explain the revival of anticommercial rhetoric and renewed appeals to state patronage by such writers as Shee and Hoare. Only with these failures in mind can we understand the "public" reaction to John Landseer's lectures on the art of engraving at the Royal Institution in 1806. First we might ask what inspired such a series on such a subject in the new British Institution's inaugural year—

[33] Pears notes "increasingly strong links between painting and a sense of patriotism" (154) even in the earlier eighteenth century, and he observes later that the "patriotic element lodged as a standard eighteenth century English response to the subject of collecting" (172). After the shock of the Revolution, this development markedly intensified. J. W. M. Hichberger's study picks up the story in 1815.

J. M. W. Turner's *Battle of Trafalgar* illustrates both the postrevolutionary development of a nationalist art and the high hopes that continued to be placed in the monarch as symbolic High Patron. Although Turner had two paintings in the inaugural (1806) exhibition at the British Institution, both were in the traditional—classical and biblical—mold of history painting. But in the same year he had at least one and probably two Trafalgar pictures (Butlin and Joll nos. 58–59) for sale in his own gallery in Queen Anne's Street. His later *Trafalgar* (Butlin and Joll nos. 250–52) was commissioned by George IV in 1822 to be part of a group with Loutherbourg's *Glorious First of June,* and to hang with a larger series (including such works as George Jones's *Vittoria* and *Waterloo*) on British naval victories to decorate the State Apartments at St. James's Palace. From the start Turner's picture was a public failure. Naval authorities, including Nelson's flag captain at Trafalgar, complained about its inauthenticity, and the king seems to have preferred pictures of military men in flashy uniforms to battle pictures. *Trafalgar* hung for about five years at St. James's; after that it was removed to Greenwich. Turner was paid £500, grudgingly it seems, in installments (Butlin and Joll 1:155–57).

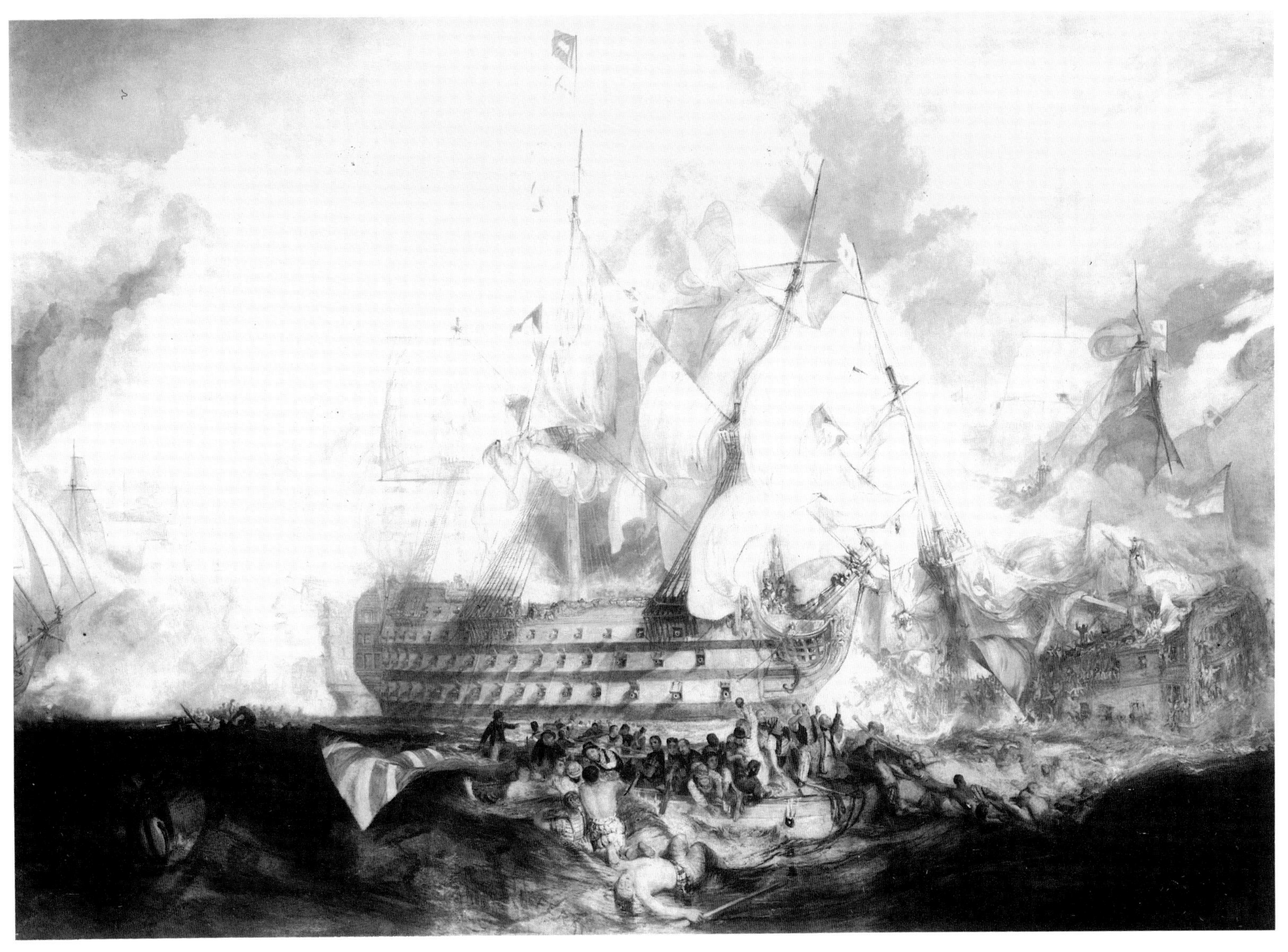

2.17. J. M. W. Turner, *The Battle of Trafalgar*, oil, 1822–1824.

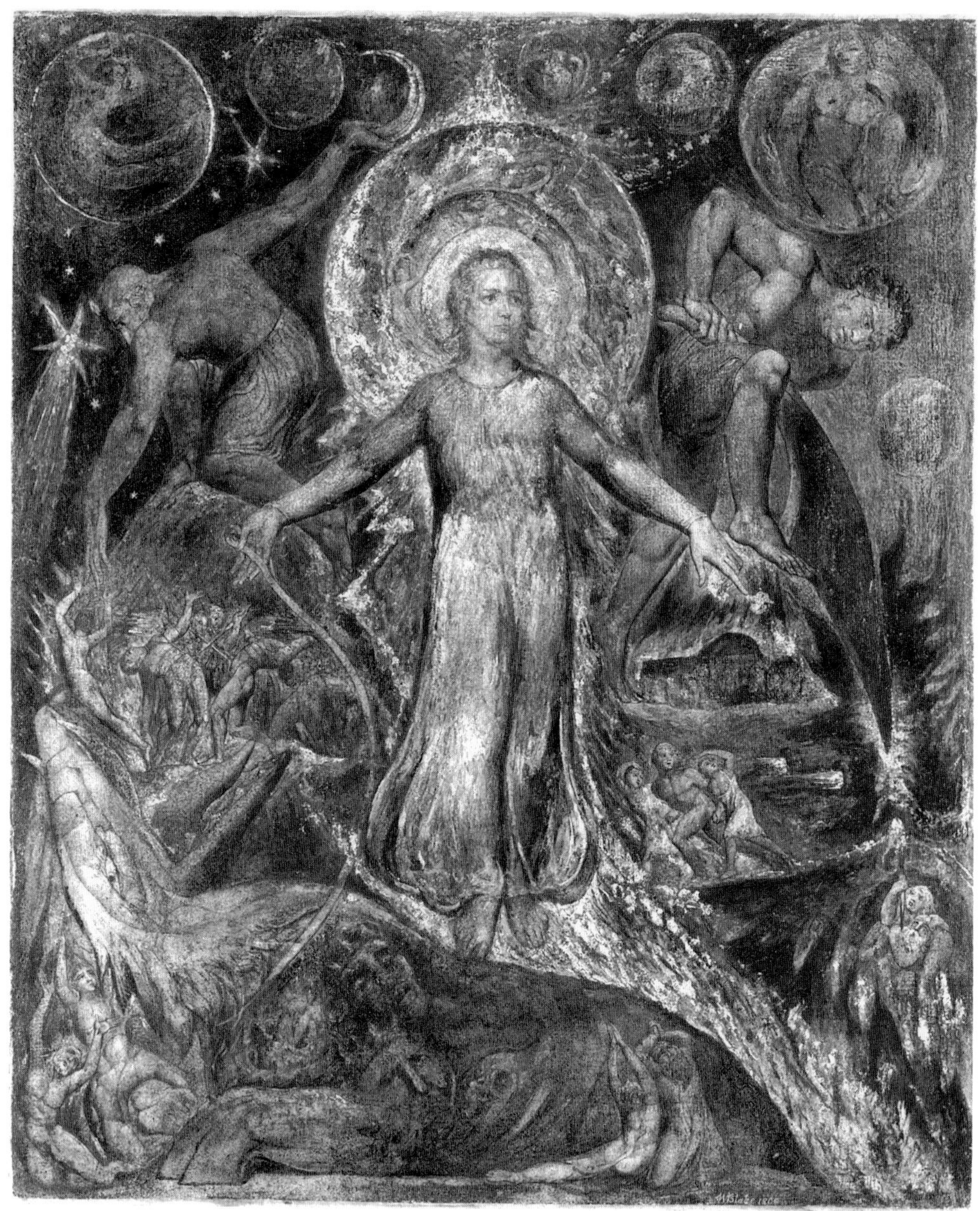

2.18. William Blake, *The Spiritual Form of Pitt Guiding Behemoth,* tempera, 1805–1809.

Geoffrey Best's *War and Society in Revolutionary Europe* shows how heroes military and political focused much of the new nationalism, and Alison Yarrington's *Commemoration of the Hero* records the effects on British sculpture after 1800. West's *Death of General Wolfe* (fig. 2.1) and Copley's *Death of Chatham* had demonstrated the power of contemporary heroes and their exploits to update the revered but chronically unprofitable imagery of history painting. In the years when artists were most absorbed in exploiting the emotion of being imperially British, Blake tried to catch this wave with "grand Apotheoses of NELSON and PITT" (E 527) that he painted from 1805 to 1809 and included in his 1809 exhibition. (Nelson died in 1805, Pitt the next year.) He displayed *The Spiritual Form of Pitt Guiding Behemoth* and *The Spiritual Form of Nelson Guiding Leviathan* as examples of *"the invention of a portable Fresco"* (E 527) that Blake, taking a page from the book of English-school wishful thinking, imagined adorning public monuments: "The Artist wishes it was now the fashion to make such monuments, and then he should not doubt of having a national commission to execute these two Pictures on a scale that is suitable to the grandeur of the nation, who is the parent of his heroes"

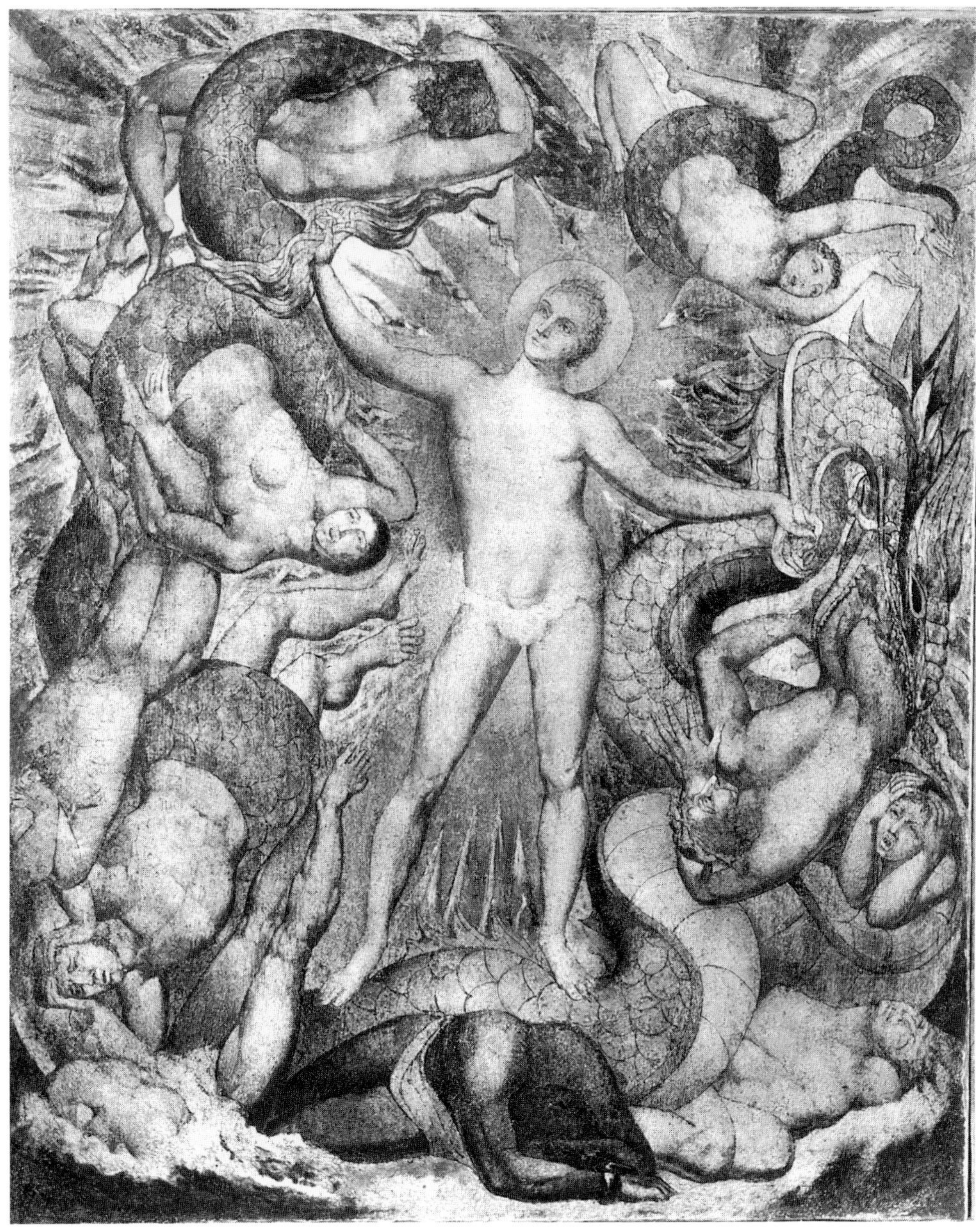

2.19. William Blake, *The Spiritual Form of Nelson Guiding Leviathan*, tempera, 1805–1809.

(*DC*, E 531). Blake's chosen position here is, typically, simultaneously inside, participating in, and beneath, challenging, the parameters of English-school discourse. Equally typical, his strategy is to work under the cloak of ironies—slyly cited as "recondite meaning, where more is meant than meets the eye" (E 531)—that few in his audience were capable of detecting. Anyone could easily read right through the entries on *Pitt* and *Nelson* in the exhibition catalogue without noticing departures from the hero worship that was the stock in trade of English-school imagery and discourse: Pitt is an "*Angel . . . pleased to perform the Almighty's orders*" (*DC*, E 530), and both men are classed among "modern Heroes" (E 531) who deserve comparison with the heroes of antiquity depicted on ancient monuments. Is Crabb Robinson's enigmatic remark that he "has seen" the pictures but "dares not describe" them a reference to the seditious hints in *Pitt* and *Nelson* (quoted in Bentley, *Blake Records* 451)? Blake may have decided not to exhibit a third painting in the series, *The Spiritual Form of Napoleon* (lost since 1882; Butlin, *Paintings* no. 652), because a "spiritual" enemy in company with two British champions would have blown the cover on his irony.

lectures on what was after all a lower-echelon reproductive art practiced by second-class members of the Academy. The general explanation is, of course, the Royal Institution's programmatic devotion to applied arts. But another equally important explanation, more specific and timely, is clearly the Boydell connection. Landseer, who had worked for Macklin and Bowyer (see fig. 2.13), was asked to lecture on the art that had made Boydell the most significant name in the history of English engraving, just as the new Institution that had taken over the emptied rooms of the old Boydell empire was launching the aspirations of the English school into the new century.

The time and subject were right for a powerful tribute to Boydell. As an engraver and historian of engraving, Landseer would have been well prepared to lay the narrative groundwork for the climactic episode that Boydell himself had told, of heroic defeat at the hands of the revolutionaries. We know the form such a narrative would take: a history of steady progress in which English engravers inherited the great line of ancient and modern engraving that ran parallel to ancient and modern painting. Boydell would play the merchant-patriot who invented a way of advantageously combining artistic skill with English commercial genius. In blocking his progress toward final victory, the French Revolution would have taken its place alongside such other time-honored obstructions as the Reformation and the Civil War. The Revolution had killed the commercial Maecenas, but there was new hope for English engraving in the spirit of Trafalgar.

As I see it, these are the essentials of the history that the English school and its promoters could have embraced, founded, as it was, in the hope of recovery from artistic failures that were fresh in the minds of its sister institution's audience. Using the familiar cyclical analogies, the history would have woven a new parallel strand, engraving, into the standard narrative of the polite arts, memorialized Boydell's additions to the narrative, and announced the renewal of opportunity that was taking place on the very spot where opportunity had first shone bright in 1789. As expected, Landseer did indeed speak to the sense of failure, rightly assuming that the members of his audience, looking back at the course of English engraving, would see a steep decline in its recent fortunes. Instead of doing the politic thing and repeating the public myth of the English merchant foiled by French radicals, Landseer blamed the commercial failure on Boydell himself and went even further, to blame him for the decline of the art of engraving as well.[34]

As soon as it became clear that Landseer was going to attack "ignorant Capital" and use the Boydells to symbolize it, the water began to heat up. Within a few appearances he had antagonized so many influential people that the public lectures had to be canceled:

> Landseer called in the evening. He told me that he had this day attended a Committee of the Royal Institution . . . [and was] charged with having in a late Lecture alluded to the late Alderman Boydell & others, denying to Him the credit of having advanced the art of engraving but on the contrary of having degraded it, & that all the merit of the popularity which English prints had at home and abroad some time ago was due to Woollet, Strange, Ryland &c. . . . In the course of the day He recd. notice by order of the Committee, that it was with regret they informed him that His assistance, as Professor, wd.

[34] Godfrey has suggested that Boydell's "failure to satisfy the home market probably contributed as much to the ruin of the project as the war's destruction of the vital export trade in prints" (47).

no longer be required. [17 March 1806, Farington 7:2695–96]

Hoare's *Inquiry* appeared in the bookstalls the day the lectures were canceled, and James Barry had died the month before. In the spirit of Barry, Landseer claimed to have been the victim of "secret machinations": "Of the means which have been employed to dismiss me from lecturing, and deter me from printing [the lectures], the most insidious and successful have been the hue and cry words *Personality* and *Attack;* which have pursued me from the committee-room [of the Institution] to the newspapers, and by which my adversaries seem to hope that I shall be hunted down" (*Lectures* xvii). Apparently undaunted, he published the lectures the next year and followed them in 1810 with "A Letter to a Member of the Society for Encouraging the Art of Engraving . . . ," then a second "Letter," and a third.

The interpretation of the history of English engraving that embroiled Landseer in controversy inverts the Boydellian plot. The story begins in the days of Hogarth, Ryland, Vivares, Strange, and Bartolozzi, an ideal past time in which an engraver could work "according to the natural bent of his own genius, uncurbed, or but little curbed, by mercantile restraints" (*Lectures* 295). In this golden age of artistic freedom, engravers published "the best of their own works" (296) in most cases.[35] In the engravings of uncurbed genius, the "mental" and "mechanical" parts of the art—conception and execution, invention and technique, content and form—are united. The public, as free to respond to these creations as the engravers were to create them, encouraged the best work. Thus the engravers themselves, not the merchants, "turned the tide and profits of the European commerce for Prints, from France and Italy to England" (296). On this promising scene arrive the Boydells. Sniffing out the trail of commercial opportunity, they lead the way for "other shopkeepers, even more ignorant" (298), to follow, "for we shall always find a sufficient number of merchants who will be ready enough to discover and follow, where profit leads the way" (xxi–xxii). Piece by piece the engravers' independence, which rests upon their free access to the public, is bought up by the merchants, reducing proud artisans to wage slaves. Landseer speaks of printsellers as "those who have interposed their opaque intellects between the Artists and the Public" (295).

In the romance of the commercial Maecenas, the merchant opens a new door, liberating engravers from their bondage to false patrons into a relationship of freedom with true patrons, the public. As Bruntjen would have it, "Boydell attempted to free artists from the traditional forms of aristocratic and state patronage by creating a public taste for reproductive prints of historical subjects. In his intermediary role between artist and consumer, he encouraged the public's taste for paintings and prints, while financially assisting both painters

[35] Pye, for all his admiration of the Boydells, also sometimes associates the prosperity of engraving, or at least the economic prosperity of engravers, with the extent of their control over publication. He claims, for instance, that Robert Strange alone among the engravers of his generation had any income to boast of because he alone "possessed the means of publishing his own works" (*Patronage* 159). And Pye's main proposal for restoring nineteenth-century English engraving to health is to restore control over publication to engravers: "And if the painter and engraver were brought together, they would publish in conjunction their own works, for their mutual advantage, which would become distributed in a degree amongst amateurs, who would pay a fair price for them, instead of their being now circulated exclusively through the trade" (*Evidence* 35, testimony of 5 July 1836).

and engravers" (245). But in interpretations of the Landseer type, the merchant prince is not the real but the "mock Maecenates" (Landseer quoted in Bruntjen 10), not the knight of the romance but the dragon, "vulgar, oppressive reptiles, who call themselves Publishers, that is, a body of worthless wretches, who rob the artists of all the honey of their labour, and stand between them and the Public, as an intermediate purgatory." This characterization, by "Anthony Pasquin" (John Williams) in 1796 ("Critical Guide" 30),[36] helps to bring out the connection between Landseer's anti-Boydell narrative and the tradition of Grub Street literature in which the merchant's opaque intellect becomes the dark dungeon that imprisons the artist. Or, in Pasquin's version, the publisher controls a purgatory that the artist must go through to reach the public in hell. A harrowing would seem to be the appropriate turn of events. When the natural relationship between artist and public is intact, the art thrives; when the dragons of commerce force artists to labor in darkness like Samson at the mill with slaves, the natural relationship of artist with public is also blocked unnaturally by a third party, and the art declines.

Landseer raises this argument to the level of a general principle governing the arts in society:

> The positions, when placed in the abstract, are these. First, *That in a Commercial Country, like ancient Greece, or modern Europe, where any degree of rivalry in the Fine Arts exists between the several states, and where the productions of any one of those arts have become an article of Commerce, the profits of that commerce will be, or will turn, in favour of that particular state where the greatest quantum and highest degrees of talent exist among the professors of that particular Art. Secondly, That if in a given Art, Ignorance shall assume, and attempt to exercise, the superintendence of Knowledge, talent in that art will, from that period, begin to decline.* [*Lectures* xix][37]

Landseer has worked commerce into the standard analogical myth of the English school as an explanation for the decline side of the cycle. He agrees with the Boydellians that England and commerce have a particular affinity; even that England "is the most commercial country in the world." He also sees a special relationship between commerce and engraving, "the most commercial of the Fine Arts" (293)—and thus, by inference, the chance for an especially fruitful relationship between England and engraving. (As early as 1775 Robert Strange had suggested that engraving, as "a profession which is now a credit and advantage to this kingdom in particular" [58], might be an especially English, or perhaps British, endeavor.) For Landseer, however, commerce starts with the maker, not the seller; with production, not marketing.

Translated into artistic terms, Landseer's position puts its faith in a natural sympathy between artist and audience and thus in a simple

[36] This is the same Pasquin who sees Boydell as the salvation of English engraving; but Pasquin is not a man to be disturbed by contradiction. Characteristically, he bites off various strands of current opinion, chews them into their most poisonous form, then spits them out again in print.

[37] In a long passage whose thesis is that "the degradation of the Roman Empire, followed or kept pace with the perversion of art" (*Lectures* 47), Landseer also claims that the fate of the empire should serve as an example to modern Europe. His history of engraving falls into two cycles, ancient, ending in the Roman decline, and modern, ending in the English decline; the former is often regarded as an object lesson for the latter.

correspondence between artistic talent and commercial success. The natural movement of an artistic "article of Commerce" in Landseer's scheme is from the individual artist's studio directly to the ultimate purchaser. The more talent the "professors of that particular Art" possess, the greater "the profits of that commerce will be." While this bipartite arrangement does not forbid third parties, it does not encourage them. The best dealer and the best system of marketing and distribution will be pure and invisible rather than opaque. Though commerce is not necessarily wicked, the commercial aspect of the transaction between artist and audience must be secondary, following naturally from the audience's direct appreciation of the artist's talents.

But the strain of hostility toward commerce that runs through Landseer's analysis—as when he describes England as "a commercial country . . . where wealth has usurped the title of *Goodness*" (*Lectures* 319)—suggests that commerce has a pattern of evolution, a progress, a goal, and presumably a history all its own. It tends to make its goal, wealth, primary, not secondary, and thus to make itself the cause of art rather than the consequence. The practical result is what Landseer calls the "ignorant superintendence" (*Lectures* xxi) of art by commerce. In the relation that Landseer considers natural, artist and public, talent, knowledge, power, and reward reside together, balanced and allied. Boydell symbolizes for Landseer the separation of talent and knowledge from power. When the opaque intellects of the dealers begin their campaign "to lead the public taste" (xv) on the one hand and to command the artists on the other, the attempt of power to dictate to knowledge corrupts the natural order of art in society. Landseer expresses this corruption by introducing the theme of conspiracy from conventional English-school discourse. The true audience of art wanders away, replaced by "mock patrons" who are the "real enemies of Engraving" (xxiv), while the true artists sink into oblivion, replaced by mock artists capable of giving mock patrons what they want. These mock artists band together in mock institutions such as the Royal Academy, in its aspect as—in Hazlitt's words—"a society of hucksters in the Fine Arts," a "mercantile body, like any other mercantile body, consisting chiefly of manufacturers of portraits, who have got a regular monopoly of this branch of trade . . . supported by authority from without and by cabal within" ("Catalogue Raisonné" 105). Hazlitt, like Landseer, has joined two fairly familiar English-school motives, the anticommercial and the conspiratorial, with new potency. (But I would add the reminder that even Hazlitt's and Landseer's rhetorical violence, like Blake's, is closer to the mainstream of art criticism in the age than gentler readers sometimes like to believe.)

According to Landseer, this system taken altogether, artists, vendors, and audience, is the house of cards that supports the art of engraving in its decadence. On one side, the subversion of craft: "In Engraving, particularly, the comparatively few noxious weeds of 1782, have grown and disseminated beyond all precedent, till the field of art is completely overspread with trivial, vulgar, unprincipled productions" (*Lectures* 286n). On the other side, the subversion of taste: "this fashionable but unfounded attachment to vague and slovenly prints which have usurped the name of Engravings" (241). In the middle, the dark intellect of "ignorant Capital" (301) that has generated the rest of the system.

Though in Landseer's history the collapse of trade inevitably follows the collapse of skill and taste, the vested interest of the merchants drives them to more and more desperate attempts to keep the truth from leaking out. It would expose "time abused, money dissipated, folly entertained, genius perverted, and the impious profanation of the divinity of Art" (286n). Thus Landseer attributes the cancellation of his public lectures to the "interested and ignorant venders [sic] of Art" such as the Boydells. (Josiah, John Boydell's nephew and partner, continued to run the firm, which was sold shortly after his death in 1817. The uproar over Landseer's lectures suggests that Josiah zealously guarded his uncle's reputation, and with it of course his establishment's.) "They are endeavouring to throw the blame of the failure of commercial profit upon the body of Engravers—amongst whom they will find one, at least, who is neither to be tamed to wrongs, nor intimidated to silence" (xvi).[38]

On the Discrimination of Anticommercialisms

> Lady Beaumont spoke with irritation of *Shee's poem & remarks;* and said the public were not to be *bullied* into patronage of the arts.
>
> This morning Hoare saw [Richard] Cumberland at his lodgings, and heard him declare that "*the Rhymes on Art*" is the best poem ancient or modern in our language. Hoare mentioned *Milton* at which Cumberland hesitated a little, but declared that *Dryden & Pope* fell before it.
>
> —Joseph Farington, 12 May 1805, 16 April 1807

Though Landseer's defense of the "divinity" of art and his fierce attacks on Boydell are pungent alternatives to the selling of Boydell as a tragic merchant hero, anticommercialism is not in itself an argument but part of one. The views of another opponent of Boydell, the painter and sometime poet Martin Archer Shee, remind us that the politics of anticommercialism is anything but monolithic. From the prefaces, notes, and texts of the various editions of Shee's *Rhymes on Art* we can sketch the essentials of a history that might even have appealed to the Institution audience that Landseer offended. The key is not anticommercialism but the context that motivates it, which is, in our terms, the narrative in which attacks on Boydell as a personification of commerce are coherent episodes.

In a note written before the demise of the Shakespeare Gallery but after its problems were well known, Shee presents the conflicting images of Boydell that had become common currency:

> Whether we consider the gigantic project of the Shakspeare Gallery, as a vast commercial speculation, . . . or whether we look on it, as a plan originating in the patriotic ambition of a man, already by a long course of honourable industry raised above the temptation of interest, and enthusiastically deter-

[38] For Landseer's lectures, see also Gage, "Early Exhibition."

mined to risk the accumulations of his life, in an effort to encourage the depressed genius, and promote the peaceful glories of his country; in either case, . . . the Shakspeare Gallery . . . has claims on our admiration, which neither malignity can misrepresent, nor prejudice deny. Whatever may be the final result . . . we shall pay our just tribute of applause to the merits of the projector." [98–99n]

Though Shee's contrast between a speculative "project" and a disinterested "plan" permits him to honor the decorum of the occasion as Landseer does not, Shee's anticommercialism is as powerful as Landseer's: "This is the true handicraft consideration of the subject—the warehouse wisdom of a dealer and chapman, who would make the artist a manufacturer, and measure his works by the yard." According to Shee, the narrative of commerce in which the character "manufacturer" creates measurable works cannot be conflated with a narrative of art in which the character "artist" creates works beyond calculation: "The principle of trade, and the principle of the arts, are not only dissimilar but incompatible. Profit is the impelling power of the one—praise, of the other. *Employment* is the *pabulum vitae* of the first—*encouragement*, of the last." As we know, "these terms are synonymous in the ordinary avocations of life; but in the pursuits of taste and genius, they differ as widely in meaning as coldness, from kindness . . ." (1st ed. Preface xviii–xix).

Shee insists that these are mutually exclusive narratives that cannot be figured one through the other: "It has of late become so much the fashion, to view every thing through the commercial medium, and calculate the claims of utility by 'The Wealth of Nations,' that it is to be feared, the Muses and Graces will shortly be put down as unproductive labourers, and the price current of the day considered as the only criterion of merit." Those who "consult Adam Smith for their theory of taste as well as of trade" and "regulate the operations of virtu on the principles of the pin manufactory" (as in Smith's famous example of divided labor) are operating under the spell of a false master analogy: "this world . . . as one vast market—a saleshop of sordid interests and selfish gratifications" (2d ed. Preface liv–lv[n]).

The turn that separates Shee's anticommercialism from Landseer's comes with the assertion that commerce really belongs in the narrative of Jacobinism whose climactic episode is the French Revolution. The claim that "there is a commercial as well as a political jacobinism" is, in our terms, a claim that the political narrative of Jacobin radicalism can be used to structure the commercial narrative of laissez-faire capitalism: "a levelling of the principles and feelings, as well as the ranks and distinctions of society" (2d ed. Preface lvi[n]). Ultimately Shee would identify the world of the Jacobin revolution with the free market of Adam Smith through the middle term "mass of society." Jacobinism and capitalism activate the same audience.

Shee's anticommercialism was implicitly responding to the pro-revolutionary arguments of commercial republicanism. Thomas Paine's *Rights of Man* (Part Second, 1792) had offered a defense of commerce as a defense of the Revolution. The charters and corporations of "old nations" such as England were hereditary obstacles to the benefits of this "pacific system, operating to unite mankind by rendering nations, as well as individuals, useful to each other." Commerce, Paine had claimed, is itself potentially revolutionary: "If commerce were permitted to act to the universal extent it is capable of, it would extirpate the system of war, and produce a revolution in the uncivilized state of governments [such as England's]." He offered a bottom-up paradigm of commerce as "no other than the traffic of two individuals, multiplied on a scale of numbers" (448–49). Seen in this way, commerce would depend crucially on interdependence and social symmetry—Shee's "levelling"—among these individuals and nations. Asymmetries of the structural and hereditary English sort could threaten the shopkeepers' livelihood only in that nation of shopkeepers.[39]

Shee's anticommercialism is an element in a more comprehensive social narrative that is reactionary in a fairly specific sense. Shee imagines the Boydell years as the time when the ownership of the arts shifted from the legitimate proprietors, the landed upper class, to the mass of society through the agency of commerce. The Boydell experiment in England and the revolutionary experiment in France are thus parallel events that trade in the same public. This is, we recall, quite the opposite of Boydell's attempt to blame the Jacobins for his gallery's commercial failure. For Shee, the Boydell failure provides the opportunity to recover the arts from "the sordid commerce of mechanics," where (in spatial metaphors) the "level of the arts" is "determined by the wants and caprices of the million," and to restore them to their original social situation in "the liberal intercourse of gentlemen" on "the summits of civilization—in the affection and admiration of minds elevated to a due sense of their value" (1st ed. Preface xix; 2d ed. Preface lv).

In their anthropology of consumption, Mary Douglas and Baron Isherwood argue that the buying and selling of art, far from the irrational activities that some have claimed, provide valuable "marking services" (198)—marking the consumer for affiliation with various social groups—on the principle that "goods . . . make and maintain social relationships" (60).[40] Shee's narrative anticipates that argument in one of its reactionary forms. It operates in three spheres, psychological, social, and national, each of which metaphorizes the others. Psychologically, he figures the arts as the internal concomitants—"principles and feelings"—of external rank. In the sphere of the individual, commercial Jacobinism is the internal version of political Jacobinism, "perhaps, in this country at the moment, the more dangerous of the two; for it works unseen and uncensured" (2d ed. Preface lvi[n]). As the enemy within, commercial Jacobinism "strikes at the ancient nobility of the mind—the privileged powers of genius and virtue . . . if our heads and hearts are

[39] The subtlest treatment of Paine's (evolving) views on commerce is Claeys, esp. 46–51, 78–82, 96–101. Claeys distinguishes classical republicanism, which was anticommercial in its fear of the effects of "luxury" on political virtue (a standard topic in civic-humanist discourse), from Paine's "commercial republicanism" (46), which has sometimes been seen as a reconciliation of democratic republicanism with economic liberalism. But, as Claeys points out, Paine was not merely an exponent of commercial Whiggism, nor did he ignore the possibility that commerce might taint political virtue.

[40] Alsop's account of art collecting, for example, is undermined by his reliance on classical economic theories of the fundamentally irrational nature of consumption to characterize collecting as a "demonstrably and fundamentally irrational" (971) activity in which extremely high prices are paid for objects divested of whatever use they might have had in some other context. More interestingly, Douglas and Isherwood maintain that "commodities are good for thinking" (62). Consumption makes fundamental sense as an "active process in which all the social categories are being continually redefined" (68).

to be overrun by a mob of mercenary sentiments, we shall have escaped to little purpose the disorganization of one revolution, to be reserved to suffer under the degradation of the other" (1st ed. Preface xxiv). The principles and feelings, the internal arts, are the mental forces empowered to engage the psychological enemy.

The counterrevolutionary psychological effects of the arts find their true match in the counterrevolutionary actions of the state. This is the symmetry through which Shee and others see the state as the new hope for the arts. Sometimes he calls on the state to intervene as if it were merely the last resort of a cause that has become desperate since "the peculiar desertion of all the ordinary powers of support" (1st ed. Preface xviii): "Thus circumstanced, the arts of the country have no resource left, but in the liberality—in the policy of the state; and unless some public exertion be made in their favour, they must sink . . ." (xvii). Even here, however, the notion that financing the arts might be an element in state policy shares the logic supporting numerous plans in the Napoleonic years to image the state through the arts. Shee draws the analogy: "The examples of her [the state's] taste and genius,—the monuments of her power and glory—all the memorials of her magnificence, are to a great state, what his dress and equipage are to a great man,—necessary to his rank, and becoming his dignity; but amongst the more trifling charges [i.e., expenses] of his establishment" (xxiv). Conflating taste and genius with power and magnificence follows from the metaphorical structure that makes military and artistic institutions into coproducers of the state's equipage.

We can see, however, that the transition from the individual to the social sphere exposes a marked shift in the supposed role of the arts in Shee's narrative. The principles and feelings through which the arts arm the mind in its war against mercenary sentiments dwindle in the outer layers of the analogy to mere dress and equipage for the aristocracy. Likewise, the nation, as a personification of its aristocracy, uses the arts as ornamental property: "The rank which Great Britain holds amongst nations . . . [where] the part she plays is of the first cast in the great drama of human affairs . . . demands that she should omit no characteristic appendage, no becoming ornament in the costume of national greatness" (2d ed. Preface lii).

The slippage originates in a contradiction. We would expect an aristocracy of the mind, based on principles and feelings that are the inner equivalents of the arts, to produce a meritocracy in the social and national spheres. But in fact Shee's psychological sphere, where art is supposed to command the troops in a war of principles and feelings, is merely a fantasy of merit projected from the social sphere. No meritocracy, artistic or otherwise, is contemplated. Rather, Shee wishes to assert that the present aristocracy *is* a meritocracy. To put it another way, the social sphere is primary. There the terms of the analogy are set, the tenors of the metaphors identified, and from there projected into their psychological and national vehicles. In the social sphere distinctions of rank, corresponding not at all, necessarily, to the merit of certain principles and feelings, are already in place, and those are the distinctions being defended against Jacobins of all sorts. Shee may attribute to the arts a special role in the hidden, fantastical war of the mind, but in the social sphere they must settle for being what they have been, the costume of rank. The key revelation is that noble principles and feelings are only ornaments in a noble costume, and among the more trifling charges.

In spite of his hollow tributes to the Shakespeare Gallery, Shee in effect turns the Boydell project into a cautionary tale framed by sharp ironies. When the prince, as the personified state, joins in a toast to the commercial Maecenas, he is gulled into collaboration with the enemy. When Boydell blames the Revolution for his failure, he blames his own collaborators. From Shee's point of view it makes sense to close the Boydell years with the announcement that "we have had great orators and great politicians—great war ministers, peace ministers, and ministers of finance; but we have had no great patrons of the arts, or protectors of the same—neither a Mecaenas [sic] nor a Colbert" (2d ed. Preface lxi).

Hazlitt's "Enquiry": A New Look at an Old Club

To see the larger pattern of entwining anti-commercialism and anti-institutionalism as it took shape in the years between the Boydell failure and the end of Blake's life, we will move in two steps, first to Hazlitt's elaborate critique of institutionalized art training and then to Cunningham's comprehensive revision of the history of English art. Hazlitt has often been dismissed as an opinionated crank in artistic matters; Cunningham has been dismissed equally often as an unreliable popularist. But of the many cranky opinions and shaky histories that the age bequeathed to us, few are as useful as those two in indicating the changing discourse of English art history.

John Brewer has studied the economic functions of eighteenth-century clubs, which included, among others, uniform training, individual financial relief, reinforcement of good business behavior, and political action (197–264). More particularly, against a background in which artists were separating themselves as a group from the painter-stainers in the old guild system and from journeymen generally, Louise Lippincott has discussed the commercial significance of the clubs that organized the art world in London before the 1760s (18–30, 42–48), and she has usefully characterized the R.A. as an institutional solution to a commercial problem: "Persistent efforts to organize painters, establish a central institution to mediate between artists and patrons and subordinate entrepreneurs [dealers, agents, auction houses] to their control led to the founding of the Royal Academy in 1768" (74).

"An Institution like this," Reynolds said in his inaugural address to the new Academy, "has often been recommended upon considerations merely mercantile" (19). He of course goes on to declare his determination to take a higher road, but it was clear from the start that the founding of the Academy had been a messy and protracted affair of mixed motives, not the virtuous expression of artistic, or for that matter patriotic, ideals that are set forth in the discourses. Later assessments of the Academy's role in the making of the English school were likewise mixed. At one pole we listen to the triumph-over-our-enemies rhetoric of the following tribute published as an anonymous *Candid Review of the Exhibition (Being the Twelfth) of the Royal Academy, M DCC LXXX:*

> Its progress has been so rapid, that . . . it has already made *Britain* the seat of the Arts, and in Painting, Sculpture, and Engraving, it rivals, if it does not excel, all the other Schools of Europe. It has been the remark of ages, that the progress of the Arts to excellence has been slow and gradual; it is however the peculiar merit of the Royal Academy of *Britain*, that it has broke through the fetters with which similar Institutions have heretofore been confined, and by one rapid stride, it has attained the pre-eminence of all Competitors. [ii]

Most observers, early and late, were more critical. Prince Hoare, whose father was one of the Academy's original members and who was himself honorary foreign secretary to the Academy from 1799, saw the institution as incomplete, or inadequately used, rather than defective. The Academy was by virtue of its national institutional status "the proper link which unites the progress of the arts with the greatness of the nation" (135). But its strength in providing training was sapped by its weakness in providing jobs, a handicap that Hoare discusses at some length (113–35). Fuseli declared that all academies "were and are symptoms of art in distress, monuments of public dereliction and decay of taste" that provide emergency shelter in a storm: "asylum . . . theatre . . . repositories" (Wornum 559).

There were always more severe critics who thought they spied an iron political and economic fist hidden in a velvet institutional glove. The annual R.A. exhibition became, among other things, a highly visible inspiration to critics. A relatively late addition to what had become a reviewers' tradition, *A Descriptive and Critical Catalogue to the Exhibition of the Royal Academy* (1823), Charles M. Westmacott saw the "injurious" arrangement of the pictures at the exhibition (by this time a venerable theme for reviewers) as evidence of "gross partiality" and a "studied neglect of genius" (11). He put his criticism of the exhibition in the context of a brief history of the Academy that associates it with the unearned privileges of social class. The exhibition exemplifies conflicts between patrician and plebeian and between private and public interest that emerge in the control of access to the exhibition: "The select few, the privileged classes of society, who are fortunate enough, from various causes, to be classed among the intimates of the Royal Academicians, have annually the secret gratification of viewing the productions of the British School on the Friday preceding the opening, before they are blown upon or tainted by the plebian's view." He points out "the peculiar advantage, in the way of *interest and connexion*, which this practice gives the R.A.'s over their less distinguished brethren" and asks "by what *right* the Academicians exhibit to . . . private friends . . . for . . . *private* advantage, the works of British artists consigned to their keeping for *public* exhibition only" (9).[41] (Shee, in contrast, would regard these "private friends" as the authentic public.)

When, seven years later, Hazlitt tacked a typically trenchant "Enquiry Whether the Fine Arts Are Promoted by Academies and Public Institutions" onto James Northcote's *Life of Titian* (1830), he was joining the well-established antiacademic discourse. As his title suggests, Hazlitt uses the Royal Academy to initiate a discussion of more general problems of patronage and education in the arts. He considers the effects of the Academy in three linked categories: its effect on the education of the artist,

[41] On admission prices as a device for controlling attendance at the exhibitions, see also Pears 127.

on the employment of the artist through patronage, and on the education of the public. His models, taken from classical and Italian art, are more familiar than his way of using them.

When he considers academic education, his paradigm is Correggio, who "saw and felt for himself," constructing "for himself, without rules and models," an "image of truth and beauty, which existed in his own mind . . . *from* the contemplation of nature"; thus "he could only hope to embody it to others, *by* the imitation of nature" (my emphasis, Hazlitt, "Enquiry" 372). In such an argument the "original genius" (370) stands in direct opposition to "what others have done" (372), an opposition between unity and fragmentation, the negative form of variety. Reynolds's opening discourse had envisioned a "seminary of learning . . . surrounded with an atmosphere of floating knowledge, where every mind may imbibe somewhat congenial to its own original conceptions." He had called such knowledge "popular" (in the sense of "public") and "useful" in contrast to knowledge "forced upon the mind by private precepts, or solitary meditation" (16). The distinctly paradoxical character of Reynolds's contrast between a mind that willingly imbibes "congenial" public knowledge and one that has its own private knowledge uncongenially forced on it in solitude demonstrates how profoundly consensual, progressive, and pedagogical Reynolds's Enlightenment commitments are.[42] Hazlitt's counterimage of original genius attending directly to nature makes the Academy by definition almost entirely intrusive and obstructionist. In place of Reynolds's pleasant classroom atmosphere of delicious floating knowledge, Hazlitt imagines a din of confusion where even the most honorable intention of "furnishing the best models to the student" can only "distract the attention by a variety of unattainable excellence" ("Enquiry" 370). In a training institution this pedagogical variety, associated with distraction (from a center) and fragmentation (of a whole), becomes prescriptive, producing the schools of painters "who have attempted to blend the borrowed beauties of others in a perfect whole" (371)—such as Carlo Maratti and Raphael Mengs, heirs of Carracci eclecticism.

At this point in Hazlitt's argument it becomes possible to understand his unexpected insistence upon a "division of labour . . . which is necessary in Art, as in all the works of man." The division of labor, a common image of fragmentation, comes in for positive treatment here because it promotes difference among individual native talents. Thus the opposite of divided labor, which makes "an almost exclusive attention to some one object" possible, is the jack-of-all-trades-master-of-none, an enforced artificial unity. Divided labor stands for undivided attention; acquisition of many skills stands for "gradual dissipation and prostitution of intellect." The image of prostitution is telling: progressive acquisition, the mainstay of English optimism in the fine arts, turns into the progressive loss of one's own will and direction to the wills and directions of multiple others. Such artistic self-betrayal—with the implication that it, like prostitution, is commercial self-betrayal—"leaves the mind without energy to devote to any pursuit the pains necessary to excel in it, and suspends every purpose in irritable imbecility. But the modern painter . . . must be 'statesman, chemist, fiddler, and buffoon.' He must have too many accomplishments. . . .

[42] Barrell (*Political Theory*) has linked these commitments, in somewhat different forms, to civic humanism.

When every one is bound to know everything, there is not time to do anything" (Hazlitt, "Enquiry" 371n).

The Academy produces another kind of fragmentation in the area of patronage. We can best understand Hazlitt by remembering that a critique of patronage is a critique of the relationship between artist and audience. Here the model of uninterrupted unity of painter and nature is expressed as uninterrupted unity of painter and public. The paradigm of "true patronage" (374) comes, as expected, from ancient Greece and Renaissance Italy, where "the religious institutions of the country" superintended the "common faith" that forged a "common link, a mutual sympathy" (376) between artists and public. It is easy to confuse Hazlitt's idealization of classical and Italian patronage with the more conventional one. In the biography of Titian to which Hazlitt's "Enquiry" is appended, Northcote had in fact taken the standard line: the fine arts reach their highest level when "the government has united with religion" (Northcote 1:395), as first in ancient Rome and Greece, then later in Italy. But Northcote is filing the stock complaint against England's Protestant religion, which makes it a "moral impossibility" (1:397) for art to make the winning three-way alliance with church and state. England's problem, then, is no "want of genius," as the foreigners say when they "exult in their triumph over us," but a "want of means" (1:398).

But where Northcote pictures in Titian's Italy an immense union of institutions "captivating the vulgar . . . to aid their grand purpose" (1:397), Hazlitt pictures a close, even intimate community where religion can give shared purpose and direction to individual efforts. The painter becomes "a public benefactor" whose duty is to "embody" sacred subjects as Correggio was said to embody nature. Besides the true patronage that emerges "from the general institutions of the country," such as the church, there is only one patronage. It emerges "from the real unaffected taste of individuals," and it too bonds producer directly to consumer. Any other patronage is "corrupted in its source," and the result again is the fragmentation of the sort imaged previously in distraction, prostitution, and dissipation, imaged here in the contrast between a patronage that operates "to rivet" artists to their work and a false patronage that operates "to divert" their gaze outward toward "the caprice of wealth and fashion" (376).

The issue of adequate patronage leads naturally to the issue of an adequate audience. Earlier writers, even such fierce ones as Barry, tended to follow Richardson in placing their hopes in "improving the public taste" ("Enquiry" 370) and "promoting a wider taste" (377). The means of improvement would be the education of an ignorant audience, and more often than not diffusion of taste was expected to follow from the improvement of taste among a core public. For Hazlitt, however, improvement and diffusion are at odds, as he explains through a fable of origins. In "the first stages of the arts" artists had "natural genius" and the audience had a corresponding "natural taste," but each group had only a few members. For the artist in this original intimacy with the public, producing paintings was "no other than the privilege of being tried by his peers" (377) in the manner of Charles V's patronage of Titian and Count Castiglione's patronage of Raphael—"true patrons, and true critics" (378).

Hazlitt's criticism of institutional education of the public parallels his criticism of institutional education of artists. In both he imagines an original, and to all intents and purposes natural, intensity and directness threatened by unnatural interruption and diffusion in the guise of education. Thus he groups "public institutions" (such as the Royal Academy) with "other artificial means" to charge that they can promote only "the diffusion of taste," not the "improvement of taste" (378). Institutions make "connoisseurship . . . a fashion" (377) and inflate the population of those operating under the labels "artist" and "critic" with incapables and "pretenders" until, once again, "the man of genius is lost in the crowd of competitors" (378). As far as the educated audience is concerned, the "public taste is . . . vitiated, in proportion as it is public," through an inverse ratio: "the decay of art may be said to be the necessary consequence of its progress" (379)—"progress" in the sense of art's traveling outward among the public at large like a monarch on a progress. (After sampling a century's worth of improvement in the moral tone of "progress," we have earned the right to be surprised by Hazlitt's reversal.)

Hazlitt's critique of the Royal Academy is in most respects the nightmare of urban alienation applied to art education. His art history purports to recall a self-sufficient community where education did not require specialized institutions, where art and taste were the natural products of everyday interactions among elite equals. A natural variety of talent was evenly distributed among the talented and matched to similarly distributed tastes. Hazlitt's criticism turns on a dread of losing talented individuals in faceless crowds of competitors indifferently but uniformly trained, all striving for the superficial attentions of an indifferently but uniformly educated mass public. The few painters of original genius who desperately seek a coterie of tasteful spectators are lost in the distracting confusion created by "the great error of British art": "a desire to produce a popular effect by the cheapest and most obvious means, and at the expense of everything else;—to lose all the delicacy and variety of nature in one undistinguished bloom of florid health; and all precision, truth, and refinement of character, in the same harmless mould of smiling, self-complacent insipidity" (380).

The dream of universal education that inspires so many plans for public art projects becomes Hazlitt's nightmare of "popular" uniformity that will lose the deep (and natural) variety of nature in the superficial (and artificial) variety of academic eclecticism. Hazlitt implies that institutional uniformity expresses itself in the English specialty, portraiture, where all is florid health and smiling insipidity cast in the same harmless mold. Through economic metaphors that tie the cheapest with the most obvious, accomplished at the expense of everything else, suggesting that what has been bad for art may have been good for business, he makes the familiar connection between urban degradation and commerce.

Insofar as it represents a new way of thinking about the academies that spread all over Europe during the eighteenth century, Hazlitt's critique is a strong sign that the artistic and commercial institutions that Boydell's Shakespeare Gallery had been designed to exploit in a forceful, efficient combination were being separated by an influential new aesthetic consensus—broadly speaking, romanticism—that would oppose the genius of the individual artist to social institutions and autonomous art to commerce. Even in the narrow precincts of his essay, Hazlitt supports his theories with historical narratives, projecting his artistic values into an abbreviated history of European art centered on Correggio. For a comprehensive application of related, though by no means identical, values to the history of British art, we have to go to Cunningham.

Cunningham's *Lives:* The Graphic Spirit of His Country

Part of the English-school problem had always been the distance between real and ideal English painting, or studio practice and narrative theory. The most influential writers could not agree to apply the label "English school" to much of what English painters were in fact painting—much of what we now arrange under that heading. George Stubbs's reception in London is a good example: he could not find engravers to reproduce what seemed to them his absurd work.[43] By giving what had heretofore been a strong undercurrent of dissatisfaction an explicit historical shape, Allan Cunningham's volumes of *Lives* (1st ed. 1829–1833) helped to reconstitute the mainstream of English-school discourse. The undercurrent is, for example, the counterhistory that we can infer from Hogarth's remarks about the situation of English art and from the subsequent history of Hogarth appreciation, since it is difficult to praise Hogarth in Barry's terms and consequently difficult to grant him a significant place in Barry's kind of history. We recall that Prince Hoare's *Inquiry* relegates Hogarth's age to the status of an untimely spring brightened not by Hogarth but only by the architect and painter of St. Paul's, Wren and Thornhill, as England awaits its artistic Aeneas, Reynolds. We may note in passing the elevation of Hogarth's father-in-law to prominence ("Venerable father of the English school!" exclaims *The Somerset House Gazette* of Thornhill in 1824 ["Ceiling Painters" 15]), but far more telling is the suppression of Hogarth, on whom turns the critical distinction between Hoare's kind of history and Cunningham's. To see on what terms and in what kind of plot Hogarth can become central to a history of English art, we must begin with Cunningham at the beginning.

In its search for a native artistic tradition, Cunningham's ethnocentric history is a distant relative of the Celtic and medieval enthusiasms of the latter half of the eighteenth century.[44] Most historians of the eighteenth century had seen no need to trace British art to British roots. The question that motivated such backtracking as there was had to do with England's failure to inherit the Italian tradition. Hence Chatterton saw an opening for his Old English inventions at the beginning of Horace Walpole's *Anecdotes.* He sent Walpole a couple of pages called "The Ryse of Peyncteynge yn Englande Wroten by T. Rowleie, 1469 for Mastre Canynge," which informs us that from Hengist came heraldry, "whyche dydde brynge Peyncteynge" (quoted in Meyerstein 255). Chatterton

[43] Bruntjen (52) quotes Ozias Humphry on Stubbs's difficulties.

[44] Newman's serviceable account of English nationalism emphasizes its literary elements—its ties to romanticism, the bardic revival, and so on. See esp. pts. 5 and 8, "The Literary Revolution, 1740–89" and "The Long Revolution, 1789–1830."

proposed that Walpole use the brief "Ryse" to complete "any future Edition of your truly entertaining Anecdotes of Painting" (quoted 254). Chatterton was faking, but faking in the vanguard of ethnocentric art history.

Cunningham's ethnocentrism is not antiquarian but religious and nationalistic, and it turns "nature" into its "native," or patriotic, equivalent. His history moves from slavery to independence—at the level of British state politics, from foreign domination by Rome to national independence. At the level of art, history begins with the fine-arts equivalent of an occupying army: "it was in the interest of Rome to supply us with painters as well as with priests" (Cunningham 1:7). It little mattered where the artists came from because art was split, for political reasons, between conception and execution. Rome controlled the primary component, ideas, and left the rest to "a mere mechanic . . . a carver of wood, a maker of figures, a house and heraldry painter, a carpenter, an upholsterer, and a mason; and sometimes . . . a tailor. Genius had not then come to the aid of art, and paintings and statues were ordered exactly as chairs and tables are now" (1:5; see also 1:10).

Thus emerges a myth of liberation: "In Britain, Painting was centuries in throwing off the fetters of mere mechanical skill" that the Catholic church forced British artists to wear, "and in rising into the region of genius" (1:5). Attributing the historically depressed status of painters to their role as technicians with no independent access to ideas is commonplace, but blaming Rome is unusual, as is the further connection with commerce. An artist without ideas necessarily becomes "a manufacturer" in a "mercantile" system, and "works of art" will be "weighed out or measured like other commercial commodities" (1:24). In Cunningham's terms, the English school of painting waits on the Reformation to free native artists from foreign ideological oppression and commercial manufacture. Liberation will allow the reunion of native ideas with native techniques.

Cunningham can admit that Rubens "gave by his works [such as the Banqueting Room at Whitehall] a visible impulse to art. . . . We had no longer forms without freedom, and faces without life" (1:34–35). But after all Cunningham's investment in a home-grown art capable of expressing "the natural spirit of our nation" leaves him with a post-Restoration history, one that can properly begin only after the "Romish" (1:193) influence departs.[45] For Cunningham, Hogarth is what the Reformation made possible, not a Protestant painter but an English painter. Before Hogarth "we relied wholly on foreign skill. With him, and after him, arose a succession of eminent painters, who have spread the fame of British art far and wide" (1:2).

Earlier writers put their hopes in the continuity of English with continental art; Cunningham moves the other way to find continuity of a different sort in the national spirit: "That his works are unlike those of other men, is his merit, not his fault. He belonged to no school of art; he was the produce of no academy; no man living or dead had any share in forming his mind, or in rendering his hand

[45] Cunningham, himself a fervently patriotic Scot, traces British Rubenism through George Jamesone (1590–1644), whom Walpole called the van Dyck of Scotland. Jamesone is reputed to have worked alongside van Dyck as a pupil of Rubens. Cunningham contends that Jamesone "stands at the head of the British school of portrait-painting . . . nor had England an artist of her own worthy of being named above him in his own walk before the days of Reynolds" (5:32).

skillful. He was the spontaneous offspring of the graphic spirit of his country, as native to the heart of England as independence is, and he may be fairly called, in his own walk, the first-born of her spirit" (1:187–88). In Cunningham's description we recognize the belated arrival of an image of Hogarth that Hogarth himself had promoted: "To Nature and your Self appeal," runs the English motto of his *Time Smoking a Picture,* "Nor learn of others, what to feel." Cunningham adapts Hogarth to his nationalistic history by equating nature with nation, the English school "a school of nature" (2:5). (Paradoxically, to certify Hogarth's independent national genius, Cunningham must join Hogarth, Barry, Hoare, and Reynolds in minimizing the Dutch-English connection.)

Revising the estimate of Hogarth predictably revises the estimate of the Academy. Speaking the language of the earlier discourse in which the progressive acquisition of skills—and thus the systematic training in skills—held a central place, Walpole had offered this thoroughly characteristic estimate of Hogarth's skills: "As a *painter* Hogarth has slender merit" (quoted in Cunningham 1:193). In light of his stress on the artist's unschooled spontaneity, it is easy to see why Cunningham would answer by demanding a broader definition of "painter": "But there seems a disposition to limit the former to those who have been formed under some peculiar course of study—and produced works in the fashion of such and such great masters. This I take to be mere pedantry . . ." (1:193–94). A decade later, by W. B. Sarsfield Taylor's time, this Hogarth had a predictable if not entirely consistent place in the standard history. Taylor treats Hogarth as an English natural who "presumed to think for himself" and to invent original skills that "could neither be taught nor acquired in any atelier" (2:99, 98). He started a "revolution in the mind of a nation" by teaching the English "to think for themselves in matters of art" (2:102). Taylor explains the time lag between Hogarth's revolutionary message and its reception as the result of an economic conspiracy by "cunning men" whose "object was to delay, if they could not prevent" the "dawn of a more auspicious day" that "was rising on the arts of England" (2:101–2).

A Hogarth strong enough to redefine "painter" and separate English from continental painting, displacing Reynolds and Barry in the process, would be strong enough to reshape English art history.[46] Endorsing training programs based on an internationalist eclecticism that values the old continental masters, the Royal Academy in effect reinforces the market for the very "religious paintings of the Romish Church," the "legions of saints and Madonnas" that kept collectors away from the "native genius" (1:193) of Hogarth: "Men who are regularly trained to the admiration of a certain class of works [through copying and studying old masters], admit few into the ranks of painting who have not a kind of academic certificate. . . . Amongst persons of this stamp,

[46] The Hogarth problem, as it were, had appeared earlier in Charles Lamb's essay "On the Genius and Character of Hogarth" (1811). In mid-course the essay turns into a point-by-point rebuttal of Barry, who had criticized Hogarth from the lofty position of one committed to the international grand style. Lamb blames Barry for "the extreme narrowness of system . . . that would make us concede to the work of Poussin . . . and deny to this of Hogarth, the name of a grand serious composition" (1:74). In a footnote (1:76) Lamb also dismisses Reynolds's similarly condescending and narrow treatment of Hogarth. The first exhibition of Hogarth's oil paintings was mounted in 1814 at the British Institution and in that same year appeared Hazlitt's essay on Hogarth.

to admire Hogarth amounts to treason against the great masters" (1:221).

The quotation comes appropriately not from Cunningham's life of Hogarth but from his life of Reynolds, who tends to become the villain of the piece. The life of Richard Wilson, for Cunningham another blighted native genius,[47] bristles with barbs aimed at "the courtly Reynolds," whose "cold, calm temper" and "cautious malignity" made him "a master in that courtly and malevolent art . . . of teaching others to sneer without sneering himself" (1:202). One of the natural by-products of fierce infighting among artists, dealers, and connoisseurs in Reynolds's time was a steady flow of pejorative gossip that soon coalesced into a vigorous anti-Reynolds tradition with antipaternal overtones. Though Cunningham drew on the tradition to spice up his popular history, it must also be said that his rough treatment of Reynolds coherently extends the democratic and nationalistic tendencies in the historical argument: "The painter who wishes for lasting fame . . . must seek to associate his labours with the genius of his country," while Reynolds attended to the "rich and the titled alone" (1:326).

The economic arguments follow suit. Cunningham disdains traditional patronage, the patronage that the rich and titled alone dole out, and links it with Reynolds: "patronage is ever ready to encourage skill such as his, exerted in such a department [portrait]" (1:223). Cunningham approves, however, the "salutary counsel" of Benjamin West's friends after West was offered the chance to decorate Lord Rockingham's Yorkshire mansion: "they advised him to confide in the *public*" (2:29) instead, and one form in which "the public" expresses itself is the subscription system (2:31). For Cunningham, wide appeal is generally a virtue. In failing "to work upon subjects for which there was a market" when he should have been "appealing more directly to the public feeling" (2:91), Barry showed that he was out of touch with the national spirit. Commercial arrangements such as the subscription system operate as mechanisms for that appeal and response: "Reynolds lectured, Barry stormed, West toiled, and Fuseli drew supernatural, and Hilton natural shapes, in support and praise of the grand style; but all would not do. The heart of the country was not with them . . ." (Pilkington, *General Dictionary* xcv).[48]

At first it may be difficult to imagine what Cunningham might mean by his further suggestion that Hogarth had laid down "a foundation," "the rudiments of future excellence" on which others might build "a perfect and lasting superstructure" (1:193–94), when Cunningham's Hogarth is otherwise so determinedly antifoundational and antirudimental. The best answer lies in Cunningham's reliance, despite his antiacademic and pro-nature biases, on a

[47] To Wilson add the unfortunate Edward Bird, whose early works Cunningham associates with the "original and unborrowed" quality of the "living world" seen by a painter who "thought for himself," but whose later despair and death were caused by "a swarm of counsellors . . . who persuaded him" to paint "fashion," found in "galleries" (2:267). Also cf. the earlier treatment of Wilson in Shee's *Rhymes*. The lack of public recognition during his lifetime exemplifies English indifference to artistic skill, but his work is praised in eclectic-internationalist terms: "the most extraordinary landscape-painter this country ever produced; uniting the composition of Claude with the execution of Poussin" (16).

[48] In his life of Fuseli, Cunningham relates the artist's failure to gain "extensive popularity" to the "poetic order" of his mind and his consequent neglect of "the grosser realities of life" (2:295) and then extends that logic to the Boydell failure.

revision of the international analogy. While, for example, he blames Barry's failure to win a following on his obsession with "the miracles of Greece and the Vatican," Cunningham transfers the analogy to his own nationalistic program: "To be truly classic he should have done for Britain what the artists of old did for Greece . . ." (2:140). He uses the analogy to establish the painter's primary relation to individual styles and national materials rather than to the international style and universal content—that other version of "nature"—promoted by Reynolds's and Barry's Enlightenment discourse. "The great artists of Greece and Rome wrought in the spirit of *their* age and country," writes Cunningham; "they sought *at home* for subjects of high character, yet *familiarly* known. But the heathen [in a painting by Barry of Jupiter and Juno] appealed to no *national* sympathy—to no national belief—to no *living* superstition" (my emphasis, 2:90).

Cunningham's history seems to combine two eighteenth-century narratives, the nurture mythos of progress and decline and the nature mythos of native genius, the former most familiar in internationalist and even scientific discourse, the latter in bard-revivalism and the like. The two come together to a certain extent in the relativistic protoanthropological discourse of comparative mythography, where cultural entities as different as ancient Greece, biblical Israel, and old Ireland can be brought into essential equivalence through their national myths. John Brown, for one, showed how to use these interests in the history of the arts. His *History of the Rise and Progress of Poetry* (1764) (and, a year earlier, his *Dissertation on the Rise, Union and Power, the Progressions, Separations and Corruptions, of Poetry and Music*) coordinates the historical pattern of cyclical analogy with the oscillation of national, or at least native, characteristics. In Brown's scheme decline is a matter not only of fragmentation but also of imitation, a downward path from "*native* Force and Vigour" to "the ineffectual Principle of *mere Imitation*" (266). This view tends to make previously unthinkable analogies thinkable: (on the rising side of the cycle) between ancient Greece and Wales, countries that invented their arts, and (on the declining side) between ancient Rome and England, countries that only imported theirs.

Cunningham and Hazlitt's revisions to the complex of history, theory, and pedagogy that had supported prevailing notions of the continuity between continental and English art are in several respects similar. Most notably, they both move away from the academic institutions that represent such continuity toward "nature," and away from eclecticism toward expressions of individualism. The old histories met the ethnocentric arguments of Montesquieu and Dubos with arguments about improvement through education; in their emphasis on indigenous genius, the new histories adapt to their purposes the very arguments that the eighteenth-century continental critics had used against British art. Despite its antiacademic component, Hazlitt's art history is finally internationalist in scope, and its core is the relation of artist to nature. Cunningham's history is written in the spirit of the British Institution. It is nationalist and its core is the relation of artist to national spirit, though that spirit tends to be identified with nature, as, further, the individuality of the original artist and the individuality of the nation are supposed to coincide.

III RELIGION

A Christian History of Engraving

The Old & New Testaments are the Great Code of Art

—William Blake, *Laocoön*

Let us hope, however, that the children of Taste, like the children of Israel, will ere long, find an establishment in the Canaan of public munificence; that some enlightened Moses will arise to lead them to the promised land of patronage and protection: already, a light [the British Institution] has dawned which omens well for their deliverance.

—Martin Archer Shee, *Rhymes on Art*

We are in a World of Generation & death & this world we must cast off if we would be Painters Such as Rafa[e]l Mich Angelo & the Ancient Sculptors. if we do not cast off this world we shall be only Venetian Painters who will be cast off & Lost from Art

—William Blake, *A Vision of the Last Judgment*

We have identified a pattern of responses to the commercial failures of the Boydell era that includes a history of English engraving formulated in the light of those failures. Let me repeat that the history of engraving took on special significance insofar as it was coupled with the commercial success of English painting. Boydell had emphasized that connection as the very key to the success he was projecting: he proposed to use the English school of engraving, the international fame of which he claimed to have established, as the basis for a second campaign on behalf of the English school of painting. Landseer's postmortem on English engraving, though its pointed attack on Boydell was upsetting to some, nonetheless fitted a pattern that had become familiar in English-school discourse over the preceding half century. It was certainly no surprise that Landseer brought Boydell into his analysis. Lecturing on English engraving in 1806 without reference to Boydell would have been manifestly negligent. Nor was the anticommercial strain of Landseer's argument unexpected. We have seen that a version of anticommercialism was routinely used by continental writers to criticize English art, and at an early stage the theme was transferred into English-school discourse as a vehicle of self-criticism. Nor was there anything particularly unusual about the engravers Landseer held up as models. When Prince Hoare reported "the return and rise of Engraving in the present reign," he named "Strange, in history and portrait, and Woollett in figures and landscape" (256) along with Bartolozzi (as a nonnative) as the trio through whose efforts "the reputation of English Engraving became . . . universally established" (260) and commercially successful. Landseer's history crests with the same group. In his critique they represent the union of the "mental" and the "mechanical" parts of the art that were subsequently severed by "ignorant capitalists" such as Boydell. This too is a familiar argument, as we recall from Barry's much earlier denunciation of "men of mean intellects" whose "entire stock of trade" is in the "mechanical principles" of art that should no more be separated from the "ideal" principles than "body" from "soul."

At this point, anyone who has read through the writings about art that Blake composed in the decade after his return from Felpham in 1803 will be able to recognize that his critique of English painting, engraving, and even poetry emerges from English-school discourse in its characteristic mood of crisis and at the intersection of several of its principal issues. Blake's analysis of the situation seems in many respects to parallel Landseer's, especially in the dire appraisal of English commerce—"Whoever looks at any of the Great & Expensive Works of Engraving that have been Publishd by English Traders must feel a Loathing & Disgust & accordingly most Englishmen have a Contempt for Art which is the Greatest Curse that can fall upon a Nation" (*PA*, E 577)—and in the connection of commerce with a forced division of labor between thinkers and doers. But if their analyses run parallel to a point, a stark and baffling divergence shows up in their exemplars. The same Woollett, Strange, and Bartolozzi who stand at the peak of achievement in Landseer's narrative represent, in Blake's, every mishap that has befallen English engraving. To understand the difference—and ultimately to understand Blake's positions on the issues of English-school discourse—we must study technology and Christian religion, the two elements that distinguish his critique of the English school and his theory of art.

In the remaining discussions, I constantly resort to the metaphors produced by the injection of religious and technological strands into artistic history and theory: art as religion, art as technology, and the offspring of those two, religion as technology. These metaphors shape yet another history of engraving that we can most usefully report in two versions, ancient and modern. The former, a Christian history of engraving, is an attempt to organize, in one plausible way, major religious elements in Blake's discourse. The latter, a technological history founded on Blake's claim that English engraving was "Lost" at the "Enterance of Vandyke & Rubens into this Country" (*PA*, E 572), is an analogous attempt to organize the major technological elements in Blake's discourse. The two narratives are separated but not isolated: each as it were remembers the other as a way of acknowledging their figural complicity.

Religion had long been a serviceable element in English-school discourse, often combining forces with the classical analogy to support the proposition that true religion deserves true art. This was the element that had brought the Reformation into focus as a major obstruction to the progress of English art and, in a different use, had given legitimacy to the artists' proposal to decorate Westminster Cathedral with English history paintings. Earlier I quoted both

Fuseli's general approval of the notion that Greek religion had been the first mover of Greek art and Barry's similar claims about the art of Renaissance Italy. Painting in the service of spiritual and moral truth was an appealing prospect with a long history. In Blake, however, religion shapes the discourse more forcefully. In *A Descriptive Catalogue of Pictures,* with tongue to some extent in cheek, he recalls his visions of the art of the ancient world, "those wonderful originals called in the Sacred Scriptures the Cherubim, which were sculptured and painted on walls of Temples, Towers, Cities, Palaces, and erected in the highly cultivated states of Egypt, Moab, Edom, Aram, among the Rivers of Paradise, being originals from which the Greeks and Hetrurians copied Hercules, Farnese, Venus of Medicis, Apollo Belvidere, and all the grand works of ancient art" (E 531).[1] Here Blake uses history as a metaphor of mind, in the romantic manner: historical firsts become standards for contemporary originality. At the end of the paragraph he notes that "the artist has endeavoured to emulate the grandeur of those seen in his vision, and to apply it to modern Heroes, on a smaller scale" (E 531). To recover historical originals he has resorted to mental visions. The archetypes of these sculptures appear to be the ones housed in the museum of human life described in *Jerusalem:*

All things acted on Earth are seen in the bright
Sculptures of
Los's Halls & every Age renews its powers from
these Works
With every pathetic story possible to happen from
Hate or
Wayward Love & every sorrow & distress is carved
here
Every Affinity of Parents Marriages & Friendships
are here
In all their various combinations wrought with
wondrous Art
All that can happen to Man in his pilgrimage of
seventy years
Such is the Divine Written Law of Horeb & Sinai:
And such the Holy Gospel of Mount Olivet &
Calvary:

[*J* 16.61–69, E 161]

Perhaps the surprise is the sudden assertion in the last two lines that the Divine Law "is" a sculpture in Los's Hall, and so is the Holy Gospel—making both of them episodes in the history of art and works of art in themselves. The biblical history of art parallels the history of Law and Gospel, those being the poles that align the sculptures in a history of fall and redemption, artistically a history of art lost and recovered. In the Blakean version of the biblical myth Moses, the mental deity of externalization and blame, embodies the loss; Jesus, the mental deity of internalization and forgiveness, embodies the recovery. In a conventional biblical typology based on a scheme of so-called progressive revelation, Jesus is the antitype, or legitimate successor, of Moses and the last in a line of prophets and priests of which Moses is the first: "I am not come to destroy, but to fulfil" (Matt. 5:17). Blake, magnifying the typological inclination to weigh similarities against differences, searches out the countertype in the antitype. He arranges Jesus and

[1] Blake's uses of ancient sculpture—ekphrastic and other—are surveyed in Paley's "'Wonderful Originals.'" His *Continuing City* is also generally relevant. Damrosch argues that Blake's passage on the sculptures, while "commonly quoted as a celebration of art," is in fact "richly ambiguous." He observes that the cherubim and Temple are "highly suspect in Blake's myth" (329).

Moses dialectically, with Jesus undoing what Moses has done, and the Gospel undoing the Law. "Jehovahs Finger Wrote the Law" (*Gates of Paradise,* E 259) on tablets of stone that Moses carried down the mountain of Sinai, thus initiating history under the Law and filling Los's Hall with bright sculptures of all things acted on earth. But Jesus calls a halt—"Cease finger of God to Write"—and writes a redemptive countermessage: "Upon his heart with Iron pen / He wrote Ye must be born again" (*EG,* E 521, 519).

Moses and Jesus as type and countertype, writer and reviser, provide the basis for a framework of oppositions that can be fairly easily expanded into at least the outlines of a dialectical history of art in the Bible, that is, in Blake's terms, a Christian history. The identification of the sculptures of Los's Hall with Law and Gospel suggests that the most appropriate biblical history of art would be a history of types as a history of sculpture—not an outrageous leap, given the derivation of *type* from Greek *tuptein,* "to incise or inscribe." As types in printing are inscribed with letters, so history is inscribed with the lessons of God's will (Kermode 91). Typological narratives, necessarily obsessed with issues of likeness and difference, are thus also obsessed with reproduction, as in type, prototype, and stereotype. That cluster will help us move from biblical histories to Blakean concepts of originality to technological histories.

To move the biblical history of art as close to Blake as possible, it helps to regard him as a sculptor. And so he was, if we accept the usual definition of engraving in Blake's time as "*a mode or species of* SCULPTURE—performed by incision," a definition that engravers are pleased to acknowledge whenever they sign *sculpsit* to their plates. Blake conflates sculpture with engraving in his address at the opening of his prose poem "Samson": "O white-robed Angel, guide my timorous hand to write as on a lofty rock with iron pens the words of truth, that all who pass may read" (E 443). Sculpture is thus the "generic term," as Landseer says and others affirm (*Lectures* 112, 113; see also, e.g., sculpture entry in James Elmes's *Dictionary of the Fine Arts*). The primary documents in our history of engraving, then, will be the Bible and the accounts of ancient engraving written by Blake's contemporaries. What in these accounts Blake credits as fact is not always apparent but not essential, either, because the rudiments, the paradigm, and its relation to Blake's ideas about the art of his time are usually sufficiently clear.

The primary perspective on the documents will be Blake's. The Bible, of course, reports the priestly version of events, the black version, as Blake calls it in *The Everlasting Gospel,* while we want the white version, which I take to be the artistic version required to authorize the assertion that "The Old & New Testaments are the Great Code of Art" (*Laocoön,* E 274). Black is the type figured on the page, a priestly garment; white is the space around the type, which figures the mental space between the lines. The black type says religion; it is my working principle that the white spaces say art. The Bible is art hid in religion. The question becomes not What does the text say? but What does the text hide from saying? Extending Blake's metaphor, I could say that the reader's job is to free the text from itself by reading between the lines. Using another metaphor, I could say that reading the Bible in Blake's manner is like looking for the outline of a face beneath a mask that intentionally blurs the outline while inevitably, necessarily revealing something about the outline in the code, as it were, used to disguise. The original is art, the code of disguise is religion.

And yet finally, Blake's metaphor wants to say that the two, so close that one is revealed in the other, are finally as different as black and white. This intention helps to explain the relationship between some key opposing pairs in Blake: Jehovah and Jesus, Urizen and Los. They are all creators in Blake's plots, and the actions of the second member of each pair are to a certain extent determined by the actions of the first member. We see the nearness of the relationship clearly in *The Book of Urizen,* for example, when Los begins to participate so deeply in a plot initiated by Urizen that it seems hard to separate them. But the difference finally accounts not just for a bit of something but for virtually everything.[2] The vexed interface of likeness and difference is, as we shall see, a central characteristic of Blake's history of art. Although, in the opening sections, I adopt as a working critical vocabulary the familiar terminology of selfsameness associated with romanticism (originality, individuality, identity, and the like), the argument ultimately turns to the unsettling character of Blakean originality itself.

The painters of Blake's day still occasionally claimed St. Luke for their patron, and Blake may have had this tradition in mind when he painted Luke holding a pen or brush.[3] Sculptors and engravers, with the same poetic logic and more poetic justice, might have staked a claim to God himself, for his work in sculpting the universe from something or nothing, Adam from clay, and Eve from a rib. Blake implies as much in *The Book of Urizen.* In any case, all the histories agree with James Elmes's *General and Bibliographical Dictionary of the Fine Arts* (1826) about the "great antiquity" ("Engraving" n.p.) of engraving, though not everyone will go all the way with Joseph Strutt's claim that "there is no art, that of music excepted, which can positively claim a priority to that of engraving . . . there is little doubt of its existence long before the flood."[4] Strutt points to Tubal Cain, son of Lamech, as a "whetter or sharpner [sic] of all instruments of copper and iron," and thus by implication a man with "great skill in metallurgy." Like a mythographer he reasons that Vulcan may even be Tubal Cain under another name (1:7–8). Thus Blake's Los, who "sings upon his Watch walking from Furnace to Furnace" and "seizes his Hammer every hour" while "flames surround him as / He beats" (*J* 86.33–35, E 245), comes by his metallurgy honestly. With a touch of skepticism Landseer—who considers the biblical history of engraving throughout his lectures—likewise refers to "some" historians who "have even supposed the art to be of antediluvian extraction: the learning or credulity of Josephus, discovered one of the engraved pillars of Seth" (*Lectures* 7; cf. *Saboean Researches* 4, 6), in reference to Josephus's claim that the children of Seth engraved two pillars, one of brick and one of stone, with astronomical principles.[5] W. J.

[2] In "Visible Language" (esp. 56ff.), Mitchell treats Urizen as a proto-artist who has more in common with Los than is generally acknowledged.

[3] See Butlin, *Paintings* no. 398, pl. 489. Without further comment Butlin quotes W. M. Rossetti to the effect that Luke holds a pen, but presumably as writing evangelist rather than drawer-painter.

[4] Ottley does not mention the biblical origins of engraving, though he does refer to stamping, etc., by "the ancients." Ottley has read Strutt, and quotes him frequently, but apparently prefers to disregard Strutt's references to the Bible.

[5] Blake engraved (after Metz and Stothard) three plates that appeared in an edition of Josephus first published in the mid-1780s. A fourth plate (after Stothard), never pub-

Stannard is repeating the same story in his *Art Exemplar* as late as 1860 or thereabouts—and adding the ornamental carving on Noah's ark to the list of antediluvian engravings.

But according to Landseer and Strutt, the oldest extant engravings are postdiluvian. Cumberland allows that "probably the Hebrews practised the art of engraving on metals" (*Essay* 26), while Landseer approves the supposition that Assyrian/Chaldean engraving is even earlier than the Hebrew patriarchs and reports that the East India Company museum owns Chaldean bricks stamped in intaglio and a Babylonian inscription engraved on stone. Since at least one of the patriarchs, Abraham, was the son of a Chaldean, Terah—whom Blake associates negatively with brickmaking (*J* 45 [31].9–12, E 194)—engraving probably came that way into Canaan. The carved images of Terah and the images (teraphim) later stolen by Rachel from Laban (Gen. 31:19) are, in the opinion of Strutt and Landseer, household gods very like engravings (Landseer, *Lectures* 9; Strutt 1:8; see also Landseer, *Observations* 7–9). Meanwhile, another essential branch of the art, gem engraving, was getting its start in India along the Ganges, far from the Fertile Crescent (Landseer, *Lectures* 18).

In Landseer's scheme, the skills developed along the Ganges and the Euphrates eventually converge somehow in what most agree is the real cradle of ancient engraving, the Nile valley. Strutt asserts that "hieroglyphical features of the Egyptians afford us perhaps the most ancient remains of engraving on metal" (Strutt 1:9; see also Landseer, *Lectures* 17–18), and Landseer claims that the earliest extant engravings might be stones in Upper Egypt said to shine with a "latent light-invisible" (*Lectures* 22). Landseer also mentions the Egyptian hieroglyphics engraved on the "sarcophagus of Alexander," which is now (he says) also called the sarcophagus of the "patriarch Joseph" (*Lectures* 28).

The Pentateuchal Plot

But this smattering of ancient history and speculation is merely a pale backdrop. It sets the stage for the event toward which, it might be said, the history of engraving has been moving: God's decision to use engraving as the medium that establishes his covenant with Israel. As Moses recalls, "the Lord delivered unto me two tables of stone written with the finger of God," that is, engraved by God: "the writing was the writing of God, graven upon the tables" (Deut. 9:10, Exod. 32:16). As an engraver, then, God is seen in his characteristic role in the poetic prologue to *Jerusalem:*

Reader! [*lover*] of books! [*lover*] of heaven,
And of that God from whom [*all books are given,*]
Who in mysterious Sinais awful cave
To Man the wond'rous art of writing gave,
Again he speaks in thunder and in fire!
Thunder of Thought, & flames of fierce desire:
Even from the depths of Hell his voice I hear,
Within the unfathomd caverns of my Ear.

---

lished, may belong to the same group. The publishing history is complicated; see Bentley, *Blake Books* 585–91, and Essick, *William Blake's Commercial Book Illustrations* 23–25.

Therefore I print; nor vain my types shall be:
Heaven, Earth & Hell, henceforth shall live in
harmony

[*J* 3, E 145]

In his *Observations on Man* David Hartley had conjectured that engraving and picture writing were both pre-Sinaitic, whereas alphabetical writing was "communicated miraculously by God to *Moses* at *Sinai*" (1:308; his reasons continue 308–15). But in *The Divine Legation of Moses* William Warburton had allowed that "at most" the finger of God might have "miraculously engraved" the ten commandments (3: 162). Landseer mentions even more doubtfully the belief that some of the commandments were engraved by God and denies outright that God gave humanity writing with the decalogue on Sinai (*Lectures* 7). Though Blake seems to find a place in the *Jerusalem* prologue for both ideas, we notice a suspiciously high incidence of unstable Blakeanisms—heaven, hell, God, mystery, Sinai, cave, harmony—embedded in an equally suspect conventional rhetoric of introduction announcing, apparently, that the muse of *Jerusalem* is the same God who in giving humanity the Law may be said to have given not only the gift of writing but also "all books," in the sense that all books worth reading must be derived from that One Book, the Law, the first book worth writing.[6] We may also wonder whether nothing in the prologue poem challenges the comfort of the reader who loves books, heaven, and the Author of both. But the worst that even the reader of most delicate religious sensibilities is likely to fear from *Jerusalem* after a glance at the prologue is the enthusiasm that excites crank prophecy.

To establish a Blakean perspective capable of putting God's meeting with Moses into the context of a biblical history of engraving, we need to know what really happened on Sinai. An infernal slant sharp enough to cut through the pious narratives of the Pentateuch comes most efficiently from *The Marriage of Heaven and Hell,* where Law and Gospel, heaven and hell, angel and devil, are "contraries." The Exodus-Deuteronomy narrative is recast in its infernal, or implicit, form as the story of the "ancient Poets" on plate 11:[7]

The ancient Poets animated all sensible objects with Gods or Geniuses, calling them by the names and adorning them with the properties of woods, rivers, mountains, lakes, cities, nations, and whatever their enlarged & numerous senses could percieve.

And particularly they studied the genius of each city & country. placing it under its mental deity.

Till a system was formed, which some took advantage of & enslav'd the vulgar by attempting to realize or abstract the mental deities from their objects: thus began Priesthood.

Choosing forms of worship from poetic tales.

And at length they pronounced that the Gods had orderd such things.

Thus men forgot that All deities reside in the human breast. [E 38]

The gift of the decalogue to Moses coincides

[6] For Blake's notions of the origin of writing in the context of eighteenth-century theories of language, see Essick, *William Blake and the Language of Adam* 33–38.

[7] Pl. 11 might be read as a pagan version of the origin of Greek religion. Since the story is about the most ancient poets, however, this interpretation would presume that Greek religion preceded Hebrew religion—against Blake's more usual presumption that the truly ancient poets were the Hebrews.

with the point in the story at which "a system was formed, which some took advantage of & enslav'd the vulgar."[8] In that context "Sinais awful cave" is awful because Moses makes it so. He returns from his forty-day journey to reveal the externalized and systemized morality said to have been graven in stone by an externalized deity shrouded in mystery at the top of a mountain. The mountain, like the cave in it, is mental, and the only God residing there is the one residing in Moses's breast. Moses sells the tribes of Israel the heavenly version of what happened.

The Marriage presents the contrary version on plates 6–7, where the narrator introduces the Proverbs of Hell with the story of how he "came home" from a trip to hell carrying proverbs the way Moses came from Sinai carrying laws. Down and up, like hell and heaven, are Blakean metaphors for inside the human breast and outside. Journeys down to hell in *The Marriage* are attempts to recoup the losses suffered by humanity as a result of trips in the other direction. Priests make the journeys up or out and ancient poets make journeys down or in. The narrator of *The Marriage* comes home to find himself not on a mountain but in an "abyss." Moses's God appeared in "thunders and lightnings, and a thick cloud. . . . And mount Sinai was altogether on a smoke, because the Lord descended upon it in fire: and the smoke thereof ascended as the smoke of a furnace, and the whole mount quaked greatly" (Exod. 19:16–18). A mighty devil appears to Blake's narrator "folded in black clouds." Moses said he hewed stones for God to engrave commands on; the etching devil of *The Marriage* writes with "corroding fires" while "hovering on the sides of the rock." He answers Jehovah's ten commands with one question, a single "sentence now percieved by the minds of men, & read by them on earth": "How do you know but ev'ry Bird that cuts the airy way, / Is an immense world of delight, clos'd by your senses five?" (E 35).

On the sound economic principle that when a need is perceived a product will be invented to meet it, it seems appropriate that, while Moses was off hatching a system to enslave the vulgar with a tale of a fiery-fingered Great Engraver in a mountain cave, another engraver and sculptor, Moses's brother Aaron, was working at his own invention, a sacred calf of gold. But Aaron's calf could not match the strong competition from Moses, who in a fit of inspired fury broke his first set of stones and refused to return for a second until he could be sure of Aaron's support. Aaron traded a promise to engrave no more sacred animals for the position of high priest.[9] Reading this plot for its

[8] Blake's history of poetry and priesthood is analogous to various other eighteenth- and nineteenth-century tales. Cf. esp. Warburton's *Divine Legation,* which fuses a narrative about writing to one about religion to report "the RISE and PROGRESS of PAGAN IDOLATRY" as a mutation from "SYMBOLIC worship of their Gods, under hieroglyphic Figures" to "*direct* worship" after "the People . . . forgot the *symbol* or *relation* . . . till at length, the animals themselves, whose figures these hieroglyphic marks represented, became the object of religious adoration" (7:298–99). Warburton also tells, out of Plato, the story of "lawgivers" who worked against "poets" to maintain religious secrets that would keep "the people in awe" for "the sake of the state" (7:156). Warburton's valuations are largely opposite Blake's. Much later, Benjamin Haydon also subscribed to the strong distinction between the art of the Egyptians before "priesthood," when artists were free, and after, when it "became a mere tool in the hands of the priests . . . the mere fac-simile of prescribed forms" ("Painting" 69).

[9] On the interplay of Moses and Aaron in relation to the complex political history of the priesthood—Mushite, Aaronid, and others—see Richard Elliott Friedman's quite readable analysis of Pentateuchal narratives, *Who Wrote the Bible?*

contribution to the history of engraving, we can see that the engraver is the archetypal Hebrew artist, or ancient poet. The artist class becomes the priestly caste because of the artist's power to externalize and fix, as "objects of worship," the deities of hearts and minds. The most powerful Hebrew engraver, Moses, may have learned from the hieroglyphics of the Egyptian priesthood a lesson about the overwhelming persuasive force of writing when it was combined with engraving and with a good subject—a mysterious but external deity who communicates in writing, but also in secret. Aaron's failure to compete successfully may be attributed directly to his lack of inventive power, the absence of the "wond'rous art of writing" from his repertory, and to his willingness to work in public.[10] He could enslave the vulgar temporarily with his rather common gold calf as an object of worship. But Moses had the priestly wit to claim direct communication with "God" and to document his claim with a sample in writing permanently sculpted on stone for all to read and in form of rules for all to obey: "Such is the Divine *Written* Law of Horeb & Sinai" (my emphasis, *J* 16.68, E 159). When the graven Sinaitic Law becomes history—when people attempt to govern lives and kingdoms according to its dictates—then the identity of the Law and the array of sculptures in Los's Hall is confirmed. Those sculptures constitute the history of art under the Law.

Blake depicts a notably Mosaic Urizen at work on the title page of *The Book of Urizen* (fig. 3.1), squatting on an open book in the

[10] Mitchell's "Visible Language" is an engaging account of Blake's attitudes toward writing. Mitchell, however, sees no irony in "Reader! [*lover*] of books! [*lover*] of heaven," whereas I see a great deal of it, alongside indecision and apprehension, in the poem and in the whole of the address "To the Public" of which the poem is a part (*J* 3, E 145). Cf. also Eaves, *William Blake's Theory* 155–62, 186–95.

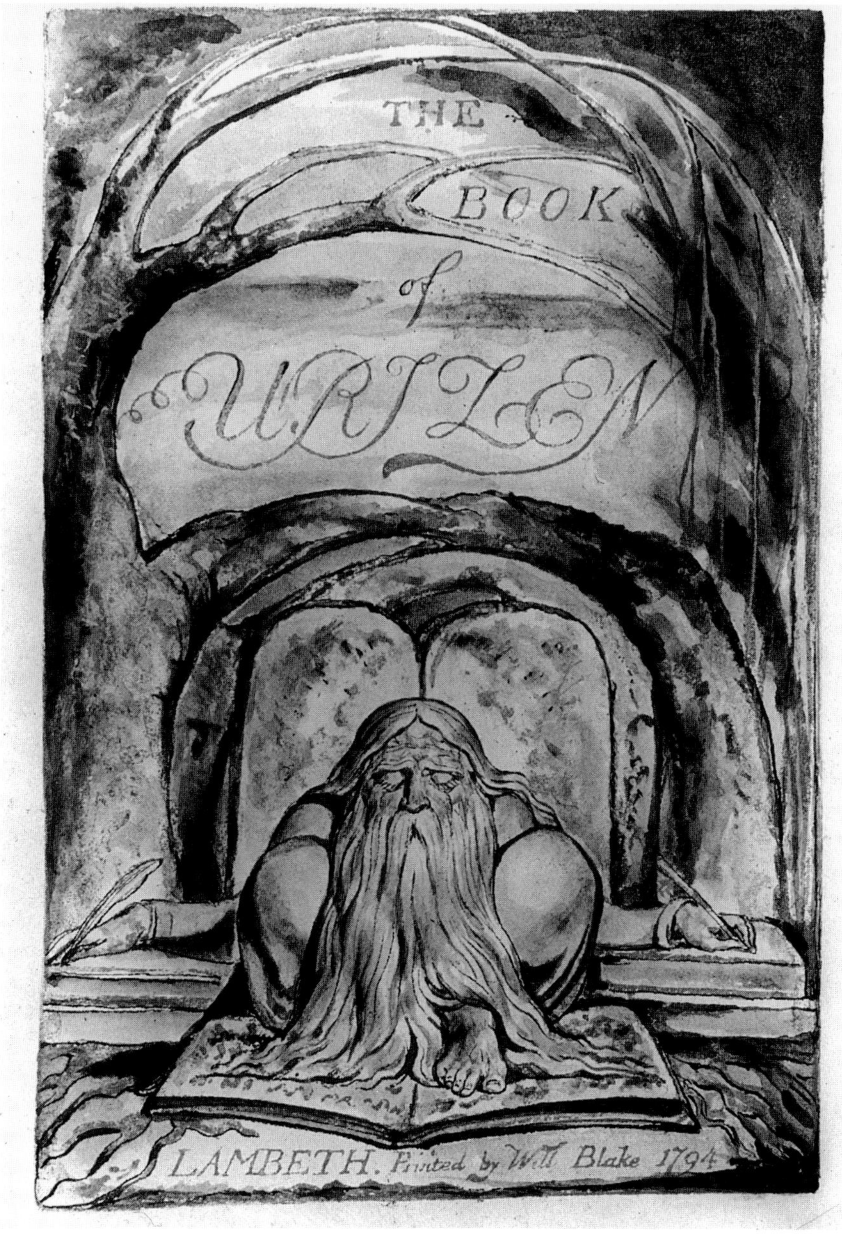

3.1. William Blake, *The Book of Urizen,* title page (copy G), relief etching, 1794.

darkness of his mental mountain cave, holding his place with his foot. He writes and/or engraves on two tablets, one with each hand, and behind him stand two more tablets—perhaps the second of the two sets that the biblical Moses engraves.[11] Blake's Urizen resembles the traditional representation not only of Moses but also of God, hinting at the truth behind the priestly myth. Since God "is" Moses, *The Book of Urizen* parodies the Creation and the Law as one.[12] Seeing that the Law is the basis of the Creation, Blake in *Urizen* restores the Pentateuchal narrative to its true order, placing the engraving of the Law (in *Urizen* chap. 2) before the Creation (chap. 3 and after).[13]

Urizen describes his lonely work in a speech on plate 4:

> 6. Here alone I in books formd of metals
> Have written the secrets of wisdom
> The secrets of dark contemplation. . . .
> 7. Lo! I unfold my darkness: and on
> This rock, place with strong hand the Book
> Of eternal brass, written in my solitude.
>
> [Pl. 4.24–33, E 72]

This is what Orc in *America* calls "The fiery joy, that Urizen perverted to ten commands, / What night he led the starry hosts thro' the wide wilderness" (pl. 8.3–4, E 54). Urizen's writings are ten rules that forbid seven fiery and joyous expressions of himself. The moment when "Eternity roll'd wide apart / Wide asunder rolling" (*Urizen* 5.5–6, E 73) is the moment when external and internal are created and, in their very creation, part. Urizen's external world of stony law is embodied self-loathing. His metal books and stone tablets are, as their shapes suggest, the geometric form of his own externalized heart.

Radical fear turned to hatred kills. The external or (in Blakean terms) corporeal law is ultimately an attempt to destroy the internal or mental. The traditional theological pattern inaugurated by Moses on Sinai or by Urizen in "Words articulate, bursting in thunders / That roll'd on the tops of his mountains / From the depths of dark solitude" (*Urizen* 4.4–6, E 71) is of sin leading to death in the stony heart of nature—the mirror image of the internal pattern of energy leading to life in the fiery heart of the person. The internal world is characterized by identity, where "One Law for the Lion & Ox is Oppression" (*MHH* 24, E 43), the external by empty solitude in collectivity. Urizen, who begins by isolating himself, generates by the end of his book a huddling community of terror. "And their thirty cities divided / In form of a human heart" (*Urizen* 27.43–44, E 83): the projection of Urizen's heart as Law produces a community that reacts as one heart to fears aroused by the Law.

[11] Eaves, "Title-Page," offers a detailed reading of the plate. Images of Moses in the later eighteenth century would itself be a subject worth studying: to Blake's *Urizen* title page compare, for instance, the outrageous 1787 caricature print *Moses, Erecting the Brazen Serpent in the Desert* (reproduced in Erdman, "Grub Street" 26), which depicts Moses struggling to control his own immense serpent-phallus as it rises (heading straight for the heavens) between his legs. Moses's hand holds his swelling organ; his foot rests on his stone tablets.

[12] Tannenbaum discusses *The Book of Urizen* as parody but with an interest in Genesis rather than the Exodus-Deuteronomy narrative and in the God-Urizen rather than the Moses-Urizen analogue.

[13] The reversal or synthesis of Creation and Fall in *Urizen* and elsewhere in Blake's work is primarily a natural revision of the biblical myth as a psychological history of projection. Possible Gnostic influences on Blake, while secondary at most, may help reinforce the pattern.

The Pentateuch relates the earliest efforts of the priestly class to displace a social order from its natural center, the human breast, into an external "God" of mystery, a vision under priestly control. Once the engraved stones are in place, other engravers find it more and more difficult to re-reveal the truth that their imaginations are God. After the engravers-turned-priests sell their claim to those who in buying it identify themselves as "the vulgar," other engravers see their own advantage in supporting the claim with their craft. The priesthood establishes a fixed mystery that forbids competing visions—as in the cunning biblical taboo against all other "graven images." Artists who once animated "all sensible objects" now ornament the Single Vision. History, in the usual sense of the term, begins with engravers taking their peripheral place as hirelings. (This is the moment when patronage becomes relevant, and painters in Blake's time begin to wonder why priests of the Church of England do not sponsor painting in a manner analogous to the Catholic hierarchy on the continent.) In the Pentateuch we see the engraver transferring allegiance and responsibility from God to God's priests in a pattern of progressive externalization: after the heart of Moses projected into the stones of the Law comes an ark for the stones, a sanctuary for the ark, and garments for the priesthood. The ratio of externalization is clear: as the heart of humanity dwells in a body, the heart of religion dwells in its temple. Projected, the mortal human body, a "worm of sixty winters" (*J* 30[34].57, E 177), becomes the corresponding "serpent temple" of which Blake often writes in connection with the druids. The gems and gold that ornament the serpent belong to the same complex of imagery.

Engravers in their new role follow intricate instructions that emanate not from imagination but from the heart of the mystery itself. The Law brings with it its own rules for taking material form: "And thou shalt make holy garments for Aaron thy brother for glory and for beauty. And thou shalt speak unto all that are wise hearted, whom I have filled with the spirit of wisdom, that they may make Aaron's garments . . . a breastplate, and an ephod, and a robe, and a broidered coat, a mitre, and a girdle. . . . With the work of an engraver in stone, like the engravings of a signet, shalt thou engrave the two stones with the names of the children of Israel" (Exod. 28:2–4, 11).

Bezaleel and Aholiab

> If we go back further than the times of Alexander, we shall find, that God himself made this art [sculpture] honourable by communicating his knowledge and wisdom to *Bezaleel* and *Aholiab,* who were to embellish the temple of *Solomon,* and make it venerable by their works.
>
> —Roger de Piles, *The Principles of Painting*

In these early stages of religious organization, the artist's role is uncertain and variable. The Pentateuch represents the victorious party, the priests, in telling how they chose to regard the artists. In Exodus we hear God explain to Moses that he is appointing a master engraver,

Bezaleel, and filling him accordingly "with the spirit of God, in wisdom, and in understanding, and in knowledge, and in all manner of workmanship, to devise cunning works, to work in gold, and in silver, and in brass, and in cutting of stones. . . . And I, behold, I have given with him Aholiab . . . that they may make all that I have commanded thee," including the tabernacle, ark, altar, priestly garments, and all the "furniture" therewith (Exod. 31:1–11). The team of Bezaleel and Aholiab is listed among the earliest engravers by Landseer, Joseph Strutt, and James Elmes.[14] Thus the engraver, the history of whose art is initiated by God, is soon executing the plans of others.

At least as reported in the priests' sacred code. The formula from *The Marriage* fits here: "It indeed appear'd to Reason as if Desire was cast out. but the Devils account is . . ." (pl. 5, E 34–35). The devil's account of Bezaleel and Aholiab appears in a Notebook poem:

If it is True What the Prophets write
That the heathen Gods are all stocks & stones
Shall we for the sake of being Polite
Feed them with the juice of our marrow bones

And if Bezaleel & Aholiab drew
What the Finger of God pointed to their View
Shall we suffer the Roman & Grecian Rods
To compell us to worship them as Gods

They stole them from the Temple of the Lord
And Worshippd them that they might make
    Inspired Art Abhorrd
The Wood & Stone were calld The Holy Things—
And their Sublime Intent given to their Kings
All the Atonements of Jehovah spurnd
And Criminals to Sacrifices Turnd

[E 501–2]

Blake's verses build on the opposition between the true religion of the Jews and classical paganism, allowing the opposition to take its biblical form: the worship of the one unimaged God, whose finger traced for Aholiab and Bezaleel subjects for art—presumably the cherubim of the Temple—versus the worship of many "graven images" or "idols." That opposition becomes the major metaphor on which Blake builds an argument between true art and false, favoring the internal, the personal, and the expressive over the external, the social, and the mimetic. The poem retells the story of the ancient poets in *The Marriage* as an anticlassical satire, with Romans and Greeks in place of priests. The implied ratio, ancient poets are to priests as biblical art is to classical art, is no surprise in Blake, of course, because (as the prophets and Jesus liked to insist) the Jewish priesthood found accommodation with various pagan authorities natural. According to Blake, the priestly and pagan interpretation of the Bible is the one passed on by the rulers of this world—the Bible read by the lamp of classical reason and morality. Under priests and emperors, artists end up in the same position—like Horace, as poetic lickspittle to some imperial majesty, or like Bartolozzi, as engraver to his insane monarch, or like Barry and Blake, as outcasts. As interpreted by priests and kings, the Bible becomes the sacred code of tyrants, its

[14] Landseer mentions Bezaleel and Aholiab in his *Lectures* 16–17; Strutt, *Biographical Dictionary* 1:9; and Elmes, *General and Bibliographical Dictionary,* "Engraving" n.p. Elmes, working I suppose from memory, claims that "Bezaleel and Aholiab are mentioned in the book of Genesis as 'filled with wisdom of heart to work all manner of work with the graver.' " In fact Bezaleel and Aholiab appear first in Exodus, and Elmes's quotation seems to be a creation of his own, yoking a rough paraphrase of Exod. 28:3 to 28:11, before Bezaleel and Aholiab are mentioned.

plot the epic allegory of military conquest described by Isaiah in *The Marriage* (pls. 12–13, E 38–39).

Blake's poem reads through the Mosaic fabrication, that Bezaleel and Aholiab are honest hirelings eager to please their employer by following the letter of his Law, to see the two engravers instead as true artists able to draw exactly "What the Finger of God pointed to their View," an interpretation faithful to the Exodus narrative insofar as (1) God's finger engraved the Law that (2) Moses delivered to the Israelites, and (3) Bezaleel and Aholiab got their artistic conceptions from that Law. Blake brings out the spiritual sense of these episodes by suppressing the priestly intermediate stage. In his verses the finger of God points, Bezaleel and Aholiab draw. The Romans and Greeks did not invent their own gods, their own artistic conceptions, but "stole" them from "the Temple of the Lord," which in the priestly tradition refers to the Temple in Jerusalem, repeatedly ransacked and looted by pagan powers until its final destruction by the Romans. But Blake's meaning depends on the meaning given to "temple" by Jesus, when "he spake of the temple of his body" (John 2:21). As Paul asks the Corinthians, "And what agreement hath the temple of God with idols? for ye are the temple of the living God" (2 Cor. 6:16; cf. 1 Cor. 3:16). The "wisdom of heart" that God in Exodus gives to Bezaleel and Aholiab is, in the Christian view, God himself. Original artists draw with the finger of God, their own, what the heart knows.

When people forget where "all deities reside" and start worshiping stocks and stones,[15] a class of kings and priests arises to rule a sacrificial religion of nature that artists are told to imitate, with the result that "inspired Art" is "Abhorrd." When self-government begins to take its cues from an external government, the defining artistic lines of character and expression that distinguish knavery from virtue become the "Roman & Grecian Rods," the various bludgeons and measuring devices of authority, including Aaron's rod as well as the scepters of kings. When imagination projects its existence into gods and kings, a new connection between the gods and governors of the culture replaces the vital connection between human identity and its artistic expressions. The imagination that expresses itself in animations of wood and stone becomes a memory instead. Memory does not animate nature; in theory, at least, the reverse is true, but dead nature cannot ani-

[15] Blake may be calling into play Milton's sonnet "On the Late Massacher in Piemont":

Avenge O Lord thy slaughter'd Saints, whose bones
Lie scatter'd on the Alpine mountains cold,
Ev'n them who kept thy truth so pure of old
When all our Fathers worship't Stocks and Stones.
[Milton, *Works* 1.1: 66]

Here the Waldenses' conservation of "truth so pure of old," especially their rejection of graven images, encourages a contrast with the idolatry of "our Fathers": thus *their* true Christian past versus *our* idolatrous heathen one. Insofar as Blake's "heathen Gods" who would eat "our marrow bones" can as well be British druids as Romans—and finally Georgians—he is working over similar material to bring home a related contemporary point. Those who massacred the Waldenses in 1655 were, in Blake's analogy, "Roman & Grecian Rods" slaughtering true Christians and eating their marrow bones.

There is also a clear artistic connection. The phrase "stocks and stones" is a standard item in Protestant iconophobia, which was identified as an obstacle to the development of a proper English school. The engraver Valentine Green ridicules the connection between paintings in churches and "a restoration of Popery" by visualizing (ironically) the community "prostrating ourselves before Stocks, Stones, or Pictures" (38–39).

mate. Memory collects and copies. The holiness that was once a property of the imagination becomes a property of the outside world. Holiness becomes a synonym for obedience, because nothing obeys law as well as nature. "The Wood & Stone," the objects rather than the subject that once animated them, "were calld The Holy Things / And their Sublime intent given to their Kings"—and taken away from the artists. The final step in this direction is the Roman and Greek identification of kingship (rod) with deity (god), which is no aberration but a natural step in the logic of projection.

Finally, the system projected from the heart turns back on it. "Atonements" become "Sacrifices": the mental process of forgiveness and self-sacrifice is spurned in favor of the sacrifice of others, a class identified by the agents of priest and king as "Criminals" who, carrying the blame for the sins of the culture, become sacrificial victims.[16] The most dangerous criminals are not those who act out bloody brutalities and are rewarded with brutality in kind, but those who keep insisting that their deities are in their breasts. All tyrants can get away with sacrificing murderers on the altar, or the cross, with the rod of their wrath and calling it a sacred meal for the gods. "Feed them with the juice of our marrow bones": but the sacrifice of an inspired criminal such as Jesus can turn into a tyrant's nightmare, because making marrowbone stew out of his body is no guarantee of extermination, as priests and emperors alike discover.

Blake imagines himself in the tradition of Bezaleel and Aholiab as he and Catherine prepare for their move to Felpham. In the optimism of the moment he adds an excited postscript to a letter to William Hayley: "My fingers Emit sparks of fire with Expectation of my future labours" (16 September 1800, E 709).[17] In the same letter he addresses Hayley, the Hermit of Eartham, as "Leader of My Angels" and claims enthusiastically that "Eartham will be my first temple & altar"—that is, his first commission as a master sculptor/engraver in the biblical manner, a "Sculptor of Eternity," as he calls his fellow laborer John Flaxman a few days later (21 September 1800, E 710). As for Catherine, she "is like a flame of many colours of precious jewels whenever she hears it [Eartham] named," indicating her fitness to be the companion of a divinely appointed metallurgist, and to play Aholiab to his Bezaleel. Blake hopes that the Leader of His Angels will lead him on the path of inspired art to ornament a temple and altar as Bezaleel did, with the finger of the artist tracing what his divine imagination pointed to his view. Blake's shattered hopes in Felpham emphasize the uncertainty of the biblical artisan's position after the installation of the priesthood; engravers who think they are hired to follow God's instructions often end up following the plans of priests and kings. As Blake learned at Felpham and never forgot, angels come from the imagination of the artist and can have no other leader. But a Blake who needs no Hayley can use a Thomas

[16] My reading of the last line is based on the assumption that all the verbs in the last four lines are parallel to the first one and thus all passive: "were called," and thus "[were] given," "[were] spurnd," "[were] Turnd." If the verb in the last line is not parallel to the other three, then the line may be read as an active construction, "and criminals turned to performing sacrifices."

[17] Cf. Coleridge's bizarre report of using "silver Light"—presumably static electricity—from "the tips of my fingers" to write "my name, Greek words, cyphers &c on my Thigh" (quoted in Bentley, *Blake Records* 73n).

Butts, "Dear *Friend* of My Angels" (my emphasis, 23 September 1800, E 711). Or, to put the lesson of Felpham in the formula that Blake would ultimately adopt for it, corporeal friends are spiritual enemies. A spiritual enemy is one who wants to pay you for the privilege of leading your angels. Blake eventually discovers that leaving London is not escaping slavery in Egypt for liberation in the Promised Land of Felpham but trading one tyranny for another. And thus he learns to abandon the useless distinction between worse and better tyrants and to make the only distinction worth making, that between imposition and friendship.

The Golden Hall of Urizen

With the Law, the ark, and Aaron's breastplate, Old Testament engraving reaches the historical stage described by Landseer: "the precepts and laws of the ancients were engraven on stone or on metal; the poems of Orpheus and Hesiod are said to have been cut in lead, and the shields of Hercules, and the heroes who distinguished themselves in the early Theban wars, as well as the more celebrated shield of Achilles, are described as having been ornamented with heraldic and historical engravings" (*Lectures* 6–7).[18] Engravers have by the end of this stage established their historical connections with law and war, while the mention of Orphism shows the association of poetry with engraving shifting ominously in the direction of natural religion. Even so, in the Bible the vision that reveals the fate of the artist in a priestly culture remains unfocused until the time of Solomon. But the outlines show with new clarity when the priesthood finally discovers its natural partner in the Davidic monarchy.

[18] Turnbull (4–5) quotes Alexander Pope on Achilles's shield as the epitome of Greek knowledge of visual, plastic, and graphic arts: "The Shield is not only described as a piece of Sculpture, but of Painting: the Outlines may be supposed engraved, and the rest enamel'd, or inlaid with various-colour'd Metals."

As the hearts and bodies of the Hebrews shrink, the body of religion swells into ever more elaborate and expensive external forms, many of which are authorized by a new ruling class, kings, who in turn support a military class that can be sent out to protect and extend the influence of the religious vision. Though the interests of the government and the priesthood may sometimes clash, the two are most effective in combination, the priests facing the source of power at the center, the government and military facing the periphery.

At this stage the skills of the engraver are on call by the ruling classes to materialize their dreams of power by bejeweling, housing, and clothing the Law on which that power rests. Artisans do not look for instruction to the deity in their breasts or even to the deity represented in the words of the Law. The ambivalence is gone. God does not speak; priests and kings speak for him. The most important artistic result is the division of the original integrity of art (artists express the deity in their breasts) into conception and execution. The artist becomes the artisan, a repository of mechanical skills of execution. The powers of invention, or conception, that were once the artist's are turned over to the ruling class, which wants art that expresses *its* ideas. These ideas are usually said to be fixed ultimately in some sacred code, the interpretation and application of which is a ruling-class privilege. In later stages of Hebrew history an iconoclastic group of outcast ancient poets called prophets arises to compete for this privilege. They are much feared by rulers, who prefer to dole out tasks to specialist artisans who work at the bidding of people with money.

Solomon, even after offering a thousand burnt offerings on "the brasen altar, that Bezaleel . . . had made" (2 Chron. 1:5)—and made according to God's own instructions—remains unimpressed by the setting in which he transacts business with the deity. So he begins planning something that will better match his fantasies of religion and power, in the manner of Blake's "Architect divine," Urizen, who "his plan / Unfolds" for a quadrangular building with three "Central Domes" that "Encompassd / The Golden Hall of Urizen." Toward the west an altar of incense: "A Golden Altar . . . with Art Celestial formd / Foursquare sculpturd & sweetly Engravd. . . ." Toward the east an altar of sacrifice: "lives of Victims" and "lives of beasts & birds" are "Slain on the Altar." Both are masterpieces of "terrible workmanship the Altar labour of ten thousand Slaves / One thousand Men of wondrous power spent their lives in its formation" (*FZ* 2.30.8–40, E 319–20).[19] Urizen's Golden Hall of geometrical magnificence can be measured, on the one hand, against the heroic public projects that English artists persisted in envisioning for themselves and, on the other, against the artistic standard for human habitation that Blake lays down in a letter from Felpham reporting to his fellow artisan Flaxman back in Tyre. The controlling metaphor of the letter is "cottages are ?": "Dear Sculptor of Eternity / We are safe arrived at our Cottage which is more beautiful than I thought it. & more convenient. It is a perfect Model for Cottages & I think for Palaces of Magnificence, only Enlarging not altering its proportions & adding ornaments & not principals." His rationale is the expected one. The cottage "seems to be the Spontaneous Effusion of Humanity congenial to the wants of Man," he exclaims, going on to describe Felpham in general as a heavenly city, "more Spiritual than London." That is, the perfect dwelling is a direct expression of "the Divine bosom . . . our Dwelling place . . . our houses of Eternity" that he mentions near the end of the same letter (21 September 1800, E 710; cf. Blake to Butts, 23 September 1800). Blake's extensive use of his cottage and garden as the visionary center of *Milton,* the artistic expression of the Felpham experience, shows more than temporary enthusiasm for the idea of a dwelling as the spontaneous effusion of humanity, proportioned to human needs; a projection of the human body that does not project itself back in forms of separation or demand anything of its projector as Urizenic palaces of magnificence demand worship and sacrifice (fig. 3.2).

Solomon's disappointment with the old spontaneous effusions of Bezaleel, however, increases. Soon he is issuing orders to artisans and—since domestic craft seems always too familiar to live up to a ruler's taste for exotic luxury—recruiting a foreigner to head the team: "Send me now therefore a man . . . that can skill to grave with the cunning men that are with me in Judah" (2 Chron. 2:7), he says to the

[19] On Solomon's temple as a work of and a gallery of art, especially engraving and sculpture, see "An Answer" in Winckelmann, *Reflections* 150–57, 160–61. Blake describes the cherubim of ancient temples as "sculptured and painted on walls" (*DC,* E 531).

king of Tyre, who obliges with "a cunning man, endued with understanding . . . to grave any manner of graving . . . with thy cunning men" (2 Chron. 2:13–14). The wisdom of heart with which God endowed Bezaleel is no longer required, only the "cunning" and "understanding" of executional skill that has nothing particularly to do with God, Israel, or Solomon and can thus be hired and imported "to grave *any* manner of graving." Bezaleel's wisdom of heart allowed him to draw what the finger of God traced; presumably Solomon's finger will suffice for the cunning artisans of Tyre. The distance from conception to execution during Solomon's reign is at least the distance that his foreign artisans, inspired by his moneybags, not by his invisible God, must travel. Blake too discovered that the spiritual journey from London to Felpham covers the miles not from Egypt to the Promised Land but from King Hiram's Tyre to King Solomon's Jerusalem, where the anticipated leader of his angels turns out to be only another boss after all.

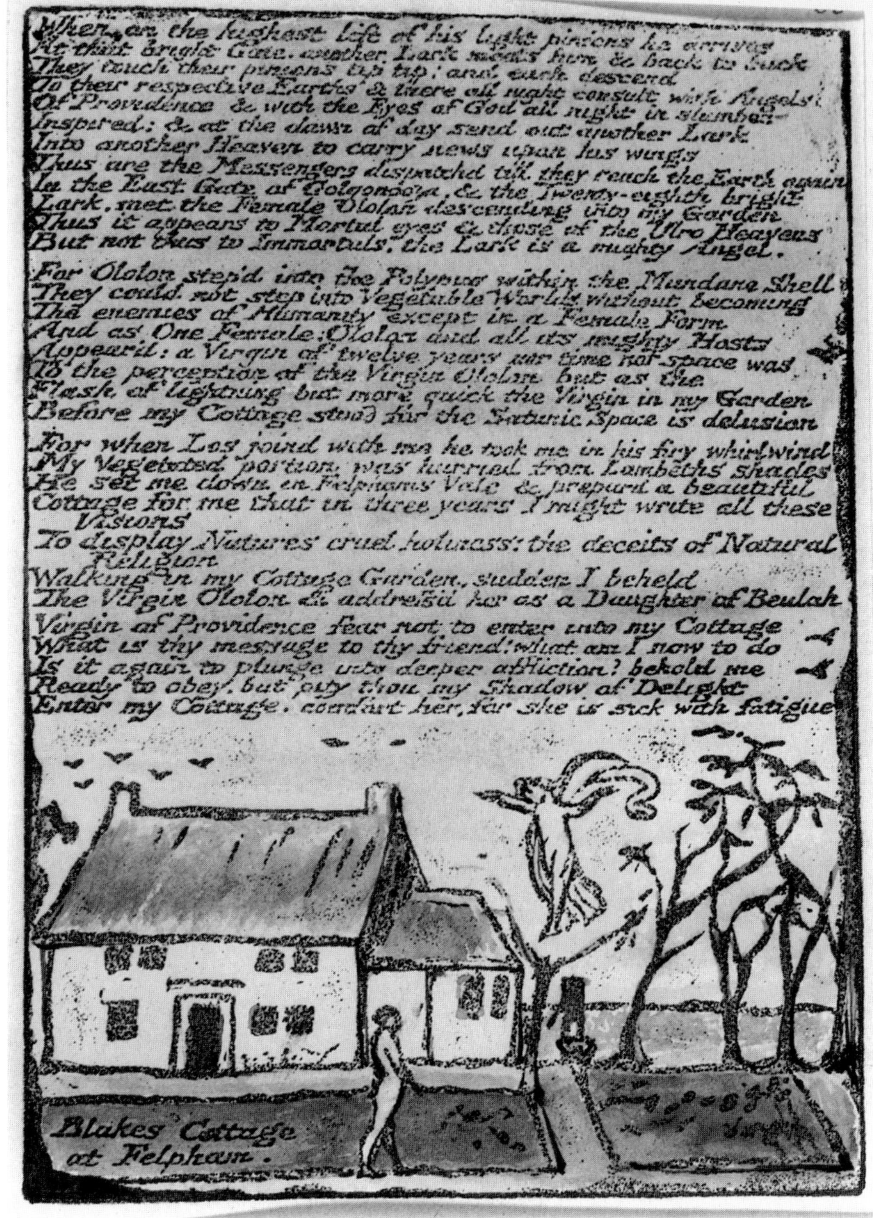

3.2. William Blake, *Milton,* plate 40 (copy A), relief etching, c. 1804–1808.

The Heart of the Pharisee

> ... the proper promise of the gospel! That he will *put* these laws in our minds, and write them in our hearts!
>
> —John Wesley, *Explanatory Notes upon the New Testament* (1754)

> *Now tho' these Graces all are* Set,
> *Our Hearts are but* White-Paper *yet;*
> *And by Adam's First Transgression,*
> *Fit only for the worst* Impression.
> *Thy Holy Spirit the* PRESS-MAN *make,*
> *From whom we may Perfection take;*
> *And let Him no Time defer,*
> *To* Print *on us Thy* Character
> . . .
> *Print our Hearts new o'er agen.*
>
> —James Watson, printer's prayer (1713)

The loss of imagination is ultimately the loss of identity. Putting its artists in thrall to the visible agents of an invisible God, Israel enthralls its identity in religion, tyranny, and war, and ends logically by losing its identity entirely. Blake frequently reads the Bible in this way, as an allegory of human identity figured as a nation. The pattern of Israel's history circulates from identity to nonentity expressed in metaphors of domestic freedom and foreign tyranny. The priestly interpretation of this pattern uses the Law as its touchstone: as the Israelites get further from adherence to the Law, they become less like "Israel" and more like a foreign nation, until they are absorbed by one. But in the artistic interpretation "Babylon" is the terminal stage of a progressive loss of imagination. Solomon brings Tyre to Israel; Nebuchadnezzar brings Israel to Babylon. English artists are thus "in Babylon" when they have no visions of their own. Their "visions" at such a point are imitations of external law, or nature. Babylon is not, as the priestly tradition would have it, the just punishment for failure to follow the Law but the state of mind, or insanity, under the Law, when human identity is exiled in nature. Accordingly, Blake's depiction of Nebuchadnezzar over the slogan "One Law for the Lion & Ox is Oppression" shows him insane in nature (fig. 3.3).

The countermovement toward recovery begins not in Israel at all, then, but in Babylon, and is based neither on the frozen priestly conceptions of the Law nor on the empty virtuoso skill of the artisans who execute them but on the potentially subversive visions of the prophets. Ezekiel, whom the priestly tradition sponsors as the great priest-prophet of the Babylonian exile, is in fact a counter-Solomon. Instead of importing goods and services from Tyre he imagines its destruction: "Thou wast perfect ... till iniquity was found in thee. By the multitude of thy merchandise they have filled the midst of thee with violence . . . and I will destroy thee, O covering cherub . . ." (Ezek. 28:15–16). Tyre's "merchandise" is the externalized and separated form of God—God as nature—that "covers" the real God with its external substitutes: stony laws for human hearts, stony temples for human bodies, religion for imagination, imposed judicial systems for self-discipline. When Ezekiel has imagined the destruction of the covering cherub in all its forms, Israelitish, Tyrian, Egyptian, Assyrian, and Babylonian, his imagination can envision the liberation of the captive Israelites from Babylon, the return of a "remnant" to Israel—which *is* imagination, in this view—and the construction of a new city, temple, and garden that are nothing if not mental (Ezek. 40–48). As a parable of redeemed identity, Ezekiel's prophecy tells of the return of the Israelites unto themselves: "and the name of the city from that day shall be, The Lord is there" (Ezek. 48:35).

Return from exile is Ezekiel's myth of national and religious reintegration; as interpreted by Blake it is a myth of the reintegrated mind by the strategy that Northrop Frye calls "recovery of projection" (*Romanticism* ad passim). Rebuilding the Temple in its true mental form and restoring the Lord to his place inside it are part of a complex of imagery whose coherence becomes evident for Blake when the prophets are interpreted in their spiritual sense. The natural sense of Jeremiah's prophecy, for example, reflects the priestly opposition between the purity of the Law and the corruption of the human heart. Measuring the heart against the tables of the Law, Jeremiah sees the irrepressible energies and desires of the Israelites as deadly sin: "The sin of Judah [the southern kingdom of a divided unity, Israel being the

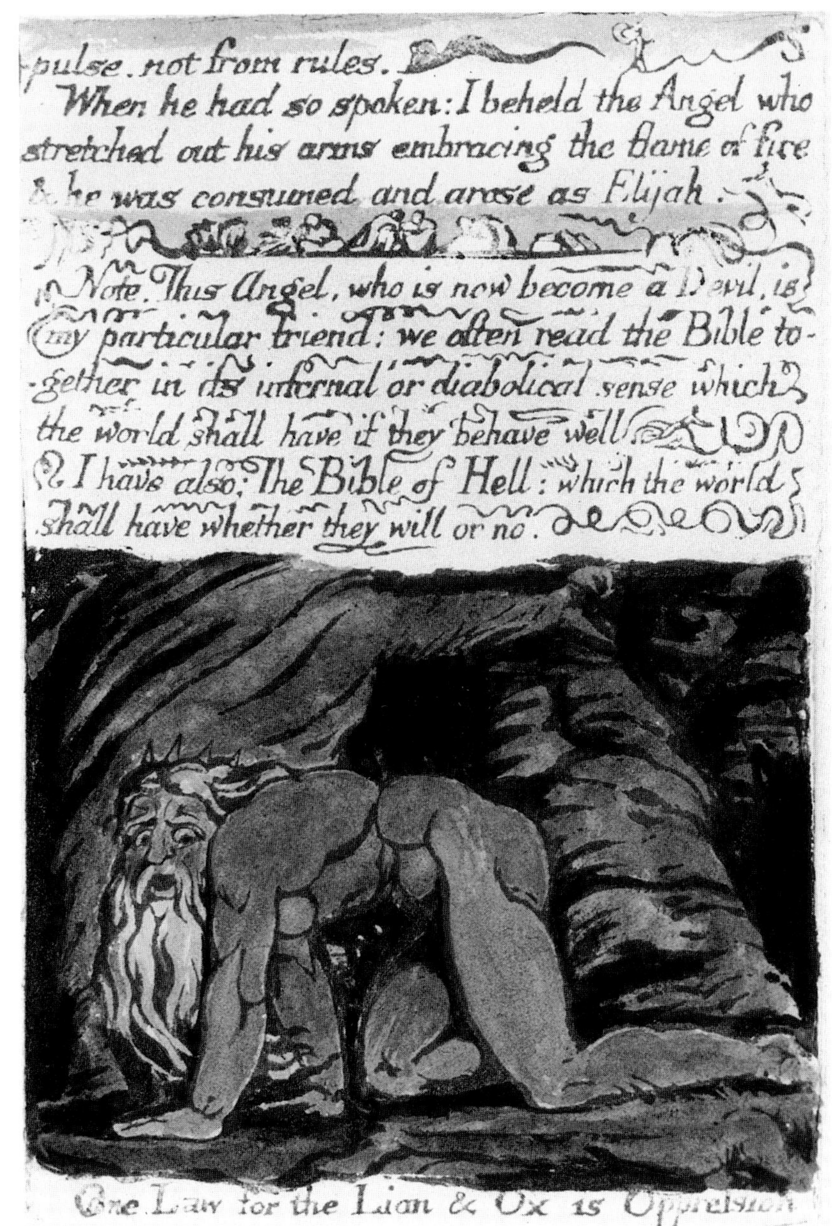

3.3. William Blake, *The Marriage of Heaven and Hell,* plate 24 (copy D), relief etching, c. 1790.

northern] is written with a pen of iron, and with the point of a diamond: it is graven upon the table of their heart, and upon the horns of your altars" (Jer. 17:1). Jeremiah's solution is replacement. Thus he imagines God as saying, "I will put my law in their inward parts, and write it in their hearts" (31:33).[20] This is what Blake calls becoming what you behold. The heart projected as Law returns as the projector, the Divine Will that projects, or in the Old Testament creates, the human breast. This cycle of externalization is the key to making sense of the oft-repeated notion that in Blake's myth the Creation is the Fall: more accurately, the Creation as reported in Genesis is the crisis point of a story that has been suppressed, and the moral polarity of the crisis has been reversed.

Blake supposes that he is restoring the true sense of Jeremiah's prophecy in *The Everlasting Gospel.* There Jesus, "When the rich learned Pharisee / Came to consult him secretly / Upon his heart with iron pen / . . . wrote Ye must be born again" (E 518–19). The Pharisee (Nicodemus—see John 3:1–15, 7:50–52, 19:39) approaches Jesus with a heart of stone because God's Law is engraved there. If he were to take to heart Jesus's counterengraving, he would be fulfilling the promise that God reveals to Ezekiel: ". . . I will put a new spirit within you; and I will take the stony heart out of their flesh, and will give them an heart of flesh" (11.19). And Paul reads Jeremiah in the spiritual sense when he reminds the Corinthians that they are "the epistle of Christ . . . written not with ink, but with the Spirit of the living God; not in tables of stone, but in fleshy tables of the heart" (2 Cor. 3:3). In the scene from *The Everlasting Gospel* the learned Nicodemus meets Jesus as Moses met God, "to consult him secretly," and Nicodemus, like Moses, brings stones to engrave on. Nicodemus, coming at a later stage in the cycle of externalization, has his stones in his heart. Moses is given the Law. Nicodemus, who already has it, expects Jesus to add one more tittle to the jots already there. But Jesus counsels eradication.

The reenactment continues in the following (parallel) section of the poem. The scribes and Pharisees bring the woman taken in adultery to Jesus, who is "sitting in Moses Chair" in the position of judge:

Moses commands she be stoned to Death
What was the sound of Jesus breath
He laid his hand on Moses Law
The Ancient Heavens in Silent Awe
Writ with Curses from Pole to Pole
All away began to roll
The Earth trembling & Naked lay
In secret bed of Mortal Clay
On Sinai felt the hand Divine
Putting back the bloody shrine
And she heard the breath of God
As she heard by Edens flood
Good & Evil are no more
Sinais trumpets cease to roar
Cease finger of God to Write

[E 521]

Jesus reengraved the Pharisee's heart. Here the

[20] Somewhat similiarly, Blake has Louis XVI complaining to the Duke of Burgundy, "My soul is o'ergrown with distress / For the Nobles of France, and dark mists roll round me and blot the writing of God / Written in my bosom" (*French Revolution* 107–9, E 290–91). The metaphor of transformed writing—the idea that old writing on the heart must be replaced by new—is a Christian commonplace. Una helps rescue Redcrosse from Despair by telling him that justice, the old Law of Moses, is "accurst handwriting" that "greater grace" will "deface" (*Faerie Queene* 1.9.53.6–8). She appeals to the strength of his "hart" and "spright" (53.2, 3).

written curses begin to disappear at the touch of Jesus's hand. Countering the uniform "Divine Written Law of Horeb & Sinai" with the variable and personal "Holy Gospel of Mount Olivet & Calvary," Jesus puts the stones back on Sinai where they belong, to replace them with a fleshy heart. Thus here, when Jesus "laid His hand on Moses Law," the earth "On Sinai felt the hand Divine / Putting back [replacing] the bloody shrine"—bloody because the stones became the altar for a religion of sacrifice.[21] The rest of this section of the poem connects the heart as the place of love ("my burning bosom") with the vagina ("Loves temple that God dwelleth in / . . . in secret hidden Shrine"). The woman taken in adultery finds in her heart "Seven Devils." They must be the seven joys that Urizen filtered through the ten commands, perverting them into seven deadly sins that have made her regard her love as sinful and herself as sinner. Her devils are a moral invasion force like the artistic "demons" that Blake complains of in his *Descriptive Catalogue:* bearing the names of dead artists such as Rubens and Titian, they "possessed his mind" and weakened "all power of individual thought" until he exorcised them. By casting out her devils the woman taken in adultery removes the external forces that have kept her mind and body in a perpetual state of self-contradiction, "repugnant to your own individual character" (*DC*, E 547).

[21] Cf. Helms 134–35, 159n. Helms's negative thesis concerning the failure of *The Everlasting Gospel* seems to divert him from the contexts and Blakean implications of this episode. For further discussion of the poem, see also Erdman, " 'Terrible Blake,' " and Hall. Paley astutely contrasts Blake's watercolor painting *The Woman Taken in Adultery* with *God Writing upon the Tables of the Covenant:* Jesus's writing on the ground replaces God's writing on the tablets (*William Blake* 56 and pls. 32, 81).

There is no agent of salvation, no second party to counsel the artist in the *Descriptive Catalogue.* But in fact the perception that Jesus is a second party is not the solution but part of the problem in *The Everlasting Gospel.* He is not, as Nicodemus comes thinking him to be, an external agent, but a power of self-scrutiny. Says Jesus to the woman, "Hide not from my Sight thy Sin / That forgiveness thou maist win." He seems to be outside, in the position of judge, because she has inscribed her true heart with the Law, and that, rather than a list of immoral acts, is her sin: "this was my Sin / When first I let these Devils in." All she must do to win forgiveness is follow Jesus's simple instruction—"What was thy love Let me see it"—because showing him is showing herself. That explains the logic of her question:

My Sin thou hast forgiven me
. . .
Canst thou *return* to this dark Hell
And *in my burning bosom dwell*
And canst thou Die [in your separated form] that I
may live
[My emphasis, E 522]

In this role Jesus fulfills, but also corrects, Job's wish: "Oh that my words were now written! oh that they were printed in a book! That they were graven with an iron pen and lead in the rock for ever! For I know that my redeemer liveth, and that he shall stand at the latter day upon the earth" (Job 19:23–25). That is, Job knows that if he could express himself to his redeemer rather than to his accuser and judge, he would be believed and understood. He imagines his problem as historical: if only he could wait for an appeal, a new judge would reverse the verdict. Job thus wishes that an engraver could build a time capsule to store Job's defense in. Blake's *Illustrations of the Book of Job* (1825) show Job, like the woman taken in adultery, learning that his problem is not history but identity; not the adequacy of some judge's conception of Job but his conception of himself. This logic derives from the radical Protestant individualism represented by the Digger Gerrard Winstanley's announcement that "*declaration* of the Gospell" by prophets and apostles will cease "when the Lord himselfe, who is the everlasting Gospell, doth manifest himselfe to rule *in the flesh* of sonnes and daughters" (122).[22] The gospel will be engraved on the heart of every individual.

The depiction of God in Blake's illustrations shows clearly that Job's judge is himself, or rather the image of himself that religion persuades him to take to heart. The cultural forces represented by the scribes and Pharisees in *The Everlasting Gospel* are represented in Job's story by the "comforters" who collect around him in his misery. These external forces have great power only because they strike a responsive internal chord, called "seven devils" in the story of the woman taken in adultery and depicted as devils from hell in plate 11 of the engraved Job illustrations (fig. 3.4).

In *The Everlasting Gospel,* as soon as the woman finds the forgiveness that can return Jesus to dwell in her bosom, the seven devils coalesce into a "shadowy Man" or false body that "Rolld . . . away / From the Limbs of Jesus." (This episode demonstrates the basic continuity of *The Marriage,* which tells how gods originally left the human breast, or rather how people forgot that gods live in the breast, with *The Everlasting Gospel,* which proposes to solve essential human problems by returning Jesus to the bosom, presumably by remembering where he has been all along.) This is the "Serpent Bulk of Natures dross," the body that Jesus "put . . . off on the Cross and Tomb." Typologically, Christ's tomb is Sinai's cave. Having sloughed the serpent bulk of his old body, Jesus emerges from the cave wearing a new "spiritual" body.

The tongue. A number of Blakean and biblical images augment the vision of a new body forming around a new heart. Any commonsense reader knows, for example, that when poets say "Jesus writes with an iron pen on a Pharisee's heart," they really mean "Jesus talked emphatically and persuasively to a Pharisee." In other words, Jesus's iron pen is also his tongue. "My heart is inditing a good matter," says the Psalmist; "my tongue is the pen of a ready writer" (45:1). Externalized, tongues become swords or the Roman and Grecian "rods" that Blake scorns in the Bezaleel poem. God applies the rod of his wrath to Job, who begs, "Let him take his rod away from me" (9:34). God promises his "son" David the king power over the heathen: "Thou shalt break them with a rod of iron" (Psalms 2:9), an image of the iron pen as kingly scepter. In such regimes, metallurgists

[22] Cf. Milton's distinction between "external" and "internal" scripture (*De Doctrina Christiana* 587; see also 584, 590). In chaps. 26 and 27 he constructs a pedagogical sequence from the one to the other. It begins with "the Mosaic Law . . . a written code . . . intended for the Israelites alone. . . . Its aim, also, was that all we other nations should afterwards be educated from this elementary, childish and servile discipline to the adult stature of a new creature" (517). In this creature the believer *becomes* the text of belief: "the Gospel . . . much more excellent and perfect than the Law . . . has been written in the hearts of believers through the Holy Spirit" (521). The old law, the "ministry of death," was "the decalogue itself" (529). Blake almost certainly never read Milton's theological credo, which was discovered and translated in the mid-1820s.

and engravers shrink to the tasks of forging and ornamenting rods and swords, while poets' tongues become propaganda organs. (Landseer claims that each Hebrew tribe had a rod engraved on its head with the tribe's symbol; thus the rod of the tribe of Judah would have shown a lion [*Saboean Researches* 66–67].) Bezaleel and Aholiab become Krupp and Wilkinson. Songs of harvest and vintage become songs of Roland. Sinai becomes Golgotha. "Cease finger of God to write"!

But the prophet Isaiah hints at the form a reversal will take when he announces that "there shall come forth a rod out of the stem of Jesse," a new kind of judge who will act not for the ruling classes but for "the poor" and "the meek of the earth": "and he shall smite the earth with the rod of his mouth, and with the breath of his lips shall he slay the wicked" (11:1, 4). The rod of his mouth is presumably what Jesus has in mind when he announces that he "came not to send peace, but a sword" (Matt. 10:34; *MHH* 16, E 40), since his tongue appears as a two-edged sword in the mouth of the messianic Christ in Revelation (1:16), indicating that corporeal acts are recovered as mental acts when swords of extermination are recovered as tongues (and iron pens) of expression. Jesus's iron pen ends the cycle of imagery that God's finger begins.

The head. The stony heart of the Pharisee parallels the stony foreheads of the Israelites—as hardheaded as they are "hardhearted," with foreheads of "adamant harder than flint," God warns Ezekiel (3:7–9). In *The Marriage,* the mighty devil who engraves words on the sides of the rocky abyss "of the five senses" engraves not on the heart but on the forehead, "where a flat sided steep *frowns* over the present world."

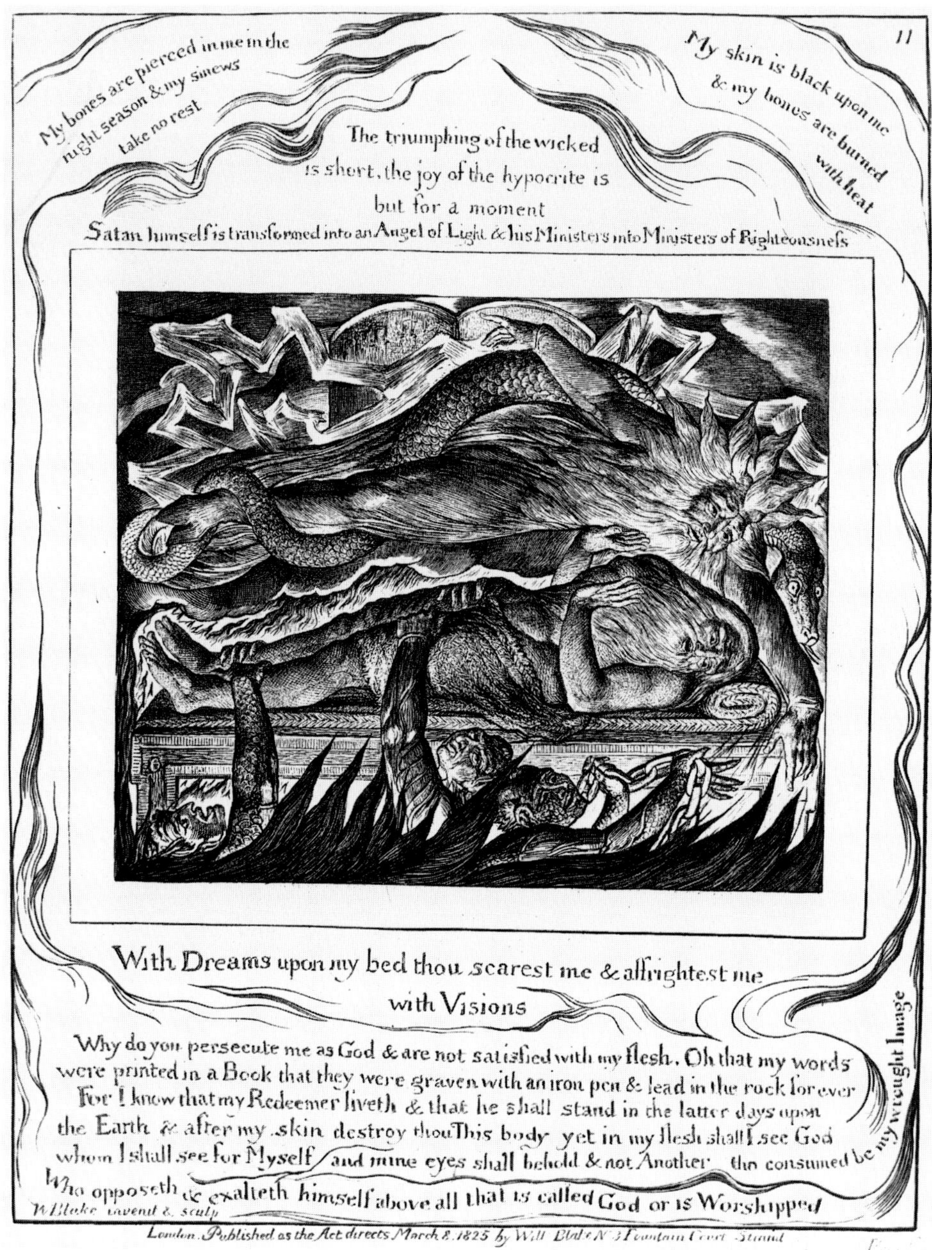

3.4. William Blake, *Illustrations of the Book of Job,* plate 11, engraving, 1825–1826.

Consequently he etches on the forehead questions about the extent of the human brain ("How do you know . . . ?") and the "clos'd . . . senses five" that cluster there. In the rocky landscape of *The Marriage* we learn that more than the Pharisee's heart has turned to stone: "For man has closed himself up, till he sees all things thro' narrow chinks of his cavern" (pls. 6–7, 14, E 35, 39). The devil's etching on the stony head of humanity is the counter-engraving to all the engraved foreheads in the Bible since the mark of Cain—the mark ostensibly of the Lord's protection doubling as the mark of accusation, blame, and mortality.

Two important kinds of ancient engraving are involved, the engraving of signets, or seals, and the engraving of gems, both discussed at length by most historians of engraving in Blake's time (and assiduously collected by connoisseurs), usually with special emphasis on the Bible, and motivating such antiquarian products as Wicksteed and Worlidge's *Specimen of a Select Collection of Drawings, from the Most Curious Antique Gems; . . . To Which Are Prefixed Observations on the Art of Engraving on Gems, with Their Nature, Composition, and Subjects in General* (1766). According to Landseer, any mention of signets is a clue to the early history of the art because "signets . . . presuppose an art of engraving" (*Observations* 7), and Abraham's father, Terah, was not only the first artist whose name is recorded but also a signet engraver and sculptor (8). Blake engraved, with Wilson Lowry, illustrations for the article on gem engraving in Abraham Rees's *Cyclopaedia*, and Samuel Palmer fondly remembered the hours passed with Blake in the examination of engravings of antique gems, by which "all his powers were concentrated in admiration" (quoted in Bentley, *Blake Records* 283). The close relation of signet, medallion, and gem engraving to copperplate engraving is still apparent during Blake's lifetime in the frequency with which the former become subjects for the latter, as we see in Blake's letter to Hayley concerning "an Engraving of that Medallion by your Sons matchless hand which is placd over his [Daniel Braithwaite's] chimney piece. between two little pretty pictures correct & enlarged copies from Antique Gems . . ." (23 February 1804, E 742).

Though the family of related images in the Bible and in Blake's illuminated books is too complicated to trace in detail here, in general the gem seems to be the externalized, or natural, form of the human brain. "What we call Antique Gems," according to Blake, "are the Gems of Aarons Breast Plate" (*Laocoön*, E 274). Aaron's ephod incorporates gems engraved "like the engravings of a signet" with the names of the tribes of Israel (Exod. 28:11, etc.), and on his forehead Aaron wears a gold plate engraved with the words "HOLINESS TO THE LORD" (28:36–38). In Blake's *Milton* these ornaments belong to Nature or Vala, the Shadowy Female, who declares, "I will put on Holiness as a breastplate & as a helmet" (pl. 18[20].21, E 111). *The Four Zoas* presents Vala "Clothed . . . with Scarlet robes & Gems / And on her forehead was her name written in blood Mystery" (8.105.14–15, E 378). Blake derives his picture of Vala from Revelation 17:3–5. She and the Whore of Babylon feature the "whore's forehead," as Jeremiah calls it (3:3), the forehead decorated with a gem that constitutes a fit ornament for a princess or a prostitute (Ezek. 16, esp. 16:12). The whore's forehead is not the exclusive property of biblical females, however. Goliath seems to have had it when David "smote the Philistine in his forehead, that the stone sank into his forehead" (1 Sam. 17:49). By associating a Philistine's forehead with a stone, David is in effect establishing the connection between false (or natural) religion, harlotry, and the externalized brain that Blake locates in the line of imagery stretching from Aaron to the great whore of Revelation. The mighty devil of *The Marriage* etches on such foreheads, "melting apparent surfaces away" with his corrosives, "and displaying the infinite which was hid" (pl. 14, E 39). As there are two opposed kinds of engraving on the heart—one that turns it to stone and another that frees it from stone—there is a signet that stamps the forehead with sin and blame and another that frees it with forgiveness. Here again the artistic meaning of the biblical texts must be read out from under the religious surface. When Blake wrote out his late illustrated manuscript of Genesis, he used the King James version of the text with few changes. But Genesis 4:15, "And the Lord put a mark on Cain," becomes "And the Lord set a mark upon Cain's forehead," and a chapter heading is invented to match: "Chapter IV How Generation & Death took Possession of the Natural Man & of the Forgiveness of Sins written upon the Murderers Forehead" (E 688). The forgiveness of sins is written upon Cain's forehead because forgiveness is an act of imagination, a mental act, and therefore in Blake's terms ultimately an artistic act. Ezekiel reports a vision of God calling "to the man clothed with linen, which had the writer's inkhorn by his side," saying "Go . . . and set a mark upon the foreheads" of those who mourn the fate of Jerusalem (9:3–4). In the priestly tradition they are the "remnant" of the righteous; in the artistic tradition they are the remnant of those who are imaginative enough to forgive sins—both their own and others'. In Revelation the implicit opposition between the two kinds of forehead engravings becomes explicit in the distinction between those who bear the mark of the beast (as in 14:9) and those who have the "seal of God in their foreheads" (as in 7:3, 9:4).[23]

Heart, mind, and the new body. Moses climbed Sinai to divide himself in secret. The engraving he produced was an act not of animation or expression but of externalization. Moses did not say of his engraving "here am I" but "here is God." As long as deity remains out of mind, the best the mind can produce is lifeless imitation of nature skillfully ornamented. Projection piles on projection, ark on tablets, temple on ark, palace beside temple, king beside priest, like an enormous sepulchral monument. As the coherence of human identity, centered in imagination, disintegrates, its projections withdraw and coalesce. What was once the identity organized by its imagination becomes a mutilated human body, its parts scattered through nature. In the priestly tradition the dismemberment of Israel punishes disobedience to the Law: "Thus saith the Lord God; . . . I have cast them far off among the heathen . . . I have scattered them among the countries" (Ezek. 11:16). The artistic tradition recognizes in the engraved stones of the Law the archetype of counter-art. The Old Testament thus narrates the history of self-division from which other divisions follow. Once the self is exiled in nature, there is no reason for the movement outward to stop at the king of Israel, and every reason to expect it to continue to the very limits of This World that Blake calls the limits of opacity and contraction. The priestly

[23] Strutt 2:11, 12 relates the signet that stamps the foreheads of the elect in Revelation to the history of engraving.

tradition interprets this history as a dialectic of obedience and disobedience, which the artistic tradition recognizes as "negations." True contraries emanate only from coherent identities: my vision versus yours. If Jesus comes to restore identity in the shape of an integrated human body, what Jesus—like any true artist—really writes on the heart of the Pharisee is his imagination. He is the deity trying to move back into the heart that projected it: "to be strengthened with might by his Spirit in the inner man; that Christ may dwell in your hearts by faith" (Eph. 3:16–17; cf. Gal. 4:6, Mark 4:14–17). Thus the tradition represented in the *Similitudes of Enoch* is true gospel: that when Enoch sees the Son of Man he is seeing the righteous form of himself, "righteous" here being the moralized form of "imaginative." A Pharisee who returns Jesus to his heart will become an ancient poet. Jesus is the reintegrated identity of Moses, as "poet" is reintegrated "priest."

The reintegration extends not only to hearts but also to minds: "This is the [new] covenant . . . I will put my laws into their hearts, and in their minds will I write them." We must read Paul as Paul is reading Jeremiah, in the spiritual sense. In a Blakean reading of his text, Paul understands that the Fall was an act of forgetting where all deities reside. When people, believing in a projected god, forget who they are, this god suddenly seems to acquire the ability to remember every sin. Salvation from the Fall will come as an act of remembrance. As they remember who they are, their god's memory accordingly fails: "And their sins and iniquities will I remember no more" (Heb. 10:17; cf. Rom. 2:15). The book of Revelation uses the image of the engraved forehead to represent rebirth of identity by reinternalization of Jesus in the mind, accompanied by forgiveness of sin: "And there shall be no more curse . . . and [the Lamb's] name shall be in their foreheads" (22:3–4). The Blakean plot behind such events is the cranial one specified in *A Vision of the Last Judgment:* "First God Almighty comes with a Thump on the Head"—thus rendering the victim unconscious—"Then Jesus Christ comes with a balm to heal it" (E 565).

In Ezekiel God promises "I will even gather you from the people, and assemble you out of the countries where ye have been scattered, and I will give you the land of Israel. . . . And I will give them one heart, and I will put a new spirit within you . . ." (11:17–19). Once the covenant is reborn in heart and mind and the rod of God's wrath is restored as the expressive tongue of imagination, the body may regain its coherence as the temple of the spirit: "And I saw no temple therein: for the Lord God Almighty and the Lamb are the temple of it" (Rev. 21:22). Paul, speaking to the Greeks from the hill of Mars in Athens, announces that "God . . . dwelleth not in temples made with hands," nor is God something "graven by art," for "in him we live, and move, and have our being; as certain also of your own poets have said" (Acts 17:24, 28–29; cf. Hab. 2:18–20). Paul would be more reluctant to honor the conclusion that Blake has God speak to Jesus: "Thou art a Man God is no more / Thy own humanity learn to adore" (*EG*, E 520). Urizen's temple, like Solomon's and Herod's, is destroyed to be replaced by the genuine form of all human shelter, the "spontaneous effusion of humanity" as described by Blake to Flaxman, a temple expressed directly by its spirit, or genius. The Mosaic Law has the spirit making rules against the body. As Moses's countertype, Jesus exemplifies the replacement of repression with expression. The devil describes Jesus to the angel in *The Marriage* as an integrated identity whose actions express his thoughts directly: "I tell you," says the devil, "no virtue can exist without breaking these ten commandments: Jesus was all virtue, and acted from impulse: not from rules" (pls. 23–24, E 43).

The Argument

Blake's attempt to introduce religious discourse into English-school discourse has suggestive precedents, some of which have been incorporated in the discussion, such as histories of engraving that trace the invention of the art to the Sinaitic covenant. These precedents, though suggestive, were peripheral. They belonged to a separate realm of cultural mythology that did not come into play when, for instance, serious questions arose about the situation of English art. In English-school discourse the functional ancient history of art was not, of course, biblical but Greek and Roman. Christianity entered the discourse more serviceably in the Italian cycle of the historical analogy. We recall Barry's comparison: as the Greeks had their intellectual arts, so the Italians had "Christian story" that was "derived from intellect" (*Inquiry* 146). Though Barry, as an Irish Catholic painting in England, may have felt either less or more conflicted than his Protestant contemporaries in arriving at a proper modern English equivalent to Renaissance Italian subject matter, his tendency to make Christian story commensurate with classical story seems typical.

What is unprecedented in Blake's theory, then, is not penetration by religious discourse but deep penetration, all the way to the metaphorical level on which the narratives of religion and art go beyond convergence into coalescence. Is *A Vision of the Last Judgment* a description of a painting about religion or about art—a history of art and science, as Blake says? Here the difference between religion figured in artistic terms and art figured in religious terms is only, as we say, a matter of point of view. The hierarchy of priorities has been leveled to such an extent that tenor and vehicle often seem interchangeable. The principal metaphors and oppositions that organize this doubled discourse have been so much the common currency of Blake criticism since the publication of Frye's *Fearful Symmetry* in 1947 that they sometimes seem in danger of disappearing from overexposure. Their significance, however, has barely been tapped, and a brief review is in order.

At the core is Blake's identification of the divine and the human:

God Appears & God is Light
To those poor Souls who dwell in Night
But does a Human Form Display
To those who Dwell in Realms of Day
[*EG*, E 493]

As this extract indicates, the metaphor of the human-divine is confrontational: it contests the opposition out of which it is itself constructed. In this instance Blake assigns the opposition to those who live in darkness; those more enlightened get the metaphor. Perhaps its most interesting feature is its length, which is extended considerably beyond the usual two terms into a verbal queue. If God is human, human is also Jesus: "man or humanity . . . is Jesus the Saviour" (*DC*, E 536). And Jesus is the imagination: "the Divine body of the Saviour . . . The Human Imagination" (*DC*, E 555). "Imagination or the Human Eternal Body in Every Man" modulates easily to "Imagination or the Divine Body in Every Man" because "Man is All Imagination God is Man & exists in us and we in him" (anno. Berkeley, E 663–64). Although these metaphors proliferate after Blake's return from Felpham in 1803, he uses them at least as early as 1788 in the tractates *All Religions Are One* and *There Is No Natural Religion* and the annotations to Swedenborg's *Divine Love and Divine Wisdom* ("the Poetic Genius which is the Lord," "God is a man," E 603).

Perhaps the most concentrated statement of this string of identifications appears in the aphoristic *Laocoön* (c. 1820 or later; E 273):

The Eternal Body of Man is The **Imagination.**
God himself
that is . . . **Jesus** we are his Members
The Divine Body

The typographically reinforced identification of Jesus with human imagination authorizes numerous further identifications. Jesus with human artists: "Jesus & his Apostles & Disciples were all Artists." Christians with artists: "A Poet a Painter a Musician an Architect: the Man / Or Woman who is not one of these is not a Christian." Christianity with art: "Christianity is Art & not Money." Sacred Christian texts with texts about art: "The Old & New Testaments are the Great Code of Art." Thus it becomes possible to speak of "Hebrew Art" and Jesus's "Works" of art, and of religious discipline as artistic training: "Prayer is the Study of Art / Praise is the Practise of Art / Fasting &c. all relate to Art." Sacred history becomes a coded history of ancient art: in the Old Testament "Israel deliverd from Egypt is Art deliverd from Nature & Imitation" in a "Spiritual War"; in the New Testament, as suggested in the opening of Revelation, the artistic works of Jesus and his apostles "were destroyd by the Seven Angels of the Seven Churches in Asia. Antichrist Science." Insofar as Jesus's life is a model for all human lives and the history of Israel an archetype of human history, the history of art and artists is "Preservd by the Saviours Mercy" (*VLJ*, E 555) in the Bible.

The conflict that propels such narratives derives from metaphors arranged in oppositions. I have already mentioned several in passing: Christianity versus money, Israel versus Egypt, art versus science. The history of art is narrated as a running encounter of the chosen people of God with God and God's enemies (at the collective level), of the individual Christian with God (at the psychological level, where Jesus is imagination), and so on. The biblical opponents of Israel and Israel's God, of Jesus, and of the early Christians "are" the opponents of art, "Divine Union Deriding And Denying Immediate Communion with God." Israel, then, versus "Egypt . . . Babylon." Israel's God versus "Gods of the Heathen," "The Gods of Greece & Egypt," who "were Mathematical Diagrams." Jesus versus those "States in which all Visionary Men are accounted Mad Men such are Greece & Rome." Christians versus "Caesar or Empire or Natural Religion." Against the visionary, the imaginative, the spiritual, the human, the artistic are set money ("Where any view of Money exists Art cannot be carried on, but War only . . . by pretences to the Two Impossibilities Chastity & Abstinence Gods of the Heathen") and its cohort law or morality ("If Morality was Christianity Socrates was the Saviour"), nature (". . . the Powers of this World. Goddess, Nature," who is "Satans Wife . . . War & Misery"), and science ("**Science** is the Tree of **Death / Art** is the Tree of **Life**"). Insofar as Jews and Christians are their own worst enemies, as the prophets and Paul are sometimes inclined to characterize them, the oppositions may divide not one nation from another but a nation, a history, or a mind from itself, generating another kind of opposition: the Old versus the New Testament, Jews versus Christians, Law versus Gospel, Moses versus Jesus, false prophets versus true. A central metaphor—take "**GOD is Jesus**"—may, as we have seen, become an opposition: ". . . the Son O how unlike the Father First God Almighty comes with a Thump on the Head Then Jesus Christ comes with a balm to heal it" (*VLJ*, E 565; all other unidentified quotations above, *Laocoön*, E 273–75). And we could extend the list considerably.

Constructed as it is from such metaphors and oppositions, Blake's history of art develops several features that deviate from the norm of English-school art history. Since his historical point of reference is biblical, and since he takes over from the Old and New Testaments their hostility toward the Greeks and Romans (as in the symbolic identification of Rome with Babylon), his theory of art is powerfully anticlassical. Thus "What Jesus came to Remove was the Heathen or Platonic Philosophy which blinds the Eye of Imagination The Real Man" (anno. Berkeley, E 664). Though Blake's anticlassicism became more explicit and elaborate after his Felpham years (1800–1803), the way was thoroughly prepared beforehand. There was no route by which George Cumberland's brand of neoclassicism could enter Blake's thought in the 1790s, for instance, that did not require translation into the lexicon, categories, and priorities of Christian discourse.

Consequently, when it came to creating a history of art, Blake was likely to depend to a certain extent upon the opposition between Christian and pagan, true art (as true Christianity) versus classical art, and to depend upon Christian formulas for working the plot toward resolution. There being no ready-made Christian theory of art to oppose to classical, Blake seems to have concocted one allegorically, as it were, from religious discourse (thus Jesus is imagination) and from neoclassical theories viewed antagonistically. That is, the terms of Blake's discourse derive partly from analogy with Christian doctrine, but also partly from opposition to neoclassicism. The spirit of opposition is not a superficial feature of Blake's thought: in a profound sense Christian art is whatever neoclassical art is not. And it is the opposition to neoclassical aesthetics that brings Blake into the romantic camp, but from an odd angle of approach.

In his search for Christian oppositions to classical artistic values, he ends up with values extracted from a burgeoning romanticism that he identifies with Christian values that have no specifically artistic referent. If a central tenet of neoclassical aesthetics is some variation on *the imitation of nature,* what is its Christian counterpart? Blake brings the oppositions into line—virtually into existence—by working not with Christianity but against neoclassicism: thus *the original expression of imagination,* which out of its Blakean context lacks religious resonance.

The opposition between the two gives us the

starting point of a dialectical history that, in its fullest form, would begin with one term, fall into a phase of conflict between the two terms ending in temporary victory for the second, and finally end in reconquest of the second by the first. That is indeed the simple symmetry of Blake's history of art. The complicating factor lies at the heart of the opposition itself, which is not, strictly speaking, an opposition but a dependent relation. The second term, imitation, names not only its difference from the first term but also its likeness. Originality, as Blake wants to conceive it, is freestanding. Imitation, however, cannot be originality's freestanding antagonist: the imitation, with only the original to imitate, depends for its existence upon the original: "those wonderful originals called in the Sacred Scriptures the Cherubim, . . . being originals from which the Greeks and Hetrurians copied Hercules Farnese, Venus of Medicis, Apollo Belvidere, and all the grand works of ancient art." This narrative kernel transfers readily to poetry: "No man can believe that either Homer's Mythology, or Ovid's, were the production of Greece, or of Latium; neither will any one believe, that the Greek statues, as they are called, were the invention of Greek Artists. . . . The Greek Muses are daughters of Mnemosyne, or Memory, and not of Inspiration or Imagination . . ." (*DC*, E 531).

Understanding this involution is essential to following the twists and turns of antagonistic relations in Blake's narratives, where the antagonism oftens depends as much on likeness as on difference. The antagonists are "plagiaries . . . lame imitators of lines drawn by their predecessors" (*DC*, E 550). Sacred history read as a history of imitation thus reports "the Poetry of the Heathen Stolen & Perverted from the Bible not by Chance but by design by the Kings of Persia and their Generals The Greek Heroes & lastly by The Romans" (inscription, E 689). In the English analogue, "England will never rival Italy while we servilely copy. What the Wise Italians . . . abhorred. . . . The Greatest part of what are calld in England Old Pictures are Oil Colour Copies from Fresco Originals" (*PA*, E 578). Imitation-as-stealing produces the difference between owner and thief but also the likeness conferred by the stolen object, while imitation-as-perversion attempts to turn sameness into difference. Greece and Persia imitate Hebrew art until the corporeal replaces the intellectual, but then the replacement is thoroughly complicated by the underlying congruence: classical art is the negation, or corporeal allegory, of Christian.

The dependent relation of imitation upon originality that is characteristic of Blake's art history shows up in several other ways. It bears, for example, a large part of the blame for making his verbal and visual narratives difficult to follow. Since all parties speak the same, or imitations of the same, languages, confrontations often seem to be staged in a hall of mirrors where lookalike, soundalike opponents challenge Blake's powers of representation and ours of discrimination. The antagonism, furthermore, seldom takes the form of direct conflict. Contraries, Blake's name for honest opposition, do not drive his plots. The strife of contraries is the desirable state that ultimately emerges from the resolution of the quite different kind of conflict typical of these plots: not action, we might say, but imitated action, such as subversion and seduction, the conspiracies of plagiarists and hypocrites, false artists, false prophets, false friends. And as this logic suggests, Blake's version of English-school history is emphatically conspiratorial—a Christian analogue being the schemes directed against Jesus by hypocritical Romans secretly in league with hypocritical priests who patronize a double cross by a member of Jesus's inner circle. In Blake's history of art, the relation of imitation to originality shows up repeatedly in his analysis of events, most memorably perhaps in the distinction he eventually learned to make between spiritual and corporeal friends: ". . . if a Man is the Enemy of my Spiritual Life while he pretends to be the Friend of my Corporeal. he is a Real Enemy—but the Man may be the friend of my Spiritual Life while he seems the Enemy of my Corporeal but Not Vice Versa" (to Butts, 25 April 1803, E 728). At one level spiritual and corporeal, like original and imitation, are the most opposed of opposites, while simultaneously they are analogues. No narrative that attempts to report the episodes of such a relationship will be easy to follow.

Again we want to note the logic of sameness-with-difference that produces this typically Blakean imagery of simulation, impersonation, mimicry, parody, and fraudulence. Especially during his periods of greatest stress and isolation, Blake often projects the imagery into a Christian romance with himself as artist-hero who has "traveld thro Perils & Darkness not unlike a Champion I have Conquerd and shall still Go on Conquering Nothing can withstand the fury of my Course among the Stars of God & in the Abysses of the Accuser" (to Butts, 22 November 1802, E 720; cf. E 729). While such statements ring with an apparent confidence that strikes some readers as self-righteousness, this is not Roland but Redcrosse or Christian speaking, a hero whose most dangerous challenges are intellectual and frequently internal. Corruption from within, becoming what he beholds, becoming the spiritual enemy of himself, are recurrent terrors that undermine Blake's self-possession with a powerful strain of self-doubt.

The standard English-school history, based on an aesthetics of imitation, emphasizes a pattern of gradual acquisition—of tastes, of skills. Blake submits instead a pattern of restoration to an original state, emphasizing the abrupt reversals of Christian discourse. Losing and relocating as problem and solution respectively are typical of Blake's art history, which tends to narrate problems in verbal metaphors that admit of solution through equal and opposite acts of redoing—rebirth, renewal, remembrance, return—to get back to a starting point. Biblical analogues come readily to mind, the return to Jerusalem being only the most obvious of geographic ones. Individualized and internalized on a Christian model, the crucial act is often the kind that happens in a flash, even if the preparation takes a lifetime. "Ye must be born again": the pattern tends to be nonacquisitional and nonprogressive insofar as the highest values are tied to broad notions of originality: what was there first, in the individual, in the group, in history.

If the standard English-school analysis of England's arts crisis imagines that local historical interruptions have impeded the pattern of acquisition that made the successes of continental painting possible and accordingly envisions solutions that reestablish broken continuities and progressions, Blake uses the Christian elements in his discourse to conceive the problem differently. Thus he organizes his *Public Address* around the claim that engraving is "lost" in England. Having lost what we had originally, we must find it again. When we do, it will be, in the special sense authorized by Blake's discourse, authentically original. The horizontal and vertical vectors of originality, the originality of historical origins and the originality of this act at this moment, are never independent. Blakean originality names the intersection of the two. Hence he advertises his 1809 exhibition "of *Paintings in Fresco*" as "Poetical and Historical Inventions" and boasts Edison-like of a technical innovation, "*The invention of a portable Fresco*," while revealing simultaneously that "the Art [of fresco] has been lost: I have recovered it." Similarly, creating "real Art" based on "THE grand style of Art restored" makes Blake "an Original Artist" whose ideas of art deserve the name "Original Conceptions" (advertisements, E 526–28) and whose original poems are "of the highest antiquity" (*DC*, E 542). For the most part he used "originality" to mean the -ality of working from the origin of significance rather than from belated copies of it, and he identified this way of working with particular artists (in the broad sense)—Milton, Shakespeare, Dürer, Michelangelo, Raphael, Fuseli, and "even" Hogarth, as he usually says. Insofar as originality of this type is conceived in temporal and spatial terms, then, the search for it will be predominantly in reverse, to get back to beginnings mistakenly abandoned.

Between the original act and the symmetrical act of recovery is what? Originals cannot just be forgotten in the wake of progress, as ignorance can be left behind by education, because imitations depend on remembering originals as hypocrisy depends on remembering sincerity: "Search O ye rich and powerful, for these men and obey their counsel, then shall the golden age return," he says of Chaucer's Parson. "But alas! you will not easily distinguish him from the Friar or the Pardoner . . ." (*DC*, E 535). Thus between original and recovery is perversion: "Fresco Painting, as it is now practised, is like most other things, the contrary of what it pretends to be" (advertisements, E 527). In such an age, painting fresco right has to be like reading the Bible right, an inversion or reversal.

This requirement is more consequential than it may seem. English-school discourse generally imagines the history of national art as a matter of being on or off the path of acquisition, not unlike being in or out of school, and indeed in these terms a knowledge of painting is a kind of literacy. Blake's history is much more symmetrical, because the periods of lost art imitate and pervert the periods of authenticity: they "turn allegoric and mental signification into corporeal command" (*DC*, E 543), and if *turn* (as if from God) is the problem, *re*turn (as if to his bosom) is the solution: "The Stolen and Perverted Writings of Homer & Ovid: of Plato & Cicero. which all Men ought to contemn: are set up by artifice against the Sublime of the Bible. but when the New Age is at leisure to Pronounce; all will be set right" (*Milton* pl. 1, E 95). The complication, however, lurks in the Christian paradox by which sin is totally different from and yet uncannily like virtue. Nothing can be less like originality than imitation, and yet the best imitation is an exact replica of the original. Blake began to explore the paradox at least as early as the paired *Songs of Innocence and of Experience* and the inversions of *The Marriage of Heaven and Hell*, and the fascination was lifelong. In his art history the paradox shows up in the form we have traced. To the extent that its roots are in Christian discourse, it not only loads his art history with the terminology of theft, depravity, and corruption, and promotes narratives of conspiracy rather than negligence, but also raises the stakes: art is not (merely) a part or even the pinnacle of education or civility; art brings salvation, and salvation must be won against powerful forces that work aggressively to prevent it, "not by Chance but by design."

In an unfinished Notebook poem Blake imagines himself being appointed at birth the hero charged with the renewal of British art:

Now Art has lost its mental Charms
France shall subdue the World in Arms
So spoke an Angel at my birth
Then said Descend thou upon Earth
Renew the Arts on Britains Shore
And France shall fall down & adore
With works of Art their Armies meet
And War shall sink beneath thy feet
But if thy Nation Arts refuse
And if they scorn the immortal Muse
France shall the arts of Peace restore
And save thee from the Ungrateful shore

Spirit who lovst Brittannias Isle
Round which the Fiends of Commerce smile
[Unfinished]

[E 479]

Common features of English-school discourse dominate: the absence of art in Britain construed as a major cultural problem, the problem formulated through opposition to and emulation of the continent, a special association of Britain with the "Fiends of Commerce," a declared lack of respect for the arts on Britain's "Ungrateful shore," and yet the anticipation of a possibly favorable outcome. But Blake has (characteristically) incorporated these elements into a plot of losing versus finding the "mental Charms" that British art originally possessed. He has doubled that opposition with an equally characteristic one between intellectual and corporeal warfare, associating British art with the former and continental militancy with the latter—in effect refusing the standard polemical correlation between recently demonstrated British military accomplishment and potential artistic accomplishment. Further Christian elements in Blake's discourse authorize the organization of these oppositions into a narrative analogous to the conversion of the heathen (in Boydell's terms the vandals), his vision of peaceful Britain conquering the invading warriors with art: "With works of Art their Armies meet." The opposition between art and commerce that seems to be surfacing in the fragmentary second stanza is authorized in turn by the opposition of God and Mammon. If commerce gets in the way of the prophesied salvation of Britannia's isle, then Blake's angel will leave Britain to the merchants and rescue Blake and France instead. Though "Now Art has lost its mental Charms" is certainly a product of the Napoleonic period, I know of no historical basis for Blake's thought that he might be saved by France if Britain lets him down. But the myth of the discourse here merges God's threats to abandon his chosen people—for serving false gods such as Mammon—with Christian universalism, by which missionaries of one nation might convert the natives of any other to a metanational faith.

Blake's inclination toward a historical narrative that proposes returns to origins raises the question of their nature. The closest English-school discourse ordinarily comes to writing such returns into art history is in the very high estimate it places on Greek and Italian art: the higher the estimate, one might say, the intenser the desire to identify the Greek or Italian cycle with the projected English one. And we have seen how Barry, for instance, prefaced the pattern of gradual acquisition that controls most of his history with a fantasy of original Greek accomplishment in which the total possible progress of art is adumbrated by one master art during one historical era. Only with considerable exaggeration, however, could we say that (in Barry's terms) all true art attempts to return to this origin. In fact the identification of modern British with ancient Greek art ordinarily remains latent. English-school narratives recall the Greek, Hellenistic, Roman, and Italian models as sources of ideals rather than as origins to which the narratives seek to return.

Blake, as we would expect, is less inhibited in pursuing these metaphorical potentials, and indeed the identification of past origins with desired future results is utterly typical of his way of structuring narrative histories. (So strong is this characteristic that he is capable of identifying all past origins with one another and with all future results, thus conferring on his work the everything-is-everything quality to which readers have sometimes objected.) If English art has lost its mental charms, it will find them again at the origins of its own history. Blake builds his histories from origin to origin, as it were, in parallel layers stacked like the floors of a building. The areas farthest from the stairs correspond to least originality, and the area adjacent to the stairs corresponds to greatest originality on that floor; the area of greatest originality is also the area in closest communication with other floors. Occupying such an area, pilgrims communicate with originality in other areas—at analogous points on other floors. The resulting pattern of arts history is potentially, at least, a teletransportation network through which original artists from different levels can exchange views, as in Milton's visits with Blake.

Early in his career Blake formulates alternative descriptions of such patterns, notably in *The Marriage of Heaven and Hell,* plates 16 (the caves in the chambers of the printing house in hell) and 17–20 (the vision of Western intellectual history in abysses, pits, seven houses of brick, and so on), prefaced by a declaration of return to paradise ("For the cherub with his flaming sword is hereby commanded to leave his guard at the tree of life"). All three episodes, plus the Memorable Fancy of the "ancient Poets" that introduces them in turn, strongly suggest that history, which may sometimes seem to be a political or military or religious history, is more fundamentally an arts history in which Blake's most distinctive medium, "printing in the infernal method, by corrosives" (E 39–43), can play a role as master art. (Noting that *The Marriage* is, after all, satirical and the picturesque use of illuminated printing opportunistic should not deter us from acknowledging that the pattern is nonetheless characteristic.)

Let us trace, from the here and now down through the passages of communication I have described, some key moments in the history of originality that supports Blake's art history.

The present. Blake locates present-day originality in the "genius" of individual artists, of whom he is one. Thus his sublime boast: "It is not the want of genius, that can hereafter be laid to our charge"—not *genius,* we know, but *opportunity*—"the Artist who has done these Pictures and Drawings will take care of that" (*DC,* E 549). Every individual has a history, however, that recapitulates the history of originality: "I have recollected all my scatterd thoughts on Art & resumed my primitive & original ways of Execution in both painting & Engraving. which in the confusion of London I had very much lost & obliterated from my mind" (to Butts, 10 January 1803, E 724). (As we shall see, the history of originality is to a large extent *only* a history of equal individual geniuses.) Here, recollecting the scattered and resuming the lost and obliterated are Blake's ways of opening an escape from the crisis of the Felpham years—and the escape is, typically, back to the future.

The juncture of old and new English art. When we consider how deeply indebted to metaphor are Blake's habits of thought, it is not surprising to find his histories of art structured as a sequence of analogous narratives, each potentially identifiable with the others: "it is the same with Individuals as Nations . . ." (*VLJ*, E 561). If "In this Plate M^r^ B has resumed the style with which he set out in life . . ." (*PA*, E 572), analogously, English engraving, now lost, should resume the style with which it set out in life, the style now best appreciated by "the admirers of old English Portraits" (*PA*, E 577; also 572). Here at the division between old and new English art Blake's history intersects with the discourse of Protestant republican dissent. Hence he injects the theme of moral decay (coordinated with a kind of visual decay) into the account of his Chaucer painting. Chaucer's description of the Prioress is "very elegant, and was the beauty of our ancestors, till after Elizabeth's time, when" (with the accession of the Stuarts) "voluptuousness and folly began to be accounted beautiful" (*DC*, E 533). We follow the decline through the Stuarts to the artistic turning point: "the Enterance of Vandyke & Rubens into this Country"—during the reign of Charles I—"since which English Engraving is Lost" (*PA*, E 572). Thus, retracing the logic that led to civil war, Blake can imagine himself in the role of "Mental Prince" pronouncing Charles guilty of "Mental High Treason" and ordering his intellectual beheading (*PA*, E 580). (Blake is Milton's mental confederate.) He shares the English-school view that the local history of art has been tragically interrupted, and his version is perhaps closest to the anti-Catholic history that blames continental intruders for thwarting the development of an indigenous school. Blake translates the Puritan opposition between the true Gospel religion of the Holy Spirit and the false popish religion of the fleshly Stuarts into an opposition between the corporeal values of false art (represented by Charles and his favorite artists) and the mental values of true art (represented, though obviously not very well, by the old English portraits).

Old English art. The history of pre-Stuart English art being a history of sustained foreign invasion that left little if anything of an English school to idealize, Blake necessarily tends to move to the art history of other nations for instances of the "original" engraving that lost English art must find. (In the *Public Address* he bridges the gap in the history of English art by drawing freely on examples from literature, where the ample history of pre-Restoration English poetry supplies the lack of visual art, with Dryden as Rubens's counterpart in the decline.) Of the modern continental schools it is nearly safe to say, on the basis of limited available evidence, that for Blake they are analogous to each other and to English art. The underlying analogous relation encourages him to declare, for instance, "Note I include the Germans in the Florentine School" (anno. Reynolds, E 662). At a higher level of generalization, English art is a microcosm of the continental schools taken together, such that the Dutch, Flemish, and Venetian schools are analogous to what Blake sees as the dominant faction of the English school, while the German, Florentine, and Roman schools are analogous to the faction that he is trying to bring into existence with the preface to *Milton.*

While of course Blake can make historical distinctions, they can always be overridden by totalizations, and those can always be expanded through metaphor and analogy. When, during his 1809 exhibition, Blake writes Ozias Humphry that "Florentine & Venetian Art cannot exist together Till the Venetian & Flemish are destroyd the Florentine & Roman cannot Exist, This will be shortly accomplishd" (E 770), we understand that Venetian art and Flemish art "are" one another and "are" also the English art Blake wants to eliminate, while the Florentine "is" the Roman, which "is" Blake's art on exhibition, "THE grand style of art restored." But further we see that the analogy is not only infinitely extendable but also total, that is, three-dimensional. It invades the line of history that separates then from now, the line of geography that separates there from here, and the line of association that separates them from me. Accordingly a fight to the finish took place (the conditions of the analogy keep us from saying that it originated) in the Florence and Venice of Michelangelo and Titian; the battle continues (following episodically, as if different) *and* repeats itself (as if the same) in the England of Blake and Reynolds; and the battle recurs in the Florence and Venice of Blake's mind: "Venetian and Flemish Demons" and memories of "Pictures of the various Schools possessed his mind . . . tormenting the true Artist, till he leaves the Florentine, and adopts the Venetian practice, or does as Mr. B. has done, has the courage to suffer poverty and disgrace, till he ultimately conquers" (*DC,* E 547).

Again we see the influence of Christian discourse—here behind the formation of Blake's urban analogies to lock two spiritual entities, a Venice-Babylon and a Florence-Jerusalem, in combat aimed at eliminating each other's existence. Blake suspends these analogies in a multileveled network of eternal essences that mirror one another: although they are about origins and departures from origins, they have no determinate existential origin. In that respect my analogy with the stories of a building on a foundation is false. As for foundational origins, it is safer to say that all the analogies are most comprehensively assembled in, even if they do not originate in, the opposition of classical/pagan to Christian/gothic, insofar as Blake is statistically most likely to transform his other metaphors into these categories. With the historical record nearly silent on the subject of old English art, he imagines a "gothic" Christian origin not in painting but in architecture, as in the inscription on his engraving of *Joseph of Arimathea among the Rocks of Albion:* "This is One of the Gothic Artists who Built the Cathedrals in what we call the Dark Ages Wandering about in sheep skins & goat skins of whom the World was not worthy such were the Christians in all Ages" (E 671). This seems to be the point of chronological transition from English to pre-English art history "among The Rocks of Albion," though the phrases "Gothic Artists" and "Christians in all Ages" suggest totalizations strong enough to displace any linear chronology.

"The British Antiquities are now in the Artist's hands; all his visionary contemplations, relating to his own country and its ancient glory, when it was as it again shall be, the source of learning and inspiration" (*DC*, E 542). The farther we trace his history of art from the present moment into the past, the more control Blake's endless loops of analogy exercise over local distinctions. In this quotation from the *Descriptive Catalogue* entry on the (now lost) painting *The Ancient Britons*, the "British Antiquities" that the artist claims to have in his hands turn out to be, upon closer examination, the artist's own "visionary contemplations." "All these things are written in Eden," after all, and "the artist is an inhabitant of that happy country." The antiquities are a "voluminous" poem by William Blake containing "the ancient history of Britain, and the world of Satan and of Adam" in a story of the original "one man, who was fourfold" until he was "self-divided" (*DC*, E 543).

Ancient arts. But as it turns out, the ancient history of Britain is not to be distinguished from other ancient histories. Not only are they equal in importance—"The antiquities of every Nation under Heaven, is no less sacred than that of the Jews"—but "they are the same thing." "All had originally one language, and one religion, this was the religion of Jesus, the everlasting Gospel" (*DC*, E 543). Ultimately the pressure of analogy threatens the opposition even of classical to Christian: "Let it here be Noted that the Greek Fables originated in Spiritual Mystery & Real Vision and Real Visions Which are lost & clouded in Fable & Alegory." Of course there is little if any undermining of Christian hegemony in Blake's willingness to include ancient Greece among the sources of real vision, since his name for that vision is the everlasting Gospel of Jesus. Consequently the texts preserved by the Saviour's mercy as "Genuine" are "the Hebrew Bible & the Greek Gospel," while classical art and learning are "not Inspiration as the Bible is" but a mere "Memory" or imitation of vision (*VLJ*, E 555). The opposition of classical to Christian is hardly collapsed before it is reinstated.

It is worth repeating that Blake's art history properly begins with the break between original and imitation, and their enigmatic antagonism reappears at each stage, as shown in our Christian history of engraving. One might expect the peculiar nature of this antagonism—imitation being the sincerest form of flattery—to diminish the conflict in the narrative, but the stress seems all the greater for the difficulty of disentangling the authentic original from the illusory imitation. Though he shares the English-school sense of cultural crisis in the visual arts, Blake replaces the standard English-school conviction that historical interruptions have prevented English artists from acquiring painting and allied arts with an energetic conspiracy theory.

Conspiracy was not unfamiliar in English-school discourse. Detractors characterized the Academy as an institutional barrier to progress, at worst a front, a whited sepulcher erected by the opposition under the name but only the name of encouragement. It is within such a narrative that Robert Strange blames the Academy for having "given a fatal check to the progress . . . of engraving" (139).[24] For Blake after a point, for Barry at times, and for many other writers on the subject now and then, this counterplot of hypocrisy—the enemy within—became especially important. If we regard the overall structure of English-school discourse as

[24] Strange's narrative of the progress of the art of engraving begins on 131; England comes into the story on 137.

a comic narrative, conspiracy is the form that the blocking forces assume as they approach maximum coherence. To put it another way, the more coherent the activity of the blocking characters is thought to be, the more prominent the conspiratorial element in the plot becomes. And it is considerably more pervasive, in any case, than is generally allowed by those who regard it as a special paranoia reserved for the likes of Barry and Blake, who are in fact only two of many who see something more than coincidence in the misfortunes of English art.

Though conspiracy is a long-lived element of the discourse, its form changes. The earliest variation with which I am acquainted appears as a development of the foreign-artist theme. Hogarth is not the first but certainly the most influential exponent of the view that foreign art and artists are a key to the English artist's dilemma. If they are regarded as simple competitors for the attentions of the public, then they are relatively weak characters and will be eliminated when the English audience is educated out of its ignorance and fickleness. They are more formidable, however, when they appear, as they usually do, in joint conspiratorial ventures with English agents. After 1800 the importance of foreign artists to the conspiracy theme decreases sharply, but the theme itself remains strong, as we were reminded earlier by the frequent references of Hazlitt, Landseer, and Taylor to cliques, cabals, cunning men, and secret machinations.

The later writers are at least as likely as the earlier to locate the roots of neglect—"various talents inadequately exerted, and genius stooping its powers to custom" (Hoare 241)—in corruption and "persecution" (267). Conspiracy becomes a standard part of the explanation for England's slow development. In 1828 J. T. Smith blames the "unprecedented depression" of art sales on "the most glaring misconduct of several speculators" who undermine the "respectable publishers" (2:253). In 1830 Cunningham writes that, though naturally "fame is still the free gift of *the people;*—it was so in Hogarth's time, and it will continue to be so" (1:92), "false instructors" and "mock patrons" (1:193) concoct an artificial economy of supply and demand, respectively, that keeps self-taught native genius out of the market and out of the historical record. Looking back and down from the relatively serene heights of English assurance in 1841, Taylor sees a turbulent history "not merely of unkindness and neglect, but of oppression and wrong," and hazards a conjecture: "It would almost seem as if some systematic plan for that purpose had been laid down, and acted upon by successive governments in England, to discourage the rising talents of the nation in works of art. . . ." He draws the foreign-artist problem into this plot: "Continental charlatans and sycophants were continually imported, to insult the native artists, and deprive them of both character and subsistence. This is the true cause why the arts have been so backward in Britain" (1:xiv–xv).

The strongest negative form of the patron is envisioned by Barry when he tries to communicate the insight that patronage has actually shaped the history of art:

> . . . this business of patronage is so big with delusion, and delusion of the most mischievous and treacherous kind, that I do most ardently wish that some man . . . would, for the public benefit, handle this subject in its full extent. . . . He would meet with matter of the most invidious, malignant kind, and yet so artfully concealed, confounded, and so politi-

> cally enveloped, with the very reverse and most amiable appearances, as would require the utmost effort of his discriminating skill and penetration, before he could strip and drag it into the light in all its native deformity. [*Letter* 41–42]

Barry personifies patronage in its conspiratorial form as a hypocrite to be unmasked and expelled.

The pattern for Blake's aggressive development of the conspiracy theme seems to derive by analogy from Christian narrative. The relation of the antagonists in Blake's narrative is not, as it often is in the mainstream of English-school discourse, the relation of knowledge to ignorance, nor does he characterize the disruptions in his art history as mere interruptions: the disruptions are exploitive and conspiratorial, fully intentional attempts to pretend, prevent, co-opt, and steal. English engraving is not just stymied, failing to progress, but conspired against, blocked through fakery, "What is *Calld* the English Style of Engraving" (my emphasis, *PA,* E 573). Blake's is, furthermore, a fully moralized history, and the force of opposition is not a mere obstacle but a fully motivated enemy—like the Philistines or the armies of Antiochus Epiphanes from the biblical point of view. As the analogue indicates, their kind of imitation aims not at flattery but at idolatry, the displacement of the real vision by the ersatz one. Thus the fierce, exclusive logic: the Venetian must be *destroyed* before the Roman can *exist.*

The opposition of original and imitation is, as I have said, the dynamic principle in Blake's historical narrative, launching it and moving it forward from episode to episode. But Blake's history also contains a static principle, an ahistorical and even antihistorical principle. Writing about the ancient Britons reminds him of the difference between artists who give "the historical fact in its poetical vigour" and historians "who being weakly organized themselves, cannot see either miracle or prodigy" but only a "dull round of probabilities and possibilities." Hume, Gibbon, and Voltaire "cannot with all their artifice, turn or twist one fact or disarrange self evident action and reality. Reasons and opinions concerning acts, are not history. Acts themselves alone are history. . . . Tell me the Acts, O historian, and leave me to reason upon them as I please. . . . His opinions, who does not see spiritual agency, is not worth any man's reading; he who rejects a fact because it is improbable, must reject all History and retain doubts only" (*DC,* E 543–44).

I submit that Blake aims his outrage at the great Enlightenment historians when his object is history itself. The "spiritual agency" that he accuses historians of ignoring is the very principle that converts history into an antihistorical network of self-duplicating analogies. Once the principle of analogy is triggered, it begins to deny the possibility of real change: "Science," or learned skill in painting, "is soon got," Blake says, while genius "never can be acquired but must be Born" (*PA,* E 575). We can see here that perhaps Blake sets out to make a distinction between what can be learned and what cannot and to insist on an interplay between nature and nurture. As he pushes the distinction harder, however—especially, though by no means only, in his annotations to Reynolds—it threatens to freeze into a mutually exclusive opposition that equates all learning with "Thieving from Others" (anno. Reynolds, E 646).

So negative an attitude toward acquisition-in-time is bound to have corollaries in attitudes toward history. When Reynolds wants to affirm that the "DEGREE of excellence [of] GENIUS is different, in different times and different places," Blake retorts, "Never!" When as proof Reynolds adduces the fact that "mankind have often changed their opinion upon this matter [of what constitutes genius and excellence]," Blake again shouts back, "Never!" (anno. Reynolds, E 656). Thinking by analogy as usual, Blake applies the principle universally. Young poets may grow old but, if original, they do not change; they may be "As Replete" with imagination "but Not More Replete" (658). The poet may change for the worse but never for the better; changes for the better can be understood only as rebirths, reversions to the state before change ever began. All intellectual activity, not just art, is covered by this principle because imagination is "the first Principle of Knowledge & its last" (647). If Blake wants to see in himself the same artist young or old, so he wants to see the same thinker: "when very Young" he read Burke, Locke, and Bacon; "on Every one of these Books I wrote my Opinions & on looking them over" many years later "find that my Notes on Reynolds in this Book are exactly Similar" (660). The same principle levels histories: "If Art was Progressive We should have had Mich Angelo's & Rafaels to Succeed & to Improve upon each other But it is not so. Genius dies with its Possessor & comes not again till Another is Born with It" (656). In short, "Ages are All Equal. But Genius is Always Above The Age" (649). Yes, but then all genius is also equal: "I cannot think that Real Poets have any competition None are greatest in the Kingdom of Heaven it is so in Poetry" (anno. Wordsworth, E 665).

In such a scheme, where intellectual change is necessarily a scandal that can be accounted for only as theft and self-betrayal, significant historical difference is assigned entirely to the intellectual crime rate. As the analogy of heaven and poetry in Blake's last comment suggests, this is the conceptual space occupied by sin in Christian discourse, which, at least in the version that Blake is adopting, may see more sinful ages and less but ultimately sees the differences as insignificant in comparison with the really significant differences of soul (original) and body (imitation), heaven and hell, and so on. In natural life the differences may be muddled, but they are always subject to ultimate clarification "Above The Age." Life and history are not an education, not a progression or gradual improvement; they are a trial in which the crime, the antagonists, and the stakes are always the same.

Time corrupts: history brings temporizing, error, and illusion. Though Blake cannot have his recollections and resumptions without history, into his history he incorporates the Christian hope for an end of history and a return to ahistorical stability at a point of origin from which nothing originates that will fundamentally alter the primitive and original ways once they are resumed. Blake deviates from some influential Christian visions of return—to paradise or heaven—in making the origin dynamic, as anyone who reads through the spirited last plates of *Jerusalem* can see. But that dynamism depends profoundly on a permanent equilibrium. "Ye must be born again"—and again and again so that, finally, being-born becomes a condition of dynamism-in-stasis, of fixed process, as it were, coincident with "Vision or Imagination . . . a Representation of what Eternally Exists. Really & Unchangeably" (*VLJ*, E 554). Blake's particular kind of dynamism, figured as "contraries" and the wars of intellect, incorporates no principle of change that would abandon, once and for all, the point of origin—which may be to say it cannot incorporate any historical principle of change whatever. More prudently we might suggest that Blake desires to see all positive historical change under the sign of originality, *as if* it were a return to a state already achieved: not the Enlightenment-style French Evolution but the truly revolutionary resumption of primitive and original ways. This proclivity to lessen the stress of change by calling it a finding of the lost is commonplace, but its formative influence over Blake's narrative structures is exceptional in English-school discourse.

The Alpha of Omega: The Old, the New, and the Original

For Blake, the major disadvantage of his analogical method lies in its tendency to imperil distinctions that he needs to be able to make. The major advantage, however, lies in its ability to create a continuum that would otherwise dissolve into unresolved contradiction. The potential contradiction resides in the two most influential applications of the term "original": to designate a primal historical position—first—and to designate novelty that is sometimes nonhistorical, but when historical, then last, or latest—newest. For convenience we can label these originality_1 and originality_2. As I have argued elsewhere (*Blake's Theory* 193–96), Blake's model here is the doubleness of Christ in Christian discourse, as in representations of the human body of a believer in which Christ can dwell and in alternative representations of a body of Christ of which we are the members, giving us individual function and unified framework. The Protestant emphasis on the individual believer helped to supply whatever the New Testament lacked in that regard. Jesus's claim to be both first and last, alpha and omega, raises the logical incongruities of originality to the status of a mystical paradox, and indeed the two are not contradictory so long as the last is the first of a new historical sequence. But when the element of contradiction is emphasized, then a family of value-laden oppositions is ready to support it: old/new, past/present, regressive/progressive, conservative/radical, and so on, including, of course, original/imitation. A central quandary in Blake's thought is the opposition between original and imitation in combination with the principle of analogy that is always trying, we might say, to assert the identification of original and imitation. The difficulties that Blake and his commentators, I among them, have had with the notion of originality and allied notions of individuality are by-products of his analogical thinking. Blake's plots of fall and redemption attempt simultaneous resolution at all levels of their analogy, psychological, social, and historical—making, in the process, great difficulties for anyone who tries to extract a single-leveled concept of originality from the narratives, and for anyone who tries to determine at which level originality originates. My own view is that it originates not at any one level but in the interplay of them all: Blake's notion of originality is an analogical notion, constituted out of analogy itself, and especially out of the attempt to think believer, community of belief, and eternity at once.

The god-terms in Blake's discourse put the individual and the public, the various and the uniform, on the same continuum, directing the theory simultaneously inward toward self (imagination, Jesus as personal savior) and outward toward a devoted audience (Jerusalem, the body of Jesus), the only place where, if anywhere, claims for the public efficacy of poetry and painting can be registered. The very centrality of religion in Blake's discourse points it toward the past, even toward civic humanism, while his manner of employing the metaphorical structures of religion points him toward the future, even toward bourgeois individualism. Theories that have polar extremes of private and public seem quite characteristic of romanticism, driven to envision audiences consisting of intimate intellectual friends, or perhaps of no one at all, but simultaneously driven to make vast claims for the public efficacy of poetry as comprehensive knowledge.

Blake's interest in framing the paradox of identity, with a mind to visions of individuation-in-community, goes back at least as far as the 1780s, to his earliest extant annotations. Lavater says, "1. Know, in the first place, that mankind agree as to essence, as they do in their limbs and senses. 2. Mankind differ as much in essence as they do in form, limbs, and senses—and only so, and not more." Blake responds, "This is true Christian philosophy far above all abstraction" (anno. Lavater, E 583–84). About the same time he tries to apply this twofold principle to artistic differences: individually, "As all men are alike in outward form, So (and with the same infinite variety) all are alike in the Poetic Genius"; collectively, "The Religions of all Nations are derived from each Nations different reception of the Poetic Genius . . ." (*All Religions Are One,* E 1). He is profoundly uncomfortable with reductions to a single essence when no provision is made for significant differences. When Swedenborg booms, "What Person of Sound Reason doth not perceive, that the Divine is not divisible; . . .—is not one and the same Essence but one and the same Identity?" Blake prefers to imagine a one that can be many: "Answer Essence is not Identity but from Essence proceeds Identity & from one Essence may proceed many Identities as from one Affection may proceed. many thoughts Surely this is an oversight. . . . If the Essence was the same *as the* Identity there could be but one Identity. which is false / Heaven would upon this plan be but a Clock but one & the same Essence is therefore Essence & not Identity" (anno. Swedenborg, E 604).

As Blake would have it, the flexibility to see one in many and many in one is characteristic of the imagination, vision, and eternity: "such was the variation of Time & Space / Which vary according as the Organs of Perception vary & they walked / To & fro in Eternity as One Man reflecting each in each & clearly seen / And seeing: according to fitness & order" (*J* 98.37–40, E 258). The individual and the collective are on the same continuum, such that "General Forms have their vitality in Particulars: & every / Particular is a Man; a Divine Member of the Divine Jesus" (*J* 91.29–30, E 251).

What is needed to make better sense of Blake is a notion of self sufficiently enriched to participate in the private-public continuum that romantic writers were attempting, stressfully and not without contradiction, to imagine. Blake conceives a deep individual life connected to a deep collective life: a class, and individual members of the class. Perhaps we can see what a Blakean version of such an enrichment looks like by examining an attempt to imagine "eternity." We find paragons not of sameness but of difference, narrated as intellectual wars of eternity in fourfold visions that can be read on multiple levels, including the individual (emanations, spectres, and zoas as constituents of the mind—"Four Mighty Ones are in every Man" [*FZ* 1.3.5, E 300]—and their actions as mental actions in a psychological history) and the social (the same elements read as social constituents of "Albion . . . Fourfold" [*J* 96.42–43, E 256], with Albion as England, for instance).

While Blake's scheme, like any other, limits differences by schematizing—omitting some differences and incorporating others, and dividing the latter into the legitimate and the illegitimate—his eternity operates on a principle of inclusion that promotes not only difference but opposition, metaphorized as the action of contraries. Jesus tells Albion that "Friendship & Brotherhood" are basic; "without it Man Is Not" (*J* 96:16, E 255). But this is not a friendship of shared lowest common denominators: "I never made friends," says Los, "but by spiritual gifts; / By severe contentions of friendship & the burning fire of thought" (J 91: 16–17, E 251). The differences Blake banishes under the term "negations" seem to be, at least as he thought of them, the differences that aim to destroy contrariety, the ongoing constructive *process* of mental opposition, and thus aim to replace useful difference with a dominance of the same. As Milton tells Ololon,

There is a Negation, & there is a Contrary
The Negation must be destroyd to redeem the
Contraries
The Negation is the Spectre; the Reasoning Power
in Man
This is a false Body. . . .
[*Milton* 40(46):32–35, E 142]

At the level of vision that Blake ranks highest, intellectual opposition is maximized. It is not a technique temporarily employed to achieve a state beyond earth and beyond opposition, as in established Christianity, but an eternal operating principle. And of course it is to flaunt that very contrast with the conventionally Christian vision of heaven—as a permanent rest home for spirits whose conception of intellectual calisthenics is loud singing—that Blake addresses the last chapter of *Jerusalem* "To the Christians" and introduces his eternity at the point where heaven would surface in an analogous Christian narrative. Once the campaign to retake eternity ends and the smoke clears over the battlefield, "the Arrows of Intellect" are still flying and the contentions "in Visionary forms dramatic . . . varying / According to the subject of discourse" (*J* 98.7, E 28–35) are just getting under way. There is indeed an achieved state of eternity or best vision such that we might justifiably speak of *the* vision toward which all Blakean artists strive. But the conformity thus achieved seems less ideological than ecological or architectural—a space where intellectual dissent can be fearlessly amplified. At the site of the original vision, there is no promise of the customary harmony but only the clarified processing of differences.

In the terms of John Barrell's argument for a civic-humanist reading of Blake's theory, which would eradicate the elements of liberal individualism and replace them with collectivities of the civic-humanist sort, individualized originality, pinned to bourgeois notions of self-interest, acquisitiveness, and privacy, must be banished.[25] For Blake, Barrell concludes, "differences among artists . . . are to be regretted and are usually the result of their relative remoteness from their visions of eternity." Since variety in the form of "different viewing positions occupied by each artist" in different relations to "the vision" is not sanctioned in Barrell's version of civic humanism,[26] difference of vision can be understood only as "relative remoteness" from a monolithic "object of vision" seen from "different points along a unilinear approach to eternity" (250). Difference is distance from *the* goal. With only one goal and one approach to it, every difference necessarily becomes a difference of quality, every artist necessarily becomes better or worse than—not just different from or complementary to—every other, and that difference in quality becomes the most important thing about the artist.

In Barrell's construction, then, originality$_1$ is utterly irreconcilable with originality$_2$. Michelangelo and Raphael are the same insofar as they are original. The more authentically Blakean reading is that, insofar as they are the same they possess originality$_1$, access to historical origins, but insofar as they are different they possess originality$_2$, individual originality. They must necessarily possess both, because one of the basic principles of originality$_1$ is a principle of individuation that produces originality$_2$. Historical origins, rather than eliminating individual origins, become the site where they prosper, differentiating intellect from intellect on the axis of contraries. At least as Blake imagines it, the individuality necessary to exercise artistic

[25] Barrell's *Political Theory of Painting* is a major contribution, and an excellent one, to the study of a chronically neglected subject, but the account of Blake is its most vulnerable point. For detailed objections to the latter, along with an appreciative critique of Barrell's book as a whole, see my review in *Studies in Romanticism.* Another fine piece by Barrell, "Sir Joshua Reynolds and the Englishness of English Art," apparently written in 1986 but not published until 1990, came too late to receive due notice here. Though focused on points of coordination between Reynolds's theories and Burke's political arguments, that essay discusses several topics covered in this book, including especially the development of a nationalistic discourse in which the special character of English art might be described and valued.

[26] Barrell locates the coherence of his account of eighteenth-century British writing about painting in a single "discourse of civic humanism" adapted largely from the work of the historian J. G. A. Pocock, whose *Machiavellian Moment: Florentine Political Thought and the Atlantic Republican Tradition* laid the groundwork for sweeping but controversial revisions in modern intellectual and political history, including the history of late eighteenth- and early nineteenth-century European and American radicalism. Historians have increasingly been taking sides on so-called republican theory. In a series of essays and in his book *Republicanism and Bourgeois Radicalism,* Isaac Kramnick has effectively criticized the efforts of Pocock and his followers to read late eighteenth-century politics through civic-humanist spectacles. The debate has tended to pit the liberal-individualist historians against the civic humanists, thus: Were the American Revolution and the Constitution liberal-individualist or civic-humanist causes? In what political discourse or discourses were the terms of the debate set? In a sense Barrell and I thus find ourselves in the position of a civic humanist arguing with a liberal individualist over Blake. I am simplifying a situation that is complicated by many factors, of course, especially by the institutional politics of civic humanism, which has been exploited in fascinating ways by both right and left on the common ground of collectivism. To the left appeals the collectivism that can make structural changes for the common good (and against the interests of powerful private individuals). But the time-honored role of civic humanism as an aristocratic ideology (the citizens of the civic humanist republic are equals, but they stand on the backs of a drone class that labors while a leisured elite devotes its time to "public" business, that is, the business of the elite), its stress on the need for a militia to conduct an effective public defense, and its distinctly nostalgic orientation to the past are only three of the features to suggest that civic humanism finally belongs to the right.

originality paradoxically flourishes only when self-annihilation flourishes (*J* 96, E 255–56).

Individuality is, as it were, real talking and self-annihilation is real listening. As listening is followed by more talking, so self-annihilation is followed by regeneration ("Jesus replied Fear not Albion unless I die thou canst not live / But if I die I shall arise again & thou with me / This is Friendship & Brotherhood without it Man Is Not" [*J* 96.14–16, E 255]). We can return to the language of *The Marriage:* "Thus men forgot that All deities reside in the human breast" and "For man has closed himself up, till he sees all things thro' narrow chinks of his cavern" (pls. 11, 14, E 38, 39) are offered as alternative diagnoses. One calls for a new focus inward and a taking back into the breast, while the other calls for a new opening up to others ("How do you know but that . . . ?").

The combined metaphorical logic is contradictory: if *all* deities are in the human breast, why look elsewhere? If we open the chinks of the human cave wide enough, there will be no cave. Where will the "breast" be, and what will "in" mean? But, as the fable on plate 11 tells it, when deities still resided in the human breasts of ancient poets, they were busy using their enlarged and numerous senses and making languages to communicate with. As dependent as the rhetoric of *The Marriage* is on strong oppositions, here a strong continuum, and even a middle way, emerges. Likewise in the later works: in *Jerusalem* eternity is not a bodiless—caveless—place. Not only are there human forms and not only do they have something to say to each other, but there is no apparent consensus of opinion.

The continuum on which individuality and community exist, associated respectively with originality$_2$ and originality$_1$, is perfectly communicated in the last five lines of *Jerusalem:*

> All Human Forms identified even Tree Metal Earth
> & Stone. all
> Human Forms identified, living going forth &
> returning wearied Into the Planetary lives
> of Years
> Months Days & Hours reposing And then Awaking
> into his Bosom in the Life of Immortality.
> And I heard the Name of their Emanations they
> are named Jerusalem.
> [*J* 99.1–5, E 258–59]

The continuum is disclosed in the doubled meaning of "identified," both difference from and likeness to, having separate identities and being identified with each other. Identity has precisely the duplicity necessary to service Blake's paradigm of a co-present individuality and collectivity with its source not in the ruins of late civic humanism but more likely in the enthusiastic rhetoric of radical Protestantism, "Awaking into his Bosom." Originality$_2$ allows "Human Forms" to *have* identity. Originality$_1$ allows them to be identified.

It is exceedingly difficult if not perverse to erase the celebration of individual expression from Blake's work—"And in Melodious accents I / Will sit me down & Cry. I. I." (*PA*, E 581). So surely does he seem to share the "fundamentally individualistic bias" of Protestantism, which Christopher Hill and many others have connected with the "insistence that each believer should look inward to his own heart" (43), that it seems finally impossible to save Blake from the house of romanticism that individualizes and internalizes Christian discourse with increasing emphasis on psychology, the creative imagination, and the connection of art ("vision") with that mental faculty, pestering older metaphors of divinity in the process: thus Blake's access to "vision" and "eternity" is through the individual imagination, though that original imagination is given status and dignity through its presumed access to ancient originals. It seems equally futile to purge from our image of Blake the elements of modern sensibility that have at times given him a twentieth-century currency that Reynolds, Barry, and Fuseli cannot conceivably be granted. But a point of maximum interest is this very enigmatic combination of apparent eligibility for assimilation with a notable resistance to it. Blake's ideals and his practices are not beyond contradiction or criticism, nor need Blake studies be an endless jubilee for the proto-Freudian-Marxist-Jungian-Joycean guru. For all that, Blake is too uncanny to remain snugly frozen into any theoretical trinity with Reynolds and Barry.

IV TECHNOLOGY
The Artistic Machine

. . . both of us cannot be in our right senses Posterity will judge by our Works.

—William Blake, *Public Address*

One of the most common responses to the aspirations and failures of the Shakespeare Gallery was technical: that the Boydells had undermined their project by resorting to fast, cheap methods of reproduction. On 26 May 1804 Benjamin West complained to Joseph Farington of the "inferior quality" of the prints: "Such a mixture of *dotting* and engraving,—& such a general defficiency in *respect of drawing,* which He observed the Engravers seemed to know little of, that the Volumes presented a mass of works which He did not wonder many subscribers had declined to continue their subscriptions to" (Farington 6:2331). As late as 1839, in an anonymous article in *The Art-Union* titled "The Comparative Merits of Line Engraving and Mezzotinto," that technical strand of anti-Boydell narrative surfaced yet again.

While praising Boydell in the expected general terms, the *Art-Union* piece blames a new export trade for having "created a new class of purchasers" whose demands compelled a "more expeditious method" of engraving—"and hence arose that flood of dotted or stippled prints which overspread the country." The author names the advantages of stipple over conventional "line" engraving. Stipple accepts coloring better, it is faster, and it takes less skill; "and as this mode includes large portions capable of being undertaken by mere mechanics . . . the workshops of Facius, Thew, and Simon were filled with assistants." There was no need to pay trained engravers "to engrave the backgrounds and draperies of dotted prints in London." Workers from the buckle factories of Birmingham would do just as well because "those who could punch holes in silver or brass, could also make holes upon copper" (57). Treated as an episode in the narrative history of English engraving, the *Art-Union*'s treatment of Boydell's techniques of production opens up new areas to inquiry by aligning the history of engraving with the history of technology as well as the history of high art. That is, students of the visual arts, wondering what the engravers were doing for Boydell in London, have not ordinarily thought they also need to wonder what the workers were doing in Birmingham buckle factories.

We can see how technological contexts point up questions of value if we consider the *Art-Union*'s account in the light of two assessments of technique, both standard intellectual subroutines within English-school discourse. The *Art-Union* author draws on a familiar anticommercialism: engraving is being cheapened and multiplied by cost-cutting measures that force it into association with common products and production methods and common workers. Technology is seen as conspiring with economic motivation to increase quantity and degrade quality. A history of engraving oriented by these values is likely to be a narrative of degradation in which an alliance of technology with commerce divides and disperses the original resources of individual artisans. In these terms, a plausible narrative of recovery might emerge from William Morris's program, perhaps with a slogan from Ruskin on the quality of work.

But in an equally familiar context, the same techniques are subject to positive assessment—one that Alderman Boydell might have offered. Adam Smith captures the mood:

> It is the natural effect of improvement, however, to diminish gradually the real price of almost all manufactures. That [price] of the manufacturing workmanship diminishes, perhaps, in all of them without exception. In consequence of better machinery, of greater dexterity [caused by greater specialization], and of a more proper division and distribution of work, all of which are the natural effects of improvement, a much smaller quantity of labour becomes requisite for executing any particular piece of work. . . . [1:260][1]

In a typical history of improvement, economic causes increase technical resources. In a virtuous cycle, new markets, creating new purchasers, spur innovation, which in turn increases productivity and profits and further enlarges the market.

Such an interpretation of technical progress is well supported within English-school discourse. After all, one venerable way of telling the history of engraving is as a record of simultaneous technological and commercial improvement (see Eaves, *Blake's Theory,* for examples). Since commercial success had been a constant object of attention for the English school, it is not surprising that principles friendly to technology had appeared in a range of narratives. As we have seen, James Barry embeds vast stretches of Vasari in his *Inquiry,* offering the Vasari canon and its program of "gradual progress" (90) as a model for the English school. The mountain journey on which painters " 'advance by little and little' " to " 'the top of perfection' " (19–20) is most easily expressed in terms of technical resources and refinements: " 'After Giotto had improved designing, those who wrought in marble grew better also . . .' " (23). There were " 'others, who worked after Giotto, following his air, design, colouring, and manner, though improving upon him in some little degree' " (26–27). Technical advances lead to efficient production: " 'that which is of the *most importance* in this art is, that it is at this day reduced to such perfection, and is so *easy;* for whosoever possesses design, invention, and colouring, that whereas the first masters made a picture in six years, the masters of our days will make six in one year' " (my emphases, 39). Adam Smith would have readily understood Vasari's concept, which plots improvements in quantity and quality on the same curve.

[1] Cf. the earlier no-lose calculation offered by the anonymous author of *Considerations on the East-India Trade* (1701): "Arts, Mills, and Engines, which save the labour of Hands, are ways of doing things with less labour, and consequently with labour of less price, tho' the Wages of Men imploy'd to do them shou'd not be abated" (589).

Blake certainly allied himself with the technical oppositions of the first of these two assessments: in painting, line versus tone and color; in engraving media, line engraving versus the tonal processes (such as stipple, mezzotint, aquatint). Who could forget that "the great and golden rule of art, as well as of life, is this: That the more distinct, sharp, and wirey the bounding line, the more perfect the work of art; and the less keen and sharp, the greater is the evidence of weak imitation, plagiarism, and bungling" (*DC*, E 550)? With most of his high-minded contemporaries, he subscribed to the theory that, as history painting rather than portraiture was the primary generic measure for the most significant visual art, so line rather than color or tone was the primary technical measure. And the merits of the drawn or painted line were usually extended to the engraved line, lending "line engraving" the cachet of history painting in oil.

The hitch, however, comes with the version of the history most often generated—by Hoare, Landseer, and others—in support of line engraving. The heroic trio of that history consists of Woollett, Strange, and Bartolozzi—the late Robert Strange and William Woollett, both survived by the long-lived Francesco Bartolozzi, who died at age 88 in 1815. They are credited with having "universally established," as Hoare said, "the reputation of English Engraving" and turned the export trade in England's favor (260), yet they show up as the chief heavies of the piece for Blake:

> What is Calld the English Style of Engraving such as proceeded from the Toilettes of Woolett & Strange . . . can never produce Character & Expression. I knew the Men intimately from their Intimacy with Basire my Master & knew them both to be heavy lumps of Cunning & Ignorance as their works Shew to all the Continent who Laugh at the Contemptible Pretences of Englishmen to Improve Art before they even know the first Beginnings of Art. [*PA*, E 573]

For Blake, the most interesting features of line engraving and the tonal processes arose not from their plain opposition but from their silent complicity—which is where he learned, as he thought from bitter experience, to fix his attention. His attack on the English school's favorite engravers is provocative but not without reason, and its reasoning involves intricate relations between English-school themes and Blakean variations. Tracing the interplay of the two demands a closer look at Blake's point of reference, the "*Toil*ettes," the toilsome workshop world of materials and organized work coupled, oddly but as we shall see meaningfully, with the feminine and the French. Here the familiar elements of the discourse take explicitly technological forms.

Hence we position ourselves to describe, instead of evolving artistic styles, evolving systems of production and reproduction in which "artistic style" is the name for a certain technical effect and "art" the name for a technology. In this frame of reference we can open up yet another view of Blake's English-school affiliations and at the same time extend the opposition developed in Chapter III: as artistic originality and its imitations find their technologies in line and its imitations, Blake develops a fascinating critique of technology from the position of his individualism.

Addressing a Public

I will concentrate discussion on Blake's so-called *Public Address.* Since it was first extracted in conjectural fragments from Blake's notebook and assembled by D. G. Rossetti for the second volume of Alexander Gilchrist's *Life of William Blake* in 1863, the *Address* has been an enigma. Editors have found in Blake's references to "this Public Address" and "The Chalcographic [i.e., engraving] Society" (*PA,* E 574, 571) tantalizing hints of a real occasion. We now have Dennis Read's groundbreaking 1981 essay, "The Context of Blake's 'Public Address': Cromek and the Chalcographic Society," to thank for documenting the brief existence of a "Chalcographic Society" (E 571) and even an allied "Society for Encouragement of Arts" (E 581) (actually Society for the Encouragement of the Art of Engraving) optimistically modeled in some respects on the plan of the British Institution, founded only five years earlier (Read, "Context" 75). Read offers reasons for supposing that the society had provided the motivation for Blake to imagine himself addressing a group ostentatiously dedicated to the encouragement of English engraving through an ambitious publishing project devised by Robert Cromek: to raise a sum of 17,000 guineas that " 'will enable the Engravers to execute, with their utmost powers, 20 plates, the size of the larger works of Strange and Woollett; making sixteen Historical and four Landscape Subjects, from the choicest Works of the best British and Ancient Masters' " (quoted in Read, "Context" 74). For Read, then, Blake's *Public Address,* though "nominally conceived as an advertisement for his proposed *Canterbury Pilgrims* engraving," is more correctly read as his "most sustained argument against this [society] project" (69).[2]

Though we must acknowledge the key role of this project in the *Public Address,* arguments are easily overcommitted to the claim that "Blake's *first* interest here is in demolishing the high-flown claims of the Chalcographic Society plan" (my emphasis, 80). It is not surprising that Read gets hung up on the "line engraving" problem in general and on Woollett and Strange in particular. He is forced to claim that Blake cannot be logical about these engravers because of "personal grievances" (77).

John Gage, unfortunately unaware of Read's essay, has similarly tried to explain Blake's demonization of Bartolozzi, Woollett, and Strange as a reaction to the Chalcographic Society's prospectus. His argument that debates over style and technique were matters of "cultural politics" and "underpinned by ideology" ("Early Exhibition" 123, 134) is unassailable, but his climactic conclusion that Blake's ideology—his favoring of line engraving over tonal processes—is "more academic than the Academicians" (138) is mistaken for reasons that will become clear in the course of this discussion. The ideology is much deeper than that. Essick's earlier proposal (*Printmaker* 199) that the *Pub-*

[2] See also Read's "The Rival *Canterbury Pilgrims* of Blake and Cromek" and, for the fullest account of the Blake-Cromek-Stothard relationship during this period, Ward's "Canterbury Revisited." These essays should be supplemented by Bentley, "Blake Reconfigured," which argues persuasively against some of Read's and Ward's key points, and by Celina Fox, "The Engravers' Battle," and John Gage, "An Early Exhibition."

lic Address is a defense of original engraving, indicating new or at least renewed commitments on Blake's part that made it easier to attack the idols of the reproductive trade, saw more clearly the broader horizons of Blake's arguments.

A series of articles on the Chalcographic Society project in the *Monthly Magazine* and in Leigh and John Hunt's immensely popular weekly, *The Examiner*—which had earned Blake's hatred for publishing a humiliating, and the only, review of his 1809 exhibition—inspired Landseer himself to respond in a series of public letters,[3] which were answered in *The Examiner* by the third Hunt brother, Robert (who had written the review of Blake's exhibition). For Blake this would have been merely the tip of a polemical iceberg, for much more was no doubt being said in the trade (as in William Sharp's letter to Charles Warren, quoted below). Here again he was joining, not starting, an argument, and one being carried on in the familiar terms of English-school discourse adapted to the ancillary art of engraving. Once again Blake's contribution is most usefully seen not as a unique aberration but as an unauthorized variant.

More than any other of Blake's writings, the *Public Address* makes it clear how central to his defense of originality is a reinterpretation of the history of art that had become a stock property of English-school discourse. In two ways the *Public Address* is one of the many belated responses to the Boydell era. First, the *Address* itself belongs with Landseer's *Lectures* among the anti-Boydell documents: "Whoever looks at any of the Great & Expensive Works of Engraving that have been Publishd by English Traders must feel a Loathing & Disgust & accordingly most Englishmen have a Contempt for Art which is the Greatest Curse that can fall upon a Nation" (*PA*, E 577; cf. "If ye will not hear, and if ye will not lay it to heart, to give glory unto my name, saith the Lord of hosts, I will even send a curse upon you, and I will curse your blessings . . ." [Mal. 2:2]). Blake is the only member of the anti-Boydell faction to track his objections so deeply that they counter, even as they exploit, the standard propositions of the discourse.

Second, unlike Hoare's *Inquiry* or Landseer's *Lectures*, Blake's *Public Address* was conceived as part of a classic commercial initiative of the English school, a project presented as a remedy for the state of English art. An inquiry into the conditions that have produced an apparent artistic crisis is initiated along with an effort to make money from the sale of engraved prints based on an exhibited painting advertised as public examples of what English art ought to be. Like Boydell's Shakespeare, Blake's Chaucer presents a true English subject that evokes the analogy of poetry and painting. Blake's project, more like Barry's than like Boydell's, exemplifies the entrepreneurial strain of English-school commercial endeavor—self-publication, self-exhibition, self-justification.

[3] Read mentions only one, which he was not able to locate (80–81). But in his bibliography Levis lists three, published as two, totaling 77 pages (both 1810).

Arts Counter Arts

> What is most important to him is that I shall be surrounded by impenetrable darkness and that his machinations shall always be concealed from me. . . . His great skill lies in his appearing to humour me while all the time maligning me, and thus giving his perfidy the appearance of generosity.
>
> —Jean-Jacques Rousseau, *Confessions*

> . . . there is a class of men, whose whole art and science is fabricated for the purpose of destroying art.
>
> —William Blake, *A Descriptive Catalogue of Pictures*

One never loses one's initial impression of the *Public Address* as a brainstorming session. But along with the barrage of incautious statements purporting to connect the author's favorite and least favorite painters and engravers with a welter of other topics, including, to name a few, poetry, imagination, imitation, machines, madness, labor, class, commerce, and empire, persistent attention eventually reveals a history of art emerging to structure other elements in the exercise. Blake launches his *Public Address* from the dramatic finding that "Engraving as an Art is Lost in England" (E 572). The public, then, is the English public, and (in typical English-school reasoning) the art is seen as a national art vying with the art of other nations: "Countrymen do not suffer yourselves to be disgracd. . . . England will never rival Italy while we servilely copy . . ." (578). Disgrace and servitude add biblical overtones. Servility suggests both the Egyptian and Babylonian captivities and the tendency of the Israelite captives to "servilely copy" the captor's religion. Jeremiah 14:20–21 expresses the fear of national disgrace: even though we and our fathers have "sinned against thee," say the Israelites, "do not disgrace the throne of thy glory: remember, break not thy covenant with us."

In accounting for the loss of English engraving, Blake remains within the structural parameters of the discourse by which the potential greatness of the school is supposed to have been blocked, with foreign artists the gainers. Accordingly, Blake's story centers on "the Enterance of Vandyke & Rubens into this Country since which English Engraving is Lost" (*PA*, E 572). A position in the structure of the discourse calls for such an explanation, and, as I have indicated, Blake's way of filling it—with a foreign painting-printmaking duo heavily patronized by the Stuarts and their allies—aligns him with the Protestant republican politics of Milton: "If all the Princes in Europe like Louis XIV & Charles the first were to Patronize such Blockheads I William Blake a Mental Prince should decollate & Hang their Souls as Guilty of Mental High Treason" (580).

Blake deepens the political connection. If the "wretched state of the Arts in this Country & in Europe originat[ed] in the Wretched State of Political Science which is the Science of Sciences" (*PA*, E 580), then political and arts histories will share plots, characters, and motivations. Rubens and van Dyck, in this scheme, are less an international team of interior decorators than political operatives. Or rather, their decoration is an ingredient in a larger political operation. In Rubens's mix of painting and politics, "commission" might as well designate a diplomatic mission for the Spanish Habsburg rulers of Flanders as a painting assignment, and often the two came together. As political agent, Rubens is sometimes credited with the peace treaty of 1630 between England and Spain, and Cambridge presented him with an honorary degree for his various services. His erstwhile assistant van Dyck, lured to England on terms generous without precedent, became part of a royalist analogy through which Charles I constructed his patronage: van Dyck would be his court painter as Titian had been Emperor Charles V's. The importation of Rubens and van Dyck was an effort to modernize in one respect—to update the nation's pathetically parochial image hoard—and a new politicization of imagery, the exploitation of foreign artistic traditions to strengthen ties between the English royalist cause and its continental affiliates. In that cause, van Dyck, Titian reborn, became the chief agent of its visualization.[4]

[4] Rubens's diplomatic assignments for the Habsburgs are well known. Commentators have explored the political function of Rubens and van Dyck in the court of Charles I. On van Dyck see Christopher Brown, the best modern account. Especially valuable are chap. 4, "Van Dyck at the Court of Charles I" (137–221), which incorporates good summaries of Charles's interests in Flemish and Venetian painting and of the early development of English portraiture, and chap. 2, "The Italian Years and the Influence of Titian: 1621–1627" (61–99). The Flemish-Venetian-English connection persisted into the Restoration: the design of Charles II's royal entry and coronation were powerfully influenced by Rubens's designs for the royal entry of the Habsburg prince Ferdinand into Antwerp in 1635 (see Ogilby, esp. 11–15). I am grateful to Paula Backscheider for calling my attention to the Ogilby volume.

To this complex politicization and commercialization Blake applies the label "Counter Arts" (*PA*, E 580). The concept is his organized extension of the conspiratorial strains in English-school discourse. Earlier the rather casual paranoia of painters and their promoters affected mood more than plot. Even Barry's deep anxieties had produced only dark suspicions and an offhand proposal for an investigation of the scandal of patronage. Blake gives conspiracy new meaning and force by integrating the counter-arts with the core of his art-historical speculation.

The counter-arts, he maintains, were "Established by Such contemptible Politicians as Louis XIV," who adopted methods "originally set on foot by Venetian Picture traders Music traders & Rhime traders to the destruction of all true art as it is this Day" (*PA*, E 580). Here, then, is Blake's reinterpretation of the internationalism that had been the hallmark of English-school hopes—by which English artists sought membership, as it were, in the extended Vasari canon through a progressive interpretation of Carracci-style eclecticism. In Blake's reading, the entrance of Rubens and van Dyck becomes not a form of "encouragement," the opening of new educational opportunities for British painters that would be tragically closed by the Civil War, but part of a larger European bid to expand commerce, stabilize the monarchy, and block republican reforms. The symbolic elements in the mix are French monarchy and Venetian commerce, and the movement is westward, from Venice to France to England, with Flemish painters as the means of conveyance and a Catholic monarch on the receiving end. With Rubens and van Dyck entered Flemish and, more important, Venetian painting and engraving but also the royalist politics of the continent. This itinerary retraces as it nullifies the westering of culture that had stirred Reynolds's and Barry's optimism for the future of English art.

In the background, as I have intimated, is the biblical pattern of a nation grown internally weak and then betrayed by its own monarchs to foreign intruders following false gods and rejecting the One True God, who finally abandons his people and leaves them under a curse. The entrances from outside are violent incursions by thieves and robbers: "As for the beauty of his ornament, he set it in majesty: but they made the images of their abominations. . . . And I will give it into the hands of the strangers for a prey. . . . My face will I turn also from them, and they shall pollute my secret place: for the robbers shall enter into it, and defile it" (Ezek. 7:20–22). Moreover, adapting another biblical pattern, Blake directs blame at an established order of court, religion, and commerce, while he addresses a public largely outside that circle.

Blake is rendering Charles and his politicized painters with a prophetic eye toward the French Revolution and its English aftermath. There is, as one expects in Blake's histories, both linear continuity and cyclical repetition. On a chronological continuum, the counter-arts survived the Civil War and the Cromwell years, were restored with the monarchy, and have flourished since—even to "this Day."

Blake captures that continuity in such emblematic post-Restoration stories as the one of Nathaniel Lee:

> An Example of these Contrary Arts is given us in the Characters of Milton & Dryden as they are written in a Poem signed with the name of Nat Lee which perhaps he never wrote & perhaps he wrote in a paroxysm of insanity In which it is said that Miltons Poem [*Paradise Lost*] is a rough Unfinishd Piece & Dryden has finishd it Now let Drydens Fall [*The State of Innocence, and Fall of Man: An Opera*, 1677] & Miltons Paradise be read & I will assert that every Body of Understanding must cry out Shame on such Niggling & Poco Piu as Dryden has degraded Milton with But at the same time I will allow that Stupidity will Prefer Dryden because it is in Rhyme & Monotonous Sing Song Sing Song from beginning to end Such are Bartollozzi Woolett & Strange. [*PA*, E 581]

Blake's example is partly structured by the English-school analogy of poetry and painting that had boosted Boydell's Shakespeare project. Most commonly, the analogy asserts the comparability of the two arts in some phase, such as production ("like Fuseli & Michael Angelo Shakespeare & Milton" [576]) or reception ("The English are as Good Judges of Painting as of Poetry" [581]). Boydell had asserted comparability in the phase of transmission, marketing words and pictures in one package. In the present instance the analogy, in a more elaborate contrastive form, underwrites Blake's uninhibited moves across the literary and visual arts: Milton is to Dryden as the "true Style of Art such as Michael Angelo Rafael Jul[io] Rom[ano] Alb[ert] Durer left it" (580) is to Bartolozzi, Woollett, and Strange.

The structure of each side of the ratio in turn derives from the opposition between original and imitation reiterated on the same page of the notebook: "To recover Art has been the business of my life to the Florentine Original & if possible to go beyond that Original. . . . To Imitate I abhore . . ." (*PA*, E 580). On the one hand, Blake uses the analogy of poetry and painting to create a combined linear history of the two arts. On the other hand, the disregard for chronology and geography built into examples—as in the leap from Dryden to Bartolozzi—signals the presence of cyclical repetition within the linear history. From that (markedly international if not universal) perspective, van Dyck is Dryden as Dryden is Bartolozzi, and the struggles of original artists in postrevolutionary seventeenth-century England are their struggles in postrevolutionary nineteenth-century England. The relationship of Dryden and Milton after the Civil War stands for the relationship of Schiavonetti and Blake after the French Revolution: there are Rubenses and van Dycks among us.

The necessary condition of the counter-arts, then, is imitation; the sufficient condition, replacement of the original by the imitation. Counter-arts politics, which originates in the effort to substitute imitations for the originals from which they necessarily derive, is defined by its fundamental duplicity. Forced, in dread of exposure, to repress the sources upon which they depend, the counter-arts exert their power in a perilous domain maintained by dissimulation. Hence Blake pictures the history of the arts since the entrance of Rubens and van Dyck as a doubled entity relating as shadow to substance with the shadow dominant.

Accordingly, he speaks not of chance but of "Subterfuge" (*PA*, E 571). Wrong opinions are not attributed to innocence or mistake but are "artfully propagated" (572) as truth by imitators, whose "robberies from me made it necessary to them that I should be hid in a corner" (582). Woollett and Strange, the most highly respected native engravers, are "heavy lumps of Cunning & Ignorance" (573), a particularly virulent Blakean kind of ignorance that we shall return to. The public has been "imposed upon" (574) by sham artists, while "Noblemen & Gentlemen" have used "Premiums"—awards—as "tricks" to "counteract" (577) the "Encouragement" that real artists might get. Blake has been relabeled a "Madman" by "Bad Men," while the public's "Error" has been relabeled "the Public Voice" (578).

A fairly consistent symmetrical pattern of three groups, artists, dealers, and public, emerges into character. The first group divides into two, original artists and imitative: "I hope this Print will . . . shew," he says of the *Canterbury Pilgrims* engraving (fig. 4.50), "that it is only some Englishmen and not All who are thus ridiculous in their Pretences [to improve art]" (*PA*, E 573). For obvious reasons the two groups tend to relate as victims to victimizers: robbers sneak and loot and lie afterward, honest citizens call for public protection. Barred from the public they deserve, original artists may double as an audience, and it is to his own group that Blake says he looks for present comfort: "I have Enough in the Approbation of fellow labourers this is my glory & exceeding great reward" (580–81). (A third kind of artist, fooled but not fooling, occasionally materializes and is addressed perhaps with hope: "The English Artist may be assured that he is doing an injury & injustice to his Country while he studies & imitates the Effects of Nature" [578].)

Blame for the crisis in English engraving rests squarely on the second group, dealers. "Englishmen rouze yourselves from the fatal Slumber into which Booksellers & Trading Dealers have thrown you Under the artfully propagated pretence that a Translation or a Copy of any kind can be as honourable to a Nation as An Original" (*PA*, E 576). Dealers are the source of the duplicity that is the modus operandi of the counter-arts: "In a Commercial Nation Imposters are abroad in all Professions these are the greatest Enemies of Genius" (582). Blake does not divide the representatives of commerce into good and bad kinds but moves instead toward a universal principle of condemnation. Employing the formula that singles out commerce as the major obstacle to English art and identifies England as a commercial nation, he reads the arts crisis as a sign of an imperial political crisis: "Commerce is so far from being beneficial to Arts or to Empire that it is destructive of both as all their History shews for the above Reason of Individual Merit being its Great hatred. Empires flourish till they become Commercial & then they are scatterd abroad to the four winds" (574). At this typically universalistic horizon of Blake's theoretical narrative, the echoes are again biblical, recalling prophecies of collapsing nations and scattered populations—"his kingdom shall be broken, and shall be divided toward the four winds of heaven"—often with strong suggestions that concentrated wealth was a contributing factor—"and the fourth shall be far richer than they all" (Dan. 11:4, 2; cf. Jer. 49:31–32; for restoration in reverse fashion see Zech. 2:6–7, Ezek. 37:9–10). The narrative is shadowed by the question put explicitly in the preface to *Milton:* "And was Jerusalem builded here, / Among these dark Satanic Mills?" (pl. 1[i], E 95).

Later, in the aphoristic *Laocoön,* the attack on commerce broadens into a blanket denunciation of money itself, with money and art explicitly opposed: "Christianity is Art & not Money / Money is its Curse." Money hauls the full metaphorical load of Blake's aversions: ". . . Money . . . that is . . . Caesar or Empire or Natural Religion." It "is The Great Satan or Reason the Root of Good & Evil / In the Accusation of Sin." Condemnation, again reflecting biblical admonitions, is total: "Where any view of Money exists Art cannot be carried on, but War only (Read Matthew CX. 9 & 10 v)" (E 274–75).

The third and final group, the public, is a product of Blake's acceptance of the saving thought that money/commerce is not metaphorically identifiable with the nation. It is essential to his case to admit that England is, as the continental critics claimed, "a Commercial Nation" (E 582), but equally essential to withhold the ultimate condemnation of the character and culture of a nation of shopkeepers. The rhetorical texture of the *Public Address* weaves beacons of hope into a sullen tapestry of anticommercial pessimism. The latter may come out in gloomy interrogations that seem to have self-evidently negative answers—"Can Anglus [Englishman] never Discern Perfection but in the Journeymans Labour"? (582)—while the former may leak into a pun, "Be-lying the English Character in that well known Saying Englishmen Improve what others Invent" (576). This is "a detestable Falshood" not just because inventions cannot be improved but also because there are those with ears to hear and eyes to see, a saving remnant, whose attention the prophetic artist may hope to engage. This is the "public" of the *Public Address,* largely exempted from imputations of guilt and made into a source of relief and, ultimately, rescue: "I call for Public protection against these Villains" (582; see also 578). As an object of faith, Blake's public embodies the future-oriented aspect of English-school discourse. Hence the strongest form of the public is its imagined future form, posterity: "but the Public will know & Posterity will know" (572).

Idealized as posterity, the public is one of the stabilizing terms in the discourse. In the *Public Address* Blake *submits* to the judgment of posterity as to no other judgment: "It is very true what you have said for these thirty two Years I am Mad or Else you ["Ye English Engravers"] are so both of us cannot be in our right senses Posterity will judge by our Works" (E 573). On posterity is bestowed the sanity to get it right in the long run: "theirs is the Contempt of Posterity" (580). The metaphorical structure through which Blake conceives the long-term role of the public in the artist's salvation derives from the Christian strain in his discourse. Sane and insane artists are as the righteous and the sinful (amended to truth and error by Blake [*VLJ*, E 563]), while posterity occupies the position of Christ as ultimate judge: "It is the same in Art by their Works ye shall know them" (*VLJ*, E 564; cf. "For the Son of man shall come in the glory of his Father with his angels; and then he shall reward every man according to his works" [Matt. 16:27]).

Thus the power of the conspiratorial strain in Blake's art history, as great as it is at this point in his life (and later, judging by the *Laocoön, On Homers Poetry,* and *On Virgil*), is limited by a faith in the narrative history of the audience. In past times and other places there have been capable audiences. In the future posterity will set things straight. Even in the present there is an audience capable of recognizing original art. Its weakest form lies in "the fatal Slumber into which Booksellers & Trading Dealers have thrown you" (*PA*, E 576). In another form its real powers have been hidden from it:

> It has been said of late years The English Public have no Taste for Painting This is a Falshood The English are as Good Judges of Painting as of Poetry & they prove it in their Contempt for Great Collections of all the Rubbish of the Continent brought here by Ignorant Picture dealers an Englishman may well say I am no Judge of Painting when he is shewn these Smears & Dawbs at an immense price & told that such is the Art of Painting I say the English Public are true Encouragers of real Art while they discourage & look with Contempt on False Art. [E 581–82]

Taking his cues from English-school discourse to entertain the old suspicion that the national audience may simply be unfit by nature or nurture, Blake shifts the optimistic analogy of painting and poetry to the area of the audience to contend that the English public judges the one art as competently as the other. He prefers to locate the problem in a commercial connection between ignorant dealers and bad foreign painters, which brought in another influx of continental rubbish, starting a new, postrevolutionary cycle of the Rubens-and-van-Dyck sort.[5] The paradigm by which "ignorance"—in producers, sellers, or buyers—blocks the free operation of the production and consumption cycle is a familiar one, growing out of answers to the charge of native inadequacy leveled by the "pious priests" of the continent. In the standard rebuttal, ignorance is to be remedied by education; thus the role of institutions—museums, galleries, academies—in eighteenth-century prescriptions for the betterment of English art.

In a way that accommodates conspiratorial logic, Blake's notion of ignorance is fundamentally different. It is a development beyond the set of original conditions, not a state prior to

[5] Reitlinger's statistics and conclusions generally support Blake's conviction that England's taste was Venetian, Flemish, and Dutch (e.g., "There have really been only three periods when Titian has been estimated at his true worth in England: in the reign of Charles I, under the Regency of George IV, and since 1929" [464]). Blake's sense of the general taste in the early nineteenth century also seems to be borne out by the subjects chosen for reproduction (e.g., Hunnisett 107) and exhibition (e.g., Herrmann 226–27, on the British Institution).

development. Metaphorically, in relation to surfaces ignorance is superficial; in relation to the sequence of events it is late. Always under it and hidden or behind it and forgotten is the original "vision" that had to be altered, hidden, or forgotten so that ignorance might be achieved. Consequently, if oddly, ignorance falls into a cluster with other belated acquisitions such as cunning and improvement. Thus Woollett and Strange can be lumps of cunning and ignorance who share "the Contemptible Pretences of Englishmen to Improve Art" (*PA*, E 573). Obeying the logic of these antiprogressive metaphors, Blake bids artists to abandon acquisitions and move downward and backward in space, time, and social status to unimproved original states: "Ye English Engravers must *come down* from your high flights ye must *condescend* to study Marc Antonio & Albert Durer[.] Ye must *begin* before you attempt to finish . . ." (my emphases, 573).

Blake tirelessly repeats the underlying principle: "There is just the same Science [i.e., learned knowledge and skill] in Lebrun or Rubens or even Vanloo that there is in Rafael or Mich Angelo but not the same Genius[.] Science is soon got the other never can be acquired but must be Born" (*PA*, E 575).[6] Ignorance comes by corrupt education: "This is like what Sr Francis Bacon says that a healthy Child should be taught & compelld to walk like a Cripple while the Cripple must be taught to walk like healthy people O rare wisdom" (580). Presumably the same principle of conditioning applies to the public. "Englishmen have been so *used to* Journeymens undecided bungling that they cannot bear the firmness of a Masters Touch" (my emphasis, 575).

The principle requires some corrupting agents to move beings from original genius to educated ignorance (why otherwise would anyone teach a healthy child to walk like anything but a healthy child?), and that requirement is indeed coherent with the ascriptions of corrupt motivation to the agents in Blake's art history: "Engravd by William Blake tho Now Surrounded by Calumny & Envy" (deleted passage, *PA*, E 571). In the terms of the *Public Address*, the English-school image of an ignorant audience in need of the educational benefits of, say, Reynolds's *Discourses* is itself a counter-arts construction intended to create ignorance through education. Hence Blake would have us recognize in the public sphere a battle for control of the public's mind: "Advertizements in Newspapers are no proof of Popular approbation. but often the Contrary" (573).[7] But to read the codes in the mirror world that Blake is trying to envision, one must realize how often the truth appears under the sign of its opposite. If the publicly apparent may be a spectacular diversion from the privately true—if "Secret Calumny & open Professions of Friendship" may mark the condition of knowledge—narratives may move in reverse: "When a Base Man means to be your Enemy he always begins with being your Friend" (572). Constructions may be known by their counter-constructions; ignorance (as to original vision) may be labeled good sense (as to imitation).

It would be fair to say that most of the intellectual energy of the *Public Address* is spent in an effort to restore the integrity of such transvalued oppositions. The central oppositions are mental; Blake assigns values to intellectual states (genius/fool, smart/dumb), us-

[6] See also the annotations to Reynolds and my more detailed treatment of the education of genius in *Blake's Theory* (93–99).

[7] He is probably referring especially to the publication of the Chalcographic Society's proposals.

ually working in extremes but implying the range in between. The basic values are coordinated by the master opposition of mental against physical, which is nowhere stated but everywhere implied, as in the contemptuous treatment of mindless physical labor. Though fundamental, the opposition is not absolute. Physical labor can be better and worse—as in the contrast between the journeyman's bungling and the master's touch—as it is more or less informed by thought. But if the ideal were an integration of the mental and the physical, then brains without work would be denigrated equally with work without brains. That symmetry is tellingly absent, and integration is unidirectional. The mental may dignify the physical; the reverse seems inconceivable.

Instead, physical labor is often portrayed as an ersatz compensation for thought. "The Lifes Labour" of this or that—of five hundred idiots, of ignorant journeymen, of ignorance and imbecility—becomes a scornful refrain. The "Lifes Labour of Ignorance and Imbecillity" opposes "the Inspired Moments of Genius & Animation" (574) as worktime versus thinktime, without consideration for the life's labor of genius that might integrate the two. Genius labors against labor toward freedom from time, space, and matter, while ignorance is bound to them. The attitude seems to be, for lack of a better term, Christian-aristocratic. It allows one to anticipate ultimate release from "the Delusive Goddess Nature & her Laws to get into Freedom from all Law of the Members into The Mind in which every one is King & Priest in his own House God Send it so on Earth as it is in Heaven" (to Cumberland, 12 April 1827, E 784), where work is pure cognition without material expression.

On the mental side of the master opposition of mental against physical, a cluster of other oppositions between desirable and undesirable mental kinds accumulates. "Imbecillity," "weak Capacities," "the Blockhead" (*PA,* E 571), the "fool" (572), "Idiots" (573), "Mental Weakness," and "Imbecillity" (574) square off against "Ordinary [mental] Capacity" (573), "Genius" (574), "the Greatest Genius" (576), the "Man of Sense" (577, 579), and "every Body of Understanding" (581), to name a few of the many. Sometimes Blake deceptively recalculates these mental oppositions in physical terms: "The Lifes Labour of Mental Weakness" is to "one Hour of the Labour of Ordinary Capacity" as "the full Gallop of the Gouty Man [is] to the ordinary walk of youth & health" (573). Here and elsewhere, however, when physical condition figures mental condition, physical state is the source of the metaphor, mental state its target.[8] Moreover, it bears repeating that the positively valued side of these oppositions is innate, the negative acquired. In this discourse idiots and cripples personify not inborn mental and physical limits but warped achievements. Physical labor without thought is what happens when thought is driven out, not a state before thought.

Since, in Blake's terms, the creative power of original artists is primarily intellectual power (thus the force of the criticism "it is a work of no Mind" [*PA,* E 578]), the duplicity attendant upon the counter-arts is represented throughout the *Public Address* in varieties of cognitive confusion and fraud: "What kind of Intellects must he have who . . . a Man who has got any brains will never . . . No Man of Sense ever supposes . . ." (578). In the Nat Lee story, for

[8] "Target" and "source" improve I. A. Richards's terms "tenor" and "vehicle." I take the better terms from Lakoff and Turner, who took them, I suppose, from the vocabulary of computer operating systems that designate "source" and "target" diskettes.

example, they show up in Blake's bitterly playful conjectures about whether Lee did or did not write the poem signed with his name and whether he was or was not sane when and if he wrote it.[9] The suppositions concerning Lee's lucidity also mock the frequent appeals by writers of Dryden's postrevolutionary generation to their own sanity and reason as against the disruptive enthusiasm of others. Thus Blake's corrective supposition of an audience divided between "every Body of Understanding" who will prefer the original Milton and readers sunk in "Stupidity" who will prefer Dryden's "degraded" imitation.

In Blake's abusive lexicon we clearly have much more to deal with than common slander. If by Blake's time Nat Lee was a nobody and Milton was hardly in danger of losing out to Dryden, in these apparently innocuous knowledge games Blake saw high stakes—ultimately, control of key mental classifications and their power to organize and value social work. Coherence derives from the claim that a counter-arts culture of imposters who are "the greatest Enemies of Genius" (582) doctors mental values. Thus we hear of "Imbecillity & Imbecillitys Journeymen . . . The Contemptible Idiots *who have been calld* Great Men of late Years," while "Rafael Mich Ang Alb D Jul Rom *are accounted* ignorant" (my emphases, 578, 579).

[9]For Lee (c. 1650–1692), see Richard E. Brown. Little is known of Lee's life. Pertinent facts include his four-year stay in Bedlam in his late years; his reputation for writing tragedies in overheated, even enthusiastic verse ("They only think you animate your Theme / With too much Fire, who are themselves all Phle'me," wrote Dryden in his commendatory verses for the 1677 quarto of Lee's *Rival Queens* [R. E. Brown 117, illus.]); and close collaborations with Dryden (including joint authorship of two plays) that support Blake's droll suspicions about Lee's real identity and Dryden's efforts to force a posthumous collaboration, as it were, with Milton.

The notion of the counter-arts freed Blake to speculate that he and his best contemporaries were the targets of a vast mental reclassification exercise signaled by the advent of Rubens and van Dyck. We have seen what powerful influence psychological and psychopathological metaphors exercise over the structure of the *Public Address*. Because their very definitions are at issue, they are wobbly; that is, they belong properly to the states of mental disturbance represented by the questions about Nat Lee. The key question, of course, is the question of insanity, and we can see that all such questions are ultimately directed at Blake himself: "I am Mad or Else you are so" (573).[10] Haunted by allegations of insanity, he had become sufficiently thin-skinned on the subject even to cast himself as Socrates betrayed by accusers: "The Painter hopes that his Friends Anytus Melitus & Lycon will percieve that they are not now in Ancient Greece & tho they can use the Poison of Calumny the English Public will be convincd that such a Picture as this Could never be Painted by a Madman" (578). Since the evidence of insanity always involved nonconformity—"O why was I born with a different face / Why was I not born like the rest of my race" (to Butts, 16 August 1803, E 733)—"insane" and "original" threatened to become synonymous, as did "sane" and "imitative." The realization that mental classification may be a mechanism of social control let him connect his life with the lives of other artists, present experience with past history, and artwork with other social work. Narrating backward, he imagined that if a realm regulated by "the true

[10]Youngquist usefully criticizes twentieth-century attempts to whitewash the issue of Blake's insanity. *Madness and Blake's Myth* is an experiment in taking seriously the notion that Blake was insane because he saw visions.

Style of Art" (*PA*, E 580) would define mental categories by artistic categories, then a nation regulated by counter-artistic forces would transpose the categories.

Of course his experience confirmed the hypothesis. The charge of insanity was leveled at him many times, and Robert Hunt even hung his devastating review of Blake's exhibition on that hook: "If beside the stupid and mad-brained political project of their rulers, the sane part of the people of England required fresh proof of the alarming increase of the effects of insanity, they will be too well convinced from its having lately spread into the hitherto sober region of Art." Though Hunt simultaneously accuses and exonerates Fuseli of insanity, he brands Blake outright as "an unfortunate lunatic, whose personal inoffensiveness secures him from confinement, and, consequently, of whom no public notice would have been taken" had he not recently found admirers to "publish his madness more largely." Hunt thus positions himself (mockingly) as a public servant only doing his public duty to arrest a "malady" spreading outward—and this is an interesting if unexpected move—from the mad monarch to the "hitherto sober region of Art" (quoted in Bentley, *Blake Records* 215–16). The immensely successful *Examiner,* known for its liberal-reformist politics, thus links Blake and Fuseli with the governmental madness symbolized by George III, while alienating them from the sane English public who know better. Hunt's attack must have injured Blake deeply.[11] We need pursue the personal connection no further than to point out how he began to narrate his own traumatic experience in the broader terms of a counter-arts conspiracy.

Blake's counter-arts are commercial products. The power at stake in these shifting mental categories is, in his reading, commercial power. In none but a "Commercial Nation" (*PA*, E 582) are enemies of genius abroad in all professions. The purpose of their imposture is to reshape the social framework. Reclassification, which produces a new language that accommodates morals, motives, and mental states to commercial ends, continues "till at length Christian Charity is held out as a Motive to encourage a Blockhead & he is Counted the Greatest Genius who can sell a Good for Nothing Commodity for a Great Price[.] Obedience to the Will of the Monopolist is calld Virtue and the really Industrious Virtuous & Independent Barry is driven out to make room for a pack of Idle Sycophants with whitlors [whitlows, finger sores] on their fingers" (deleted passage, 576). Blake imagines an invasion of the body snatchers that leaves all the old cultural bodies superficially the same—there continue to be arts and geniuses and virtue—but altered profoundly beneath the skin.

The basic shift resituates authority in commercial hands to bring art production in line with the general truth recommended by James Mill in his keen response to Thomas Spence and William Cobbett, "that nothing creates wealth but the hands of our industrious countrymen, set to work by the means, and regulated by the skill and judgment of others" (Mill

[11] Not that the *Examiner* was alone in associating Blake's exhibition and catalogue with lunacy. In a letter to his son, Cumberland called the catalogue "truly original—part vanity part madness—part very good sense." See also Robert Southey's memories of the exhibition ("great but insane genius") and of a visit to Blake in 1811 ("a decided madman") (quoted in Bentley, *Blake Records* 219, 226, 229). By 1808–1810 the label of insanity had begun to stick, and it was circulating freely even among Blake's greatest admirers.

109). A system of production controlled by individual artists and sustained by a moral order that locates virtue, including the workplace virtues of industry and independence, in those individuals gives way to a system controlled by "the Monopolist." (The *OED* usefully cites George Eliot's *Felix Holt:* "We know what monopolists are: men who want to keep a trade all to themselves, under the pretence that they'll furnish the public with a better article" [chap. 30].)

The two systems obviously cannot be upheld by the same values. The independence of a Barry comes to look like temperamental obstreperousness or even insanity, and the name of virtue is accordingly reassigned to the worker's compliance with the monopolist's will. The genius label is transferred from worker to trader—"the Greatest Genius who can sell"—while a customer-centered economic standard of good value for money is replaced by a mercantile trinkets-for-the-natives standard of maximum return on minimum investment. At worst, an entire transvaluation and displacement occurs: "the really Industrious Virtuous & Independent Barry is driven out to make room for a pack of Idle Sycophants with whitlors on their fingers."

Vulgar Fellows and Ignorant Journeymen

> Who knows his trade is a Journeyman;
> A Master is he that invents the plan;
> An Apprentice, each and every man.
>
> —Motto over Theodore Steinway's workbench

> Division of labour only becomes truly such from the moment when a division of material and mental labour appears.
>
> —Karl Marx, *The German Ideology*

That fierce little narrative of virtue expelled by sycophancy depends upon a vision of class alignments that emerges from the *Public Address.* Students of English art history have begun to pay increased attention to class. Iain Pears, writing about an earlier period, has argued that a new framework of common values accompanying "a process of cultural unification of the upper ranks of English society" became the basis for a consensus on "taste, the body of aesthetic prescriptions which provided the intellectual framework through which the [visual] works themselves were interpreted" (3, 26). As part of the consolidation at the top of the class hierarchy, painters and dealers furthered their interests by advocating these values and of course expressing and marketing them as paintings. Painting became a liberal art—that is, free of manual labor insofar as labor was deemphasized in an overwhelmingly intellectual procedure—while painters became the liberal practitioners of a profession on the order of architecture or medicine, not, as the term was, mechanics.

Pears is describing major socio-theoretical developments in the earlier eighteenth century. Blake's vision emerges from them and yet against them. He makes no radical move to return painters to the status of house painters or to raise house painting to the level of history painting. If anything, he insists on making distinctions even more rigid. But he looks far more critically than Barry ever did at the class alliances that, as Blake thought, had undone English painting and engraving.

In one of the familiar anticommercial strains in English-school discourse, the villains are in the middle, are indeed "middlemen" of the Boydell sort, blocking the free flow of production and reception. The *Public Address* supplements that strain with new discursive positions that establish new points of view. They allow Blake to occupy the middle position and report his story from it, thus creating, in a meaningful if not a classical economic sense, a potential bourgeois tragedy in its view of the "really Industrious Virtuous & Independent" artist's imperiled post between upper and lower.

If the concept of class that structures Blake's narrative has its center of gravity at the middle, from which both just and unjust power emanates, one might indeed say that the upper and lower classes are themselves treated as the products of the unjust occupation of the middle by the monopolizing traders of commerce and the exile of the true middle class. Blake had been thinking in terms of such usurpations and displacements at least as far back as the early 1790s, when he composed the story of the "just man" displaced by "the villain" who drove the just man into "barren climes":

> Now the sneaking serpent walks
> In mild humility.
> And the just man rages in the wilds
> Where lions roam.
>
> [*MHH* 2, E 33]

In this and later versions, Blake's narrative is about the shape of exile and homelessness, powerfully influenced by the multiple expulsions, diasporas, and promised returns of biblical story. The original art of imagination in the one replaces the true religion of Yahweh in the other, with the Greeks and Romans as the shared third term:

> Rouze up O Young Men of the New Age! set your foreheads against the ignorant Hirelings! For we have Hirelings in the Camp, the Court, & the University: who would if they could, for ever depress Mental & prolong Corporeal War. Painters! on you I call! Sculptors! Architects! Suffer not the fashionable Fools to depress your powers by the prices they pretend to give for contemptible works or the expensive advertizing boasts that they make of such works; believe Christ & his Apostles that there is a Class of Men whose whole delight is in Destroying. We do not want either Greek or Roman Models if we are but just & true to our own Imaginations, those Worlds of Eternity in which we shall live for ever; in Jesus our Lord. [*Milton* 1[i], E 95]

The better days these narratives want to recall—before the gentlemen connoisseurs above and the journeymen below united at the expense of the true artists in the middle—are a fabrication. If Blake's retrospective alibi asks to be read as a critique of historical developments, it must simultaneously be read as an exercise in middle-class self-construction: a prospective expression of ambition, in which a utopian Christian vision legitimizes the desire to penetrate the confederation of devouring upper, controlling middle, and exploited lower classes at its midpoint to make economic room for autonomous middle-class artist-heroes who see the possibility of combining in themselves the aesthetic judgment of an elite and the technical skills of a working class.

As it criticizes the exploitive class hierarchy built around the "Arts of Trading Combination" (*PA*, E 577), it implicitly promises a classless society upon the model of integrated labor. Here the middle class is all classes in one, and all can be one in the bosom of imagination: "The whole Business of Man Is The Arts & All Things Common"; "A Poet a Painter a Musician an Architect: the Man / Or Woman who is not one of these is not a Christian" (*Laocoön*, E 274). Though the expression is certainly a middle-class one, it constructs itself partly by robbing the repertory of upper-class attitudes: toward the body and manual labor, toward the "ignorance" of "journeymen," and, in an arresting paradox, toward the "vulgarity" of all attempts to imitate the inimitable original.

Again, this is not the most familiar version of class warfare. The contest is envisioned not as a battle of higher against lower but as a fight for the middle position, art counter art or, better perhaps, Art counter "art." Upper and lower classes come into play chiefly as they are drawn into alliances at the middle, where power is held and wielded. Blake draws the battle lines between artists such as himself and the traders, denounced for molding an alliance with middle-class "artists" and lower-class laborers to produce goods for a largely upper-class market.[12] That is, he situates himself in an intermediate position alongside, but alienated from, the salvageable public to which he appeals. That middling station is invaded and devalued, and those who occupy it are "driven out to make room" (cf. Blake's own "Starve me out," E 577). Their one place is filled by three groups: the traders themselves; the "Blockhead[s]" who devise ideas for art "Suited to the Purposes of Commerce" (573) and lend their names to projects actually carried out by others; and the journeymen who do the work. Thus "the Monopolizing Trader . . . [Manufactures Art by the Hands of Ignorant Journeymen]" (passage in brackets deleted; 576), but under the names of a puppet class of artists for hire.

On the axis of class distribution above, along with the "Fools" in the "Houses of Commons & Houses of Lords" who are "something Else besides Human Life" and the equally foolish "Princes" (E 580) who for their patronage deserve mental hanging are the "Noblemen & Gentlemen" (577) who offer prizes for imitations, "Gentlemen of Fortune who give Great Prices for Pictures," and "Gentlemen Critics" who "may rage" (575) against Blake's revelations. "Gentlemen" rarely appear with Blake's proper public, though he occasionally concedes the existence of at least a few whose first-rate fortunes are matched by first-rate intellects, as when he claims that "Gentlemen of the first Rank both in Genius & Fortune have subscribed their Names" to his "Inventions" without objecting to "the Executive part" (582).

The central rhetorical tradition of English-school discourse being tutorial, painter-

[12] Pears notes that in the early part of the eighteenth century, "the dealer frequently drew the lightning of social criticism from the painter, partially separating him from the taint of lucre and thus allowing the more idealised, intellectual aspects of the painting profession to attain greater emphasis" (96). Blake inherits and transmits this idealization but takes up the heavy additional burden of protecting the engraver from taint.

theorists typically address their knowledge to an upper-class audience, perhaps best symbolized by the monarchy, with defective tastes. At one extreme this rhetoric modulates into one that might be called prophetic, as an inferior class issues dire warnings to its superiors. Barry, for one, often exemplifies these central tendencies. However, they overlap and compete with a bourgeois version in which the object is to have one member of the class supply knowledge and taste to others of the same class in a kind of self-improvement exercise, as one might turn out for Coleridge's or Hazlitt's lectures. The *Public Address* mixes features of both rhetorics. Although Blake not infrequently breaks into the language of an inferior speaking to superiors, more often he imagines a public on his level, like "most Englishmen" who have (understandably) lost their respect for art because of the engravings published by "English Traders" (E 577).

As the upper class constitutes the major art market, the essential alliance is the one Blake mentions in his description of the origins of the "Contemptible Counter Arts": such "contemptible Politicians as Louis XIV" in league with "Venetian . . . traders" (E 580). The toast to the Boydell project illustrates this compact of monarch and trader, with the work force of journeymen outside and below, as it were. What kind of art do they conspire to sell? Almost all of Blake's significant metaphors for the counter-arts product have their source in familiar critiques of upper-class behavior: vacant, artificial, insincere, pretentious, superficial, trivial. Critiques of the class become critiques of the work that it wants to buy. Insofar as that class implicitly seeks to purchase mirrors of itself and its world (mythologized as Blake's "nature"), we can lump all these features under vanity and pride (mythologized as Blake's "selfhood"), which, with ignorance, were typically blamed for most of the failings in English artistic taste, including the notorious preference for portrait over history.

Thus, we are told, noblemen and gentlemen understand "Artifice"—in the double sense of decoration and hypocritical disguise—but not "Art" (E 576). Their frivolity is mocked in feminizing, francophobic terms. The feminine and the French are, of course, confederates in the discourse. (Conceding the unquestioned superiority of French engraving over English in the 1750s, Campbell's *London Tradesman* named "Softness" and "Delicacy" as the leading virtues of the former [113].) Blake's gentlemen are "English Connoisseurs" (E 580), "silly Fellows" (577) who patronize "Toilettes" (573) such as Woollett's where engravings are dressed, with great labor and effect but little thought, for display.[13] The works are themselves figured as

[13] Pears outlines the history of the virtuoso and the connoisseur for the period before c. 1760 in his chap. 7 (181–206). In a related vein, Bindman discusses the interplay of positive and negative stereotypes of the French as they appeared in British reactions to the Revolution (*Guillotine* 42–47). "Toilette" is a particularly interesting lexical intersection, recalling, of course, the lucubrations of eighteenth-century toilets, which required an array of special equipment for dressing and thereby created a spectacle of vanity and a fashionable eighteenth-century ritual of visitation, such as the toilet of Belinda memorialized in Pope's *Rape of the Lock.* But "toilette," as the name for a stage of cleansing organs in surgery, became powerfully associated with the tools and technologies of death and hence with the preparation for execution, particularly by the French mechanism, the guillotine ("the ghastly ceremony of his toilette": *OED* def. 8c). That association was cemented during the Revolution. It became useful to Blake as he played on the connection between execution as a terminal stage of engraving and execution as the termination of life, as when Schiavonetti, the engraver of Blake's designs for Robert Blair's *The Grave,* becomes "Assassinetti" in a poem so fixed on the connections between violent death and engraving that Blake has himself shed tears of aqua fortis to

snatches of drawing room trifling and fakery, "Fribbles" (573), "Epigrammatic Wit in Art," a "Fashion" (579), and the commerce between the connoisseurs and their painters is represented accordingly as an exchange of *bons mots* at a modish venue, a "Modern Exhibition" (579). Rembrandt's etchings made the "Vulgar Epigram" (579) a stylish substitute for sound conversation, while painters who shun the repartee are "accounted ignorant" (579) and excluded, as if socially unfit. "Vulgar" here seems intended to designate mental class, especially the abject dependence that defines the intellectual parasite. Rubens and Correggio were in that respect "very weak & Vulgar fellows" (580). The *OED* quotes the *Monthly Magazine* for 1797—"So, the word *vulgar* now implies something base and groveling in actions" (def. 13a)—and offers an instructive citation from Marvell: "The mean malice of the same Vulgar Scribler, hired by the Conspirators at so much a sheet" (def. 13b). For his vulgarity Reynolds is similarly branded the connoisseurs' "Doll" (E 580), their feminized—empty-headed, frivolous, infantile—boy toy.[14] Vulgar fools such as Rubens, we might say, are ignorant journeymen who have risen above their station by stealing their knowledge from others.

Below the traders on the class axis, then, but bound to them by economic interests, are the journeymen, semiskilled day laborers, "a pack of Idle Sycophants with whitlors on their fingers," blamed for "Journeymens undecided bungling," lacking the "firmness of a Masters touch" (E 576, 575). These laborers on whom Blake heaps so much scorn are "Idle" not physically—they have sores to show for their pains—but mentally. Sycophants by definition, they are profoundly *hired* hands, bodies without minds, incapable of individual action. They are spiritually allied with, and sometimes metaphorically collapsed into, the imitative painters whose names go on the work. Together these two groups are "Imbecillity & Imbecillitys Journeymen . . . The Contemptible Idiots who have been calld Great Men of late Years" (578). Blake's contempt for the work and the ignorance of journeymen reveals something of his own class allegiances and helps to show where the economic lines are drawn. On the one hand, "if the Art is no more than this [copying from nature] it is no better than any others Manual Labour any body may do it & the fool often will do it best" (578). On the other hand, there are the "fellow labourers" whose "Approbation" is Blake's "glory" (580–81).

The journeymen's separation from the class of minds that directs them is reflected in Blake's principled opposition to the separation of conception from execution, which in class terms might be seen as a separation of ruling upper-class minds from working lower-class bodies.[15] The work of art thus reproduces the class structure that produces it. The emptying of the structure at the center—the replacement of real

etch the epitaph on an enemy's tombstone ("And his legs carried it like a long fork," E 503–4).

[14] "Doll" derives from a pet form for "Dorothy." The *OED* lists among its meanings "the image of a human being (commonly of a child or lady) used as a plaything," a "pretty, but unintelligent or empty person," and (in "doll-common" and "dolly-mop") a "prostitute" (recalling, for instance, Dol Common in Ben Jonson's *The Alchemist* and Doll Tearsheet in Shakespeare's *2 Henry IV*).

[15] See Pears on the social advantages of this division, as in the painters' attempts to raise their status by separating their arts into "liberal" and "mechanical" components (see esp. chap. 4, 107–32). He argues accordingly that the Academy is the "final triumph of the intellectual component of the painter's art over the technical aspect" (120).

artists with frauds and hirelings—leaves paintings and engravings likewise empty. Hence Blake's conceits for such works attempt to capture the notion of labored physical surfaces without mental depth, as in the identification of Rembrandt's Hundred-Guilder Print (fig. 4.40) with witty linguistic display and the comparison of a highly finished Woollett engraving with "a fool or a Knave. in an Embroiderd Coat" (573)—made for gentlemen of fortune by ignorant journeymen. (And here again emerges the anti-aristocratic topos of empty vanity.)

The coat, he claims, "is an Emanation from Ignorance itself & its finishing is like its master The Lifes Labour of Five Hundred Idiots for he never does the Work Himself" (E 573). We want to note carefully the object of Blake's anger here, "masters" who do none of their own work, and the relevant middle-class values of independence and self-sufficiency. The criticism is directed, furthermore, at both masters, prince and trader: the upper-class wearer of the coat, surrounded by five hundred slavish needleworkers, and their middle-class master tailor.

Blake can thus be expected to favor a strategy of integration (called reintegration). As his own craft of engraving falls on the socially inferior side of the division between conception and execution, integration has obvious social advantages: he, as a specialist in devalued skills of execution, can only gain. In this respect the master behind the "firmness of a Masters Touch" to which he appeals is as much an old-fashioned artisan standing for the return to artisanal values as a proto-romantic artist-hero. The underlying persuasion is that the commercial system of production has bypassed masters for journeymen and introduced a division of labor by shifting values away from what once had to be "Drawn with a firm and decided hand at once" by one person to what now has only to be "smoothd up & Niggled & Poco Piud" (E 576).[16] The complaint is issued in part from the position of an experienced artisan replaced by scab labor, a middle-class worker whose livelihood is threatened simultaneously by upper-class exploitation and gullibility (to the outrageous appeal of empty fashions imposed by the merchant-traders) and lower-class encroachments (of the unskilled on the skilled). In this position Blake's stand-in is his own old master Basire, contrasted to imposter masters such as Woollett, who ridiculed "Basires knife tools" but who "did not know how to grind his Graver" (E 575). Removing the master's touch has removed the heart of engraving, leaving only lower-class bodies and upper-class minds in a false union around the heartless heart of the monopolizing trader.

By and large the *Public Address* tends to project the counter-arts onto a class structure in which the upper-class connoisseurs are gulls, the lower-class journeymen thoughtless hands, and the middle-class traders a center of illegitimate power based on mental theft. Blake suggests that this power structure has been created at the expense of two alienated groups, a public who have been "imposed upon for many Years"

[16] In Blake's time "niggling" retains overtones of feminine licentiousness (1809, "My little pet . . . niggled, nudged, toyed, and romped, like a school-girl in vacation," *OED*) that may have disappeared by the mid–nineteenth century (the *OED* quotes Ruskin from 1860: "So long as the work is thoughtfully directed, there is no niggling"). "Poco piu" (for *poco più o poco meno*, the little more or less that might make all the difference), a common term of connoisseurship, suggests the foreign-feminine. Jean Hagstrum was the first to correct the customary reading, "poco pen," to "poco piu" (see E 882, textual note).

(E 574) and whose experience of the counter-arts has led them to conclude that they have "no Taste for Painting" (581) and original artists who have been robbed of their ideas and left to die in cultural exile. Though he is not explicit about the class assignments of these two groups, numerous features suggest that they both belong in the middle. But with a caveat: the very class structure seems to be a product of the counter-arts venture. Blake's vision of the alternative is itself, from what we can tell, classless, but the imagined state of classlessness is a projection from the middle. Insofar as the *Public Address*'s trenchant criticisms of divided labor are criticisms of the class structure itself, they point toward reintegration at a newly legitimated middle that would eliminate the need for (any other) class.

That classlessness returns us to the question of originality in its personal form, individuality, for the kind of classlessness implicated in the *Public Address* seems to resolve itself in the integrated individual, capable of the kind of merit excluded by commerce. Blake's middle-class dream of integrated action takes the form of a robust individualism. The touch of a master promises to reconnect show with substance, body with mind, at the center, in the middle class, where substance lies. Journeymen are "suited" to commerce because "Commerce Cannot endure Individual Merit its insatiable Maw must be fed by What all can do Equally well" (E 573). Worse, commerce is "destructive" of both arts and empires "for the above Reason of Individual Merit being its Great hatred" (574). Obviously the standard of individuality in this unique, unacquirable form provides epistemological support for the artistic standard of originality. Imitation and translation can produce only "contemptible Copies" (578) in an individualist ethos where works of art are essentially creations of the unique individual in "Inspired Moments of Genius & Animation" (574).

It is tempting to label this, even at the risk of anachronism, a *bourgeois* individualism. Certainly the world Blake imagines seems open to criticism as, at worst perhaps, an idealization and hence an ideological prop for the notorious atomistic, possessive individualism of Marxist discourse. The criticism would be just to a point, but some elementary distinctions between individualisms are called for. Modern liberal-democratic movements have on occasion found relief from their fears of the unknowable individual other—leaving no basis for collective knowledge, let alone action—in a Lockean psychology by which individuals are thought to be constituted largely by an environment strong enough to write them into existence. So long as the environment is stable, individual beings remain (consolingly) connected because they are made of overlapping collections of atomic impressions.[17]

Blake's individualism is powerfully antipathetic to that atomistic kind. His is backed up not by notions of mental development but by fantasies of the precedence of birth over technical education. To that extent his individualism adapts aristocratic values, hence his ready disdain for the supposed vulgarity of artists admired for their technical skills: mere copyists, he complains, envisioning a class that can only ape the manners of an authentic nobility that knows how to be original because it was born that way. The prospect of a spiritual nobility

[17] Blake's anti-Lockean individualism is another element that distances him from English-school discourse. See, for example, Gibson-Wood on the Lockean basis of Jonathan Richardson's rational, learnable connoisseurship.

of birth (proved, say, by the continuity of the worlds of the living and the dead-eternal through the conversations of our nobility with theirs) recommended Blake to Yeats and other early modernists. His uses were limited, however, because his nobility is potentially unrestricted. Everyone is born into it or, more accurately, born from it into the world of "generation," where the Argument of *The Marriage of Heaven and Hell* takes over. As original art must be recovered, so original selves must be reborn. Salvation is available to all, but it turns out to be largely a matter of self-consultation—thus self-construction—as illustrated in Blake's designs for the book of Job, dominated by a series of confrontations between Job's generated (imitative) and spiritual (original) selves, whose images are virtually identical (fig. 3.4).

The artistic line, like the individual who makes it, is not divisible and measurable by "Newtons Doctrine of the Fluxions of an Atom" but "is Itself & Not Intermeasurable with or by any Thing Else Such is Job"—that is, Job *and* Blake's Job engravings as paradigms of individual merit—"but since the French Revolution Englishmen are all Intermeasurable One by Another . . ." (to Cumberland, 12 April 1827, E 783). The English reaction to the Revolution produced intermeasurability by allowing the ruling and commercial classes to suppress the incalculable differences that constitute originality. Thus in the *Public Address* Blake dwells on "my Character," "my character as an Artist" (E 572), as the unit of consideration. His best metaphor for the integrated individual character is melody: "And in Melodious accents I / Will sit me down & Cry. I. I." (581), the song of himself.

The melody of I/aye as opposed to the harmony of we? Yes: Blake deploys melody and harmony as strictly opposed rather than complementary metaphors (e.g., *contra* Reynolds, E 659). But again it would be rash to conclude that his nonconformist individualism spurns community, especially since the couplet ends the very sentence in which he has exalted his craft solidarity with others: "I have Enough in the Approbation of fellow labourers this is my glory & exceeding great reward I go on & nothing can hinder my course" (580–81). The juxtaposition of collective plurals with first person singulars in that sentence reminds us of the baffling union of individualism and communalism at the heart of his thinking. This is no "problem" we can hope to "solve." But we can trace it through another useful context, this time the technology of engraving, where harmony names a set of visual rather than musical conditions.

The Space of Translation

The core of the art history that Blake cultivated in the postrevolutionary, post-Boydell years is his concept of the counter-arts, which amplifies conspiratorial themes that had played an erratic and underdeveloped role in English-school discourse. In important respects, as we have seen, the counter-arts emerge in the social terms that produce claims about art's relation to empire and the hierarchical interdependencies of kings and journeymen. That social side of the counter-arts idea and its associated art history rests in turn upon a technological argument. Although Blake applies it across a broad range of arts—to poetry, painting, and music as well as engraving—that often seem metaphorically interchangeable, to bring out the argument's clarity and shape I shall assemble yet another history of engraving and move a bit beyond the *Public Address.*

The most imposing contention of the *Public Address* is that original English art had been superseded by a counter-art of imitation adapted to commerce, "Suited" to its "Purposes" and "Subservient" to the "interest" of the "Trader" (E 573, 576). This adaptation had generated two competing art histories, one centering on "the Florentine original" (580)—to which Blake assigns such symbolic counters as Dürer and Milton—and the other on the "Venetian" (580) conspiracy to steal the original, counterfeit it, and spread it abroad: thus "Wooletts and Stranges works *are like those* of Titian & Correggio . . . Suited to the Purposes of Commerce." The adaptation is founded on a deep, extensive division of labor—"Wooletts and Stranges works are like those of Titian & Correggio *the Lifes Labour of Ignorant Journeymen* Suited to the Purposes of Commerce"—that he blames for having leveled art production to "What all can do Equally well" (573). What interests us here is the technological keys that open the possibility of this exchange of many for one.

The argument: (1) The divisions of class apparent in the *Public Address* are, among other things, part of a division of labor that makes production more efficient and profitable. The system might, for example, help meet demand (for portraits, say) and correlate the production of images (slow) with other kinds of production, such as printing (fast). Efficiencies are gained largely by the shifting of values away from intellectual toward physical labor expressed in sane—that is, uniform and predictable—technical features (thus the direction and purpose of mental reclassification discussed earlier). Journeymen can supply cheap labor but they cannot, by themselves, make acceptable pictures under the terms of the arrangement.

(2) The division of labor in which journeymen participate depends upon a rational division of production, which in turn requires a rational division of the product, which naturally requires a divisible product. The ideal is a macrosystem capable of unifying labor, management, marketers, and markets through interlocking structures that coordinate the ideological (such as a consensus about "taste," to supply ideas that legitimate material outcomes), the institutional (such as the Royal Academy and the British Institution, to supply formal education and display space), and the technological (such as the methods and machines discussed below, to supply techniques of production) with the overarching socioeconomic framework.

(3) Blake in effect contends that the standard English-school program of pedagogy and principle, as outlined in Chapter I, had been adapted to "suit" these integrative commercial "purposes": as formulated in English-school discourse, the Carracci ideal of gradualism and eclecticism is in large measure a technical ideal easily translated into the arrangements of the system, and Blake's critique in the *Public Address* is in like measure technical. Hence, as a visual response to standard English-school pictorial syntax, the style of his *Canterbury Pilgrims* engraving—the major visual subject of

the *Public Address*—is predicated on a technological regression to originality, backing up through the history of engraving to the Old English portraits and thereby rejecting, as he supposes, public displays of consensus virtuosity, and embracing a one-artist/one-style concept of expression (fig. 4.50).

How does the history of art read when it is narrated from these premises? We can answer, in effect, by using cues from the *Public Address* to complement the "Christian" history of engraving in Chapter III with the necessary technological perspective. As a point of departure, we might note how, in the brief anecdote of Nat Lee, Blake manages to introduce four technical concepts, "Niggling" and "Poco Piu" from the terminology of the visual arts, "Rhyme" and rhythm ("Monotonous Sing Song Sing Song") from poetry (E 581)—a striking indicator of the degree to which technical issues shape his critique.

Behind the terminology stands the guiding theoretical ideal of the *Public Address*, the correlation of the mental and material phases of production. Though I have discussed it at length elsewhere, some reiteration seems indispensable.[18] In brief, at the level of technology—of art production—the relation of conception to execution determines the difference between original and imitative art for Blake. (Needless to say, the riddles that attend all claims about conception and execution, content and form, internal and external world, and so on attend Blake's effort to establish that relation as a first principle.) He desires this relation: in original art thought and deed are necessarily integrated, while in imitative art they are equally necessarily unintegrated, because that separation makes imitation possible. That is, the separation of conception from execution is the first principle of imitation as their integration is the first principle of originality, and from their twisted relation are generated the complicitous, troubled histories of "Florentine" and "Venetian" art.

The purveyors of the counter-arts establish their legitimacy in the illegitimate space between conception and execution—execution of what?—that is the space of translation where all imitations become possible. Moreover, they treat the intermission as valuable commercial property, because in it thoughts become marketable products. The value of those products rises in a system that privileges execution by, for instance, promoting the notion that "a Copy Could be better than an original" (E 582). In this view translations are not secondhand copies but necessary second steps in the process of turning crude materials into technically refined, polished commodities.

A view of the original artist follows: Milton may, in the throes of religious enthusiasm, have come up with the germ of a good idea, "a rough Unfinishd Piece" (E 581) that required Dryden, a poet of eminently sane taste, judgment, and technical skill, to correct and thus "finish" it. The impostors who are abroad in all professions in a commercial nation "sedulously propagate an Opinion that Great Inventors Cannot Execute. This Opinion is as destructive of the true Artist as it is false by all Experience" (582). The proposition is that commerce, to decrease costs, seeks modes of production that accommodate cheap labor—Blake's "journeymen." This practical advantage is promoted ideologically by an aesthetic preference for their work—as technically correct—over the execution of the conceiving artist. To put it crudely, mad-

[18] See "form and content" in the index to Eaves, *Blake's Theory.*

ness is tolerable only in a context of sanity. The inability to execute is like the inability to function in society. Great inventors are imaginative, think interesting thoughts, but require the control of the sane complement. Imagination must be channeled. This is indeed a way of rationalizing a mode of production by means of the venerable idea that the wild horse of inspiration must be broken; we want its energy but not its chaos. Imagination is associated with the early stages of art production, invention, while control is associated with the later stages, execution. The transition stage installed between these two is imitation. The great executor imitates the great conceiver, as Dryden imitated Milton.

In response Blake makes three drastic modifications to the theory that he attributes to the counter-arts and blames for prejudicing his chances of success with the public: he claims that imagination is individualistic and autonomous, inverts the priorities of conception and execution, and tightens the sequence of the two to cancel the space that makes imitation possible. These changes make it possible to recategorize Dryden's virtuosity as "Niggling & Poco Piu," at best a belated and superfluous trifling, at worst an attack of alienated technical violence that "has degraded Milton" (E 581).

The opening sentence of the *Public Address* puts the fundamental opposition front and center, even at this early point already astride the opposition of mental states: "If Men of weak [mental] Capacities have alone the Power of Execution in Art M[r] B has now put to the test" by doing his engraving of the Canterbury pilgrims:

> If to Invent & to Draw well hinders the Executive Power in Art & his Strokes are still to be Condemnd because they are unlike those of Artists who are Unacquainted with Drawing is now to be Decided by The Public[.] M[r] B s Inventive Powers & his Scientific Knowledge of Drawing is on all hands acknowledgd it only remains to be Certified whether Physiognomic Strength & Power is to give Place to Imbecillity In a work of Art it is not fine tints that are required but Fine Forms, fine Tints without, are loathsom Fine Tints without Fine Forms are always the Subterfuge of the Blockhead. [E 571]

Indicatively, inventing *and* drawing, ordinarily separate mental and physical actions, appear twice in this passage as a single phenomenon that calls for a singular verb ("hinders," "is"). This practice compresses the more traditional idea that, for artists, drawing is the physical neighbor of mental invention. Blake moves further toward identification. So when he quickly goes on to claim that "Drawing" and "nothing Else" is the "Foundation" (E 572) of both engraving and painting, we should be prepared to understand *drawing* as *invention-drawing.* Although even this claim remains the compressed reformulation of a commonplace, it signals aggressive moves to come.

Come they do, in more striking declarations that drawing "is" not only the foundation but also "indeed the Superstructure" (E 572). Conception and execution are locked together:

> I have heard many People say Give me the Ideas. It is no matter what Words you put them into & others say Give me the Design it is no matter for the Execution. These People know Enough of Artifice but Nothing Of Art. Ideas cannot be Given but in their minutely Appropriate Words nor Can a Design be made without its minutely Appropriate Execution[.] The unorganized Blots & Blurs of Rubens & Titian are not Art nor can their Method ever express Ideas

> or Imaginations any more than Popes Metaphysical Jargon of Rhyming[.] Unappropriate Execution is the Most nauseous of all affectation & foppery He who copies does not Execute he only Imitates what is already Executed Execution is only the result of Invention [E 576]

Blake returns yet again to the subject at the end of the *Public Address.* The context is his despair over the frequent charge that "he can concieve but he cannot Execute." He injects the counter-arts theme and turns to the public: "this Absurd assertion has done me & may still do me the greatest mischief I call for Public protection against these Villains." As a defense he offers the fusion of idea and act: "I am like others Just Equal in Invention & in Execution." Why have lookers failed to see? Their eyes have been fooled by techniques of execution, as "absurd Nonsense about dots & Lozenges & Clean Strokes" has been "made to occupy the attention." He reaches out to claim a technical mastery of his own: "I defy any Man to Cut Cleaner Strokes than I do or rougher when I please." And finally he, a "Master of Drawing" addressing his public over the heads of fools, blockheads, knaves, and robbers, fires off the most impudent and audacious rendering of his theory yet. It arrives, characteristically, as a charged series of metaphorical equivalences: "Painting is Drawing on Canvas & Engraving is Drawing on Copper & nothing Else Drawing is Execution & nothing Else & he who Draws best must be the best Artist & to this I subscribe my name as a Public Duty" (E 582).

The identification is complete: conception is drawing, drawing is execution, conception is execution, and their shared sign is drawing. The apparent leveling, however, is to a great extent polemical. In fact Blake's value system is strongly at work orienting the items in the series toward conception and away from execution, toward the "Mental" and away from the "Corporeal" (*Milton* 1, E 95). His investment in the bifurcation of mind from nature is simply too powerful to allow mental invention to be made interchangeable with physical expression. The positive value assigned to conception may be mapped onto execution by metaphorical transfer. But the metaphor is not reversible, or rather, reversal would produce one of those characteristically catastrophic Blakean plots based on the loss of originality.

Hence the danger in separating conception from execution is not that execution will fail to influence conception but the other way around: "Execution is only the *result* of Invention" (my emphasis, E 576) conveys the true and irreversible sense. While leaving open the possibility that one might *have* ideas without voices or writing and designs without engraving or painting, he proposes that one cannot communicate, or *give,* them: "People say Give me . . . others say Give me," but words and pictures "cannot be Given" without the "minutely Appropriate Execution" on which adequate communication depends. Interference with it creates a space of mental confusion. When the dangerous intervals, the spaces of translation, are squeezed out of the process, however, it reorients itself not toward the center as it might, balancing conception with execution, but toward the "first Beginnings of Art" (E 573): "Let a Man who has made a Drawing go on & on & he will produce a Picture or Painting but if he chooses to leave off before he has spoild it he will Do a Better Thing." This kind of spoiling by going on—not making a picture "Drawn with a firm and decided hand at once" but making one "smoothd up *&* Niggled *&* Poco Piud *and* all the beauties pickd out *&* blurrd *&* blotted" (my emphases, 576)—is the kind that naturally happens in a life lived over the abysses of space and time, where the external world lures the artist out away from origins into extension, expenditure, and exertion.

Both the structure and the economics of scrutiny in the *Public Address* submit to this hierarchy of value because Blake understood that notions of conception and execution were helping to harmonize viewing practices with economic consequences. A key rhetorical goal of the *Public Address* is to persuade members of a viewing public that their optical habits have been constructed by and thus adjusted to the purposes of imperial commerce. Blake compares viewers who allow their attention to be occupied by Titianesque coloring techniques with a monkey before a mirror: he "Admires all his colours brown & warm / And never once percieves his ugly form" (E 578). The monkey here emblematizes the imbecilic mentality of the viewer, the prioritized sequences of commercialized viewing, and the self-regard at the heart of imitation. Colors in painting correspond to "what is calld Tints" in engraving, and the structure of scrutiny is the same: "The Modern Chalcographic Connoisseurs & Amateurs admire only the work of the journeyman Picking out of whites & blacks . . . they despise drawing which despises them in return. They see only whether every thing is coverd down but one spot of light" (577).

The alignment of viewing habits with buying habits generates Blake's (rather optimistic) analogy: "A Jockey that is any thing of a Jockey will never buy a Horse by the Colour & a Man who has got any brains will never buy a Picture by the Colour" (E 578). (The monkey is, as it were, buying himself by the color.) Whatever may be true of English jockeys, English connoisseurs go at it the other way around, bringing along "Gentlemen of Fortune who give Great Prices for Pictures" (579). The question is raised repeatedly: What will an English picture buyer "lay out his money upon" (579)? And repeatedly Blake returns with warnings of the "immense price" put on "Smears & Dawbs" (581–82) whose value is established by counter-looking.

As the analogy between horses and paintings suggests, his counter-proposal depends upon an inversion of structure and value represented as a reversion to a prior original structure and value. Thus he "invites the admirers of old English Portraits to look at his [*Canterbury Pilgrims*] Print" (E 577). In contrast to the habits of the ordinary connoisseur, their kind of looking is an overlooking of technique in favor of concept, an inversion of commercially established orders and priorities. In a revised viewing sequence that would revise cash value, features of execution, dots and lozenges and points of light, move into second place, after primary characteristics of conception. If his work were viewed in that new-old original way, Blake imagines, his losses would turn into gains.

"I in my own defence Challenge a Competition with the finest Engravings & defy the most critical judge to make the Comparison Honestly" (E 582). He supposes that he could win the contest if the viewing public would transfer the virtues that they credit to his conception over to his execution. But he seems to understand that they will do so only if they learn to look for execution last, and to look at it as a sign of conception: "My Conception & Invention are on all hands allowd to be Superior My execution will be found so too" (582). Will be found so *if* "Drawing is Execution & nothing Else" (582), that is, if only drawing qualifies as execution; *and if* the meaning of drawing is restricted to the aspect of a picture that allows the viewer to draw conclusions about the rather mysterious thing called "conception," and often treated in Enlightenment aesthetics as a kind of public script that the painting performs.

By and large, Blake's estimates have been borne out historically. He has consistently benefited from theories and viewing formulas that privilege conception. Under their influence he has won accolades as one of the most "inventive" or most "imaginative" of artists. He would benefit most from a theory that prized conception exclusively—as by proposing that conception is (the only) execution, but not the other way around. But his desire to extend the metaphorical reach of invention to take in drawing has met sustained resistance from influential theories that privilege drawing indeed, not as he wanted to conceive it—as synonymous with original invention—but as a system of execution with public standards of "quality" or "technical merit." In the company of those notoriously normative "great draughtsmen of the Renaissance," revered as the "final touchstone" of virtuosic skills comparable with those of operatic sopranos and classical violinists, Blake has fared poorly. Traditional art historians and connoisseurs, who are generally sympathetic with if not entirely loyal to these standards, have been apologetic in their dealings with Blake, feeling the pressure of a double standard: "A rather strange criterion in assessing the authenticity of works by Blake is that quality of execution is relatively immaterial. Blake was a very uneven artist . . . one can justifiably argue that a drawing too bad to be by, say, Flaxman or Stothard can nevertheless . . . be by Blake" (Butlin, "Cataloguing Blake" 80–81).[19] Whenever poetry, painting, and engraving have been defined by analogy with public performances, Blake has tended to lose out. Arts of performance that value (shared) virtuoso skills typically take for granted a rift between conception and execution because a performance is one of many possible executions of a prior conception—a script, a score, choreography. That is, performances are strong analogues to translations and imitations.

It cannot be that Blake eliminates elements of performance and translation in his theory. Dangerous spaces remain at the point where original artists get their original conceptions, as if from a pure reservoir known to artists but not to dealers; and, at the other end of the process of production, where artists publish for an audience whose own viewings and readings are so easily described as performances of scripts. He holds these dangers at bay by trading in the paradoxes of originality at one end—"the Human Imagination / Which is the Divine Body of the Lord Jesus" and "the Poetic Genius, / Who is the eternal all-protecting Divine Humanity" (*Milton* 3, 14[15]; E 96, 108) collapse others into selves—and in intensely social and religious rather than theatrical metaphors for the artist-audience relationship at the other: "Mark well my words. they are of your eternal salvation" (*Milton* 3.3–5, 14[15].1–2; E 96, 108). Dryden may imitate Milton. Blake closes the space: Milton enters his foot (*Milton* 21[23].4, E 115).

Among the consequences of Blake's reinter-

[19] For further discussion of technical merit as an operative category in connoisseurship, see my review of Butlin's *Paintings and Drawings of William Blake.*

pretation of conception and execution is support for the values of independent artisanry (and, implicitly, independent publication—as with the illuminated books and the *Canterbury Pilgrims* print) over the values of the workshop system supervised by manager-masters in commercial alliance with printshop middlemen. Of course this opposition is as much a manner of thinking as a reality: the shop of Blake's master, Basire, was probably not all that different from Woollett's. At most Basire might have encouraged the spirit of intelligent independence in his apprentices. He did, after all, manage to carry his apprentice Blake to term—though the tales of Blake's isolation in Westminster Abbey indicate that it may not have been easy—and to win his lifelong respect. Blake's own assessment is not to be lightly dismissed: his picture of Basire as an intelligent artisan and Woollett as a cunning manager ignorant of the craft and dependent upon other people's skills may not be entirely fabricated from fantasies of revenge against the system that had excluded Blake. But both shops were participating in that system.

Technohistory

> In society, once, a cultivated stranger, as a mark of polite attention, was showing him the first number of *The Mechanic's Magazine.* "Ah, sir," remarked Blake, with bland emphasis, "these things we artists HATE!"
>
> —Alexander Gilchrist, *Life of William Blake*

> Clearly, "art" is still primarily a cottage industry. As opposed to most architectural, film and TV works, which need constant infusions of client capital to happen, "art" can remain relatively unmediated by the armies of "collaborators" whose desires must be considered and wallets stroked.
>
> —Barbara Kruger, "What's High, What's Low—and Who Cares?"

We need to know what characterizes Blake's awareness of and attitude toward this system. Perhaps "machine" was the most telling noun to emerge in his reflections during the stormy period of his 1809 exhibition and its aftermath. Although he seems to have had little if any use for the term or concept previously, it suddenly takes a central role in focusing his attack on the "Venetian" and "Flemish" ascendancy in the English school, first in the *Descriptive Catalogue* (twice in the entry for *Satan Calling Up His Legions,* E 547) and then even more forcefully and frequently in the *Public Address.*[20] He

[20] In Blake's lexicon, the machine is clearly a later and a primarily negative item. In the extant prose writings before the *Descriptive Catalogue* and *Public Address,* "machinery" occurs just once as a conventional designation for the supernatural agents in epic: "the Persons & Machinery intirely new to the Inhabitants of Earth" (to Butts, 25 April 1803, E 728). Machines have no place in the vocabulary of the illuminated books of the 1790s. Later there are a couple of "dark machines" and "immense machines" in *The Four Zoas* (8.101.7, E 373; 7.96.10, E 361), though we cannot easily tell when they were written into the manuscript, which Blake worked over for at least the better part of a decade.

employs the term over a broad range from most to least tangible. At its narrowest, "machine" designates a subset of the tools of Blake's trade, such as the ruling machine that efficiently produces a "Ruled Sky that is quite Even" but never a "Natural Sky" that is "Ever varying."[21] The engraver is not waxing Wordsworthian. He means that even the imitative aim of copying "Natures Shadows" (575)—a telling phrase—cannot be well served by such machines. The point is small, we might say a technicality. But he moves straightaway, by means of an attack on the technical "Ignorance" of Woollett, to the sublime heights of abstraction: "A Machine is not a Man nor a Work of Art it is Destructive of Humanity & of Art the Word Machination" (E 575)—and leaves off in mid-sentence with this connection between machines, devices that hide their users' ignorance behind mechanical procedures in a kind of hypocrisy of technique, and machination as the behavioral context of that hypocrisy in the counter-arts.

To put it bluntly, in Blake's argument machines are seen as forms of artificial intelligence that promote what has been called the dumbing down of the work force, "What all can do Equally well" (E 573). At the same time they draw attention away from instantaneous mental life ("the Inspired Moments of Genius") toward corporeal life in the extended world of time and space ("the Lifes Labour of Ignorance" [574]). Thus Blake dwells on the interruptive nature of production, in which many dispersed little steps—the "fumble & Bungle . . . which Doubts & Hesitates" (575)—try to imitate the continuously expressive motion that can be concentrated in the firmness of an original master's touch.

This is the antitechnological germ of Blake's case against "Venetian" art. Much of the significance of his argument lies in its power of prognostication: it soars high above the average level of English-school discourse, anticipating some of the most acute critiques of mechanization associated with the Industrial Revolution. Thus a few colorful Blake quotations have become stock ornaments in that repertory.[22] But the implications of his argument may be too readily dissolved into a generalized suspicion of technologies. We would want to distinguish his argument from some others. For one thing, it follows from his middling social vision, where a few masters fear replacement by many workers. That is, his criticism of machines expresses fears of losing work not to machines, Luddite fashion, but to "ignorant journeymen." Despite meaningful overlap, antimachine arguments are launched at different levels in the social hierarchy and diverge at key points. From the assembly line, for example, one might seriously entertain the counter-argument that the march of technology can improve employment opportunities by multiplying and leveling jobs—many journeymen for one master. Blake's argument would strongly resist such appeals, be-

Then there are three others, all located within fifty lines of one another, in chap. 2 of *Jerusalem:* "a Sexual Machine: an Aged Virgin Form" vegetating out of Hyde Park, Africa's "dark / Machines" of slavery, and Albion's "machines . . . woven with his life" (*J* 39[44].25, 40[45].22, 25; E 187–88).

[21] Wilson Lowry, whose portrait Blake engraved with John Linnell, invented a ruling machine in 1790. In improved versions it was used throughout the nineteenth century in various graphic media (Wakeman 30–31, 171; Stannard 45–46). Landseer applauded Lowry's invention in his *Lectures* (141–42), and Ruthven Todd claimed Blake used it for his last project, the Dante plates. See also Essick, *Separate Plates* 207–8.

[22] I think of the works of J. Bronowski, Lewis Mumford, and Marshall McLuhan, for instance. One could name many others.

cause its attitude toward machines is bound up with a range of other intellectual ideals, pitting "destructive" mechanism against life, soul, humanity, and art. The leveling potential of the argument is all toward the middle: no one a journeyman or a gentleman connoisseur, everyone a master artist and a Christian, "Would to God that all the Lords people were Prophets" (*Milton* 1, E 96).

In general the arguments favored in English-school discourse had been progressive, based profoundly on visions of gradual, systematic improvement—on technical and aesthetic education for English artists and audiences—and they had strongly opposed the arguments from fixed native ability that had been used to characterize England as irremediably backward in the visual arts. The Vasari canon, the associated pedagogical program, and the ideals of Carracci eclecticism—harmonizing the several virtues of invention and, especially, execution in a single presentation—had seemed very attractive under the circumstances. Painters might be less well trained than they should be, potential purchasers might have poorer taste than they should have, but all such defects could be remedied by institutions that would provide training, practice, encouragement, and opportunity.

Blake's argument, by contrast, is technologically so regressive—so given to notions of recovery and return—that it comes close to opposing tools and materials per se. This may not be apparent at first glance: after all, it is just here in the attack on ruling machines that Blake, with the pride of an artisan, scorns Woollett for not knowing how to grind his graver. If he had known, the argument suggests, he would not have needed to rely on the compensations of ruling machines. Still, the same logic that seeks to lessen the distortions of time and space by finding the most immediate communication between artist and viewer and the shortest path between mind and matter; that idealizes an intellectual world free of Adam and Satan, the natural limits of contraction and opacity; that sees history as largely the story of repeated efforts to reascend from nature into mind; and that blames a rather simple engraver's work saver for being "Destructive of Humanity & of Art" is not far from blaming even the burin that Woollett never learned to sharpen.

It is possible to advance a more moderate argument about Blake's attitudes toward his media. Robert Essick has envisioned a Blake who conducted technical experiments in the spirit of exploratory interactions of mind with material medium; each would make its own contribution. The conceptions of Joseph Viscomi's Blake take shape in the medium of execution (Essick, *Printmaker* 35; Viscomi, *Idea;* cf. Eaves, *Blake's Theory* 151). As attractive as these transactional models of creativity are to (what is left today of) the romantic spirit, they risk sentimentality and anachronism. They tend to sentimentalize "the medium," thus confusing Blake's Platonistic if not Platonic theorizing with the kind of Wordsworthian naturalism that promotes the deep engagements of human subjects with natural objects. In practice, of course, Blake may have accepted the contributions his media could make to his messages. But in theory such interactive ideals seem more typical of twentieth-century expressionistic painting than of late eighteenth- and early nineteenth-century engraving, and insufficiently answerable to the severe oppositions that structure Blake's theorizing, especially after his return to London from Felpham in 1803. Certainly, within the terms of Blake's argument such simple tools as burins, quills, brushes, and graphite pencils are more responsive to acts of mind than ruling machines, which have a limited range of repetitive action within a confined mechanical system, but all tools signify compromises that This World makes necessary. There are no burins in eternity.

Even if the ultimate artistic freedom is "Freedom from all Law of the Members" (E 784), nevertheless we see here the great appeal that illuminated printing must have had, less as an escape from nature than as a worthy compromise with it: an autographic medium close to drawing, responsive to the hand and thus to the "melodious accents" of a single mind and imagination; a medium in which lines drawn onto the plate by a human hand holding a simple tool such as a quill or brush loaded with a simple paintlike fluid would become printable lines without the intervention of (more) mechanical transitional processes.[23] Even the requisite technical procedures could be turned to symbolic effect: acids in relief etching purge the matter left unmarked by mind ("I will pour Aqua fortis on the Name of the Wicked & turn it into an Ornament & an Example" [E 579]), and reverse writing suggests the difficulties of representing the realities of intellect in a "sexual" world of "generation" that inverts them (fig. 4.1).

Though it may be idle to fantasize that Blake invented illuminated printing to practice theories expressed two or three decades later, it is

[23] After decades of floundering by his predecessors, Essick was the first to describe accurately the technical basis of illuminated printing (*Printmaker* 85–164). Viscomi confidently amends significant details, adds a wealth of facts and contexts, and constructs an imposing new set of arguments about the dating and editing of the illuminated books. For a useful critique of Blake's attitudes toward his medium (or rather, the medium of his that has been favored by posterity) in a commercial context, see Mann.

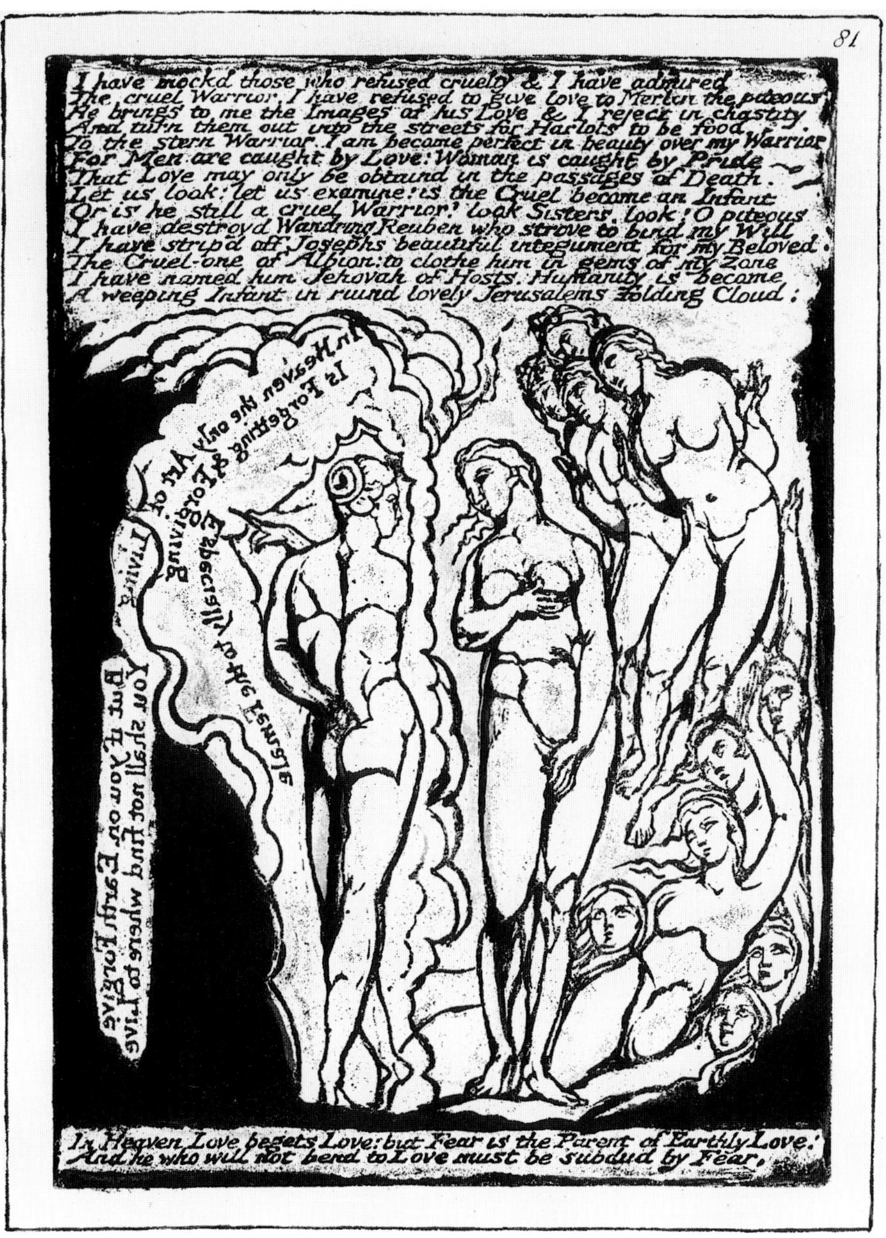

4.1. William Blake, *Jerusalem,* plate 81 (copy D), relief etching, c. 1804–1820.

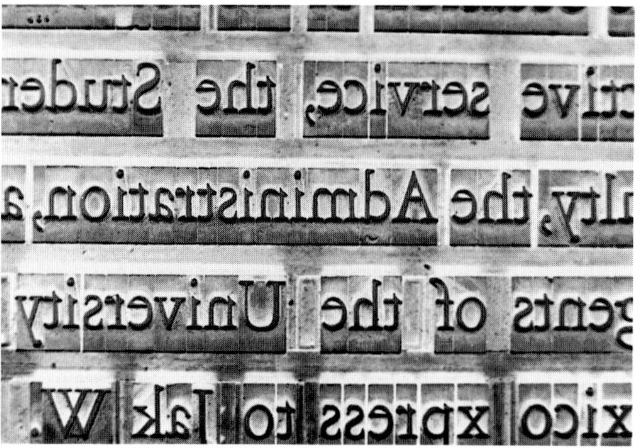

4.2. Type in chase.

worth noticing why he never needed to abandon the medium: the technical features of illuminated printing correlate well with the technical values that produce such works as the *Canterbury Pilgrims* print and such polemical defenses as the *Public Address.* Projected into a technological history of engraving, they shape a narrative with the "Enterance of Vandyke & Rubens" at its English turning point. Although Blake never systematically related that history and perhaps never fully formulated it, we can recapture the broad outlines.

The technological key to the history is what Blake castigated as "division"—namely, the principle that complex operations can be mechanized by being broken into simpler operations. In many cases more efficient divisions depend upon some binary or "digital" segment by which all things can be reduced to two bits, 0–1, on–off. As I shall construe it here, digitization is not a notion confined to electronic devices but a technological norm that operates across a spectrum of materials and processes. As a rule of thumb, the more deeply digitization penetrates, the more efficient the process becomes. The history of engraving recapitulates within print technology one version of the discovery of a workable digital principle that could be efficiently applied to the intractable problems of reproducing paintings.[24]

The situation of engraving in Blake's time and before was roughly as follows. Technically, engraving is a family tree of which printing is (only) one branch. But the discovery of movable type altered the outlook for letterpress printing so favorably that the technological basis common to the reproduction of both words and pictures became hard to discern: words were "printed," pictures "engraved." Alphabetic technology, the division of all words into a small set of uniform letters—twenty-six in the Latin alphabet, plus ten numerals and a few "accidentals"—made efficient letterpress printing possible. Typesetters set their type in letters, not in words or sentences, and a handful of little metal blocks could print every sentence. Technologically those uniform letters had the efficiency of interchangeable parts, and they were reusable: once a book had been printed, the types could be unlocked from their chases and shelved for the next job.

By comparison engraving was slow, inefficient, and expensive. "Engraving is of so slow Process . . . ," Blake commented to William Hayley, "Endless Work is the true title of Engraving . . ." (27 April 1804, E 747). For a painter such as John Singleton Copley, who was selling history painting by tying it to contemporary history and simultaneously using engraving to increase the profits generated by a single cluster

Letterpress printing is a relief process, like the relief etching that Blake used to produce most of his illuminated books. The units of reproduction here, geometrically coordinated blocks, one per letter, were molded from molten metal by a Linotype machine in the 1970s, but they could have been produced in several other ways, including relief etching.

Part of the top left quarter of the copperplate for (canceled) plate *a* of *America* is the only surviving fragment of any of Blake's relief-etched plates. The unit of reproduction here is the plate. Subunits, such as lines (of designs) and letters (of words), are produced as part of one process.

[24] The following discussion is indistinctly but profoundly indebted to a range of suggestive work by Walter Benjamin, William Ivins, Marshall McLuhan, and Lewis Mumford, pioneers in tying the evidence of technology to the visual arts, as well as to subsequent studies by Hyatt Mayor and Estelle Jussim.

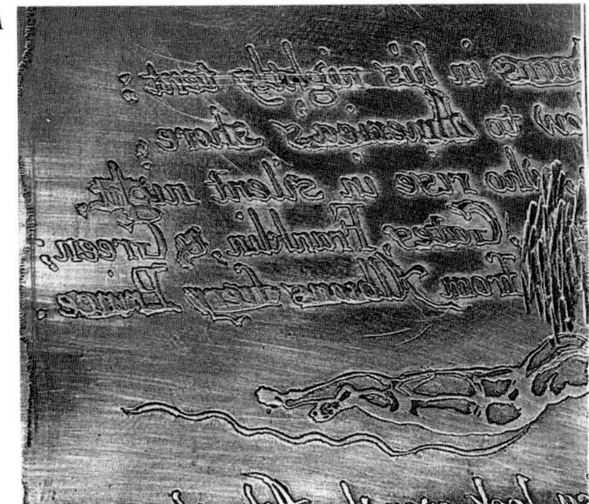

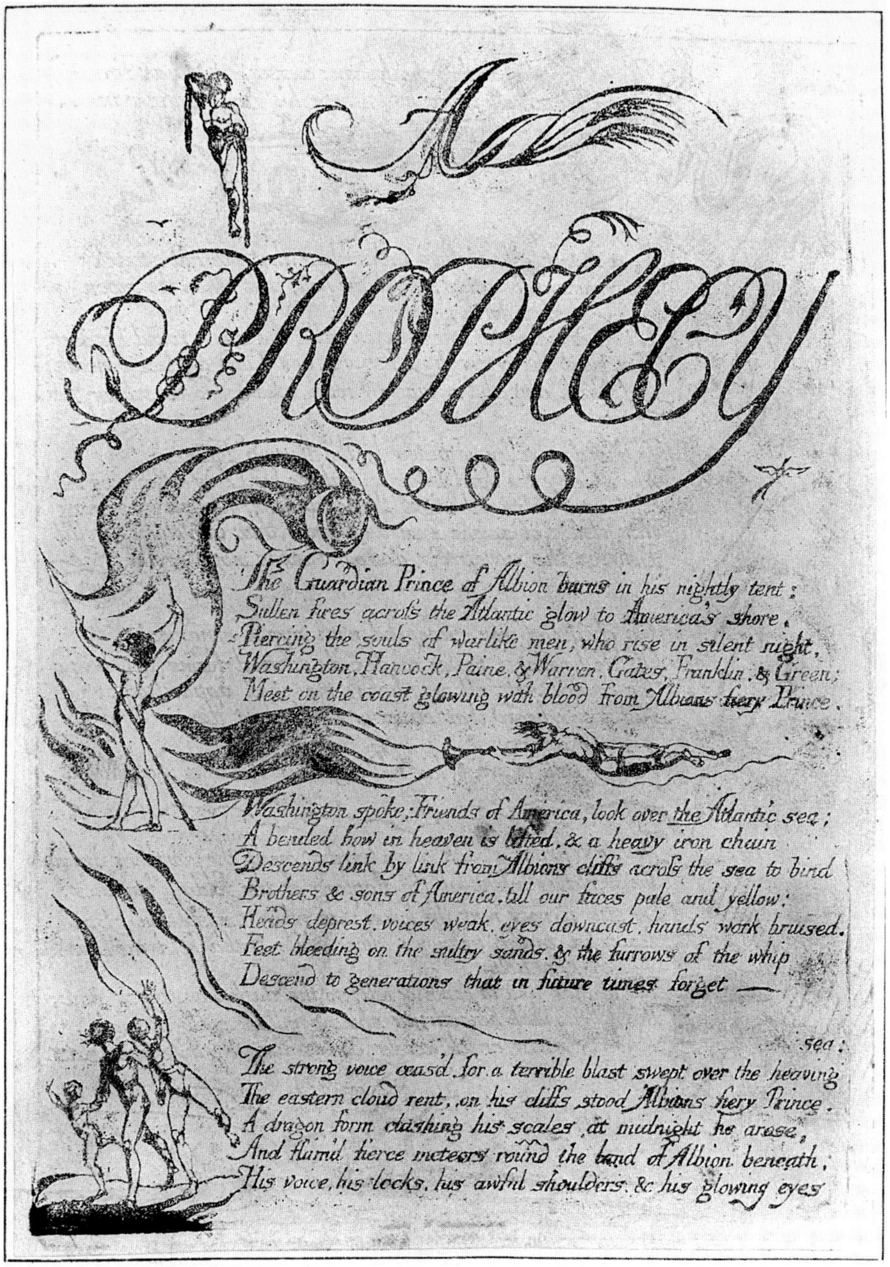

4.3. William Blake, *America a Prophecy,* 1793: (*A*) fragment of relief-etched copperplate, detail; (*B*) plate *a,* printed impression.

of imagery, the technological frailty of engraving was devastating. Copley's *Death of Chatham* had three engravers, first John Keyse Sherwin briefly and then, for an inordinately long time indeed, Bartolozzi, who worked on the plate until 1791, more than a decade after subscriptions were first taken. Because Bartolozzi's plate turned out to be so expensive and its commercial potential thus so reduced, Copley hired Jean Mari Delattre, one of Bartolozzi's assistants, to engrave a smaller, cheaper version. Upon its completion Copley rejected it as unmarketable, thus inspiring a lawsuit that was not resolved until 1801 (Landseer and Bartolozzi were among those who testified for Delattre) and delaying the print's publication until 1820. Copley's dealings with engravers were so miserable that when he was soliciting subscriptions for *The Siege of Gibraltar* in 1789, the engraving for neither *The Death of Chatham* nor *The Death of Peirson* had been delivered to subscribers (Prown 2:289–90). The wretched list of postponed and suspended commissions could be extended indefinitely.[25]

Engraving's technological and economic ties to printing generated relentless pressures to speed up, systemize, and cheapen. Ideally engraving would have been in perfect technological harmony with its neighboring systems, painting and printing—so well coordinated as to extract maximum advantage from its ability to translate the terms of the one system of representation into the very different terms of the other. But it regularly suffered the disadvantages of both and received the social, economic, and technological benefits of neither. It seemed terribly poky and unsystematic by comparison with the printing press that was setting the pace, and yet harshly mechanical by comparison with the imagery it was trying to reproduce. The ultimate result was oblivion. Today it is difficult to explain the cultural role of a Basire or a Woollett because methods of reproduction more efficiently coordinated with the printer's press and painter's palette replaced engraving as Blake knew it. The craft now survives largely, if marginally, as a minor vehicle for "original" work in the "graphic arts" tier of the "fine arts" departments of art schools and universities. But in the stress of the relationship that once bound the fortunes of engraving to those of painting and printing lies the sum of its interest to us.

The success of letterpress print technology relied heavily upon uniformities and simplifications that yielded great gains in efficiency. *All* printable expressions in languages written in the Latin alphabet combine those twenty-six letters, the meanings of which do not depend

[25] See, for example, Fox's revealing list of the engravers' failures to meet their deadlines for the project to reproduce paintings from the new National Gallery in the 1830s (14).

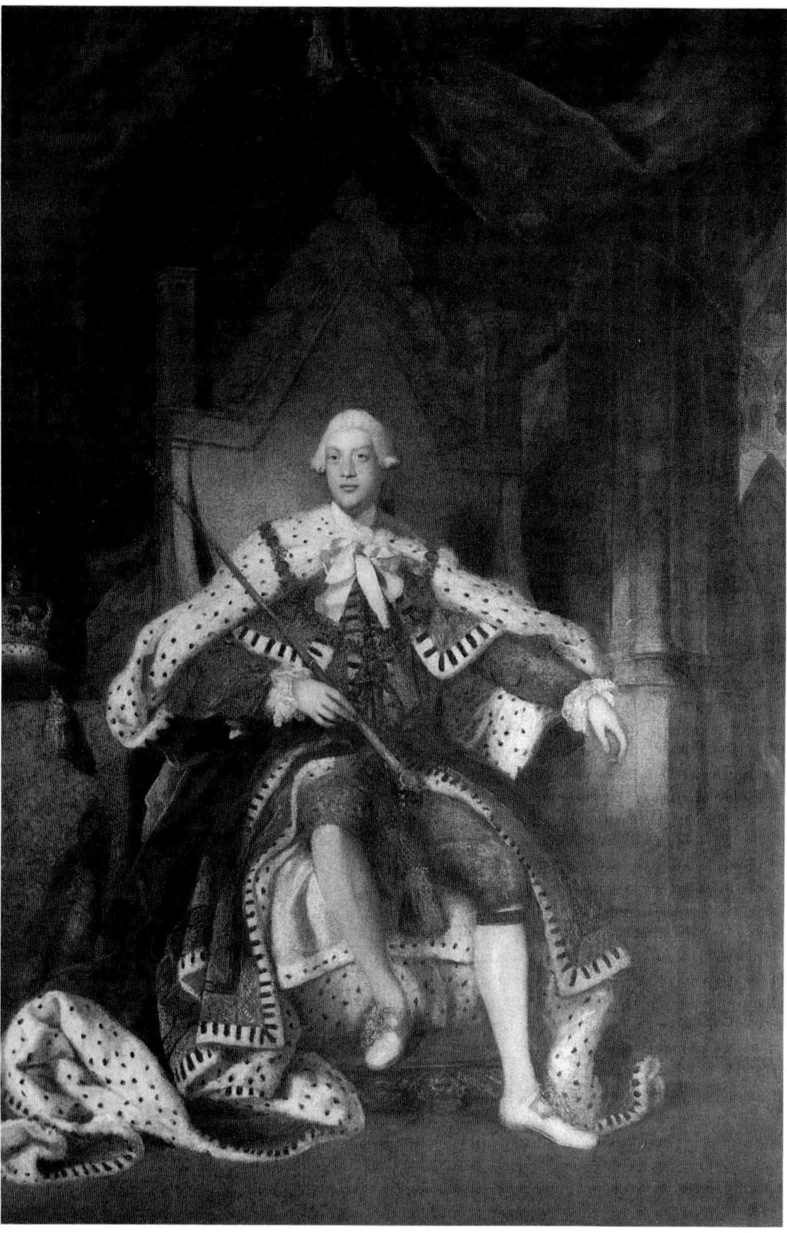

4.4. Joshua Reynolds, *King George III,* oil, 1780.

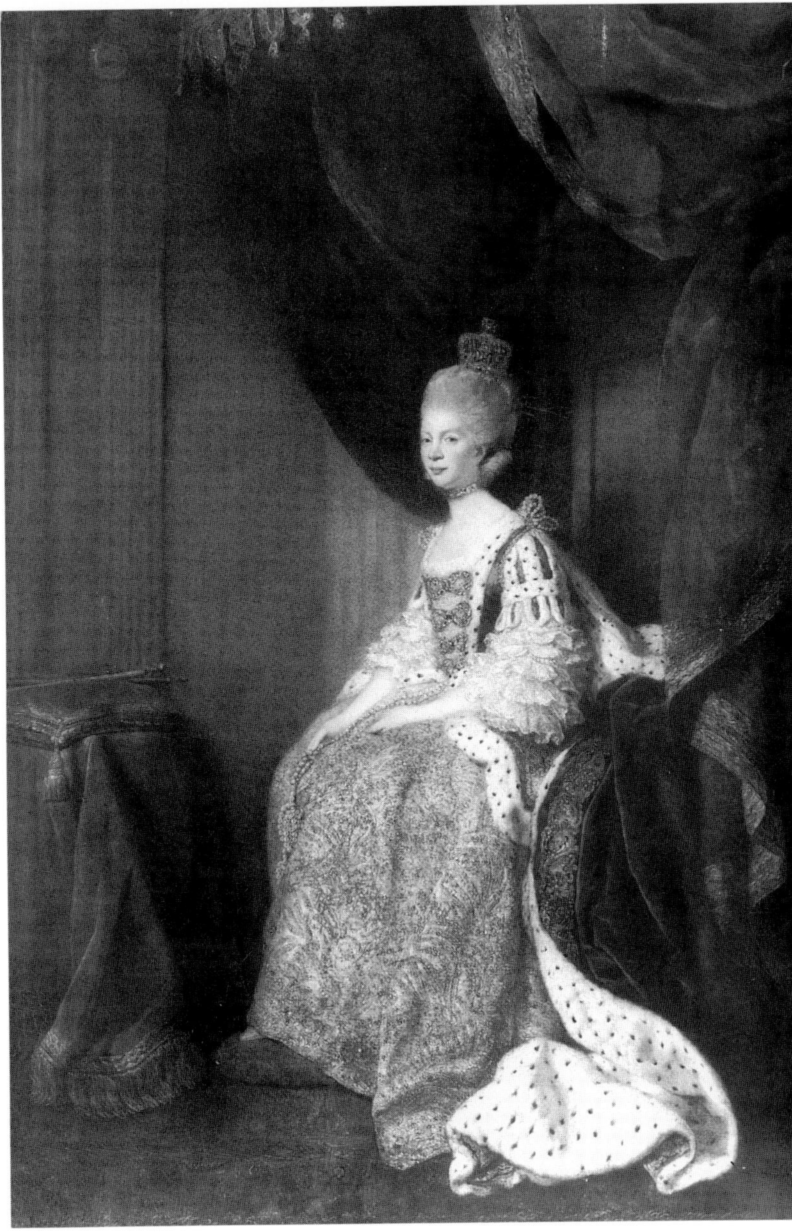

4.5. Joshua Reynolds, *Queen Charlotte*, oil, 1780.

If pictures could be divided into something parallel to letters in words, then they could easily be reproduced. Long before photography and the halftone screen, picturemakers in most branches of the enterprise sought a mechanical basis for the reproduction of images. A focus on this aspiration helps to organize data that typically have been beyond the attention span of mainstream art histories. The history of the visual arts in England is littered with revealing anecdotes that might be filed under Blake's phrase "machine of art": about the one-man painting factory who adhered to a method so efficient that he could paint the twelve apostles while his wife got supper; the warehouse of partly finished commissions left by Sir Godfrey Kneller at his death; the cartel of leading portraitists whose monopoly depended upon the services of a single drapery painter; and the mistakes made by portrait painters when their system seemed so efficient that the human operators dozed, producing an admiral with two hats or a lady in shepherdess garb who had intended to be displayed in finery (Whitley 1:23–24, 22, 53–55, 104). *The London Tradesman* cautioned parents in search of an occupation for their children that

> the Drapery-Painter is but the lowest Degree of a liberal painter. . . . A Portrait-Painter, who is well employed, has not Time to cloath his Figures, and therefore employs a Drapery-Painter to finish that Part of the Work. . . . [H]is chief Skill consists in his Knowledge of Colours . . . for the Painter

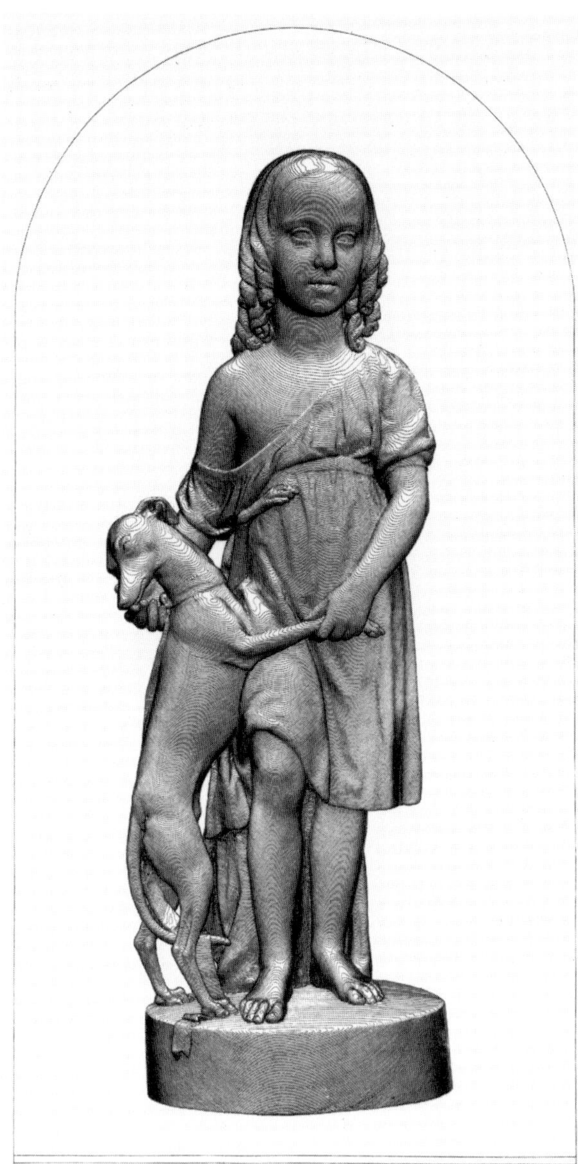

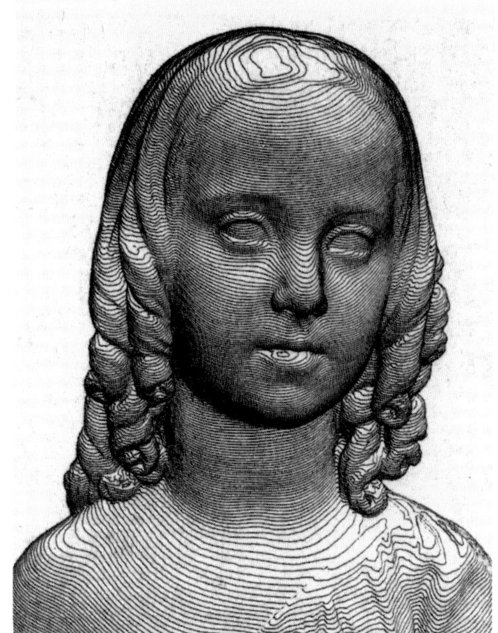

4.6. Bate's New Process: engraving of *The Friends,* 1848, after a statue by William Behnes, and detail.

on unique characteristics but on general configuration. A printer's *n,* it turns out, is an *n* rather than a *u* or an *m* across a wide range of styles and sizes. Since authorship depends not on the representation of unique characteristics but on generalized images, it may efficiently detach itself from the technology of reproduction on which it depends for extended representation in time and space. Books have authors to write them, while in separate cultural compartments they have other specialists—designers, printers, publishers—to reproduce them.

Hence we reflect separately on the aesthetic sense represented through book design and the aesthetic sense represented through the text, which is a general or abstract entity located in all particular instances: *The Pilgrim's Progress* is a text, a sequence of words, not a particular

generally draws the Out-lines, and leaves him to fill up the empty Space with proper Colours. The Drapery-Painters . . . have commonly but a dull Genius, and a mere Mechanic Head. [R. Campbell 101]

The situation is easier to understand when one studies the problem Reynolds faced when he became principal painter to George III in 1784 and was expected to turn out dozens of royal portraits for government offices. His studio carried out this formidable but profitable task according to set formulas of procedure.

The interlocked histories of engraving and sculpture come together outlandishly in *The Friends,* an engraving of a statue by a process announced in the article "On the Applications of Science to the Fine and Useful Arts" in the *Art-Union Monthly Journal* in 1848. The patented process mapped three-dimensional images onto copper with a uniform system of topographical representation. Most interestingly, the technology of translation produced a style that fits neatly into the history of engraving, highlighting the mechanical basis of that history. The *Art-Union* extolled our

real pleasure in witnessing those mechanical appliances which have for their object the multiplication of the beautiful. . . . Every invention which enables the artist to give to his public copies of his works at an economic rate, benefits alike the producer and the purchaser. . . . The question, indeed, of the advantages of economy of production,

printing "of" that text. A poorly printed *Pilgrim's Progress* is *The Pilgrim's Progress* still. Authors who want control over the printing of "their" texts have to have the surplus influence to exert control in a technological arena not considered properly theirs. Their power must be sufficient to flow across the cultural space that Blake identified as the space of imitation or reproduction, which is, however, a very well-established institutional frontier in the arts and economics of word processing. Authors who attempt to move the boundary, as by making the page, for instance, a unit of authorial significance in their novels, fly in the face of established power relations based on alignments of money and technology. If the page is among other things an economic unit to be packed uniformly with type—white space is a luxury commodity—then sacrificing that uniformity to some unfamiliar notion of significance, such as the significance of the top of the page or the right edge, calls for an economic decision to invest more money per unit.

"Photo-offset lithography"—photography and lithography combined with traditional methods of typesetting—transformed the technology of printing during the first half of the twentieth century. Lithography and photography are graphic processes that do not distinguish words from images; hence the reproduction of printed pictures as "halftones" alongside the text became a routine event in printing at all levels from the illustrated daily to the book of fine photographs. More recent alternatives to traditional letterpress and offset printing that involve computer technology and laser printing (a form of xerography), such as "desktop publishing," put the history of printing in yet another perspective. Desktop publishing, as the name suggests, may also offer new opportunities to redistribute the traditional spaces in the production process by bringing more of the technology under the supervision of computer-wise authors and, in some cases, by connecting authors in an electronic network that could conceivably shed the customary distinction between author and audience for an "interactive" relationship. At least that is one vision of the post-print age that has animated the latest generation of electronic prophets, including even such formerly sober scholars as Richard Lanham.

However computers may shape the future of what has been the four-part process of writing, printing, publishing, and reading/viewing, it is important to see that deep digitization makes these forecasts possible: digital processes in the computer's central processing unit, of course, but also in the sending and receiving of bits of digitized information over connecting lines, and, most important for our understanding of engraving in Blake's time, in the digital reproduction of visual information on the monitor. Pixels, the building blocks of information that make coherent pictures on the screen, visualize the digitized flow of electronic signals. The size and density of pixels determine the optical resolution; the more pixels per square centimeter, say, the higher the resolution. The higher the resolution, the less the human eye can perceive the pixels that make up the image (fig. 4.7).

Electronic pixels exemplify principles of reproduction that we can trace through the history of picturemaking. The pixel matrix of modern printing, as it were, is the halftone screen, where resolution is gauged in vertical and horizontal lines that create the characteristic "dots" of the halftone. The process is digital in the broad sense: the halftone screen translates all images, no matter what their constitu-

has been plainly answered by the stream of wealth which in many cases has poured in to the producer. Beyond this, the benefits to be derived from it are great in a moral point, and these demand the attentive consideration of all who are interested in the well-being of their race. [363]

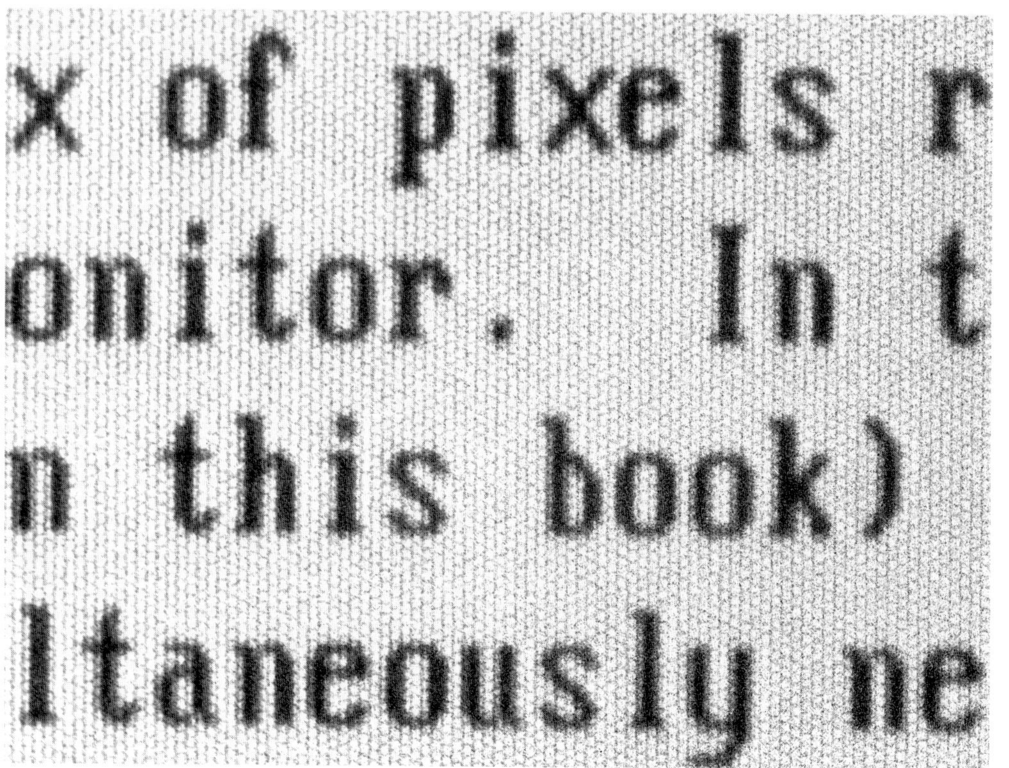

4.7. Printed text in pixels.

A uniform matrix of pixels reproduces the letter images on a computer monitor. In this illustration (as in most illustrations in this book) at least three reproductive layers are simultaneously nested: the halftone screen reproduces a photograph reproducing a monitor screen. These are the three closest to the surface; they bear the historical traces of several others.

tion, into combinations of dark and light dots of varying density (fig. 4.8). Since the light areas are already present—they come from the paper itself—the printing press needs to perform one simple action, print dots of ink. Though at first glance a halftone may appear complicated, with its areas of light and dark subtly ordering the tones and lines of the image, in fact the ordering is an automatic outcome. The screen, placed between the image (say a painting, but more likely a photograph of a painting) and the camera, breaks up the image into constituent dots without reference to the makeup of the image. No matter what—dots, lozenges, lines, tones, colors—makes the image, the halftone translates it into dots (fig. 4.9).

The success of the system depends partly upon its relation to the threshold of human vision. If the dots are small enough, they disappear beneath that threshold. If they are not, the units of translation visibly compete with the message being translated; the result is optical noise that increases as the units of reproduction grow larger. Consider "block portraits," computer-generated images devised in the early

Here the common halftone screen is caught in the uncommon act of reproducing only itself. This enlargement makes it easy to spot the intersecting lines, so many per inch, that create the dots characteristic of the system.

The analog tones of a familiar oil painting are converted into the digital reproductive terms, dark and light bits, of a halftone screen (*A*). A "line shot" of the same painting (*B*) shows what happens when the halftone screen is not present to reorganize the image into printable bits. When the bits diminish in relation to the threshold of vision (*C*), they disappear, recreating the smooth tonal effects of the painting.

4.8. Halftone screen.

B

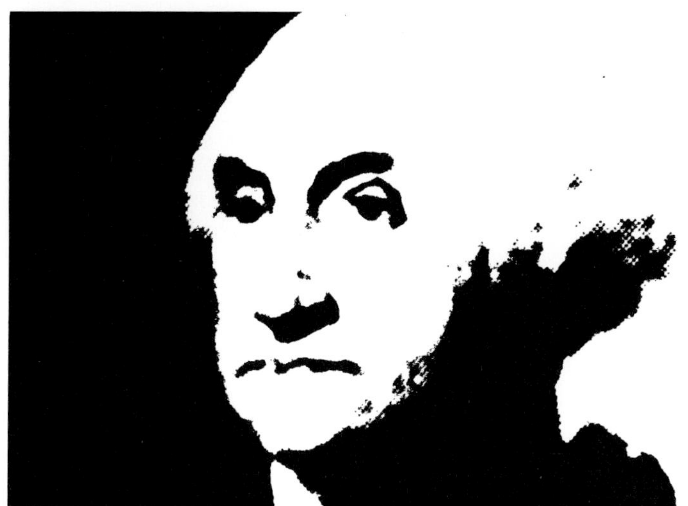

A

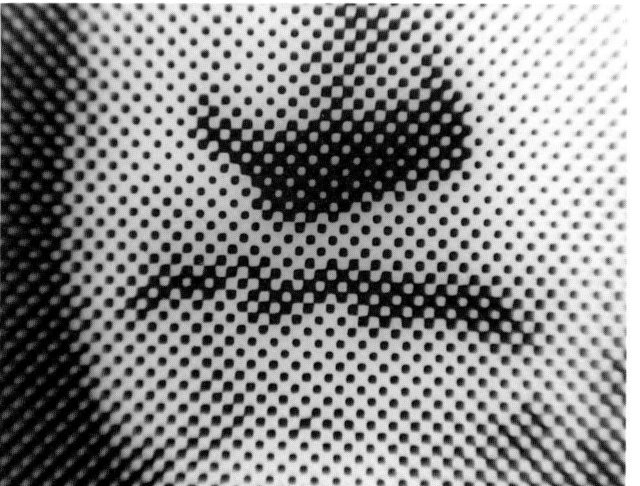

C

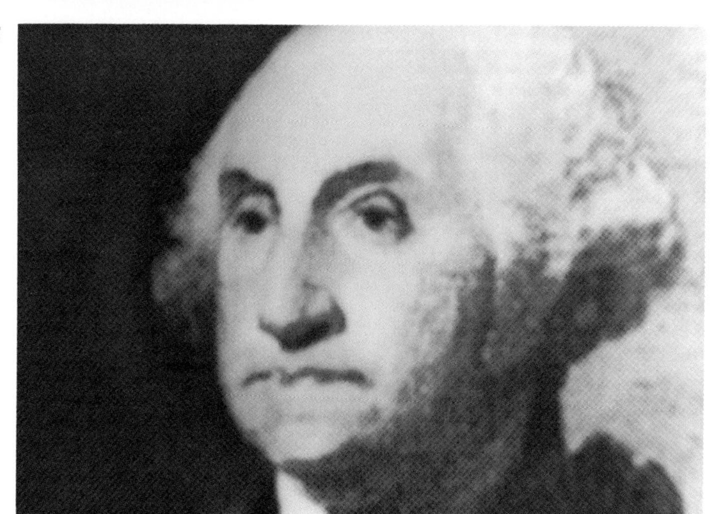

4.9. Gilbert Stuart, *George Washington,* oil, detail: (*A*) magnified halftone; (*B*) line shot; (*C*) halftone. White House Collection.

1970s for experiments testing the human ability to recognize faces, as in police sketches (figs. 4.10, 4.11). Now ubiquitous, block portraits show up regularly in their static printed form on book jackets and in their dynamic video-tronic form as the masks that simultaneously conceal and divulge the faces of subjects being interviewed on television news programs. The principle of reproduction is the one we have been discussing, the only difference being that

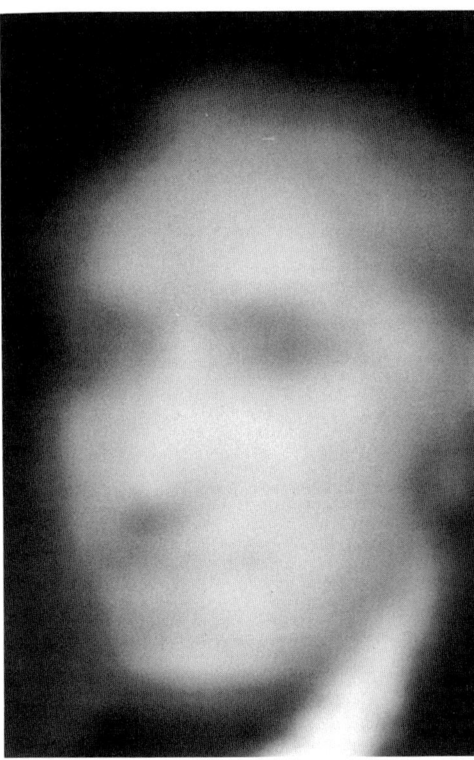

4.10*A*. Computer-generated block portrait of George Washington: (*A*) out of focus; (*B*) in focus. Courtesy of Leon D. Harmon, by permission of the estate of Leon D. Harmon.

the objective is to produce a deliberately degraded image, a bad translation. "Bad" in this instance means, technically, that the unit of reproduction, analogous to the pixel and the halftone dot, dominates the image being reproduced, raising the optical noise produced by the system itself to a level high enough to interfere with recognition.

The block portrait can be manipulated so as to help explain the generalizing that is fundamental to optical reproduction. To reproduce an image, one bit of the system generalizes the particulars in one area of the image created by another system. In block portraits a uniform grid is imposed on a face, and a computer averages all the tones within a single square (which might be a dot in a halftone or a pixel on a monitor) to a single figure. The average is rounded off to the nearest step on a gray scale—the steps from the lightest light available in the system to the darkest dark through steps of gray. The bigger the squares of the grid and the fewer the steps on the gray scale, the higher the level of generalization to which the image is carried. Imagine this system at its most extreme, a grid with one square and a gray scale with one step. The translation of the entire image, whatever its configuration in the original, would appear as a single area of one uniform tone. Furthermore, *all* images fed through the system would translate into a single uniform image.

"This is quite Perfection, one Generalizing Tone" ("To Venetian Artists," E 515). And this is, I believe, about as close as we can get to a technological model of Blake's argument against generalization—"General Knowledge is Remote Knowledge. . . . General Masses are as Much Art as a Pasteboard Man is Human" (*VLJ*, E 560)—in its links to mechanical systems, translation, and the history of reproduction. These are the terms by which he interpreted the commercial and political significance of English-school discourse. In the aesthetic sphere, Enlightenment generalization authorized such idealizations as Joshua Reynolds's "central forms," images averaged out of their singularity in pursuit of the tulip relieved of its streaks—not the English or Abyssinian

A computer-generated block portrait (*A*) reveals more about the principles that make halftone reproduction work. Here the portrait seems grossly out of focus and hence obscure, though the tones are smooth to the eye. Instead of improving its intelligibility, focusing the portrait (*B*) merely shifts its obscurity into another register. *B* is, of course, a halftone reproduction of the block portrait, in which the large units of its grid are dispersed into bits so small that they are nearly indistinguishable. Reproduced here in monochrome, the original (as it were) appeared as a color reproduction in Leon Harmon's article "The Recognition of Faces" (1973).

tulip but the tulip, and the flower, behind both. In Blake's reading of the situation, to value that form of generalization is to value approximations, the indefinite, indeterminate, and indistinct, over precisions, the definite, determinate, and distinct; translations over originals. In some more familiar versions of this attack on Enlightenment ideals, the opposition is between general ideas of things and things themselves in all their natural factness and presence. But Blake seems to have been quite certain that he was not opposing ideas to realities, or the human to the natural, but was opposing two different mental constructs to each other, while acknowledging that they related as original to translation. Burke, in ranking generalization first among the powers of the human mind (and provoking Blake's famous retort that "To Generalize is to be an Idiot" because "General Knowledges are those Knowledges that Idiots possess" [anno. Reynolds, E 641]), was in this context supplying ideology for commercial ventures that stand to gain from mechanized systems that require the average of human effort and ability. A work force and an art based in what all can do equally well are always available. Avoiding costly labor shortages and self-aggrandizing special-case geniuses, the system strives to coordinate a technology of interchangeable parts with its human complement.

The halftone screen is, on one side, a technical descendant of the reproductive engraving that it replaced. (Some screens are named after engraving techniques and media; thus "mezzotint" screens.) For the sake of a point we might say that reproductive engraving strove through most of its history to achieve the condition of halftone reproduction.[26] Seeing the familiar face on the dollar bill [fig. 4.12] in relation to the block portraits in figures 4.10 and 4.11 makes the technological connection plain. Again focusing disintegrates the image into its components, not in this case a grid of averaged tones but the engraver's dots, dashes, and lozenges, which the eye averages into tones and lines (as at the border of Washington's cheek on the right, a line suggested by the intersecting tonal systems used to create the face and background). In the eighteenth century Robert Dossie criticized this technique in a complaint about the popularity of "high finish": outlines in small engravings, he said, "ought not to be obscure, but distinctly visible. Much pains is now taken to form them only by strokes, which approach to the place of them [the outlines]. This manner may, perhaps, be good in larger works; but it is very faulty in small, because it gives too much softness to the outlines" (2:143–44).

The halftone screen exemplifies another principle of reproduction relevant to Blake's critique of the history of engraving. Not all halftone screens divide pictures into dots; almost any binary pattern that will reduce tones to dark ink on light surfaces will do (fig. 4.13). And no halftone provides a perfect translation

[26] Although John Pouncy's *Dorsetshire Photographically Illustrated* (1857) was the first English book with photolithographed halftones (Wakeman 89), a satisfactory halftone screen was not available until the 1880s (Wakeman 95), and photolithography was not in general use until some years after that. The roadside of nineteenth-century book illustration is littered with such inventors' dreams as photoglyptic engraving, collotype, photogalvanography, heliogravure, photogravure, photomezzotint, woodburytype, photoaquatint, and zincography, not to mention leggotype, luxotype, hyalography, ink-photo, wharf-litho, scratchboard, and chromotypography, to name only a few gleaned from Wakeman (passim).

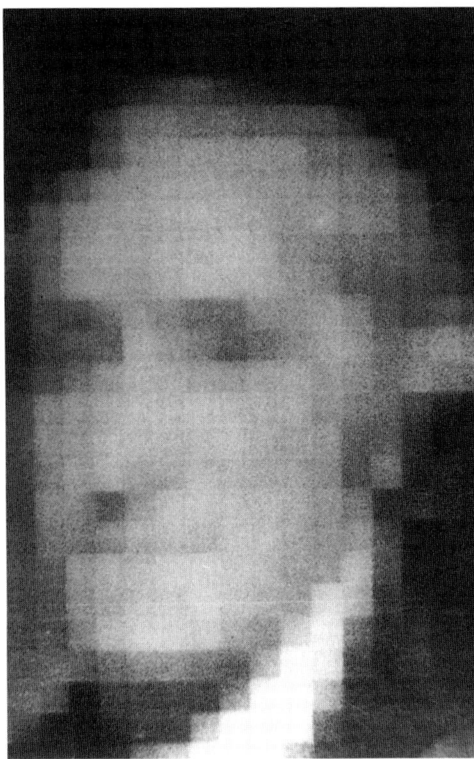

4.10*B*.

of any image except itself. Curiously, that image, from the system of translation, is often best dealt with when the technician purposely works it into the image being translated, thus using what is at worst a technical failure, at best a surplus extraneous to the aim of accurate reproduction, to provide an element of aesthetic display. A mezzotint halftone might look best in a book on Victoriana; a circular halftone in an advertisement for new-age religion. These methods of reproduction "call attention to themselves," we say, because they displace

A

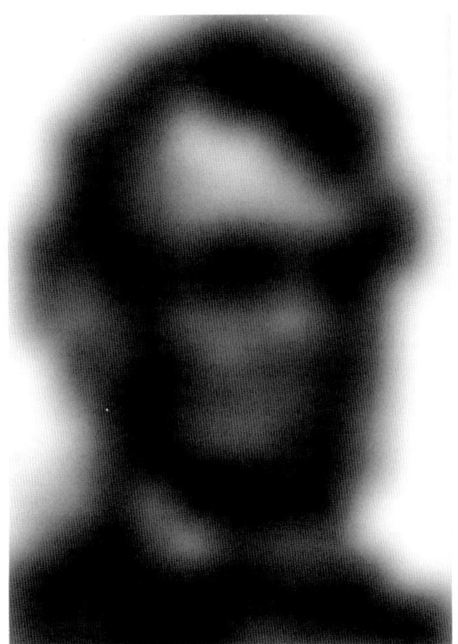

B

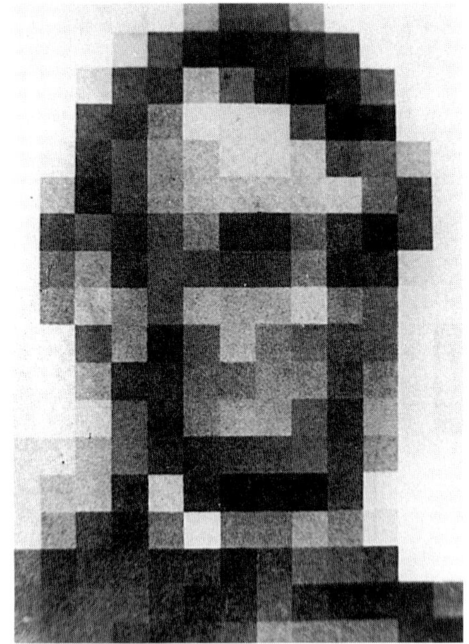

If we repeat the process with a simplified example, the principles of the reproduction method become clearer. A coarser grid and a gray scale with fewer steps show how a unit of translation generalizes an area of the image being translated. Notice, for example, how many squares of the grid are simply, and uniformly, the darkest tone available in the system. The simplification can proceed considerably further. Imagine the portrait with a grid of four squares and a gray scale of two steps (dark and light). Simplification brings out the paradoxes that burden these reproductions. The closer one looks, the more obscure they get—the worse one's vision is, the better one can see—because the ability to read such degraded imagery requires one to overlook the particulars of the system for a general effect, a common denominator that can then be matched to the features of a remembered image, such as the face of Lincoln. If we were to magnify the reproduction—that is, move the optical threshold from the level of the block portrait to the level of the halftone that is delivering it here on this page—we would discover that in fact the entire area is built up from two tones, black ink dots on a white ground.

4.11. Computer-generated block portrait of Abraham Lincoln: (*A*) out of focus; (*B*) in focus.

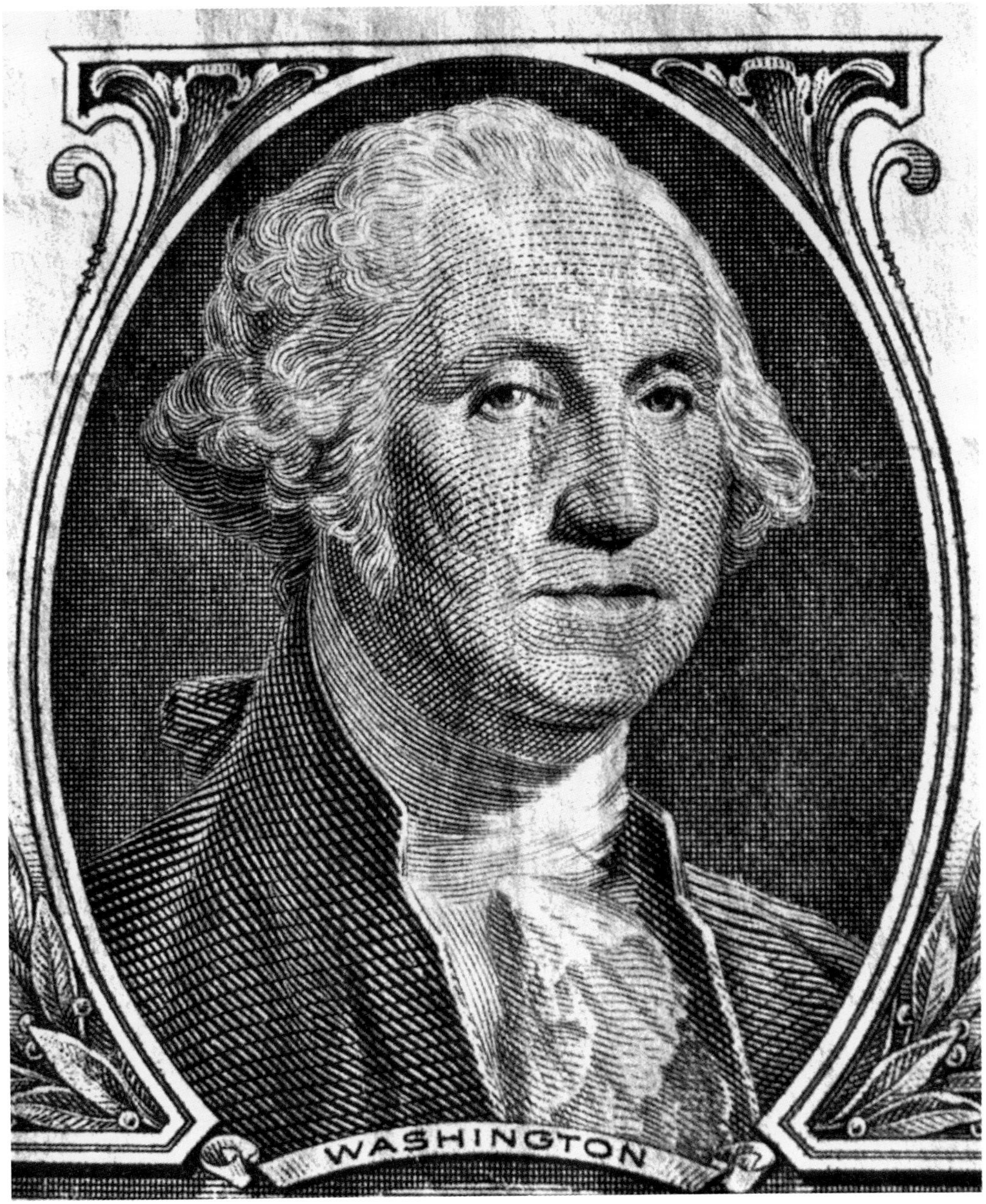

4.12. A dollar bill, magnified; normal size.

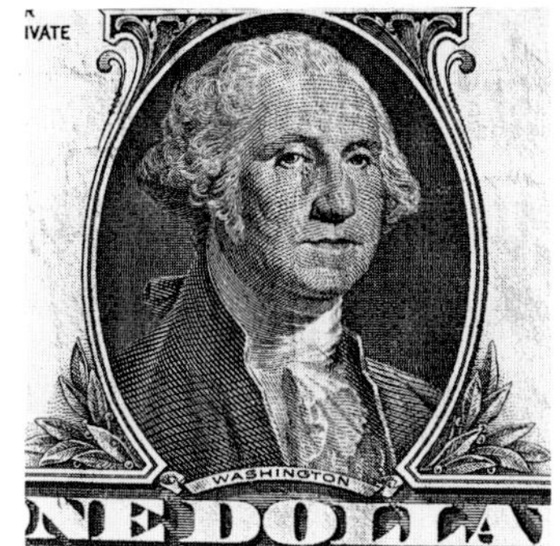

In 1918 George Smillie, an engraver with the Bureau of Engraving and Printing in the U.S. Treasury Department, copied Washington's face for the dollar bill from one of the Gilbert Stuart portraits (or, more than likely, from some reproduction of it). To make the translation, Smillie used reproductive conventions of an earlier era when engraving had been the mainstay of picture reproduction. Magnification makes this familiar image strange by shifting its customary relation to the threshold of vision, a critical point of reference in all reproductive media. At the usual arm's length at which one exchanges dollar bills for merchandise, Smillie's dots and lozenges, like halftone dots, blur into slightly grainy tones. The effect of distance is duplicated here by reduction in size rather than defocusing.

(OVERLEAF)
In "novelty" screens, such as this circular one, the basis of reproduction is switched from the dot to other digital units.

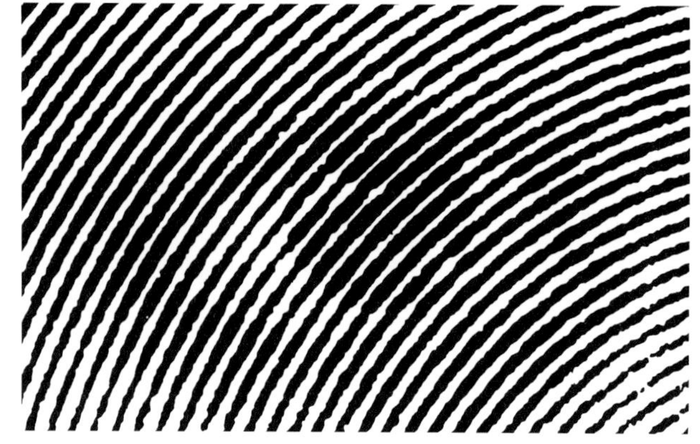

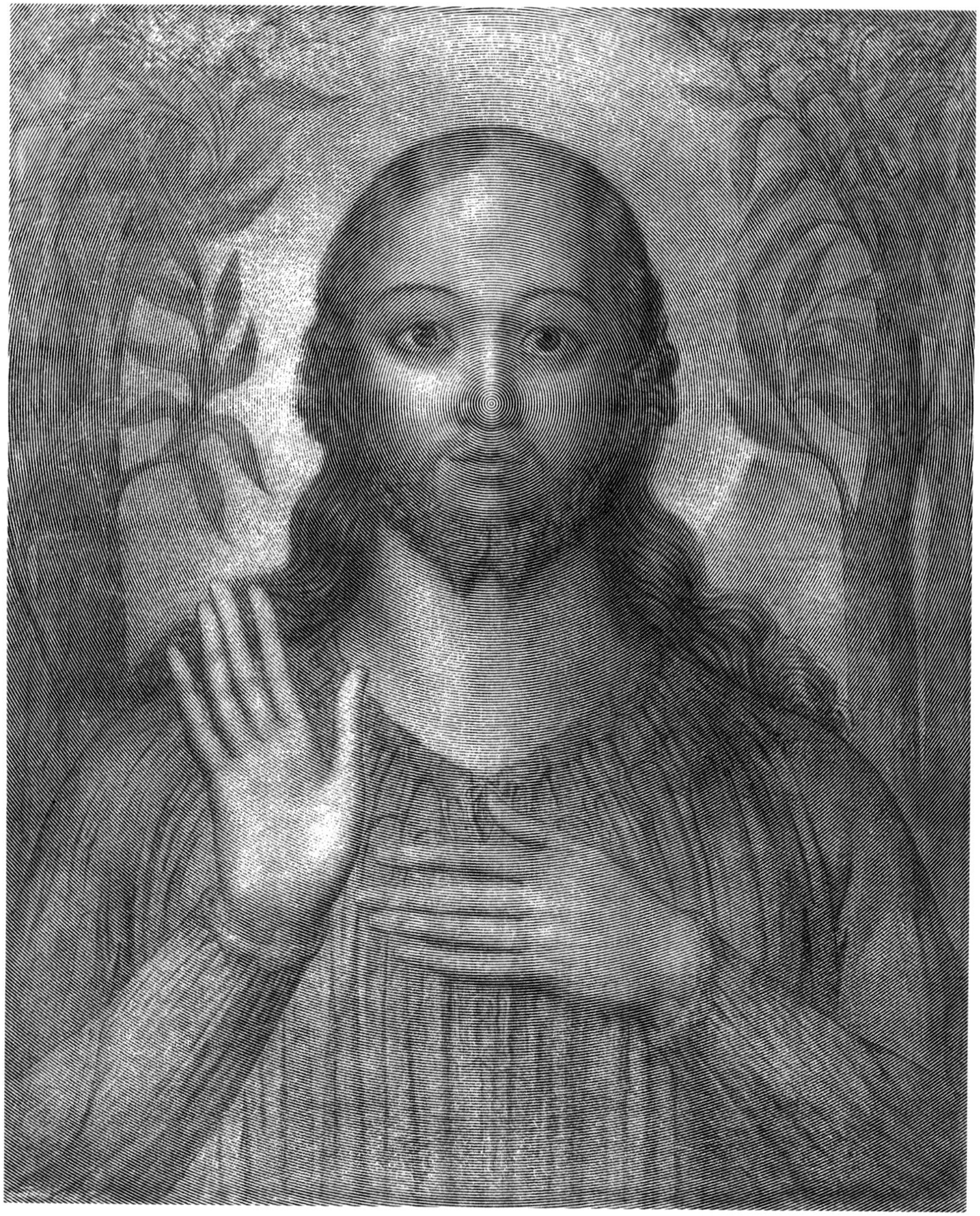

4.13. William Blake, *Christ Blessing,* tempera, c. 1810, reproduced by circular screen, and detail.

the viewer's attention from the object of translation to the system. This phenomenon is familiar to those who buy high-fidelity speakers. Because reproduction is imperfect, speakers display different variations from the norm of accurate reproduction. As speakers have different audial flavors that appeal to different tastes, so do halftones, and those flavors can themselves become sources of optical interest—thus (to misapply R. P. Blackmur and Jacques Lacan) adding to the stock of available reality by supplementing a lack.

Engraving offers ample evidence of such technical compensation, perhaps most memorably in Claude Mellan's famous seventeenth-century print of St. Veronica's veil (figs. 4.14–4.17). The automatic halftone screen is hard to distinguish from Mellan's single-line system because he developed his technique to a nearly mechanical pitch of uniformity with two aims, accurate reproduction and display. His technical system serves both, though it is finally hard to say whether it extends his powers or he serves his system. His highly refined technique intentionally never quite refines itself out of existence. The threshold of vision, the point of reference that makes the optical magic possible, is anchored to the tip of Christ's nose at the center of the print (located at the center of an X—for Christ and his cross—drawn from the four corners of fig. 4.16), where the engraver's spiraling line begins, its stealthy windings encompassing every aspect of the image. Thus another technical paradox: although the technique depends entirely upon a line, there is no coherent outline, no point at which line corresponds with image, anywhere in the print, not even in the signature (fig. 4.17).

A great deal of Mellan's ingenuity has gone into matching technique to occasion, so that it is impossible to notice the print without noticing the technique and its master. The inscription—*formatur unicus una,* "by one the one is formed"—names neither subject nor engraver but points at both. The tonal richness of the single-line technique venerates Christ and his devoted saint on the far side of the threshold of vision, while, on the near side, at a blink, the technique offers itself up for veneration: "Who has not beheld with admiration the incomparable burin of Claudius Melan. . . . The Sudarium of St. Veronica, where he has formed a head as big as the life itself, with one only line, beginning at the point of the nose, and so by a spiral turning of the graver, finishing at the utmost hair, is a prodigy of his rare art and invention, because it is wholly new, and performed with admirable dexterity" (quoted from John Evelyn's *Sculptura* [1662] in Stannard 20).

What do the admirers admire? *Truth to nature,* of course, and that aim is boldly advanced in the lifesize scale of the face. Also *control,* however, and we always wonder to see something so complex as the natural human face reduced to one unnatural thing—the spiraling line—and yet still recognizable. As we can see the circular halftone in Mellan's single-line Christ, we can see the machine in the human being. Much of the pleasure derived from such reduction comes from seeing a human being act like a mechanism. We marvel at the engraver's simplemindedness and sheer durability as his line winds and winds, expressing the concentration of all resources into one. In one way, Mellan and his system are bizarre mannerist spectacles, freaks of human mechanism akin to the fattest woman, the tallest man, and flagpole sitters.

But more significant, the lesson of Mellan is

(OVERLEAF)

That kind of "novelty" is not new, but the product of a potential for display in all processes of mechanical reproduction, as Claude Mellan's seventeenth-century experiments with single-line engraving stunningly reveal.

Legend has it that St. Veronica, having wiped Christ's bleeding face on the road to Calvary, came away with an image on her sudarium, veronica, napkin, veil, or vernicle. Her name, which is also the term for her cloth, may signify *vera icon,* "true image." She is both a second mother of Christ, the feminine vehicle for accurate impressions of masculine divinity, and a kind of painter-printmaker, hence a highly eligible subject for the artist's ingenuity. The painter Girolamo Muziano combined Veronica with a study in textiles (veil and drapery) and circles (her halo, Christ's, and the base).

More resourcefully, Claude Mellan eliminated Veronica and fixed instead on his print of her print. He tied a naturalistic (and lifesize) representation to the spiritual mathematics of the circle by adapting the artist's amusement of single-line drawing (how long can you draw without lifting your pencil from the paper?) to his own technique, which replaced the lozenges of common crosshatching with a system of swelling and shrinking parallel lines running in only one direction. The visual conceit seems to be that contact

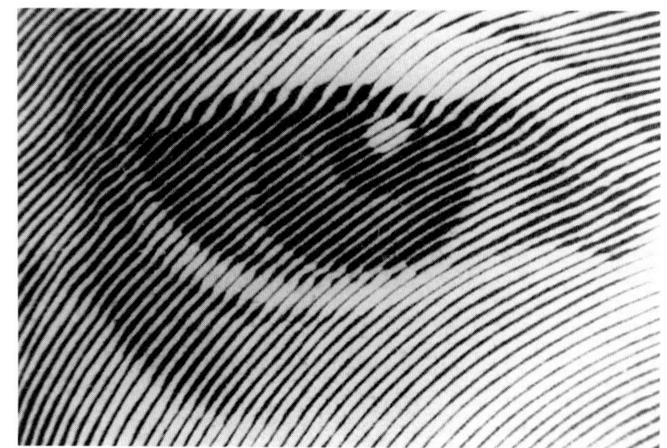

4.14. Dudesert after Claude Mellan (1649), *The Sudarium of St. Veronica,* engraving, 1735, detail.

not about the "wholly new" and the unique but about the systematic deployment of skills that are the opposite of biological sports, including the sport of genius. The skills are thoroughly communicable—teachable and learnable—and they belong, furthermore, to a pedagogical tradition that had been transmitting and improving them for centuries by the time Mellan came along to learn them, improve them, show them off, and pass them on. To say that Claude Mellan is, in Blake's sense, one of the master journeymen of the history of engraving is not to deny his undeniable skill but to affirm it as skill of a certain quite mechanical kind. There are good imitations of his *Veronica* by various hands not just because the print was popular but also because it was imitable, and it was imitable because it evolved technically from an organized set of imitable skills. Mellan belonged not to the genius wing of engraving but to the research-and-development wing, where imitable systems and technical models are the center of attention. Histories of engraving fre-

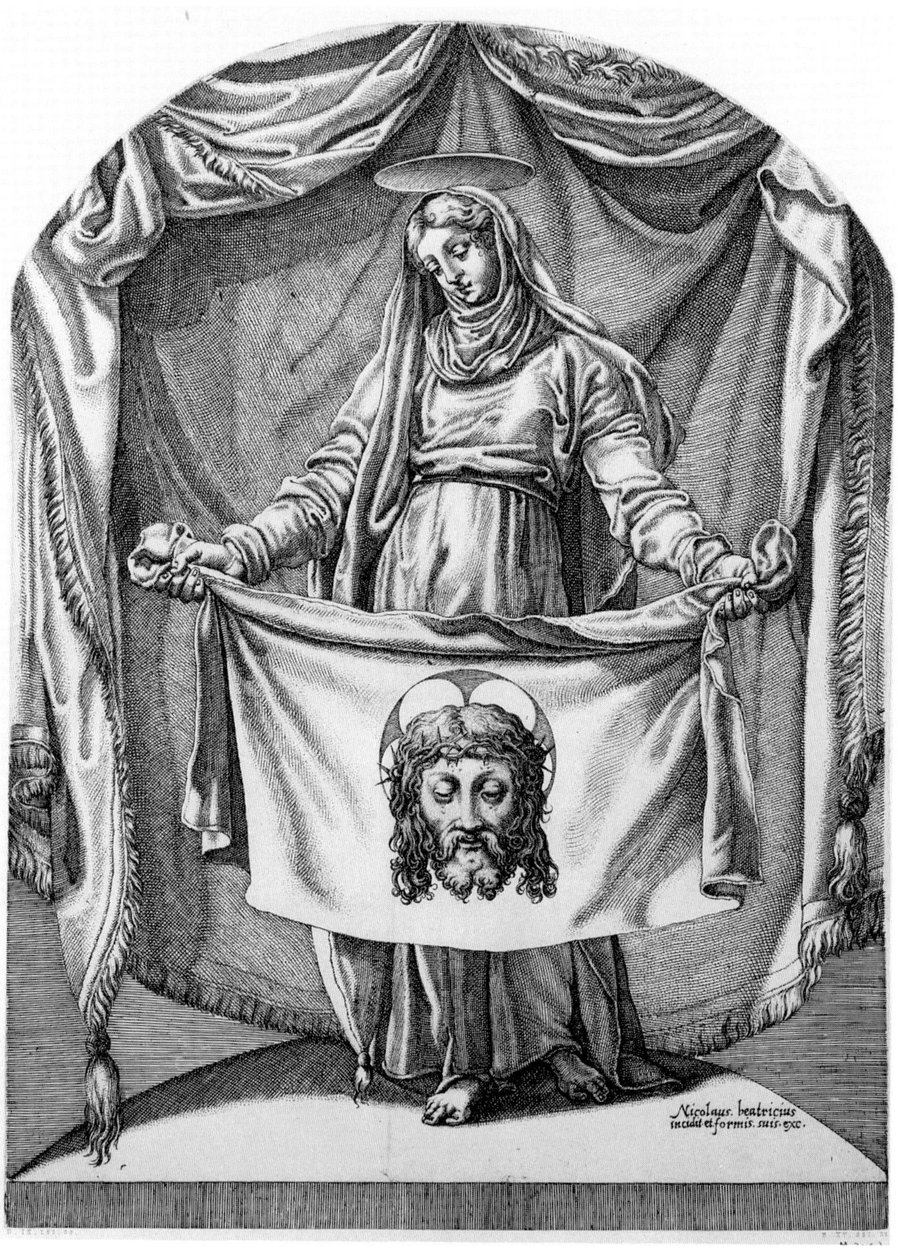

4.15. Nicholas Beatrizet (active 1540–1568) after Girolamo Muziano, *The Sudarium of St. Veronica,* engraving.

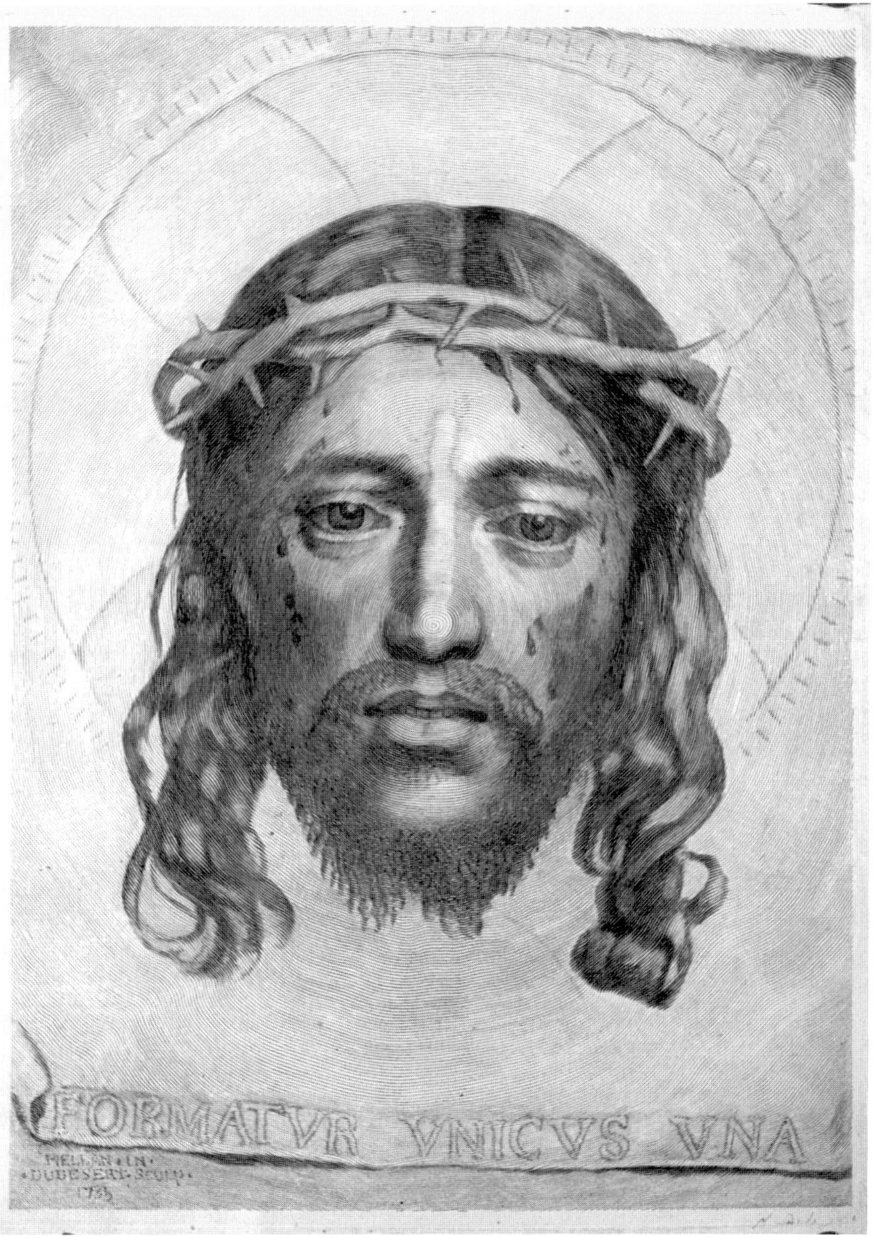

4.16. Dudesert after Claude Mellan (1649), *The Sudarium of St. Veronica,* 1735.

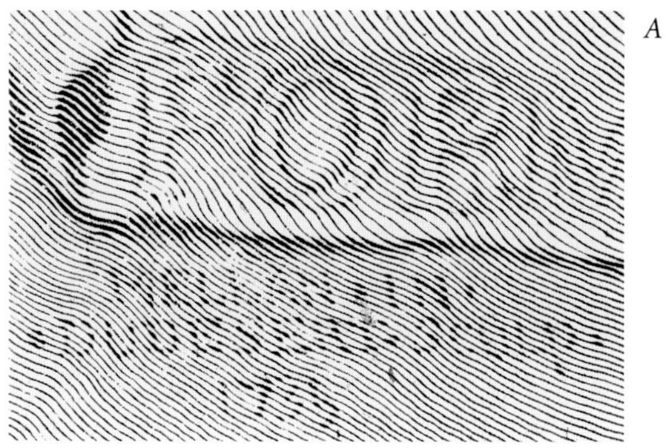

A

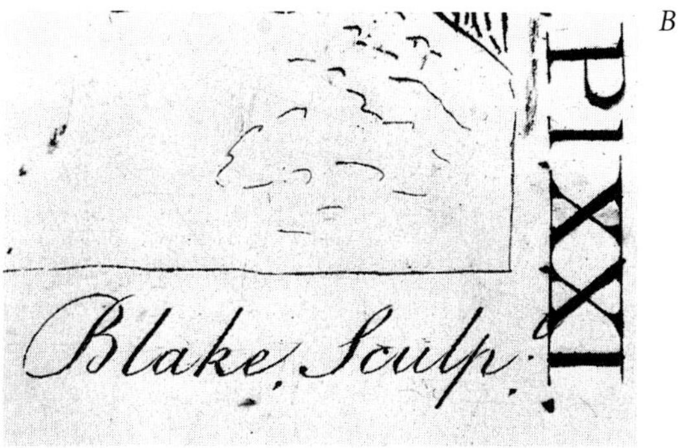

B

4.17. Signatures: (*A*) Claude Mellan, *The Sudarium of St. Veronica,* detail; (*B*) William Blake, *The Antiquities of Athens,* 3:16, plate 21, 1792, detail.

with Christ's face transformed the crisscross weave of common cloth into a spiral textile of a single thread. Interestingly, the impression reproduced here is not Mellan's but a good eighteenth-century copy by Dudesert (an otherwise unknown engraver). The British Museum also owns a second copy published by the Fleet Street printseller Robert Sayer, an indication of the lasting appeal of Mellan's invention.

Christ occupies the center of Mellan's work, but the engraver, signing himself

quently organize themselves from this angle. Rembrandt's manner "is even more wonderful in its penetrating genius than the work of Van Dyck; only it is essentially inimitable, and has perhaps never succeeded except in the hands of the master himself. Van Dyck, on the other hand, has remained the pattern to the best of modern portrait etchers" (Hind, *History* 142).[27] These questions of mechanism, skill, display, and imitation are at the heart of the objections Blake made to the labor of journeymen and the connoisseur's preoccupation with technique.

Though the standard accounts brand Mellan's print as "mannerist" (Hind, *History* 143), they can seldom resist the opportunity to display it, and they must simultaneously concede its place in the technical logic of the central traditions of engraving. However mannered, Mellan was no outsider but an engraver's engraver with numerous pupils and imitators, including Robert Nanteuil, engraver to Louis XIV. According to Strutt (2:143), Charles II greatly admired Mellan and tried unsuccessfully to lure him to England. His way there did not finally require emigration: Abraham Bosse, a Parisian practicioner of Mellanesque technique, wrote *Traicté des manières de graveur en taille douce* (1645), an influential engraving handbook that was translated into English by William Faithorne as *The Art of Graveing and Etching* (1662) after it had already been translated into German and Dutch. Faithorne, the best-known English engraver of his time and the first to be known widely outside of England, worked in the style of Mellan and probably met both Nanteuil and Bosse in Paris.[28]

We can most conveniently trace the historical narrative in which Mellan's technique is a significant episode to the engraving shops of Renaissance Italy, where painters learned to invest in reproduction to multiply commercial value. When Raphael hired the engraver Marcantonio Raimondi (figs. 4.18–4.20) to work under his supervision, he was simply extending a practice already widely followed in painters' studios, where assistants were regularly employed to execute the conceptions of their masters.[29] This fact about Renaissance studio practice was well known in Blake's time: Reynolds had observed that any artist less accomplished than Raphael might have been intimidated by having "under his direction the most considerable Artists of his age" (dis. 12, 212) in his work at the Vatican. Landseer had marked the teamwork of Marcantonio and Raphael as a key shift in the organization of work as it affected the history of engraving. Whereas in less advanced economies a painter might also be a sculptor, engraver, and architect, wrote Landseer, even-

through his system at the margin, signals that this is the house that Mellan built. Blake's signature, from an engraving of Flaxman's design for his Nelson monument, shows what is ordinarily expected to happen when a burin engraves lines in copper.

[27] Cf. John Opie's characterization, from his Royal Academy lecture on design, of the value of Michelangelo and Raphael: "The first undoubtedly stands highest, but the last is probably the more eligible and safe model for *imitation*" (Wornum 268).

[28] See Jacob Kainen's introduction to the facsimile ed. of Faithorne (ix). In 1764 Robert Dossie declared that, since French engravers were technically superior, Bosse/Cochin remained the manual of choice for "conveying the greatest part of the general rules of the art" and "imparting also the peculiar inventions and improvements of the French which could be hitherto known only to those who had the opportunity of studying it in France" (2:vi). How many engravers used handbooks we cannot guess, but the trail of technique and pedagogy is apparent. Dossie also saw his own treatise, published before Boydell's first great successes in the following decade, as a means to "advance that progress we are making towards a rivalship of the French in this art" (2:vii).

[29] Vasari describes the procedures of the workshop. For modern accounts that correct Vasari's emphasis on rampant individual competition, see Wackernagel, Sheard and Paoletti, and, most recently, Dunkerton et al.

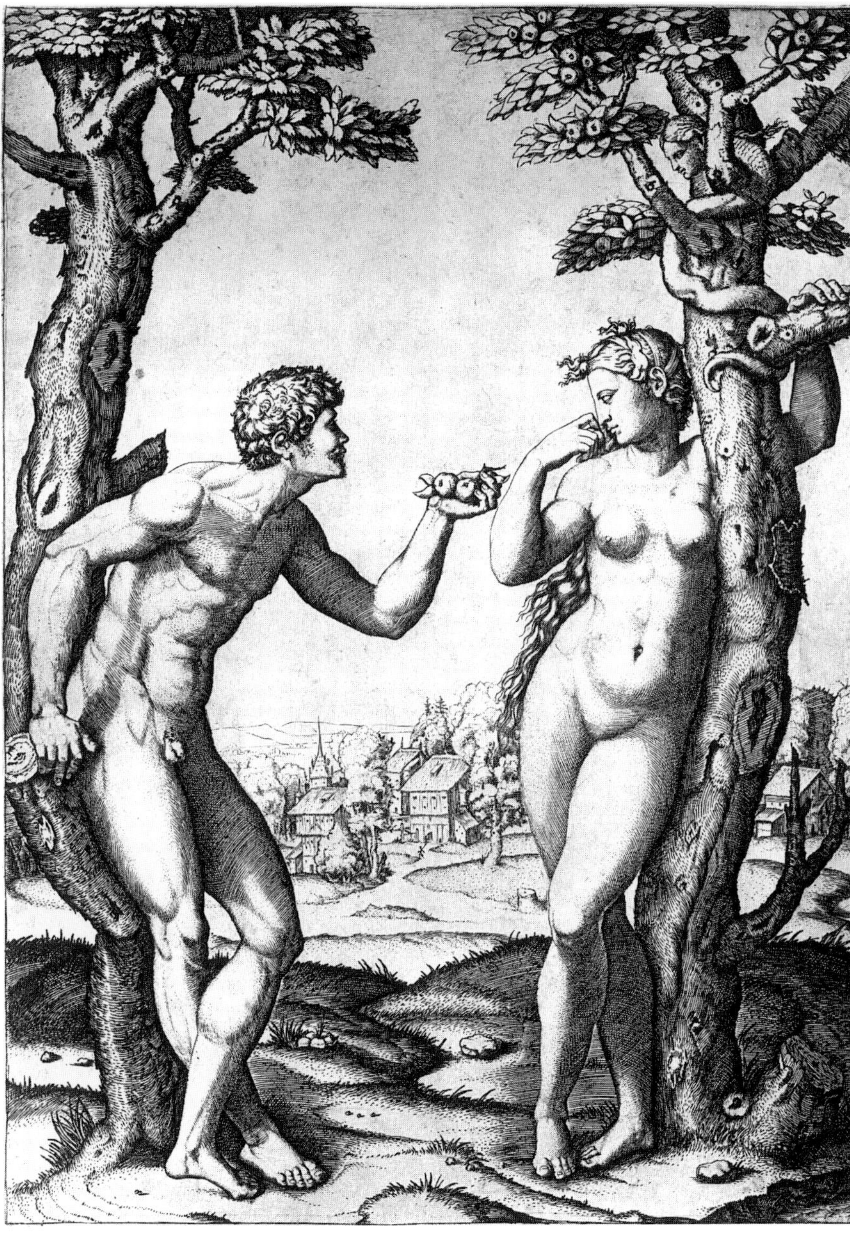

4.18. Marcantonio Raimondi (c. 1480–1530) after Raphael, *Adam and Eve,* c. 1512–1514.

Blake associated Dürer, perhaps his favorite engraver, with Marcantonio—"Ye English Engravers must come down from your high flights ye must condescend to study Marc Antonio & Albert Durer" (E 573)—casting them as heroes of a golden age when imagination and outline had been first principles. An alternative interpretation closer to the facts would be that Marcantonio simplified and regularized Dürer's already quite uniform style into a commercially efficient system of translation.

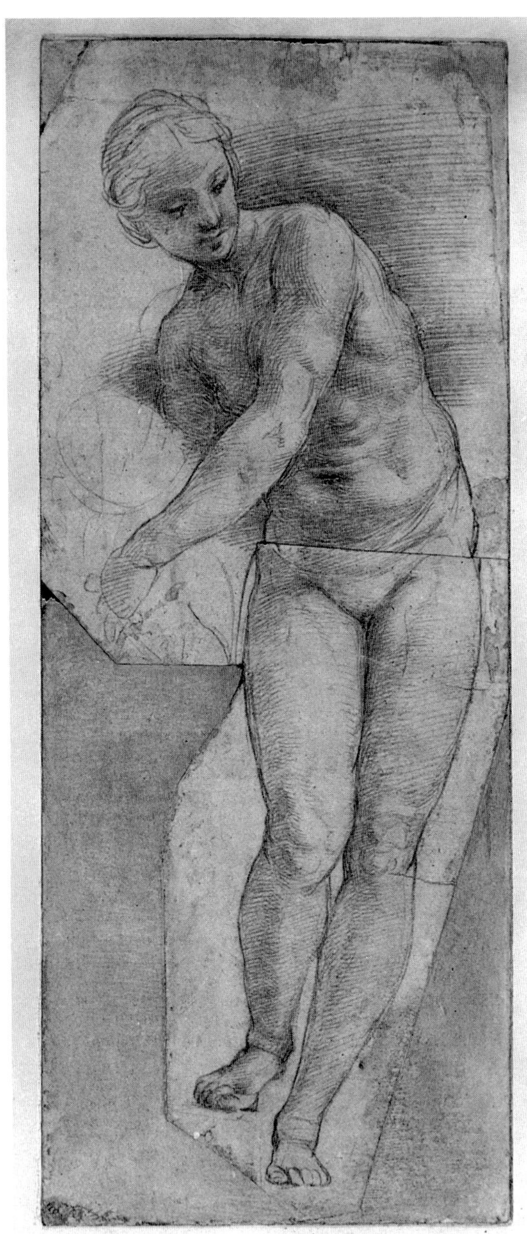

4.19. Raphael, *Venus*, drawing, c. 1512.

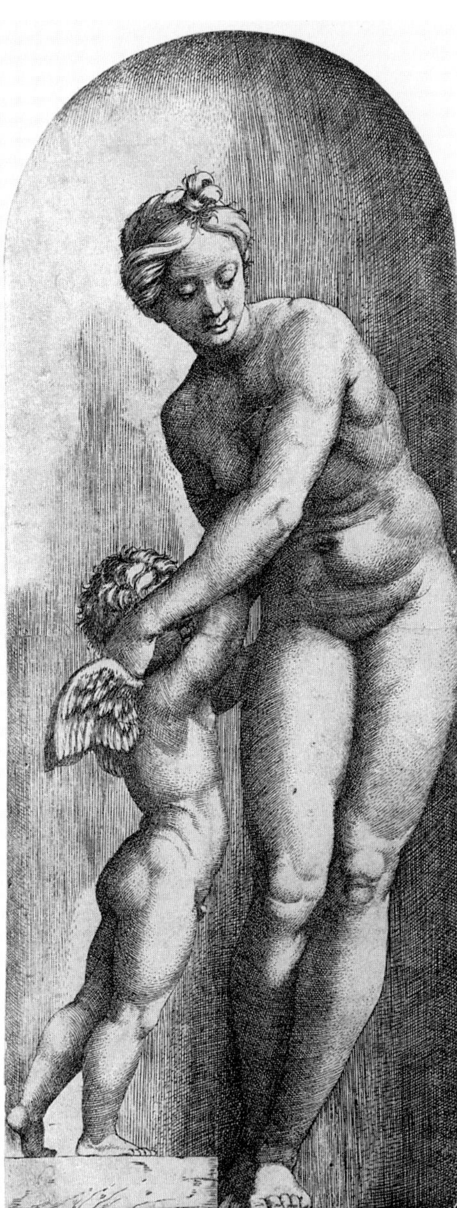

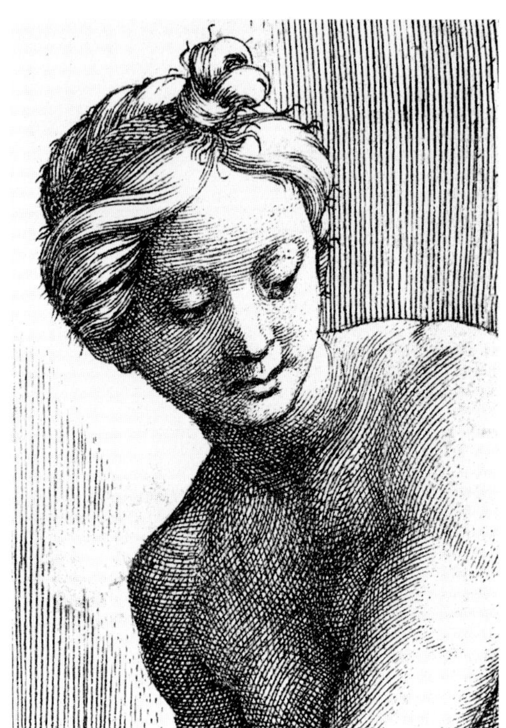

4.20. Marcantonio Raimondi after Raphael, *Venus and Cupid*, engraving, c. 1512–1514, and detail.

Raphael, the principal exemplar of line (thus of drawing) in Blake's time, found his match in Marcantonio, who sparsely augmented lines with regular crosshatching in his engravings; hence the venerable tradition that Marcantonio worked from Raphael's drawings rather than from his finished paintings (see Fréart 22–23 and Baker 47–78). To eyes of the eighteenth and early nineteenth centuries, the pure and graceful outlines that Landseer praised seemed more often, as to William Gilpin, "harsh, and formal to the last degree" (51). Strutt quoted Bernard Picart's complaint about Marcantonio's "hard" outlines and "neat, but meagre" hatch-

tually a "more wise, because more useful economy of distribution"—specialization—develops: "Hence, when the general good of Society called for subdivision, the sister Arts [here painting and engraving], whose object is that general good, found pleasure in obedience. . . . Thus Raphael painted, and Marcantonio translated" (*Lectures* 266, 267).

Most histories of engraving have offered variations on Landseer's proposition, the underlying principle of which we might understand as follows. A division of labor that can accommodate multiple laborers requires a system to connect their labors in a coherent outcome. These connections appear in various mutually supporting forms. As translator of Raphael, Marcantonio must have a system of translation, which appears most obviously at the level of "style," narrowly construed as a set of technical practices that are possible, and preferably efficient, in the medium of translation. To put it simply, because painters can do things in paint that engravers cannot do on copper, engravers must find stylistic approximations to the techniques of painting. As Blake noted, translations thus generalize the object of translation. If they are sufficiently systematic, they will generalize the same thing the same way each time, thus creating not only predictability and efficiency but also the desired look of uniformity rather than patchwork across the surface.

Histories of engraving treat Marcantonio as such a systemizer. Dürer and Marcantonio are typically paired as host to parasite, originator expressing "inner power" to brilliant assimilator of that power imitated, simplified, and refined in a "system" capable of "formal beauty." We may be reassured that Marcantonio was "always original in his assimilation" (Hind, *History* 91–93; see also 72, 97). He was, in effect, averaging Dürer's style, opening it up technically to make room for others, such as Raphael. Marcantonio also aimed to make room for others in another way. His own assistants could be *his* assistants only if they contributed to the reproduction of a single style capable of accepting their multiple contributions without disintegrating visually. To be shared the style had to be teachable, and teachable in something less than a lifetime to make it feasible to replace workers who left with their skills. Thus Hyatt Mayor has pictured Marcantonio, with some exaggeration, as the sole progenitor of reproductive engraving:

> Marcantonio synthesized the main printmaking styles of his time with a logic so teachable that his assistants could blend their engraving indistinguishably on one copperplate. His mostly anonymous crew composed the first internationally important engraver's shop and perfected a system of collaboration that spread uninterruptedly until about 1875, when reproductive printmaking began to give way to the cheaper and more accurate photomechanical processes. [n.p., near figs. 341–43]

But Landseer, even as he praised the ability of Marcantonio's system to reproduce the "truth, purity, and spontaneous grace" (*Lectures* 269) of Raphael's outlines, had identified the chief failing of Marcantonio's system. It could translate only "those masters who did *not* unite their pictures by any pervading system of Light & Shade, nor add the fascinations of harmonious colouring" (*Lectures* 268–69; cf. Strutt 2:3, 8). It was *too* well matched to Raphael or, let us even say, to Raphael's system. If one art-historical narrative pits line against color, Roman against Venetian, another, with a ing, which "lacks roundness, or gradation of light and shadow" (2:3; cf. 2:8). In 1793 Blake's friend George Cumberland had responded to Gilpin's disparagement of Marcantonio:

> In these times, when he who can cut the clearest stroke on a copper-plate, or dot out the softest shadow, and not he who makes the purest outline, is esteemed the best engraver; when those who write essays on prints prefer the French school to the Italian, and find fault with Mark Antonio, it may be deemed hazardous to point out to public notice engravings . . . which have neither the merit of clear strokes, fine effect, or finishing, to recommend them. . . . [*Anecdotes* 26–27]

To "*real artists,*" he concluded, "Mark Antonio is still unrivalled as an engraver." These are clearly the terms that Blake later adopted for the *Public Address,* where they are, however, assimilated to an individualistic, visionary aesthetic at some remove from Cumberland's neoclassicism.

special place in English-school discourse, sees each as the necessary complement of the other. This logic, which I have associated with the Carracci program,[30] is what caused Barry to declare Raphael only half a painter, his works "in the coloring part . . . short of the perfection and of the superiority they possess in almost every other" (Wornum 222; cf. Reynolds dis. 5, 81). Sharing the inadequacy, Marcantonio had brought to Raphael the "emaciated dryness" and "Gothic gloom" of Dürer (Fuseli in Wornum 403; cf. Landseer, *Lectures* 234).

Some suggestion of the problem appears even in Marcantonio's partnership with Raphael. It has often been said that Raphael gave his engraver drawings rather than paintings to work from. If so, Raphael understood the limits of the system and was responding to the pressure to increase efficiency by generalizing the object along with the translation, to conceive the message in the terms of the medium, since those are the only terms that finally matter. The most useful system of translation would be universal. Since no system is universal, what typically happens is an accommodation, a movement toward the center, where the systems of production and reproduction overlap in their capabilities: Raphael moves toward Marcantonio's system.

The technological goals of engraving, which would set its course of improvement, become clear: practitioners would need to seek a roomier system that could house not only outline but also tone and color, and at the same time offer increases in productivity through better use of the studio system. A brief series of illustrations will reveal this path of progress.

As Raphael had reproduced his sparse drawings through Marcantonio's system, Titian reproduced the sumptuous fleshes and fabrics of his paintings (much less successfully) through Cornelis Cort's enhanced system of crosshatching (figs. 4.21, 4.22). Cort's task was not simply to find a style most suitable to Titian's paintings but also to integrate his system into a studio system that included Titian as only one of its elements. His studio comprised an elaborate division of labor. Blake could have learned from Pilkington's *Dictionary,* for example, that "it was the custom of this great master [Titian] to repeat the same subject, sometimes by his own pencil [brush], and often by the hands of his disciples, who carefully copied them; yet he always retouched them, adding only a background, or some trifling alteration, by which management they had the look of originals, and were in all probability very little, or perhaps in no degree inferior" (1805, 602). Within the system Titian's job, then, was to conceive subjects that could be "copied" by assistants yet remain recognizable as "the same" subject in each repetition, and by a minimum of "management" to bring them up to the "look" of "originals." Such accounts of Titian's studio practices can be correlated with narratives of his development as a painter. Drawing largely on Joachim von Sandrart, Pilkington relates how Titian's obsession with the particular in a "dry, stiff" manner gave way to techniques of "blending and uniting the colours" in a way that made the "force and beauty" of his paintings appear to greatest advantage only "at a more remote view, and they pleased less when

[30] Blake's only references to "Carrache" occur in a letter to Butts (22 November 1802, E 718–19). He associates the name with Raphael, though also with Correggio, for whom see below.

they were viewed more nearly" (600–601).[31] If Blake's conception of the original intellectual line is our point of reference, Titian's stylistic development appears to be a clever adaptation to the demands of production that shows him learning to paint for reproduction, generalizing his "originals" so that they may be more convincingly copied. "Titian" names a construction of the system (fig. 4.23).

Despite the direct pedagogical and technical evolution from Dürer to Marcantonio to Cort to Hendrik Goltzius of Haarlem (1558–1616), the range of development had been sufficiently great for Fuseli to see the "emaciated dryness" of Dürer in direct contrast to the "bloated corpulence" of Goltzius (Wornum 403), whose scintillating network of lines begins to approach the limit of tonal possibility in so-called line engraving (fig. 4.24). In Goltzius's technique the line was in fact almost totally assimilated to the lozenge, the infinitely adjustable quadrilateral figure that came closest to translating the opulence of colored and modeled surfaces into the harsh environment of engraved metal. Goltzius's virtuosity points the way to Mellan's in its ability to focus attention alternatively on or away from itself by exploiting the relation between reproductive techniques and the threshold of vision. His control over that threshold is so finely developed that a blink can tip the delicate balance from imitator to imitated, from captivating technique to ravishing subject.

Joseph Strutt, who published his history of engraving in the mid-1780s, tracked Goltzius's style from Haarlem to the Bolswert brothers in Antwerp, who then, "under the instruction and patronage of Rubens, changed their [Goltzian] style for one, better adopted to represent the finished and picturesque beauties of the paintings by that great master" (2:7–8). Antwerp had been prepared for that transition by decades of specialization in reproduction by engraving: such words as "organization," "manufacture," and "efficiency" occur regularly in the literature on these shops. Shaping Marcantonio's methods to the larger demands of an international market, the engraving dynasties of Antwerp improved standardization on all fronts. Most important, in order to close the most troublesome gap in the production process, that between media, they worked to standardize the adjustment of conception to execution. In the Antwerp shops, interlocking systems evolved to a new level of integration as artists learned to meet engravers halfway by drawing for the system of execution.

Robert Strange—of Blake's fiendish trio Bartolozzi, Woollett, and Strange—observed, accurately enough, that under the hands of Rubens's engravers, copper became gold (135). Rubens understood, better than anyone else had, how to avail himself of the opportunities presented by an international art marketplace. Blake identifies (but of course overstates) the fundamental method: "All Rubens's Pictures are Painted by Journeymen" (anno. Reynolds, E 655), and, he might have added, drawn by journeymen and engraved by journeymen. A Blakean account of Rubens is easily assembled out of contemporary and later sources from Sandrart to the present, which virtually always split their narrative voices between the active

[31] In an extended note to the entry, Fuseli seconded this account, adding to the narrative a "competition of finish" that Dürer supposedly lost to the young Titian, who soon, however, adopted a "freer and less anxious method" from Giorgione (602n).

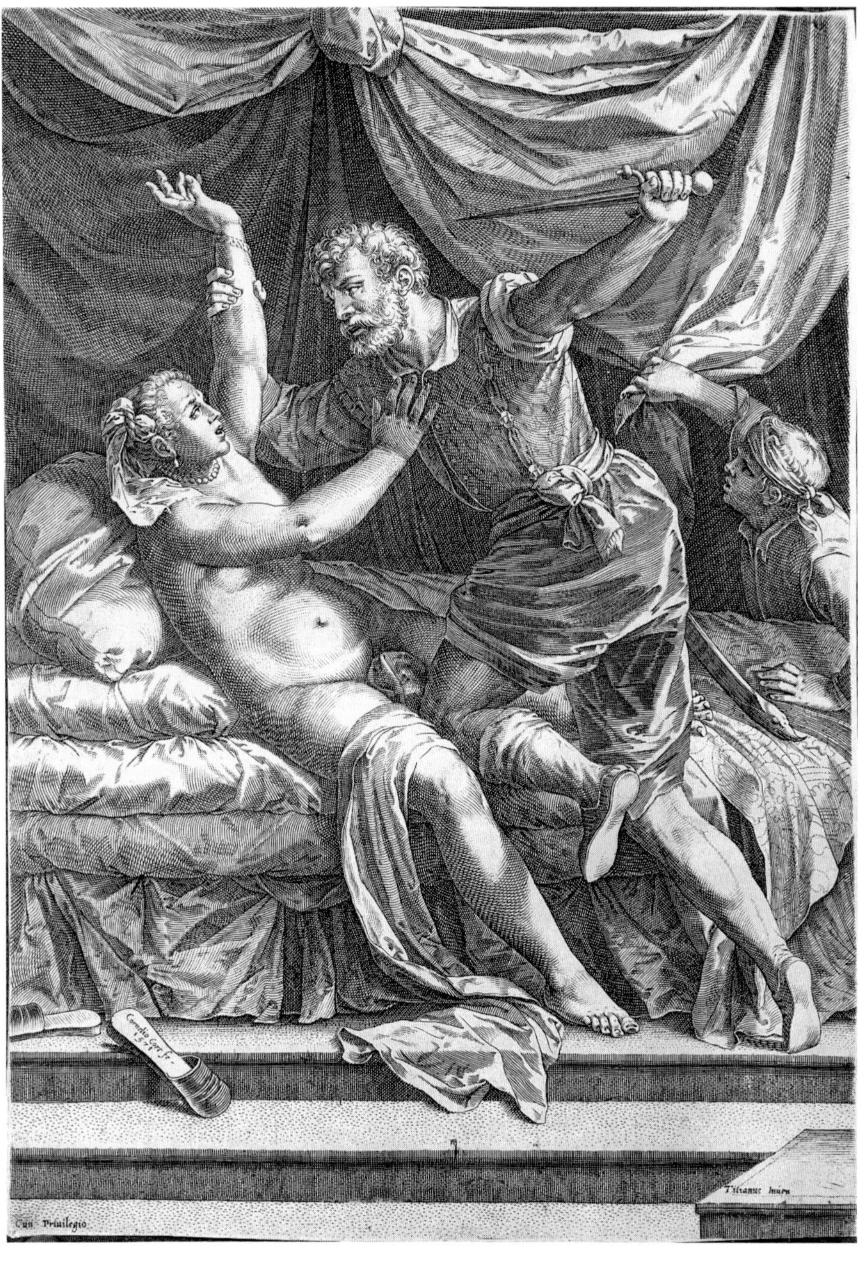

4.21. Cornelis Cort after Titian, *Tarquin and Lucrece,* engraving, 1571.

The pedagogical and technological principles that structure histories of engraving emerge clearly in descriptions of Cornelis Cort, best remembered as engraver to Titian beginning in 1565. In Bryan's *Dictionary* Cort is seen as an improver of Marcantonio. He "sought to graft on the simple manner of Marcantonio a more brilliant and broader style" capable of communicating the brilliant, broad style of Titian. In turn, Cort's style is said to have been "adopted and extended by Agostino Carracci" (1:334; cf. Mayor near fig. 408).

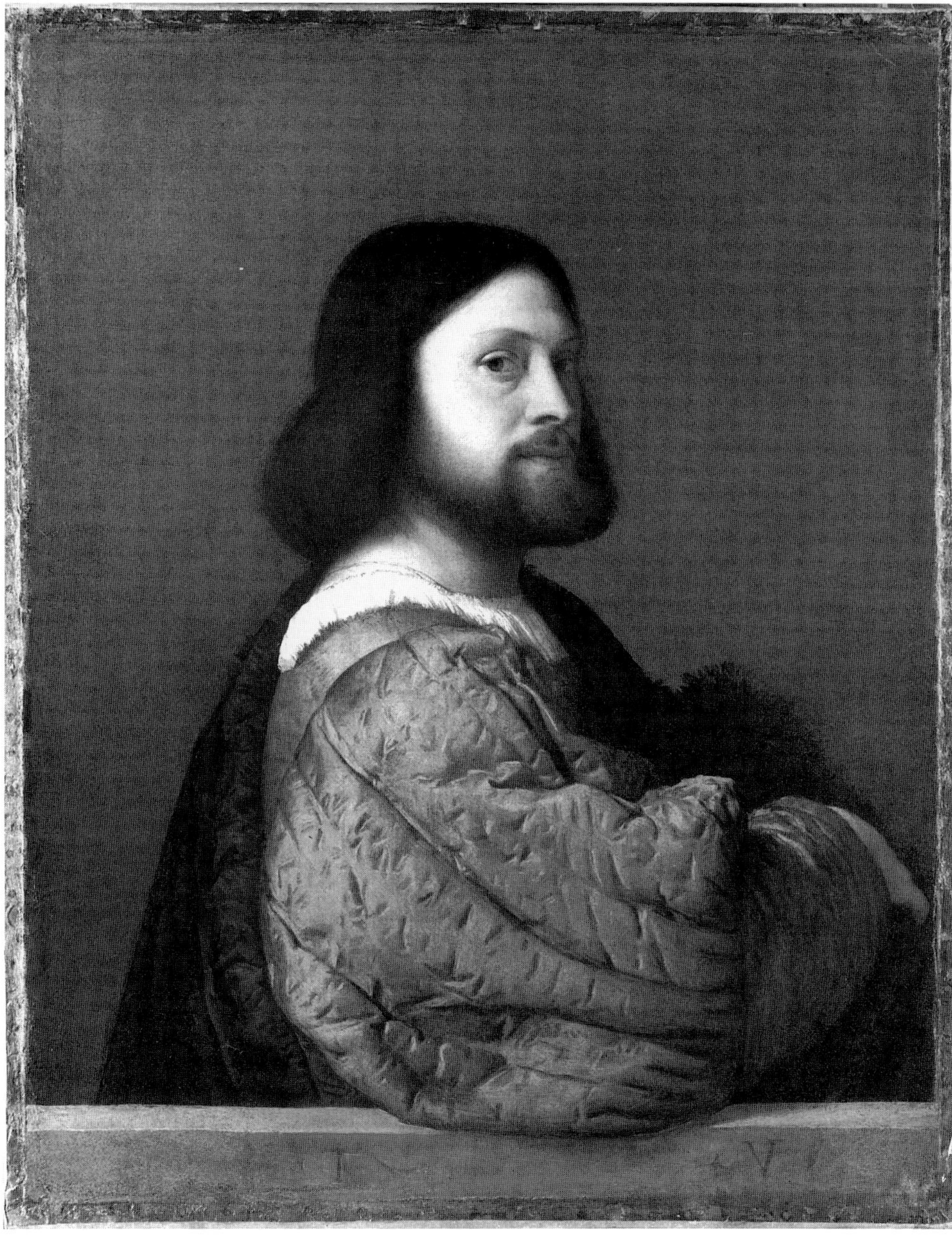

4.22. Titian, *Portrait of a Man,* oil, c. 1512.

But a comparison of a sample of Cort's engraving with a sample of Titian's painting instantly confirms the vast distance that remains between the two. Engravers needed to capture the continuous tones of Titian's velvety harmonies of flesh, hair, fur, and satin with burins, needles, and acids on copper. That formidable technological challenge motivated much of the history of engraving.

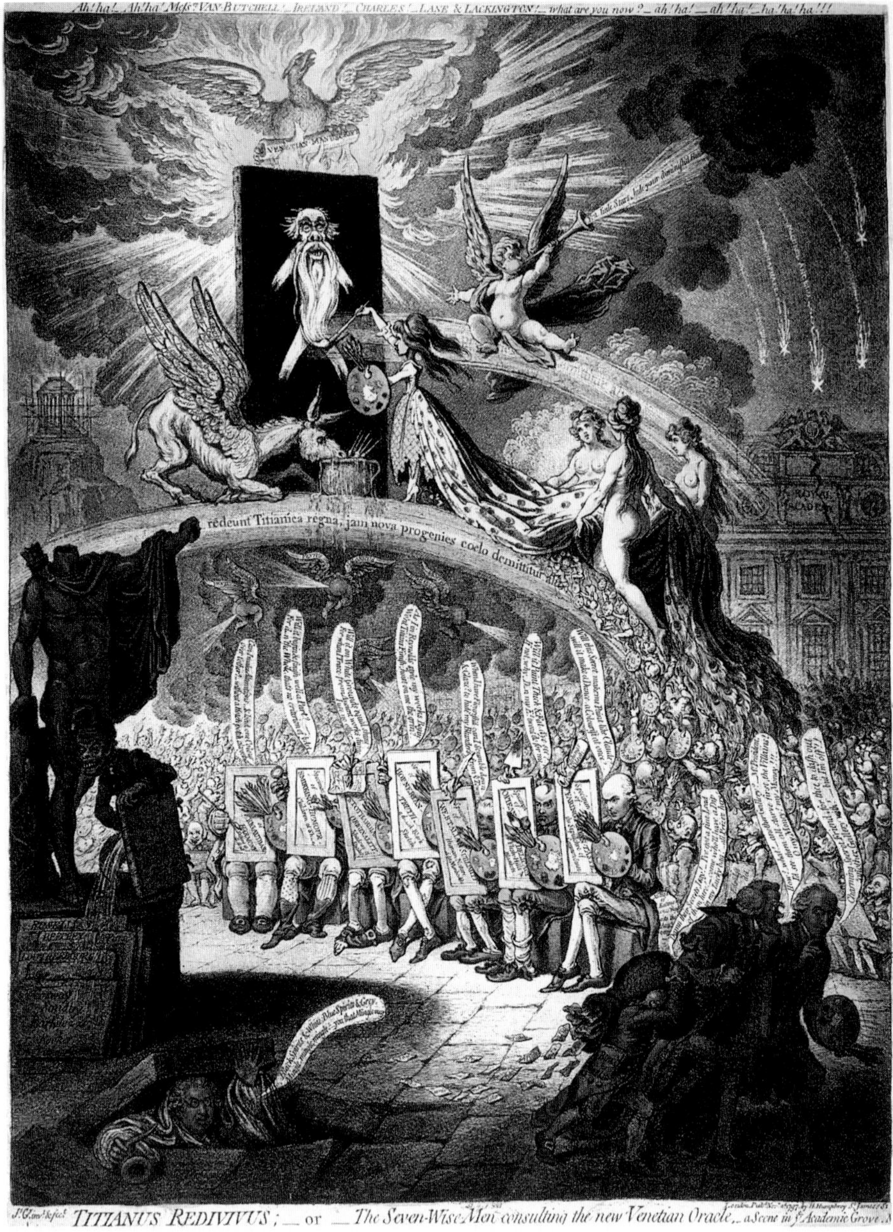

4.23. James Gillray, *Titianus Redivivus,* etching and aquatint, 1797.

Titian's *Portrait of a Man* inspired self-portraits by Rembrandt and van Dyck. In the English school, the materials and methods by which Titian had achieved his brilliant effects of color and light were sources of much rumor and some humiliation. Reynolds's experiments with Titianism were blamed for causing his pictures to fade into ghosts of their former selves. And as late as 1797 the incident of the "Venetian secret" inspired Gillray's *Titianus Redivivus;—or—The Seven Wise Men Consulting the New Venetian Oracle.* In the top half the twenty-year-old art student, who, with her father, was supposed to have given Titian's secret to Benjamin West and sold it to others for ten guineas each, paints Titian's portrait from a rainbow. Fittingly female, given the gendering of color and harmony, she wears a peacock gown. Across the middle, Royal Academicians associated with the ruse are lined up with canvases and suitable slogans about "beginning" and "finishing" and hiding faults behind paint. The ghost of Reynolds rises from a grave in the foreground. Macklin, Boydell, and West, worrying about profits and competition, head off to the right, leaving a trail of cash. (See also Gage, "Magilphs"; Dorothy George 126; von Erffa and Staley nos. 22, 133, 356, 543.)

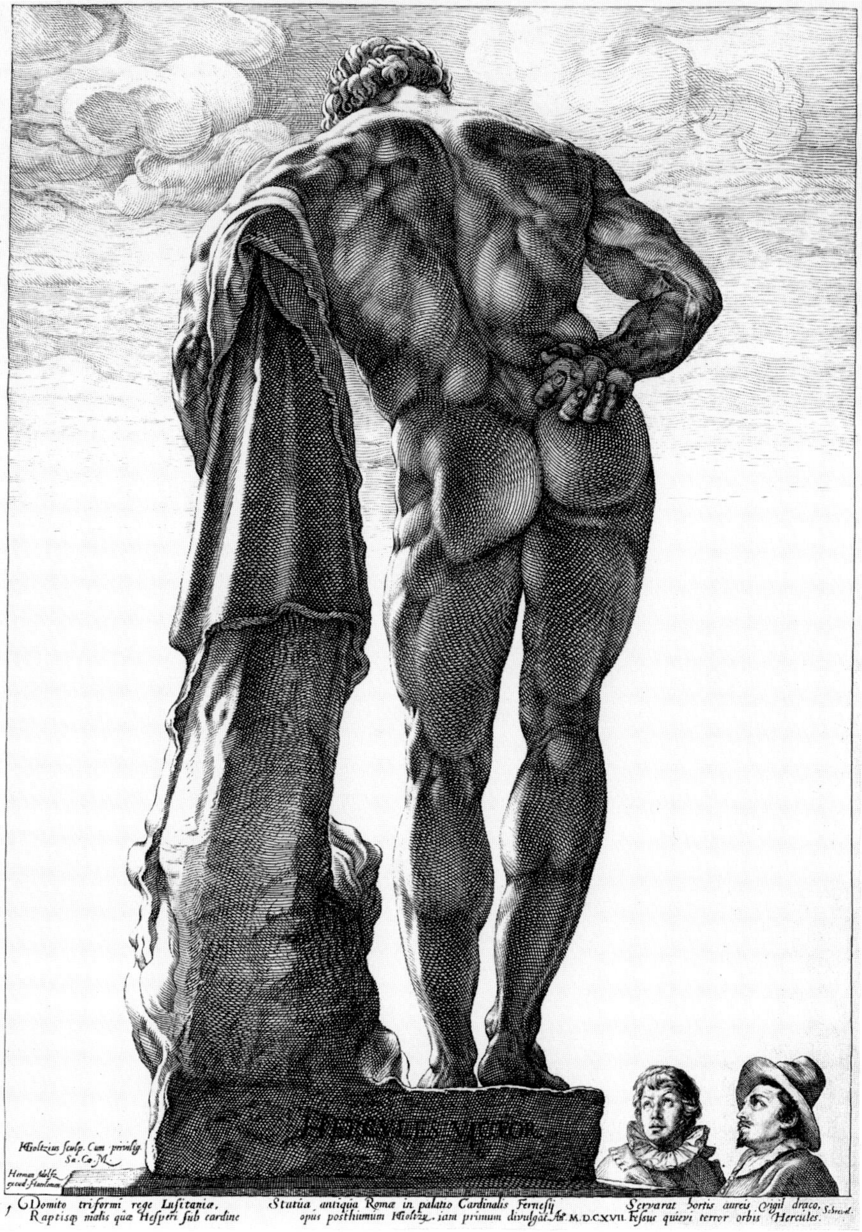

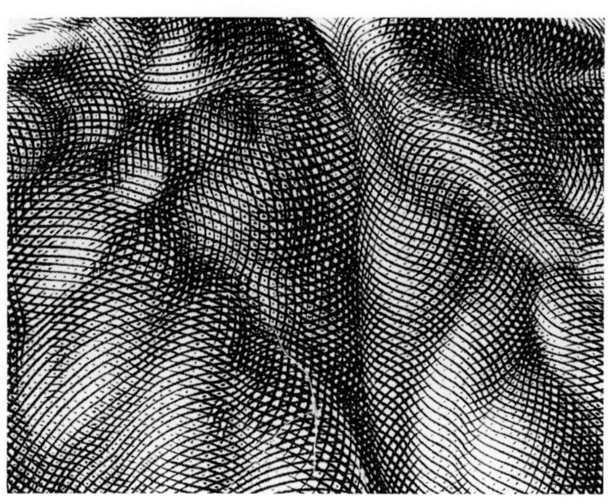

4.24. Hendrik Goltzius, *Farnese Hercules,* engraving, c. 1591 (pub. 1617), and detail.

Goltzius's control of the continuous network of lozenges makes it possible to give an engraving the topographic modeling of a painting or, here, a statue. The displays of musculature and of chalcographic virtuosity strike the viewer together. The spectators at lower right get to see only the statue; we spectators of the print get to see the technical brilliance of Goltzius as well. Paradoxically, with a matrix of lines Goltzius can obey the painter's dictum that there is no outline in nature. As Hogarth wrote, "Even prints, by means of lights and shades alone, will perfectly inform the eye of every shape and distance whatsoever, in which even lines must be consider'd as narrow parts of shade, a number of them, drawn or engrav'd neatly side by side, called *hatching,* serve as shades in prints, and when they are artfully managed, are a kind of pleasing *succedaneum* to the delicacy of nature's" (107).

and passive: "It was the habit of Rubens to paint, or to cause to be painted . . ." (Stevenson 93, 105). They report, on the one hand, the story of a master who could force his irresistible artistic will on an entire "picture factory"; on the other, the even more compelling story of the shrewd methodology that made the displacement possible.

Out of the procedures of the studio system and the Antwerp engraving factories Rubens devised a rational system of production sufficiently consolidated to manufacture a full product line ranging from single canvases—easel and cabinet pictures, portraits and landscapes—to prints and altarpieces. Engraving offered, as always, a technology of reproduction that could disseminate the images of the Rubens studio more cheaply and efficiently than "original" works. But the international distances that had to be spanned made engraving, the photocopying and fax technology of the time, far more critical to the marketing of his products than it had ever been to a relatively parochial artist such as Raphael.

Rubens imposed on the increasingly standardized shop styles of Antwerp new demands of uniformity, simplicity, rationality, repeatability, and learnability at the same time that he extended the velvet harmonies of the engraved surface (figs. 4.25, 4.26). The surface had to remind the viewer of a painting but also had to absorb the extensive division of labor by which it was produced. It did so in two ways, by closing gaps in production and by assigning positive values to the characteristic results of the system itself. Paintings and engravings became rationally *designed* products whose configuration could be known ahead of time, so that all the workers, from painters to engravers to printers, could contribute their labors to the image that summed up those contributions. As R. A. M. Stevenson astutely observed in his early study, it was necessary for Rubens to "adopt a reasoned and formal system of work" that included "regulation figures," "a method made to order, and a conventional line of treatment" (94).

In the end, of course, signs of the rational fragmentation that is fundamental to the system inevitably remained on the face of the image. Systems of finishing evolved to disguise them under hatched networks that blended—averaging, as it were, the surrounding sums—the transitions into an approximated unity of effect. In both painting and engraving, "high finishing," though never invulnerable to suspicion, became a valued effect, a high-priced commodity, and the last in a standard sequence of artistic construction. The value placed on finishing is well signified by the frequency with which writers on Rubens have imagined how he must have reserved that special responsibility to himself, "by his own free, spirited, and judicious retouching" giving "the whole an appearance of being only the work of one hand" (Pilkington [1805], 481). In his marginal encounters with Reynolds, Blake takes up the incongruity. Reynolds says he sees in Rubens "a remarkable instance of the same mind being seen in all the various parts of the art. The whole is so much of a piece . . . ;" Blake claims to penetrate the illusion: "All Rubens's Pictures are Painted by Journeymen & so far from being all of a Piece. are The most wretched Bungles" (anno. Reynolds, E 655).

As Rubens elaborated it, the system required of its labor force a combination of virtuosity in the parts and compliance with the whole. The virtuosi he employed to paint animals, figures, flowers, drapery, and landscape backgrounds had to exercise their specializations in compliance with some general effect, some conventional notion of what a "Rubens" looked like. We might characterize these conditions by analogy with recent theories of mechanization: Rubens was in effect standardizing "parts" and storing them in a "file," the file in this case being the very techniques of his programmable, that is, teachable, workers.[32]

We can restate this observation in terms of Blake's strict opposition of individual merit to what all can do equally well. If deadlock is to be avoided in a system of production such as Rubens's, individual merit and average ability must be differences of degree rather than kind, such that individual merit can be built up from what all can do equally well, that is, from communicable skills polished to a high degree. Information can then be stored and shared. Hence the great value of van Dyck to Rubens was not at all in the way his "special skill . . . preserved him from slavish emulation of Rubens" and gave him "a distinct identity" but rather the opposite, in the "advantage to be had in employing an assistant whose work could pass for that of the master himself," and pass so well that works from the period of their association in Antwerp often cannot be told apart.[33] There is nothing uncanny about the parity. Rubens's own methods of generalizing his style to make it sharable and repeatable made duplication inevitable and made even van Dyck replaceable. The more learning and practicing required to fill a position in the system, the less efficient the system, because skilled workers are expensive to replace—though by definition never, in such a system, irreplaceable.

The core principle is intermeasurability. Where agreement is essential, so is intermeasurability. It is the common denominator of what all can do equally well that makes the division of labor feasible, ideally allowing the worker to add a single unskilled operation to a rational sequence of other operations executed by other workers, culminating in a finished product that, without the system, would have demanded the skills of an artisan. Of course, the division of labor in Rubens's system fell far short of that goal. Because he depended upon a highly coordinated team of skilled workers, he, like Wedgwood later, found himself in a constant battle against the agitations of genius—or the simulacrum thereof typical of such a system. The manager's impatience with the employee's temperamental disruptions of the system may remind us of nineteenth-century factory managers for whom the erratic human worker seemed the greatest impediment to productivity: "I have wanted above all that my

[32] Analyses of mechanization have tended to concentrate on managing "the flow of information" (Gunn 119) in the system. Though Thomas Gunn's 1982 study concerns itself with machine tools and automation, some of the principles are relevant even to systems of production as relatively small and primitive as Rubens's: "The ready accessibility of the design throughout the company tends to break down the institutional barriers between the design and manufacturing departments" (120–21). But it is also true that "in most instances the design of the product itself is modified to facilitate automatic assembly" (127). That is, an efficient system integrates conception and execution (as design and manufacture); the more information they share, the more accessible each is to the other, and the more smoothly the system operates. Zuboff captures the strange backward adjustment of conception to execution in her phrase "anticipatory conformity" (345). Her study also offers useful sketches of Taylorism and other theories of management that have developed in efforts to control systems of production based on divisions of labor and mechanization.

[33] McNairn 17, 16. The narrative tension, verging on contradiction, between van Dyck's uniqueness and his repeatability surfaces in most accounts, including McNairn's.

(OVERLEAF)

Rubens's engravers, such as the Bolswert brothers, Boetius and Shelte, learned to "finish" their prints by extending harmony from the main figures right to the margins.

Whatever the origin and training of the engravers who came to him, they had first of all to set about learning to draw as he understood drawing; their burin, their etching needle, leaving Goltzius far behind, had to learn to render that modelling of forms, that texture of materials, that gradation of light and shade, of foreground and background and finally that disposition of the whole which were the master's in a host of sometimes very crowded scenes.

[Burckhardt 33]

The paradox in the often-repeated claim that Rubens's engravers were duplicating the master's touch is that the master was managing a system that had defined the role of master.

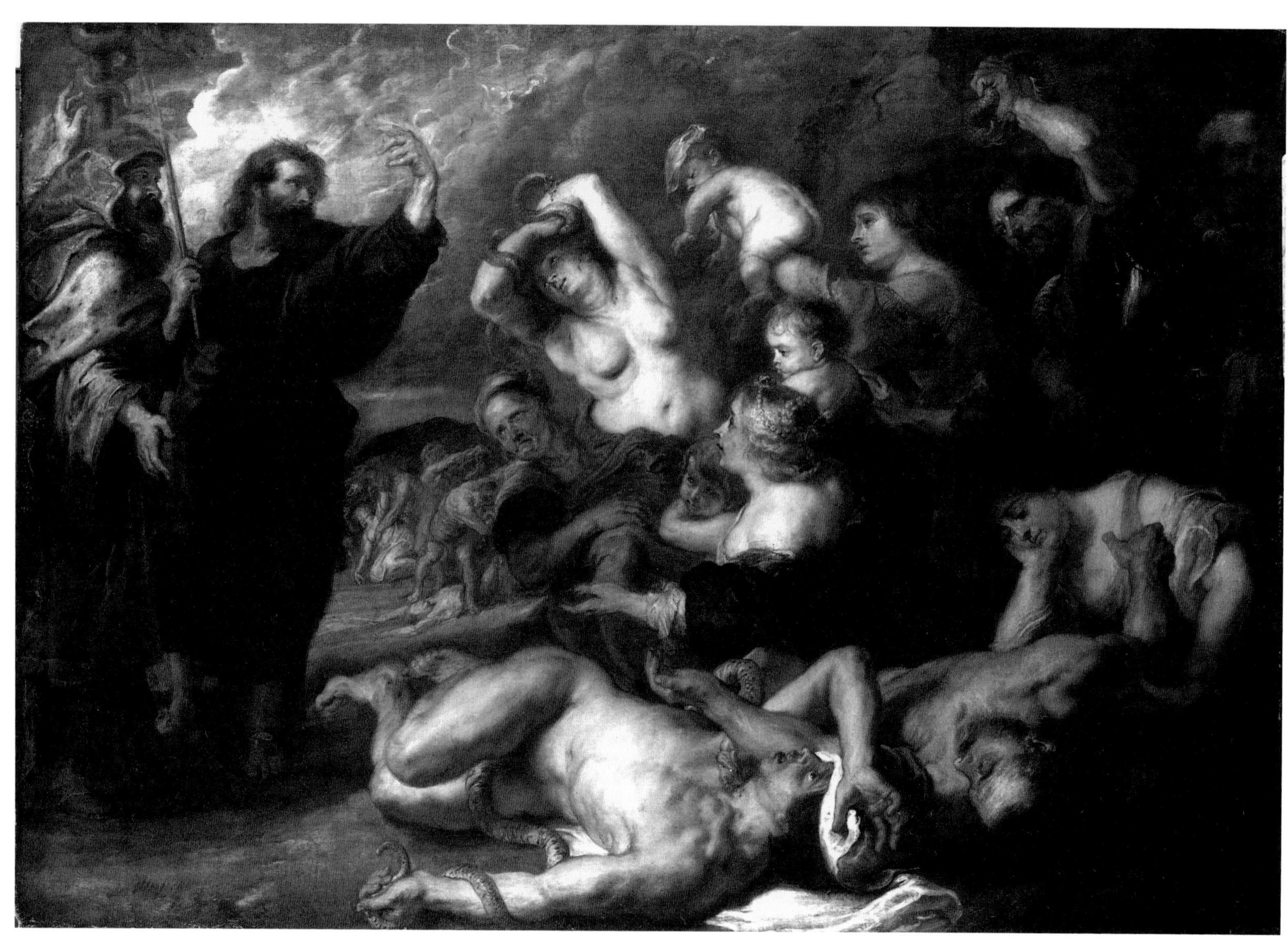

4.25. Peter Paul Rubens, *Moses with the Brazen Serpent,* oil, c. 1630.

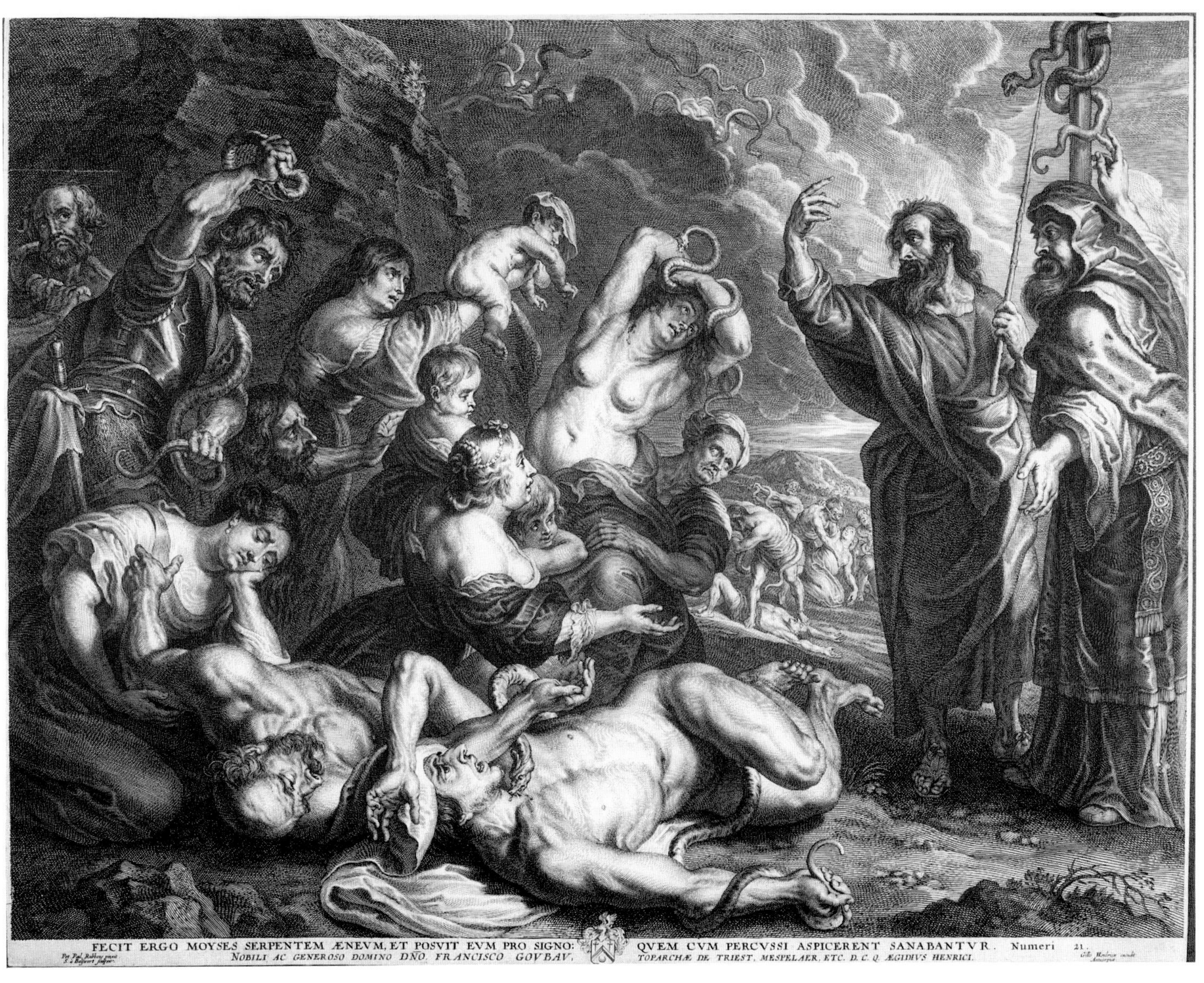

4.26. Schelte Adams van Bolswert after Peter Paul Rubens, *Moses with the Brazen Serpent,* engraving, probably after 1633.

engraver was capable of imitating well the model given to him, and it seems to me better to have them made in my presence by the hand of a youth of good intentions than by some great virtuosi according to their own caprice" (Rubens quoted in Held 114–15).[34]

We have seen that Rubens, like Wedgwood, grasped the commercial advantages of incorporating a myth of individual artistry into a systematic production scheme, and of presenting that myth as the public face of the system. Additionally, like Alderman Boydell, Rubens grasped the commercial value of publicity in the literal sense. His erstwhile assistant van Dyck fell into the role of successful English court painter to Charles I, but Rubens resisted such solicitations, including Charles's, and cast himself instead as a public figure, taking on diplomatic assignments that doubled as art junkets in and around the courts of Europe. His letters tell of a frantically busy middleman with many irons in the fire as he settled disputes in the shop back home, coordinated its work with the collaborative execution of large wall and ceiling paintings on location across the continent, lobbied for international copyright legislation to protect the profits from his prints, delivered state secrets along with paintings, and negotiated treaties along with new commissions.

He understood that markets are made, not born, and in England he vigorously shaped his market by shaping (through advice and consultation) the very collections of which his own paintings would seem the natural extensions, most notably the collection of Charles I—still regarded as the most impressive single picture collection ever assembled in the West. In a collection heavy with as many as fifty-five works attributed to Titian, it comes as no surprise that Rubens and van Dyck were the modern masters most advantageously positioned to be "the King's chief bets on the old masters of the future" (Alsop 462). The king was not gambling alone. The Earl of Arundel, himself a great Rubens collector, the Earl of Pembroke, and the Duke of Buckingham, who bought part of Rubens's personal collection, raised the stakes considerably. While Rubens was in England he was knighted by Charles, and Cambridge conferred on him its Master of Arts degree: "I Rubens am a Statesman & a Saint / He mixed them both & so he Learnd to Paint" (deleted reading, E 871; cf. 513).[35]

Some historians maintain that the style associated with Goltzius and others in Haarlem and Antwerp reached France by way of such Italian intermediaries as Francesco Villamena. Be that as it may, the styles of seventeenth-century French engraving can be seen in useful relation to the elements of virtuosity and compliance in the productions of the Rubens manufactory. Mellan's mannerism evolved from the virtuoso elements that were always needed to lend touches of brilliance to shop styles such as those cultivated by Rubens. This was the heritage of Goltzius. After a period of fascination with Mellanesque virtuosity, however, students and followers of Mellan, such as Robert Nanteuil (figs. 4.27–4.29), Abraham Bosse, and Bosse's English translator William Faithorne, retreated toward the norm: a style dominated

[34] For the Vorsterman affair, see Held. Cf. Burckhardt 215, Avermaete 104, Mayor near fig. 427.

[35] My sketch of Charles's collection derives from the sources and conclusions of Alsop 453–65. He counts, in addition to the Titians, about thirty van Dycks (454). After Charles's execution, the West's greatest art collection was dispersed at the West's largest art sale, the so-called Commonwealth sale: "Half the greatest museums in the world today take pride in superb paintings from Charles I's collection" (163).

This portrait of Charles Benoise, Conseiller au Parlement de Paris, 1651, after a painting by Philippe de Champaigne, a teacher of the engraver Robert Nanteuil, shows Nanteuil's early attraction to Mellan's variable line technique. He softened its mathematical severities, especially in the face, into luxurious realism by "crossing the strokes as occasion required, and harmonizing the lights with dots" (Strutt 2:178–79). Later, as engraver to Louis XIV, Nanteuil turned out likenesses of court figures. The visual decorum called for the high style of line engraving, while the magnitude and repetitiveness of the task brought out the utilitarian elements in that style as it had developed from Marcantonio to Mellan. At the same time, by avoiding abrupt, explicitly linear transitions and lowering his lineal matrix in relation to the threshold of vision, Nanteuil refined the range of realistic tonalities in etching and engraving. The king, playing Saul to Nanteuil's David, expressed his satisfaction. "Partez content Monsieur de Nanteuil, car je suis très content de vous" (Petitjean and Wickert 25; cf. 1 Sam. 16:22), he declared as he officially promoted engraving from an industrial to a liberal art.

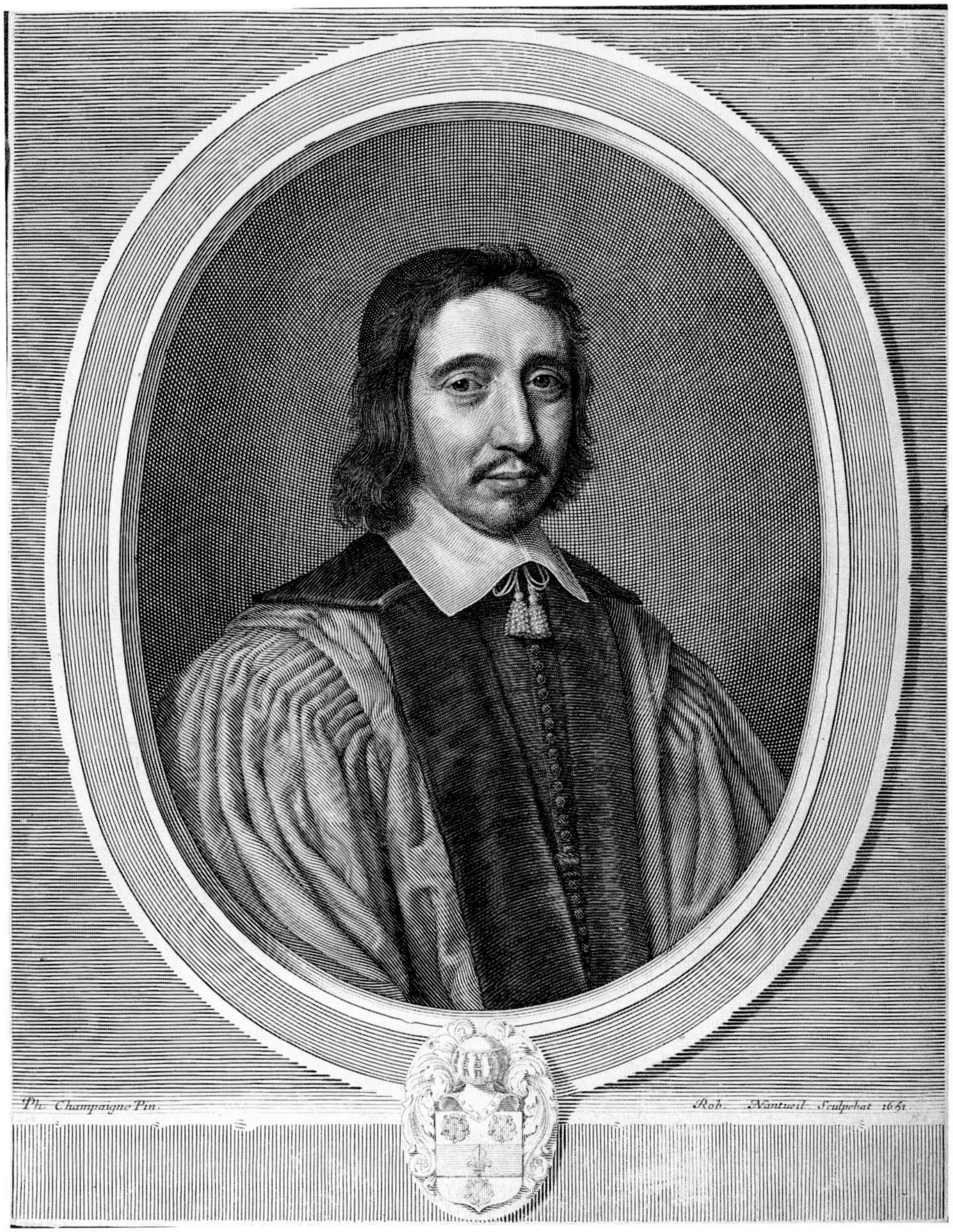

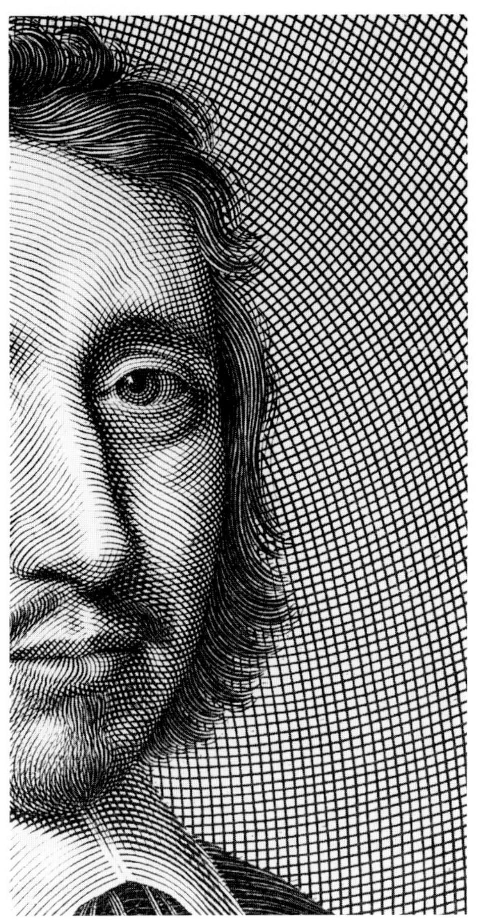

4.27. Robert Nanteuil after Philippe de Champaigne, *Charles Benoise, Conseiller au Parlement de Paris,* engraving, 1651, and detail.

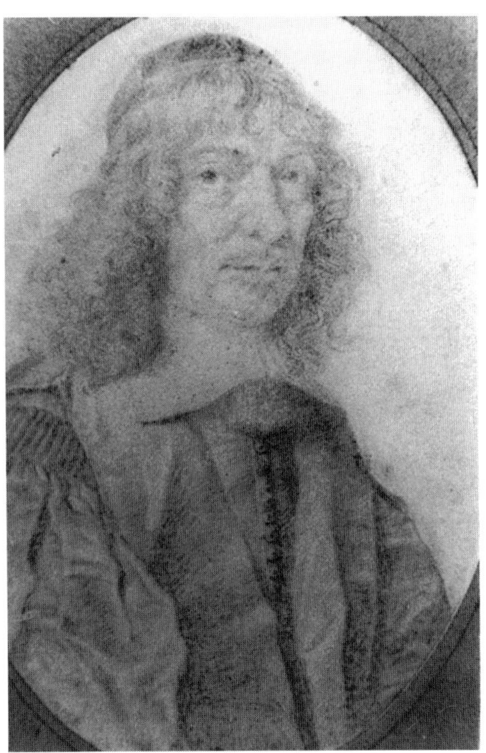

4.28. Robert Nanteuil, preliminary drawing for *Marin Cureau de la Chambre,* c. 1656.

by elements of compliance and moderation for the sake of utility. The variations were less important than the common base, the principle being, once again, that Mellan's virtuosity was the imitation of individual merit that the system, based in what all can do equally well, made available. From that point of view, Mellan's procedures were anything but individual in Blake's sense; their mannerism consisted in being even more uniform and mechanical than the composite style from which they derived.

Rubens's and van Dyck's services to Charles and his circle, Nanteuil's service to Louis XIV,

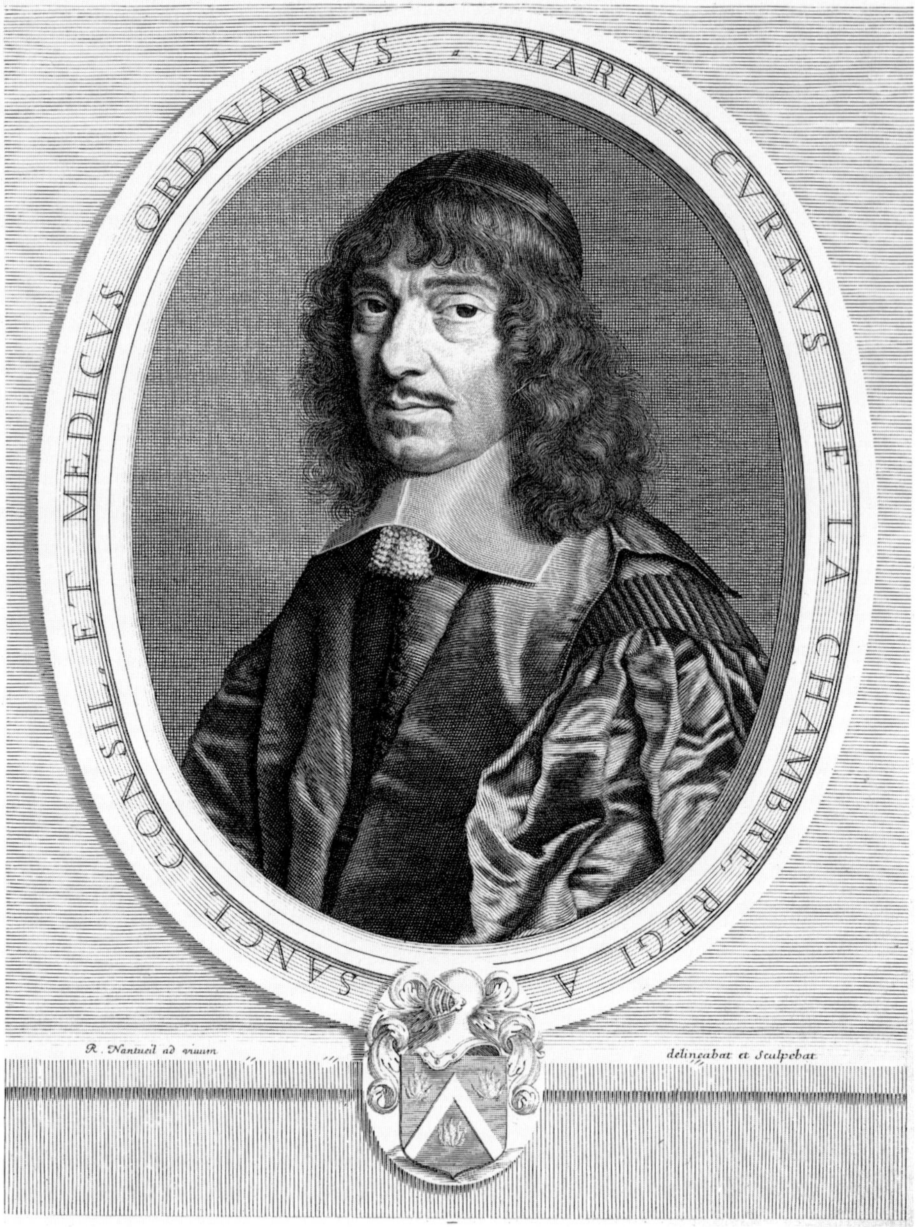

4.29. Robert Nanteuil, *Marin Cureau de la Chambre,* engraving, 1656.

Faithorne's translation of Bosse's handbook into English: they provide multiple ways to shape a satisfying narrative around Blake's conclusion that the entrance of van Dyck and Rubens set English engraving on a ruinous course that we can follow to Blake's time.

Again consider the technological challenge the engravers faced. Reynolds's former assistant James Northcote incorporated this delicious description of Venetian technique into his *Life of Titian:* ". . . blended, softened, woven together into a woof like that of Iris. . . . Every colour is melted, *impasted* into every other. . . . Everywhere tone, not form, predominates—there is not a distinct line in the picture,—but a gusto, a rich taste of colour is left upon the eye as if it were the palate, and the diapason of picturesque harmony is full to overflowing. 'Oh Titian and Nature! which of you copied the other?' " (2:358–59). Rubens's shop methods had been based entirely upon the coordination of divided labor with a systematic application of the methods of traditional "line" engraving. But the very term suggests that if the harmonies of tone and color are the primary ends, line may not be the optimum means. Technologically, other resources needed to be exploited. "The effects indeed of the division of labour" are indeed "surprising and almost miraculous," James Mill observed in 1808, but then "the same is the case with machinery. How much the production of commodities is accelerated and increased by the invention and improvement of machines, requires no illustration" (29). Those journeymen bucklemakers of whom Boydell's detractors complained would not have fitted easily into Rubens's shop because the requisite level of skill had been too high. To accommodate them, some "invention and improvement of machines" were called for.

Innovative processes needed to be better translators of the colorist and chiaroscurist effects achieved so laboriously through the technical displacements—lines used to avoid linearity—of line engraving. Consequently, while the prestige associated with slowness, skill, indirection, and expense allowed line engraving to hang onto its prime position as the translator of choice for masterpieces, new technologies improved the accuracy of translation and slashed the cost of more ordinary work.

Engravers whose livelihood depended upon the increasingly old-fashioned skills of line engraving tried to protect themselves with hostile assessments of the popular tonal processes, stipple, mezzotint, and aquatint. Robert Strange raged against "manufacturers" who, using stipple, had "deluged" the country with "a superfluity of inferior productions" by the "ignorant and unskillful" (quoted in Dennistoun 2:256). He described mezzotint as "an art in which lack of real artistic power is easily hidden in the delightful results that even unpractised hands can achieve" (Strange 8). Landseer said aquatint was so popular that "every booby who could hold a pencil and pour gum and spirit over a plate of copper" was doing it, and he blamed the "rage for dotting" and the singlemindedness of print dealers for the decline of English engraving (*Lectures* 136, 128). In this vein, the best overall appraisal known to me appears in a letter solicited from Blake's fellow engraver William Sharp by Charles Warren, president of the Chalcographic Society and himself a minor engraver. Since the occasion of Sharp's informative letter, dated 29 May 1810, coincides with the occasion of Blake's *Public Address*—the Chalcographic Society's proposal to issue a series of engravings after "the choicest Works of the best British and Ancient Masters"

The shadowy tones of Nanteuil's preliminary sketch for his engraved portrait of a physician consulted by Louis XIII and XIV show that Nanteuil thought of his portraits as (to quote de Piles on Titian) "an opportunity of shewing all his skill and address in the *claro-obscuro*" (119).

(OVERLEAF)

Blake's commitments to elevated, even elitist Art kept him from assenting fully to the postrevolutionary reappraisal of Hogarth. There is a persistent note of condescension in Blake's references: "This *Even* Hogarths Works Prove a detestable Falshood. No Man Can Improve An Original Invention . . ." (my emphasis, E 576). But he reluctantly follows the inclinations of his decade in granting Hogarth's originality, his self-identity, and in valuing that above all: "Even Hogarths Execution cannot be Copied or Improved" (579). One of its stylistic markers is irregularity, including even the spots and blemishes that earlier generations took for technical inadequacy. "[T]he same with every Object in a Picture its Spots are its beauties[.] Now Gentlemen Critics how do you like this" (575).

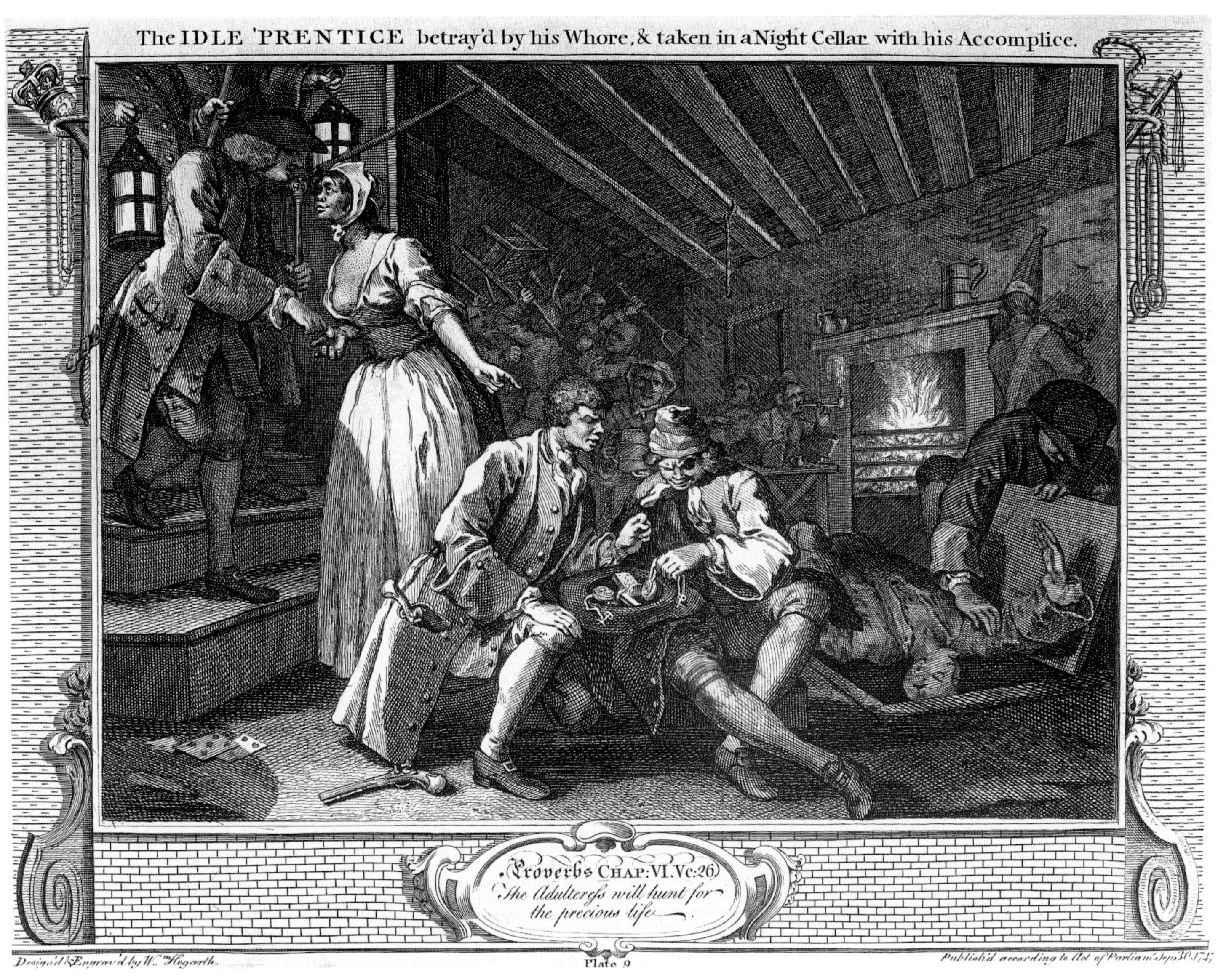

4.30. William Hogarth, *The Idle 'Prentice Betray'd by His Whore,* plate 9 of *The Idle Apprentice,* engraving, 1747.

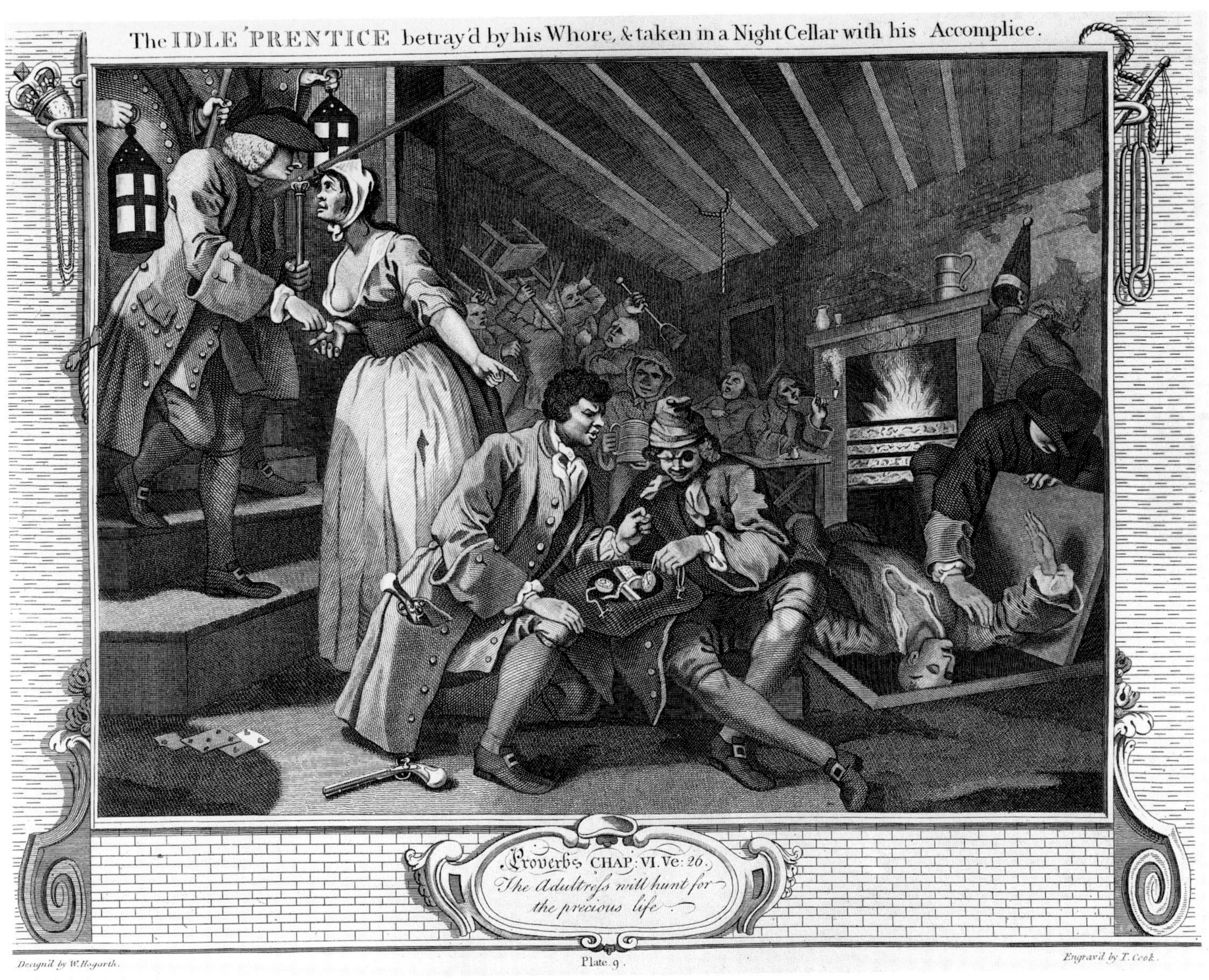

4.31. Tom Cook after William Hogarth, *The Idle 'Prentice Betray'd by His Whore*, 1795(?), from *Hogarth Restored*, 1806 (folio volume, but published in separate prints over several years).

A

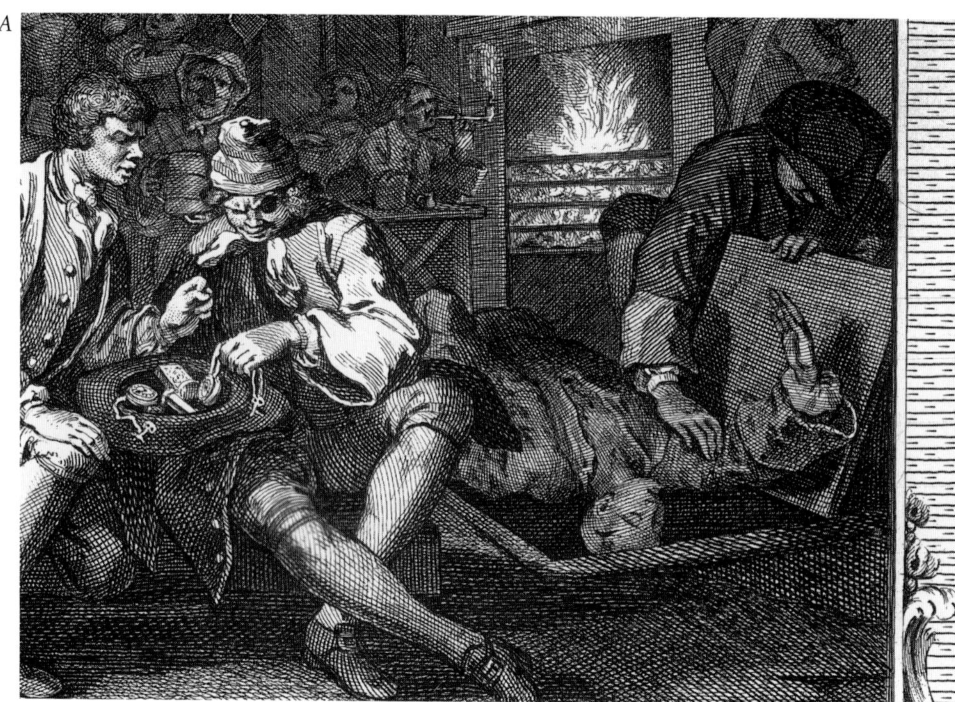

4.32. Details: (*A*) Hogarth, *The Idle 'Prentice;* (*B*) Cook after Hogarth, *The Idle 'Prentice.*

If even Hogarth is Hogarth, then he cannot be altered for the better. In 1786 Strutt acknowledged that Hogarth's prints, despite mechanical ineptitude, are preferable to the best copies (2:21–22), and in 1792 Gilpin, with a similar mixture of condescension and the urge to preserve Hogarth's "spirit" and "imagination" from "cold correctness," suggested only a few improvements (124–25). Blake, in rejecting Tom Cook's charitable efforts to improve Hogarth by finishing what Hogarth had only started, rejects the English-school eclecticism that authorized Cook's remedial program: "Tom Cooke who Engraved after Hogarth wished to Give to Hogarth what he could take from Rafael that is Outline & Mass & Colour but he could not" (E 574). Despite Blake's veneration of Raphael, under the terms of his argument he must read Cook's attempts to add Raphael to

(quoted in Read, "Context" 74)—the one can be instructively read alongside the other. In fact Sharp wrote his letter as a kind of public address ("after you have read it to the Gentlemen who have done me the honor to desire my opinion"). As it has seldom if ever circulated beyond the little-known pages of Howard Levis's specialized bibliography and is not cited in Dennis Read's study of the Chalcographic Society, I shall quote from it at some length.[36]

[36] Levis quotes Sharp's letter, from his own collection, in full on 96–99, from which all the following quotations come.

Sharp addresses the interplay of labor, skill, and price in engraving. His point of reference is conventional line engraving—"regular" engraving, he oftens calls it, or the "old regular mode." He begins by calculating the relative values of line engraving and mezzotint:

> I shall begin with the Second resolution wherein is mentioned the 20 plates to be engraved in various ways. First I shall notice the Art of Mezzotinto . . . The Mezzotinto being almost as quick as drawing. Many of them can be begun and finished at the same time that one Engraved Plate can, in a greater proportion than Twenty to One. . . . Ten Engravings . . .

B

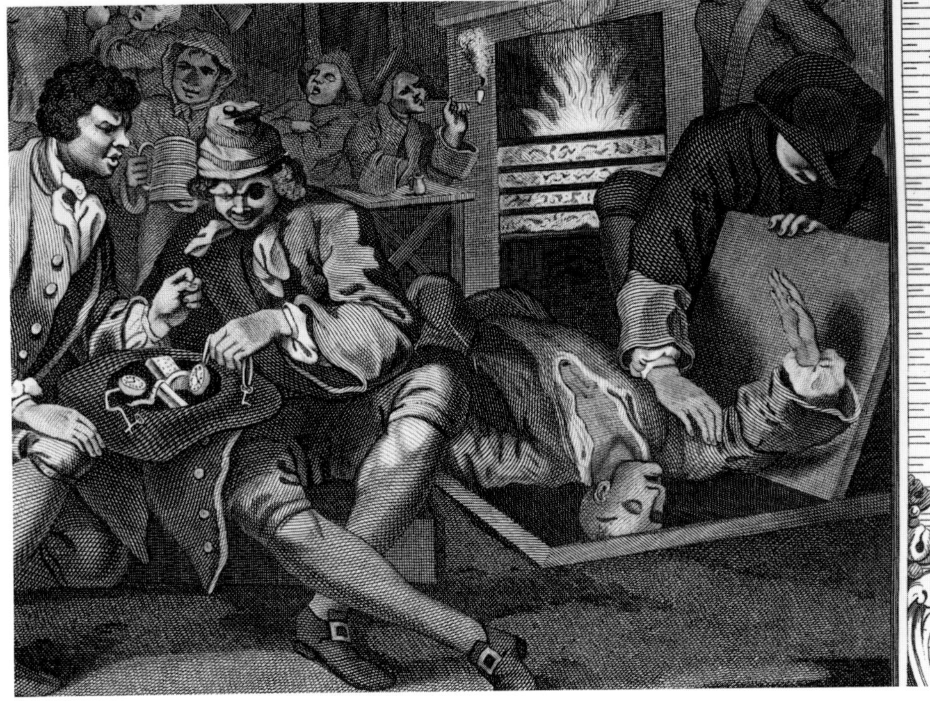

Hogarth as blotting and blurring the Hogarth already present; or, as Blake has it in a jingle, Cook cut Hogarth down to his own size as he cleaned him up: "Tom Cooke cut Hogarth down with his clean graving / Thousands of Connoisseurs with joy ran raving" ("Blakes apology," E 505). The stylistic indication of the presence of blotting and blurring is the immaculate uniformity of Cook's technique, the "System & Monotony" that can turn a Hogarth into "a Piece of Machinery" (E 579). During the first quarter of the nineteenth century, a dawning recognition of the "autograph importance"—as Cunningham phrased it in the *Lives* (1:107)—of Hogarth's prints, and his claim on the newly created cultural post of national artist, transformed the context in which complaints about his skills of execution had to register.

would employ one Individual at least 30 years allowing Three Years to each, and the four Mezzotintos may be completed in less than two years of the Size of Wooletts [Death of] Wolfe, the process being so rapid that four Plates can only employ one person for a short period—*and that only for one person.*

"There are subjects much better adapted for Mezzotinto in preference to any other" and "great advantages in a pecuniary way"—offset somewhat by the "less than 200" impressions that a mezzotint plate could produce (until the introduction of more durable steel plates a few years later). Sharp identifies in mezzotint a set of features matched to a set of market conditions. If the subject is large, timely, and tonal, and if only a few impressions will meet the demand, then the medium fits the market. But to "encourage" mezzotinters equally with line engravers in the Society's project, the ratio would have to be twenty mezzotints to one engraving.

Moving from mezzotint to stipple, the "dotted manner," he again acknowledges "in respect to expidition great advantages over the Old established engraving." The prime advantage of stipple is its adaptability to what all ignorant journeymen can do equally well,

which is evidently proved by the Numbers who are employed in that mode, and who are daily increasing. It is not only easy in its process, but they [the

> stipplers] have advantages over either the Line manner of Engraving, or Mezzotinto, by assistants which can be easily procured, and which assistants can without any knowledge of drawing, or any Natural taste perform the great part of the labour: The Principal Artist who employs them . . . may produce many subjects at nearly the same time, and by the advantage of such assistants can produce as many, and even more than Mezzotinto can. . . . The dotting engraving has a considerable advantage over Mezzotinto in regard to the number of Impressions which may far exceed 1000, and I believe may be easily retouched by persons of inferior Abilities. . . . In a trading point of view the advantages . . . is prodigeous.

Like Blake and Strange, Sharp envisions teeming hordes of ignorant dotters: "some of these Men are dying away but their Numbers are increasing all over these Kingdoms." And portraits of the clergy alone, he says, can provide them with "inexhaustible" work. No need, in other words, to encourage the dotters.

The mention of stipple sends Sharp back to the heyday of the 1790s and the "late plan of the Boydells Shakespere, the greater part" of which was, he has to admit, "executed in the dotting way." But Sharp reminds Warren that Boydell's method was to unlock a market with the prestige of line engraving and only afterward to supply the ensuing demand with stipples: "When Boydells Fame as a Print Merchant was well established abroad in Foreign Countries by means of Wolletts finely engraved Prints—He of course resorted to every means to produce a quantity of Prints for sale." Sharp leaves his auditors to draw the obvious conclusion: Boydell's early successes were due to the quality of line engraving; his later failures may have been due to the quantity of stipple.

Aquatint, like mezzotint and stipple, has been "encouraged by Trade and Commerce and . . . by the Public." But what of the old regular mode? As if in answer, Sharp constructs a brief and nostalgic history whose course was set "particularly at the Time of Louis the 14th. & since" by engravers such as Nanteuil, who were followed by "Great Men" such as Strange and Woollett, who

> considered the Quality more [than] the quantity. The latter best suiting the purposes of Trade, and the former for excellence. It is well known if a Person can get assistants and engage subjects of various sorts, Plates may be so Manufactured as to produce a large Fortune, One Gentleman an Engraver informed Me, that He has gained 20,000£ only by the Labour of others during the prime of his Life, and all this was tottally independant of his own labour.

Sharp's story is the standard lament for the replacement of an old two-way alliance between artisans and an elite class by a new three-way association between a broader public, innovative producers who could supply affordable goods, and merchant-middlemen through whom supply could meet demand. So told, the history of engraving becomes part of the decay of aristocratic patronage, of the made to order, and the flourishing of the street trade, of shopping for the ready-made from inventories of stock on hand: "Print Merchants live by the Quantity as much as by the quality and as some Mode of Engraving . . . being easier of execution together with that dispatch frequently so necessary in Trade, gave them the prehemінence."

Sharp's construction may usefully recall some commonplaces of intellectual history. With metaphors of quantity and pace he pic-

Robert Strange's *Miserere* (1753), after a painting by Guido Reni (pupil of the Carracci and later rival of Caravaggio), appropriates French technique for "What Is Calld the English Style of Engraving" (*PA*, E 573). The intricate tonal work illustrates Strutt's contention that the inferiority of old engravers to moderns could be expressed as the inferiority of mere "neatness" to "high finishing," which created "the harmony and powerfulness of the effect, and a judicious distribution of light and shadow" (1:2). Of English "line" engravers associated with high finishing, Strange was often regarded as the greatest—"by far," wrote John Thomas Smith in 1828, "the first Historical-engraver, this or any country has produced" (2:247). "Harmony and union" constituted Strange's highest aesthetic value, for which he praised Correggio's *St. Jerome* as "the finest picture I have ever seen" (quoted in Dennistoun 2:141). When Strange was criticized, it was usually for the mechanical uniformity of his meticulous technique and for the assistants that such manual labor demanded. Pasquin said Strange "managed" the "harmonious conjunction of strokes" so that they "worked like automata, without souls" (107). Blake said that "Stranges Prints were when I knew him all done by Aliamet & his french journeymen whose names I forget" (*PA*, E 574). Strange did have lifelong French connections, first because of his Jacobitism (as engraver to the prince he escaped to France when the cause collapsed) and

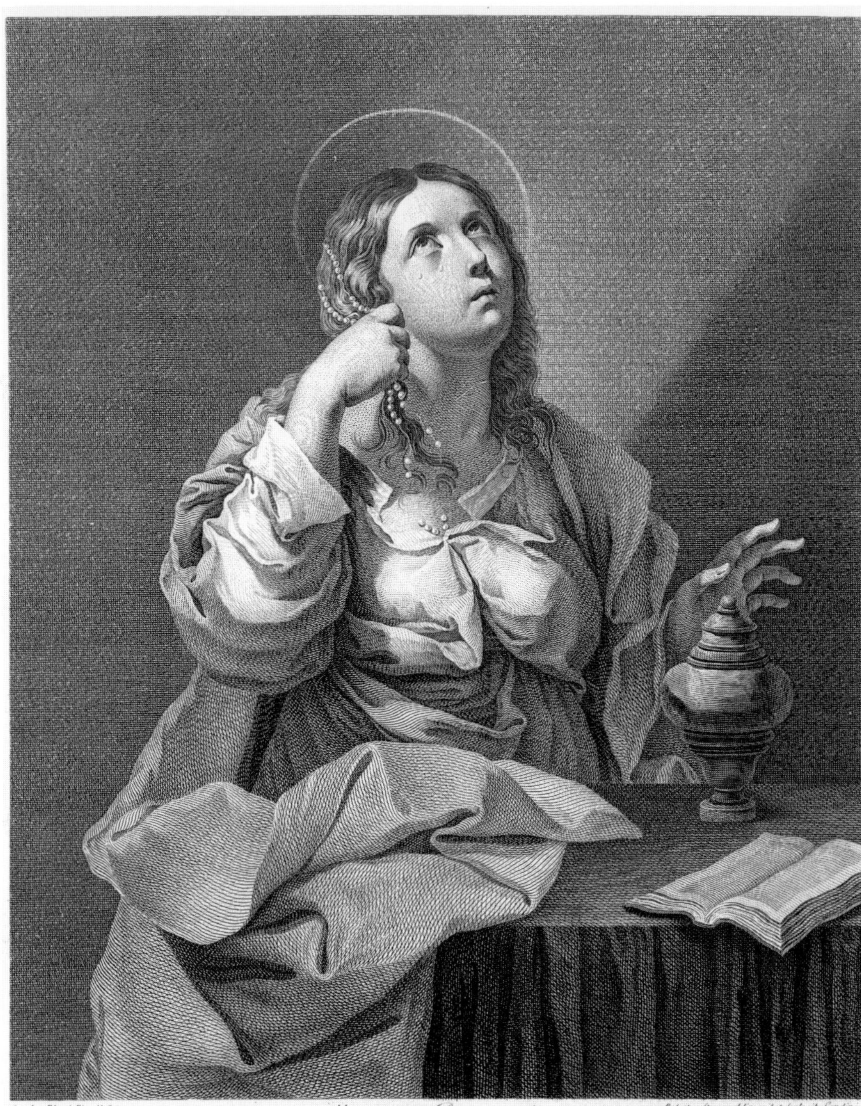

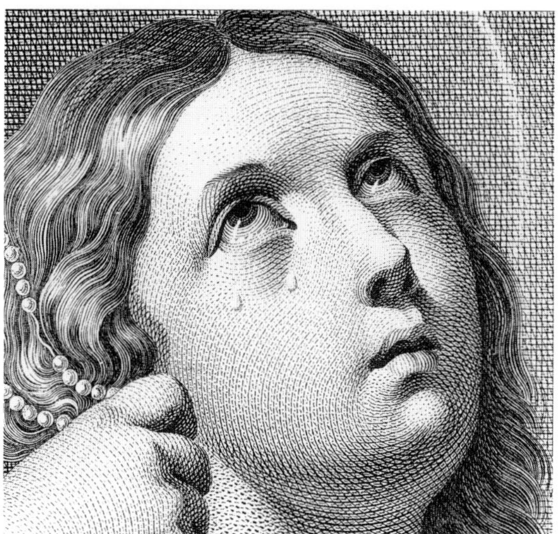

4.33. Robert Strange after Guido Reni, *Miserere,* engraving, 1753, and detail.

then later as a pupil in Paris of Jacques-Philippe Le Bas, a tutelary spirit of eighteenth-century reproductive engraving. Le Bas was known for his vast and mediocre output, his economical and quick methods, and his large assembly of pupils. Diderot singled him out as the engraver who killed *la bonne gravure,* according to Lady Dilke (93).

Strange, who regularly complained about the extent of the contribution he had to make to his prints because of unreliable assistants, typifies the role of a virtuoso technician in such productions. While he would explain how he was "retouching . . . purposely to bring in my hand," he would also become defensive when newspapers drew attention to his foreign assistants—"as if," he wrote to Lord Bute (who had refused to patronize him), "it had been a matter of importance whether the background . . . [or] drapery were to

tures the shift from an old world of craft to a new one of manufacture through changes in time, space, and the flow of events. In the uncrowded past one had time and room to reflect and make and the patience to wait for quality. Relationships were direct. Encouragement was in the hands of a few—tellingly symbolized by a single monarch—who knew enough to command the best from a few skilled artisans. In Sharp's modern world, time to train and to make have shrunk. Money is time, time has become all expedition and dispatch, packed with shorter and shorter intervals.

As time, so space. The space of production grows crowded with "numbers . . . daily increasing," assistants laboring over their fragments of the total design. The space of merchandising is the same. As anyone quickly learns who reads through descriptions of London, contemporary passers-by registered impressions of ever more, newer, faster: streets more crowded with customers converging on more shop windows crowded with more merchandise, all circulating faster. Even the merchandise is, so to speak, faster, as when Sharp acknowledges the special ability of the cheap and easy tonal processes to capture "any event of the day, that may suddenly engage the attention of the Public." What chance can any old regular mode have of surviving an impatient, impermanent world such as this?—"for there is no patronage at all adequate to the trouble & time." The old single patron with much encouragement to offer has been distributed over many faceless customers with a little for each, while the old regular engraver with much skill to offer has been distributed over the many hands of many assistants.[37]

No wonder, then, that the social vision that emerges from Sharp's analysis encourages no hope for useful association: "And I am decidedly convinced, in considering all the various Methods of producing prints which are called Engraving that it is impossible to form any Society whatever to unite them together—They never can at all be in Harmony." No effective Chalcographic Society or Society for Encouragement, only a multitude of societies of "opposite interests": "I shall now conclude by recommending an immediate Seperation. . . ." One wonders to what extent Sharp's religious inclinations—he was a follower first of Richard Brothers, Prince of the Hebrews, and then of Joanna Southcott[38]—prepared him to find differences outweighing similarities and discover a moral necessity for sectarianism. Despite ecumenical gestures—"every Man has an undoubted right to give the preference where he thinks proper, and leave others to enjoy their own opinions"—he grants line engraving a superior moral position. His fundamental princi-

be dead-coloured either by an Englishman or a Frenchman" (quoted in Dennistoun 2:27, 35). In the division of labor that had become virtually *de rigueur,* faces were set aside as sanctuaries for the master's hand, but backgrounds and drapery could be, so to say, handed to assistants.

In his early bid to turn the English school of engraving into a marketable commodity, Boydell published Francesco Bartolozzi's "nearly incomparable *Clytie*" (Pasquin 106), a dot-and-lozenge line engraving, in 1772. Though Bartolozzi did not leave his native Italy for England until 1764, he was usually credited as being one of two or three engravers who carried the English school of engraving to the commercial success that helped inspire the Shakespeare Gallery project: "Previous to the publicity of Bartolozzi (excepting Woollett, and Ryland's works,) our prints were inconsiderable, and of little value; but since that period, they formed a great article of commerce" (Pasquin, "Royal Academicians" 106).

[37] Cf. Barbara Kruger's use of these by now standard metaphors in one of her warnings about the new world we inhabit:

> Times have changed, and the world comes to us in different ways. Narrative has leaped . . . computers have jumbled . . . and television has merely changed *everything.*
>
> Now things feel as if they're moving *really* fast. . . . We are soaked in sales pitches and infotainments that make history when they do business.
>
> Running in place at the speed of light, we defensively cling to categories, our dilapidated signposts in a bleak landscape. They make things simple again. Reflections of control, they reassure us that there's a time and a place for everything. [43]

[38] Paley, "William Blake," surveys Sharp's attachments to Brothers and Southcott, including Sharp's failure to make Blake a Southcottian.

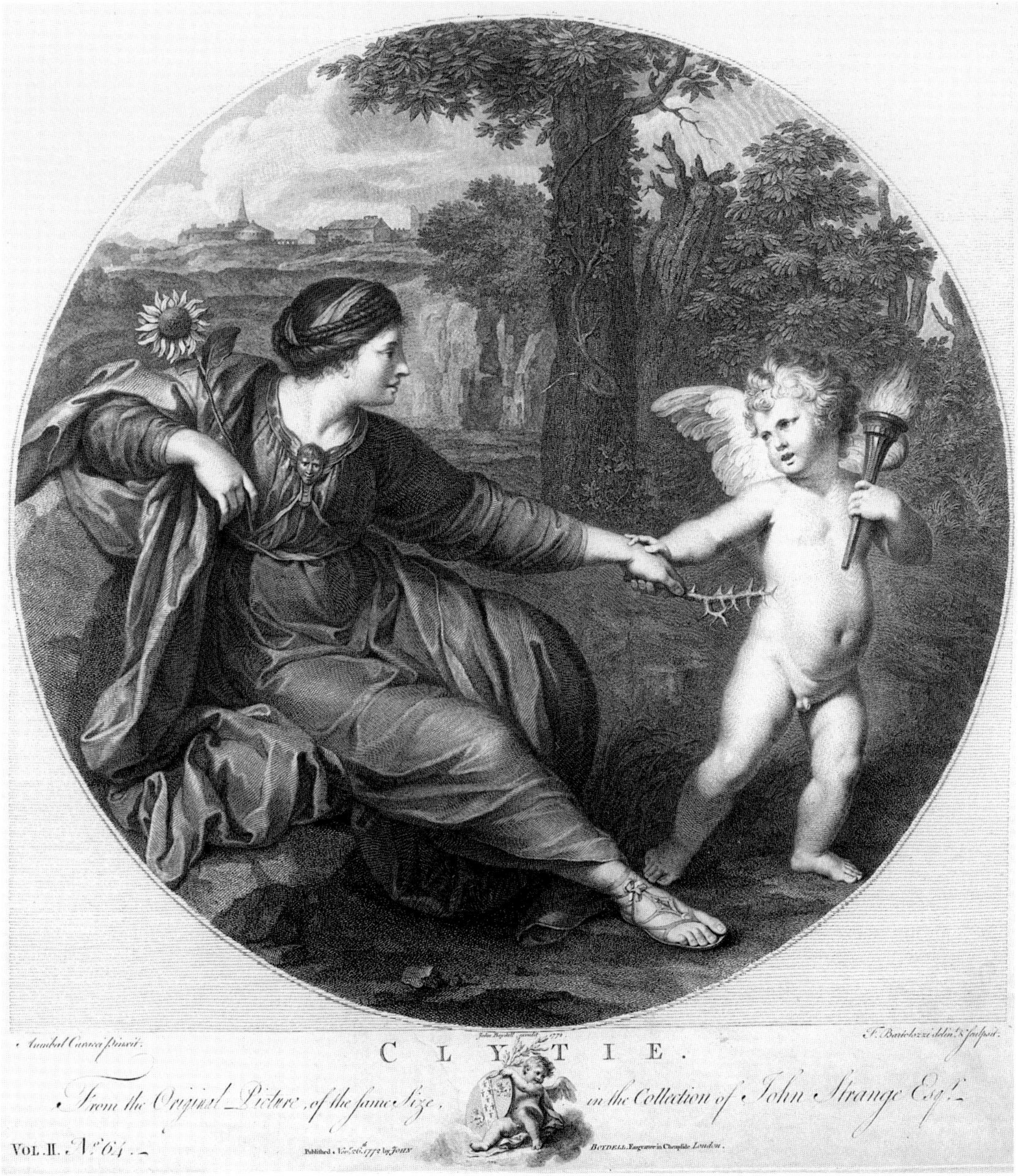

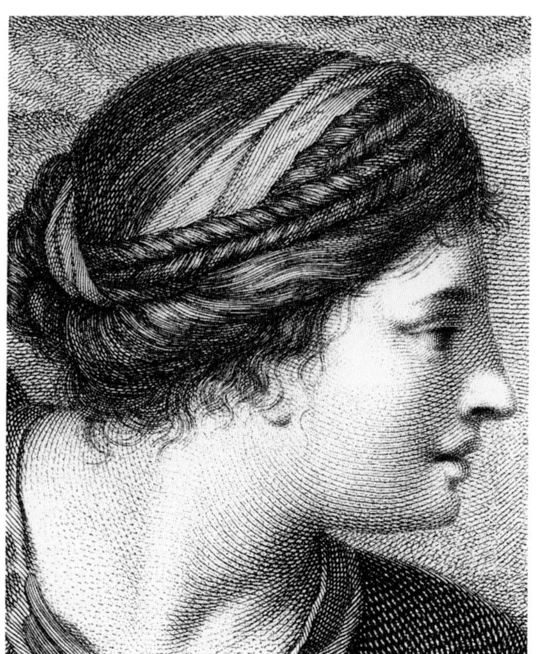

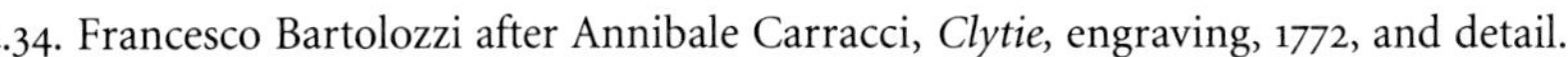

4.34. Francesco Bartolozzi after Annibale Carracci, *Clytie,* engraving, 1772, and detail.

Like Strange, Bartolozzi would add his "touches" with the burin ("graver")—the engraver's chief instrument—to "finish" a base of acid-etched preliminary lines, concentrating his skill on the faces of the main figures. The practice was widely understood and accepted. In an anonymous review of Blake's illustrations for Robert Blair's *Grave,* the reviewer praises the engraver Schiavonetti's portrait of Blake (after Phillips) for being "etched with spirit," then remarks that the "head is finished with the graver, and is an excellent specimen of art" (*Monthly Magazine,* 1 December 1808, quoted in Bentley, *Blake Records* 210).

A

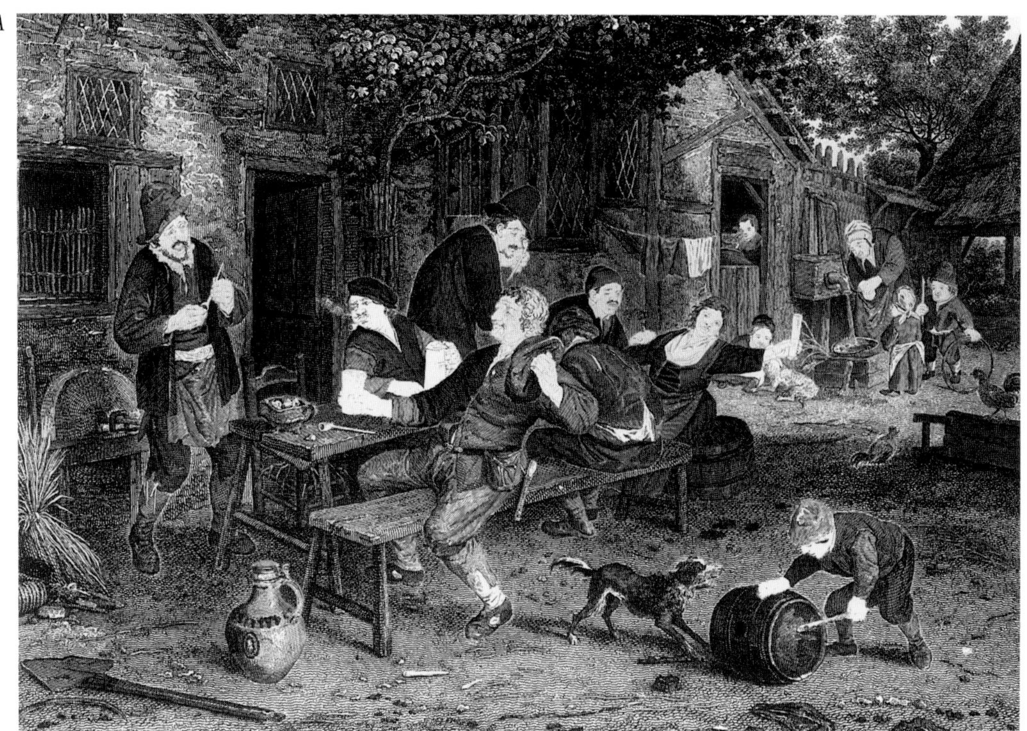

4.35. William Woollett after Cornelis Dusart, *Jocund Peasants,* engraving, 1767: (*A*) early state, detail; (*B*) published state.

ple would demote every other method and promote line engraving because the difference between them corresponds to "the difference between the Trading Artist and adventurer, & those whose principal desire is for excellence in his Art—It is very difficult for these two characters to be found in One Person." To promote gain will always be to "undermine Industry & real merit."

Finally, however, his criticism miscarries because line engraving never earns the special virtue he wants to claim for it. He is never able to demonstrate that "All these different methods" whose prolific reproduction threatens to smother the old regular mode are meaningfully inferior. Line engraving is slower and takes more skill. That is the basis of Sharp's best point: a publishing project must acknowledge that different methods occupy different niches in the commercial economy, as a handmade automobile, product (partly) of an artisanal economy, differs from an automobile produced on an assembly line with cheap labor. Those differences may be tied to differing significations: in engraving "line" may symbolize the craft of the maker, "stipple" the science of the

William Woollett's popular print *Jocund Peasants* makes an appearance in Blake's *Public Address:* "Wooletts best works were Etchd by Jack Brown Woolett Etchd very bad himself. . . . Jocund Peasants . . . [&] all that are Calld Wooletts were Etched by Jack Browne & in Wooletts works the Etching is All tho even in these a single leaf of a tree is never correct" (E 574). John Browne had been a fellow apprentice with Woollett under the master John Tinney. An early state of *Jocund Peasants* in the British Museum carries credit lines for the painter and etcher only: *Browne Aqua forte fecit* ("Browne did the aqua fortis") (lower right) tells us that, if he followed customary procedure, Jack Browne etched, in multiple stages and with assistants of his own, a fairly dense network of preliminary lines over a sparser network of even more preliminary lines. Working by the program shared widely by engravers but also portrait and history painters, he or they left faces and hands unfinished, awaiting the arrival of the master. More extreme divisions of labor were not unusual: *The Children in the Wood* (1786) was designed by J. Hodges Benwell, with a landscape engraved by William Byrne and Thomas Medland and figures by William Sharp. (Sharp's biographer highlights the master's "power of adaptation": "did we not know otherwise, the same hand would seem to have produced the whole plate" [Baker, *William Sharp* 16].) To illustrate his *One Hundred Fables, Original and Select* (1828–1833), James Northcote cut figures out of prints and pasted them

B

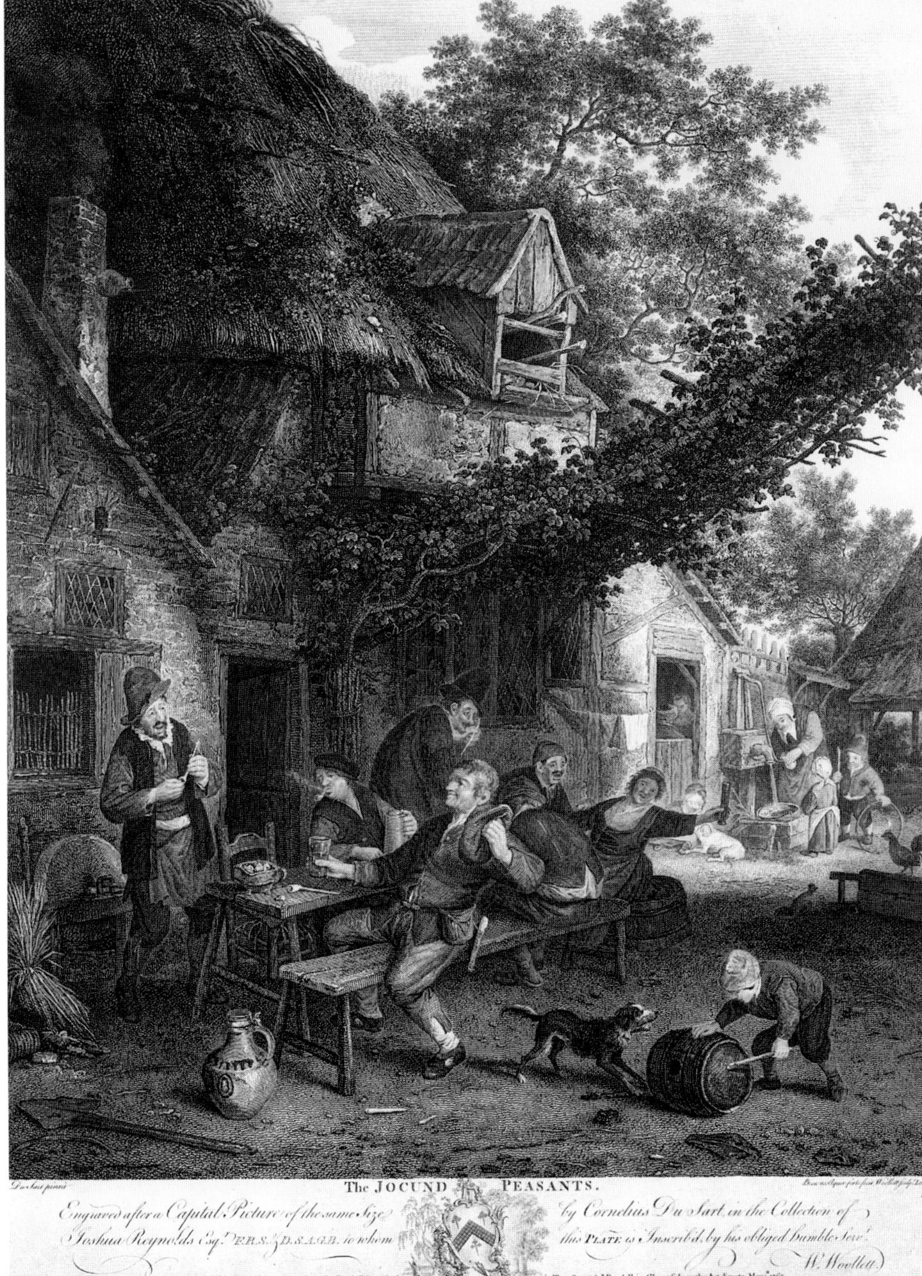

together into a composition that was drawn on wood blocks by William Harvey and then cut into the wood by several engravers. An engraving of A. E. Chalon's *Prophet of St. Paul's,* published in *The Keepsake* annual for 1830, was divided among four engravers, though it was scarcely larger than three inches by four. Only one engraver, Charles Heath—son of the engraver James Heath—is credited on the print. As master, he took responsibility for the "flesh" (Hunnisett 54–55). And of course several unnamed assistants would also be involved at these stages, not to mention the printing (by a specialist in printing engravings) and coloring (sometimes by stencils, with colors divided among several "washers," often women).

Early arrivals are low in the pecking order; the master arrives last. The published state of *Jocund Peasants* shows how faces and hands are identified with, and arrive with, the master's hand: *Woollett sculp* ("Woollett sculpted it"). The theory of painted faces runs parallel with the practice. Faces and hands are ultimate tests of the artist's highly prized powers of character and expression (see Eaves, *Blake's Theory* 46–54). Woollett's powers of producing what one French admirer called "*miracles d'harmonie*" (Charles-Clément Bervic quoted in Godfrey 44) were indeed prized. A sale catalogue of 1786 shows Woollett's prints bringing in more than a Raphael drawing and Rembrandt etchings.

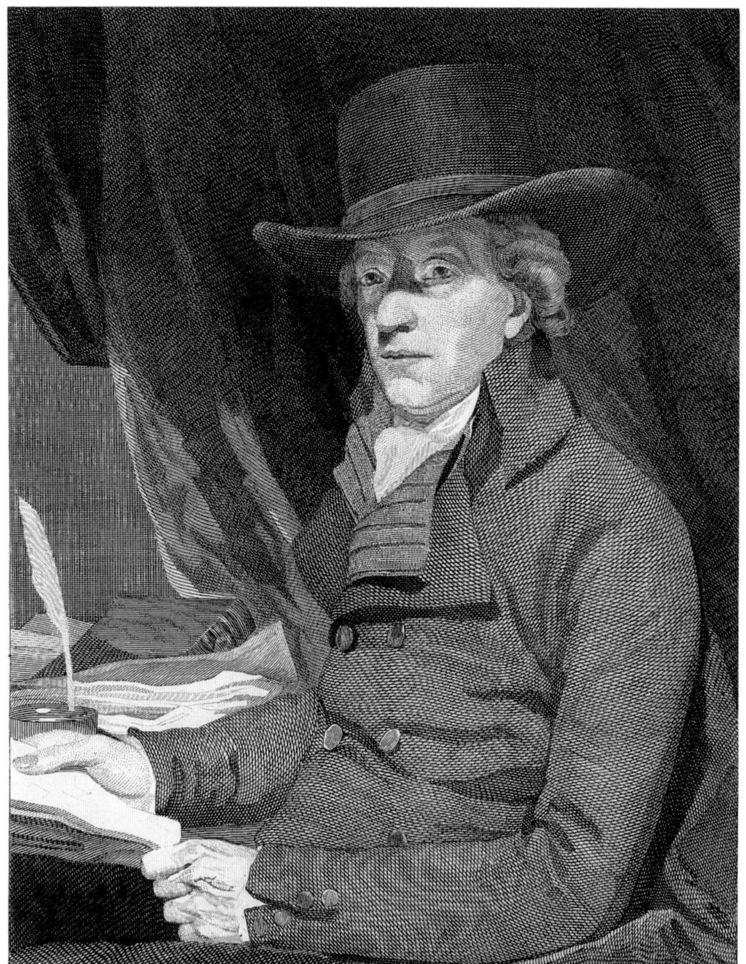

A

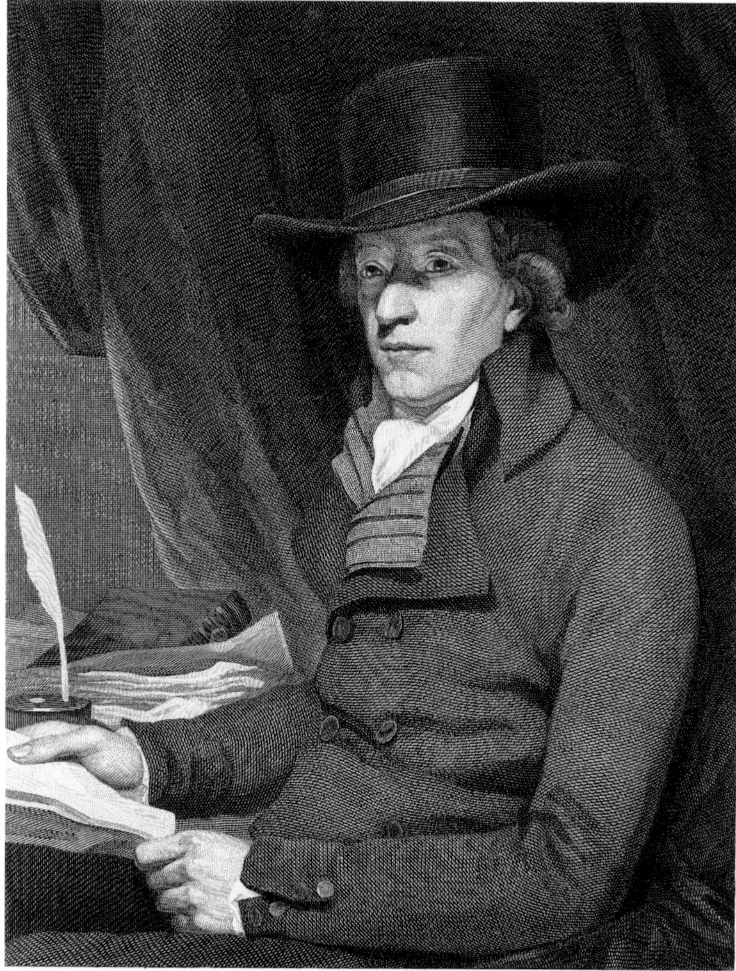

B

4.36. William Sharp after John Opie, *Edward Long:* (*A*) preliminary etched state; (*B*) before all letters, after insignia; (*C*) before letters, after frame and insignia; (*D*) published state, 1796.

natural world, the accurate imitation of nature by the best means available.

But Sharp concedes that the tonal processes, like line, can achieve beautiful and striking effects. He never faces the hard fact that mezzotint, stipple, and aquatint were bona fide technical advances that became popular for good reason. They allowed gains in accuracy, resolu-

Engraving, like painting, depended heavily on portrait commissions. Sitters and their families often wanted multiple copies, and paintings were very expensive to copy. Engraving was usually the medium of choice. A typical collaboration is seen in William Sharp's engraving of Edward Long after a painted portrait by John Opie. Any

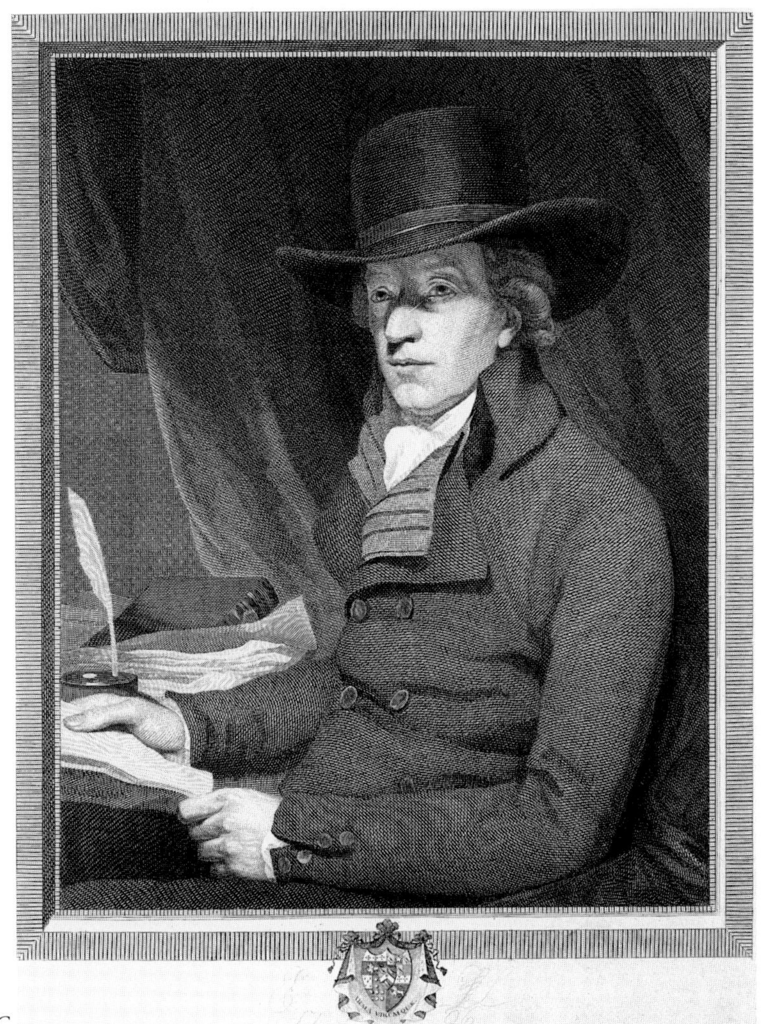

C

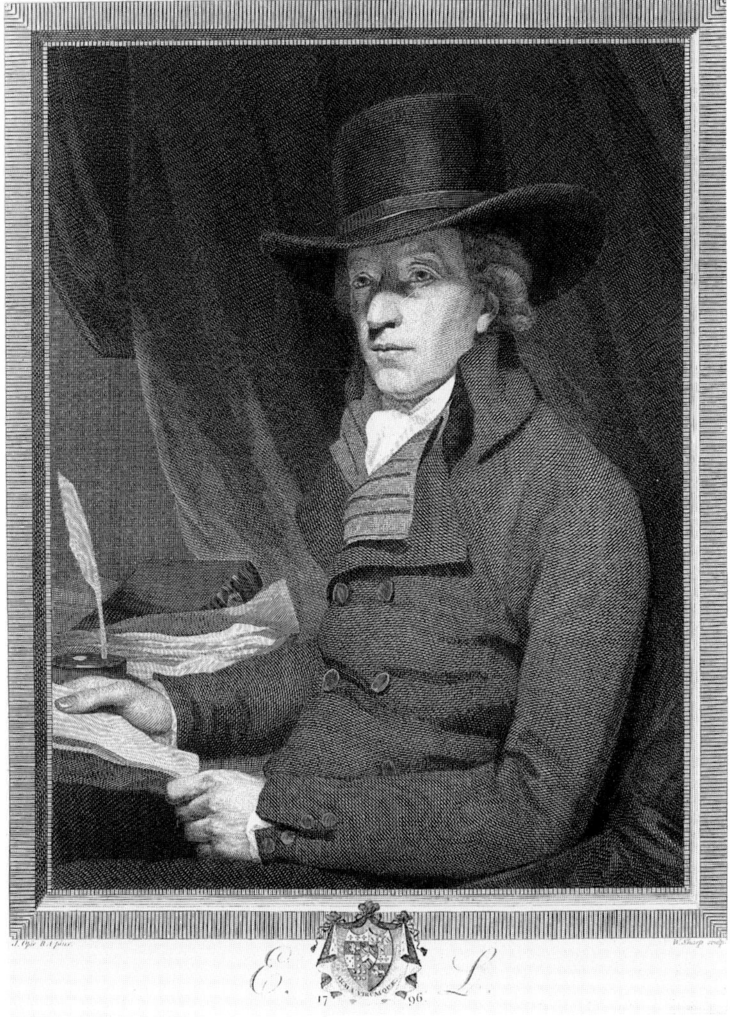

D

efficient collaboration requires a meeting of minds or systems. The extent to which the latter made the former possible is revealed here in a progression of states: first a proof, before all letters, of the preliminary etching, mostly crosshatching of varying density; then another proof before letters showing

tion, and productivity in the areas of greatest demand. Accuracy and expedition made a practically irresistible commercial pair that spoke to eye and pocketbook in one voice.

Sharp's analysis obviously shares with Blake's not only its occasion but also themes and a framework. Both certainly belong to an anti-commercial tradition of complaint about the decline of English line engraving that had been firmly established in the wake of the Boydell failure by Landseer's *Lectures.* But pressing the comparison between Blake's assessment and Sharp's reveals the former to be, in effect, a revisionary critique of the latter.

We know craft matters to Blake. He too focuses blame by opposing mastery to incompetence (and its personification in the opposition of expert master to ignorant journeymen). But craft is the key to Sharp's history as it is not to Blake's. The differences register in their accounts of changes in time and space. If Sharp finds a world short of time for the labor of craft, Blake finds one that measures value in terms of labor: thus the question becomes how to "*make use* of either Labour or Care" (my emphasis). Time and space are overloaded, but with the extension, repetition, and monotony that offer cheap substitutes for mental life and crowd out the real thing, as if "Five Hundred Idiots" (*PA*, E 573) could add up to one genius. The criterion of mastery is not a repertory of time-consuming skills—"dots & lozenges," "clean strokes & mossy tints," and so on (572–73)—but a single skill, drawing, represented by a single unit, line, which is taken to be the product in space-time of an "eternal" mental activity. If "leave off" is better than "Lifes labour" (576, 574), the measure of an artist's work cannot be the years that Woollett could spend over a fancy line engraving of West's *Death of Wolfe* for Boydell in the good old unhurried days before the Revolution. Blake was thinking of such legends of labor when he countered with his *Canterbury Pilgrims* engraving:

> The Artist engages to deliver it, finished, in One Year . . .—No Work of Art, can take longer than a Year: it may be worked backwards and forward without end, and last a Man's whole Life; but he will, at length, only be forced to bring it back to what it was, and it will be worse than it was at the end of the first Twelve Months. The Value of this Artist's Year is the Criterion of Society: and as it is valued, so does Society flourish or decay. [Prospectus, E 567–68]

Hence Woollett and Strange, among the champions of Sharp's and Landseer's stories about the loss of craft, can turn into the scoundrels of Blake's story of the loss of mind. (And as he worries acutely about the loss of his own mind, this artist's year is a discipline of imagination from which he is not exempt, as he indicates when he evaluates his failed chiaroscurist experiments in the *Descriptive Catalogue* [fig. 4.59; see also Eaves, *Blake's Theory* 117–18].) Woollett and Strange can be vilified alongside Bartolozzi because in Blake's analysis all three belong to the counter-arts tradition of the artistic machine and intermeasurable technique. The established distinction between the evolved atelier style of line engraving and the newer tonal processes is in effect branded false. Likewise, the two opposing halves of the narrative join in a continuous tale of progressive improvement: accepting the inheritance of van Dyck and Rubens, Woollett, Strange, and Bartolozzi cultivated techniques and attitudes that created the present situation, "Suited to the Purposes of Commerce no doubt" (E 573).

Blake's stake in the continuity of that story explains why he often writes as if Woollett, Strange, and Bartolozzi—the first two dead, the third in his eighties and in Portugal since the turn of the century—were still active, certainly not heroes of a more heroic age but the mean spirits who animate the present generation of bucklemakers from the factory towns. The continuity of his story also accounts for his refusal to accept the usually strict division between the boom of the prerevolutionary Boy-

the harmonizing effects of dots (here tiny slashes) in the lozenges; a third proof, after insignia and border but before letters and signatures (the subject's initials are sketched in); and finally the published state of 1796.

Perhaps the family never liked Long's headgear—or perhaps the change of fashion made a once-dapper chapeau look slightly absurd. In any case, after his death in 1813, someone sought out a restyled image. The engraver duly hammered up the plate from the back and then reworked the flattened copper to liberate head from hat, delete shadows, add hair, and execute a few other posthumous modifications: no stripes on the collar, new motto, new letters. Perhaps most remarkable for those weaned on the ratio of one artist, one work, it appears that not Sharp but Robert Graves (1798–1873) made the alterations. A complete change of hands was made feasible by the standardized system of production, including a standard repertory of representational techniques, in which all line engravers participated. Systems of harmony, applied in the final stages, hide the deletion of the hat by blending fragmented surfaces back into a uniform *tout-ensemble.* As the hat was made from the same building blocks of the system as the surrounding surfaces, they all belong to a system of interchangeable parts. Those blocks had only to be rearranged by shared techniques of arrangement.

A

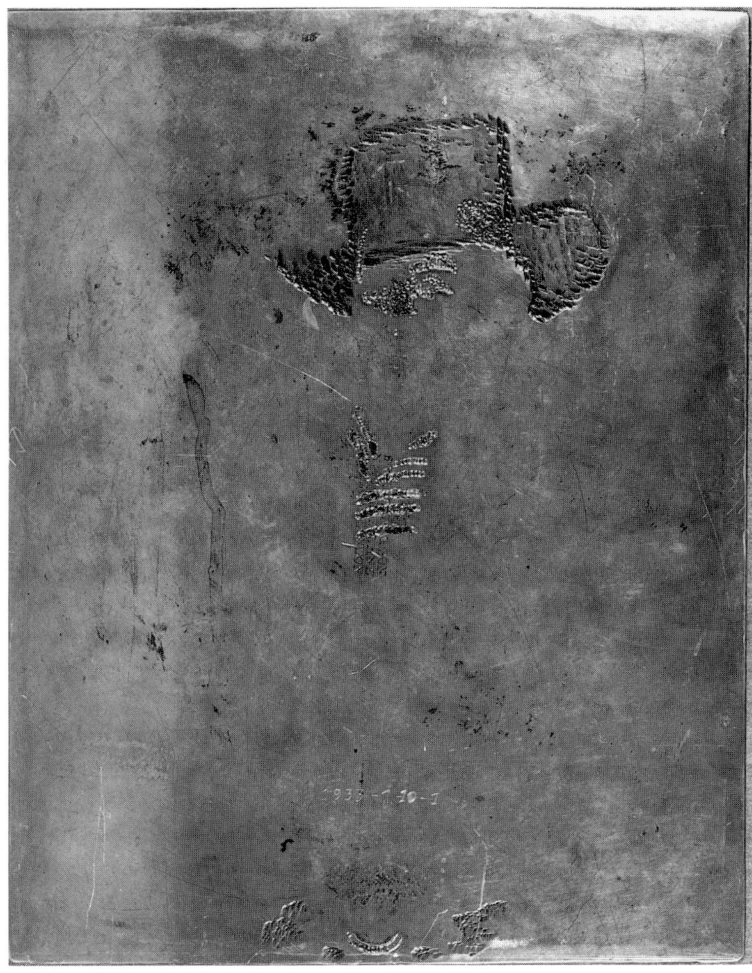

B

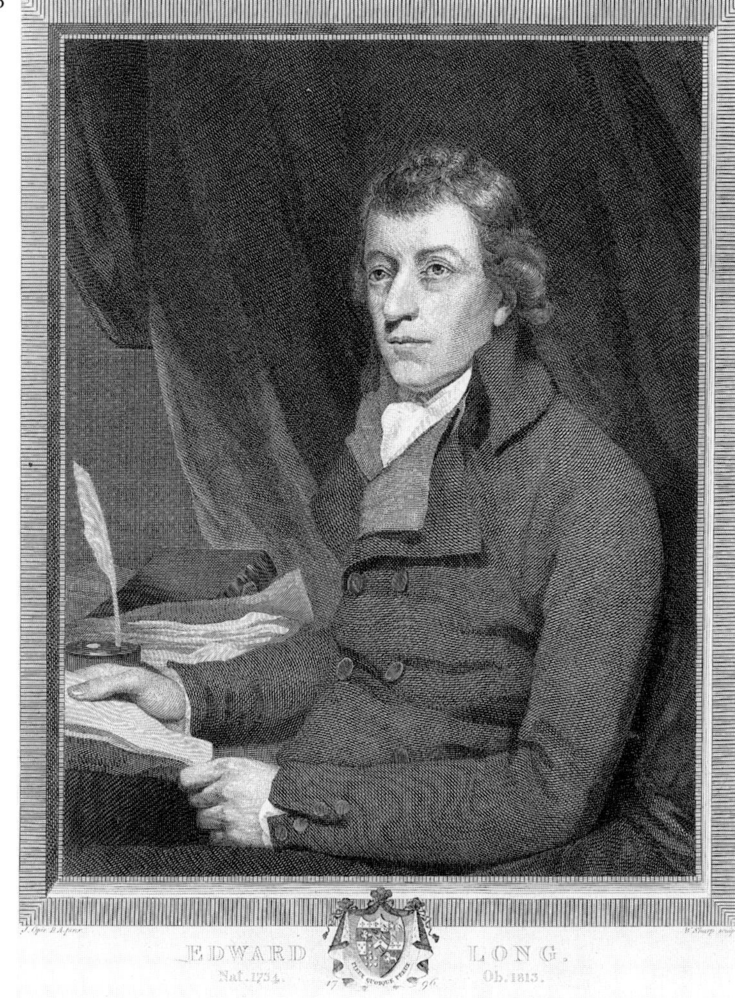

4.37. Robert Graves after William Sharp after John Opie, *Edward Long:* (*A*) copperplate (back); (*B*) engraving, c. 1813.

dell era and the bust ever since. To Blake business appeared better than ever; the dividing line was not between decades but between him and other engravers. Upon returning to London from Felpham in 1803, he wrote Hayley that "Art in London flourishes. Engravers in particular are wanted. Every Engraver turns away work. . . . Yet no one brings work to me" (7 October 1803, E 736).[39]

[39] Though the dearth of work is a standard engravers' complaint after 1800, Gage seems to agree with Blake that work was abundant ("Early Exhibition" 126). More research is needed.

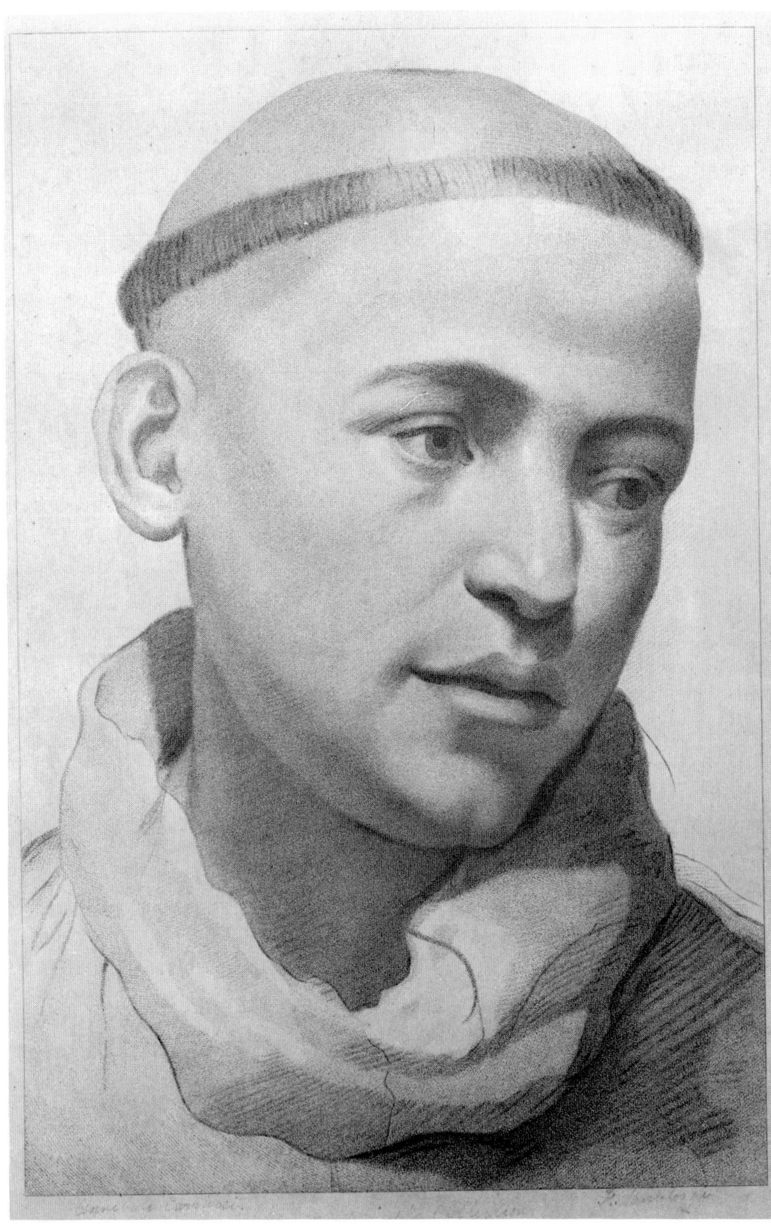

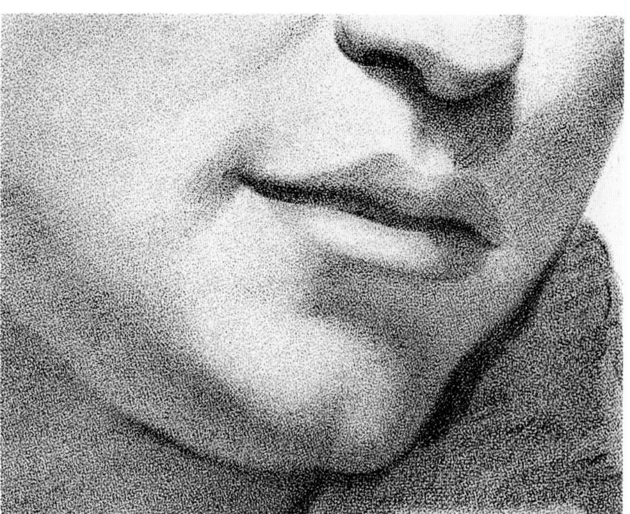

4.38. Francesco Bartolozzi after Annibale Carracci, *Head of a Young Monk,* stipple in imitation of chalk, unpublished state and detail, c. 1796.

The very virulence of attacks on the tonal processes by line engravers such as Robert Strange and William Sharp suggests that the tonal media had technical, economic, and aesthetic merits that were hard to get around. Critics often observed that stipple and mezzotint were so well adapted to prevailing tastes that they were the preferred media for reproducing the tonal harmonies of the English school—so much so that both earned the same appellation, the "English manner." A glance at one of Blake's own reproductive line engravings, *Head of a Damned Soul* (fig. 4.47), and one of Bartolozzi's stipples in imitation of chalk drawings, as different as the two are, reveals how threatening stipple could be to its technical competitors. The gray scale is more refined, the residual evidence of reproduction above the threshold of vision—the optical noise—is less, and the manufacturing process, requiring

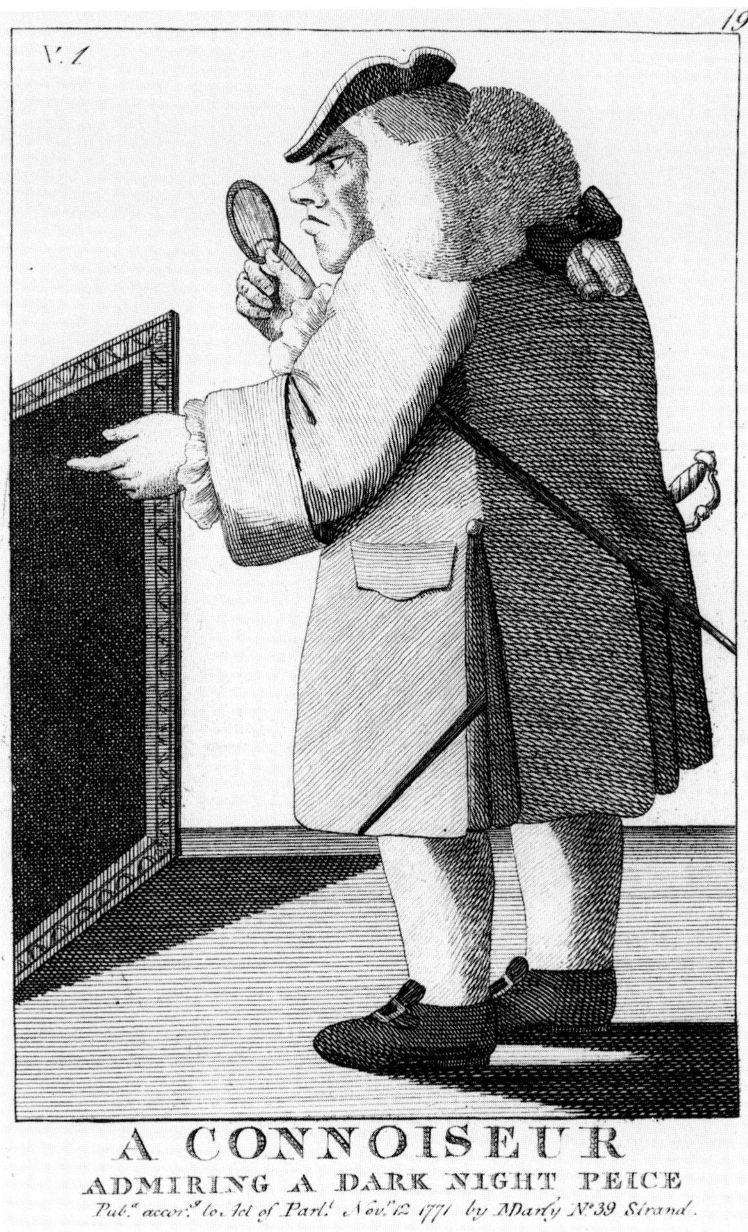

4.39. Anonymous, *A Connoiseur [sic] Admiring a Dark Night Piece*, engraving, 1771.

less labor and less skill, is cheaper. And after all, the basis of reproduction is comparable: where the one systematically deploys networks of lozenges softened with dots, the other deploys dots only, but with the same aim.

Fascination with the almost scientific—yet almost magical—powers of chiaroscurist harmony to represent the diffusion of natural light over natural surfaces led to an enduring fashion for so-called candlelight subjects or fire pieces: "Most Englishmen when they look at a Picture immediately set about searching for Points of Light & clap the Picture into a dark corner" (*PA*, E 579). This is a familiar and durable accusation. In 1842 we hear it in ridicule directed at a printseller for "shutting out God's daylight from the exhibition of his pictures, and in a room covered with red baize, lighting up his pictures by gas-light, with a mirror and a showman to point out to the 'ignorant' English public what they are to admire!" (quoted in Fox 21). Perhaps the most interesting aspect of the fashion is its apparently paradoxical double association with the status-seeking of an elite audience and the sensation-seeking of a mass audience. While the connoisseurs were off in dark corners looking for points of light, spectators were filing in off the street to experience the chiaroscurist effects of Teniers, Rembrandt, Correggio, Reynolds, and others adapted to stained glass, needlework, and xylopyrography (hot poker on wood) (see, e.g., Altick 111, 400).

The power to reconfigure the commonplace history of engraving comes, of course, from capitalized Genius, Originality, Imagination, and Art, a cluster of metaphors absent from Sharp's account and vestigial in Landseer's but fundamental to Blake's. So radical are their effects that the *Public Address,* despite its emergence from English-school discourse, can seem less at home with the statements of Hoare, Landseer, Sharp, and Pye than with the new romantic literary manifestos. In such position papers as Wordsworth's prefaces, craft, lowercase art, had been getting short shrift. Links with performance (of someone else's script or score), imitation, artificiality, superficiality, patronage, consensual rules of procedure, manipulation, display, and the like were making artisanal virtuosity an unattractive model in an individualized environment of inspired, spontaneous expression. Blake can thus readily adapt to his purposes the literary history of Wordsworth's prefaces to *Lyrical Ballads,* rejecting the polish and refinement of neoclassical tradition for the presumably original poets of an unimproved earlier age. And, like Wordsworth, Blake finds no use for musicians in his (otherwise latitudinarian) notion of art, because music was still the most artisanal of arts and the most dependent upon an aristocratic patronage system. In spite of republican gestures toward the lower reaches of the social structure, Wordsworth's poetic contributions to *Lyrical Ballads* find remarkably little use for active, contemporary rural artisans, weavers, smiths, builders, masons, stone carvers. Dreams of the Middle Ages can be somewhat more productive in this line, as when Blake idealizes the "Gothic Artists . . . of whom the World was not worthy such were the Christians in all Ages" (E 671) (fig. 4.49).

As learning how to write poetry becomes a matter less of apprenticeship than of self-reflection, the skills and techniques adequate to the expression of original vision will not be discovered in academies or other artists. Since, conversely, other artists' skills are more likely to obstruct than to clear the path to one's own, there is almost always some refusal of craft in romantic decrees. Technical flaws may signify authenticity, whereas technical facility may be taken for slickness, a kind of cunning superficiality: "I do not mean smoothd up & Niggled & Poco Piud . . . but Drawn with a firm and decided hand at once [with all its Spots & Blemishes which are beauties & not faults] like Fuseli & Michael Angelo Shakespeare & Milton" (passage in brackets deleted, E 576).

As the ratio of one unique poet to one unique poem comes into play, the problem of recognizing merit increases. How is the public to identify good poets? As the task of gaining recognition for one's skills becomes increasingly personalized, it becomes increasingly strenuous and threatening for the artist. Without publicly articulated standards of craft, the grounds for confidence in the ability of the meritorious artist and the understanding audience to locate each other shrink. The ideal audience likewise shrinks, perhaps to the one best friend, and withdraws in time, perhaps to the posthumous future, Blake's "posterity." The construction of time and space in the *Public Address* should be seen in this light. The contraction and withdrawal of the audience are threats but also opportunities that make certain kinds of communication more likely to succeed. If, for example, one sees the commercial history of engraving as the response to a set of commercial initiatives to increase consumption and production, one might read the result as a thinning out of substance through extension, mediation, and substitution. What counted as artistry and what counted as spectatorship had both been radically reduced to what all can do equally well, the common denominators of demand and supply.

One conceivable response to this analysis of the crisis is Blake's agoraphobic theorizing, which retreats from a crowded public world of consumers and producers to the private comfort of bare essentials: instead of going on and on, he advocates pulling back and back until all skills drop away except the essential one, drawing; all units of execution are stripped away except line; all time vanishes except the moment, the pulsation of an artery; and all resubmit to the authority of the one essential faculty, imagination. Movement out into the world is cautiously restricted and highly ritualized. The world itself, nature, as the spatiotemporal form of these extensions, tends to vanish, leaving the essential self, of which nature was (only) the projection. This theory of an art of unextended moments and unelaborated beginnings rests in a kind of Christian primitivism, conceived, science-fiction style, as an exodus from the fraudulent center of the civilized world to the peripheral wilderness where a hardy congregation of individualistic survivors increase their chances of spotting one another, hoping to gain in immediacy and depth what they have sacrificed in extension. That seems to be the consolatory understanding behind Blake's claim that "I have Enough in the Approbation of fellow labourers" (E 580).[40]

In the context of English-school discourse Blake's primitivism, thus understood, attacks the eclectic ideal of a composite "finished" whole by which the English school answered charges of native deficiency with proposals for better education. If England was visually backward, not stupid, its school of painting, including the market to support it, could be educated into existence. The pedagogical initiative could promise more than a chance for English art to catch up with the continent. As the Royal Academy lectures of Reynolds and his successors show in their breadth of reference and their avoidance of narrow sectarianism, the English school might aim to synthesize the best of the national schools without losing sight of decorous distinctions. But Blake's *Public Address* in effect responds that an eclectic ideal is simply a commercial ploy to authorize an academic curriculum—to ensure an abundance of specialized expertise in the arts of imitation that are basic to all systematic pedagogy—that could in turn support a system of production organized to multiply copies through cheap divided labor.

(OVERLEAF)

Blake blames the popularity of chiaroscurist formulas on "That Vulgar Epigram in Art Rembrandts Hundred Guelders . . . all both Morning & Night is now a dark cavern" (*PA,* E 579). And it is true that the Hundred-Guilder Print (named after a price supposedly paid for it while the artist was alive) was most likely *the* Rembrandt print of Blake's time in price and reputation. The engraver who most effectively parlayed Rembrandt's status into immediate profits by imitation was Captain William Baillie. He also invested in Rembrandt in other ways. In 1775 he bought the original but exhausted copperplate of the Hundred-Guilder Print, "restored" it, and offered 100 expensive impressions with a money-back guarantee of satisfaction. After he had exhausted the restored plate, he cut it into four parts, reworked them, and issued separate impressions. (See White et al. 75, 83, 96.)

The *Tout-ensemble*

Perhaps this analysis seems to project the theories of the *Public Address* too far beyond their local targets. We can see why it does not by taking a closer look at this composite ideal as it appears in the *Public Address.* The relevant

[40] Hughes and Allen, *Illusions of Innocence,* provides useful contexts for what I am calling Blake's Christian primitivism.

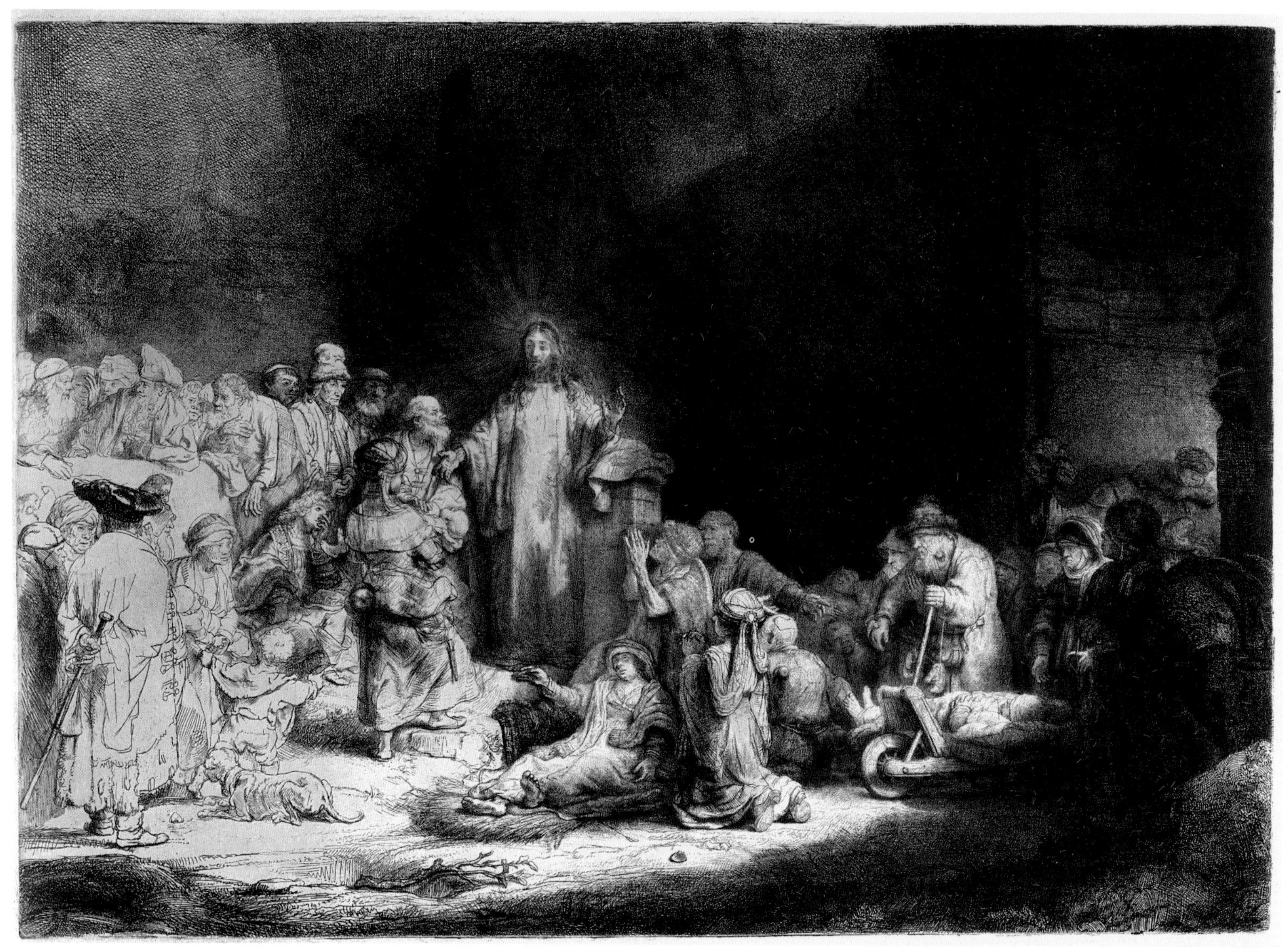

4.40. Rembrandt van Rijn, *Christ Healing the Sick* (the Hundred-Guilder Print), etching and drypoint, c. 1649.

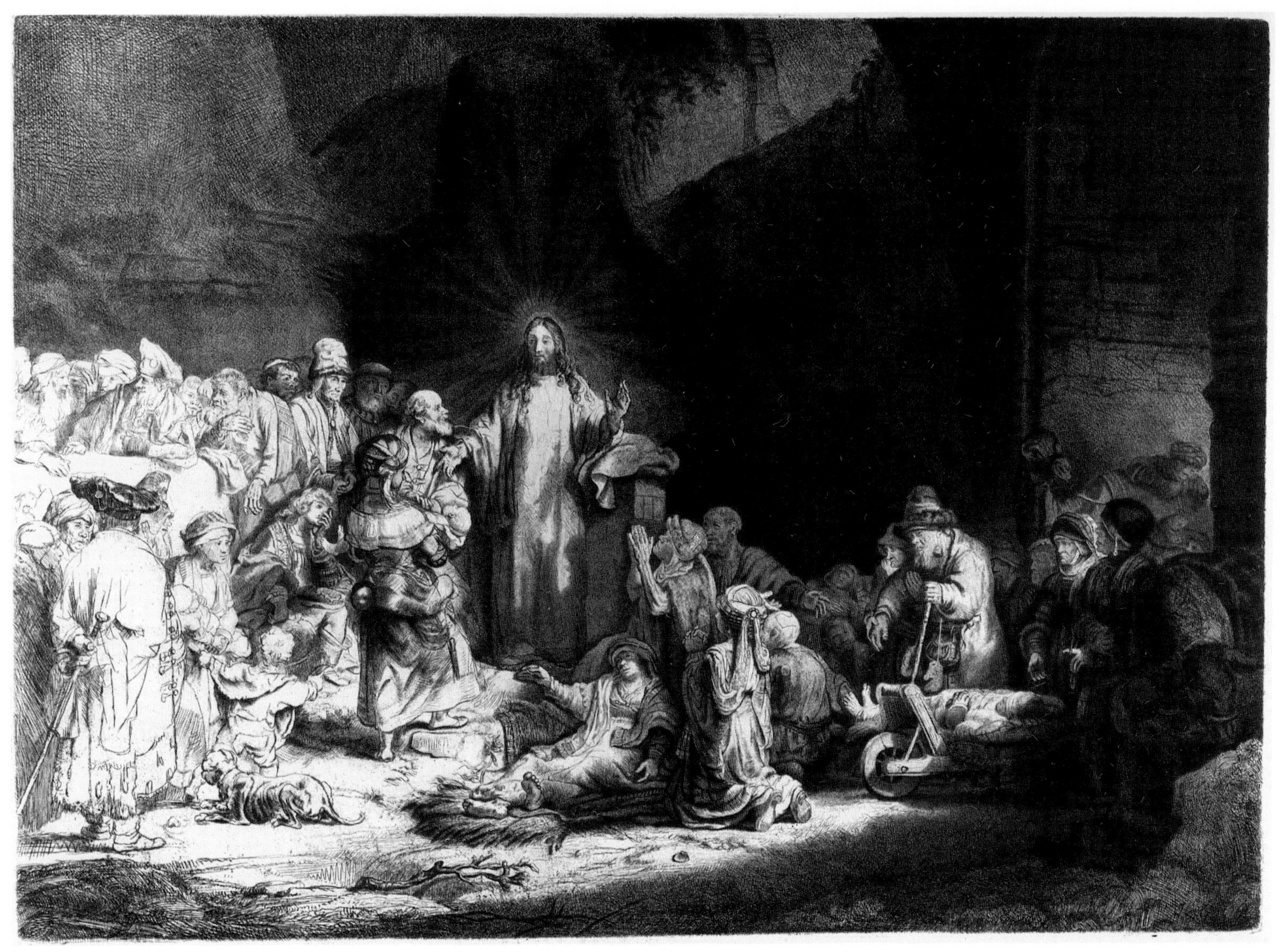

4.41. Captain William Baillie's restoration of Rembrandt's Hundred-Guilder Print, 1775.

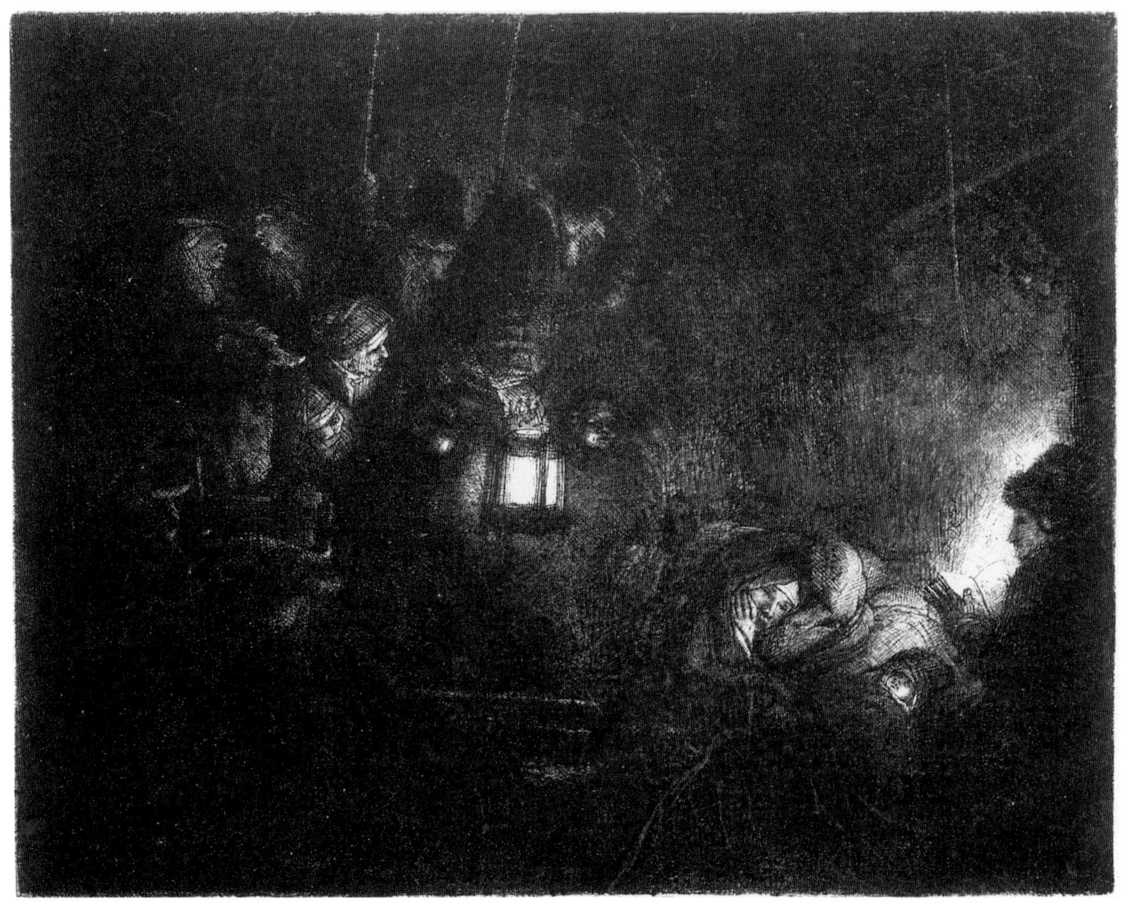

4.42. Rembrandt van Rijn, *Adoration of the Shepherds,* etching, c. 1652.

The Rembrandt spurned in Blake's *Public Address* for having caused "Every Picture" in a "Modern Exhibition" to have "the same Effect. a Piece of Machinery or Points of Light to be put into a dark hole" (*PA*, E 579) is not immediately recognizable to twentieth-century readers because he is a particular creation of the eighteenth and early nineteenth centuries. Blake's attacks are aimed at the Rembrandt who was supposed to have visited Venice and painted portraits in Yorkshire and to have learned about coloring and chiaroscuro from Rubens (Slive 138, Whitley 1:10–11, Barry in Wornum 228–29). (Slive [116–33] discusses the fit between Rembrandt's work and the academic standards that were at stake in debates between the linearists and colorists. The catalogue by White, Alexander, and D'Oench is the most useful account of the understanding of Rembrandt in eighteenth-century England.) Though he was routinely criticized for his unidealized nudes and other "singularities," Rembrandt's works were exalted as models of visual harmony. The preeminence of that value is shown in Fuseli's tribute, which compares Rembrandt with Shakespeare and puts him in charge of "the full empire of light and shade, and of all the tints that float between them" (Wornum 403). Rembrandt's mastery of harmony could be read as a commercial skill that coordinated his methods of production. The author of the entry on Rembrandt in Rees's *Cyclopaedia* comments on the "many pupils . . . whose copies

technical concept is "harmony." When Reynolds lamented that Poussin had not attended to "harmony of colouring," Blake answered that "One Species of General Hue over all is the Cursed Thing calld Harmony it is like the Smile of a Fool" (anno. Reynolds, E 662). Though he does not name harmony in the *Public Address,* it is everywhere by implication. Without it we could not explain his jingle "And in Melodious accents I / Will sit me down & Cry. I. I." (E 581), which builds on a ratio of strong oppositions, melody:harmony::I:we. He depends on the opposition of melody and harmony to figure the difference between individualistic, originary expression and consensual imitation. In that context, "Melodious accents" mark a precise

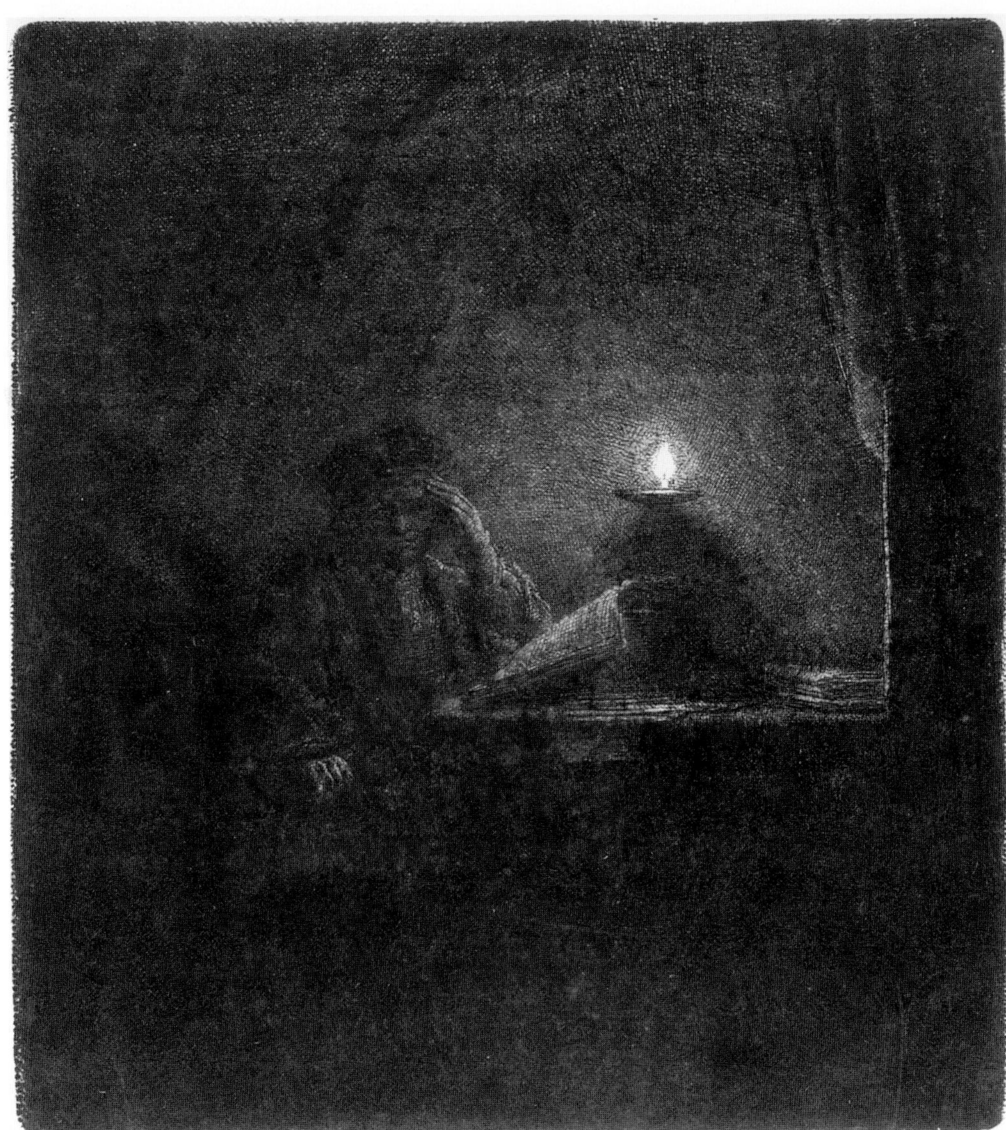

of his pictures he not unfrequently sold as originals, after bestowing a short time upon them himself. By these means, aided by incessant industry, and the sale of etchings . . . he accumulated great wealth." The "effect he desired" depended on a viewer who stood "at a proper distance, disregarding the appearance of the work upon a closer inspection" (vol. 29). In his lecture on chiaroscuro, Barry does criticize Rembrandt, among others, for the "magic-lanthorn-like and too artificial contrivance which sometimes offends" (Wornum 183). That is also the basis of Blake's intolerance, which is directed especially at "dark manner" etchings such as the two shown here.

4.43. Rembrandt van Rijn, *Student at a Table by Candlelight,* etching, c. 1642.

curve of articulation as against their implied opposite, an orchestrated mass of sound overwhelming individual distinctions:

> . . . Harmonies of Concords & Discords
> Opposed to Melody, . . . Lights & Shades, opposed
> to Outline
> . . . Abstraction opposed to the Visions of
> Imagination
>
> [*J* 74.24–26, E 229]

"Sit me down" declares Blake's obstinate refusal to join in. We are now in a position to examine the difference between melody and harmony in terms of the technological progress of engraving.[41]

Harmony was never an uncontested value, and the grounds of contestation in music and words will help us follow the arguments over harmony in pictures. In literary theory, where it was most strongly identified with regular poetic rhythm and, especially, rhyme, there were important precedents for rejecting harmony, chiefly on two grounds: renouncing the siren song of sensuality in favor of purified expressive and intellectual values; and renouncing imposed mathematical regularities—the machinery of verse. The two are less contradictory than they may seem, in view of the extent to which metaphors of mechanism dominate eighteenth-century discussions of the senses. Milton's rejection of rhyme in *Paradise Lost,* Wordsworth's agonizing reappraisal of versification in the preface to *Lyrical Ballads* and Coleridge's response in the *Biographia Literaria,* and Blake's diatribe against both rhyme regular meters in *Jerusalem* supply a compact review of the subject.

In musical theory, from which, of course, the metaphor of harmony derives, harmony and melody were as color and line in painting, often rivals in a history of antagonism that stretches at least from the humanist aversion to polyphony—and the preference for music attached to words—to the romantic reassociation of music with verbal expression.[42] In unfavorable dialectical interpretations, melody was tied to the purity of original expression, harmony to secondary ornamentation, meretricious beauty, and mathematical system. John Brown claimed that the "complex and varied Harmony" that allowed music to become a "compleat Species" separate from poetry also "gave it an artificial and laboured Turn; . . . a pompous Display of Art, to the neglect of *Expression* and true *Pathos*" (*Dissertation* 198). Harmony was traditionally taken as the best demonstration of how music reveals the mathematical basis of all things in nature (hence the otherwise puzzling inclusion of music in the medieval quadrivium of arithmetic, geometry, and astronomy). Hence Rousseau, in his *Musical Dictionary* (as quoted extensively in the entry on harmony in Rees's *Cyclopaedia,* vol. 17), could associate the "beauties" of harmony with "learning," "pedantry," and European corruption, as opposed to the "music truly natural" based on melody. To the common charge that English music had "too much harmony"—Rousseau said that only northerners really needed it, to penetrate their

[41] Though not directly relevant to my treatment of the idea of harmony in the visual arts, the studies by Hollander, Spitzer, and Winn provide a usefully broad background.

[42] See Winn's *Unsuspected Eloquence* for a useful history of melody and harmony as they relate to music and language. The quotation from Liszt on 275, despite the continental-romantic rather than Blakean vocabulary, bears interestingly on the case.

gross organs—Goldsmith had been able to retort only that "deficiency of genius" (2:163) caused equally disastrous failures of expression on the continent.

In the jargon of the painting and engraving trades, "harmony" became a standard term for the final stage of the artist's efforts that would integrate chiaroscuro (light and shadow), color, and composition. Harmony began to appear in English-school discourse as early as Aglionby's *Observations* in 1685, which speaks of "Union *in* Painting, *which makes up an* Harmony *to the Eye, and causes the* Whole *to appear one, and not two or three* Pictures" (20; see also 113). As it came to stand for "union" in painting, harmony was routinely offered not only as a set of technical recipes for painters but also as something close to an ultimate standard of judgment for critics. In 1719 Jonathan Richardson had presented it as one of the connoisseur's chief criteria:

> There must be one principal light, and this, and all the subordinate ones with the shadows, and reposes, must make one intire, harmonious mass; the several parts must be well connected, and contrasted so that the tout-ensemble must be grateful to the eye; as a good piece of music is to the ear. By this means the picture is not only more delightful, but better seen, and comprehended. [113][43]

Visual harmony should coordinate chiaroscuro with composition:

> In a figure, and every part of a figure, and indeed in every thing else, there is one part which must have a peculiar force, and be manifestly distinguishable from the rest, all the other parts of which must also have a due subordination to it, and to one another. The same must be observed in the composition of an entire picture; and this principal, distinguished part ought (generally speaking) to be the place of the principal figure, and action: and here every thing must be higher finished, the other parts must be less so gradually. . . . Nothing must start or be too strong for the place where it is; as in a concert of music when a note is too high, or an instrument out of tune; but a sweet harmony and repose must result from all the parts judiciously put together, and united with each other. [54–55]

Moreover, color should be harmonized with chiaroscuro and composition:

> Whatever are the predominant colours of the principal figure, the same in kind . . . must be diffused over the whole composition . . . ; for subordinate colours as well as subordinate lights serve to soften, and support the principal one, which otherwise would appear as spots, and consequently be offensive. [59]

Like the lights and figures, the colors must be duly subordinated "so as to be mutually assistant to each other . . . so as that every part, and the whole together may have a pleasing effect to the eye; such a harmony to it as a good piece of music has to the ear . . ." (67).

Well into the nineteenth century, the essentials of harmony are reiterated endlessly in technical manuals, critical treatises, specialized dictionaries, and universal encyclopedias. In their Academy lectures, Reynolds, Barry, Fuseli, and Opie all incorporated passages of boilerplate wisdom on harmony-as-unity to let their listeners know why the "principal object"

[43] See my n. 10, chap 1.

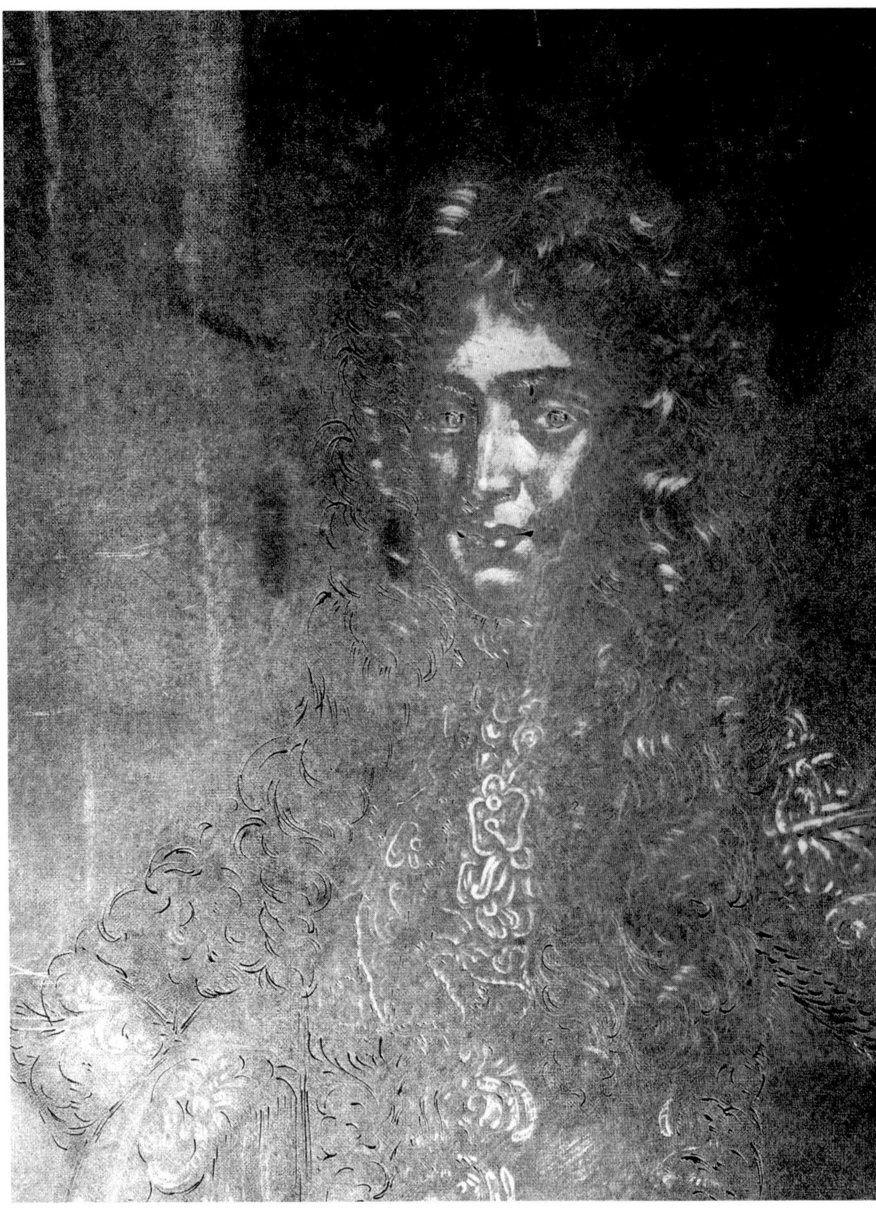

4.44. R. Williams after Godfrey Kneller, *Theophilus Hastings, Seventh Earl of Huntingdon,* mezzotint copperplate, 1687, detail.

Some critics thought that Rembrandt's dark-manner etchings represented his attempts to imitate mezzotint with "interesting scratches" (Gilpin 39). Certainly mezzotint, etymologically identical with "halftone," became the medium of choice for copies of Rembrandt's etchings (see the list at the end of Daulby). Immensely popular in England, mezzotint produced both the "dark manner" and (with stipple) a second "English manner." Like stipple, mezzotint uses the dot to overcome what Gilpin shrewdly termed "the prejudices of cross lines, which exist on no natural bodies: but *mezzotinto* gives us the strongest representation of the real *surface*" (38). (Though the analogy is crude, it may help to think of lines as algorithms and dots as digital units. In the line engravings of Strange and Sharp, lines were being used as if they were digital.) Often regarded as the simplest and fastest of all graphic processes (e.g., Dossie 2:173), mezzotint makes it easier to produce no line than to produce a line. Hogarth's description of the process (which moves from darks to lights) as the coming of dawn over a landscape is irresistible:

> I have often thought that a landskip, in the process of this way of representing it, doth a little resemble the first coming on of day. The copper-plate . . . is wrought all over with an edg'd-tool, so as to make it print one even black, like night: and his whole work after this, is merely introducing the lights into it; which he does by scraping off the rough grain . . . artfully smoothing it

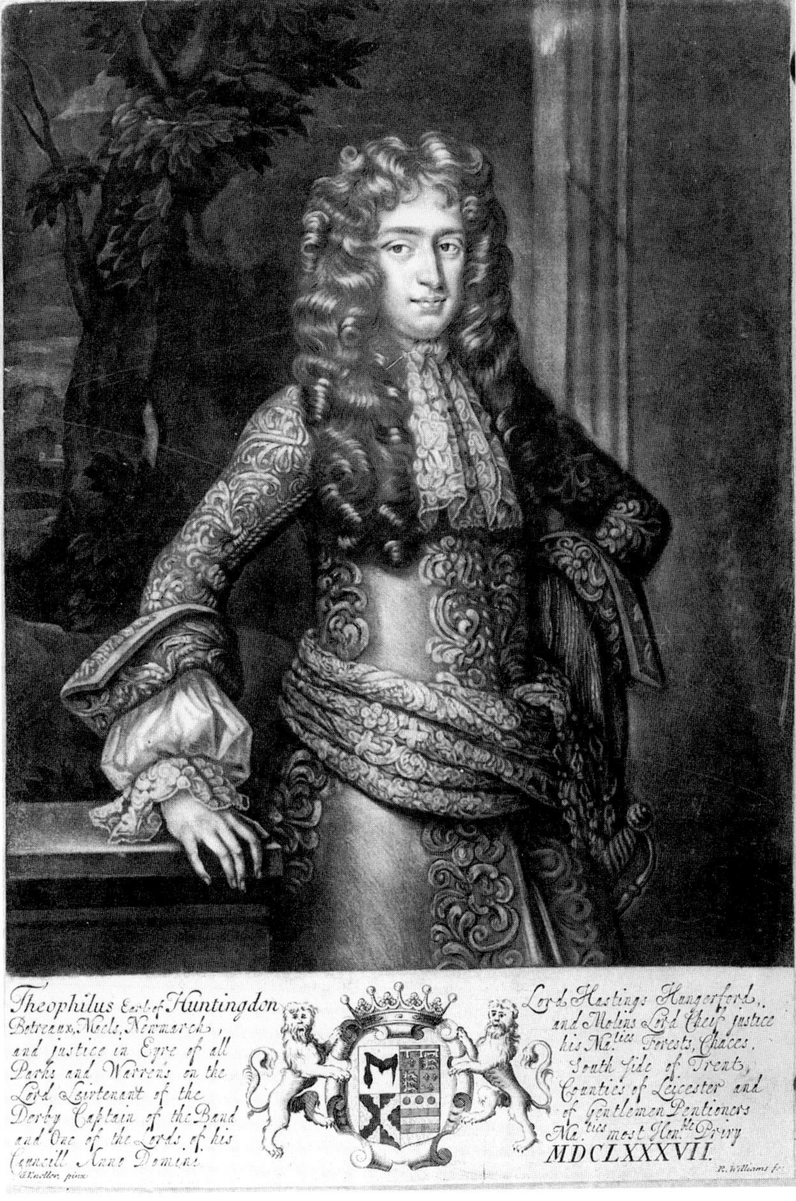

4.45. R. Williams after Godfrey Kneller, *Theophilus Hastings*, mezzotint (strengthened with the burin), 1687.

most where light is most required: but as he proceeds in burnishing the lights . . . each proof appears like the different times of a foggy morning, till one becomes . . . a daylight piece. . . . I think the whole operation . . . shews what lights and shades alone will do. [108]

Even the political affiliations of mezzotint are not irrelevant to our arguments, such as the often-repeated story that it "was first invented by Prince *Rupert*, Nephew to King *Charles* the first, during the Time of the Troubles in *England*" (R. Campbell 112). The technique is well illustrated by the copperplate used to produce the late seventeenth-century mezzotint portrait of Theophilus Hastings.

of the painter should be "the character and management of the whole" (Reynolds dis. 11, 202). "Management" properly took the form, said Reynolds, of "contriving various methods of composing the work,—in trying different effects of light and shadow,—and employing the labour of correction in heightening by a judicious adjustment of the parts the effects of the whole" (dis. 11, 197). Ignorant viewers, he said, often looked for finishing in the painter's details when they should have been looking for these more subtle adjustments—contrivances, effects, corrections, heightenings—that make parts appear to be parts of something.

Barry, similarly, envisioned the goal of chiaroscuro as that "general result . . . effected by the several co-operating gradations of the light and dark objects of a picture"—technically accomplished by "the judicious and happy management of the middle tint," through which "those fierce opposite extremes of light and dark are brought to co-operate and harmonise" (Wornum 177, 183). In his lecture on coloring, Barry emphasized the role of "dirty and broken colors" (212)—those compounded from secondary colors, which have in turn been compounded from the primary colors of yellow, red, and blue—in creating the unity of effect associated with harmony. The goal of color is to establish the "general hue, or first tone of the picture," which "must necessarily predominate, and hold all the other tones of colour in a graduated subordination" (217; see also 182, 188, 191). Barry, like Reynolds, construed such unifying techniques as signs of the intellection that, in making painting more than the imitation of nature, made painters the mental equals of poets (217).

Fuseli later offered up more of the stock wisdom in the standard technical categories of chiaroscuro and color to which are attributed great powers of unification conceived by analogy with music. In color "a sovereign tone must pervade the whole . . . as the first instrument in a regular concert tunes all the rest" (Wornum 479). He describes "that harmony which is produced by what the ancients called the *corruption* of the colours, by mixing and breaking them till there is a general union in the whole" (516). As color, so light: the "two extremes of light and shade" can "make a whole" when they are referenced to "one . . . point of light" from which, "in all directions, the existent parts advance or recede" (505–6).

As artists had given the terminology of harmony prominence in a regularized pedagogy that sought to explain how, technically, to achieve a unity of effect in the last stages of production, critics had come to depend on harmony for a framework of observation and description, and, most significantly, for an ultimate standard of evaluation: "The production of a *whole* is the great effect, that should be aimed at in a picture" (Gilpin 14). The standard proved eminently adaptable to the systems of reproductive engraving. Hence a description such as the following, from Henry Tresham and William Young Ottley's *British Gallery of Pictures*, an engraving project of 1818 much like the one that Cromek and the Chalcographic Society had tried to launch a decade earlier, can actually do double duty as an account of a painting (*The Village Festival* by Philip Wouwerman) and of its engraved reproduction (by John Scott), which was itself based not on the painting but on a drawing of it (by W. M. Craig). Despite the reference to "canvas," it is impossible to tell whether the description is of the painting or of the engraving, or whether the author has had any more experience of the painting than the engraver had. That is precisely the point. The business of harmony is to organize wholes out of the fragments of visual representation produced by systems of divided labor, and at the same time to manage an aesthetic of translation, approximation, and generalization.

> The group on the right, more especially the admirable figure of the gentleman seen in a back view, and the white horse whereupon he is mounted, receives the principal light. The light is conducted, by means of that reflected on the distant river, to the more central parts of the foreground, where it strikes with less vivid rays upon two or three of the more prominent figures of the carousing peasantry: the remainder of that group, together with the hovel on the left extremity of the piece, being judiciously represented in a low and subdued tone of colouring, which is accounted for by a dark overshadowing cloud, seen in part at the top of the picture at that side. The result of this arrangement of the clair-obscure is favourable to the whole: the delicate tints of the sky and the distant landscape, recede with the greater truth of effect, whilst the group on the right, which the painter intended to be the focus of his picture, acquires additional brilliancy, and starts from the canvas with increased force. [n.p.]

Harmony, then, is strong enough to serve a multitude of purposes in the system. Dignified accounts of chiaroscuro and color in the service of harmony most often associated them with that final burst of compensatory "industry that conceals the artifice" (de Piles 221; see also Pilkington [1805] xvii) to achieve the traditional aim of making the artificer invisible and the artifice transparent. But a less exalted purpose was commonly acknowledged. Harmony built techniques of error correction into the system; it promised last-minute technical compensation for the early conceptual failures that, according to Blake, were inevitable. If "we should have only a piece of patch-work," wrote Gilpin, "such is the power of *light*, that by an artificial management of it we may even harmonize a bad disposition [i.e., arrangement]" (13). Barry's *Letter to the Dilettanti Society* had connected the technical powers of harmony to the studio practice of the Venetian and Flemish schools: "Titian, Rubens, Vandyk, or any other great colourist, may with advantage retouch and complete any work of their scholars [i.e., students], or other inferior artist, by scumbling over, tinting, and uniting the whole . . ." (4). Contemporaries regularly pointed to Reynolds's opportunistic use of light and color to hide failures of invention. "In light and shade, in colouring and expression, the late President stands without a rival," exclaimed a commentator of 1790. "His lights display the drawing he knows, and his shades conceal his defects . . . in the captivating parts of painting" that he had learned from Titian, van Dyke, Rembrandt, and Rubens (*Observations* 13).[44]

From the standard technical divergence between conception and execution—between the Roman and Florentine schools, which produced lines and hence parts, and the Venetian and Flemish schools, which produced harmony

[44] Similarly, Reitlinger has noted how Reynolds matched an ideology of generalization to his commercial practices: "The 'broad free manner,' which Reynolds so astutely commended, blinded the client to the fact that large areas had been filled in by studio-hands and apprentices" (1:60).

and hence wholes—one could draw surprising conclusions: "And indeed . . . the masters of the Roman school were more studious of those essentials of painting, which regard the *parts;* and the Flemish masters, of those, which regard the *whole.* The former therefore drew better *figures;* the latter made better *pictures*" (Gilpin 48). In the literature on printmaking we see this reasoning taken another logical step: "If the picture [i.e., painting] has no harmony . . . , which is often the case in the works even of reputable painters, a good print from such a picture, is more beautiful than the picture itself. It preserves what is valuable, . . . and removes what is offensive" (Gilpin 23). Though Gilpin's conclusion, which followed directly from the practices and theories we have analyzed, was not widely shared by painters, it was often repeated by printmakers and their allies.[45] Ateliers had dispersed production, assembly-line fashion, from a point of origin (in its most concentrated form the moment of imaginative conception in the artist's mind) out into a sequence of operations by various hands. This organization of work, though not a response to theory, was coherent with a body of theory that promoted the general and universal over the particular and local. (Blake read that theory as a "natural" allegory of commercial practice.)

These workshop practices are well supported by much of Reynolds's *Discourses.* Take his telling proposition that true wit "preserves itself when translated. That wit is false, which can subsist only in one language" (dis. 7, 134). This is only a step from suggesting that translation itself might improve wit by raising it from parochial to universal. Translation causes idiosyncrasies to fall away (if they are peculiar to the mental habits of one person they cannot be remembered) and a general version to emerge. Likewise, Reynolds told his young charges, the best ideas for paintings came not from singular minds but from a common stock of general ideas that had passed the survival test of time and space (in this sense, nature).

Such theory, at ease with the general and uneasy with the singular, accords well with the processes of extension, fragmentation, repetition, and collaboration entailed in divisions of labor. Reynolds's analogy applies just as well to execution as to conception. It suggests that the master artist's "original" contribution, whether idea or technique or both, may be usefully checked and balanced by reference to a wider human community of labor organized in a system of production, which may even provide the means of processing the general out of the particular. This kind of Enlightenment thinking can recognize "degradation" of the image as a type of universalization and "blurring" as a type of generalization: blurring may be to sight what distance is to immediate impressions—a way of attaining, paradoxically, greater clarity and unity. As Gilpin indicated, reproductive engraving may be a beneficial extension of the process: an additional medium, like another language, affords a new opportunity to generalize and thus improve the original. An engraving may, as many spokespeople for the trade maintained, have its own special dignity not as a copy but as a translation (e.g., Landseer quoted in Hutchison 90).

As harmony brought the redress of technical grievances, it was thought to bring other important advantages. A response to Winckel-

Joseph Wright of Derby became the leading English exponent of candlelight subjects in the latter half of the eighteenth century. (Blake engraved a portrait of Wright for the *Monthly Magazine* in 1797, and the two are connected in other indirect ways, especially through their mutual patron William Hayley.) Wright painted Arkwright's cotton mills by night, girls reading by candlelight, a blacksmith's shop, an alchemist discovering phosphorus, Vesuvius erupting by night (repeatedly), fireworks displays, cottages on fire, landscapes by moonlight, and various grottos. In one way the paintings certainly epitomize Blake's complaints about the mechanical and formulaic means used to degrade lights from one central point over an entire picture, and the dreary uniformity of the "harmonious" results. But at his most profound Wright of Derby was indeed a kind of scientific painter who allied his chiaroscurist techniques with scientific, technological, and industrial subjects to probe a characteristic eighteenth-century subject: the transactions of mind and nature via the human optical system. In *The Air Pump,* as the natural philosopher conducts an experiment in oxygen deprivation, the painter conducts one in epistemology and optics. Valentine Green's masterly mezzotint rendition demonstrates the medium's power to imitate artificial harmony *and* natural imagery, making it a nearly ideal technical match for Wright's paintings, concocted of both. In this monochrome reproduction the print is

[45] James Dennistoun, Robert Strange's Victorian biographer, remarks of Strange's engraving of Raphael's *St. Cecilia,* "indeed, the original may be almost said to gain in the engraving" (2:143).

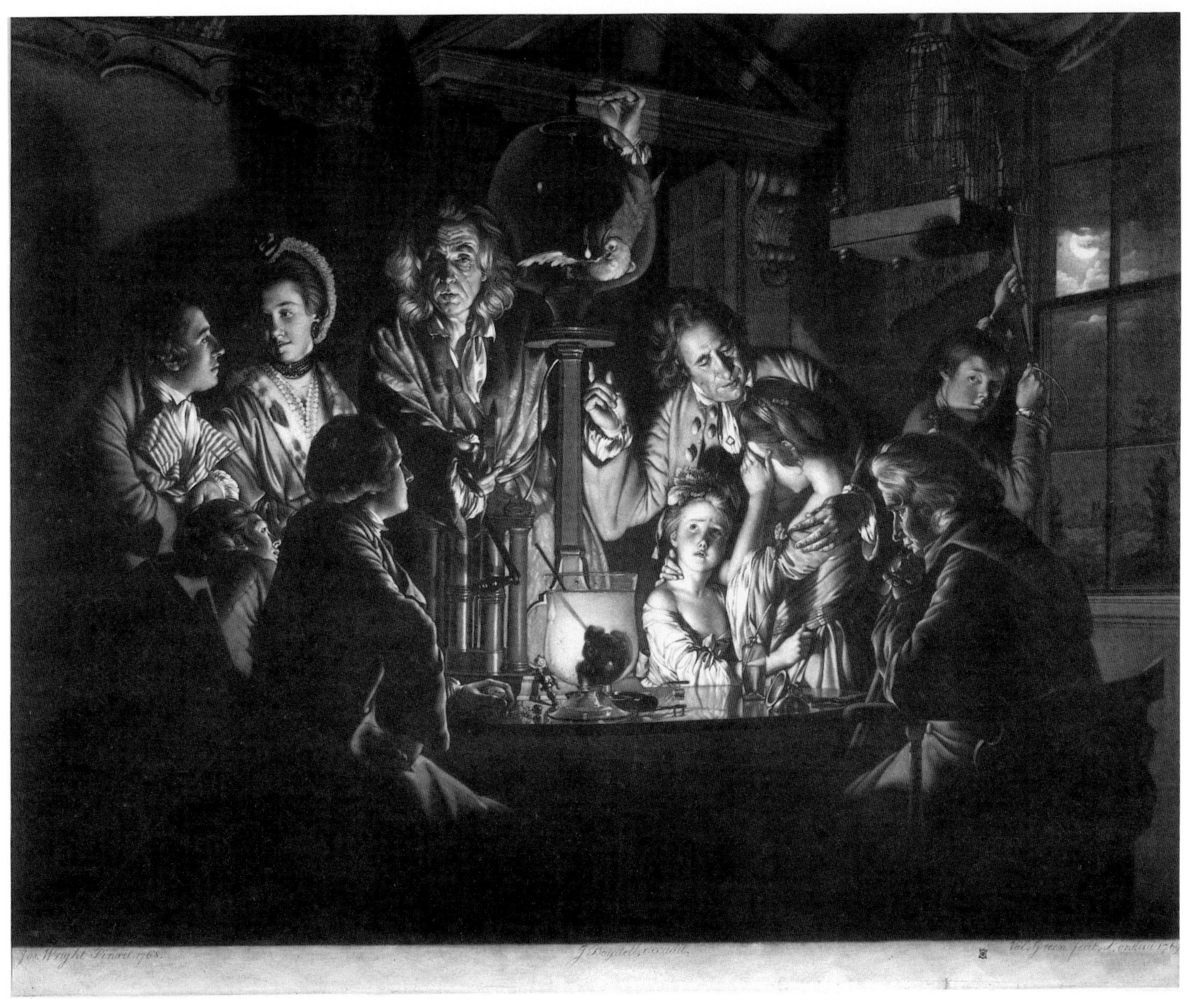

4.46. Valentine Green after Joseph Wright of Derby, *Experiment on a Bird in the Air Pump,* mezzotint, 1769.

mann's *Reflections* mounted this defense of color:

And indeed are not colours so essential, that without them no picture can aspire to universal applause? Do not their bewitching charms cover the most grievious faults? They are the harmonious melody of painting; whatever is offensive vanishes by their splendor, and souls animated by their beauties are absorbed in beholding . . . so as to find no faults. These, joined to that important science of Chiaro-Oscuro, are the characteristics of Flemish painting. ["Letter" in Winckelmann, *Reflections* 105–6]

In the dominant Western construction, line is the brains of painting and color the body; in eclectic theories they are complementary, in dialectical theories opposed. In this metaphoric context harmony, emphatically gendered and sexually activated, becomes the feminized body of visualization, strongly associated with the form but not the content of a painting, and possessing the power of optical "beauty" to move the spectator. Harmony presents the "bewitching . . . splendor" that a late stage of execution can add to the mental stock of conception, maximizing its impact on the senses of the beholder. Harmony gives a painting the erotic power to "call to the spectator" (245), says de Piles. It "introduces" the painting and "procures . . . a gracious reception" (281) by its seductive presentation of the all-together. It draws the gaze into the painting, establishing "the repose and fascination of the eye" (Pilkington [1805] xvi; for "repose" see also Richardson above, 243, and Opie below, 254.)

Physical allure can compensate for mental deficits or cover mental deformities (as it conceals drawing, the technique that was believed to test inventive intellection).[46] Harmony is the female body simultaneously hidden and revealed in a veil, a net, a web of technical manipulations that pleasure the senses of the viewer with light and color, drawing him (advisedly him) closer while simultaneously hiding its designs from him: "diffusing a kind of thin vapor," Pilkington says of one of the elements of harmony, "that deceives the eye agreeably" ([1805] xv).

This agreeable deception operates by softening the intellectual basis of a painting, the outlines. The approved technique calls for systematic blurring. When de Piles defines it, he might be describing a body on display: "The turn of the parts, and the outlines, which insensibly melt into their grounds, and artfully disappear, bind the objects, and keep them in union . . ." (214–15; cf. Gilpin 114). He projects his approval of melted outlines into a pseudohistorical narrative: modern painters of Raphael's time and before mistakenly observed "regularity and preciseness in their outlines" only because they were unaware of "the passages of antient authors, in praise of melting one object into another" (216). These warm and liquid harmonies are coherent with the metaphorical construction of the sensual and emotional body. The *OED* quotes to good effect Pope's *Rape of the Lock* (1714)—"What guards the purity of Melting maids / In courtly balls, and midnight masquerades?"—and a poem of 1771: "How weak fair faith and virtue prove / When Eloisa melts away in love." Melting harmonies execute the painting's designs

[46] For Blake's relation to traditional concepts of line and color, see Eaves, *Blake's Theory* chap. 1.

nearly indistinguishable from the painting. Such an effect produced by line or even stipple would be unimaginable.

on, and allow it to have its way with, the audience.

Writing and reading the female body into visual representation in this way are, as we now hardly need to be reminded, aspects of larger social projects. As commentators conceived harmony in terms of features and powers attributed to the female body, they conceived harmony at its most sublime as the body of society in a female form, that is, as nature. De Piles expounds visual harmony as a representation of the unified social, religious, political, and commercial order:

> It is certain, that all beings tend to unity, either by relation, or composition, or harmony; and this as well in things human as divine, in religion as politicks, in art as nature, in the faculties of the soul as the organs of the body. God is one, by the excellence of his nature: the world is one. Morality brings every thing into the compass of religion, which is one; as politicks makes every thing subservient to the government of a state. All nature preserves . . . an unity . . . ; and art assigns various precepts for making one only work. The several conditions of men fit them for commerce and society, as the several wheels of a machine act for a principal motion. . . . Thus, as in a picture there ought to be an unity of subject for the eyes of the understanding, so there ought to be an unity of object for those of the body. This unity is only to be procured by the knowledge of the *claro-oscuro*. . . . [226–27]

Before one could ascend to this step in the paradigm, of course, dreadful attributes of the body had to be tamed and more ennobling ones activated. Here de Piles invokes the system of hierarchical analogy that structures the metaphor of the great chain of being to organize the otherwise threatening energies of harmony-as-woman into a unity of unities based on a strict mathematics of subordination: "So that we may define *the whole together* to be, *Such a general subordination of objects one to another as makes them all concur to constitute but one*" (65). The terminology of "subordination," "declension," "degree," and "degradation" is an orthodox element of the discourse of harmony, as heard in Dryden's epistle to Sir Godfrey Kneller:

> Where light, to shades descending, plays, not
> strives,
> Dies by degrees, and by degrees revives.
> [Quoted in Hogarth 118]

De Piles, no less than Dryden, reads the subordination of visual parts as a type of social subjugation, sanctioned in the name of political, moral, and divine order. Though the gender of harmony still emerges in the "unity . . . procured" through the "eyes . . . of the body," de Piles defends it with the standard correspondences of she:him::he:God. She, here, is the sexualized body of nature itself, on which is inscribed the book, or at least the primer, of patriarchal God and state. (It is in such quasi-political forms that visual harmony finds its way into English romantic discourse as a metaphor of choice for expositions of organicism. Thus Coleridge uses the harmonies of Washington Allston's paintings to focus his own essays in *On the Principles of Genial Criticism* [1814], his first attempt to take a comprehensive view of art.)

Harmony, so explicated, was by Blake's time virtually identified with the English school. Prince Hoare put it succinctly: "The foreign

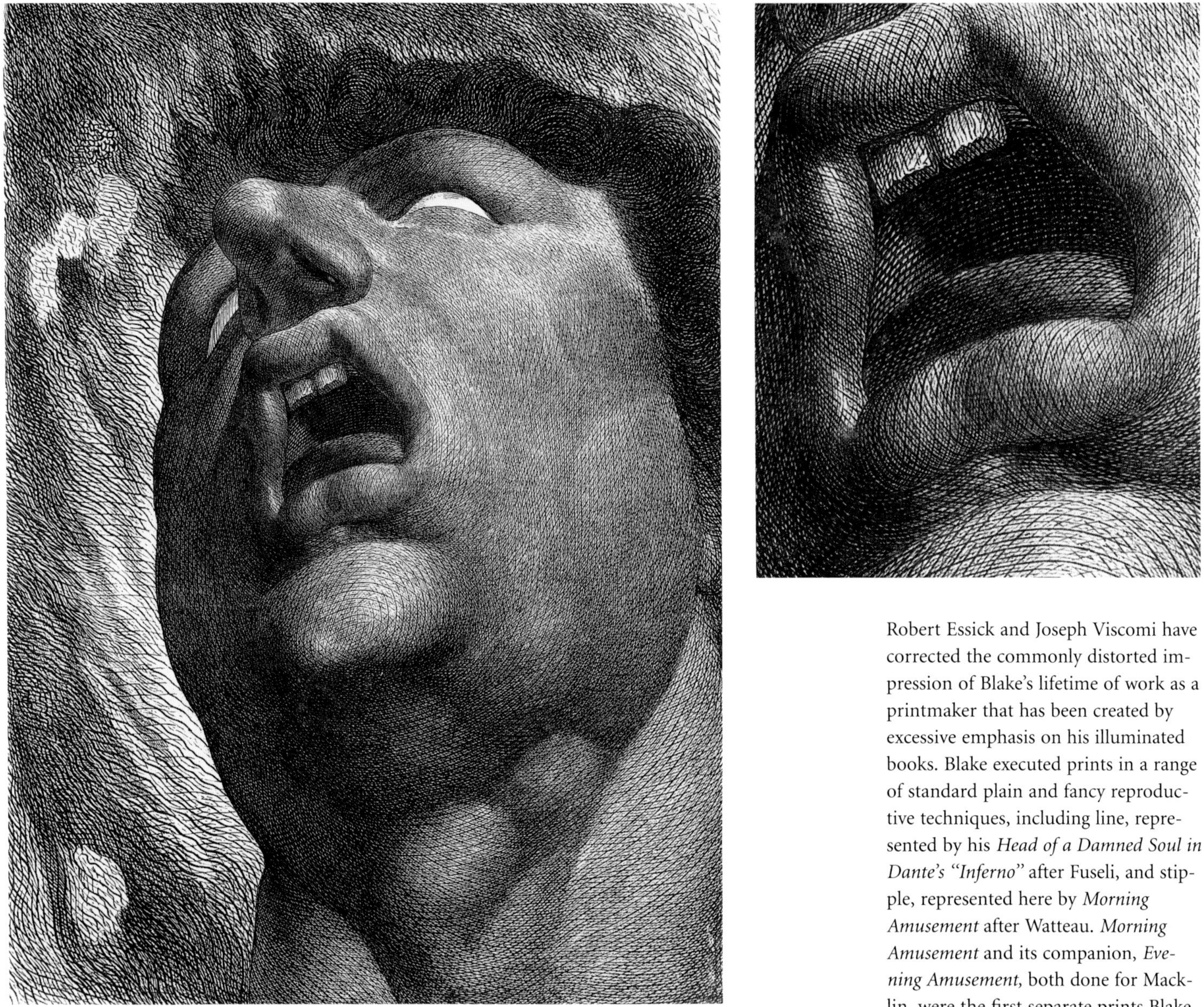

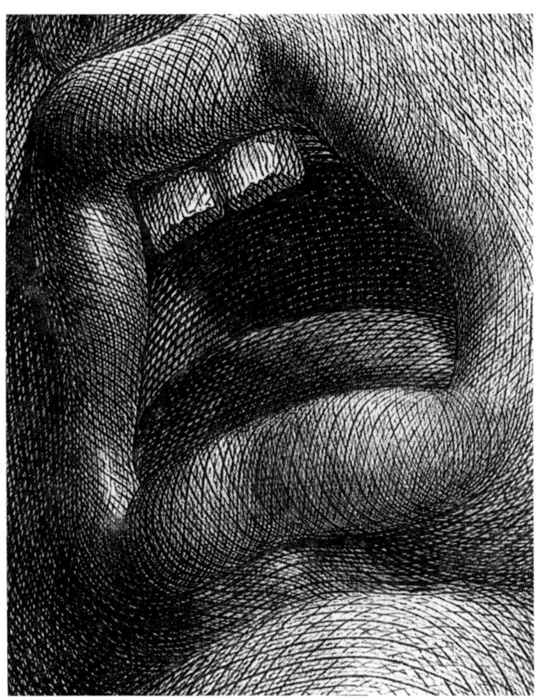

4.47. William Blake after Henry Fuseli, *Head of a Damned Soul in Dante's "Inferno,"* line engraving, first state, c. 1789, and detail.

Robert Essick and Joseph Viscomi have corrected the commonly distorted impression of Blake's lifetime of work as a printmaker that has been created by excessive emphasis on his illuminated books. Blake executed prints in a range of standard plain and fancy reproductive techniques, including line, represented by his *Head of a Damned Soul in Dante's "Inferno"* after Fuseli, and stipple, represented here by *Morning Amusement* after Watteau. *Morning Amusement* and its companion, *Evening Amusement,* both done for Macklin, were the first separate prints Blake executed after his apprenticeship ended in 1779, and the Fuseli print (never published) came a few years later. Blake

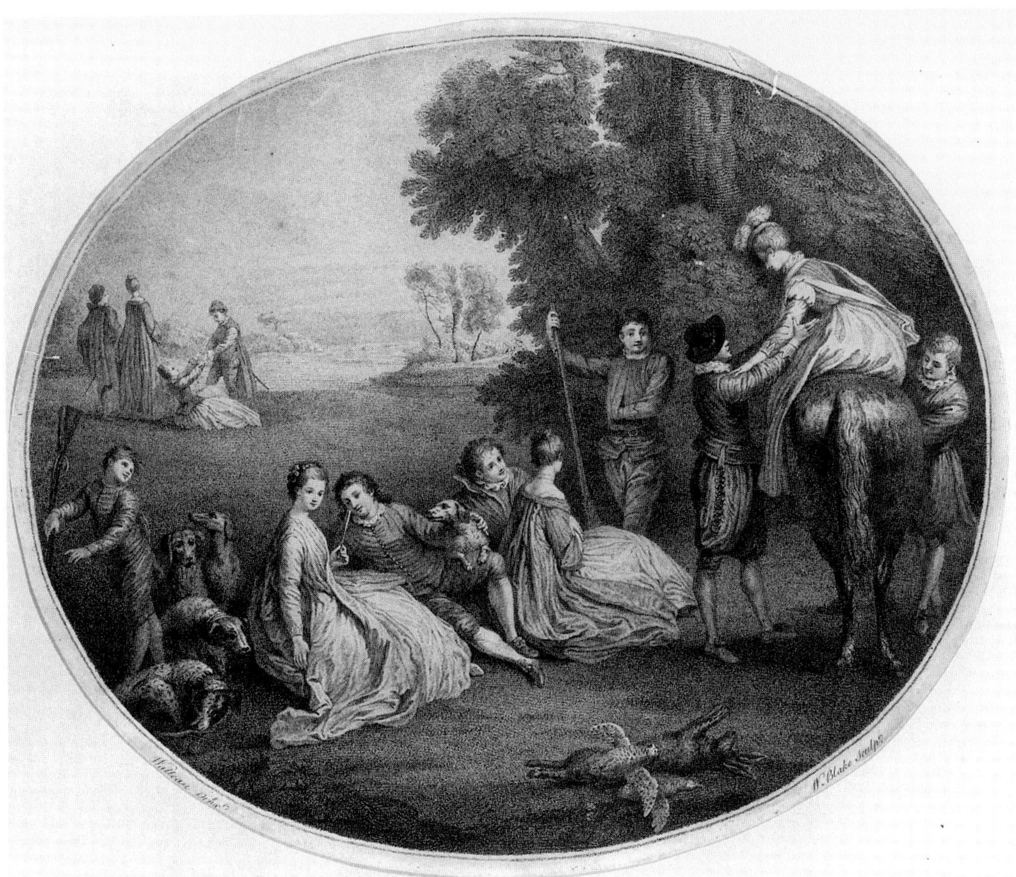

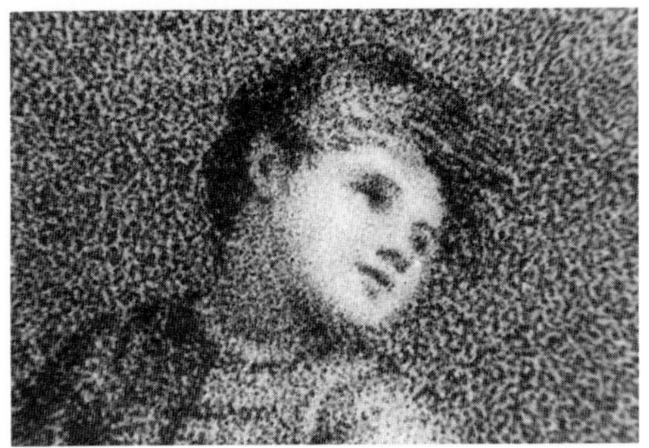

4.48. William Blake after Jean-Antoine Watteau, *Morning Amusement,* stipple with line and flick work, second state, 1782, and detail.

schools of Engraving are, in general, more remarkable for the correctness of their drawing . . . and the English for the breadth of light and shadow." In that feature English engravings follow the "prevailing character" of English paintings (261, 142). Clearly it is to this aspect of English-school theory and practice that Blake is reacting when he renounces modern viewing habits: "Most Englishmen when they look at a Picture immediately set about searching for Points of Light & clap the Picture into a dark corner" (*PA*, E 579). (Compare the anonymous *Candid Review* that rapturously pronounced West's *Raising of Lazarus* "one of the most systematic paintings we ever saw. . . . Having examined it both in the full glare of day, and in the dusk of the evening, I am persuaded that when a few years have mellowed the tints, they will fall into a perfect harmony" [22–23].)

also participated in the divisions of labor common to his craft. Although he worked in a sizable shop alongside other assistants as an apprentice for James Basire, as a master he worked mostly alone. But as a reproductive engraver he accepted as a matter of course the division between *invenit* and *sculpsit,* or inventing and making, and often other divisions, as between the engraver of pictures and the engraver of inscriptions, and between the engraver and the printer of plates. Several of Blake's prints were published in colored and uncolored impressions. The colors were sometimes varied in the inks before the plates were printed; sometimes watercolors were added afterward. With stencils and a fairly extensive division of labor, colorists could produce colored impressions on a scale sufficiently vast to allow the publisher Rudolph Ackermann to insert a hand-colored aquatint in every copy of his *Repository of the Arts* magazine, despite the challenge of very large print runs. Blake's wife, Catherine, printed and watercolored some of his "original" work, and a professional engravers' printer printed the *Job* plates.

Perhaps the best measure of Blake's alienation from this orthodoxy is his reaction to the artists most closely associated with it. The author of the entry on harmony in Rees's *Cyclopaedia* names Titian, Giorgione, and Correggio as the "great original exemplars" (vol. 17) and adds van Dyck and Reynolds. Fuseli had said that "every work of Correggio is an illustration" (Wornum 479) of harmony, and Opie had furnished purple prose on Correggio's seductive power:

> By classing his colours, and judiciously dividing them into few and large masses of bright and obscure, gently rounding off his light, and passing, by almost imperceptible degrees, through pellucid demi-tints and warm reflections, into broad, deep, and transparent shade, he artfully connected the fiercest extremes of light and shadow, harmonised the most intense opposition of colours, and combined the greatest possible *effect* with the sweetest and softest *repose* imaginable. [Wornum 304]

As denounced by Blake, Correggio appears among the "very weak & Vulgar fellows" (E 580) in several categories of the defective:

> When I see a Rubens Rembrant Correggio
> I think of the Crippled Harry & Slobbering Joe
> And then I question thus are artists rules
> To be drawn from the works of two manifest fools
> [E 514]

It is Correggio whose paintings, along with Titian's, Blake likens to Woollett's and Strange's engravings as the life's labor of journeymen suited to commerce and opposed to individual merit (E 573). To malign Correggiesque harmony, Blake, always hypersensitive to metaphorical textures, takes his cue from the negative potential already latent in its construction. Reynolds's critics had drawn on this potential when they mocked his notorious fascination with the "captivating parts of painting." His devotion to "Venetian" coloring, they said, had produced paintings so delicate and frail that they were fading into thin air in his lifetime: "I hear 'em at the exhibition cry / P'shaw! Reynolds daubs, so—then his colours fly" (*More Lyric Odes* n.p.; cf. Blake's jingle anno. Reynolds, E 641). Obviously the technical idiom we have rehearsed—of "dirtying" and "breaking" and "corrupting" colors, "scumbling" with the brush, "degrading" tones—though normally positive, responds readily to invective against "Smears & Dawbs," "unorganized Blots & Blurs," and "broken lines, broken masses, and broken colours" (*PA*, E 581, 576; *DC*, E 538), and against Rubens's coloring, with shadows "a Filthy Brown somewhat of the Colour of Excrement . . . filld with tints & messes of yellow and red" and lights "all the Colours of the Rainbow laid on Indiscriminately & broken one into another" (anno. Reynolds, E 655).

Similarly, instead of suppressing the negative potential in the feminization of harmony, Blake hyperbolizes it. He also extends it from Correggio's techniques to Correggio himself, whom the *Descriptive Catalogue* transforms into a seductive and sinister androgynous personification of harmony, "a soft and effeminate and *consequently* a most cruel demon" (my emphasis). The laborious techniques normally associated with harmony here become the discipline enforced by a mental bondage queen, "whose whole delight is to cause endless labour to whoever suffers him to enter his mind." Correggio will "take possession" of the artist's "affections" and infuse "a love of soft and even tints without boundaries." The possessed painter toils in a feminized world of narcissistic beauty, of "endless reflected lights, that confuse one another," a blurry, indeterminate mirror world of "reflections and refractions" (*DC*, E 548). (We recall the "Toilettes of Woolett & Strange," boudoir-factories where servant-journeymen struggle to attire and adorn their mistress-copperplates with "Fribbles.")[47]

From the orthodox discourse Blake has also collected the spatiotemporal metaphors that put harmony last in a production sequence. That process permits him to imagine escape from harmony's enchantments to recover some prior state of the painting—and, historically, a prior state of painting—that survives beneath the harmonized surface. Thus he hypothesizes: "for if one of Rafael or Michael Angelo's figures was to be traced, and Correggio's reflections and refractions to be added to it, . . . it would be weak, and pappy, and lumbering, and thick headed, like his own works; but then it would have softness and evenness, by a twelvemonth's labour, where a month would with judgment have finished it better and higher. . . ." Drawing produced immediately with judgment is the original, and figuratively masculine, state. Femininity and idiocy figure debased, learned departures produced in the extensions of time and space. That construct, at least, is the basis of hope for real artists—"I say again, O Artist, you may disbelieve all this, but it shall be at your own peril" (*DC*, E 548). Exorcise the Venetian and Flemish demons, skin your paintings of their harmony, and reexpose their naked melodies: "The flush of health in flesh, exposed to the open air . . . cannot be like the sickly daubs of Titian or Rubens" (545). These bodies of the ancient Britons are—in metaphorical tendency, at any rate—male, and their sickly, adorned, and belated forms are toiling in the darkness of Vala, or Nature, or the Female Will. In other words, the technological discourse of harmony in the English school should become a more important touchstone in arguments over the gender bias of Blakean mythology than it has been to date. (The bias is, unsurprisingly, masculine, but biases should not be mistaken for seamless garments.)

But, of course, this optimistic forecast of recovering the stable lines of the male drawing beneath the refracted surface added under the influence of the Female Will (as transmitted through effeminate demons) cannot apply to all painters in Blake's dialectically conceived world, where "there is a Class of Men whose whole delight is in Destroying" and "Hirelings" to "depress Mental & prolong Corporeal War" (*Milton* 1, E 95). Harmony has a central, seldom understood role in Blake's argument to that end—against the dominance of the "Venetian" counter-arts in the English school and the dominance of a suitable commercial and political order in the state—and it will serve to return us to the mental and political themes with which we began.

In the *Public Address,* the assaults on niggling, poco piu, points of light in dark caverns, sing song sing song, dots, lozenges, clean strokes, high finishing, smoothing, smears, dawbs, blots, blurs, colors brown and warm, mossy tints, and the picking out of whites and blacks are all directed against standard ways of achieving harmony, which is, in brief, the kind of unity that the new tonal processes could produce. For Blake's purpose—of narrating a

[47] More mundanely, the print historian Arthur Hind used the opposition of female and male to rank graphic media and their exponents. Stipple engraving is "an essentially feminine art" that "has appealed to few artists of robust genius" (*Bartolozzi* 5).

plot that explains his isolation in particular, but also conceived to stand for the isolation of true art in the English school—the point more important than discovering original drawings is exposing the absence of original drawings behind that ostentatious veil. In their place will be, he assures us, the shards of secondhand stolen originals. "Talk no more then of Correggio, or Rembrandt, or any other of those plagiaries of Venice or Flanders. They were but the lame imitators of lines drawn by their predecessors, and their works prove themselves contemptible dis-arranged imitations and blundering misapplied copies" (*DC,* E 550).

At its most daring, Blake's counter-arts narrative incorporates a mental crime, plagiarism, as its fundamental transgression. As he represents the system legitimized by Rubens and van Dyck, counter-art begins with an act of imitation or mental theft instead of an idea. The full mind is evacuated, and the process of production moves almost entirely outside the mind into nature, where "idiots" live. At that illegitimate point of origin, a credibility gap opens that the system must ever after attempt to close, as if backfilling to cover its tracks. As the conception end of the sequence empties of intellectual labor, the execution end compensates with physical labor, applying techniques for calculating approximate relations among plagiarized fragments to create the manufactured appearance of a whole on the site of intellectual incoherence. Harmony names the sum of that compensatory labor and assigns a high value to it.

Since the organization of methods and materials is crucial to the efficiency of the process, an inverse dynamic develops whereby conception may follow from execution rather than the reverse, with the end dictating the appearance of a beginning. Despite Blake's rebuke—"Ye must begin before you attempt to finish or improve & when you have begun you will know better than to think of improving what cannot be improvd" (*PA,* E 573)—any modern system of production builds from the understanding that maximum efficiency must involve the adjustment of conception to execution, even the conception of conception by execution. A "new" automobile design, for example, is many things besides an idea that originates in the heads of designers who then figure out how to execute it: it is much more significantly an accommodation to the materials and methods of production at hand and to the perceived demands of consumers. "Begin" and "finish" are not linear but cyclical: one cannot begin until one knows what the system can finish, and one builds that knowledge of executing into one's way of conceiving. Rubens, it has been noticed repeatedly, learned to draw for the engravers. Likewise, Richard Godfrey has suggested, following the lead of eighteenth-century authorities, that Reynolds's "predilection for broad effects of light and shade was partially conditioned by the requirements of the mezzotint" (48). In this externalized technological environment, "anticipatory conformity" (Zuboff 345), reading the end into the beginning, is a necessity. In this, the worst case, harmony is not a superfluous addition to melody but a mechanical substitute for it. In other terms, harmony is the sum of the sounds the system of production makes.

Gilpin's anatomy of prints, based firmly on the notion that "the production of a *whole* is the great effect, that should be aimed at in a

The two states of Blake's engraving of *Joseph of Arimathea among the Rocks of Albion,* created at least thirty years apart and probably forty or more, show him revising backward, against the customary system—back toward a "new" beginning, imagined as simpler in technique, instead of forward toward a more finished product. Instead of working toward harmony, which operates chiefly on the transitions among component images, he worked against and away from it, taking away areas of hatching, eliminating the evidence of systems of representation, and making transitions harsher instead of softer. The ideology that justifies such subtractive or restorative revision is originality, here expressed biographically and technically, that is, in a biography of technical development that seeks to end in beginnings, as if going backward in time will cause time to shrink into a timeless eternal moment. The biotechnical regression is coordinated with a regressive historical subject, "One of the Gothic Artists who Built the Cathedrals in what we call the Dark Ages Wandering about in sheep skins & goat skins" (E 671). The technical regression is even more interesting in *Joseph of Arimathea* than in, say, *Satan Calling Up His Legions* (fig. 4.59), because the original state of 1773 was apparently not original enough, unless Blake imagined that his revisions were restoring some earlier state of work beneath the "finished" state of 1773.

A

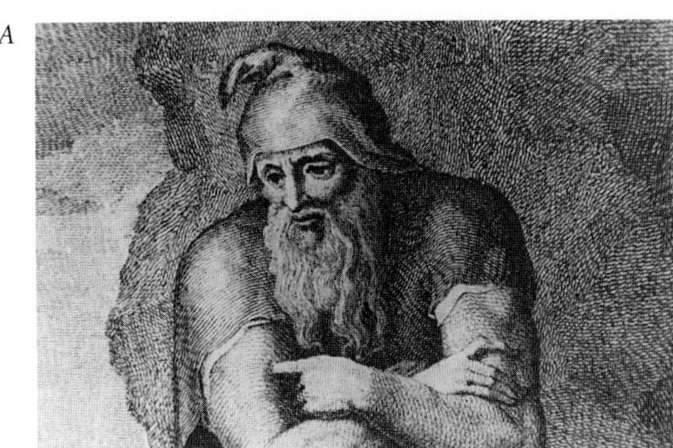

B

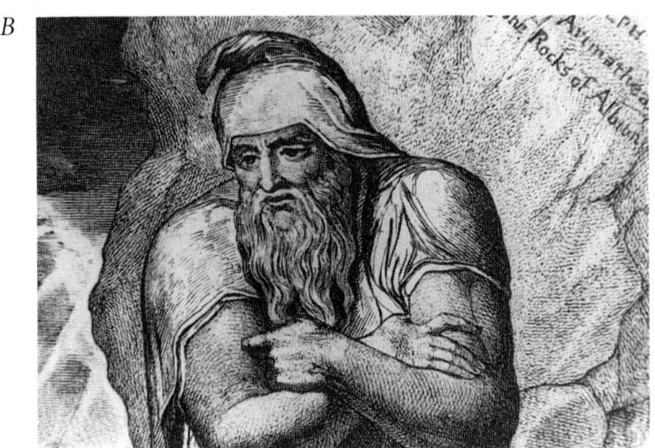

C

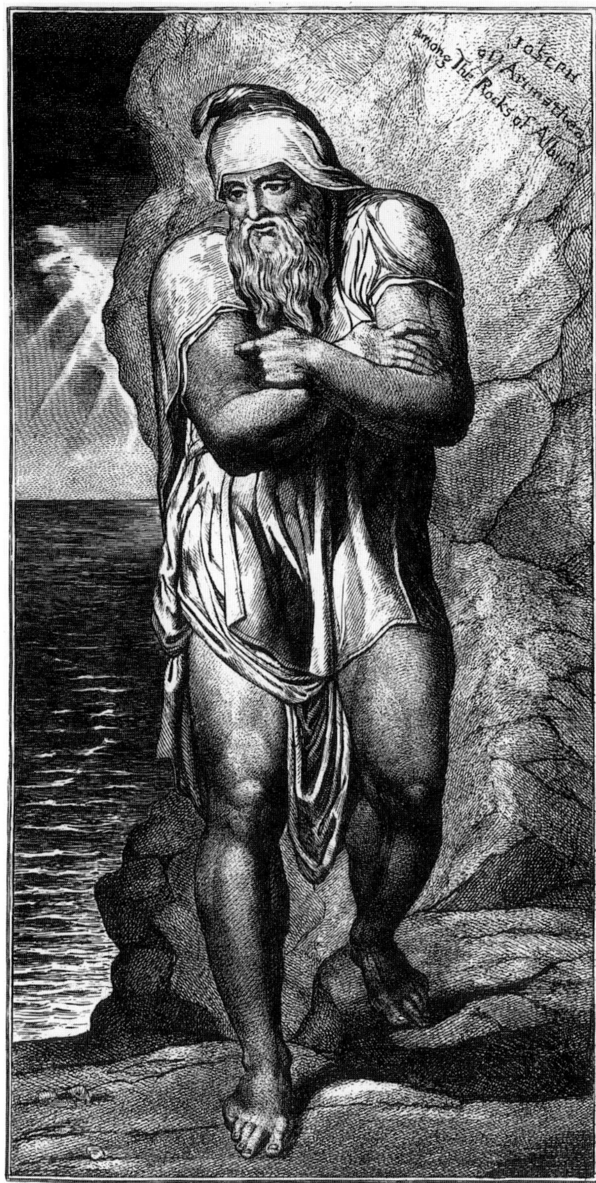

4.49. William Blake, *Joseph of Arimathea among the Rocks of Albion,* engraving: (*A*) first state, 1773, detail; (*B*) second state, c. 1810–1820, detail; (*C*) second state.

picture" (14), recommends such a cycle. If parts refuse to cooperate in their own subjugation, the technical solution is to "consider the *whole* before it's *parts*": "the painter first forms his general ideas. . . . His last work is to finish the several parts" (2). Although that sounds like a simple inversion of standard practice, in fact the colorist and chiaroscurist techniques on

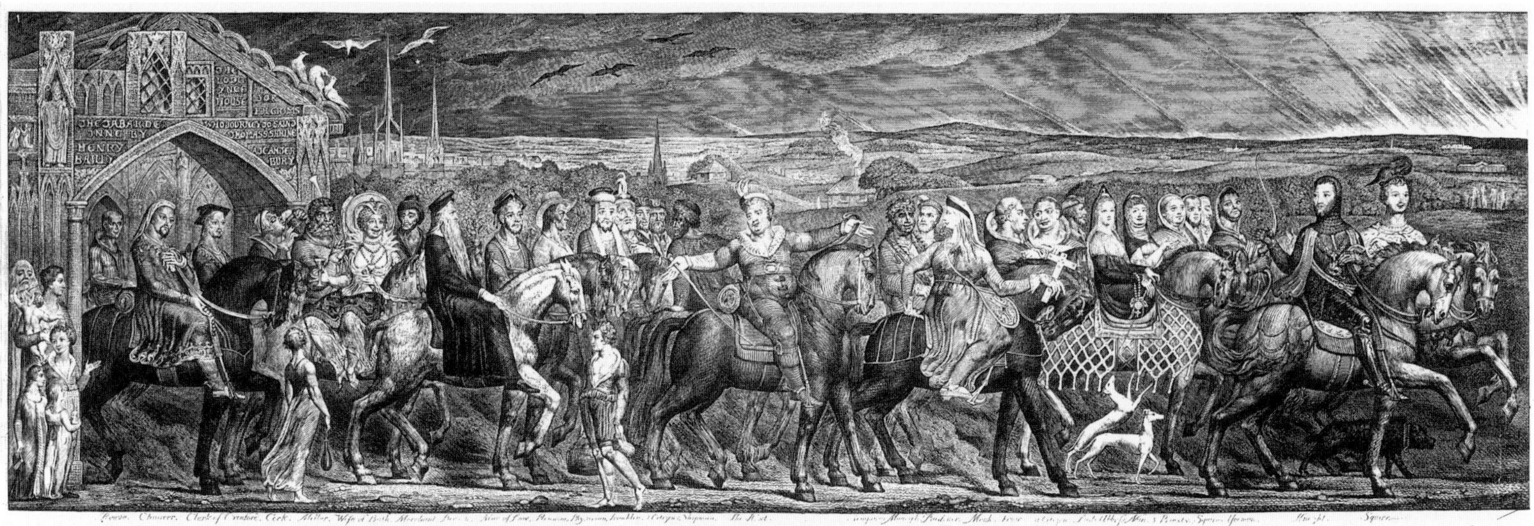

4.50. William Blake, *Chaucers Canterbury Pilgrims,* engraving, third state, c. 1810–1820, and detail.

which Gilpin depends to achieve his ultimate value are applied in the ultimate stage of production—"The last thing, which contributes to produce a *whole,* is a proper *distribution of light*" (13)—so that the effect of the whole can be brought in at the end to salvage a picture defective in its parts, as we have seen. Gilpin's model of production is the polar opposite of Blake's. As Blake builds the prime values and techniques of conception cyclically into execution so that nothing qualifies as authentic execution except drawing, Gilpin builds the prime values and techniques of execution cyclically into conception so that ultimate effect is the first thing an artist considers. "General ideas," initial generalizations, open the way for "general effects," final generalizations: "The painter first forms his general idea . . . in such a manner as to receive . . . the most beautiful effect of light" (2).

Critiques of technology have often presented nightmares of a mechanized world that conceives products somewhere besides the conceiving mind of those doing the executing. There are two significant variations. The first, generally more benign, imagines that consumers have gained the power to demand certain products and thus certain conceptions and executions. In the *Lyrical Ballads* prefaces and his appendix on poetic diction, Wordsworth claims that eighteenth-century poetry had become the product of a one-sided contract in which poets had agreed to supply readers with vicarious excitements. The system of production that supplies these pleasures—the popular organs of a commercialized print culture—are

The styles of Blake's original engravings make especially conspicuous his rejection of visibly polished, virtuoso technique and the standard of harmony. Transitions from part to part, figure to figure, figure to ground, which had provided generations of engravers with treasured opportunities to exhibit their mastery in blending and covering with a shimmering skein of tonal effects, are by Blake relentlessly exposed and preserved. In the *Canterbury Pilgrims* print he combined various modes of representation at a single stylistic level instead of blending them with a uniform system. By contemporary standards the effect would have been harshly eclectic. Curiously, this horizontal eclecticism,

culpable by implication; Wordsworth's analysis focuses on poets and readers with the goal of restoring the power of initiative to the former.

The second variation moves the focus of illegitimate power from consumption to production. Blake's analysis, in its willingness to exempt the public from blame and in its attacks on the booksellers and trading dealers and on the power of production to turn soul or life into a mill or machine, falls here. Accordingly, harmony is treated less as a response to corrupt consumer desires than as an effect of production that consumers, "imposed upon for many years" (*PA*, E 574), must be fooled into desiring. Furthermore, if as practice harmony is a mechanical substitution for something the machine cannot produce, as theory it is an effort to make a virtue of technical and commercial necessity.

In this construction, the "ignorance" and "pretense" that Blake so often names with harmony are not by-products but integral factors. Pretension, like plagiarism, is located in the gap between appearance and reality so as to account for the ability of the counter-arts to fool—"A Pretence of Art: To Destroy Art" (anno. Reynolds, E 642)—while plagiarists are ignorant by definition in not knowing their own minds because their minds are not their own. In Blake's narrative the ideology of the counter-arts is as plagiaristic as the practice it ratifies. As he embraced the widespread suspicion of "plagiarism" (*Observations* 12) in Reynolds's paintings—the "borrowed fragments" hidden under "the thick-strewn graces of his execution" (Cunningham s.v. Reynolds 1:323), Blake also adopted the epidemic hunch that the ideas in Reynolds's discourses were not his own: "The Contradictions . . . are Strong Presumptions that they are the Work of Several Hands But this is no Proof that Reynolds did not Write them" because plagiarism is a state of mind: "The Man . . . who Learns or Acquires all he Knows from Others. Must be full of Contradictions" (anno. Reynolds, E 639; see also 651, 657, and the similar comments on Wordsworth's prefaces, 665–66).

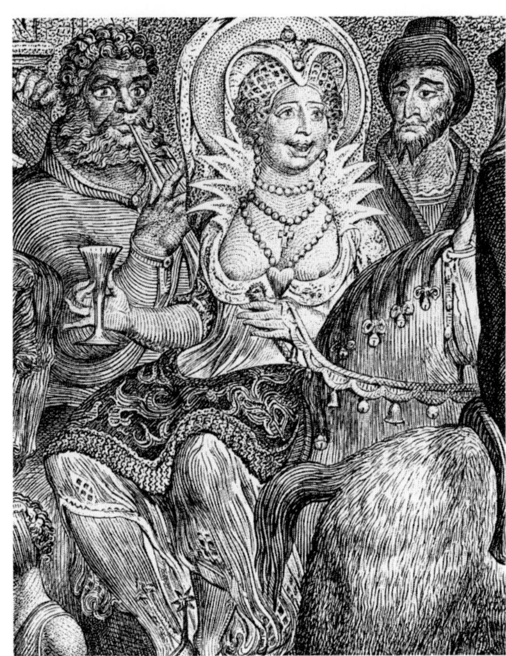

A Republican Art

> Rome & Greece swept Art into their maw & destroyd it a Warlike State never can produce Art. It will Rob & Plunder & accumulate into one place, & Translate & Copy & Buy & Sell & Criticise, but not Make
>
> —William Blake, *On Virgil*

In his 1798 edition of the *Discourses,* Edmond Malone expressed relief that Reynolds (d. 1792) had not lived to witness these seditious times and proclaimed that the "complete answer to all the SEDITIOUS DECLAMATIONS" lay in the fact that "England is at present in an unparalleled state of wealth and prosperity" (quoted in E 641). "This Whole Book," Blake

as we might call it, is one result of rejecting the sanctioned vertical eclecticism: the drawing of Raphael plus the coloring of Titian, and so on.

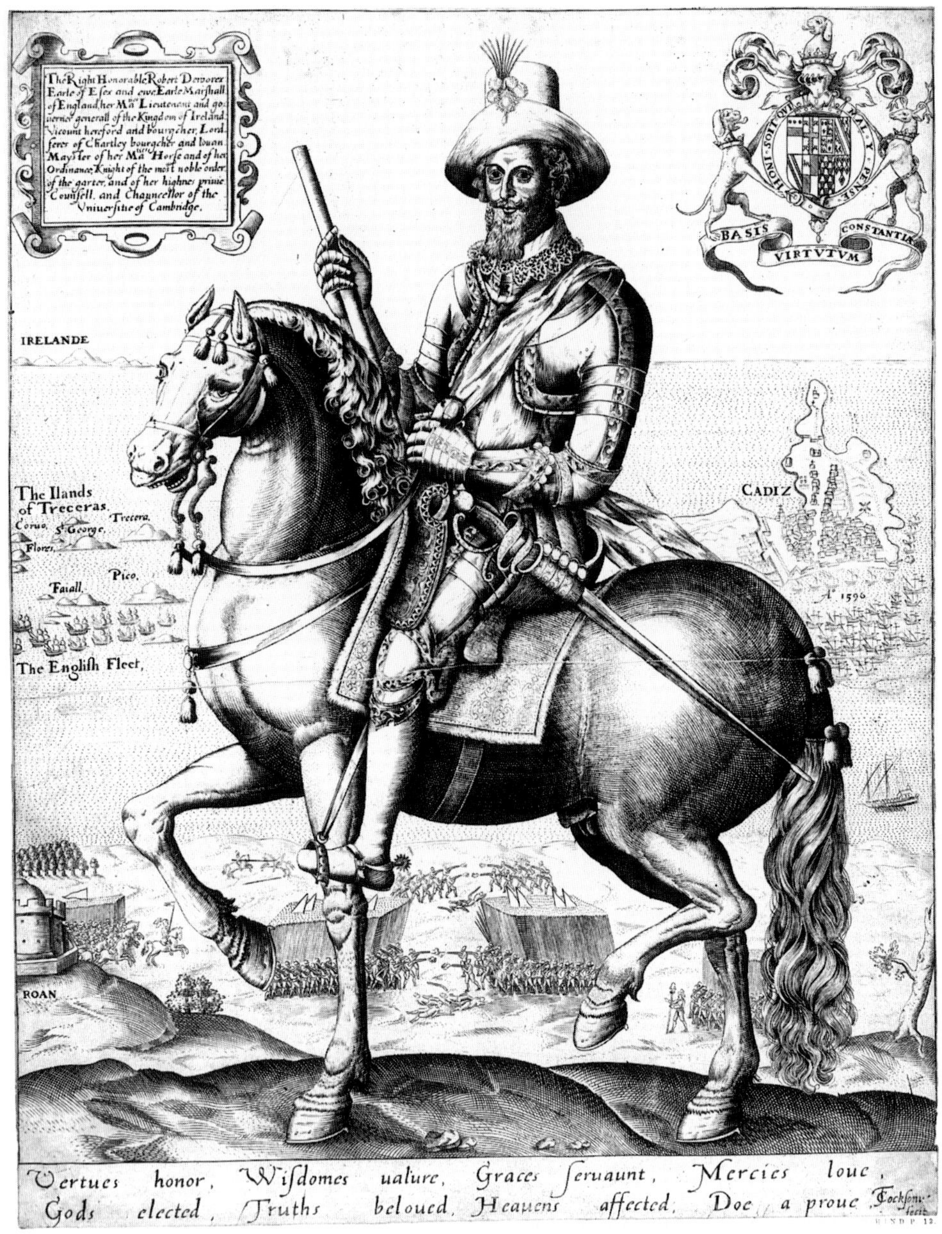

It is not easy to tell what images Blake had in mind when he asked the members of the Chalcographic Society to compare his *Canterbury Pilgrims* engraving with old English portraits, but probably something like Thomas Cockson's engraving of Robert Devereux, second Earl of Essex, Elizabeth's favorite. According to Arthur Hind, Cockson worked from about 1591 to 1636, producing "wooden" and "very awkward" equestrian portraits that "reflect no great skill" (*Engraving in England* 1:239, 315). Those very characteristics, along with strong outlines and severely restrained tonal systems, might have recommended them to Blake in his search for old English alternatives to the technical flights of the new English school of engraving. Several features of such old English work, furthermore, turn up in the *Canterbury Pilgrims* print (fig. 4.50). The equestrian portrait seems to be the foundation of its composition and iconography, and Cockson's barbaric Tudor heterogeneity in layering words with images to communicate Essex's public history reappears in Blake's labeling of the pilgrims, the sign carved on the front of the inn, and the slogans added to the inscription in the fourth state of the plate. By plugging in a new head, changing coats of arms, altering inscriptions, and rubbing out some of the background, Cockson later transformed Essex into Ernest, Count Mansfield, who served with the Protestants in the Thirty Years' War. Though sometimes surprising to modern sensibilities, these were the

responded, "was Written to Serve Political Purposes" (anno. Reynolds, E 641), in the sense that Reynolds's theory was intended to quell seditious malaise and encourage satisfaction with things as they are. I have indicated that Blake saw the combined technical and ideological mechanisms of the English school conspiratorily, as part of a substantial enterprise with commercial and political dimensions. (With a caveat: as Reynolds's plagiarism is no proof that he did not write his discourses, so conspiracy is no proof of conscious plotting. What is true of Reynolds in particular—"the Mischief is just the same, whether a Man does it Ignorantly or Knowingly" [anno. Reynolds, E 642]—is true of the counter-arts in general.)

In Blake's analysis, the technological principle shared by war machines, political machines, commercial machines, and art machines is intermeasurability, which simultaneously makes possible, through the organization of materials, the mechanical devices that produce acceptable translations and reproductions, and, through the organization of human work, the divisions of labor that unite with mechanical devices to produce marketable products (such as pictures) or services (such as battles). Products that are translations and copies benefit from an ideology that sets a high value on acquisition (by which the work force is trained) and imitation.[48] As we have seen, the "degradations" of visual harmony satisfy technical, commercial, and more comprehensive political aims as well:

Advice of the Popes who succeeded the Age of
Rafael

Degrade first the Arts if you'd Mankind degrade,
Hire Idiots to Paint with cold light & hot shade:
Give high Price for the worst, leave the best in
disgrace,
And with Labours of Ignorance fill every place.
[Anno. Reynolds, E 635]

The political dimension of harmony shows up clearly in Blake's consistent characterization of it as a "trick," a term that even then had the strong political overtones with which we became familiar during the dirty-tricks campaigns in the Nixon era of American politics. With that use in mind, we can hear the common political assumptions that inform otherwise disparate remarks about established religion, government, and art. As Blake labels Bishop Richard Watson "a State Trickster" (anno. Watson, E 612) and challenges Thomas Paine's claim "That the Bible is all a State Trick" (anno. Watson, E 616), so he brands the work of Salvator Rosa (the "Quack Doctor of Painting" who was "precisely what he Pretended Not to be") the "Production of Labour & Trick" (anno. Reynolds, E 654); urges "exposure" of the "vile tricks" of the Venetian and Flemish demons (*DC*, E 547); and calls the financial encouragement offered by the aristocracy an "endeavour to counteract by tricks" (*PA*, E 577).

[48] Benjamin's "Work of Art in an Age of Mechanical Reproduction" is a classic and still stimulating analysis, if somewhat dated and overapplied, of the differing kinds of commercial efficacy that originality and reproduction possess. Kibel formulates a strong answer to Benjamin's notion that reproduction would overcome "the systems of physical access through which society attempts to regulate our approach to works of art" (249). He focuses on "levels of articulation" in relation to "transcription" (of the original in a reproduction) and "meaning" (transmitted from the original to the transcription or not) (248). His discussion is relevant to intermeasurability and the manipulation of the threshold of vision. standard expedients of portraitists and engravers.

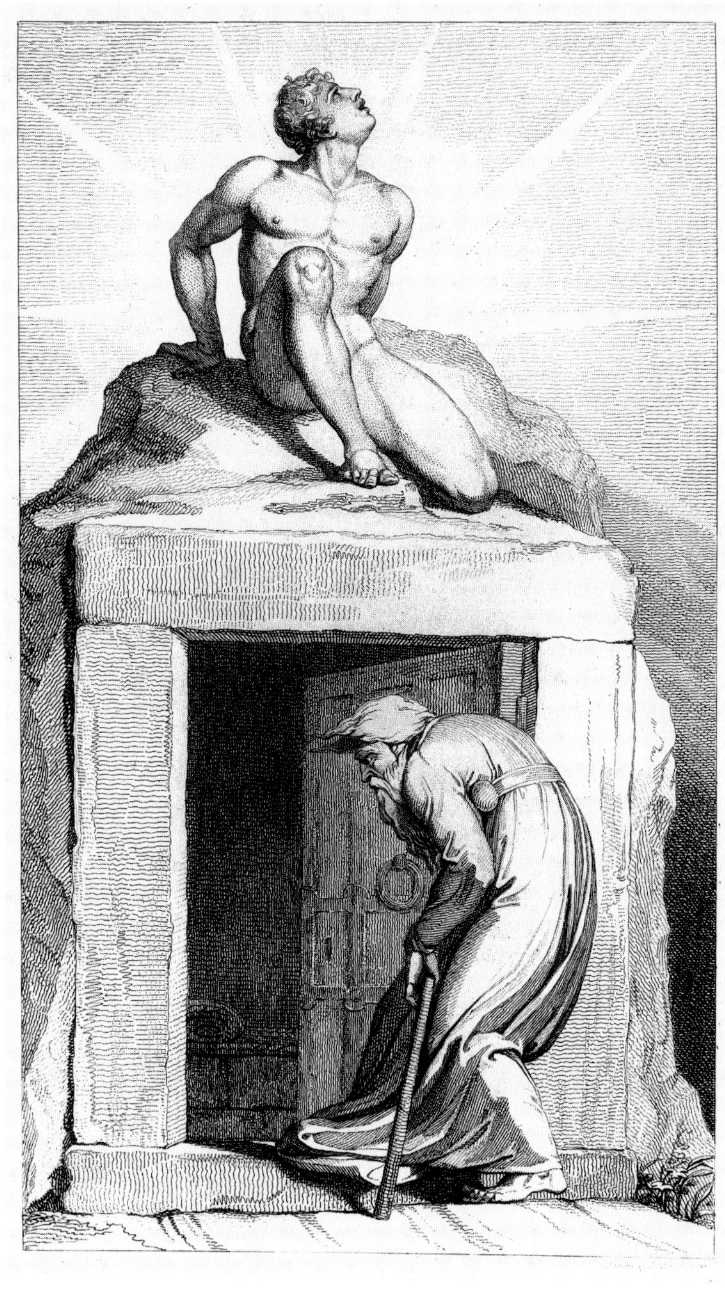

4.52. Louis Schiavonetti after William Blake, *Deaths Door,* engraving, from Robert Cromek's 1808 edition of Robert Blair, *The Grave.*

Blake's biographer Alexander Gilchrist suggested that if Louis (Luigi) Schiavonetti instead of Blake had executed the *Canterbury Pilgrims* engraving and "doctored" it "by correct smooth touches . . . a different fortune would have awaited the composition" (1:231–32). Robert Cromek, who in 1805 had commissioned Blake to do both the designs and the engravings for an illustrated edition of Robert Blair's *Grave* (1808), eventually turned the engraving over to Schiavonetti, whom Blake named "Assassinetti" ("And his legs carried it," E 504) for his skills. The Edinburgh painter David Scott declared that the "disappointment" to Blake was a "benefit to the work" (quoted in Gilchrist 1:377). A vexatious issue surfaces: what is "the work" and where are its borders? Blake would have had little doubt that it did not include Schiavonetti's neat and trim engravings *of* "the work." But Gilchrist termed Schiavonetti's "a graceful translation, and, as most would think, an improvement" (1:265).

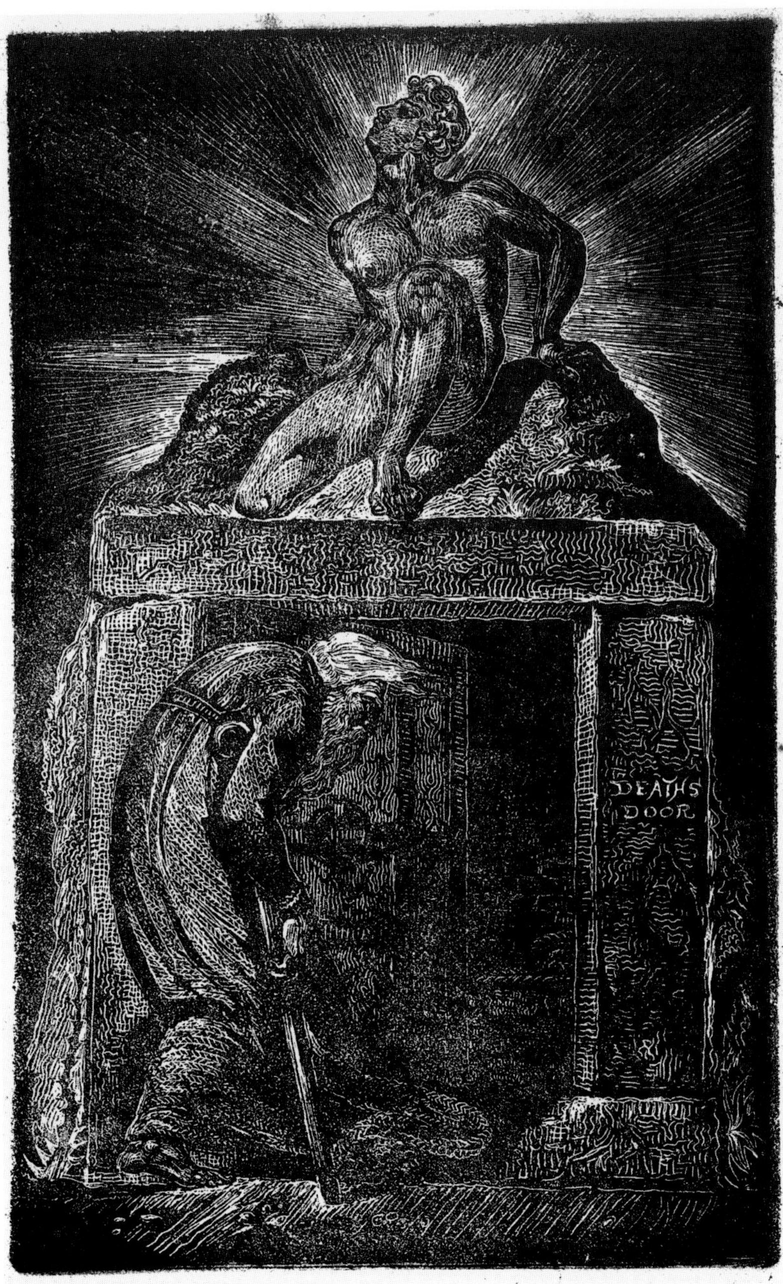

4.53. William Blake, *Deaths Door,* white line etching, only known impression, 1805.

If this white line engraving was indeed the "Specimen of the Stile of Engraving" on exhibition with "the Original Drawings" (quoted in Essick, *Separate Plates* 49) at Cromek's, as the *Grave* prospectus suggests, then we can easily see why Cromek sought out a more presentable form in which to present Blake's designs to the public. In discussing them, Gilchrist introduces such words as "extremes" and "ravings" to locate Schiavonetti's diplomatic role in presenting a tamed, "modified version" of Blake's "wild" style to the public (1:233). To understand Gilchrist's position, it may be helpful to think of Schiavonetti as an editor and of his engravings in the context of editorial acts—including, of course, all forms of "doctoring," "censorship," "normalization," and "improvement" of originals as well as "accuracy" and "fidelity" to them. As Gilchrist's language indicates, the nomenclature of mental illness has played an important role in authorizing editorial approaches to Blake. In editions, posterity takes a hand, sometimes a strong one, in representation. Here we should not be distracted by the inconsequential circumstance that Schiavonetti was not as posterior to the artist as posterity sometimes is. The "original" edition of a book is an edition nonetheless and often involves many individuals, institutions, and technologies far beyond the understanding, much less the control, of the author.

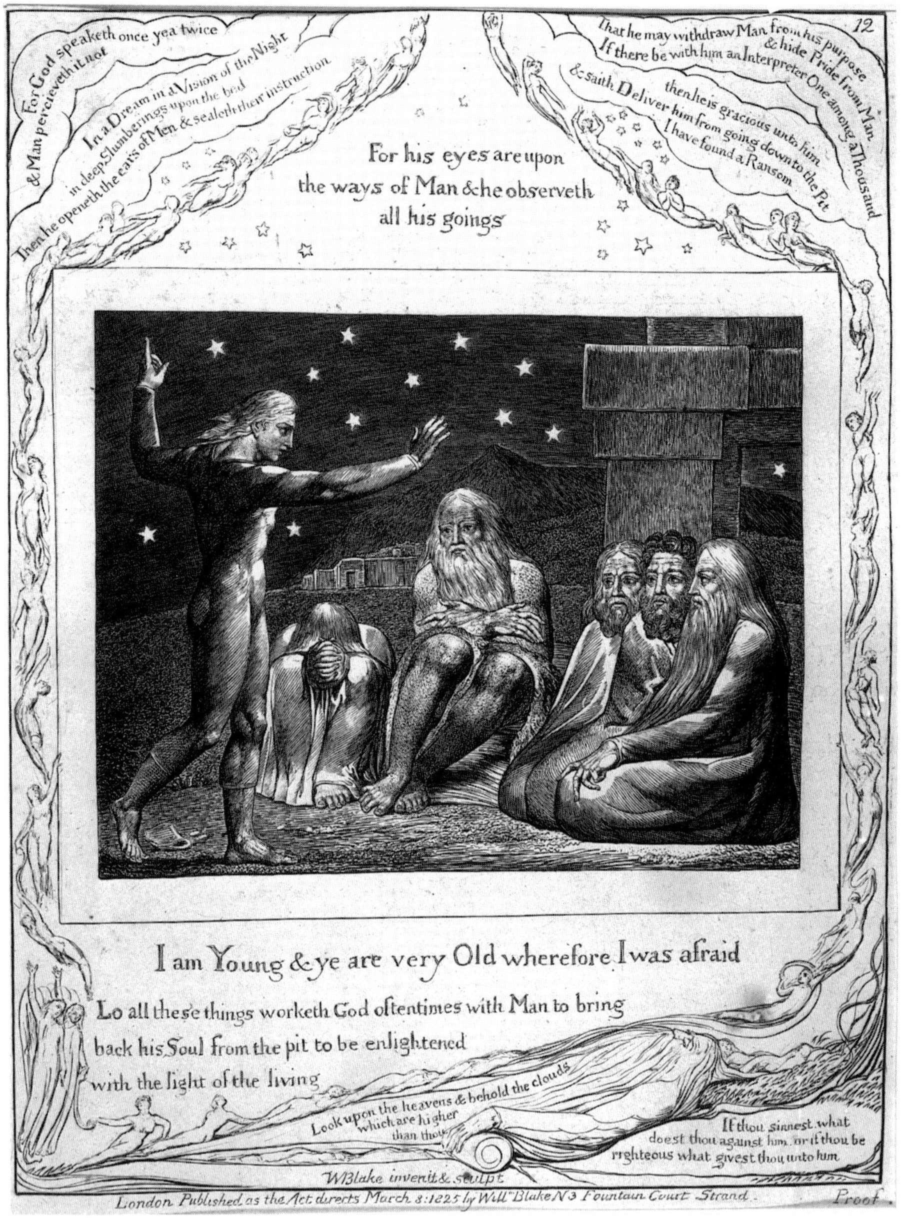

4.54. William Blake, *Illustrations of the Book of Job*, plate 12, engraving, 1825–26, and detail.

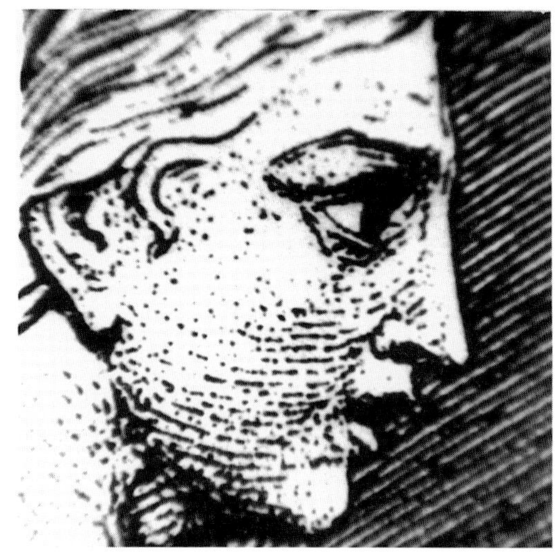

Blake represented the *Job* engravings (1825–1826) to Cumberland as a republican project. Technically, their politics emerges through Blake's individuality of style, frankly exposed in firm burin lines, clear transitions, and a restricted gray scale (cf. Essick, *Printmaker* 249). The influence of John Linnell, however, may have been responsible for Blake's abandonment of the mock-gothic, or old English, eclecticism of the *Canterbury Pilgrims* print for hatching sufficiently dense and uniform to accommodate greater fascination with light and shade, while he relied on strongly engraved outlines to establish the priority of drawn forms (Essick has argued for Linnell's influence on Blake's late engraving style [*Printmaker* 234–54, *Separate Plates* xxvi–xxvii]). Here a magnified halftone simulates how "the old regular mode"

A

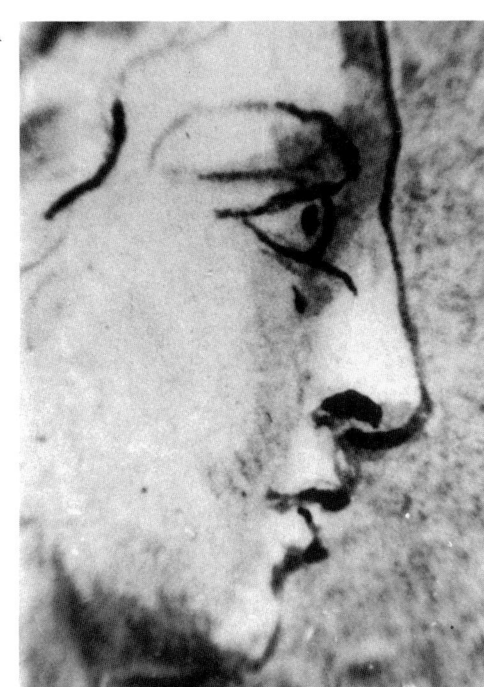

B

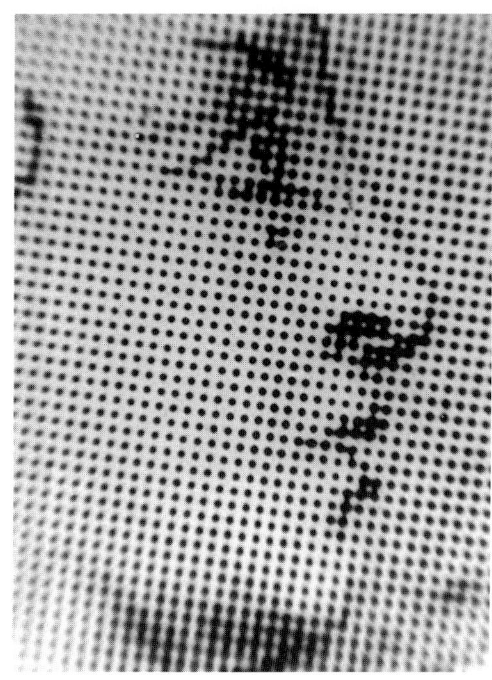

4.55. William Blake, *The Wrath of Elihu,* pen and watercolor drawing, 1821: (*A*) detail; (*B*) detail, magnified halftone.

Harmony is thus a state trick with low-order technological and high-order ideological applications, doubling as a recipe for production and as a paradigm of repressive social order calling for the "sweet harmony" of "due subordination" (in Richardson's words) that can accommodate and exploit that recipe. The ignorant journeymen hired by such hirelings as Reynolds have their Blakean niche alongside the chimney sweepers who need not fear harm if they only do their duty and the little black boys who will be free in heaven if they agree to stay slaves on earth. The rose that is sick is not just the eroticized body of the individual woman but the body of this society, "the Flower of the English Nobility & Gentry" who let Barry "Give them, his Labour for Nothing . . . Suffering an Artist to Starve while he Supported Really what They under pretence of Encouraging were Endeavouring to Depress" (anno. Reynolds, E 636).

The analogy of Israel seems largely responsi-

of line engraving might have harmonized Blake's style by destabilizing the outlines. It may seem odd that Ruskin could later have chosen *Job* to exemplify chiaroscuro. "In expressing conditions of glaring and flickering light," he wrote, "Blake is greater than Rembrandt" (342). In Blake's time that judgment would have identified him with the Venetians as a master of harmony. But this was apparently not the contemporary effect of the *Job* prints, the manner of which Cunningham, for one, characterized as "in the earlier fashion of workmanship," with "no resemblance whatever to the polished and graceful style which now prevails" (2:177). Ruskin's Victorian Rembrandt is one revised after new ways with light on canvas by Turner (among others) had transformed the old orthodoxy of harmony.

(OVERLEAF)

Although it would be impossible to apprehend Blake's attitude toward visual harmony or to fix his place in the history of engraving and painting without consideration of his illuminated books, it is not entirely clear how he thought of them. None was included in the exhibition of 1809, which he seems to have designed around a technical notion of reviving fresco; the *Canterbury Pilgrims* engraving, rather than *Milton* or *Jerusalem,* inspired the notion of a Public Address; and Viscomi has demonstrated that Blake spent far less time producing illuminated books than we

ble for the syntax of Blake's counterclaim: "Let us teach Buonaparte & whomsoever else it may concern That it is not Arts that follow & attend upon Empire but Empire that attends upon & follows The Arts" (*PA*, E 577). This is, of course, the lesson that biblical Israel kept having trouble learning. Blake's "republican" answer to English-school ideology was largely amalgamated from biblical narrative—with true art metaphorically double-bound to the everlasting Gospel so that each can be offered to explain the other—adjusted to an ethics and politics of individual merit, in religious terms the salvation of the individual soul. In Blake's analysis, the opposition to liberated individuality is less repressive collectivity, as we might ordinarily expect, than a pincer-like alliance between a totalitarian body politic above and atomization below: the one a ruling class dominating the individual from above—allied, as it were, with the starry worlds—the other dividing the individual from below, at the level of intermeasurable constituents (atoms, Lockean impressions, interchangeable parts, interchangeable workers, money as the measure of all things). The two cooperate in a two-pronged system of natural and supernatural law that Blake associates with deism.

Once again his fear and suspicion, or call it paranoia, emerge from the (seditious) middle position, as between kings and fools, where the individual soul must hold the line against disintegrative forces from below that would turn the integrated imagination into the sum of the parts it can acquire ("When a Man talks of Acquiring Invention & of learning how to produce Original Conception," he is a "Hired Knave" whose "Eye is on the Many. or rather on the Money" [anno. Reynolds, E 655]) and at the same time resist the "Rich Men of England" (E 642) who would sell off the divided labor hour by hour and piece by piece. Blake was commenting on the coordination of low-order intermeasurability with high-order harmony in his cranky late letter to Cumberland. Blake comments that most "Englishmen" will not like the severe linear style of the *Job* engravings because they are "fond of The Indefinite"—that is, the tonal values of harmony—"which they Measure by Newtons Doctrine of the Fluxions of an Atom. A Thing that does not Exist." He is criticizing harmony by way of its conventional association with mathematical regularity. "These are Politicians & think that Republican Art is Inimical to their Atom." Republican art is based on line, which "is Itself & Not Intermeasurable with or by any Thing Else Such is Job."

"Job" here refers both to Blake's thematic treatment of the character Job in his illustrations and to the engravings as such. Thematically, the illustrations expose Job's identity to the repressive powers of natural religion from above and the divisive powers of nature from below. His ability to withstand this attack, which is followed by a phase of self-doubting reinforced by the doubts of others, depends on his recognition that he and God are not separate but identical, as the designs make evident (the hair is erect in points, for instance, first on Job in pl. 9, then on his mirror-image God in pl. 11). As he explains to his daughters, he came to realize that his story is an exercise not in religious morality but in art (pl. 20).

Stylistically, Blake represents the clarity of his vision of Job through the definitive clarity of a republican engraving technique, the articulate lines of liberated individual merit rather

have sometimes imagined—and he spent most of his last twenty years without conceiving a new one. After his death, however, the illuminated books served the absolutely essential function of providing the texts that allowed sponsors such as Swinburne to assert Blake's significance as a poet—the literary canon being the base on which his posthumous significance was ultimately built. And when we members of posterity have pondered Blake as an original engraver, the main evidence has been his illuminated books in illuminated printing. Among other striking points of originality is the technology of their base medium, which is (with a couple of exceptions) relief etching. Since relief etching has been subjected to considerable critical fantasizing, we might take a brief but hard new contextual look by means of three of Estelle Jussim's useful categories, which use the terminology of information theory to describe the transition from engraving to photography in the nineteenth century. *Molecular codes:* The molecule of the halftone is the halftone dot; the molecules of line engraving are the lozenge and dot. Relief etching, as Blake usually employs it, spurns molecular codes as the basic channel of visual information. Early and late examples of illuminated printing, *The Approach of Doom* (fig. 4.56*B*) and *Jerusalem* 99 (fig. 4.57*A*), show how Blake could use relief etching to produce images organized by rugged surfaces (which are sometimes thin

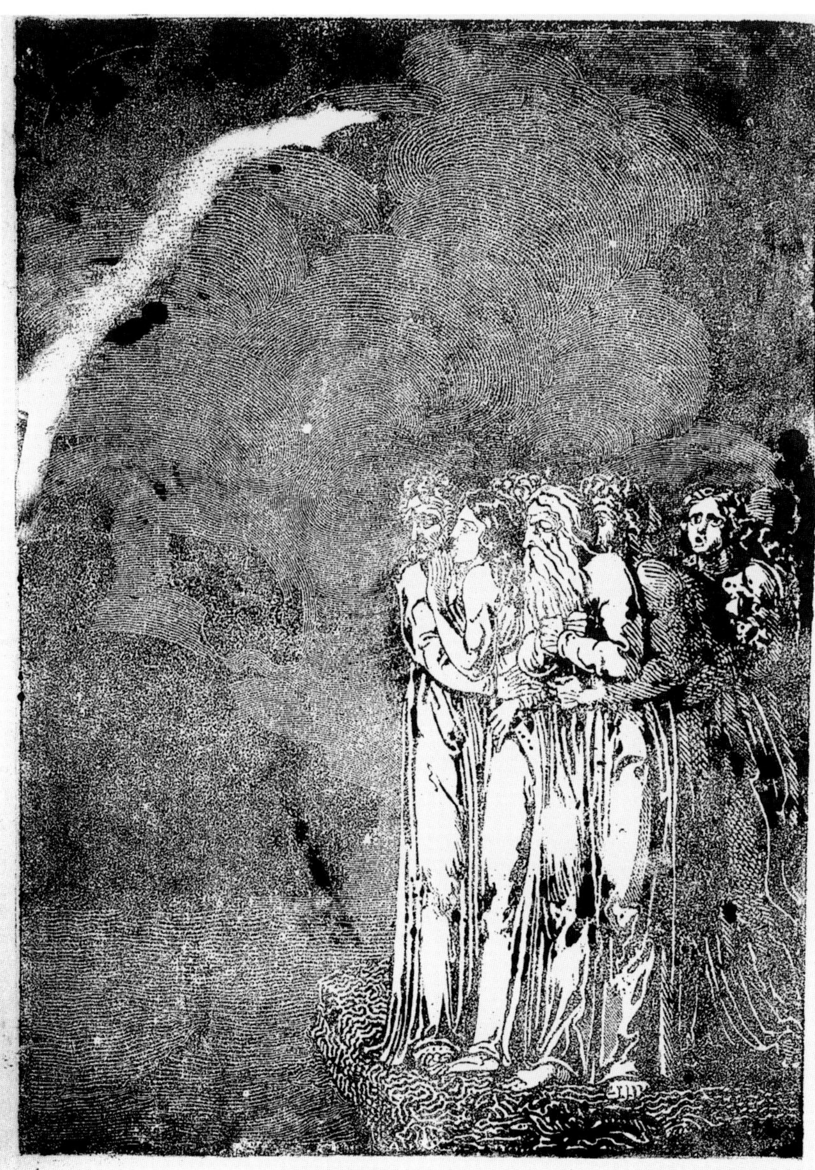

4.56. William Blake after Robert Blake, *The Approach of Doom,* relief etching, only known impression, c. 1792, and detail.

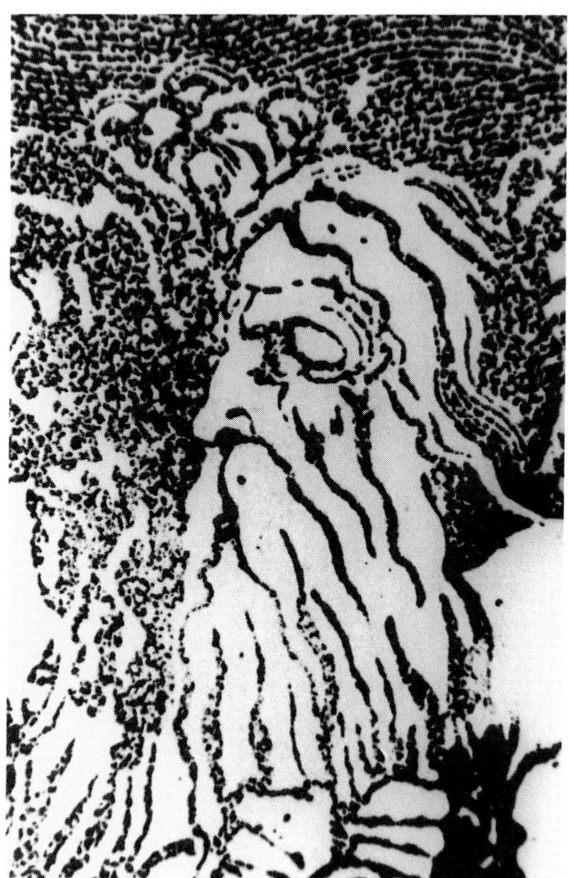

enough to be called lines). Molecular codes are not banned, but they are usually firmly contained—as local variations—by this rugged environment. *Compression index:* Mezzotint and photography have a higher compression index than line engraving; that is, they can squeeze more visual information into a designated space. The higher the compression index, the broader the spectrum of images that

A

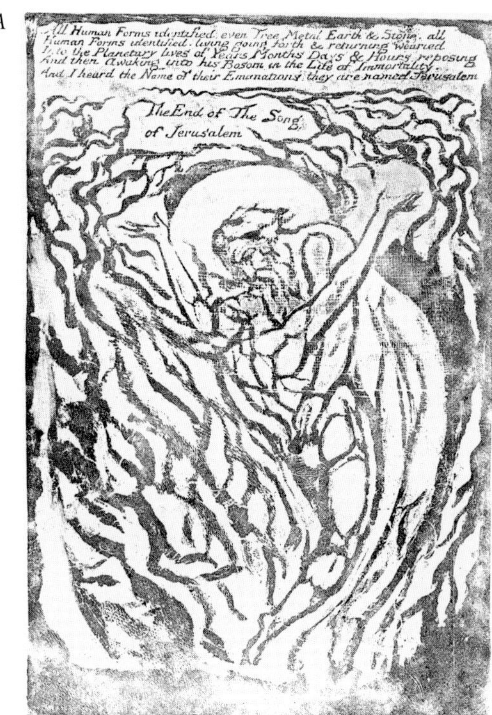

B

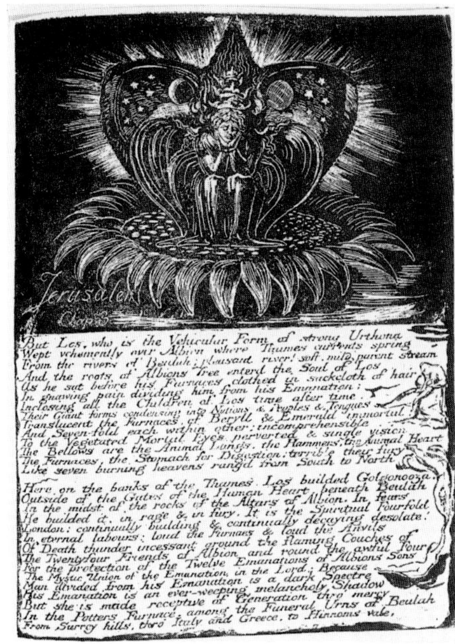

C

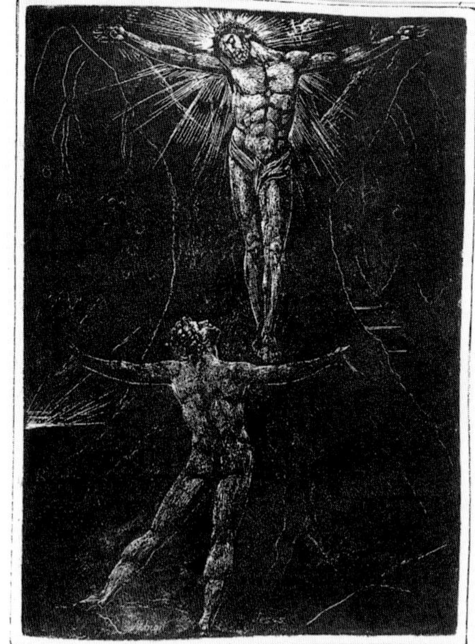

4.57. William Blake, *Jerusalem,* relief etchings, c. 1804–1820: (*A*) plate 99 (copy J); (*B*) plate 53 (copy A); (*C*) plate 76 (copy A).

the medium of reproduction can adequately copy. In Blake's hands, relief etching has a very low compression index. Imagine trying to copy one of Reynolds's paintings with it. Hence images in the medium tend to look as if they originated there rather than as if they were brought there from some other information channel. *Subliminal codes:* Basically, codes are subliminal when the units cannot be perceived: scale and distance locate the point at which a code becomes subliminal. As we have seen, the threshold of vision is a critical measure when artisanal skills are the means and a delicate combination of display and reproduction is the goal. Moreover, techniques of achieving harmony manipulate the threshold to hide the evidence of codes and procedures. In illuminated printing subliminality ceases to be an issue because the threshold of vision, the intelligible middle distance between the microscopic and the macroscopic, is so wide. Much of the time, the middle distance is all there is. Of course, these are generalizations. Blake experimented with a range of ways of using relief processes, which Essick and Viscomi have authoritatively described.

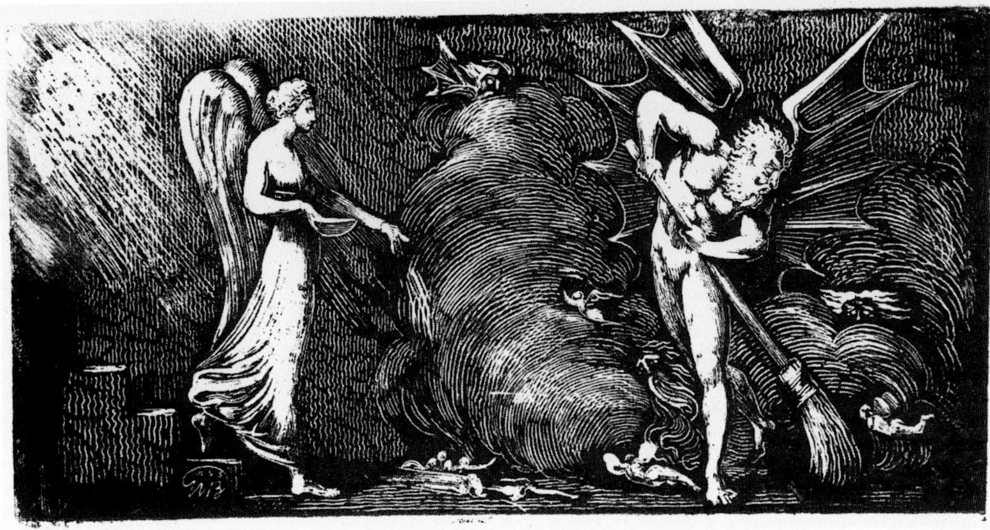

4.58. William Blake, *The Man Sweeping the Interpreter's Parlour,* relief etching and/or engraving, second state, c. 1822.

than the intermeasurable atoms of divided labor blended into indefinite harmony. "Such is Job but since the French Revolution Englishmen are all Intermeasurable One by Another." Antirepublican forces turned the Revolution into an opportunity to associate individual distinction with sedition and thus to impose the harmony of uniformity, "Certainly a happy state of Agreement to which I for One do not Agree. God keep me from the Divinity of Yes & No too" (12 April 1827, E 783) (figs. 4.54, 4.55). Blake's egalitarianism, like Thomas Paine's, operates very much in the service of a meritocracy, conceived as the liberation of real distinction from the absurdities of a "hereditary system" of discrimination "repugnant to human wisdom," as Paine says. In this construction egalitarianism is a way of "giving to genius a fair and universal chance": "I know not whether Homer or Euclid had sons; but I will venture an opinion that if they had, and had left their works unfinished, those sons could not have completed them" (Paine 410–11).

On these grounds, Blake's rebuttals to Reynolds on pictorial harmony also apply to the political fate of individual merit. Reynolds insists that "all smaller things, however perfect in their way, are to be sacrificed without mercy to the greater." When Blake retorts, "Sacrifice the Parts. What becomes of the Whole" (anno. Reynolds, E 650), he is reading the social agenda embedded in Reynolds's technical discourse. The smaller things, famously cherished as Blake's "minute particulars," are not merely separable images in a picture but individuals in the polity whose identities, however perfect in

(OVERLEAF)

The most interesting feature of Blake's discussion of Correggio in the *Descriptive Catalogue* is its immediate purpose: to explain why one of Blake's own paintings on display, *Satan Calling Up His Legions,* illustrating *Paradise Lost,* was ruined while he labored under the demonic influence of Rubens and Correggio, then was "with difficulty brought back again to a certain effect, which it had at first, when all the lineaments were perfect." He blames in particular "that infernal machine, called Chiaro Oscuro" (E 547). Chiaroscuro, he says,

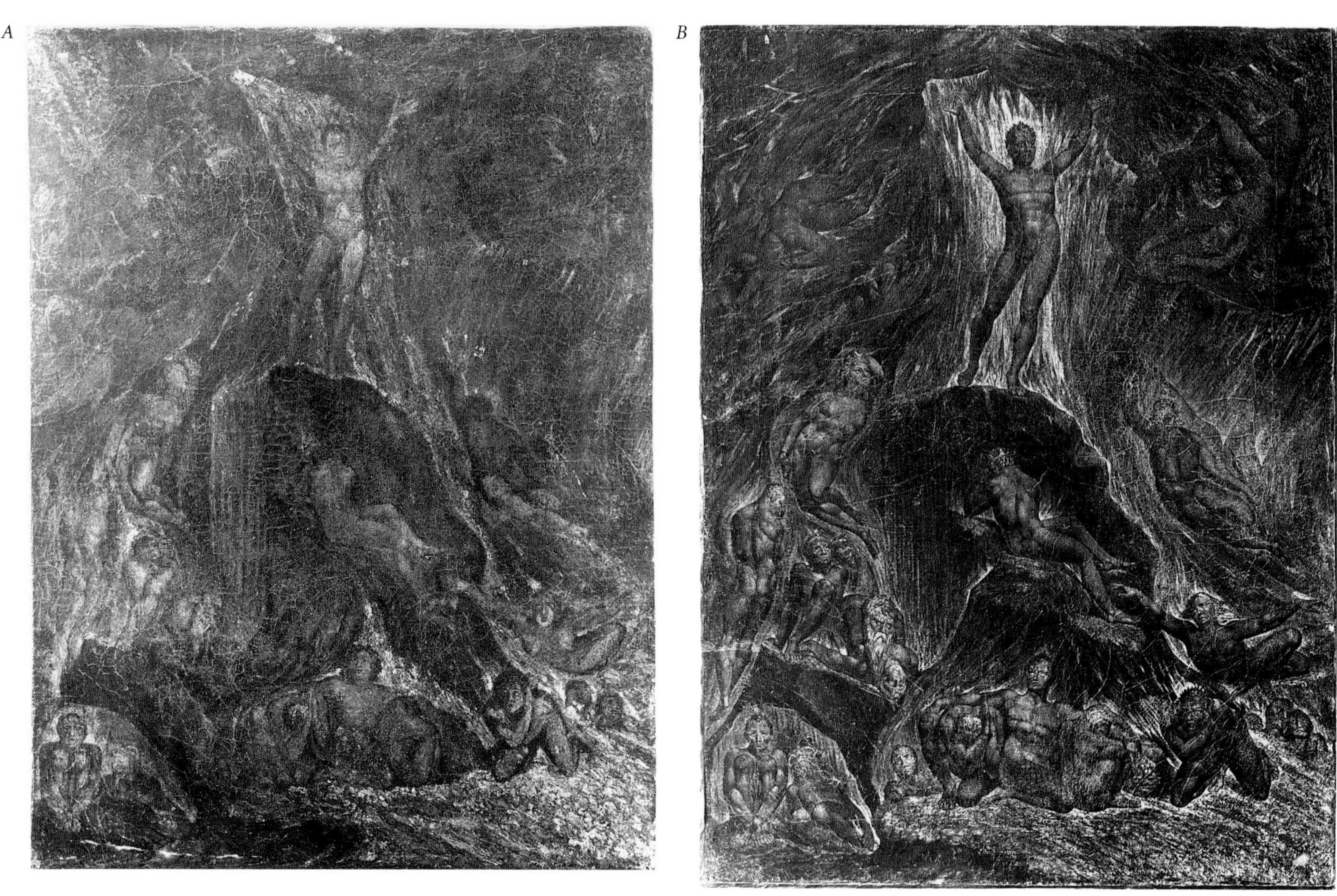

4.59. William Blake, *Satan Calling Up His Legions:* (*A*) tempera, c. 1795–1800; (*B*) tempera, c. 1800–1805.

their way, must be mercilessly sacrificed to the harmony of the *tout-ensemble.* What kind of social vision, Blake is asking, demands that sacrifice?

Much more of the substance of *Jerusalem* than readers often realize is woven from just such English-school issues. If, as I contend, Blake shapes his contributions to that discourse with a range of commercial, political, and biblical narratives, those contributions in turn shape his layered mythopoetic narratives. The feedback is what makes possible such wonderful concatenations as this kaleidoscopic account: of a painting upon which the degradations of harmony have been imposed; of the disarticulated souls of English folk; and of slavery among ancient Hebrews. Exploring the artistic and social interiors of Albion with his lamp, Los detects

> . . . every Minute Particular of Albion degraded & murderd
> But saw not by whom; they were hidden within in the minute particulars
> Of which they had possessd themselves; and there they take up
> The articulations of a mans soul, and laughing throw it down
> Into the frame, then knock it out upon the plank, & souls are bak'd
> In bricks to build the pyramids of Heber & Terah. But Los
> Searchd in vain: closd from the minutia he walkd, difficult.
>
> [*J* 45(31).7–13, E 194]

Both Blake's later visual styles and his later attempts to imagine fragmentation and wholeness are, I suggest, responses to his technological, aesthetic, and political understanding of harmony (fig. 4.50). In rejecting harmony, the lofty intersection of material practice and metaphysics, as a paradigm of artistic and social unity, he apparently felt compelled to offer a revision. It is not extravagant to claim that *Jerusalem* is, among other things of course, a considered reply to English-school discourse, and hence it is not surprising that when it ends, unity is the subject. Combining the Pauline metaphor of the mystical body of Christ with the iconography of Renaissance humanism, Blake arrives at the Human Form Divine as his figurative alternative to the mechanistic naturalism of orthodox aesthetic harmony. His attempt to describe living fourfold Form as an emanative rather than supersessive unity based on individual merit, original art, and republican politics comes in the glorious final plates, which, curiously but perhaps inevitably, owe as many literary debts to his encounters with the discourse of the English school of painting as to those loftier conversations with the likes of the St. John of Revelation, Swedenborg, and Milton: "revealing the lineaments of Man / . . . In the Four Senses in the Outline the Circumference & Form" (98.19–22, E 257). So conceived, a republican art banishes the harmony that represses melody and voice and puts its faith in the reemergence of "original" melodies: the recovered art of individuals who participate in deep structures of imagination by birth, not by education, or, more palatably, by birth followed by an education that honors the birthrights of imagination rather than represses and distorts them for the sake of commerce. Imagining a society expressed into diversity instead of harmonized into uniform efficiencies, Blake expresses his noble and chal-

puts *Satan Calling Up His Legions* among his "experiment Pictures," which have been "bruized and knocked about, without mercy, to try all experiments" (548). The connection between chiaroscuro and experiment is not idle. Harmony was frequently linked to nature as an image of natural law. George Turnbull claimed in his *Treatise on Ancient Painting* (1740) that "Harmonies of Phaenomena . . . reduce Appearances to general Laws" (x–xi) that explain the unity of the natural world. Painting, being to natural science as music is to mathematics, thus "aims at visible Harmony, as Musick at Harmony of Sounds." Pictures become "Samples and Experiments to help and assist us in the Study of those Laws [of light and color], as any Samples or Experiments are in the Study of the Laws of Gravity, Elasticity, or of any other Quality in the natural World" (146). The progress of painting parallels the progress of scientific demonstration. One experiment begets another as lessons are learned, generalizations are made, and a path of progress is defined. The very point of Blake's experiments, on the contrary, is to separate art from nature and to demonstrate artistic failure. They are experiments against experiment. In the *Catalogue* Blake mentions two versions of *Satan,* the first (on display in his exhibition) a "composition" for the second, "more perfect Picture, afterwards executed for a Lady of high rank" (E 547).

lenging faith—in the face of troubling evidence to the contrary—that there exist structures of imagination capable of providing reliable order in diversity when more forceful economic and technological uniformities are removed. "Nature has no Tune, but Imagination has!" (*Ghost of Abel*, E 270). Our own inquiry will end off-key if Blake's secret jester, the Idiot Questioner, makes a last-minute appearance to ask: What is this "imagination"?

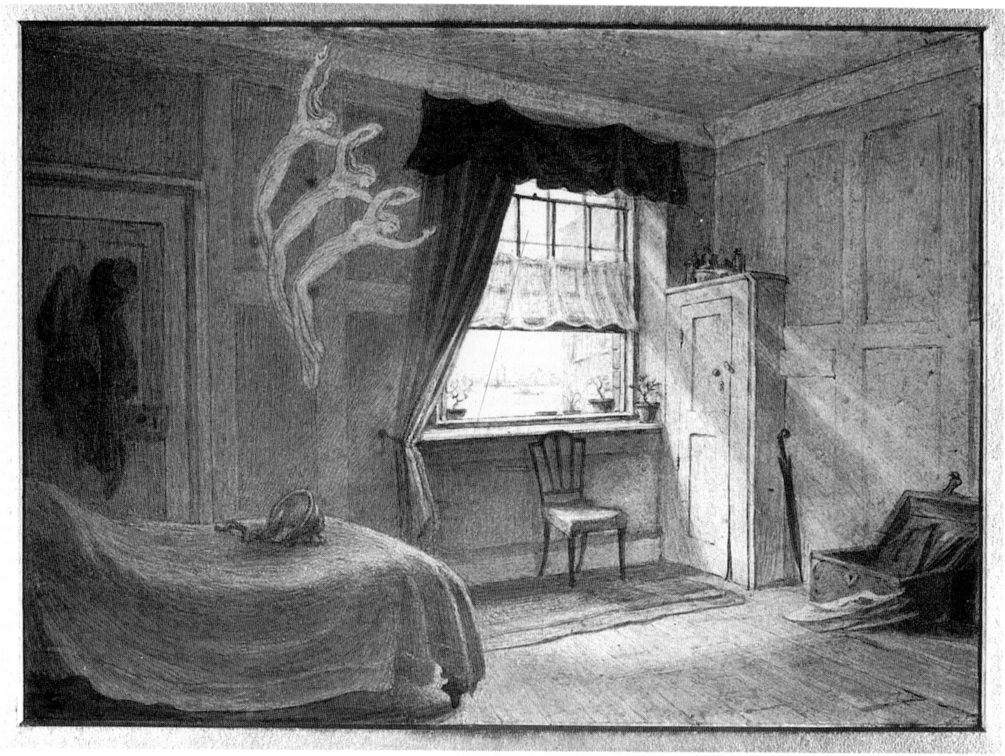

4.60. Frederic Shields, *Blake's Work-Room and Death-Room*, monochrome wash drawing, c. 1880–1890.

WORKS CITED

Aglionby, William. *Choice Observations upon the Art of Painting. Together with Vasari's Lives of the Most Eminent Painters, from Cimabue to the Time of Raphael and Michael Angelo. With an Explanation of the Difficult Terms.* 1685. London, 1719.

Alexander, David. *Retailing in England during the Industrial Revolution.* London: Athlone, 1970.

Alexander, David, and Richard Godfrey. *Painters and Engraving: The Reproductive Print from Hogarth to Wilkie.* New Haven: Yale Center for British Art, 1980.

Alsop, Joseph. *The Rare Art Traditions: The History of Art Collecting and Its Linked Phenomena Wherever These Have Appeared.* London: Thames & Hudson, 1982.

Altick, Richard D. *The Shows of London.* Cambridge: Harvard University Press, 1978.

Ashton, John. *A History of English Lotteries.* London, 1893.

Avermaete, Roger. *Rubens and His Times.* Trans. Christine Trollope. New York: Barnes, 1968.

Baker, W. S. *The Origin and Antiquity of Engraving, with Some Remarks on the Utility and Pleasures of Prints.* Boston, 1875.

——. *William Sharp, Engraver: With a Descriptive Catalogue of His Works.* Philadelphia, 1875.

Balston, Thomas. "John Boydell, Publisher: 'The Commercial Maecenas.'" *Signature* n.s. no. 8 (1949): 3–22.

Barrell, John. *The Political Theory of Painting from Reynolds to Hazlitt: "The Body of the Public."* New Haven: Yale University Press, 1986.

——. "Sir Joshua Reynolds and the Englishness of English Art." In *Nation and Narration,* ed. Homi K. Bhabha, 154–76. New York and London: Routledge, 1990.

Barry, James. *An Account of a Series of Pictures, in the Great Room of the Society of Arts, Manufactures, and Commerce, at the Adelphi.* London, 1783.

——. *A Call to the Connoisseurs, or Decisions of Sense, with Respect to the Present State of Painting and Sculpture, and Their Several Professors in These Kingdoms . . . Intended to Vindicate the Genius and Abilities, of the Artists of Our Own Country, from the Malevolence of Pretended Connoisseurs, or Interested Dealers.* London, 1761.

——. *An Inquiry into the Real and Imaginary Obstructions to the Acquisition of the Arts in England.* London, 1775.

——. *A Letter to the Dilettanti Society, Respecting the Obtention of Certain Matters Essentially Necessary for the Improvement of Public Taste, and for Accomplishing the Original Views of the Royal Academy of Great Britain.* London, 1798.

——. *Proposals for Publishing by Subscription, Six Engraved Prints, from the Above-Mentioned Series.* London, 1783.

——. *See also* Wornum.

Barryte, Bernard. "Francis Wheatley's *Death of Richard II* (1792–1793): Content and Context." *Porticus* 10–11 (1987–1988): 31–45.

Benjamin, Walter. "The Work of Art in an Age of Mechanical Reproduction." In *Illuminations,* ed. Hannah Arendt, trans. Harry Zohn, 216–51. New York: Schocken, 1969.

Bennett, Shelley M. *Thomas Stothard: The Mechanisms of Art Patronage in England circa 1800.* Columbia: University of Missouri Press, 1988.

Bentley, G. E., Jr. *Blake Books.* Oxford: Clarendon, 1977.

——. *Blake Records.* Oxford: Clarendon, 1969.

Best, Geoffrey. *War and Society in Revolutionary Europe, 1770–1870.* Leicester: Leicester University Press, 1982.

Bindman, David (with Aileen Dawson and Mark Jones). *The Shadow of the Guillotine: Britain and the French Revolution.* London: British Museum, 1989.

——, ed. *John Flaxman.* London: Thames & Hudson, 1979.

Blake, William. *The Complete Poetry and Prose of William Blake.* Ed. David V. Erdman. Commentary by Harold Bloom. Newly rev. ed. Berkeley and

Los Angeles: University of California Press, 1988. [Cited throughout as E.]
Boase, T. S. R. *English Art, 1800–1870.* Oxford History of English Art. Oxford: Clarendon, 1959.
Boydell, John. "An Autobiography of John Boydell, the Engraver." Introduction by W. Bell Jones. *Flintshire Historical Society Publications* 9 (1925): 79–87. [This publication apparently reproduces either the lost original notes that Boydell showed to Joseph Farington in the mid-1790s or Farington's heretofore lost transcription of them. Jones says only that he "recently acquired the following MSS auto-biography, written by John Boydell himself."]
Brewer, John. "Commercialization and Politics." In *The Birth of a Consumer Society,* ed. Neil McKendrick et al., 197–264. London: Europa, 1982.
Brown, Christopher. *Van Dyck.* Ithaca: Cornell University Press, 1983.
Brown, John. *Dissertation on the Rise, Union and Power, Progressions, Separations and Corruptions, of Poetry and Music.* London, 1763.
——. *The History of the Rise and Progress of Poetry, Through It's Several Species.* London, 1764.
Brown, Richard E. "Nathaniel Lee." In *Restoration and Eighteenth-Century Dramatists, First Series,* ed. Paula R. Backscheider, 114–25. *Dictionary of Literary Biography,* vol. 80. Detroit: Gale Research, 1989.
Bruntjen, Sven H. A. *John Boydell, 1719–1804: A Study of Art Patronage and Publishing in Georgian London.* New York and London: Garland, 1985.
Bryan, Michael. *Bryan's Dictionary of Painters and Engravers.* Ed. G. C. Williamson. 4th rev. ed. London: G. Bell, 1925.
Burckhardt, Jacob. *Recollections of Rubens.* Ed. H. Gerson. Trans. Mary Hottinger (Burckhardt's essay), R. H. Boothroyd, and I. Grafe (Rubens's letters). London: Phaidon, 1950.
Burke, Edmund. *The Correspondence of Edmund Burke.* Ed. Holden Furber. Vol. 5. Cambridge: Cambridge University Press and Chicago: Chicago University Press, 1965.
Burke, Joseph. *English Art, 1714–1800.* Oxford History of English Art. Oxford: Clarendon, 1976.
Bury, Shirley. "Flaxman as a Designer of Silverwork." In *John Flaxman,* ed. David Bindman, 140–48. London: Thames & Hudson, 1979.
Butler, Marilyn. *Romantics, Rebels, and Reactionaries: English Literature and Its Background, 1760–1830.* New York: Oxford University Press, 1981.
Butlin, Martin. "Cataloguing William Blake." In *Blake in His Time,* ed. Robert N. Essick and Donald Pearce, 77–90. Bloomington: Indiana University Press, 1978.
——. *The Paintings and Drawings of William Blake.* 2 vols. New Haven: Yale University Press, 1981.
——. *William Blake.* London: Tate Gallery, 1978.
Butlin, Martin, and Evelyn Joll. *The Paintings of J. M. W. Turner.* 2 vols. Rev. ed. New Haven: Yale University Press, 1984.
Campbell, Colin. *The Romantic Ethic and the Spirit of Modern Consumerism.* Oxford: Basil Blackwell, 1987.
Campbell, R. *The London Tradesman, Being an Historical Account of All the Trades, Professions, Arts, Both Liberal and Mechanic, Now Practised in the Cities of London and Westminster. . . .* 3d ed. London, 1757.
A Candid Review of the Exhibition (Being the Twelfth) of the Royal Academy, M DCC LXXX. Dedicated to His Majesty. By an Artist. London, n.d.
"Ceiling Painters." *Somerset House Gazette* 1 (1824): 15.
Chalmers, Alexander, ed. "Boydell, John." In *The General Biographical Dictionary . . . ,* 6:301–10. Rev. ed. London, 1812.
Claeys, Gregory. *Thomas Paine: Social and Political Thought.* Boston: Unwin Hyman, 1989.
Coleridge, Samuel Taylor. *Collected Letters of Samuel Taylor Coleridge.* Ed. Leslie Griggs. 6 vols. Oxford: Clarendon, 1956–1971.
"The Comparative Merits of Line Engraving and Mezzotinto." *Art-Union,* 15 May 1839, 57–58.
"Considerations on the East-India Trade." 1701. In *Early English Tracts on Commerce,* ed. J. R. McCulloch, 541–629. Cambridge: Cambridge University Press, 1954.
Constable, John. *John Constable's Discourses.* Comp. R. B. Beckett. Ipswich: Suffolk Records Society, 1970. [Vol. 14 in a series of records published by the Society.]
Cumberland, George. *An Essay on the Utility of Collecting the Best Works of the Ancient Engravers of the Italian School, Accompanied by a Critical Catalogue. . . .* London, 1827.
——. *Some Anecdotes of the Life of Julio Bonasoni . . . To Which Is Prefixed, A Plan for the Improvement of the Arts in England.* London, 1793.
Cummings, Frederick J. "The Problem of Artistic Style as It Relates to the Beginnings of Romanticism." In *Irrationalism in the Eighteenth Century,* ed. Harold E. Pagliaro, 143–65. Cleveland: Case Western Reserve University Press, 1972.
Cunningham, Allan. *The Lives of the Most Eminent British Painters, Sculptors, and Architects.* 2d ed. 6 vols. in 3. London, 1830–1846. [Vols. 1–3, 1830; vol. 4, 1831; vol. 5, 1833; vol. 6, 1846.]
——. *See also* Pilkington, *General Dictionary.*
Cunningham, Hugh. "The Language of Patriotism, 1750–1914." *History Workshop Journal* 12 (1981): 8–33.
Damon, S. Foster. *A Blake Dictionary: The Ideas and Symbols of William Blake.* Providence: Brown University Press, 1965 [and later printings].
Damrosch, Leopold, Jr. *Symbol and Truth in Blake's Myth.* Princeton: Princeton University Press, 1980.

Daulby, Daniel. *A Descriptive Catalogue of the Works of Rembrandt, and of His Scholars. . . .* Liverpool, 1796.

Dempsey, Charles. "The Carracci Reform of Painting." In *The Age of the Correggio and the Carracci: Emilian Painting of the Sixteenth and Seventeenth Centuries,* ed. various hands [none named on title page], 237–54 [catalogue by various hands, 255–324]. Washington and New York (etc.): National Gallery and Metropolitan Museum (etc.), 1986.

Dennistoun, James. *Memoirs of Sir Robert Strange, Knt., Engraver . . . and of His Brother-in-Law Andrew Lumisden, Private Secretary to the Stuart Princes. . . .* 2 vols. London, 1855.

de Piles, Roger ["Du Piles" on title page]. *The Principles of Painting.* Trans. anon. ["And now first Translated into English. By a Painter."] London, 1743.

Dilke, Lady [Emilia Frances (Strong)]. *French Engravers and Draughtsmen of the Eighteenth Century.* London: George Bell, 1902.

Dillenberger, John. *Benjamin West: The Context of His Life's Work with Particular Attention to Paintings with Religious Subject Matter.* San Antonio, Tex.: Trinity University Press, 1977.

Dodd, Thomas. *The Connoisseur's Repertory; or, A Biographical History of Painters, Engravers, Sculptors, and Architects. . . .* 6 vols. only (A–Barr). London, n.d. [1824–1828?].

Dossie, Robert. *The Handmaid to the Arts.* 2d ed. rev. 3 vols. London, 1764.

Douglas, Mary, and Baron Isherwood. *The World of Goods: Towards an Anthropology of Consumption.* New York: Basic Books, 1978.

Dubos ["Du Bos" on title page], Jean Baptiste. *Critical Reflections on Poetry, Painting, and Music. With an Inquiry into the Rise and Progress of the Theatrical Entertainments of the Ancients.* Trans. Thomas Nugent. 1719. 5th ed. rev. London, 1748.

Dunkerton, Jill, Susan Foister, Dillian Gordon, and Nicholas Penny. *Giotto to Dürer: Early Renaissance Painting in the National Gallery.* New Haven: Yale University Press (with National Gallery Publications), 1991.

Earland, Ada. *John Opie and His Circle.* London: Hutchinson, 1911.

Eaves, Morris. "Blake and the Artistic Machine: An Essay in Decorum and Technology." *PMLA* 92 (1977): 903–27.

——. Review of *The Paintings and Drawings of William Blake,* by Martin Butlin. *Studies in Romanticism* 25 (1986): 147–54.

——. Review of *The Political Theory of Painting from Reynolds to Hazlitt: "The Body of the Public,"* by John Barrell. *Studies in Romanticism* 27 (1988): 429–42.

——. "The Title-Page of *The Book of Urizen.*" In *William Blake: Essays in Honour of Sir Geoffrey Keynes,* ed. Morton D. Paley and Michael Phillips, 225–30. Oxford: Clarendon, 1973.

——. "What Is the 'History of Publishing'?" *Publishing History* 2 (1977): 57–77.

——. *William Blake's Theory of Art.* Princeton: Princeton University Press, 1982.

Edwards, Edward. *Anecdotes of Painters Who Have Resided or Been Born in England, with Critical Remarks on Their Productions.* London, 1808.

Ellis, Edwin J., and William Butler Yeats, eds. *The Works of William Blake, Poetic, Symbolic, and Critical.* 3 vols. London: Quaritch, 1893.

Elmes, James. *A General and Bibliographical Dictionary of the Fine Arts. Containing Explanations of the Principal Terms Used in the Arts of Painting, Sculpture, Architecture, and Engraving, in All Their Various Branches. . . .* London, 1826.

Erdman, David V. "Grub Street behind the Skirts of Margaret Nicholson." *Factotum* no. 12 (July 1981): 25–27.

——. " 'Terrible Blake in His Pride': An Essay on *The Everlasting Gospel.*" In *From Sensibility to Romanticism: Essays Presented to Frederick A. Pottle,* ed. Frederick W. Hilles and Harold Bloom, 331–56. New York: Oxford University Press, 1965.

Essick, Robert N. *The Separate Plates of William Blake: A Catalogue.* Princeton: Princeton University Press, 1983.

——. *William Blake and the Language of Adam.* Oxford: Clarendon, 1989.

——. *William Blake, Printmaker.* Princeton: Princeton University Press, 1980.

——. *William Blake's Commercial Book Illustrations.* Oxford: Clarendon, 1991.

Faithorne, William. *The Art of Graveing and Etching.* 1662. Introduction by Jacob Kainen. New York: Da Capo, 1970.

Farington, Joseph. *The Diary of Joseph Farington* [1793–1821]. 16 vols. to date. Vols. 1–6 ed. Kenneth Garlick and Angus Macintyre; vols. 7–16 ed. Kathryn Cave. New Haven: Yale University Press, 1978–.

Flaxman, John. *A Letter to the Committee for Raising the Naval Pillar, or Monument, under the Patronage of His Royal Highness the Duke of Clarence.* London, 1799.

Fox, Celina. "The Engravers' Battle for Professional Recognition in Early Nineteenth Century London." *London Journal* 2 (May 1976): 3–31.

Fréart, Roland. *An Idea of the Perfection of Painting.* Trans. John Evelyn. London, 1668.

Friedman, Richard Elliott. *Who Wrote the Bible?* New York: Summit, 1987.

Friedman, Winifred H. *Boydell's Shakespeare Gallery.* New York: Garland, 1976.

Frye, Northrop. *Fearful Symmetry: A Study of William Blake.* Princeton: Princeton University Press, 1947.

——. *A Study of English Romanticism.* New York: Random House, 1968.

Fullerton, Peter. "Patronage and Pedagogy: The British Institution in the Early Nineteenth Century." *Art History* 5 (1982): 59–72.

Fuseli, Henry. *See* Knowles; Wornum.

Gage, John. "An Early Exhibition and the Politics of British Printmaking, 1800–1812." *Print Quarterly* 6 (1989): 123–39.

——. "Magilphs and Mysteries." *Apollo* 80 (1964): 38–41.

Gainsborough, Thomas. *The Letters of Thomas Gainsborough.* Ed. Mary Woodall. Greenwich, Conn.: New York Graphic Society, 1963.

Gay, Peter. "The Emancipation of Art: Burdens of the Past." In *The Science of Freedom,* vol. 2 of *The Enlightenment: An Interpretation,* 216–48. London: Weidenfeld & Nicholson, 1970.

George, Dorothy. *Hogarth to Cruikshank: Social Change in Graphic Satire.* New York: Walker, 1967.

George, Eric. *The Life and Death of Benjamin Robert Haydon, 1786–1846.* London: Oxford University Press, 1948.

Gibson-Wood, Carol. "Jonathan Richardson and the Rationalization of Connoisseurship." *Art History* 7 (1984): 38–56.

Gilchrist, Alexander. *Life of William Blake, "Pictor Ignotus."* 2 vols. London and Cambridge, 1863.

Gilpin, William. *An Essay on Prints.* 4th ed. London, 1792.

Godfrey, Richard T. *Printmaking in Britain: A General History from Its Beginnings to the Present Day.* New York: New York University Press, 1978.

Goldsmith, Oliver. *An Enquiry into the Present State of Polite Learning in Europe.* 2d ed. rev. London, 1774.

Graves, Algernon. "A Light on Alderman Boydell and the Shakespeare Gallery." *Magazine of Art* 21 (1897): 143–48.

Green, Valentine. *A Review of the Polite Arts in France, at the Time of Their Establishment under Louis the XIVth, Compared with Their Present State in England: . . . in a Letter to Sir Joshua Reynolds. . . .* London, 1782.

Greene, Donald. " 'Sweet Land of Liberty': Libertarian Rhetoric and Practice in Eighteenth-Century Britain." In *The American Revolution and Eighteenth Century Culture,* ed. Paul J. Korshin, 127–55. New York: AMS Press, 1986.

Gunn, Thomas G. "The Mechanization of Design and Manufacturing." *Scientific American* 247 (September 1982): 115–30.

Hagstrum, Jean. *The Sister Arts: The Tradition of Literary Pictorialism and English Poetry from Dryden to Gray.* Chicago: Chicago University Press, 1958.

Hall, Jean. "Blake's *Everlasting Gospel.*" *Blake Studies* 4 (Autumn 1971): 61–72.

Harmon, Leon D. "The Recognition of Faces." *Scientific American* 229 (November 1973): 70–82.

Hartley, David. *Observations on Man, His Frame, His Duty, and His Expectations.* 2 vols. London, 1749.

Haydon, Benjamin. "Painting." In *Painting, and the Fine Arts.* Edinburgh, 1838. [This edition reprints Haydon's article for the 7th ed. of the *Encyclopaedia Britannica,* along with Hazlitt's "Fine Arts" for the same edition.]

——. *Some Enquiry into the Causes Which Have Obstructed the Advance of Historical Painting, for the Last Seventy Years in England.* London, 1829.

Hazlitt, William. "The Catalogue Raisonné of the British Institution." In *The Complete Works of William Hazlitt,* ed. P. P. Howe, 18:104–11. London: Dent, 1933.

——. "An Enquiry Whether the Fine Arts Are Promoted by Academies and Public Institutions." In *The Life of Titian,* by James Northcote, 2:370–83 (app. 8). London, 1830.

Held, Julius S. "Rubens and Vorsterman." In *Rubens and His Circle,* ed. Anne W. Lowenthal, David Rosand, and John Walsh, Jr., 114–25. Princeton: Princeton University Press, 1982.

Helms, Randel. "The Genesis of *The Everlasting Gospel.*" *Blake Studies* 9 (1980): 122–60.

Herrmann, Frank, ed. *The English as Collectors: A Documentary Chrestomathy.* New York: Norton, 1972.

Hichberger, J. W. M. *Images of the Army: The Military in British Art, 1815–1914.* Studies in Imperialism. Manchester: Manchester University Press, 1988.

Hill, Christopher. "Protestantism and the Rise of Capitalism." In *Essays in the Economic and Social History of Tudor and Stuart England in Honour of R. H. Tawney,* ed. F. J. Fisher, 15–39. Cambridge: Cambridge University Press, 1961.

Hind, Arthur M. *Bartolozzi and Other Stipple Engravers Working in England at the End of the Eighteenth Century.* New York: Frederick Stokes, n.d. [1912].

——. *Engraving in England in the Sixteenth and Seventeenth Centuries: A Descriptive Catalogue with Introductions.* 2 vols. Cambridge: Cambridge University Press, 1952.

——. *A History of Engraving and Etching from the Fifteenth Century to the Year 1914.* 3d ed. Boston: Houghton Mifflin, 1923.

——. *John Raphael Smith and the Great Mezzotinters of the Time of Reynolds.* New York: Frederick A. Stokes, n.d. [1911].

Hoare, Prince. *An Inquiry into the Requisite Cultivation and Present State of the Arts of Design in England.* London, 1806.

Hogarth, William. *The Analysis of Beauty: With the Rejected Passages from the Manuscript Drafts and Autobiographical Notes.* 1753. Ed. Joseph Burke. Oxford: Clarendon, 1955.

Hollander, John. *The Untuning of the Sky: Ideas of Music in English Poetry, 1500–1700.* Princeton: Princeton University Press, 1961.

Holt, Elizabeth Gilmore, ed. *The Triumph of Art for the Public: The Emerging Role of Exhibitions and Critics.* Garden City, N.Y.: Doubleday/Anchor, 1979.

Hudson, Derek. *Sir Joshua Reynolds: A Personal Study.* London: Geoffrey Bles, 1958.

Hughes, Richard T., and C. Leonard Allen. *Illusions of Innocence: Protestant Primitivism in America, 1630–1875.* Chicago: University of Chicago Press, 1988.

Hunnisett, Basil. *Steel-Engraved Book Illustration in England.* London: Scolar, 1980.

Hutchison, Sidney. *The History of the Royal Academy, 1768–1968.* New York: Taplinger, 1968.

"Irish Artists II." *New Monthly Magazine* 10 (1824): 513.

Ivins, William. *Prints and Visual Communication.* London: Routledge, 1953.

Jones, W. Bell. *See* Boydell.

Jussim, Estelle. *Visual Communication and the Graphic Arts: Photographic Technologies in the Nineteenth Century.* New York: Bowker/Xerox, 1974.

Kermode, Frank. *The Classic.* London: Faber & Faber, 1975.

Keynes, Geoffrey. "Blake and the Wedgwoods." In *Blake Studies: Essays on His Life and Work,* 2d ed., 59–65. Oxford: Clarendon, 1971.

Kibel, Alvin C. "The Canonical Text." *Daedalus,* Winter 1983, 239–53.

Knowles, John. *The Life and Writings of Henry Fuseli, M.A.R.A.* 3 vols. London, 1831.

Kramnick, Isaac. "Children's Literature and Bourgeois Ideology: Observations on Culture and Industrial Capitalism in the Later Eighteenth Century." *Studies in Eighteenth-Century Culture* 12 (1983): 11–44.

——. "The 'Great National Discussion': The Discourse of Politics in 1787." *William and Mary Quarterly* 45 (January 1988): 3–32.

——. *Republicanism and Bourgeois Radicalism: Political Ideology in Late Eighteenth-Century England and America.* Ithaca: Cornell University Press, 1990.

——. "Republican Revisionism Revisited." *American Historical Review* 87 (June 1982): 629–64.

Kruger, Barbara. "What's High, What's Low—and Who Cares?" *New York Times,* 9 September 1990, sec. 2 (Arts & Leisure): 43.

Lakoff, George, and Mark Turner. *More than Cool Reason: A Field Guide to Poetic Metaphor.* Chicago: University of Chicago Press, 1989.

Lamb, Charles. "On the Genius and Character of Hogarth; with Some Remarks on a Passage in the Writings of the Late Mr. Barry." In *The Works of Charles and Mary Lamb,* ed. E. V. Lucas, 1:70–86. London: Methuen, 1903.

Landseer, John. *Lectures on the Art of Engraving, Delivered at the Royal Institution of Great Britain.* London, 1807.

——. *Observations on the Engraved Gems, Brought from Babylon to England by Abraham Lockett, Esq. . . . Considered with Reference to Early Scriptural History.* London, 1817.

——. *Saboean Researches, in a Series of Essays . . . on the Engraved Hieroglyphics of Chaldea, Egypt, and Canaan.* London, 1823.

Lanham, Richard A. "Digitizing Some Keywords." *Computers and Composition* 6 (August 1989): 123–28.

Leith, James A. *The Idea of Propaganda in France 1750–1799: A Study in the History of Ideas.* University of Toronto Romance Series, 8. Toronto: University of Toronto Press, 1965.

Leppmann, Wolfgang. *Winckelmann.* New York: Knopf, 1970.

Leslie, Charles Robert, and Tom Taylor. *Life and Times of Sir Joshua Reynolds: With Notices of Some of His Contemporaries.* 2 vols. London, 1865.

Levis, Howard C. *A Descriptive Bibliography of the Most Important Books in the English Language Relating to the Art and History of Engraving and the Collecting of Prints.* 1912. London: Dawson's of Pall Mall, 1974.

Lipking, Lawrence. *The Ordering of the Arts in Eighteenth-Century England.* Princeton: Princeton University Press, 1970.

Lippincott, Louise. *Selling Art in Georgian London: The Rise of Arthur Pond.* New Haven: Yale University Press for the Paul Mellon Centre for Studies in British Art, 1983.

Locquin, Jean. *La Peinture d'histoire en France de 1747 à 1785.* Paris, 1912.

Mann, Paul. "Apocalypse and Recuperation: Blake and the Maw of Commerce." *ELH* 52 (1985): 1–32.

Martz, Louis L., ed. *The Anchor Anthology of Seventeenth Century Verse.* 2 vols. Garden City, N.Y.: Doubleday, 1973.

Marx, Karl, and Frederick Engels. *The German Ideology: Part One, with Selections from Parts Two and Three, Together with Marx's "Introduction to a Critique of Political Economy."* Ed. C. J. Arthur. New York: International Publishers, 1970.

Mayor, A. Hyatt. *Prints and People: A Social History of Printed Pictures.* New York: Metropolitan Museum of Art, 1971.

McCulloch, J. R., ed. *Early English Tracts on Commerce.* Cambridge: Cambridge University Press, 1954.

McKendrick, Neil. "Commercialization and the Economy." In *The Birth of a Consumer Society,* by McKendrick et al., 9–196. London: Europa, 1982.

——. "Josiah Wedgwood and Factory Discipline." *Historical Journal* 4 (1961): 30–55.

——. "Josiah Wedgwood: An Eighteenth-Century Entrepreneur in Salesmanship and Marketing Techniques." *Economic History Review* 12 (1960): 403–33.

McKendrick, Neil, John Brewer, and J. H. Plumb. *The Birth of a Consumer Society: The Commercialization of Eighteenth-Century England.* London: Europa, 1982.

McNairn, Alan. *The Young van Dyck.* Ottawa: National Gallery of Canada, 1980.

Meyerstein, E. H. W. *A Life of Thomas Chatterton.* London: Ingpen & Grant, 1930.

Mill, James. *Commerce Defended.* 1808. Reprints of Economic Classics. New York: Augustus M. Kelley, 1965.

Milton, John. *De Doctrina Christiana.* Ed. Maurice Kelley. Vol. 6 of *Complete Prose Works of John Milton,* ed. Don M. Wolfe. New Haven: Yale University Press, 1973.

——. *The Works of John Milton.* Vol. 1. pt. 1. Ed. Frank Allen Patterson et al. New York: Columbia University Press, 1931.

Mitchell, W. J. T. "Visible Language: Blake's Wond'rous Art of Writing." In *Romanticism and Contemporary Criticism,* ed. Morris Eaves and Michael Fischer, 46–86. Ithaca: Cornell University Press, 1986.

Montesquieu, Charles de Secondat, baron de. *The Spirit of Laws by Montesquieu: A Compendium of the First English Edition.* Ed. David Wallace Carrithers. Berkeley: University of California Press, 1977. [An abridgement based on the 1750 translation by Thomas Nugent.]

More Lyric Odes to the Royal Academicians, by a Distant Relation to the Poet of Thebes, and Laureat to the Academy. London, 1786.

Newman, Gerald. *The Rise of English Nationalism: A Cultural History, 1740–1830.* New York: St. Martin's Press, 1987.

Northcote, James. *The Life of Titian; with Anecdotes of the Distinguished Persons of His Time.* 2 vols. London, 1830.

Observations on the Present State of the Royal Academy: With Characters of Living Painters, by an Old Artist. London, 1790.

Ogilby, John. *The Entertainment of His Most Excellent Majestie Charles II in His Passage through the City of London to His Coronation.* Ed. Ronald Knowles. Medieval and Renaissance Texts and Studies, 43. Binghamton, N.Y.: Center for Medieval and Early Renaissance Studies, 1988.

"On the Applications of Science to the Fine and Useful Arts." *Art-Union Monthly Journal* 10 (1 December 1848): 363–64.

Opie, John. *See* Wornum.

Osborn, James M. "New Poems by John Denham." *Times Literary Supplement,* 1 September 1966, 788.

Ottley, William Young. *An Inquiry into the Origin and Early History of Engraving on Copper and in Wood. . . .* 2 vols. London, 1816.

Paine, Thomas. *The Rights of Man* (with Edmund Burke, *Reflections on the Revolution in France*). Pt. 1, 1791; pt. 2, 1792. New York: Doubleday/Anchor, 1989.

Paley, Morton D. *The Apocalyptic Sublime.* New Haven: Yale University Press, 1986.

——. *The Continuing City: William Blake's "Jerusalem."* Oxford: Clarendon, 1983.

——. *William Blake.* Oxford: Phaidon, 1978.

——. "William Blake, the Prince of the Hebrews, and the Woman Clothed with the Sun." In *William Blake: Essays in Honour of Sir Geoffrey Keynes,* ed. Morton D. Paley and Michael Phillips, 260–93. Oxford: Clarendon, 1973.

——. "'Wonderful Originals'—Blake and Ancient Sculpture." In *Blake in His Time,* ed. Robert N. Essick and Donald Pearce, 170–97. Bloomington: Indiana University Press, 1978.

Pasquin, Anthony [John Williams]. *An Authentic History of the Professors of Painting, Sculpture, and Architecture, Who Have Practiced in Ireland; Involving Original Letters from Sir Joshua Reynolds, Which Prove Him to Have Been Illiterate. To Which Are Added, Memoirs of the Royal Academicians; Being an Attempt to Improve the Taste of the Realm.* London, n.d. [1796?]. [Includes several works cited separately: "Addenda; or, Sir Joshua Reynolds Developed," "A Liberal Critique on the Exhibition for 1794," "The Royal Academicians," and "A Critical Guide to the Exhibition of the Royal Academy, for 1796."]

Paulson, Ronald. *Book and Painting: Shakespeare, Milton, and the Bible: Literary Texts and the Emergence of English Painting.* Knoxville: University of Tennessee Press, 1982.

Pears, Iain. *The Discovery of Painting: The Growth of Interest in the Arts in England, 1680–1768.* New Haven: Yale University Press for the Paul Mellon Centre for Studies in British Art, 1988.

Penny, Nicholas, ed. *Reynolds.* New York: Abrams, 1986.

Petitjean, Charles, and Charles Wickert. *Catalogue de l'oeuvre gravé de Robert Nanteuil.* Paris: Loys Delteil & Maurice le Garrec, 1925.

Pilkington, Rev. Matthew. *A Dictionary of Painters from the Revival of the Art to the Present Period.* Ed. Henry Fuseli. Rev. ed. London, 1805.

——. *A General Dictionary of Painters.* Ed. Allan Cunningham. Rev. ed. London, 1840. [Cunningham added an introductory essay, "Modern Painting," and 26 new lives, and he omitted all the technical terms defined in earlier editions.]

The Plan of an Academy for the Better Cultivation, Improvement and Encouragement of Painting, Sculpture, Architecture, and the Arts of Design in General. . . . London, 1775.

Plan of the Shakespeare Lottery. London, 1804.

Pliny. *Natural History.* Trans. H. Rackham. 10 vols. Loeb Classical Library. Cambridge: Harvard University Press, 1952.

Pocock, J. G. A. *The Machiavellian Moment: Florentine Political Thought and the Atlantic Republican Tradition.* Princeton: Princeton University Press, 1975.

Pointon, Marcia. "Portrait-Painting as a Business Enterprise in London in the 1780s." *Art History* 7 (1984): 187–205.

Pressly, William L. *James Barry: The Artist as Hero.* London: Tate Gallery, 1983.

——. *The Life and Art of James Barry.* New Haven: Yale University Press for the Paul Mellon Centre for Studies in British Art, 1981.

Prown, Jules David. *John Singleton Copley.* 2 vols. Cambridge: Harvard University Press for National Gallery (Washington), 1966.

Pye, John, II. *Evidence Relating to the Art of Engraving Taken before the Select Committee of the House of Commons, on Arts, 1836. . . .* London, 1836.

——. *Patronage of British Art, An Historical Sketch.* London, 1845.

Quintilian. *The Institutio Oratoria of Quintilian.* Trans. H. E. Butler. 4 vols. Loeb Classical Library. Cambridge: Harvard University Press, 1922.

Read, Dennis M. "The Context of Blake's 'Public Address': Cromek and the Chalcographic Society." *Philological Quarterly* 60 (1981): 69–86.

——. "The Rival *Canterbury Pilgrims* of Blake and Cromek: Herculean Figures in the Carpet." *Modern Philology* 86 (1988): 171–90.

Rees, Abraham, et al. *The Cyclopaedia; or, Universal Dictionary of Arts, Sciences, and Literature.* 39 vols. London, 1819.

Reilly, Robin. *Wedgwood.* 2 vols. New York: Stockton, 1989. [Vol. 1 comprises Josiah Wedgwood's life and work.]

Reitlinger, Gerald. *The Economics of Taste.* 3 vols. Vol. 1. London: Barrie & Rockliff, 1961.

Reynolds, Sir Joshua. *Discourses on Art.* Ed. Robert R. Wark. San Marino, Calif.: Huntington Library, 1959.

——. *The Letters of Sir Joshua Reynolds.* Ed. Frederick W. Hilles. Cambridge: Cambridge University Press, 1929.

Richardson, Jonathan. *The Works of Jonathan Richardson . . . Intended as a Supplement to the Anecdotes of Painters and Engravers* [by Horace Walpole]. Strawberry Hill and London, 1792.

Robinson, Henry Crabb. *Diary, Reminiscences, and Correspondence of Henry Crabb Robinson, Barrister-at-Law, F.S.A.* Ed. Thomas Sadler. 2d ed. 3 vols. London: Macmillan, 1869.

Roscoe, William. *On the Origin and Vicissitudes of Literature, Science and Art, and Their Influence on the Present State of Society. A Discourse, Delivered on the Opening of the Liverpool Royal Institution, 25th November, 1817.* Liverpool, 1817.

Rouquet, André. *The Present State of the Arts in England.* 1775. Facs. rpt. London: Cornmarket, 1970.

Rowlandson, Thomas, and A. C. Pugin. *The Microcosm of London.* London, 1808–1811.

Ruskin, John. *The Elements of Drawing.* London, 1857.

Saunders, J. W. *The Profession of English Letters.* Studies in Social History. London: Routledge & Kegan Paul, 1964.

Schama, Simon. *Citizens: A Chronicle of the French Revolution.* New York: Knopf, 1989.

Sheard, Wendy Sherman, and John T. Paoletti, eds. *Collaboration in Italian Renaissance Art.* New Haven: Yale University Press, 1978.

Shee, Martin Archer. *Rhymes on Art; or, The Remonstrance of a Painter: . . . Including Strictures on the State of the Arts, Criticism, Patronage and Public Taste.* London, 1805 (1st and 2d eds.), 1806 (3d ed.).

Slive, Seymour. *Rembrandt and His Critics, 1630–1730.* The Hague: Martinus Nijhoff, 1953.

Smith, Adam. *An Inquiry into the Nature and Causes of the Wealth of Nations.* 1776. Ed. R. H. Campbell, A. S. Skinner, and W. B. Todd. 2 vols. Oxford: Clarendon, 1976.

Smith, John Thomas. *Nollekens and His Times: Comprehending a Life of That Celebrated Sculptor; and Memoirs of Several Contemporary Artists, from the Time of Roubiliac, Hogarth, and Reynolds, to that of Fuseli, Flaxman, and Blake.* 2 vols. London, 1828.

Spitzer, Leo. *Classical and Christian Ideas of World Harmony: Prolegomena to an Interpretation of the Word "Stimmung."* Ed. Anna Granville Hatcher. Baltimore: Johns Hopkins University Press, 1963.

Stannard, W. J. *The Art Exemplar: A Guide to Distinguish One Species of Print from Another. . . .* London, n.d. [1860?]. [Ten copies printed.]

Stevenson, R. A. M. *Peter Paul Rubens.* 2d ["new"] ed. London: Seeley, 1909.

Strange, Robert. *An Inquiry into the Rise and Establishment of the Royal Academy of Arts. To Which Is Prefixed, A Letter to the Earl of Bute.* London, 1775.

Strutt, Joseph. *A Biographical Dictionary Containing an Historical Account of All the Engravers from the Earliest Period of the Art of Engraving to the Present Time. . . .* 2 vols. London, 1785, 1786.

Tannenbaum, Leslie. *Biblical Tradition in Blake's Early Prophecies: The Great Code of Art,* 201–24. Princeton: Princeton University Press, 1982.

Taylor, Gary. *Reinventing Shakespeare: A Cultural History, from the Restoration to the Present.* New York: Weidenfeld & Nicolson, 1989.

Taylor, W. B. Sarsfield. *The Origin, Progress, and Present Condition of the Fine Arts in Great Britain and Ireland.* 2 vols. London, 1841.

Todd, Ruthven. "Blake's Dante Plates—Revised Version." *Book Collecting and Library Monthly* no. 6 (1968): 164–71.

Tresham, Henry, and William Young Ottley ["the executive part under the management of Peltro William Tompkins, Esq., Historical Engraver to Her Majesty"]. *The British Gallery of Pictures, Selected from the Most Admired Productions of the Old Masters, in Great Britain; Accompanied with Descriptions, Historical and Critical.* London, 1818.

Turnbull, George. *A Treatise on Ancient Painting, Containing Observations on the Rise, Progress, and Decline of That Art amongst the Greeks and Romans . . . To Which Are Added Some Remarks on the Peculiar Genius, Character, and Talents of Raphael, Michael Angelo, Nicholas Poussin, and Other Celebrated Modern Masters. . . .* London, 1740.

Vasari, Giorgio. *See* Aglionby.

Vertue, George. *A Catalogue and Description of King Charles the First's Capital Collection of Pictures, Limnings, Statues, Bronzes, Medals, and Other Curiosities. . . .* London, 1757.

Viscomi, Joseph. *Blake and the Idea of the Book.* Princeton University Press, 1992.

von Erffa, Helmut, and Allen Staley. *The Paintings of Benjamin West.* New Haven: Yale University Press, 1986.

Wackernagel, Martin. *The World of the Florentine Renaissance Art Market: Projects and Patrons, Workshop and Art Market.* 1938. Trans. Alison Luchs. Princeton: Princeton University Press, 1981.

Wakeman, Geoffrey. *Victorian Book Illustration: The Technical Revolution.* Newton Abbot, Devon.: David & Charles, 1973.

Walpole, Horace. *Anecdotes of Painting in England, with Some Account of the Principal Artists; and Incidental Notes on Other Arts; Collected by the Late Mr. George Vertue; and Now Digested and Published from His Original Mss. by Mr. Horace Walpole.* 2d ed. 4 vols. Strawberry Hill, 1765–1771.

——. *Catalogue of Engravers, Who Have Been Born, or Resided in England; Digested by Mr. Horace Walpole from the Mss. of Mr. George Vertue; to Which Is Added an Account of the Life and Works of the Latter.* Strawberry Hill, 1763.

——. *The Correspondence of Horace Walpole.* Ed. W. S. Lewis. Vol. 33, pt. 2. New Haven: Yale University Press, 1965.

Warburton, William. *The Divine Legation of Moses in Nine Books.* 4th ed. 6 vols. London: 1755–1788. [Vol. 1, 1755, contains pt. 1, bks. 1 and 2, and pt. 2; vol. 2 is missing; vol. 3, 1765, bk. 4; vol. 4, 1765, bk. 5; vol. 5, 1765, bk. 6.]

Ward, Aileen. "Canterbury Revisited: The Blake-Cromek Controversy." *Blake/An Illustrated Quarterly* 22 (Winter 1988–1989): 80–92.

Waterhouse, Ellis K. *Three Decades of British Art, 1740–1770.* Memoirs of the American Philosophical Society, 63. Philadelphia: American Philosophical Society, 1965.

Watson, James. *The History of the Art of Printing.* 1713. English Bibliographical Sources, ser. 3, Printers' Manuals. London: Gregg, 1965.

Weber, Max. *The Protestant Ethic and the Spirit of Capitalism.* Trans. Talcott Parsons. London: Unwin, 1930.

Wesley, John. *Explanatory Notes upon the New Testament.* 1754. New York, 1818.

Westmacott, Charles M. *A Descriptive and Critical Catalogue to the Exhibition of the Royal Academy.* London, 1823.

White, Christopher, David Alexander, and Ellen D'Oench. *Rembrandt in Eighteenth Century England.* New Haven: Yale Center for British Art, 1983.

Whitehouse, Rev. John. *An Elegaic Ode to the Memory of Sir Joshua Reynolds, Late President of the Royal Academy.* London, 1792.

Whitley, William T. *Artists and Their Friends in England, 1700–1799.* 2 vols. London: Medici Society, 1928.

Wicksteed, J., and T. Worlidge. *A Specimen of a Select Collection of Drawings, from the Most Curious Antique Gems; Etched in a Peculiar Manner by T. Worlidge, Painter. To Which Are Prefixed Observations on the Art of Engraving on Gems, with Their Nature, Composition, and Subjects in General.* London, 1766.

Williams, Raymond. *Communications.* 3d ed. rev. Harmondsworth: Penguin, 1976.

Wimsatt, W. K., Jr., and Cleanth Brooks. *Literary Criticism: A Short History.* New York: Random House, 1957.

Winckelmann, Abbé Johann Joachim. *History of Ancient Art.* Trans. G. Henry Lodge. 4 vols. in 2. New York: Ungar, 1968.

——["Winkelmann" on title page]. *Reflections on the Painting and Sculpture of the Greeks: With Instructions for the Connoisseur, and An Essay on Grace in Works of Art.* Trans. Henry Fuseli. London, 1765. [Contents: *Reflections,* 1–64; "A Letter, Containing Objections against the Foregoing Reflexions," 65–126 (initialed "AN"); "An Answer to the Foregoing Letter, and a Further Explication of the Subject," 143–247; "Instructions for the Connoisseur," 249–70; "On Grace," 271–87. Though the essays following *Reflections* are anonymous, they are also by Winckelmann.]

——. *Winckelmann: Writings on Art.* Ed. David Irwin. London: Phaidon, 1972.

Winn, James Anderson. *Unsuspected Eloquence: A History of the Relations between Poetry and Music.* New Haven: Yale University Press, 1981.

Winstanley, Gerrard. *The Works of Gerrard Winstanley.* Ed. George Sabine. Ithaca: Cornell University Press, 1941.

Wordsworth, William. *The Poetical Works of William Wordsworth.* Ed. Ernest de Selincourt and Helen Darbishire. 4 vols. Oxford: Clarendon, 1940–1949.

Wornum, Ralph N. *Lectures on Painting, by the Royal Academicians: Barry, Opie, and Fuseli.* London, 1848.

Yarrington, Alison. *The Commemoration of the Hero, 1800–1864: Monuments to the British Victors of the Napoleonic Wars.* New York: Garland, 1988.

——. "Nelson the Citizen Hero: State and Public Patronage in Monumental Sculpture, 1805–18." *Art History* 6 (1983): 315–29.

Youngquist, Paul. *Madness and Blake's Myth.* University Park: Pennsylvania State University Press, 1989.

Zuboff, Shoshana. *In the Age of the Smart Machine: The Future of Work and Power.* New York: Basic Books, 1988.

INDEX

Page references to illustrations appear in **boldface type.**

Aaron, 114–15, 117, 119, 121, 130, 131
Abraham, 112, 130
Ackermann, Rudolph, 24, 77, 253
Acquisition, pattern of, 8–9, 17–19, 20–25, 28–31, 79, 103, 137–38, 140, 145–46. *See also* Eclecticism; Improvement
Acts, Book of, 132
Aglionby, William, 3, 9, 21, 28, 42, 243
Aholiab, 118–20, 129
Alexander, David, 33, 72
Alexander the Great, 12, 26
Allston, Washington, 251
Alsop, Joseph, 10n
Altick, Richard D., 53
Analogy in art history, 25–27, 44, 52, 80, 90, 139–43, 147–48. *See also* Painting: and poetry
Anticommercialism. *See* Commerce: opposition to
Antiquarian Society, 40, 142
Aquatint. *See* Engraving: tonal processes of
Art, history of: Barry's, 8–14, 17, 22–23, 26–31; Blake's, 135–47; Boydell's, 54–55; Cunningham's, 101–5; Hazlitt's, 96–101; primacy of, 140. *See also* Conspiracy; English school of painting; Engraving: histories of
Art-Union, 153–54, 190
Arundel, Thomas Howard, Earl of, 216
Audience: as Blake's "public," 162–63, 170; as community, 148–52; as consumers, 67–69, 224, 235, 259; and dealers, 89–92, 169, 224; Hazlitt's critique of, 99–100; as objects of seduction, 250–51; as patrons, 104; vulgarity of, 99, 114, 172. *See also* Education; Exhibitions; Patrons and patronage

Babylon, 124–25, 158
Bacon, Francis, 44–45, 146, 164
Baillie, Capt. William, 237, **239**
Balance de la peinture, 17–19, 23
Banks, Thomas, 52
Barrell, John, 149–50
Barry, James, xxiii; Adelphi paintings of, 47–49; on art history, 8–15, 17, 19, 20n, 22, 26–31, 62, 133, 139–40, 154, 160, 206; Blake's view of, 167–68, 171; on engraving, 69; on harmony, 243, 246–47; on Hogarth, 101, 103; on patronage, 99, 104–5, 108–9, 143–45, 159; on public collections, 79–80; on Rembrandt, 240–41; *Commerce or the Triumph of the Thames,* **47–48;** *Inquiry,* **4–6**; self-portrait, **7;** mentioned, 36, 74, 82, 89, 118, 152, 169
Bartolozzi, Francesco, xxiii, 15, 40, 53, 74, 89, 107–8, 118, 155–56, 161, 187, 207, 232, 255n; *Clytie,* 226–**27;** engraved ticket, 52–**53;** *Head of a Young Monk,* **234**–35
Basire, James, xxiii, 173, 182, 188, 253
Bate's New Process, **190**–91
Beatrizet, Nicholas, **200**
Behnes, William, **190**–91
Bennett, Shelley M., 26n
Bentley, G. E., Jr., 59, 120n, 130, 167, 227
Bentley, Thomas, 38
Benwell, J. Hodges, 228
Best, Geoffrey, 86
Bestland, C., 15, **16–17**
Bezaleel, 118, 119–20, 122–23, 129
Bible as code of art, 109–21, 134–36, 265–66. *See also* Christianity; Engraving: Christian history of, in New Testament, *and* in Old Testament; Gospel
Bindman, David, 65, 171n
Blair, Robert, 2, 171, 227, 262–63
Blake, Catherine, 120, 253
Blake, Robert, 267
Blake, William: and Boydell, 34n, 36, 58–59; and exhibition of 1809, 2, 157, 167, 265; fears insanity, 166–67; after Felpham, 1–3, 232; at Felpham, 122–23; technical repertory of, 252–53
—annotations: to Lavater, 148; to Reynolds, 25, 141, 145–46, 175, 195, 207, 212, 240, 259, 261, 269; to Swedenborg, 134, 148
—*Public Address:* argument of, summarized, 176–77; class in, 168–74; conspiracy in, 136, 145, 158–64, 176; harmony in, 240, 255; history of art and engraving in, 141, 155, 158–60; mental and physical oppositions in, 164–68, 177–82, 184–85, 256; occasion for, 1–2, 156–57; originality defended in, 141, 145, 174–75, 205; politics of, 158–60, 266; and romanticism, 236; time and space in, 236–37
—other works: *All Religions Are One,* 134, 148; *America,* 116, 186–**87;** *Approach of Doom,* 265–66, **267,** 268; *Book of Urizen,* 111, **115,** 116, 122, 132; *Chaucers Canterbury Pilgrims,* 156, 161, 176, 180, 182, 186, 232, **258–59,** 260, 262, 265–66; *Christ Blessing,* 197–**98;** *Deaths Door,* **262–63;** *Descriptive Catalogue* 1–2, 109, 127, 136, 138, 140, 142–43, 145, 155, 158, 182, 232, 254; *Everlasting Gospel,* 110, 126–28, 133; *Four Zoas,* 130, 149, 182n; *Gates of Paradise,* 100; Genesis manuscript, 131; *Graphic Muse,* **5,** 6–7; *Head of a Damned Soul,* **252**–53; "If it is True What the Prophets write," 118–20; *Jerusalem,* 109, 111–13, 115, 146, 148–50, **185,** 265–**68;** *Job* engravings, 127–**29,** 175, **264**–66; *Joseph of Arimathea,* 142, 256–**57;** *Laocoön,* 15, 130, 134–35, 162–63, 170; *Last Judgment* painting, 1; *Man Sweeping the Interpreter's Parlour,* 265–**69;** *Marriage of Heaven and Hell,* 113–14, 116, 118, 124–**25,** 128–32, 138, 140, 150, 169, 175; *Milton,* 122–**23,** 130, 138, 142, 149, 162, 169, 179, 181, 184, 255, 266; *Morning Amusement,* 252–

Blake, William (*cont.*)
53; *Naval Pillar,* **82;** *Nelson,* 86–**87;** "Now Art has lost its mental Charms," 139; *On Homers Poetry,* 163; *On Virgil,* 163, 259; *Pitt,* **86**–87; *Portland Vase,* **39**–40; *Romeo and Juliet,* 58–**59;** *Satan Calling Up His Legions,* 269, **270,** 271; *Songs of Innocence and of Experience,* 138; *There Is No Natural Religion,* 134; *Vision of the Last Judgment,* 1, 132–33, 141, 143, 163, 194; *Wrath of Elihu,* **265**
Blake's Work-Room (Shields), **272**
Block portraits, **193–96**
Bluck, J.: *Great Room of the Society,* **24**–25; *Interior of the British Institution,* 76–**77**
Body, 117, 119, 121, 125, 128–33, 134. *See also* Gender; Physical labor
Bolswert, Boetius and Shelte, 207, 213, **214–15**
Bosse, Abraham, 202, 216, 219
Boulton, Matthew, 56
Bowyer, William, 35–36, 59, 62, 74, 81, 88
Boydell, John, xxiv, **71;** as dealer, 43, 67–68, 224; designs Shakespeare Gallery, 33–62; as hero, 63–73; and technology, 153–54, 219, 224; as villain, 70–101, 107–8, 157, 210; mentioned, 28n, 139, 160, 171, 216, 226, 232. *See also* Shakespeare Gallery
Boydell, Josiah, 35, 52, 61n, 70–**71,** 75, 92
Brewer, John, 67n, 96
British Institution, 74–78, 76–**77,** 83–84, 88, 103n, 103, 156
British Mercury, 35
Brothers, Richard, 226
Brown, John, 8, 242
Browne, John, 228
Bruntjen, Sven H. A., 34n, 35, 41, 46, 49, 55–59, 61n, 63, 65–66, 68, 70, 72, 78, 89
Bryan, Michael, 208
Buckeridge, Bainbrigg, 3
Buckingham, George Villiers, 1st Duke of, 216
Bulmer, William, 35
Bunyan, John, 190–91
Burke, Edmund, 15, 30, 34, 38, 52, 66, 146, 150n, 195
Burke, Joseph, 65
Bute, John Stuart, 3d Earl of, 225
Butler, Marilyn, 34n
Butlin, Martin, 111n, 181
Butts, Thomas, 122, 137, 141, 166, 182n, 206n
Byrne, William, 228

Cain, 131
Calonne, Charles Alexandre de, 65
Campbell, Colin, 67n, 171
Caravaggio, Michelangelo da, 224
Carracci, Annibale, 17, 19, 21–22, 79, 98, 159, 176, 184, 206, 208, 224; *Clytie,* 226–**27;** *Dead Christ Mourned,* 10–**11;** *Head of a Young Monk,* **234**–35
Catherine II (the Great), 40
Chalcographic Society, 2, 64, 156, 164n, 180, 219, 226, 246, 260
Chalmers, Alexander, 63, 68, 73
Chalon, A. E., 229
Chambers, William, 49
Champaigne, Philippe de, 216–**17**
Charles I, King, 13, 14, 66, 141, 159, 163n, 216, 218
Charles II, King, 202
Chatham, William Pitt, 1st Earl of, 49, 81, 86
Chatterton, Thomas, 101–2
Chaucer, Geoffrey, 138, 141. *See also* Blake, William, other works: *Chaucers Canterbury Pilgrims*
Chiaroscuro. *See* Engraving: tonal processes of; Harmony; Tone
Christianity: in Blake's history of art, 109–10, 133–52, 158, 160, 162, 265–66, 271; in English-school discourse, 28–29, 81, 102–3, 105, 108–9, 133, 237; and technology, 108. *See also* Engraving: Christian history of, in New Testament, *and* in Old Testament; Gospel; Protestantism
Chronicles 2, Book of, 122–23
Church, Albert Herbert, 40
Cimabue, Giovanni, 10n, 21
Civic humanism, 148–51
Class, social, 168–76, 265–66, 269
Classicism and anticlassicism, 118, 135–36, 143. *See also* Greek and Hellenistic art; Roman art
Claude Lorraine, 61
Cobbett, William, 167
Cockson, Thomas, **260**
Coleridge, Samuel Taylor, 70, 120n, 171, 242, 251
Color, 9–10, 180, 210, 240, 242–43, 246, 250, 254
Commandments. *See* Law, biblical
Commerce: Blake's view of, 159–62, 167–77; as English specialty, 47, 67, 90–91, 162, 167; generalization in, 195; Landseer's view of, 90–92; narratives of, 27, 30, 38, 62, 66–70, 73, 102; opposition to, 63, 73–74, 89–96, 107–8, 139, 169; and patronage, 25, 33, 40, 56, 62, 67–68, 224; Reynolds's view of, 20; Sharp's view of, 224, 231–32; Shee's view of, 92–96; and technology, 153–54. *See also* Dealers and middlemen
Community. *See* Audience
Conception: adjusted to execution, 207, 213, 256; divided from execution, 108, 121–22, 172–73, 177–82, 247–48; Hogarth's, 219; reunited with execution, 173, 177. *See also* Division of labor
Connoiseur [sic] Admiring a Dark Night Piece, **235**
Connoisseurs, 171, 173, 180–81, **235**
Conspiracy: in Barry's art history, 31; in Blake's art history, 136–47, 163–68, 260–72; as counter-arts, 159–61, 167, 171, 173–77, 255–56; in English-school discourse, 143–45; in Landseer's history of engraving, 89, 91
Constable, John, 61, 74
Consumption, 67–69, 94–95. *See also* Audience; Patrons and patronage
Contraries, 113, 132, 136, 146–47, 149
Cook, Tom, **222–23**
Copley, John Singleton, xxiv, 15, 58, 82, 86, 186–87; *Death of Major Peirson,* 49, **50–52;** *Siege of Gibraltar,* 52–**53**
Corinthians 2, Epistle to, 119, 126
Correggio, 98–99, 101, 172, 176, 235, 254–56, 269
Cort, Cornelis, 206–7, **208,** 209
Counter-arts. *See* Conspiracy
Craig, W. M., 246
Creation, 116, 126
Cromek, Robert, xxiv, 2, 156, 246, 262–63
Cromwell, Oliver, 160
Cumberland, George, 2, 38, 49, 79, 112, 135, 165, 167n, 175, 205, 265
Cunningham, Allan, xxiv, 15, 30, 43, 61, 63, 73, 75, 78, 84, 96, 101–5, 144, 223, 258–59, 266

Damer, Anne, 52
Damrosch, Leopold, 109n
Dance, George (the Younger), 35, 52
Daniel, Book of, 162
Darwin, Erasmus, 39
David, King, 121, 128, 130–31
Davy, Humphry, 74
Dealers and middlemen, 26, 72; Blake on, 161–62, 169–71, 173; Landseer on, 73–74, 89–92; Sharp on, 224. *See also* Boydell, John: as dealer
Decalogue. *See* Law, biblical
Decline, pattern of, 22, 90
Delattre, Jean Mari, 187
Dempsey, Charles, 10
Denham, John, 67
de Piles, Roger, 3, 17, **18–19,** 23, 117, 247, 250–51
Deuteronomy, Book of, 112
Devereux, Robert, **260**–61
Diderot, Denis, 225
Digitization, 191, 244
Dilke, Lady, 225
Division of labor, 10, 30–31, 93; in Blake's argument, 170, 173, 176–82, 219–23, 237, 226–72; in Enlightenment theory, 248; in history of engraving, 88–91, 153–54, 205, 212–14, 219–33, 253
Dodd, Thomas, 64
Dodsley, Robert, 35
"Doll," 172
Dollar bill, **197**
Dossie, Robert, 195, 202, 244
Douglas, Mary, 94

Drawing, 178–79, 232, 237, 255–56, 264
Dryden, John, 141, 160–61, 177–78, 181, 251
Dubos, Jean Baptiste, 4, 7, 18n, 105
Dudesert (engraver), **200–201**
Dürer, Albert, 138, 160, 176, 203, 205–7
Dusart, Cornelis, **228–29**
Dutch art, 163n

East India Company, 112, 154n
Eaves, Morris, 10n, 115n, 116n, 147, 154, 164n, 177n, 229, 232, 250n
Eclecticism, 10, 15, 18–19, 88, 100, 103, 105, 159, 176, 184, 206, 237; Blake's rejection of, 222, 258–59
Education: of artist, 15, 19, 43, 88–89, 200, 205, 236; of audience, 18, 22, 45, 47, 144, 170–71, 224; Blake's idea of, 271; as English-school strategy, 237; as ignorance, 164, 258. *See also* British Institution; Exhibitions; Royal Academy
Edwards, Edward, 3
Edwards, Richard, 2
Egypt, 112, 115, 121, 123, 134, 158
Eliot, George (Mary Ann Evans), 168
Elizabeth I, Queen, 13, 14, 260
Elmes, James, 110–11, 118
Encouragement, 7, 26, 42, 46–47, 53, 64, 140
English Civil War, 14, 159–61, 243
English school of engraving: and English school of painting, 88; histories of, 56, 64–69, 72–74, 88–92, 107–8, 137–47, 158–82; situation of, 155, 158, 231–33
English school of painting: Blake's history of, 139–47, 157–82; in Blake's *Jerusalem*, 271; commerce in, 27, 157; continental critics of, 2–8, 105, 163; discourse of, summarized, 21–25; foreign artists intruding on, 42, 81, 102, 141, 144, 163; founding of, 14–15; government neglect of, 6, 14; and harmony, 251, 253; interrupted history of, 13–14, 25, 66, 102; and nationalism, 75–88; problem of, 2–8, 20, 23, 41, 54, 144, 184; religious discourse in, 108–10, 133, 264, 271; in Shakespeare Gallery scheme, 34, 41–55
Engraving: and body, 126–33; Christian history of, 107–47; commercial role of, 68–69; "dark manner" of, 240–41, 244; of gems, 130–31; harmony in, 205, 209–10, 213, 219, 224, 226, 229, 234–35, 237–41, 246–47, 262; histories of, 64–69, 72–74, 88–92, 107–8, 110–33, 182–237; line, 153, 155–56, 199, 204–5, 216, 219–35, 260–61, 264–65; market for, 59–60, 64–65, 72–73, 223, 226, 233; mechanization of, 182–272; in New Testament, 126–33; in Old Testament, 112–26, 158; and painting, 3, 47–49, 65, 88, 234; and printing, 186, 188–91; and sculpture, 110, 190; technological disadvantages of, 34, 53, 57, 153–54, 186–88; tonal processes of, 7, 153, 155–56, 219–35, 244–45, 248–49, 255–56, 268; as translation, 206, 262–63. *See also* English school of engraving
Enoch, 132. *See also* Originality: in engraving
Ephesians, Epistle to, 132
Essick, Robert N., 15, 17, 58, 59, 113n, 156, 183–84, 185n, 252, 263, 265, 269
Eternity, 149–50
Execution. *See* Conception
Exhibitions, 35; Barry's, **24**–25, 47–**48**; Blake's, 2, **86–87**, 157, 167, 265; British Institution's program of, 83–84; Copley's, 49, **50–53**; Cumberland's, 79; early English, 46–53; educational, 47, 79; nationalistic, 78–88; Royal Academy's annual, 28–**29**, 46, 49, 97; in Shakespeare Gallery scheme, 35, 46, 49–52, **54–55**; for Wedgwood pottery, 38–40. *See also* British Institution; Royal Academy; Shakespeare Gallery
Exile-and-return narrative, 125–26, 158, 169
Exodus, Book of, 112, 114, 117–18
Externalization, 116–22, 125–33
Ezekiel, Book of, 124–26, 129, 130–32, 160

Faithorne, William, 202, 216, 219
Fall, 116, 126, 132, 147
Farington, Joseph, 15, 68, 75n, 153
Fawkes, W. R., 84
Felpham, 2, 108, 120, 121–23, 134–35, 141, 184, 233
Feminization. *See* Gender
Fielding, Joseph, 60
Finishing, 195, 212–13, 224, 256
Flaxman, John, xxiv–xxv, 38–40, 79, **82**–83, 120, 122, 132, 181, 202
Flemish art, 142, 163n, 182–83, 247–48
Florentine art, 142, 176–77
Forgiveness, 127, 131–32
Foundling Hospital, 46, 49
French art and patronage, 3, 14, 64n, 22, 26–28, 72, 80, 139, 171–72, 224–25
French Revolution, 6, 10, 26, 34, 60, 65–66, 70, 75, 78, 82, 88, 147, 160, 266
Friedman, W. H., 57, 59, 63, 65, 72–73
Friendship, 121, 149
Frye, Northrop, 125, 133
Fuseli, Henry, xxv; *Lectures,* 9–10, 12, 15, 25, 97, 109, 206–7, 240, 243, 246; Milton Gallery of, 35, 81; possible insanity of, 167; *Head of a Damned Soul,* **252;** mentioned, 2, 36, 104, 138, 152, 160, 236

Gage, John, 2n, 156, 233n
Gainsborough, Thomas, 19, 28, 61, 83
Galleries. *See* Exhibitions
Gallery of British Honour, 80–82
Gay, Peter, 3
Gender, 171–73, 250–51, 254–55
Generalization, 194–95, 205–6, 212–13, 247–48, 254–56, 258
Genesis, Book of, 112, 131
Genius: Blake's ideal of, 140–41, 145–46; Cunningham's ideal of, 105; in English-school discourse, 7, 9; Hazlitt's ideal of, 88, 100; imitations of, 213–14; life's labor of, 165
George III, King, xxv, 14, 15, 20–21, 25, 38, 47n, 68, 78, 167, **188**–90
George IV, King, 28, 34
George, Eric, 6
Gibbon, Edward, 145
Gibson-Wood, Carol, 17n, 174n
Gilchrist, Alexander, 156, 182, 262–63
Gillray, James, 49n; *Design for the Naval Pillar,* 82–**83;** *Shakespeare Sacrificed,* **36;** *Titianus Redivivus,* **210**
Gilpin, William, 204–5, 222, 244, 246–48, 250, 256, 258
Giorgione, 254
Giotto, 10n, 154
Gnosticism, 116n
God, 110, 112–19, 123–29, 131–35, 138–39, 251
Godfrey, Richard, 34, 256
Goldsmith, Oliver, 33, 243
Goltzius, Hendrik, 207, **211,** 213, 216
Gospel, 109–10, 127–28, 143
Gothic art, 142
Graves, Robert, 232–**33**
Greek and Hellenistic art, 8–9, 10, 12, 22–23, 28, 38–40, 79, 99, 109, 118–20, 121n, 136, 139–40, 143, 169
Green, Valentine, xxv, 4, 7, 14, 27–28, 44, 49, 119n; *Experiment on a Bird,* 248, **249,** 250; *John Boydell,* 70–**71**
Greene, Donald, 67n
Greuze, Jean-Baptiste, 23
Gunn, Thomas, 213

Hagstrum, Jean, 44
Halftones, 191, **192–93,** 194–96, 244, 264, **265,** 266
Harmon, Leon D., 194
Harmony, 210, 219, 238–59; Blake's view of, 175, 232, 254–59, 269–72; in music, 22n, 242, 271; in Rembrandt, 237–41; social theory of, 226, 251–72; as stage of technical production, 18, 232, 240–41, 243–48, 255–59. *See also* Engraving: harmony in
Hartley, David, 113
Harvey, William, 229
Hastings, Theophilus, 245
Haydon, Benjamin, xxv, **6**–7, 13, 60, 72, 114n
Hayley, William, xxv–xxvi, 2, 35–36, 58–59, 82, 120, 130, 186, 233, 248
Hazlitt, William, xxvi, 91, 96–101, 103n, 105, 144, 171
Head, 129–31
Heart, 116, 120, 125–28, 131–33
Heath, James, xxvi, 34, 49, **50–51,** 52, 229

Hebrews, Epistle to, 132
Hercules, 121
Herod, King, 132
Heroes, 82–83, 86–87
Hesiod, 121
Hieroglyphics, 8, 114n, 115
Hill, Christopher, 151
Hind, Arthur M., 4, 202, 205, 255n, 260
Hiram, King, 123
History, 37, 43, 60, 80–81, 140, 142, 145–47
History painting, 34, 37, 41, 43–44, 47, 53, 55–56, 60–62, 80, 155
Hoare, Prince, xxvi, 25, 28n; on English-school themes, 4, **5,** 7, 13–15, 60–62, 107, 144; on engraving, 69, 108, 155, 251, 253; revives naval monument proposal, 78–82; and Royal Academy, 75n, 97; mentioned, 53, 84, 89, 92, 101, 103, 157
Hogarth, William, 46, 144, 64–65, 69–70, 89; on graphic processes, 211, 244–45; as national painter, 61, 101–4; *Idle 'Prentice Betray'd by His Whore,* 219, **220–23;** mentioned, 19, 46, 49, 83, 138
Holbein, Hans, 19
Homer, 9
Hume, David, 35, 145
Humphry, Ozias, 142
Hunt, John, 157
Hunt, Leigh, 157
Hunt, Robert, 167
Hussey, Giles, 22
Hutchison, Sidney, 7, 23n, 248

Identity, 124, 148
Ignorance, 163–64, 258
Illuminated printing, 185–87, 265–68
Imagination, 124, 131–32, 134–35, 146, 151–52, 178, 237, 271–72
Imitation, 124; vs. originality in Blake's history of art, 135–47, 160–61
Improvement: commercial uses of, 41–42, 45, 47, 54–55, 68–69, 88; in English-school discourse, 9–10, 20–25, 105, 143n; resistance to, 84, 100; technological, 154, 184, 200, 205–35, 242–48
Individualism, 128, 147–52, 174–75, 178, 205, 263–72; as individual merit, 175, 218, 269–72. *See also* Genius
Insanity, 124, 164–68
Institutionalization. *See* British Institution; Exhibitions; Royal Academy; Shakespeare Gallery
Intermeasurability, 213, 232, 266, 269
Internalization, 125–33, 137
Internationalism in art, 9, 15, 43, 162
Isaiah, Book of, 129
Isherwood, Baron, 94
Italian art and patronage, 9–13, 21–23, 28–29, 80, 99, 109, 133, 139–40, 247

Jeremiah, Book of, 124–26, 130, 132, 158
Jesus, 109, 111, 119–20, 126–27, 132–35, 143, 147–48, 271
Job, Book of, 127–28
John, Book of, 119, 126
Johnson, Joseph, 2
Jones, W. Bell, 71
Jordaens, Jakob, 22
Journeymen, 172–73, 177, 183, 223, 232, 265

Keynes, Geoffrey, 39
Kneller, Godfrey, 189, **244–45,** 251
Kruger, Barbara, 182, 226

Labor. *See* Blake, William, *Public Address:* mental and physical oppositions in; Body; Division of labor; Journeymen; Physical labor
Lamech, 111
Landscape painting, 61
Landseer, John, xxvi, 73–74, 129–30; *Angel Binding Satan,* **76;** mentioned, 53, 187, 236, 248
—*Lectures:* on ancient engraving, 110–13, 118, 121; on aquatint, 219; on conspiracy, 89, 92, 144; on dealers, 1, 73–74, 89–92; on division of labor, 202, 204–6; on English engraving, 64, 107–8, 155, 232; occasion for, 70, 74, 83, 88; mentioned, 157
Lanham, Richard, 191
Lavater, Johann Kaspar, 148
Law, biblical, 109, 112–21, 124–28, 131–33
Le Bas, Jacques Philippe, 225
Lee, Nathaniel, 165–66, 177
Leicester, John, 84
Leith, James A., 80–81
Leonardo da Vinci, 12
Leppmann, Wolfgang, 7
Levis, Howard, 222
Liberty, 12, 27, 45, 67, 78
Lincoln, Abraham, **196**
Line, 9–10, 242, 250, 255. *See also* Engraving: line
Linnell, John, 183n, 265
Lipking, Lawrence, 3n, 17n
Lippincott, Louise, 26n, 33, 46, 56, 96
Locke, John, 10, 17n, 21, 45, 146, 174
Los, 109–11, 115, 149, 271
Lotteries, 37, 53, 58–59, 70, 74
Louis XIV, King, 27, 33, 159, 202, 216, 218, 224
Louis XVI, King, 34, 66
Loutherbourg, Philippe Jacques de, **76**
Lowry, Wilson, 130, 183n
Luke, Saint, 111

"Machine" metaphor, 182–84, 189, 199, 223
Macklin, Thomas, 35, 45, 53, 59, 62, 74, 76, 81, 88, 210, 252
Malachi, Book of, 157
Malone, Edmond, 259
Mammon, 139
Maratti, Carlo, 98
Marcantonio Raimondi, 202, 205–8, 216; *Adam and Eve,* **203;** *Venus and Cupid,* **204**–5
Marketing and markets, 10–11, 56, 59–60, 64, 216, 232; schemes to improve, 34–35, 38–40, 157, 160
Martini, Pietro, 28–**29**
Marx, Karl, 168, 174
Matthew, Book of, 109, 129, 163
Mayor, Hyatt, 205
McKendrick, Neil, 35, 38, 40, 57n, 67n, 70
Mechanism and mechanization, 31, 102, 213, 182–272. *See also* Division of labor
Medici family, 13, 52
Medium, artistic, Blake's attitude toward, 184–85. *See also* Translation
Medland, Thomas, 228
Mellan, Claude, 199, **200–201,** 202, 207, 216, 218
Melody, 175, 240, 242, 271
Memory, 119–20, 132
Mengs, Raphael, 98
Metaphor, Blake's use of, 109, 133–35, 142–43, 165
Meteyard, Eliza, 40
Mezzotint. *See* Engraving: tonal processes of
Michelangelo, 10, 13, 19, 21, 44, 79, 138, 142, 146, 150, 160, 164, 202, 236, 255
Middlemen. *See* Dealers and middlemen
Militarism, 61–62, 75–88, 139
Mill, James, 167, 219
Milton, John, 44–45, 119n, 128n, 242; as original artist, 160–61, 166, 176–78, 236; mentioned, 92, 138, 140, 271
Milton Gallery, 35
Mind and body. *See* Blake, William, *Public Address:* mental and physical oppositions in
Mirabeau, Honoré-Gabriel Riqueti, comte de, 80
Mitchell, W. J. T., 111n, 115
Montesquieu, Charles de Secondat, baron de, 4, 7, 25, 105
Moses, 109, 112–17, 126, 131, 132
Music. *See* Harmony; Melody
Muziano, Girolamo, 199–**200**

Nanteuil, Robert, 202, 224; *Charles Benoise,* 216–**17;** *Marin Cureau,* **218**–19
Napoleon Bonaparte, 78, 80, 139
National Gallery, 49, 188n
Nationalism, 22, 37, 43, 47, 49, 61–62, 68, 75–88, 95–96, 101–5

Nature, 102, 105, 251; Blake's idea of, 119–20, 124–25, 130, 135, 171, 237, 266
Naval monument, 47, 78–81, **82–83**
Negations, 132, 149
Nelson, Horatio, 34, 47, 82–83, 86–**87,** 202
Neoclassicism, 38–40, 58, 79, 135
Nicodemus, 126–27
"Niggling," 173, 177
North, Frederick, 82
Northcote, James, 7, 15, 36, 43, 60, 72–73, 78, 97, 99, 219, 228

Opie, John, xxvi, 41; *Lectures,* 10, 202, 254; proposes naval monument, 47, 78, 80–83; *Edward Long,* **230–31,** 232, **233;** *Romeo and Juliet,* 58–**59;** mentioned, 15, 36, 243
Opportunity. *See* Encouragement
Orc, 116
Originality: Blake's idea of, 109, 156–57, 164, 174–75, 177–79, 181, 240–41, 256, 263–72; in engraving, 156–57, 248, 262–69; and imitation in Blake's history of art, 136–47, 147, 177, 206; and individualism in Blake's history of art, 147–52; and virtuosity, 236
Orpheus, 121
Ottley, William Young, 111n, 246

Paine, Thomas, 93–94, 261, 269
Painting: line and color in, 155; mechanization of, 189–90, 207, 212–16; and poetry, 8, 44–46, 60–61, 160, 163, 246. *See also* English school of painting; History painting; Portrait painting; *names of individual painters*
Paley, Morton, 76, 109n, 226
Palmer, Samuel, 130
Pantheon, 80–81
Parry, J., **72**
Pasquin, Anthony (John Williams), 63, 90, 226
Patriotism. *See* Nationalism
Patrons and patronage: Barry on, 144–45; commercial, 33, 67–68, 91; Cunningham on, 104; English, 12–13, 25–31, 56, 144–45; French, 26–28; Hazlitt on, 99; mock-, 144–45; religious, 13–14, 25–26, 46, 117; Sharp on, 224, 226; state, 14, 26–28, 84, 95–96; in Wedgwood's scheme, 40
Paul, Saint, 126, 132, 135, 271
Paulson, Ronald, 43n
Pears, Iain, 23n, 26n, 38, 63–64, 84, 169, 170–72
Pembroke, William Herbert, 3d Earl of, 216
Penny, Nicholas, 7
Pentateuchal history of engraving, 109–21
Pharisees, 126–30, 132
Physical labor, 165, 168, 172–73, 184–85
Picart, Bernard, 204
Pilkington, Rev. Matthew, 15, 104, 206, 212, 247, 250
Pitt, William (the Elder), 1st Earl of Chatham, 49, 81, 86
Pitt, William (the Younger), **86**–87
Pixels, 191–**92**
Plagiarism, 259
Plato, 9, 135, 184
Platonism, 21
Plumb, J. H., 67n
Pocock, J. G. A., 150n
Poco piu, 173, 177–78, 180, 236
Poetry, 4, 108. *See also* Painting: and poetry
Pointon, Marcia, 26n, 30
Pond, Arthur, 33
Pope, Alexander, 121n, 250
Portrait painting, 28, 30, 41–43, 60, 62, 81, 100, 141, 171, 180, **188–90, 230–31,** 232, **233**
Poussin, Nicolas, 10n, 61, 103–4, 240
Pressly, William L., 46–47, 49
Priesthood, 4, 112–22, 124–33, 163
Primitivism, 237
Printing, letterpress, **186,** 188–91
Production, 57–58, 67–68, 160, 212; methods of, 153–54, 167–68, 237, 248, 256–59, 260–61. *See also* Division of labor; Engraving; Technology
Progress. *See* Improvement
Prophets, 122
Protestantism: in Blake's history of art, 141; and commerce, 67n; images in, 13, 46, 81, 102, 99, 119n; and individualism, 128, 147, 151; and republicanism, 141, 158
Prown, Jules D., 53
Psalms, Book of, 128
Pugin, A. C.: *Great Room of the Society,* **24**–25; *Interior of the British Institution,* **76–77**
Pye, John, II, xxvii, 59, 64–67, 69, 72, 74, 89, 236
Pythagoras, 9

Quintilian, 12

Rachel, 112
Raimbach, Abraham, 67
Raimondi, Marcantonio. *See* Marcantonio Raimondi
Raisons naturelles, 4, 7, 25
Ramberg, J. H., 28–**29**
Raphael, 10, 13, 19, 22, 45, 79, 99, 138, 146, 150, 202, 206, 210, 222, 229, 250, 255, 258, 261; *Adam and Eve,* **203;** *Venus,* **204**–5; *Venus and Cupid,* **204**–5
Rasselas, 33
Rawle, S., **54**
Read, Dennis, 2n, 156–57, 222
Rees, Abraham, 15, 130, 240, 242, 254
Reilly, Robin, 38n, 39, 41, 65
Reitlinger, Gerald, 163n
Rembrandt van Rijn, 15, 19, 22, 172–73, 202, 210, 229, 235, 244, 247, 256, 266; *Adoration of the Shepherds,* **240;** *Christ Healing the Sick,* 237, **238–39;** *Student at a Table by Candlelight,* **241**
Reni, Guido, 224, **225,** 226
Repton, Humphrey, 41
Republican politics, 20, 93–95, 141, 158, 259–72
Resolution. *See* Threshold of vision
Revelation, Book of, 129, 131–32
Reynolds, Joshua, xxvii; in Blake's narratives, 142, 150, 160, 172; as colorist, 210, 246, 247, 254, 256, 259; as English-school figurehead, 15, 28, 30, 41, 101–4, 261; English-school themes in *Discourses* of, 19–21, 25, 28, 44, 61, 98, 105, 194, 237, 248, 259, 261; exhibition arranged by, 47; on Shakespeare Gallery, 33, 34–36; *Graphic Muse,* **5**–7; *King George III,* **188**–90; *Queen Charlotte,* **189**–90; mentioned, 1, 23, 60, 84, 152, 235, 243. *See also* Blake, William, annotations: to Reynolds
Richards, I. A., 165n
Richardson, Jonathan, 3, 15, 17, 22, 60, 99, 174n, 243, 264
Robinson, Henry Crabb, 76, 87
Rockingham, Charles Watson-Wentworth, 2d Marquess of, 104
Roman art, 23, 80, 90, 102, 118–20, 139–40, 169
Romanticism, 67n, 100–101, 111, 135, 148, 236, 242
Romney, George, 58, 63
Roscoe, William, 35, 69
Rossetti, Dante Gabriel, 156
Rossetti, W. M., 111n
Roubillac, Louis François, 40
Rouquet, André, 13, 27
Rousseau, Jean-Jacques, 158, 242
Rowlandson, Thomas: *Great Room of the Society,* **24**–25; *Interior of the British Institution,* **76–77**
Royal Academy: and Boydell, 34, 41, 66; and British Institution, 75; in English-school program, 19–20, 23, 25–26, 28, 30, 43, 46, 49, 78–79; engravers in, 74, 88; reaction against, 72n, 91, 96–97, 101, 210, 237; *Exhibition . . . 1787,* 28–**29;** *Royal Academicians,* 15, **16–17;** mentioned, 6, 82
Royal Institution, 74, 88
Rubens, Peter Paul: in Blake's history of art, 141, 158–59, 161, 163–64, 166, 172, 186, 218–19, 232, 240; in English-school discourse, 13, 102; harmony exemplified by, 247, 254–56, 269; systemization of production by, 207, 212–16; *Moses with the Brazen Serpent,* 213, **214–15;** mentioned, 10n, 15, 19, 22, 83, 108, 127
Rumford, Benjamin Thompson, Count, 74
Ruskin, John, 266
Ryland, William Wynne, 88–89, 226

Ste-Geneviève, Church of, 80

St. Paul's Cathedral, 47, 49, 52, 82, 83
Salviati, Francesco de' Rossi, 19
Samuel 2, Book of, 130–31
Sandrart, Joachim von, 206
Saunders, P. W., 68n
Schiavonetti, Luigi ("Louis"), xxvii, 161, 171n, 227, **262,** 263
Science, 39, 45, 61, 271
Scott, David, 262
Scott, John, 246
Scribes, 126–28
Sculptors and sculpture, 82–83, 109–10, 115, 190
Shakespeare, William, 43–44, 61, 138, 236
Shakespeare Gallery: design of, 34–35; English-school discourse exploited by, 41–47, 49, 52, 56, 160; failure of, 56–60, 74, 78; reactions to, 60–69, 73, 78, 81, 88, 92–93, 96, 100, 153–54; *Opening of the Shakespeare Gallery,* **55;** *Romeo and Juliet,* 58–**59;** *Shakespeare Sacrificed,* **36;** *View of the Shakespeare Gallery,* **54.** *See also* Boydell, John; British Institution; Landseer, John
Sharp, William, xxvii, 157, 219, 222, 224, 226, 228, **230–31,** 232, **233,** 234, 236, 244
Shee, Martin Archer, xxvii–xxviii, 20–21, 56, 75, 79, 84, 92–96, 107
Sherwin, John Keyse, 187
Shields, Frederic, **272**
Sin, 146
Singleton, Henry, 15, **16–17**
Sister arts. *See* Painting: and poetry
Smillie, George, **197**
Smith, Adam, 68, 93, 154
Smith, Anker, **37**
Smith, J. T., 144, 224
Society for the Encouragement of Arts, 23, **24**–25, 49
Society for the Encouragement of the Art of Engraving, 156
Solomon, 121, 122–24, 132
Southcott, Joanna, 226
Southey, Robert, 46, 167
Specialization. *See* Division of labor
Spence, Thomas, 167
Spenser, Edmund, 126n
Stevenson, R. A. M., 212
Stipple. *See* Engraving: tonal processes of
Stothard, Thomas, xxviii, 2, 15, 26n, 111n, 181
Strange, Robert, xxviii, 88–90, 107–8, 143, 155–56, 161, 164, 176, 207, 219, 224, **225,** 226–27, 232, 234, 244, 248n, 254–55
Strutt, Joseph, 111–12, 118, 131n, 202–4, 207, 224
Stuart, Gilbert, 34, **193**
Stubbs, George, 40, 101
Swedenborg, Emanuel, 134, 148, 271
Swinburne, Algernon Charles, 267

Tannenbaum, Leslie, 116n
Tatham, Frederick, 15
Taylor, Gary, 43n
Taylor, W. B. S., 4, 7, 46n, 65, 74–75, 78, 83–84, 103, 144
Technology: Blake's argument about, 176, 182–85, 256; in English-school discourse, 153–55; in engraving, 153–54, 206; generalization in, 195; romantic critiques of, 258–59; teachability of, 200, 205
Temple, 118–19, 122, 132
Teniers, David, 235
Terah, 112, 130
Thales, 9
Thornhill, James, 15, 101
Threshold of vision, 191–92, 194, 196–98, 207, 216, 234, 241, 248, 250, 253, 268
Time and space, 177–82, 184, 226, 232, 236–37, 248, 255
Tinney, John, 228
Tintoretto, 10n
Titian, 10, 15, 19, 22, 79, 99, 127, 142, 176, 206–10, 219, 247, 254–55, 258; *Portrait of a Man,* **209;** *Tarquin and Lucrece,* **208;** *Titianus Redivivus* (Gillray), **210**
Todd, Ruthven, 183n
"Toilettes," 155, 171, 255
Tone, 9–10, 207, 216, 219. *See also* Engraving: tonal processes of; Harmony
Tone, Wolfe, 26n, 33, 34, 57, 86, 232
Tongue, 128–29
Translation, 177–82, 191, 194, 205–6, 248, 261–63
Tresham, Henry, 246
Tubal Cain, 111
Turnbull, George, 9–10, 27, 44–45, 61, 121n, 271
Turner, J. M. W., 83n, 84–**85,** 266
Type in chase, **186**
Tyre, 122–25

Unity. *See* Harmony

Vala, 130, 255
van Assen, Anthony, 58, **72**
van Dyck, Anthony: in Blake's history of art, 141, 158–59, 161, 163, 166, 186, 218–19, 232; in Charles I's court, 13–14, 216; in English-school discourse, 13–15, 19, 22; as engraver, 202; harmony exemplified by, 247, 254, 256; in Rubens's system, 213; mentioned, 83, 108, 210
Vasari, Giorgio, 3, 9–10, 15, 21, 23, 27–28, 45, 154, 159, 184, 202
Venetian art, 142, 163n, 176–77, 182–83, 219, 247, 255
"Venetian secret," **210**
Veronese, Paolo, 10n
Vertue, George, 3
Villamena, Francesco, 216
Virtuosity, 177–78, 181, 196, 199–200, 211–13, 216, 218, 225, 232, 236, 258
Viscomi, Joseph S., 184, 185n, 252, 266, 269
Voltaire, 80, 145

Waldenses, 119n
Walpole, Horace, 3, 33, 101, 103
War, 139, 146–47
Warburton, William, 8, 113
Ward, Aileen, 2n, 156n
Warren, Charles, 157, 219, 224
Washington, George, **193–94, 196, 197**
Waterhouse, Ellis K., 25
Watson, James, 124
Watson, Richard, 261
Watteau, Jean-Antoine, 252–**53**
Weber, Max, 67n
Wedgwood, Josiah, xxviii, 28, 38–41, 56, 58, 65, 68, 70, 79, 213, 216
Wesley, John, 124
West, Benjamin, xxviii–xxvix, 15, **32**–34, 36, 38, 47n, 49, 67, 82, 84, 86, 104, 153, 210, 232
Westering of culture, 20–21, 159–60
Westmacott, Charles M., 97
Westminster Abbey, 82, 108, 182
Wheatley, Francis: *Death of Richard II,* 36–**37;** *Opening of the Shakespeare Gallery,* **55**
Whitehouse, Rev. John, 28n
Whore of Babylon, 130–31
"Whore's forehead," 130–31
Wicksteed, Joseph, 130
Williams, R. (engraver), **244–45**
Williams, Raymond, 68n
Wilson, Richard, 23, 57, 61, 83, 104n
Winckelmann, Abbé Johann Joachim, 4, 7, 12, 25, 44, 248, 250
Winstanley, Gerrard, 128
Woman taken in adultery, 126–27
Woollett, William, xxix, 57, 88, 107–8, 155–56, 161, 164, 173, 176, 182–84, 188, 207, 224, 226, 232, 254–55; *Death of General Wolfe,* **32**–34; *Jocund Peasants,* **228–29**
Wordsworth, William, 70, 146, 236, 240, 258–59
Worlidge, T., 130
Wouverman, Philip, 246
Wren, Christopher, 15, 101
Wright, Joseph, of Derby, xxix, 248, **249,** 250
Writing, 113, 127–29

Yarrington, Alison, 83, 86
Yeats, William Butler, 175
Young, Edward, 2
Youngquist, Paul, 166

Zoffany, Johann, 83

Library of Congress Cataloging-in-Publication Data

Eaves, Morris, 1944–
The counter-arts conspiracy : art and industry in the age of Blake / Morris Eaves.
p. cm.
Includes bibliographical references and index.
ISBN 0-8014-2489-5 (alk. paper)
1. Art and industry—England. 2. Art, Modern—17th–18th centuries—England. 3. Art, Modern—19th century—England. 4. Blake, William, 1757–1827—Criticism and interpretation. I. Title.
N72.I53E28 1992
709′.42′09034—dc20 92-52749